Business in the Canadian Environment

Third Edition

Peter H. Fuhrman

Department of Business Administration
Fraser Valley College

Prentice-Hall Canada Inc., Scarborough, Ontario

To my father and mother

Canadian Cataloguing in Publication Data

Fuhrman, Peter Harry
   Business in the Canadian environment

3rd ed.
Includes bibliographical references and index.
ISBN 0-13-091877-6

1. Business.   2. Canada — Commerce.   I. Title.

HF5349.C2F84 1989   380.1'0971   C88-094660-1

Prentice-Hall, Inc., Englewood Cliffs, New Jersey
Prentice-Hall International, Inc., London
Prentice-Hall of Australia, Pty., Ltd. Sydney
Prentice-Hall of India Pvt., Ltd., New Delhi
Prentice-Hall of Japan, Inc., Tokyo
Prentice-Hall of Southeast Asia (Pte.) Ltd., Singapore
Editora Prentice-Hall do Brasil Ltda., Rio de Janeiro
Prentice-Hall Hispanoamericana, S.A., Mexico

ISBN 0-13-091877-6

Production Editor: Peter Buck
Production Coordinator: Sandra Paige
Typesetting: Q Composition Inc.

Cover: "Day View," by Katherine Hanley. Courtesy AT&T
Graphics Software Labs
Part Opening Photos: The Financial Post, except Part IV
photo courtesy Public Archives of Canada

1   2   3   4   5   JD   93   92   91   90   89

Printed and bound in Canada by John Deyell Company

Contents

PART III The Business Functions 297

PART IV Business and Its Environment 545

Preface

The saying, "In like a lion, out like a lamb," could apply to the Canadian economy in the 1980s. The serious recession at the beginning of the decade gave way to healthy economic growth. Although the forecast for the 1990s is a continuation of prosperity for most Canadians, there are always dark clouds on the horizon. The economies of many nations are interdependent and events anywhere in the world can have a profound effect on the well-being of Canadians. Since business is so central to our way of life, it is important to understand how the system operates.

A business career as a manager or owner can be rewarding, but getting started in a business program is not easy. An introductory business course that covers many fields can provide a good overview of what is involved. This textbook is designed to make such a course interesting.

The third edition of *Business in the Canadian Environment* is completely updated but retains the structure of the first two editions. The section on starting and operating a small business has been expanded with information about franchising and the development of a business plan. The production chapter has been completely rewritten, and information has been added to the chapters on marketing, finance and personnel. The chapter on government and business has been completely revised to reflect the impact of the Progressive Conservative government, with emphasis on tax reform, deregulation, privatization and free trade. A section on career planning has been included in Chapter 15. Additional cases have been added to various chapters and existing cases updated where necessary.

The book is organized to present the various aspects of business in a logical manner. The three chapters that make up Part I, Foundations of Business, examine how the Canadian business sytem works in comparison with the other economic systems in operation today. Particular emphasis is placed on the changing economies of China and the U.S.S.R. In Chapter 2 the basic concepts of capital, entrepreneurship, profit and competition are discussed in detail, since these are the forces responsible for the development of our business system over the past two centuries. Chapter 3 examines small business — the requirements for starting and operating a business and the factors that contribute to its success. It also looks at the forms of business ownership.

Part II, Business and Management, examines the role of managers and their importance in the effective operation of any organization. The three chapters in this section provide a comprehensive picture of the functions of management — planning, controlling, organizing, and directing people in order to achieve organizational goals. An important addition is a discussion of the use of microcomputers by managers in their daily decision-making.

Part III, The Business Functions, looks at the four functional areas of business — production, marketing, finance, and personnel. The four chapters in this section focus on the major responsibilities of managers in these areas and the problems they are most likely to encounter. As it is essential to understand the interdependence of these four functions, particular emphasis is placed on the cooperation between production and marketing in producing goods and services with the aid of financial and human resources. Particular attention is also given to the increasing role of computers in the business functions. Chapter 7 includes a discussion of the elements and history of the computer, the use of computers in production, the advantages and disadvantages of automation, and the human problems of computerization.

Part IV, Business and Its Environment, examines the relationship between business organizations and other groups in our society. Since one third of all Canadian workers belong to labour unions, we examine the relationship between unions and business. We also examine the relationship between business and government — how government regulates business on the one hand, and how it provides financial incentives and services to encourage business growth and economic expansion on the other. Since almost one quarter of everything Canadians produce is sold to people living in other countries, we also look at international business, and in particular the impact of foreign ownership on Canada's economy. The last chapter in Part IV looks at the responsibility of business to society. By placing this topic at the end of the book, one can get a better appreciation of the meaning of responsibility in business after learning about the system and the problems faced by management.

Finally, Part V, Business in Canada: The Future, takes a brief look at the forces responsible for our rapidly changing world. The more accurately management can forecast changes to the environment and the more quickly it can respond to these changes, the more assured it will be of survival. The last section in Chapter 15 provides an overview of career planning, particularly for people entering the job market from a college or university program.

Each chapter begins with a comprehensive outline, a short preview of the major points in the chapter, and specific learning objectives — the concepts and ideas you should know or be able to explain. At the end of each chapter is a summary, a list of key terms, review and discussion questions, as well as cases for analysis. The emphasis is on providing a thorough overview of how business operates, as well as how it interacts with society and other nations. You are introduced to business vocabulary and to the basic principles and practices involved in the management of any organization. Illustrations are used wherever possible to clarify difficult concepts. In addition, a number of issues suitable for class discussion are raised to encourage awareness of the complexities involved and the need for careful examination of all sides in any debate.

Acknowledgements

I am indebted to my colleagues and students who have helped in the development of this book. I would like to thank specifically Bill Beattie, Barry Bompas, Brian Coulter, Janet Falk, Malcolm Harvey, and Ian McCaskell, who have contributed greatly to the third edition. I would also like to thank the individuals who have taken the time to review and comment on the first and second editions. Among them are Joseph O'Brien, Douglas College; Rick Jackson, Queen's University; Patrick Northey, Ryerson Polytechnical Institute; Jim McCutcheon, Sir Wilfrid Laurier University; Gary Veaks, Southern Alberta Institute of Technology; Don Whitely, East Kootenay Community College; Brahm Canzer, John Abbott College; Thomas Lynch, Seneca College; Greg Streich, DeVry Institute of Technology; Musetta Thwaites, Mount St. Vincent University; and Fred White, University College of Cape Breton.

I would also like to thank the many people at Prentice-Hall Canada who have contributed their time and skills to this book, especially Yolanda de Rooy, editor, David Jolliffe, project editor, and Peter Buck, production editor, whose help and attention to detail are very much appreciated.

Peter H. Fuhrman
January 1989

THE PLAN OF THIS BOOK

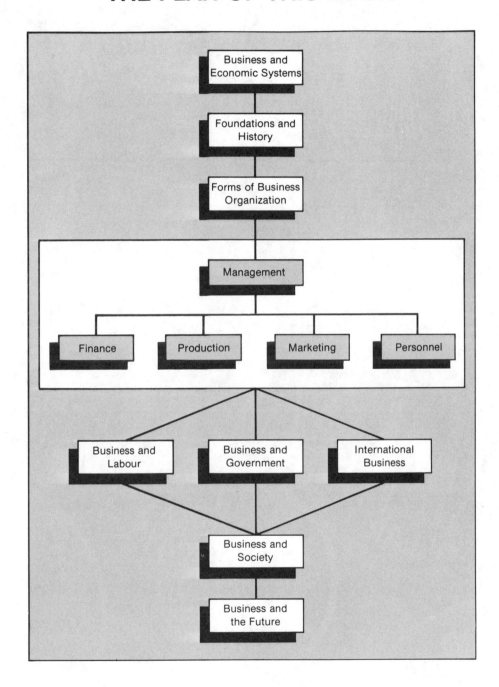

Part One

Foundations of Business

Human beings are generally industrious and most strive to improve their lot in life. Unfortunately, many people do not have the freedom to do as they please. They also may lack resources, or the knowledge to convert resources into useful goods for production or consumption. Some people live under such fragile conditions that a natural disaster, such as a flood or drought, is enough to destroy what little food they can produce. As a result, the vast majority of humanity lives in poverty, and each year millions die of starvation because they lack the capability to produce food or other necessary goods.

Production is the key to prosperity. Business organizations produce goods and services using raw materials, human labour, and machines and equipment. Nevertheless, choices must be made in determining what to produce, how to produce it, and how to distribute the product among individuals. To make these decisions, different countries have adopted different systems.

In Chapter 1 we examine the three major types of economic systems and how each attempts to resolve the economic problems of production and distribution. We also consider the role of business organizations in economic systems.

In Chapter 2 we look at Canada's economic system, a modified form of capitalism, also called free enterprise. In the latter part of the chapter we trace the development of business and the Canadian economy over the past 150 years.

In Chapter 3 we look at how to start and operate a small business successfully. In the latter part of the chapter we consider the characteristics, advantages and disadvantages of each of the three private forms of business ownership and briefly look at cooperatives.

Business and Economic Systems

West Edmonton Mall

CHAPTER OUTLINE

CHAPTER PREVIEW

What do the words capitalism, socialism and communism really mean? In Chapter 1 we examine these economic systems and the importance of business organizations to our way of life. We look at the role of private businesses within Canada's capitalistic economic system and examine how this system has been modified through government intervention in an attempt to serve us better. The Canadian system is also compared to the other two economic systems — democratic socialism and communism — to determine the strengths and weaknesses of each. The chapter then ends with a discussion of the reasons for studying business.

LEARNING OBJECTIVES

After reading this chapter you should be able to explain:

1. How the standard of living in a given country is affected by the total population and the amount of goods and services it can produce;

2. What business organizations are, and how they contribute to the production of goods and services;
3. The three basic functions of an economic system;
4. The three major economic systems and the differences between them;
5. The principles underlying capitalism;
6. How capitalism in Canada differs from pure capitalism;
7. The advantages and disadvantages of each of the three major economic systems;
8. The importance of understanding how business in general — and the Canadian business system in particular — operates.

What does the future hold in store for Canadians? Will there be another energy shortage as there was in the 1970s? Will there be a serious depression in the 1990s? Will there be high unemployment? Will our standard of living drop or continue to rise? Will free trade with the United States help Canadians? These are only a few of the many questions that we as Canadians may ask. It is unlikely that economists, business people, politicians, academics, and others who have intimate knowledge about these matters would agree as to what may happen in the future. They would almost certainly disagree as to the economic policies government should implement. Nevertheless, while the future is uncertain, we enjoy, for the present at least, a fairly high standard of living.

OUR WAY OF LIFE

The average Canadian probably sees little of the poverty that exists in the world. Of the five billion people on earth today, an estimated two billion live in a continual state of hunger. In excess of three-and-a-half million die of starvation each year. Extreme poverty exists in many countries in, for example, Asia, Africa and South America. In Calcutta, one of India's largest cities, an estimated 600 000 people live in the street, drink contaminated water and pick through the roughly 2000 tons of garbage that litters the street for their food. More than 70% of the city's people live at or below the poverty line, calculated as an income of less than $8 a month. The average earnings of a family of five are $34 per month. For at least 200 000 people, begging is the only source of income.[1]

Even in countries such as Canada and the United States, there are people who have no homes and go hungry most of the time. Poverty does exist in Canada and in other parts of North America, but there is no equivalent to Calcutta on this continent. In Canada we speak of low-income families — officially, families at or below a cutoff where basic expenditures for food, clothing and shelter amount to 58.5% of their income. These cutoffs were determined for various family sizes and living areas in Canada in 1978 and reviewed in

1982. In 1988 this cutoff income level for a family of three in Canada was approximately $19 000. Of course, what we class as a low or poverty income in Canada would be considered undreamed-of luxury by many people in other parts of the world. Few Canadians die of starvation: private and government agencies ensure that those in need are provided with at least the basic necessities of life. Simple diseases are routinely cured and we generally live to a ripe old age.

When we examine the Canadian family more closely, we find that the average household in 1988 consists of 3.3 persons and has an estimated average income of $38 000 per year. This income is partly earned by wives since more than half of all married Canadian women work outside the home. The average family lives in a six-room suburban house with most modern conveniences and owns a fairly well equipped car. While the family budget does not allow for extravagant spending, the average Canadian family does have all the necessities and time for leisure activities.[2]

The average family has approximately 74 hours of free time per week. Approximately 29 hours of this time is spent watching television; much of the rest is spent watching movies, reading newspapers and books, listening to the radio, records and tapes, or pursuing various recreational activities.[3]

Canadians are generally happy with their life and confident about the future. Nevertheless, a recent *Maclean's/Decima* survey, which polled 1500 Canadians about Canada's pressing problems, indicated that Canadians were concerned about a number of major issues. The Free Trade Agreement between Canada and the United States is a major concern with one third of those polled. They feared that it would result in fewer jobs for Canadians. Other concerns were unemployment, government deficits, and inflation. However, Canadians seemed overall to be in a confident and optimistic mood — 78% of the respondents were satisfied with their own economic situation, and 85% indicated that they were optimistic about their own futures.[4]

Standard of Living and Production

Why is life so much better in Canada than in Calcutta? Certainly the size of the population is a major factor. The essential problem, however, is that countries where living conditions are poor have neither the knowledge nor the means to produce enough of such basic necessities as food, let alone luxury goods and services. We can express the relationship between the standard of living and what a country can produce by the following equation:

$$\text{Standard of living} = \frac{\text{Production}}{\text{Population}}$$

The equation shows that the material well-being, or **standard of living**, of the people in a particular country depends directly on the amount of goods and services produced and the number of people that must share them.

To calculate the standard of living we must first calculate the value of production, also known as **gross national product** or **GNP**. We could do this by adding up the final value of all the goods and services produced in a country for a given time, such as one year. When the GNP is divided by the total population, the result is a **per capita GNP** which can be compared with those of other countries.

To make the calculation of the GNP easier we can take advantage of the fact that GNP is equal to **gross national income.** Remember that everything produced in the country represents income to someone in the form of wages, rent, interest or profit. Since both businesses and individuals must file tax returns it is not difficult to determine the gross national income or **GNI**.

Table 1.1 shows how this calculation is performed in Canada. In the top half of the table **gross domestic product** at market prices is calculated by adding the income of the various economic sectors in Canada. Following that is another way of arriving at gross domestic product based on who purchased the goods that were produced. You can see that the various levels of government accounted for almost 25% of total direct expenditures for investment and for goods and services produced by the economy. Finally, at the bottom of the table we transform gross domestic product to gross national product by adding investment income received from non-residents and deducting investment income paid to non-residents.

In industrialized countries a fairly accurate GNP is not difficult to calculate. However, in many third world countries getting an accurate GNP is virtually impossible. Most of the people in these countries earn little in wages and may toil from dawn to dusk simply to provide enough food, clothing and shelter for their families. Furthermore, there may be a high rate of illiteracy, and business records may be non-existent or, if they exist, their accuracy may be questionable. Getting an accurate population count may also be a problem because of illiteracy. In these countries, therefore, a standard of living figure will not be accurate.

Similarly, the per capita GNP of many third world countries is a crude measure at best. Because of the absence of accurate records, the per capita GNP may provide no information as to how income is distributed among people or how readily goods and services are available to the average person. For example, a high GNP could mean that the top 40% of the population lives very well while the bottom 60% lives in extreme poverty. On the other hand, another country with the same GNP could have more evenly distributed income and virtually no poverty.

TABLE 1.1
Calculation of Canada's Gross National Product, Income and Expenditure Based, 1985-1986

Income based	1985	1986
Wages, salaries, and supplementary labour income	$257 493	$273 978
Corporation profits before taxes	47 673	45 384
Interest and miscellaneous investment income	40 357	40 784
Accrued net income of farm operators from farm production	3 931	5 127
Net income of non-farm unincorporated business, including rent	28 493	32 351
Inventory valuation adjustment	− 2 260	− 1 124
Net domestic income at factor cost	375 687	396 500
Indirect taxes less subsidies	47 456	53 923
Capital consumption allowances	54 182	57 634
Statistical discrepancy	2 121	1 841
Gross domestic product at market prices	$479 446	$509 898

Expenditure Based		
Personal expenditure on consumer goods and services	$275 844	$298 747
Government current expenditure on goods and services	96 374	101 198
Government investment		
Fixed capital	12 749	12 708
Inventories	− 64	− 35
Business investment		
Fixed capital		
Residential construction	25 739	31 925
Non-residential construction	26 901	24 964
Machinery and equipment	29 104	32 363
Inventories		
Non-farm	1 924	2 345
Farm and grain in commercial channels	633	1 389
Exports of goods and services	135 358	138 265
Deduct: Imports of goods and services	− 122 995	− 132 130
Statistical discrepancy	− 2 121	− 1 841
Gross domestic product at market prices	$479 446	$509 898
Add: Investment income received from non-residents	7 649	7 194
Deduct: Investment income paid to non-residents	− 21 983	− 24 080
Equals: Gross National Product at Market prices	$465 112	$493 012
Gross National Product at 1981 prices	$374 793	$388 192

SOURCE: *Canadian Statistical Review* (Ottawa: Statistics Canada), Cat. 11-003E Monthly. Reproduced with permission of the Minister of Supply and Services.

Using machines, the Canadian farmer can cultivate large areas
of land

Nevertheless, the per capita GNP is the best measure we have
and does allow some comparison of productivity in different countries (See Figure 1.1). For example, individuals in countries with a
low per capita GNP are not as productive as their counterparts in
countries with a high per capita GNP. This does not mean that the
former individuals do not work as hard as the latter, but rather that
the latter get more out of a given amount of effort. For example, we
can compare a Chinese worker with a per capita GNP of $310 per
year, to a Canadian worker with a per capita GNP of 13 700 per
year. Assume that both work an equal amount of time during the year,
expending an equal amount of effort. On a per capita basis, then, the
Canadian produces approximately 44 times more than his counterpart in China.

Figure 1.1 Per capita GNP, 1980 and 1985, selected countries

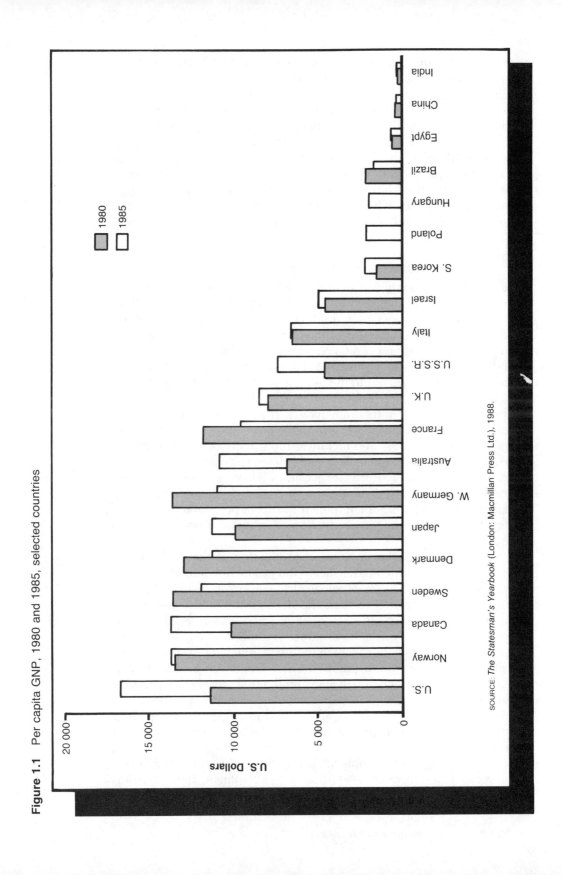

SOURCE: *The Statesman's Yearbook* (London: Macmillan Press Ltd.), 1988.

How can the Canadian worker produce so much? Obviously production can be increased either by working longer hours or by putting out more effort. But even longer hours and greater effort would not account for the great difference between the Canadian worker's standard of living and that of his Chinese counterpart. The major reason for the difference lies in the large quantities of machines and equipment available to the Canadian worker, which greatly increase his capacity to produce. With the help of machines the Canadian farmer is able to cultivate large areas and produce enough food for large numbers of people, while the Chinese farmer may work most of the year to produce only enough to feed his family.

Factors of Production

Before considering how a nation's standard of living could be raised, we must examine more closely the meaning of the term **production**.

Goods and services are produced by combining human effort, raw materials and various equipment and machines. Economists call these labour, land and capital respectively, and they represent three of the five **factors of production. Labour** refers not only to human beings able to work, but to the human effort, both mental and physical, required in the production process. **Land** means natural resources such as oil, iron ore and forests. The third factor of production, **capital**, refers to equipment used in the production and distribution of goods and services, and includes simple tools as well as complex equipment such as automobile assembly lines, railroads and computers.

We in Canada are fortunate because we have great quantities and varieties of natural resources, a well-educated labour force, and a large amount of capital equipment available per worker. All these factors contribute to the production of complex products in large quantities.

Technology, a fourth factor of production, is the practical application of scientific knowledge to the production and distribution of goods and services. Technological advances can increase the productivity of individual workers, result in greater output and reduce manufacturing costs and consequently prices. Henry Ford's invention of the assembly line, for example, significantly reduced the cost of producing automobiles which in turn resulted in lower prices and allowed more people to purchase cars. The development of computers allowed automation of many production processes, increasing efficiency and leading to the development of many new products. As more products become available and as consumer prices drop due to more efficient production processes, the standard of living rises.

Technological development is the direct result of research and development programs established by government, industry, universities and private foundations. Firms continuously strive to earn a profit and they must therefore offer consumers a better product, better service or a lower price than the competition. Thus, they must develop better manufacturing processes or better products or both. **Education** is the foundation of research and development. As more people are educated and the level of education per person rises, more consumer and industrial products are developed. At the same time a highly educated population is necessary to use the complex products that an industrialized society produces.

The **entrepreneur** — the fifth factor of production — is the risk-taker who with effort and financial resources brings together all the other factors of production — land, labour, capital and technology. If the venture proves successful, the entrepreneur reaps great financial rewards as well as prestige in the community. Failure, on the other hand, usually means a loss of the entire investment. The entrepreneur may be an individual, the government or an existing business firm.

Raising the Standard of Living

How can a nation such as India raise the standard of living of its people? Because the huge, largely unskilled and poorly educated population continues to grow rapidly, any small increases in the country's productive capacity are cancelled out and the standard of living does not rise. Compared to industrialized countries, India has little capital equipment. And even when complex modern machinery is provided through foreign aid, few of its people have the training required to use it.

Bearing in mind that solutions to such vast problems are easier to suggest than to implement, some of the essential steps are clear. The rate of popuation growth must be reduced, and the level of education raised. Then the country's resources must be developed and channelled into the production of capital goods. If all these steps can be accomplished, then the standard of living may slowly start to rise.

BUSINESS

Every country in the world has **business organizations** that bring together the factors of production to produce goods and services to satisfy the needs and wants of the population. Private businesses are out to make a profit (we look at profit in more detail in Chapter 2). Simply put, **profit** is the money left over after expenses have been deducted from the money received from sales. To make those sales a business provides either goods or services. Regardless of whether a business produces a product such as ice cream or provides a service such as air transportation, both need to acquire the appropriate resources to produce the product or service, and then make potential customers aware of them.

While some businesses produce only **consumer goods** such as food, clothing and television sets, others create **capital goods** — agricultural equipment, machines, assembly lines, trucks, locomotives, computers and so on. Capital goods are not intended for the final consumer, but to help in the production and distribution of consumer goods and services.

Not all businesses are privately owned. The federal government and the various provincial governments own businesses called **Crown corporations**. The Post Office and Canadian National Railways, for example, are Crown corporations. Ontario Hydro is a provincial Crown corporation, as is Alberta Government Telephones. Water works, sewage and garbage disposal plants, and the fire and police departments are often municipal corporations or departments. Some of these government services are entirely supported by taxpayers, as are the fire and police departments, while Crown corporations charge for their services. However, if the revenue from these services is not enough to cover costs, then the government must make up the shortfall from taxes.

There are also businesses that provide a variety of services but do not make a profit. Charities, for example, depend on donations to carry on their work, while a business such as an automobile association is primarily interested in providing the motorist with a variety of services. These organizations may in some years have a surplus of revenue over expenditures, but they are basically **non-profit organizations.**

Business and Economics

Business revolves around the practical matters of producing goods and services. Business managers are concerned with the efficient combination of workers, machines and raw materials to ensure that the firm is profitable. They concentrate on the internal workings of the firm — developing new products and improving existing ones, motivating employees toward better performance, controlling expenses and so on. While they may be deeply concerned with society and its problems, their primary objective must always be profit.

Economics, on the other hand, sees business units as basic particles of the economic world. Economists are interested in the behaviour of these units and their interaction with each other; they are not concerned with what goes on inside individual firms. If the price of gasoline goes up, the economist will attempt to analyze how the price increase affects the consumer demand for gasoline and for cars. Economists are interested in such matters as the distribution of income, trends in prices and wages, total national income, and business cycles.

Business cycles are a fundamental problem in the capitalistic system and it is virtually impossible to eliminate them completely. When the economy is in an upswing business looks forward to increased production and greater profits. An economic downswing, on the other hand, results in decreased sales, increased unemployment and a decline in profits. Economists study both the causes of these cycles and their effects on national income, unemployment and inflation. Through **economic forecasts** economists can help business managers to predict cyclical swings in business and thus help to prevent firms from incurring large losses. Government too uses economic forecasts, to design economic policies that will help to smooth out the income inequalities and lessen the impact of business cycles.

ECONOMIC SYSTEMS

While individuals' desires for material goods appear to be unlimited, economic resources are scarce. Therefore a nation needs some mechanism to help make the following decisions:

1. What goods and services are to be produced;
2. How they are to be produced;
3. How they are to be distributed among the people.

A country's economic system is precisely such a mechanism. First, the **economic system** determines what should be produced, and what proportions of the basic factors of production — land, labour and capital — should be allocated to manufacturing consumer products and capital goods. In some cases private individuals vote in the marketplace by buying the products they prefer. But the decision can also be left to the state, in which case the government decides on the type, quantity and quality of goods to be produced.

The second decision can again be left to either private firms or to government planners. In either case, decisions have to be made regarding plant location, the type of equipment and machines to use, and the degree of automation. If private firms make these decisions, the results are likely to be quite different from decisions made by government planners because the objectives of the two sectors are different. Businesses are concerned with profit, while government is more concerned with the needs of society and employment.

The third problem that an economic system must resolve is the equitable distribution of goods and services among the nation's people. This is generally accomplished by allowing consumers to purchase whatever goods and services they require with their monetary income — the greater their income, the more they can buy.

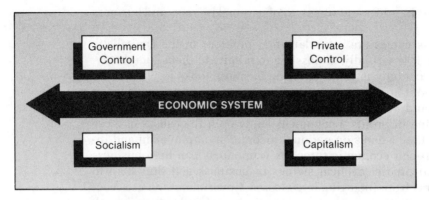

Figure 1.2 Control of economic systems

How Economic Systems Differ

Even though all economic systems perform the same functions, as Figure 1.2 indicates, no two countries have an identical system. In fact, many countries have vastly different systems. Essentially the difference lies in the proportion of economic decisions made by government as opposed to private individuals — in other words, who controls the three tasks that all economic systems must resolve.

An economic system under private control is called capitalism, while one under government or state control is called socialism. To better understand these two major systems, we must examine their development.

The Historical Roots of Capitalism and Socialism

Capitalism is an economic philosophy that emphasizes the right of individuals to pursue their own self-interests. Underlying capitalism is the principle that private ownership of the means of production — implying the profit motive and competition among producers in the absence of government controls — is the most effective method of allocating the factors of production to provide people with the goods and services they want.

Capitalism evolved from the feudal system in England and Europe and was later transplanted to the North American continent. The capitalist system developed because of social and economic changes that occurred during the 16th and 17th centuries and these changes laid the foundations for the Industrial Revolution in the 18th century. One major change was the monetization of many aspects of life — money was used to buy goods and services, and labour was bought and sold in the marketplace. Goods and services were no longer exchanged in kind. Another major factor was the change in the religious climate in England and Europe. The new Protestant religions diffused the power of the Catholic church and made the pursuit of commercial activities honorable and legitimate, an attitude that the Catholic church strongly disapproved of during the feudal era.[5]

Thus the social climate allowed ambitious entrepreneurs to become industrial giants through the invention of new machinery or manufacturing processes that greatly increased the production of existing goods. The ownership of private property, together with the freedom to compete in the marketplace in any way they deemed necessary to sell their products, gave the early industrialists the incentive to build and expand their factories and to accumulate wealth. Government did not interfere in business, nor did it protect the consumer or worker since the prevailing philosophy held that the individual was best able to make decisions on matters affecting his daily life. The lack of government intervention in the economy is also termed **laissez-faire**, which means "let it be."

While initially most goods produced in England were exported to other countries, particularly to the "New World," a growing English middle class increased the demand for new and existing goods and services. The industrial revolution raised living standards to levels unlike any the world had known before.[6] However, during the late 18th and early 19th century, living and working conditions for the majority of people were terrible.

One individual who observed the misery of the working class was Karl Marx, who in 1848, together with Friedrich Engels, wrote the *Communist Manifesto*. Based on their observation of the English industrial system, Marx and Engels held the private ownership of property and the profit motive to blame: the working classes were being exploited by capitalists (industrialists) for monetary gain. In Marx's view, abolishing private ownership of property and substituting the state as owner would permit all members of society to live in peace and channel all of their efforts towards improving their society.

Marx looked toward a revolution in which the hereditary nobility and wealthy industrialists would be overthrown. A temporary regime known as the dictatorship of the proletariat would be established to govern during the transition from capitalism to **socialism**. Then a planned socialist economy would emerge. In this new state goods and services would be produced on a voluntary basis, through the cooperation of all citizens. Since all would be equally and adequately rewarded for their work, society as a whole would be free for more humanistic pursuits.

The economic systems that exist today are a mixture of these two philosophies — complete state ownership of the means of production on the one hand, and complete private ownership on the other. Needless to say, no nation operates under a pure form of either system. Countries with capitalistic economic systems — also known as free enterprise, private enterprise, or mixed economies — all experience considerable government intervention. The purpose of intervention is to eliminate the most undesirable aspects of the capitalistic system, as well as provide a more stable economic environment. Socialism can also have many variations, as described in the article "Forms of Socialism."

All forms of socialism share two basic tenets. First is the belief that if the means of production remain in private hands, the worker will be exploited. Second is the belief in egalitarianism, the conviction that all individuals should enjoy political and social equality.

Capitalism, Communism and Democratic Socialism — An Overview

Having looked at economic systems in more detail, we can now modify Figure 1.2 somewhat, and indicate where the economic systems of selected countries might fall on the continuum. As you can see in Figure 1.3, we have introduced another type of economic system, **democratic socialism**, which represents a middle ground between capitalism and communism in the amount of control the state exerts over economic decisions.

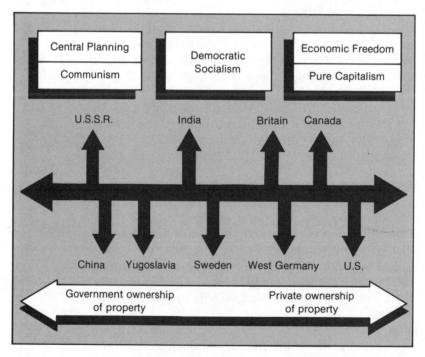

Figure 1.3 Range of economic systems from pure communism to pure capitalism (neither extreme exists in the world today)

Forms of Socialism

Marxism-Leninism, commonly known as **communism**, is the political ideology of the Soviet Union and its East bloc satellites, as well as of China, Mongolia, North Korea, Vietnam, Laos, Cambodia, Cuba, Albania and Yugoslavia. In its drive to establish a classless society, communism seeks ultimately to abolish private property and nationalize the means of production. Almost total power is concentrated in a tightly structured party with its leaders forming a dictatorship of the proletariat. Communism is repressive and allows its citizens little freedom.

The most liberal version of socialism is **social democracy**. Social democrats consider Moscow's leaders dictators who do not live up to the humanistic vision of Marxism. Social democrats believe in achieving their socialist goals gradually and peacefully.

Rather than restructuring society into a classless, collectivized whole, they concentrate more on rectifying the hardships brought on by capitalist economies, such as unemployment, poverty, and wage and salary inequities. Countries ruled by social democrats are generally mixed economies: they have state ownership or direction of key industries, but also retain many elements of private enterprise competition.

Social democrats work within a multi-party system. Most European countries have had social democrats in power over the years. For example, Sweden's social democrats were in power for 44 years before being defeated in 1976 by a centre-right government. They subsequently regained power in 1982. Norway, Portugal, Spain and France each currently have a social democratic government.

Third world socialism comprises a number of disparate systems, including the Islamic socialism of Algeria and Libya, Baathist (Renaissance) socialism of Syria and Iraq, the *ujamaa* (familyhood) socialism of Tanzania, as well as the cooperative societies of some Caribbean nations such as Jamaica and Guyana. Although these societies call themselves socialist, their beliefs are rooted less in Marxist dogma than in nationalism or in the communalism practised in tribal Africa. Many of these nations have also had bad experiences with colonialism and thus equate capitalism with imperialism and exploitation. These countries are also intent on decreasing the importance of private property in the economy as well as sharply curbing foreign investment by private firms.

SOURCE: Based on "Socialism: Trials and Errors," *TIME*, March 13, 1978, pp. 18-31.

CAPITALISM: Under this economic system the productive capacity of the country is basically privately owned. Businesses compete with one another to produce goods and services on the basis of consumer needs and wants. Private business firms decide in the main how raw materials, labour and capital are to be used to produce consumer and capital goods alike. Individuals may work were they choose; they may establish their own businesses and compete with others to produce and sell their goods to consumers. Individual income may be derived from a number of sources, including wages and salaries, rent, interest or business profits. After paying income taxes to the various levels of government, individuals may spend their

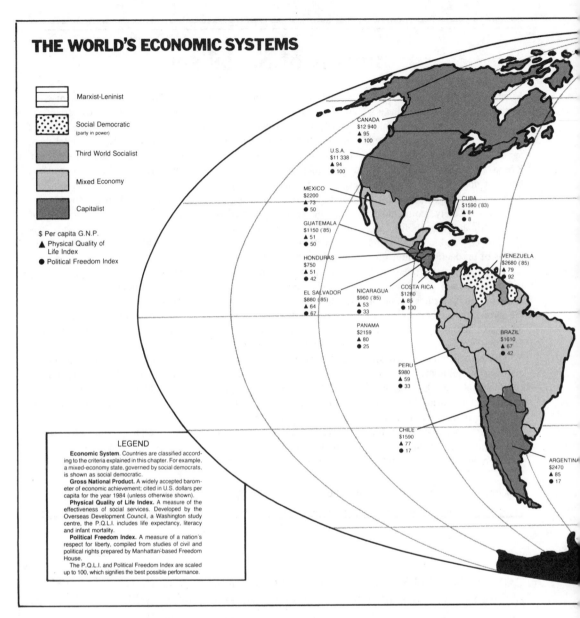

THE WORLD'S ECONOMIC SYSTEMS

Marxist-Leninist

Social Democratic
(party in power)

Third World Socialist

Mixed Economy

Capitalist

$ Per capita G.N.P.
▲ Physical Quality of
Life Index
● Political Freedom Index

CANADA
$12 940
▲ 95
● 100

U.S.A.
$11 338
▲ 94
● 100

MEXICO
$2200
▲ 73
● 50

CUBA
$1590 ('83)
▲ 84
● 8

GUATEMALA
$1150 ('85)
▲ 51
● 50

VENEZUELA
$2680 ('85)
▲ 79
● 92

HONDURAS
$750
▲ 51
● 42

EL SALVADOR
$880 ('85)
▲ 64
● 67

NICARAGUA
$960 ('85)
▲ 53
● 33

COSTA RICA
$1280
▲ 85
● 100

PANAMA
$2159
▲ 80
● 25

BRAZIL
$1610
▲ 67
● 42

PERU
$980
▲ 59
● 33

CHILE
$1590
▲ 77
● 17

ARGENTINA
$2470
▲ 85
● 17

LEGEND

Economic System. Countries are classified according to the criteria explained in this chapter. For example, a mixed-economy state, governed by social democrats, is shown as social democratic.

Gross National Product. A widely accepted barometer of economic achievement; cited in U.S. dollars per capita for the year 1984 (unless otherwise shown).

Physical Quality of Life Index. A measure of the effectiveness of social services. Developed by the Overseas Development Council, a Washington study centre, the P.Q.L.I. includes life expectancy, literacy and infant mortality.

Political Freedom Index. A measure of a nation's respect for liberty, compiled from studies of civil and political rights prepared by Manhattan-based Freedom House.

The P.Q.L.I. and Political Freedom Index are scaled up to 100, which signifies the best possible performance.

Figure 1.4 The world's economic systems

SOURCES: *TIME*, The Weekly Newsmagazine, March 13, 1978; *The Statesman's Yearbook* (London: Macmillan Press Ltd.), 1988.

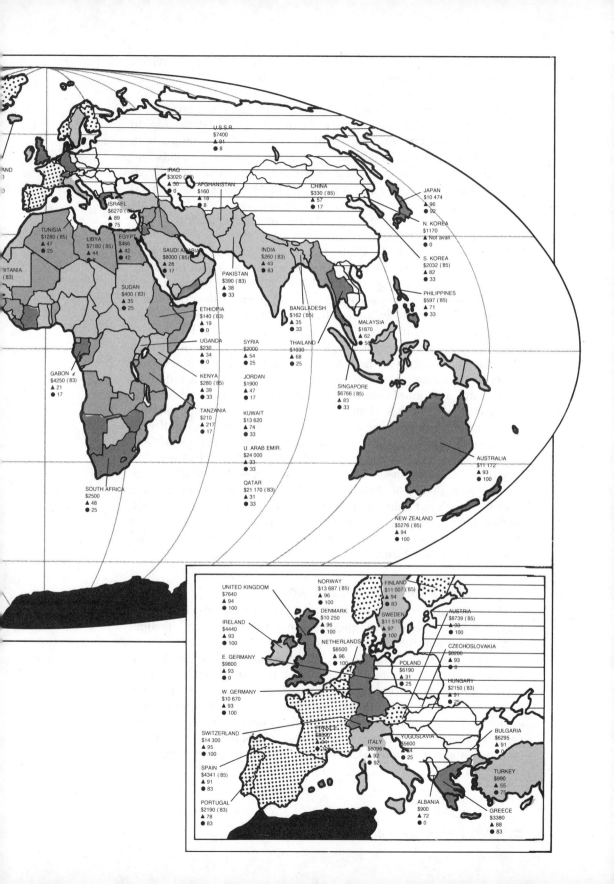

remaining income as they wish on consumer goods and services; they may save it, or they may reinvest it in business.

COMMUNISM: Under this system government (the state) owns all of the country's productive capacity. Government officials decide on how the factors of production will be combined to produce both consumer and capital goods, as well as the types of products and services to be produced. Since property is state-owned, virtually all income is derived from wages and salaries that are largely determined by the state. The individual has few choices as to how to allocate his limited income among the goods and services available.

DEMOCRATIC SOCIALISM: Under this system government generally owns basic industries — mines, utilities, sometimes major industrial complexes — that are important to the development of the country's economy or that employ a large number of people. Most other production is carried out by privately owned firms. The governments in general do not aim to eliminate private ownership of business or property. They are concerned with the collective welfare of the people. Philosophic aims of the government may include equal opportunity for the citizens to employment and education, stable economic growth and high employment, reduction of poverty, social housing and a strong welfare system. To ensure stable economic growth, government, industry and labour together determine overall economic goals for the nation and plan on how to achieve them. Government may therefore set overall wage and price guidelines, but producers and consumers interact in the marketplace to determine the type and quality of consumer goods to be produced. Individuals have the freedom to choose their occupations and the way in which they acquire their income. Citizens also elect their government in the hope that it will exercise the degree of control over economic matters that they desire.

Principles of Capitalism

Capitalism rests on four basic principles: **private ownership of property, freedom of choice, free competition** in the market, and **freedom from government interference.**

No country in the world today operates according to pure capitalistic principles. In most modern nations government is actively involved in ownership of economic enterprises and in managing the economy to protect individuals from the severe swings in business cycles and other undesirable aspects of capitalism. These modified capitalistic systems are known as **mixed economies.** We now focus on the capitalistic system in Canada and see how it has been modified by government.

Capitalism in Canada

How does the Canadian economic system compare to pure capitalism? To answer this question we must examine the four underlying principles of pure capitalism and see how closely Canada adheres to each of them.

Private Property

In North America particularly, individual ownership of property is considered almost sacred. The government cannot take away private property without due process of law. The possibility of ownership provides an incentive for individuals to work hard and save money to acquire property. Ownership becomes a source of pride that helps to ensure that property is well maintained and creates respect for the property of others. Private ownership of property extends to the ownership of business and underlies the profit motive, which encourages business owners and managers to strive to provide new products and services to consumers. Often profits are reinvested in a firm to ensure its growth.

While most business, housing and farmland in Canada remain in private hands, the federal or provincial governments own the remainder. Government may sell or lease this land, or give it away under such legislation as the Homestead Act. Since the mineral rights are owned by the provinces, a large part of provincial government revenue is derived from the leasing of mineral rights and collection of royalities on the raw materials mined.

In addition to owning sizable amounts of land, both the federal government and the provincial governments own a large number of Crown corporations. Many of these Crown corporations, such as Canadian National Railways, compete directly with private companies. Another Crown corporation, the Post Office, is a virtual monopoly for delivering mail. Canals, bridges, roads and airports are all government owned and operated as are power generation and water works. To keep people employed, the federal and provincial governments often buy out private corporations which threaten to close for economic reasons. At other times the government will create a Crown corporation to control a vital economic resource. Between 1976 and 1978, the Saskatchewan government bought out a number of private potash companies because it believed that such a vital enterprise should not be left entirely in the hands of private companies who may not always operate in the best interests of the public. Another example is the automobile insurance industry, which in three western provinces — Manitoba, Saskatchewan and British Columbia — are government owned and operated.

Since the late 1970s, however, the concept of **privatization** — selling government-owned companies back to private investors —

has become popular. This move was based on the belief that under private ownership these enterprises would be managed more efficiently because of the emphasis on profit and also because of the competition from other private companies. In 1979, Premier Bennett of British Columbia returned a number of companies to private ownership with the establishment of the B.C. Resources Investment Corporation. Each B.C. resident was given five free shares in the corporation, the remaining shares being sold to the public and to private institutions. We discuss privatization further in Chapter 12, "Government and Business."

Even when property is in private hands, the government may restrict the owner's right to use it. Municipal governments, for example, have zoning laws to specify which parcels of land may be used for high-rise development, single family dwellings or industrial activity.

Freedom of Choice

The right to own property goes hand in hand with the right to do as one pleases with that property as long as one does not harm others. For the owners of land, resources and capital it means that they have the right to sell it, rent it, trade it or even give it away. Similarly, individuals are free to use their skills and talents as they see fit. Any individual is relatively free to open a business, producing and selling whatever he or she feels will earn a profit. People may change jobs or occupations whenever they wish; they may choose to work or not to work. They are free to spend what they earn, or they may save, invest or dispose of it otherwise.

While Canadians are generally free to pursue their own interests, they also face many restrictions. For example, the federal government regulates how certain industries operate. Television stations must broadcast a certain amount of Canadian content and otherwise conform to regulations. Until recently, the transportation industry was tightly controlled. An airline could not simply start a new route or drop an unprofitable one, nor could a trucker start delivery into any town without approval from a government board. Government also specifies the standards products must meet before they can be sold to the public. Provincial legislation specifies minimum wages, health and safety standards, hours of work, statutory holidays, and minimum annual vacations that employers must provide for their employees. Municipalities require licensing of all business activity.

Government may also restrict entry into an industry such as the delivery of mail, or the operation of a private taxi cab in a city, which is often tightly controlled. In British Columbia the government has decreed that certain lands are to be used for agricultural purposes and cannot be developed for housing or industry, leaving some farmers unable to sell their land for other than farm use. In addition, all B.C. motorists must purchase their auto insurance from the Insurance Corporation of British Columbia, a government-owned monopoly.

Federal, provincial and municipal governments take a large part of our income through taxes, spending it on programs and services that may not always be in accordance with the wishes of all or even most Canadians. Thus, individual choice in the allocation of income is less than complete.

A considerable amount of property and resources is owned or controlled by large corporations. While corporations are theoretically owned by many individual shareholders who elect a board of directors to oversee professional managers, in practice, individual shareholders have little ability to influence what the corporation does. Instead, the professional managers, often with little ownership themselves, determine how the corporation's resources are used, depriving many small owners of this choice.

Other organizations also limit a person's freedom of choice. Often workers are compelled to join labour unions and pay union dues. Their freedom to work may be restricted by seniority rules, and some may be required to go on strike against their will. Various professional organizations limit the number of individuals who may practise a given profession and specify how they should conduct themselves in their business affairs. The medical and legal professions, for example, do not allow their members to compete with one another by advertising or lowering prices.

Freedom of Competition

Competition among businesses that provide similar goods and services ensures that consumers receive the best possible product at the lowest possible price. Competition also provides an incentive for businesses to produce superior products at an affordable price since higher sales revenues usually mean higher profits and ultimately business success.

The private enterprise system, however, does not always ensure that free competition exists. The more successful firms often buy out smaller firms or force them out of business because they cannot compete for various reasons. Unchecked, this activity could ultimately lead to a few large firms controlling product quality and prices, leaving consumers at their mercy.

To protect consumers, the Canadian government has established agencies that monitor and often regulate product quality, prices, and price increases. Sometimes it is in the consumers' interest to have a private company, such as a telephone or utility company, operate as a monopoly. In this instance, competition may result in a wasteful duplication of services unnecessarily increasing the costs of the competing companies. Higher costs would be reflected in higher prices to consumers without necessarily providing better service.

In some instances regulatory agencies may keep prices artificially high to ensure that all Canadians receive adequate service. For example, before deregulation of the airline industry began in 1984, regulatory agencies ensured that air fares on the most often travelled routes were considerably higher than they should have been under free competition. This was done to offset the cost of providing regular air service to Canadians living in northern communities and in cities and communities across Canada where there was considerably less demand for air service. The higher air fares from the popular routes gave Canadian air carriers the revenue and consequently the profit to provide regular air service on the less profitable routes.

Freedom from Government Interference

According to pure capitalism, the role of government is very narrow: to promote free competition and free trade and to provide services — such as national defence, police and fire protection — that private industry would be unlikely to provide because of low or non-existent profits. Government should not interfere by regulating business or manipulating the economy, nor should government provide social welfare to its citizens, since all individuals would be expected to look after themselves.

As we have seen, government in Canada does not adhere to pure capitalism. The capitalistic system, although highly efficient in allocating resources and capable of providing an abundance of goods and services, by its nature rewards only those who are industrious and gifted. Those who are handicapped or unable to find work receive no income. As a result, many people may suffer severe hardship and when competition is curtailed, the consumer has little choice but to accept the quality and price of products and services offered.

Government regulation of business and its intervention in managing the economy are designed to minimize the impact of the capitalistic system's defects. Government has thus instituted programs for unemployment insurance, old age pensions, social welfare and low-cost medical insurance, and it has legislated minimum wages, hours of work, working conditions and fringe benefits. Government also protects the consumer through various agencies that monitor the quality of products and protect against health hazards, for example.

Too much government involvement, however, can interfere with individual freedom of choice, reduce the incentive to work and invest, and make citizens more dependent on the state. The more services, subsidies and regulations that private individuals request the more personal income the government has to take in the form of taxes. Tremendous power has become concentrated in government, which is now both the largest employer and largest purchaser of goods and services in Canada. With this economic power, the danger always exists that government might exert pressure on those that are dependent on it for their livelihood to conform or support its policies.

There has been considerable debate over the size and influence of the public sector in Canada. Issues centre on the efficiency of government in managing tax revenue, allocating resources and providing necessary services. In private firms, the profit motive controls the firm's objectives and influences the performance of its managers. Those who operate government enterprises and provide services, however, often do not have to make a profit, and political objectives may therefore dominate. In addition, as government deepens its social involvement, it requires more detailed information about its citizens. Another major issue, therefore, is the amount of personal information that must be revealed to government officials. We examine the government sector and its relationship to business and private individuals in Chapter 12.

OTHER ECONOMIC SYSTEMS

The majority of people in the world live under an economic system that is not capitalistic, but socialistic. Such systems range from democratic socialism, as in many European nations, to communism, as in the U.S.S.R. and the People's Republic of China. We now examine these systems to see how they attempt to increase the prosperity of their people.

Communism

Communist countries rely on centralized planning to achieve their economic goals. Since the state owns the means of production — land, mines, factories and communication facilities — planners can establish priorities as to what goods and services are needed, and then provide the necessary resources to produce them. Because of this control over the factors of production, communist countries can achieve a rapid build-up of their productive capacity. Poor living conditions can be improved quickly by channelling resources into the production of basic necessities and services. Thus housing, though it may be poorly constructed, is relatively cheap, while social services such as medical care and education are exceptionally good. In fact, extensive social welfare services are the most distinctive achievements of communist countries.

In many communist countries, there is no visible unemployment or inflation because the state has artificially eliminated them. As a consequence offices are often heavily overstaffed, and factories overflow with workers who are rarely fired for not producing. The state controls wages, prices and the kinds of goods available for sale. Thus the official price of an item may remain stable for years, but the item may be available only on the black market at a substantial premium.

A major problem experienced by communist countries is the inability to produce a large variety of quality consumer goods at a price people can afford. In a market economy an increase in price usually signals that the demand for a particular product is greater than the supply. There is no automatic mechanism in a communist country that tells planners of consumer demands. Even when shortages become evident, the bureaucracy and rigid economic planning do not lend themselves to quick shifts in the production of goods. Furthermore, innovation is discouraged since incentive systems for both workers and managers are based primarily on quantity produced. Shifts to new products could slow production and jeopardize bonuses. In addition, consumer goods often take second place to capital goods and to the requirements of the military. As a result, in many communist cities, long lines may form in front of any shop rumoured to have received a shipment of consumer goods, whether it be shoes, fresh fish or fruit.

No doubt the greatest disadvantage of most communist countries today is the loss of political and economic freedom. There is no choice of government, limited career choice and no opportunity to open a private business. In addition, there is little freedom of speech and newspapers and other communication organs are used for the propaganda of the state. Critics of the state are silenced through imprisonment or threat of execution. Strikes rarely occur and are generally quickly suppressed as they have been in Poland over the last decade. In almost all cases there is political and social pressure on individuals to work hard and otherwise conform to the wishes of the state.

The U.S.S.R.

In the Soviet Union, the state owns virtually all means of production in both agriculture and industry. A comprehensive planning process allocates economic resources with primary emphasis on military requirements, capital goods and basic necessities. Planning boards set production targets for more than 70 000 items and set some 200 000 prices of consumer goods, as well as the salaries and wages of the workers. Consumers have little say in the types of consumer goods and services to be produced, or in the choice of their jobs and careers.

In the past, a centralized planning system was clearly helpful to the Soviet Union, enabling it to channel abundant human and material resources into the production of capital goods and the postwar rebuilding of the country. However, this centralized planning, collectivized agriculture and emphasis on heavy industry has produced a rigid and inefficient system. The Soviet economy was growing at an average rate of only 2% by the mid 1980s, lower than any other industrialized country except Britain. Agricultural output grew less than 1% per year between 1971 and 1979 because of a combination of bad weather and bad management. Industrial production has been chronically hampered by supply bottlenecks, absenteeism and equipment failures. Most Soviet industrial goods remain far below worldwide standards in quality and design. For example, a recent Moscow newspaper article noted that 40% of the 28 056 fires reported in the city in 1986 were caused by faulty television sets.[7]

The quota system, which stresses quantity over quality, has disadvantages. Quotas discourage innovation. A manager attempting to change existing practices might fail to meet his production quota, and thus jeopardize his bonuses, benefits, and ultimately his job. For example, no factory has been willing to manufacture corrosion-ressistant plastic instead of cast-iron pipes for fear of falling behind production quotas, which are based on weight.[8]

Another major failure of the Soviet system is in the field of agriculture. Although the U.S.S.R. has the world's largest agricultural area, the agricultural sector, which employs 23% of the labour force and recieves 25% of all investment capital, is unable to feed the population. The blame has been placed on collectivization, which has apparently deadened the initiatives of workers, who have little concern for increasing production. In contrast, while less than 3% of farmland is privately owned, this small area produces approximately 25% of all agricultural output.[9]

With Mikhail Gorbachev taking over as leader of the Soviet Union, change appears to be taking place in this immense country. Although a superpower in terms of weapons, the Soviet Union is a third world country in economic terms. Gorbachev introduced two new words to the Western world; *glasnost*, meaning openness, and *perestroika*, meaning restructuring. He is intent on modernizing the Soviet economy by encouraging small-scale free enterprise and introducing the profit principle in state-owned industries. In 1987 he won backing from the powerful Central Committee plenum to give greater independence to factory and farm managers and leave less power in the hands of the central planning bureaucracy. Furthermore, local managers must be elected by the workers and the state's 48 000 enterprises must fund new and continuing operations from their own profits.[10]

In the speech to the Central Planning Committee he stated that "it is particularly important that the actual pay of every worker be closely linked to his personal contribution to the end result, and that no limit be set." Gorbachev also applied the profit principle to agriculture, calling for a sharp increase in small-scale private farming to supplement the inadequate output of the collective farms. He declared that "competition is central to activating the motive forces of Socialism."[11]

Already, major changes have been made in the Soviet Union. A system of factory inspectors can reject substandard products. The new high-tech factories that combine research and production are mostly run by the Academy of Sciences instead of the ministries, and they are allowed to keep part of the profits they earn. The Academy of the National Economy also functions as a management training institute offering case studies and seminars similar to business schools in North America.

Novosti Photo Service

A fruit and vegetable store in downtown Moscow

The election of plant managers has already happened at several hundred of the state-owned firms. Some firms have also been allowed to buy and sell products abroad without going through the Foreign Trade Ministry, which has been a bureaucratic bottleneck. There is also a new law permitting joint ventures with foreign companies where a Western firm may hold up to 49% interest in a venture with a Soviet company.[12]

One of the first Western companies to take advantage of this change is McDonald's, which signed a joint-venture agreement in 1988 after 12 years of negotiations with the food-service division of Mossoviet (Moscow's City Council). According to the agreement, 20 pairs of golden arches will eventually rise over the Soviet capital. Other fast food chains, including Kentucky Fried Chicken and Pizza Hut, are also negotiating contracts with the Soviets to open restaurants in the city.

Changes are also happening in the agriculture and service sector. Collective farms are beginning to sell produce through their own outlets as well as through state stores. Private-enterprise restaurants are being set up in competition with state-owned establishments. A new law allows small-scale service businesses that are run by an individual or family. For example, owners of private automobiles are allowed to use their cars as taxis during their time off from regular state jobs, and skilled workers like carpenters and plumbers may legally take on private work. In all, some 137 000 of these private enterprises have been registered across the country.[13]

China

In 1949 the communists came to power in China. The communist government immediately implemented strong, centralized controls compelling everyone to work in some productive capacity. The major objective of the communist government was to improve farm output. In the 1970s the whole of China was organized into 50 000 communes, each with about 13 000 people in them. The land was farmed collectively, with local officials telling the farmers what crops they should plant, when and where, even though many of the officials knew little about farming. This so-called great leap forward that established the communes was followed in 1960 by the worst famine of the 20th century when 25 million people starved to death. Nevertheless, the communes remained the most important economic unit in China until 1978 when Deng Xiaoping took over as Chairman of the Communist Party and China began another revolution. A contract system was instituted that makes farmers individually responsible for grain production and gives them permission for sideline occupations. The new policy has freed most rural communities from subsistence existence, bringing prosperity and sometimes wealth to peasant farmers.[14]

In the nine years following 1978, rural income tripled, an increase greater than that which occurred after the first thirty years of communist China. In the more prosperous regions of eastern China, some 5% of the households earn more than 10 000 yuan ($2700) each year. Now so-called super-rich families that earn more than 100 000 yuan per year ($27 000) are starting to appear. As collective farms are returned to private ownership, farmers are producing surpluses to sell in the marketplace for their own profit. Most of the new prosperity comes from so-called sideline work — raising crops for sale on the open market, animal husbandry, fish ponds and so on. Even with these diversions from raising rice and wheat, grain production reached a record high of 405 million tons in 1984, slipping only slightly in 1985 and 1986.[15]

Something akin to the consumer age has now arrived in China. In the cities, new productivity incentives for factory workers have doubled wages and increased bank accounts. The people now eagerly seek out goods such as sunglasses, radios, bright clothing and colour televisions.

To ensure that uncontrolled population growth would not jeopardize economic growth, in the early 1980s the government also launched a campaign to induce each couple to have only one child. The government thus hopes to stabilize the population at 1.2 billion by the end of the 20th century. The campaign includes financial incentives for families who have only one child and financial penalties such as a 10% wage cut for those who have more.[16]

For the present leaders, China's economic growth is not fast enough, even though the government must now cope with some inflation and unemployment. The present rulers have realized that the country's problems cannot be solved by adhering strictly to communist doctrine and are admitting that overemphasis on socialism caused China's economy to suffer.[17] Therefore, they are encouraging a gradual move towards more private ownership. In fact, since 1976 China's communist government has been encouraging its people to open private businesses. From 1978 to 1983 the number of people engaged in private enterprise jumped from 140 000 to 7.54 million. These businesses include retail shops, handicrafts, restaurants and service industries such as automobile repair, cleaning and maintenance. China's government says that private enterprise is not only tolerated but regarded as part of the path to common prosperity.[18]

Hungary

Among the East bloc communist countries — Poland, East Germany, Czechoslovakia, Hungary, Romania and Bulgaria — Hungary has become the most progressive lately in terms of economic and political reforms. In a visit in 1988 to Toronto, Hungary's prime minister expressed the desire to create a dynamic country, in the forefront of scientific development, with an economy that can adjust to the fast changing world economy, and which makes the best use of its human and material resources. Along with economic reforms, Hungary is also cautiously looking to political reform by overhauling its 40-year-old constitution.[19]

In October 1988, the Hungarian parliament approved changes that would allow private companies to employ up to 500 people, permit foreign investors to own 100% of Hungarian companies, and allow individuals to buy stock on the Hungarian stock exchange, which opened in January 1989. Although Hungary has been one of the most progressive East bloc communist countries in the past, 40% of its state-owned businesses are losing money. To make them more competitive, and to reduce the country's huge foreign debt, Hungary wants to introduce private enterprise into its central planning system. While the change is sure to raise unemployment from its current level of 1% and cause inflation to rise even higher than the present rate of 18%, most Hungarians agree that there is no option but to press ahead. Hungary is hoping that foreign investment will help them out, and a number of joint ventures with U.S. companies are already being considered. To help Hungarians learn Western management skills, a management training school is being established. While no one expects immediate results, if Hungary succeeds, it could lead the way for other Eastern European nations.[20]

Democratic Socialism

Having looked at both extremes — capitalism and communism — it is easier to understand the underlying objectives of social democratic governments.

A social democratic government must be elected by the people who can choose from a number of political parties. Once in power the government tries to direct the economy to serve the general interest of the people. Major emphasis is place on providing comprehensive welfare programs, minimizing unemployment and creating an egalitarian society by reducing the gap between rich and poor. To support these policies the state has to control economic decision-making and emphasize economic planning which often means nationalizing major industries.

While social democrats are cautious about revolutionary changes such as rapid nationalization of major industries, they try to accomplish their objectives through steeply progressive taxes on income, capital gains, profits and inheritances. Government revenue is used to finance cradle-to-grave welfare services and provide benefits such as child allowances, free tuition for universities and colleges, generous sick pay, free hospital care and high retirement pensions. To ensure high employment, jobs are often created in government, while labour legislation in a number of European countries makes it difficult for private firms to lay off workers. In addition, many social democratic governments also actively encourage worker participation in management and ensure that private business organizations provide generous benefits to their workers.

Democratic socialism is practised in countries as diverse as Sweden, Austria, Norway, Egypt, and the Netherlands. In Sweden, for example, basic industries such as the postal service, railways, telecommunications and most utilities are government-owned, while most steel, automobile, shipbuilding and consumer goods industries remain in private hands. Representatives of labour, government and industry serve on a central planning board which attempts to allocate resources and money to industry. Although Sweden's main goal is to ensure high employment as opposed to high economic growth, supply and demand work to determine what consumer goods will be produced.

The objectives of social democratic governments are largely humanitarian and what the leaders believe to be in the best interests of the people. However, socialist policies tend to reduce individual initiative because the high taxes, and the policies that act as a curtailment of the rights of private ownership take away private incentive. As a result, investment in private business is discouraged and technological innovation, capital replacement and ultimately the productive capacity of the economy are limited. The lack of incentive to work and invest is a major reason why social democratic countries also experience economic stagnation and inflation. The economy does not grow fast enough to produce the goods and services demanded by the people. Increasingly, social democratic governments are realizing that to finance the costs of social welfare, they must increase productivity and provide an incentive to work.[21]

Choosing an Economic System

How does a country choose an economic system? For many impoverished third world nations, the choice is difficult. People who are starving need food and shelter. A capitalistic business system can work to eliminate poverty, but it takes time, since fundamental social, economic and political changes are required. Often nations that have tried to emulate Western capitalist countries have found themselves with a dictatorship in which a few members of the ruling class become wealthy, while the majority of the population remains poor. The people may therefore come to regard capitalism as exploitative, and eventually revolt in favour of some form of socialism.

TABLE 1.2
A comparison of economic systems

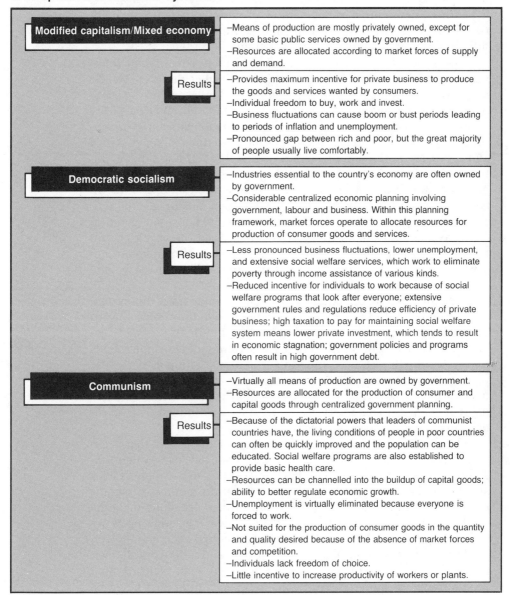

Modified capitalism/Mixed economy	—Means of production are mostly privately owned, except for some basic public services owned by government. —Resources are allocated according to market forces of supply and demand.
Results	—Provides maximum incentive for private business to produce the goods and services wanted by consumers. —Individual freedom to buy, work and invest. —Business fluctuations can cause boom or bust periods leading to periods of inflation and unemployment. —Pronounced gap between rich and poor, but the great majority of people usually live comfortably.
Democratic socialism	—Industries essential to the country's economy are often owned by government. —Considerable centralized economic planning involving government, labour and business. Within this planning framework, market forces operate to allocate resources for production of consumer goods and services.
Results	—Less pronounced business fluctuations, lower unemployment, and extensive social welfare services, which work to eliminate poverty through income assistance of various kinds. —Reduced incentive for individuals to work because of social welfare programs that look after everyone; extensive government rules and regulations reduce efficiency of private business; high taxation to pay for maintaining social welfare system means lower private investment, which tends to result in economic stagnation; government policies and programs often result in high government debt.
Communism	—Virtually all means of production are owned by government. —Resources are allocated for the production of consumer and capital goods through centralized government planning.
Results	—Because of the dictatorial powers that leaders of communist countries have, the living conditions of people in poor countries can often be quickly improved and the population can be educated. Social welfare programs are also established to provide basic health care. —Resources can be channelled into the buildup of capital goods; ability to better regulate economic growth. —Unemployment is virtually eliminated because everyone is forced to work. —Not suited for the production of consumer goods in the quantity and quality desired because of the absence of market forces and competition. —Individuals lack freedom of choice. —Little incentive to increase productivity of workers or plants.

Let us briefly review the advantages and disadvantages of each of the three major economic systems

Communism is often commended for raising the standard of living in poor countries in a relatively short period of time, improving living conditions dramatically and providing numerous social welfare services. However, communism almost inevitably seems to be accompanied by totalitarianism — the government requires enormous power over individuals in order to achieve its sweeping goals. Even then, communist states cannot provide sufficient consumer goods for their citizens, nor can they eliminate unemployment or inflation except by concealing both artificially.

Most capitalistic systems have considerable government intervention and are therefore better labelled "mixed economies." While they still face problems of unemployment and inflation, mixed economies have less severe business cycles, virtually eliminating severe depressions because of a variety of social programs such as unemployment insurance and fiscal and monetary government policy. (Fiscal and monetary policy are discussed in Chapter 12.) Capitalist countries encourage private ownership of property, considerable freedom of choice for individuals, and active competition among firms. In conjunction with the profit motive, the system encourages the production of large quantities and many varieties of consumer goods at a quality that consumers want. The gap between the very rich and the very poor remains wide, but the vast majority of people fall into a middle income range, while social legislation and extensive welfare systems help those in need.

It is unlikely that Canadians would ever want to trade this system for communism. But what about moving more to the centre, toward a social democracy like Sweden's? With a middle-of-the-road economic system, Sweden produces a wide variety of consumer goods for its people. In fact, according to various international yearbooks, per capita income in Sweden is among the highest in the world, and the cradle-to-grave welfare system is better than most. There are few poor people, and some earn very high incomes indeed. Is a social democracy not a superior system?

Opinions would probably vary widely. Many believe that eventually all countries will adopt this middle-of-the-road system, regardless of which system they have today. But social democracies also have disadvantages. Ambitious social and economic programs have created huge bureaucracies, and arbitrary decisions made by the bureaucracies restrict individual initiative. The high taxes required to pay for social services reduce individual economic power, while the services themselves reduce the incentive to work. In fact, the motivation to work has been curtailed to such a degree that productivity has suffered. And since workers can almost never be fired, absenteeism is high. Social democracies have had some success controlling unemployment, but only through make-work programs and job creation in the public serivce. The resulting bureaucracy tends to reduce efficiency in government operations and is responsible for a high level of waste. Social democracies are also not immune to inflation and economic stagnation.

Issue: *Is Canada Moving Toward Socialism?*

We often hear it said that Canada is becoming a socialist country. The evidence most often cited is the increase in the number of social welfare services available — unemployment insurance, old age pensions, welfare, low-cost medical insurance, housing grants and subsidies to low-income families.

However, the provision of these benefits does not reflect the true meaning of socialism. Socialism means public rather than private ownership, a government-planned economy as opposed to individual economic choice, and government monopoly rather than free competition among firms.

The increasing number of social welfare benefits introduced by the federal government is simply an acknowledgement that the capitalistic system has some shortcomings, which can be tempered. Thus some of the excess that the system is capable of producing is channelled to reward those who have contributed a life's work to society, and to provide temporary relief to those who are unable to provide for themselves. In effect, these social welfare benefits help to level the inequalities caused by business cycles. Without reducing everyone's income to a common level, they ensure that a basic level of necessities is available to all.

Thus these measures help to strengthen the system by keeping the economy at a higher level of production than might otherwise be the case, which in turn ensures a high level of employment. At the same time, social welfare as practised in Canada refutes the standard accusation that capitalism rewards only the rich, and not the poor. Indeed, it shows that the traditional communist motto — "From each according to his ability, to each according to his need" — can also apply to capitalism, without the dictatorship and loss of freedom associated with the communist system.

SOURCE: See George Hogan, "Free Enterprise," in K.J. Rea and J.T. McLeod, eds., *Business and Government in Canada*, 2nd ed. (Toronto: Methuen Publications, 1976), p. 69.

This democratic socialism does not appear to be significantly "better" than the present Canadian system, and may not even be as good. However, as government continues to impose more regulations, spend more money on social programs, take a more active role in job creation and tax more heavily to pay for government services, Canada may drift towards a greater degree of socialism. Once there, it may be difficult — if not impossible — to return to a position with less government intervention in the economy.

On the other hand, if social democratic countries like Sweden can find ways to restore the incentive to work and increase productivity, social democracy may yet become the most workable economic system.

WHY STUDY BUSINESS?

At the beginning of this chapter we saw how well the average Canadian lives. Since then, we have seen how the high standard of living in a capitalistic system depends on efficient and effective use of the factors of production by organizations. If our standard of living — indeed, our entire way of life — depends on our business system, it makes sense that we should understand how it works.

To understand how a business system operates, we must examine business organizations and the way they function in the economic system as a whole. We must understand how a firm produces goods and services, how it raises the money required to build manufacturing plants and purchase machinery and equipment, and how it recruits and pays people for their work. If we study the marketing function of a business, we will be better equipped to understand the importance of advertising, as well as the roles of the wholesaler and retailer. At the same time, we must also examine the function of managers: how they coordinate raw materials, labour, capital and technology for the efficient production of goods and services.

While the study of business is generally recommended, it is particularly important for those who intend to go into management in a large Canadian corporation or open their own small business. The principles of business and management remain the same regardless of the company's size, although the method of operation may be different. Large corporations tend to have highly formalized organizational structures, with many specialists to perform the tasks that owners of small businesses must do themselves. It is therefore necessary that anyone intending to operate a small business acquire a more general business education and then hire specialists when appropriate, while those planning to enter large corporations should acquire more specialized training and education in their field of interest.

Finally, understanding our business system enables us to better evaluate the effectiveness of existing as well as proposed government policies. We can examine the claims made by business people, politicians, government officials and labour leaders and we are not likely to be easily persuaded by individuals who blindly condemn the system, demanding change at any cost.

NOTES

1. "Calcutta: India's Maligned Metropolis," *National Geographic*, Vol. 143, No. 4, April 1973, p. 534. See also, "And if Mexico City seems bad . . .", *TIME*, August 6, 1984, p. 26.

2. Kathy Farrel, "Your Average Canadians," *Weekend Magazine*, Vol. 28, No. 26, July 1, 1978, pp. 4-7. See also *Canada Yearbook 1988*, (Ottawa: Minister of Supply and Services), Chapter 5.

3. *Ibid.*

4. "The *Maclean's*/Decima Poll," *Maclean's*, January 4, 1988, p. 35.

5. Robert L. Heilbroner, *The Making of Economic Society*, 6th ed. (Prentice-Hall: Englewood Cliffs, N.J. 1980), Chaps. 3-4.

6. *Ibid.*, p. 87.

7. "Can he bring it off?", *TIME*, July 27, 1987, pp. 20-6.

8. See "Inside the U.S.S.R.," *TIME*, June 23, 1980, pp. 44-7.

9. See "Socialism: Trials and Errors," *TIME*, March 13, 1978, pp. 18-31.

10. See "Can he bring it off?", *TIME*, July 27, 1987, pp. 20-6.

11. *Ibid.*

12. *Ibid.*

13. *Ibid.*

14. "A World Turned Upside Down," *The Economist*, "A Survey of China's Economy," August 1, 1987.

15. *Ibid.*

16. "Population nears billion," *Vancouver Sun*, April 30, 1981.

17. "China says private enterprise part of path to prosperity," *Vancouver Sun*, March 3, 1984, p. A8.

18. Fred Harrison, "Consumer Age arrives in China," *The Financial Post*, May 23, 1981.

19. Andrew Phillips, "The Scent of Freedom," *Maclean's*, August 22, 1988, p. 17. The above is a lead-in article, followed by a separate discussion of the social and economic condition of each of the six East bloc communist countries.

20. Gail Shares and Rose Brady, "Hungary vaults into the free market," *Business Week*, October 10, 1988, p. 56.

21. Bob Kuttner, "Sweden/Denmark Trials of Two Welfare States," *The Atlantic Monthly*, December 1983, pp. 14-22.

CHAPTER SUMMARY

A country's standard of living depends on the production of goods and services by the business organizations that are basic entities of its economic system. An economic system is a mechanism that regulates the production and distribution of goods and services in a country by helping to make three basic decisions — what goods and services are to be produced, how to produce them, and how to distribute the product among the people.

The Canadian economic system is basically capitalistic; but the principles underlying pure capitalism — freedom of choice, private property, freedom of competition, and freedom from government intervention — have been influenced in varying degrees by the actions of government or other social institutions. In many other countries, the economic system is socialist and ranges from communism, in which government directs all economic and most social matters, to democratic socialism, in which government intervenes extensively in the nation's economic affairs, but holds power only as long as it is elected by the people.

All three systems have their advantages and disadvantages. Capitalism, because of the market system, is particularly well-suited to the production of capital goods and a wide range of consumer goods and services. However, capitalist systems are subject to business cycles which can hurt economic activity and cause large-scale unemployment. While most industrialized capitalist countries can protect their people from the ups and downs of the market system through comprehensive social welfare systems, people in less wealthy capitalist countries may suffer.

In a communist system, government controls the factors of production and can therefore channel resources into the production of goods or services deemed necessary. Therefore, business cycles are eliminated and unemployment and inflation closely controlled. Communism can quickly improve subsistence living conditions that exist in third world countries, educate the population relatively quickly, and provide basic social welfare services, housing and medical care. However, the system is unable to increase living standards substantially because market forces are not allowed to allocate resources based on consumer demand. Since private individuals generally cannot go into business, there is no competition and little incentive to provide consumers with the goods and services they need and want. Most importantly, as communist systems are basically one-party dictatorships, the political and economic freedom of the people is drastically curtailed.

Social democratic countries are a blend of the two extremes. Major industries are usually owned by government while most businesses that produce consumer goods are privately owned. However, economic freedom is often restricted through high taxation and government regulations, which discourage private incentive. Extensive social welfare services tend to reduce the incentive to work as well, contributing to low productivity and slow economic growth.

As both consumers and workers, it is important for us to understand the Canadian business system in order to make informed judgments about the country's future.

KEY TERMS

Standard of living
Gross national product (GNP)
Gross national income (GNI)
Gross domestic product
Per capita GNP
Production
Factors of production
Labour
Land
Capital
Technology
Entrepreneur
Business organizations
Capital goods

Consumer goods
Non-profit organizations
Business
Economics
Business cycles
Economic systems
Capitalism
Laissez-faire capitalism
Mixed economy
Privatization
Socialism
Communism
Social democracy

REVIEW QUESTIONS

1. How is the standard of living determined? What does it indicate about the material well-being of people in a particular country?
2. List the five factors of production. Briefly explain how each factor contributes to the total production of a country.
3. How can a knowledge of economics help business people?
4. What is an economic system?
5. What is the relationship between a country's economic and political systems?
6. Outline the basic differences between the three major economic systems: capitalism, democratic socialism and communism.
7. What are the four basic principles underlying pure capitalism? How does the economic system in Canada differ from pure capitalism?
8. Why is private property so central to capitalism?
9. What are the advantages and disadvantages of each of the three major economic systems?
10. Why should every citizen have some knowledge of the Canadian business system?

DISCUSSION QUESTIONS

1. If you were the head of government in a third world country with a large population, how would you attempt to raise the standard of living?
2. Discuss the following statement: "It is inevitable that Canada will become a social democratic country like Sweden, since capitalism simply does not work."

3. There is no doubt that government intervention in our economic system has helped to make individuals' lives more secure. However, deepening government intervention means more regulation of the activities of individuals and businesses; it also means that government requires an increasing amount of information about its citizens. What are your views on government intervention in the economy and in the private lives of individuals?

4. Can a communist system, such as in the U.S.S.R. or China, continue to exist, or is there a natural tendency to move toward the centre on the continuum of economic systems, toward social democracy? Is this tendency to move toward the centre also true of capitalist countries?

CASE 1-1 Raising the Standard of Living

India, with the second largest population in the world, is one of the poorest nations. Millions of people suffer from malnutrition and many die each year from starvation. The Indian government is interested in improving the well-being of its people, and has commissioned various

TABLE 1.3
Economic statistics for four countries (1985 unless otherwise indicated)

	India	U.S.	U.S.S.R.	People's Rep. of China
GDP (billions 1985 US $)	$190.0	$3988.5	$2062.6	$1042.4
GDP (per capita 1985 US $)	$250	$16710	$7400	$354.3
Real growth	3.5%	2.3%	1.2%	12.0%
Population (millions)	767.7	238.6	278.9	1042.4
Annual increase in population	2.1%	0.8%	0.9%	0.9%
Labour force				
engaged in agriculture	72%	2.9%	19.4%	66%
engaged in industry	11%	24.6%	25%	13%
engaged in trade and services	17%	72.5%	55.6%	21%
Literacy	36%	99%	98%	76.5%
Life expectancy (years)	46	73	70	67
Infant mortality per 1000 births	90	11	27.9	n.a.
GNP spent on education	2.5%	7.5% (1976)	7.6% (1974)	n.a.

n.a. = figures not available

SOURCES: *Handbook of Economic Statistics, 1986* (Washington, D.C.: U.S. Government Printing Office), 1986: *The Statesman's Yearbook* (London: Macmillan Press Ltd.), 1986-87.

agencies and individuals to study the country's problems and recomment some possible corrective measures. The following figures provide data for comparing India with the United States, the U.S.S.R. and the People's Republic of China.

QUESTIONS

1. To raise the standard of living of its people, India must do two things almost simultaneously. What are they? (Refer to the standard of living equation for this answer.)

2. Under what circumstances would it be possible for India to increase its GNP without increasing its standard of living? Explain clearly, again referring to the standard of living equation.

3. List and discuss the arguments that can be presented for and against a communist system in India.

4. Compare the data presented for each country in Table 1.3.
   a) What factor or factors can you see to account for the differences in per capita GNP of the four countries?
   b) Does the type of ownership of business (private or government) have any effect on the difference in standard of living? If so, explain why this might have an effect.

5. Briefly explain how each of the five factors of production can contribute to raising the standard of living for the people of a country.

6. Outline briefly the steps the Indian government should take to achieve its economic goals.

CASE 1-2 Business Careers in Favour Again

If your children want to take economics or business at university rather than sociology or political science, they're in the new wave. Our best and brightest young people are planning business careers, a major attitudinal shift that's one of the most bullish signs for the longer-run development of Canada's economy.

As usual, the swing started in the U.S. Since 1980, enrollments in business-related disciplines at major colleges and universities have been soaring. The trend is so advanced there that, at Harvard, the traditional breeding ground for liberal social activists bent on government careers, economics majors now outnumber majors in any other field by a huge margin.

But these days a business career is compatible with any undergraduate discipline you care to name. Roger Smith, CEO of Detroit's General Motors Corp., recently spoke to students at Yale about the potential of a liberal arts degree. Smith indicated that training in the arts prepares students for management positions, that innovators with broad perspectives will help companies compete internationally.

Regardless of whether an arts degree or a business or economics degree is obtained, students can learn to adapt their knowledge to the work environment, and it's clear that more and more Canadian university students are getting ready for careers in the private sector.

This is a dramatic break with the past. In the '60s and '70s, many of the smartest students scorned business. Their hero was Ralph Nader, and they sought careers in government and universities where they could help build a social democratic society in which benign, enlightened governments would redistribute wealth and set national priorities. All of it was to be based on the insights of bright, energetic, generous rulers.

The liberal enthusiasts said that business was the refuge of the mediocre, the self-interested and the well connected, and they weren't all wrong. Indeed, the second tier of management at some of Canada's biggest companies includes considerable deadwood that never did look like good lumber.

Which goes to show that, at any given time, there is only so much good talent to go around. If you are building a society based on ever-expanding government, you need to recruit smart people to run it. If you are building a society based on ever-expanding productivity and wealth creation, you need to recruit smart people to run the large and small companies that will propel the economy.

Much of the agonizing about Canada's pitiful productivity record in recent years ignored the reality that the public sector was attracting a disproportionate amount of our talent as well as our economic wealth. In addition to struggling along with an increasing burden of regulation and a diminishing share of total resources, the private sector has had its middle-management ranks clogged up with dullards.

Things are different now for two reasons: first, the limits on government's ability to create an earthly paradise have become obvious, even to utopians; secondly, governments are collectively broke.

The Canadian economy has grown faster in the past two years than it has for most of the past decade, yet the combined deficits of our governments continue at extraordinarily high levels. As a result governments are struggling to find the money to fund existing programs, and there's almost no room to consider shiny new proposals for imaginative government intervention. Civil servants who once redistributed wealth now must spend much of their time redistributing poverty.

As this financial tourniquet tightens, we're seeing a massive shift in spending priorities: knowledge jobs such as university professorships are receiving minimal pay increases, while public-sector workers, thanks to powerful unions able to inconvenience society with strikes, are still making real gains. The rest of the money goes for the most basic universal programs. All the creativity and idealism that went into disigning the programs is history: computers now burp out the cheques.

This government poverty, which looks to be permanent, is wonderful news for the Canadian economy. Without a rich, ambitious government, society will have to meet more of its needs through the market. Without a rich government that's able to entice top-notch people, Canadian business should become a tougher competitive force in a tougher competitive world. With that in mind, here's to today's and tomorrow's grads: may you become great entrepreneurs and executives. Your country needs you.

SOURCE: Donald Coxe, "Sectoral Magnetism," *Canadian Business*, August 1986, p. 98.

QUESTIONS

1. According to the author, what has been the central problem with Canada's economy in the recent past?
2. Why had business fallen out of favour with Canada's young people? Why are they now once again flocking to take business at colleges and universities?
3. Why does this author believe that "government poverty" is good for Canada?

CHAPTER 2

Foundations of the Canadian Business System

CHAPTER OUTLINE

CHAPTER PREVIEW

In Chapter 2 we examine four factors central to the capitalistic business system: capital, entrepreneurship, profit and competition. We also survey the development of the Canadian economy, from the original fur trade to the complex industrial economy of today.

LEARNING OBJECTIVES

After reading this chapter you should be able to explain:

1. The role of capital, entrepreneurship, profit and competition in the capitalistic business system in Canada;

2. How profit and competition act as regulators to ensure that consumers receive the best possible product at the lowest possible price;
3. How the modern market system differs from the system that existed during the time of the industrial revolution;
4. The major phases in the history of Canada's economic development;
5. The gradual change from a manufacturing to a service economy;
6. The effect of government involvement on the Canadian economy today.

As we saw in Chapter 1, Canada's capitalistic economic system provides us with the goods and services we need and want. But to understand how this happens, we must examine the crucial factors — capital, entrepreneurship, the profit motive and competition — on which capitalism is based. The profit motive and the entrepreneurial drive provide the incentive for individuals to establish businesses. Capital enhances the productivity of labour so goods can be produced in quantity, and competition ensures that consumers get the best quality product at the lowest possible price.

THE IMPORTANCE OF CAPITAL

Many people think of capital as money, and indeed the term is often used in that context. But in the economic sense, **capital** refers to the tools, machines and equipment used in the production of consumer goods and services. Money is a medium of exchange. It can be used to purchase capital goods, but cannot be used directly in the production process. For example, if an individual becomes bankrupt, he or she cannot carry on with the business, because there is no money to buy materials or pay salaries. On the other hand, the capital goods that exist in the business — machines and equipment — are still available for production.

Capital is important for two reasons. First, without capital, many products could not be produced at all. Tools, machines and equipment provide human beings with the ability to perform operations that would otherwise be impossible. Second, capital makes human labour more productive, as it facilitates the specialization of labour in the production of goods. For example, a complex product such as an automobile can be built even by unskilled workers with the help of an assembly line. Each complex manufacturing operation is broken down into small, easily learned tasks that unskilled or semi-skilled workers can perform rapidly with the help of appropriate machines and equipment. This is known as **specialization of labour**. When individuals are trained to perform simple tasks rapidly, the total output of a group of workers is much greater than it would be if each individual worker was required to make the entire item. It is estimated that each manufacturing worker in Canada today has approximately $60 000 worth of capital goods at his or her disposal.

Capital Formation

Capital formation refers to a country's accumulation of capital stock for the purpose of production. This means that capital formation requires saving on the part of individuals and businesses. A certain portion of gross national income must be saved to ensure that, first, worn out capital can be replaced and, second, that we an add to our stock of capital goods as technology advances and as new capital and consumer goods are developed. Not spending all of our income on consumer goods, in other words saving a certain portion of gross national income, frees resources for research and development and the production of capital goods. The more that is saved, the greater is the rate of capital formation, which can significantly increase future productivity and GNP and consequently the standard of living.

Capital Formation: A Historical Perspective

The industrial revolution in Britain was not a pleasant time for industrial workers. The pitiful wages they received for long hours of work under the most terrible conditions imaginable were barely enough to allow them to buy the bare essentials for themselves and their families. Entire families, including children, had to work to make ends meet. The goods they produced were generally exported or bought by the wealthy upper class. Because of the low wages paid to their workers and the high prices charged for their goods in the British colonies and other foreign countries, the early industrialists earned large profits. Although many lived in great style, they all had one thing in common — investment for investment's sake. They were above all interested in technological progress and increasing manufacturing output. Most of the profits were reinvested into plant expansion, capital goods and improvement of production processes.

This rapid capital formation was responsible for an immense increase in the output of goods and in productivity. Although this great increase in output did not benefit the average worker immediately, by 1870 the long-run effects were making themselves felt. Weekly earnings were higher than the price of necessities, and hours of work were shorter. While Britain was still a far from abundant society, and certainly not an affluent one, the tide had turned. The standard of living was subsequently to rise quickly. As the working classes earned more money the had more to spend, and as basic needs were increasingly fulfilled, more luxury goods were demanded. As England's middle class grew, more consumer goods were demanded. As businesses responded to the increased demand, their profits rose, which provided more money for expansion of production facilities. This in turn provided more jobs, resulting in more income and even greater consumption expenditures, which started the whole cycle anew.

In North America the capital formation process was similar. Together with vast amounts of land and natural resources, Canadians and Americans could develop their economies quickly and raise their standard of living.

Capital Formation and Productivity

Productivity is a term that describes the relationship between output and input. Output represents the goods and services produced, while input refers to the quantity of labour, capital and resources used to produce that output. By increasing productivity we are in effect producing a greater quantity of output — goods — from the same amount of input. We can measure productivity by calculating output per person-hour. The three most important factors that help to increase the output per person-hour have been found to be capital investment, technological innovation and change, and the quality of labour. Thus, a growth in capital investment and consequently in capital formation increases productivity.

Inflation and the Effect on Capital Formation

As long as an adequate amount of total GNP is saved to replace worn-out capital and provide funds for research and development of new capital, productivity should continue to rise along with economic output. However, if consumers suddenly decide to save less and spend more on consumer goods, fewer dollars would be available for investment in capital goods and research and development. If this trend continues for any length of time it can hinder capital formation and affect productivity, since worn-out capital goods are not replaced with new and more efficient ones to meet the increased consumer demand. If demand for consumer goods continues to increase, ultimately the production capacity of the economy will be reached. If investment dollars are still not available to increase production capacity, the result is a general rise in the prices of all goods. This is known as **inflation**.

Once inflation has taken root it can become a vicious cycle as consumers attempt to stay ahead of it. Their incomes increase but so do the prices of goods. As inflation rises further, people rush to buy goods in an attempt to beat further price increases. Saving money becomes rarer as money saved quickly loses its value. Businesses that want to raise money for expansion and capital renewal are faced with high interest rates, which either threaten most new ventures with failure or make the cost too high in relation to the return. Furthermore, the cost of renewing machinery, plants and equipment rises as quickly as that of consumer goods. Unless checked, inflation gets worse — the demand for goods increases further, yet the capacity for production remains the same or even decreases because of lower productivity due to worn-out equipment that becomes increasingly expensive to replace.

Inflation exists in any economy where money is used as a medium of exchange. When it amounts to only a few percent per year, its effect on the economy is minimal. However, if inflation begins to increase and nothing is done to reverse the trend, it can become a serious problem as it erodes savings and investment and ultimately affects productivity and the standard of living. Most industrialized nations experienced high inflation in the 1970s and early 1980s.

Capital Investment in Canada

Figure 2.1 shows total capital expenditures in Canada for the years 1969–1986. Although there appears to be a tremendous increase in

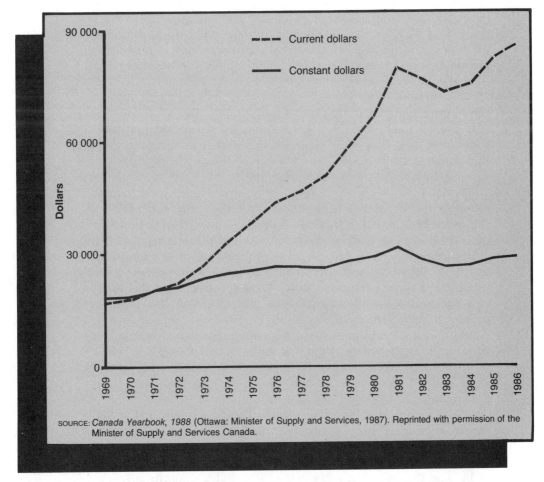

SOURCE: *Canada Yearbook, 1988* (Ottawa: Minister of Supply and Services, 1987). Reprinted with permission of the Minister of Supply and Services Canada.

Figure 2.1   Capital expenditures, Canada, 1969–1986 ($000 000), current vs. constant (1971) dollars

capital investment in terms of current dollars, when inflation is taken into account, that is, when we compare capital investment in 1971 constant dollars, the increase is only slight.

The large drop in capital investment after 1981 was due to the recession, which seriously affected business. Many smaller businesses become bankrupt and most others operated at a loss for a few years. Without a healthy profit outlook, businesses do not commit themselves to large capital expenditures. Figure 2.1 shows only capital expenditures for new construction, equipment and machinery; spending for repairs, which can amount to 25% of expenditures for new items, is not taken into account.

ENTREPRENEURSHIP

An **entrepreneur** is an individual who brings together the factors of production — land, labour, capital and technology — to produce goods and services for consumers. Entrepreneurs transform ideas into concrete products often using their own money to establish a business. Success may be rewarded handsomely; on the other hand, the entire investment could also be lost.

It is this ability to take risk, either financial or personal, that sets the entrepreneur apart from other individuals. But why does the entrepreneur take risks? No doubt some are like poker players — sometimes they win, and sometimes they lose, but the appeal is in the gambling itself. As soon as the suspense is over, regardless of success, they move on to something else.

Various studies of the entrepreneurial character have yielded different results. Some have shown that the entrepreneur is an achievement-oriented individual, someone who will work tirelessly until the project at hand is completed. Other studies have found that entrepreneurs do not readily fit into organizations. They are restless, unable to submit to authority and unskilled at solving managerial problems. A more persuasive study, however, has found that many entrepreneurs were individuals whose ideas could not be developed in their former companies, and so they started out on their own.[1]

Although all entrepreneurs presumably hope to be rewarded for their efforts, in many cases their primary objective is simply to create. As in the arts, where authors, painters and filmmakers may go for years without any significant reward, for many entrepreneurs it is the creative process itself that is most important.

We often hear that the entrepreneurial spirit is lacking in Canada, and that we leave the risk-taking to people from other countries, primarily the United States. While this charge is debatable, there is some evidence that Canadians tend to be conservative in their risk-taking and thus are slow to exploit new business opportunities. Canadian financiers have been criticized for their conservative attitude toward financing new ventures for Canadians, yet appear willing to lend money to foreign companies and individuals who want to establish new ventures in Canada.

Can entrepreneurship be taught? Some universities and colleges have introduced programs to stimulate and develop the entrepreneurial spirit in Canadians. Certainly, the specific knowledge and skills required to establish a new business can be taught, along with the principles of good management. However, whether the risk-taking ability, drive and creativity can be taught is another question. There are those who claim that entrepreneurs, like poets, are born, not made, and cannot be developed.

In any event, there are definite advantages to supporting the development of entrepreneurs. Government intervention can stimulate new businesses, which are the greatest generators of new jobs in the course of their rapid expansion and growth. Large corporations, on the other hand, usually grow at a much slower rate, and are often more concerned with reducing costs by exchanging human labour for capital equipment. We will examine the importance of small business to the economy in Chapter 3.

THE IMPORTANCE OF PROFIT

It sometimes seems that the term "profit" has become a dirty word. Many individuals, including some politicians, equate profit with profiteering — making excessive profits by charging exorbitant prices for products or services. Of course profiteering does occur. Some businesses are set up precisely to sell a shoddy product or service at high prices for a short time, then close shop and move on. But the majority of businesses do not operate in that manner. Their owners establish them with permanency in mind, to produce and sell goods and services expecting to earn a profit.

What is Profit?

A **profit** is a surplus of revenues over expenditures. It is what remains after all expenses associated with operating the business have been deducted from the revenue received from customers. However, a consistent surplus (profit) is by no means guaranteed. In fact, many firms incur periodic losses due either to the seasonal nature of their businesses or to the swings of business cycles.

We have stated what is meant by profit, but we have only hinted at its importance to our economic system. Why is profit so crucial to capitalism? Profit provides incentive to establish a business and thus creates jobs. Channelled into the purchase of capital goods, it helps make the production process more efficient and helps to raise the standard of living. It is also a regulator of business activities — firms that do not produce a needed product do not make a profit and thus go out of business. Profit is also used by firms to pay investors for the use of their money. Finally, since almost half of all profits realized by business is paid to government in taxes, profit can be used for social services that benefit society in general.

Profit is an Incentive

Profit is the major incentive for establishing a business. Profitable small businesses can provide their owners with a good income and prestige in the community, while allowing them independence. Many of the benefits that apply to owners of small businesses also apply to professional managers whose careers and income depend on the corporation's success and survival. Because managers gain personal benefit from a successful business, they strive for growth and compete with other firms for sales and profits. In this process they develop and produce new, often better, products and services, benefiting consumers and creating new job opportunities.

Profit as a Measure of Efficiency and Effectiveness

To understand how profit helps to measure the efficiency and effectiveness of a business, we must first define the terms. **Efficiency** refers to the relationship between input and output. Greater efficiency means that a greater output can be achieved from the same amount of input. If, for example, two firms produce the same product but one is more profitable than the other, we could say that the more profitable firm is more efficient. Efficiency may be due to newer machines, better-trained production workers, better management or a better sales force. Ultimately the more efficient firm will likely survive, whereas the less efficient one will disappear.

Aside from helping to gauge the efficiency of a business, profit also gauges the success of an operation. A company that shows only marginal profits over the years, perhaps even requiring government assistance, cannot be considered successful. The firm or industry is probably not producing what consumers want; it is not **effective** in serving the needs of the people. The factors of production would be put to better use if the firm produced some other good or service.

Thus, profit acts as a **regulator**. To survive over a period of years, a business must be profitable and thus both efficient and effective. It must offer a product that people want at a price they can afford and produce that product at the lowest cost in terms of raw materials, labour and capital. The quest for profit thus ensures that the factors of production are properly allocated.

Profit for Expansion and Capital Formation

Firms are continuously striving to become more profitable by offering consumers a better product, better service or a lower price than the competition. To remain ahead of the competition and remain profitable, they must develop better manufacturing processes, or better products, or both. A large part of business profit is therefore used to replace manufacturing plants and equipment that have become obsolete or worn-out, increase the existing capital stock to expand production, and conduct basic research to develop new products and processes or improve existing ones.

Profit as a Return to Investors

A portion of business profits is used to pay shareholders — individuals who have invested their money in a business. Their per share-based payment is called a **dividend**. If a firm is profitable it can pay dividends. A well-managed firm with a consistent dividend payment record attracts buyers and the increased demand tends to raise the price of the firm's shares. People invest in a business because they hope that the potential return — dividends plus appreciation of a firm's share prices — will be greater than the return they would get by putting their money in a bank savings account or Canada Savings Bonds, for example.

Profits Contribute to Society

A business' drive for profit is not harmful to society — it is an effective method of allocating society's resources. The profit motive ensures that businesses are effective in what they do and efficient in the way they allocate the factors of production. When profits are available for reinvestment, society benefits from increased productivity by a rise in the overall standard of living. In addition, almost half of all profits are paid in the form of taxes to the federal, provincial and municipal governments. Tax revenue can be used to finance social programs or to produce goods or services that might otherwise not be produced by private firms because there is little chance of making a profit.

Thus, profit stimulates the private sector of our economy, increasing output and employment, and at the same time helps to keep that sector in check. A similar control mechanism for non-profit organizations and government operations would be helpful to measure their effectiveness and efficiency.

How High are Profits?

Firms that report a high profit are often criticized or charged with gouging the consumer. While profiteering should be exposed, of course, there are often valid reasons for a firm showing extraordinarily high profits in a given year. For example, it may be the first time that profits earned by a newly purchased subsidiary firm have been included with those of the parent company. High profits might also reflect the sale of a piece of real estate that has appreciated significantly.

Sometimes firms earn high profits simply because they have the right product at the right time. A firm may have been struggling for years until a sudden change in consumer tastes puts its product in demand and makes the business profitable. At other times, a firm may profit because it is quick to perceive a new market and take advantage of the situation by providing a needed product or service. In both of these instances, however, excess profits are soon eliminated as new firms offer similar or even improved products to the consumer, often at lower prices.

Perhaps the major reason businesses show a high profit during particular years, is that business cycles can cause substantial fluctuations in profits over time. During a recession, many firms actually lose money, sometimes for several years. These losses incurred during the bad years must be recovered with higher profits during the good years.

For example, the profits of 173 public companies rose 74% in the last quarter of 1983 over the same period a year earlier. Though this rise seems outrageous, one has to consider that many of these companies suffered severe losses during the previous years while continuing to employ workers. Ford Motor Co. of Canada, for example, reported a 1983, fourth-quarter profit of $84.3 million compared to a $56.6 million loss a year earlier. During the same period, Stelco showed a $5.4 million profit compared to a $36.5 million loss.[2] Similar changes in profit could be cited for many other companies that are slowly recovering from a recession. Thus it is inaccurate to compare profits between years or single out individual companies for particularly profitable years without taking all factors into consideration.

How Canadians See Profits

In a survey conducted in the 1970s, Canadians generally estimated profits to be much higher than they actually were, and the majority of Canadians believed profits were excessive (see Figure 2.2). Some Canadians believed that profits ran as high as 40¢ on the sales dollar. Whether or not these views are still widely held is difficult to say. However, the concept of profit is generally not well understood and the public is often unaware of the general level of profits and how and why they fluctuate.

In general, actual profits for manufacturing industries fluctuate between 7¢ and 11¢ per dollar on average. For individual industries,

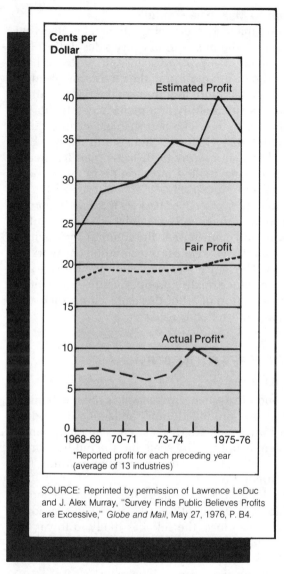

Figure 2.2 Public attitudes to manufacturers' profits

profit margins vary from 2.5¢ per dollar for food processors, for example, to 13.5¢ per dollar for communications and pipe manufacturing. In any event, actual profits are well below the level estimated by the general public; in fact, they are less than what the public believes a fair profit for manufacturers would be. Nevertheless, over the last half century profits have gradually increased, as the article "Distorted Profits" indicates.

Do Businesses Attempt to Maximize Profits?

Every business owner and manager has profit as the major objective. But do businesses in fact get the most out of every sales dollar? Not often. Managers cannot maximize profits because they do not have complete knowledge of the future or of how the environment might affect the firm. Planning is an attempt to minimize the risks of future uncertainty, but even the most carefully laid plans may fall short as conditions change from day to day. The best managers can do is to plan for a profit that will satisfy investors and the firm's need for capital replacement and long-term growth. If firms plan for steady earnings in the long run, the inevitable short-term profit fluctuations are less likely to damage their operation.

Firms thus have many other objectives besides maximizing profit. Since they want to become permanently established, they want to be good corporate citizens and contribute to the community in which they operate. They also want loyal, well-trained employees working in pleasant surroundings. They are concerned about their image and reputation; they want to produce quality products and be innovators in their industry. The realization of all of these objectives increases the cost of doing business and reduces profit.

PROFIT, COMPETITION AND THE MARKET

Under a capitalistic economic system, the market is the mechanism that regulates what goods are produced, how the factors of production are allocated, and how goods are distributed. The operation of a country's **market system** is not readily seen, but the public market where sellers and buyers gather to exchange money for produce, fish and meat provides an illustration.

Although public market prices are usually marked on the goods, sellers are not inflexible. If large quantities of a perishable product are left as the day draws to a close, the seller is likely to lower the price to induce people to buy. On the other hand, when a particular commodity is in short supply, it is likely to be sold quickly. The seller has no need to reduce prices nor do buyers expect it.

To some extent then, a public market allows the interaction between buyer and seller to determine the prices at which existing goods are sold. If a particular product is in demand, prices for the existing quantities will rise and indicate that production should be increased. As producers bring greater quantities to market, the price will eventually drop again as demand is satisfied. If quantities cannot be easily increased, then prices of existing quantities will rise and remain at a level where only those who absolutely want the product will buy it.

Distorted Profits

Profit has become one of the great shibboleths of modern times, separating the sheep from the goats, capitalists from marxists, rich from poor, boss from employee. It is at the centre of our economic system, and certainly shapes the priorities of business as no other objective does. The newspapers, even the sophisticated *Report on Business*, still seem unable to distinguish between profit as a proportion of revenue (or assets) and growth in profits; both are expressed as percentages, and headlines leave the impression that a 50% increase in profits is no different from a 50% profit. The fact that profits may have grown from an 8% return on investment to 12% to make that 50% increase is, at best, buried deep down in the columns of newsprint.

So what does profit look like historically? The chart shows profit and other investment income as a percentage of gross domestic product, a relationship chosen to cover a wide ground but exclude some controversial side issues. And we can see that over the past half century profit has been grow-

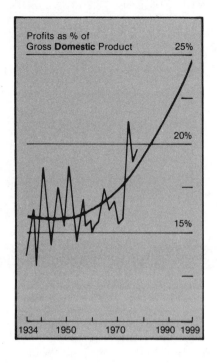

Profits as % of Gross **Domestic** Product

ing as a percentage of GDP. Figures before 1934 are excluded because the bad results of the Depression would have pointed the forecast even higher. Note that the trend from 1934 to 1973, that is, before the recent era of what have been called inflation profits

(including the all-time peak of 21.5% in 1974), is still a rising curve, though not so spectacular in slope. So here is a reasonable way of reckoning profits that shows they are indeed on the increase.

SOURCE: Reprinted by permission of *Executive*, Sept. 1979, p. 18.

Figure 2.3 shows this interaction between buyers and sellers by a **demand and supply schedule**. The schedule shows the various quantities that will be demanded depending on the price charged. If the price of peaches is low, for example, then people will buy more than if the price were high. Different individuals have different wants, so each person has a unique demand schedule, but the total

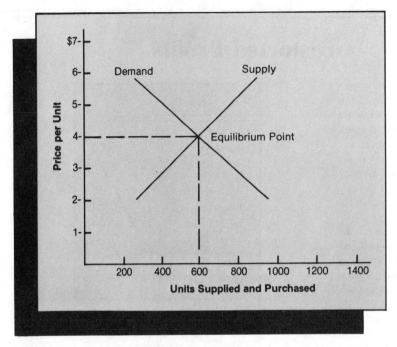

Figure 2.3 Product supply and demand

demand schedule for a particular product is an average for all consumers. The supply schedule, on the other hand, shows the opposite. When prices are high, producers would be happy to produce and supply larger quantities as opposed to when prices are low.

When these two schedules are superimposed over each other, the point at which they cross — the **equilibrium point** — indicates the quantity that will be bought at the given price. Both consumer and producer are satisfied with the product price indicated at the equilibrium point. Keep in mind that there are always some people who will pay a high price for any product, while others are unable to pay even a very low price.

The market system works well when there are many producers. With only one or a few producers, however, the orderly working of the system is disrupted, since a few producers can easily control the amount of product supplied to consumers and keep prices artificially high. You can see from the supply and demand schedule that if less product is supplied, the price per unit is higher. This kind of control over supply and price can be detrimental to consumers, particularly if the product or service is a necessity. In this case, the consumer must accept what the producer offers regardless of quality or price.

Hence the market system requires competition between producer and consumer in order to function properly. Without competition as a counterforce, the drive for profits could be detrimental to individual consumers and to society as a whole. Imagine a situation in which there were only one producer in each industry. Consumers would be compelled to purchase what each produced, regardless of price or quality. Chances are that there would be little product variety, while the producer would have no particular incentive for innovation in product design or increased efficiency in the production process. Consumers would have only one alternative — refusal to purchase the product at all.

Effective and Responsible Competition

An ideal market system would consist of many small firms, each competing with the other to provide the best products at the lowest possible cost. Under this system, one seller's gain is another seller's loss. Everyone is actively striving to gain a greater share of customers.

Unfortunately, **effective competition** is not often present in the private enterprise system. A few giant firms produce steel, automobiles and electrical products, while there is often only one producer for such services as electricity, water and telephone. In addition, groups such as marketing boards and producers' co-ops can reduce competition by setting prices and limiting quantities. Labour unions and employers' association also impede the competitive forces of the market system.

Responsible competition should be practised by firms that compete among themselves. Competition should not be so aggressive as to destroy viable businesses through dishonest advertising and the discrediting of competitors. Unfair methods of competition could damage a firm's reputation to the point of bankruptcy and they may border on criminal acts which society cannot condone.

In an attempt to maintain effective and responsible competition, the federal government has introduced legislation under the Combines Investigations Act. This legislation allows the government to press charges should violations occur with respect to mergers, agreements, monopolies, price discrimination, false and misleading advertising or price maintenance. Where monopolies are necessary because competition would mean higher prices and possibly poorer service, the government regulates prices, quality of service, and various other aspects of operation. We will examine competition legislation in more detail in Chapter 12.

Types of Competition

We can classify competition under four main types depending on the number of firms that exist in an industry and how they behave toward other firms. These categories are perfect or pure competition, monopolistic competition, oligopoly and monopoly.

Perfect or Pure Competition

Although economists distinguish between **perfect** and **pure competition**, we will consider the two terms as one and the same. Under this competitive situation, there are many small firms in a particular industry, each producing a virtually identical product. There will be a good number of competing firms because the cost of establishing a small business is relatively low. And since each firm is small, it can never produce a sufficient quantity to influence the current market price.

The agricultural industry is a good example. Products are identical and no single producer has the power to influence the price of the product in the marketplace by withholding production. As prices of commodities are established in the market, producers enter or leave the industry depending on their ability to operate. High beef prices, for example, induce people to raise beef cattle, while low prices cause a drop in beef production.

During the last decade, however, the federal and provincial governments have allowed various segments of this industry to establish marketing boards, to which all producers of a particular product must belong. The objective is to protect individual producers from excessive competition and fluctuations in demand for the product, while ensuring orderly distribution for a particular commodity. Although marketing boards may guarantee steadier earnings for the producer, they have been accused of artificially restricting output and raising consumer product prices. They may also cause problems in other facets of the agricultural industry. The Issue in this chapter discusses marketing boards in more detail.

Monopolistic Competition

Under **monopolistic competition**, a large number of relatively small firms produce a product or provide a service which is slightly different, or at least perceived as different by the consumer. As a result, each firm exerts some influence on the prices charged. Retail operations such as service stations are a good example. The different gasoline and automotive products sold by each station, along with the various services each provides, serve to distinguish one station from another. Again, access to the industry is relatively easy.

Oligopoly

Under an **oligopoly**, there is only a small number of producers. Whether the product is different, as in the case of automobiles, or similar, as in steel, entry into these industries is virtually impossible because of the great amounts of investment capital required. While the producers have considerable control over prices, they all stand to lose

TABLE 2.1
Summary of the four main types of competition

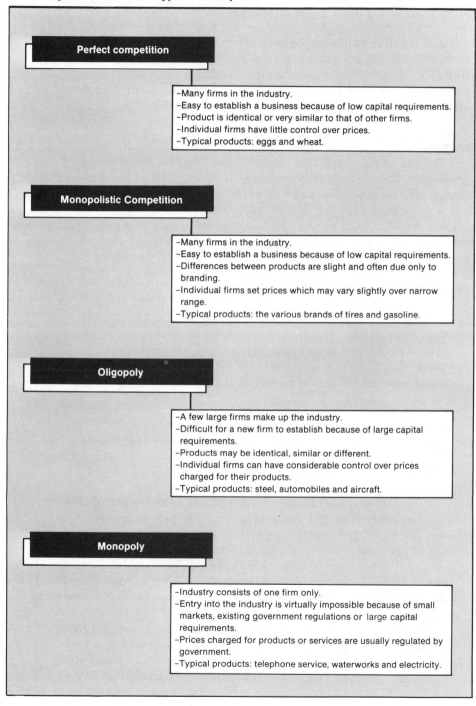

Perfect competition

–Many firms in the industry.
–Easy to establish a business because of low capital requirements.
–Product is identical or very similar to that of other firms.
–Individual firms have little control over prices.
–Typical products: eggs and wheat.

Monopolistic Competition

–Many firms in the industry.
–Easy to establish a business because of low capital requirements.
–Differences between products are slight and often due only to branding.
–Individual firms set prices which may vary slightly over narrow range.
–Typical products: the various brands of tires and gasoline.

Oligopoly

–A few large firms make up the industry.
–Difficult for a new firm to establish because of large capital requirements.
–Products may be identical, similar or different.
–Individual firms can have considerable control over prices charged for their products.
–Typical products: steel, automobiles and aircraft.

Monopoly

–Industry consists of one firm only.
–Entry into the industry is virtually impossible because of small markets, existing government regulations or large capital requirements.
–Prices charged for products or services are usually regulated by government.
–Typical products: telephone service, waterworks and electricity.

if price competition is intense, since, if one firm were to reduce prices, all the others would soon be forced to follow.

To attract customers away from other firms, businesses use non-price methods of competition such as advertising, consistent upgrading of existing products, or offering new products and better customer service. In the case of automobile companies, for example, each tries to gain customers by offering extended warranties, quality construction and constant product changes, whether technical or simply cosmetic.

Monopoly

When there is only one seller or producer, the situation is known as a **monopoly**. Often a monopoly exists because the total market may be too small for more than one producer to operate profitably. Even when a monopoly exists, however, consumers usually do have a choice as to whether they will buy the product. If the only beef producer in the area charges too much, for example, consumers can always switch to chicken or pork. Where there is no substitute available, such as telephone, utility or transportation services, the government regulates product quality, price and service.

A **monopsony** is the term given to a monopoly on the buyer's side. Examples are giant supermarket chains that buy from small suppliers, or small manufacturers that depend on government contracts. These small companies are virtually at the mercy of the buyer and have little power to demand higher prices for their products. Often their only alternative is to refuse the order, which usually means severe hardship or bankruptcy.

Issue: *Do Marketing Boards Impede Competition?*

While the net income of non-farm unincorporated businesses rose fairly smoothly over the years 1955 to 1975, net income of farm operators fluctuated wildly. A major factor contributing to fluctuations is the weather, which can lead to either a large or a small harvest. In either case, the farmer's income is likely to be affected. Another factor is the investment required by today's farmer which is usually substantially greater than that required by many other small businesses.

The objective of **marketing boards** is to operate in the best long-term interests of the producer and consumer by smoothing out seasonal and cyclical supply irregularities and providing farmers with a fair return for their labour and investment. Marketing boards also

---

attempt to promote marketing efficiency through centralized coordination of product and market research, transportation and selling.

Every province has marketing boards for each major commodity, and the provincial boards differ widely in their authority over the control of both marketing and production. With the institution of the National Farm Products Marketing Act in 1972, the first national marketing boards were established — the Canadian Egg Marketing Agency and the Canadian Turkey Marketing Agency. Although operating under separate legislation, the Canadian Dairy Commission and the Canadian Wheat Board are also national boards.

Marketing boards are criticized for their attempt to manage supply, even though only a few operate comprehensive supply management systems (dairy products, eggs, turkeys and tobacco). Some charge that the boards are government-mandated cartels (monopolies) designed to raise prices above competitive levels, which amounts to a tax to consumers on eggs, broilers, turkeys and milk. Estimates place this "tax" at a total of $500 million to $1 billion annually, not including direct government subsidies to these producers. This tax is not imposed by a legislature but by those who benefit directly from it such as farmers. In addition the tax is not visible as is a sales tax so it is difficult to measure. Finally, the cost of collecting the tax is high for both consumers and producers. In a recent study of the B.C. Egg Marketing Board, it was found that every dollar transferred from consumer to producer cost the consumer $1.25 and the producers as much as 65¢.[1]

By intervening in the normal operation of the market system, marketing boards create two major problems. First, the cost of operating the marketing boards is added to the farm price of the product, and the consumer actually pays proportionally more than the original cost added to the farm price because the retail price is calculated as a percentage of the wholesale price. Second, the production quota system, which has to go along with any supply-management system, restricts farmers from freely expanding their production according to their ability to run an efficient operation. For example, all egg producers have quotas on egg-laying hens. Without such a quota, a farmer cannot sell eggs. If he produces more than the quota allows, the board can have the excess hens destroyed. Fluid milk producers are required to fulfill their quotas in both summer and winter even though fluid milk is less costly to produce in the summer. Those farmers who do not comply are faced with penalties. Since quotas are a must to be in business, they actually acquire value over time. The quota can be sold to someone else who wants to go into business or to another farmer who wants to increase production and needs a higher quota. Unfortunately, their high cost often deters new entrants to the industry. It is also charged that the security of a fixed income based on a fixed output will deter producers from putting forth the extra effort and cost needed to increase output.

In 1981 the Economic Council of Canada called for the deregulation of the agricultural industry. The marketing boards replied that deregulation would force many farmers out of business and plunge the rest back into a dog-eat-dog system of competition. Making more quotas available for the various products would reduce the price of those goods, but it would also create a surplus of product, leaving some producers with a market and some without one. Those who would like to see the powers of marketing boards stripped away suggest that they should exist as a producer association to seek new export markets, to increase domestic demand by advertising and to help avoid shortages and surpluses by spreading current market information to producers.[2]

[1] Thomas E. Borcherding and Gary W. Dorosh, "The Egg Marketing Board, A Case Study of Monopoly and its Social Costs" (The Fraser Institute, 1981).
[2] Rick Ouston, "Think Tank Director raps marketing boards," *Vancouver Sun*, June 12, 1981.

How Competition is Limited

Although new businesses are continually being established, many go bankrupt. Those that are successful or have a product with a promising future are often bought by larger companies. For example, in the early 1920s there were at least 300 automobile manufacturing companies in the U.S., but by 1960 the industry had consolidated into four big firms. A similar trend appears to have started in the computer industry. The number of computer manufacturers dropped from 200 to 150 between 1983 and 1985, and the number of major software producers dropped from 200 to 50 in the same period. Thus the market system has a natural tendency to reduce the number of firms in a given industry, ultimately resulting in an oligopoly.

In 1975, the federal government established a royal commission to determine whether large corporations were detrimental to Canadian society and whether they had the power to influence official government decisions and public policy. The commission found that large corporations were not detrimental.

But corporate size can and does influence competition. Because of the large amounts of capital required, few new firms are able to enter industries such as automobile or steel production, oil refining and chemical manufacturing. In addition, large companies usually have strong engineering, marketing and service organizations, with which new companies find it difficult to compete. Large companies also have the financial resources for large-scale advertising and sales promotion, giving them a substantial competitive edge. IBM, for example, did not introduce its personal computer until many other companies had introduced personal computers and were well established. Even though IBM's model was not as advanced as those of other companies, it quickly gained an almost 30% market share within two years primarily because of IBM's advertising resources and its dominance and reputation in the mainframe computer industry.

At the same time, despite efforts to promote competition, government can also adversely affect it. For example, the imposition of tariffs keeps the prices of domestic goods higher than they would be if international companies could compete freely with Canadian firms. Various governments agencies can affect competition as well, by establishing regulations that companies must follow. In the broadcasting industry, for example, the Canadian Radio-Television and Telecommunications Commission (CRTC) can affect competition through its power to grant or withdraw licences for radio or television stations. Finally, perhaps the greatest factor limiting competition is a firm's lack of knowledge concerning its competitors — what their plans are, what their markets are like, and how high their production costs are.

THE MARKET SYSTEM IN THE EARLY DAYS

During the time of the industrial revolution in Britain, the market system operated unhampered by government regulations. Individuals depended entirely on themselves for survival, and government did not intervene. While a few wealthy individuals led an opulent life, it was at the expense of often appalling conditions for the working classes.

One notable observer of the situation was Adam Smith, an economist at the University of Glasgow. Engaged in an overall study of the social and economic life of the time, Smith was mainly concerned with how a modern economic system produced national wealth. He outlined the workings of that system, which had as its ultimate aim the production of goods and services for consumption by society, in his book *An Inquiry Into the Nature and Causes of the Wealth of Nations.*

Adam Smith's View of the Market System

Published in 1776, Smith's wide-ranging work was an economic recreation of life in his time. He saw individuals pursuing their own self-interest with no traditional authority to guide them or tell them what to do — yet out of this seeming confusion a certain order emerged. Smith termed the unseen force that seemed to create this order the "invisible hand of the market." Smith viewed the market mechanism basically as competition between individuals, each in pursuit of his own self-interest. However, he also saw that this competition resulted in the production of goods that people wanted, in the quantity they wanted, and at a price they were prepared to pay. It allowed businessmen to strive for higher profits and labourers for higher wages, while the exchange of services and property provided individuals with greater benefits than either group had known before the transaction.

Hence the market system — where self-interest and competition among individuals appeared to work to the benefit of society — could not tolerate interference by any group, especially by government. The system depended on freedom of action for all, or "laissez-faire." Although Smith believed government should provide defence, justice and various public works — services which would not otherwise be provided because of the lack of profit — he believed that any other interference would seriously impair the system's operation.

The Market System and Economic Growth

There was one further advantage to the Smithian system — economic growth. Many other economists of the time considered the existing system to be static, incapable of expansion. In their view, workers would always remain at a subsistence level. The only hope of escape would be an eventual revolution of the working class, to overthrow the capitalist system and replace it with another in which everyone would contribute and share equally. Smith, however, explained that economic growth could come about through the capital-enhanced specialization of labour, which would increase productivity, leading to greater output, higher profits and ultimately a larger fund from which higher wages could be paid. Once workers could afford to support larger families, the growing population would require an increased supply of goods and services, resulting in still further division of labour. The cycle would continue to repeat itself in its entirety.

Thus Adam Smith's world was one of optimism, even though it was conceived during one of the most dismal times in the history of industrial society. Through the self-interest motives of individuals and the free operation of the market mechanism, society could pull itself up by its own bootstraps.

THE GROWTH OF BUSINESS IN CANADA

The capitalistic economic system and its underlying principles were ideal for the development of North America. Here was a vast, unexplored territory where an individual could strike out on his own and easily acquire land or establish a business. As more settlers came to North America and the population increased, formerly small businesses also grew. As transportation systems developed, the market for many products expanded further still, contributing all the more to industrial growth.

Industrial development and economic growth in Canada and the United States differed markedly, however, even though the two countries shared the same language and a similar cultural background. Business and industry in the United States expanded largely through private initiative, with little government interference until the late 19th century. Canada's economic development, on the other hand, depended almost from the beginning on public funds and government policy, and that dependence has shaped Canada's economic development to the present day.

We will examine Canada's economic and business development in more detail in the remainder of this chapter, comparing it, where appropriate, with that of the United States.

Canadian Business Development: From the Beginning to Confederation

The first settlements in Canada were established by Europeans, drawn to North America by the fertile fishing waters off the Atlantic coast. International rivalry for the products of these waters was intense, though it was somewhat resolved when the Spanish and Portuguese left the continent to the French and English. However, rivalry between the two latter factions deepened with the subsequent discovery of the new land's rich fur resources.

The French quickly established an efficient trading organization in the St. Lawrence region which by 1763 had extended westward to the Saskatchewan River. However, the network encountered severe competition from the English Hudson's Bay Company, established in 1670. Operating out of Hudson Bay gave the English the advantage of easier access to the West.

Although France surrendered its Canadian possessions to Britain in 1763, rivalry between the Hudson's Bay Company and the Montreal merchants continued. In 1787, some of the Montreal merchants combined with other, smaller trading groups to form the Northwest Company, and as competition intensified, it occasionally resulted in violence. Finally, in 1821 the Northwest Company was forced to merge with the Hudson's Bay Company. Nevertheless, because of the fur trade, by the early 19th century Canada had become a continental entity reaching from the Atlantic to the Pacific. The article "From Fur Traders to Takeover Kings" traces the development of the Hudson's Bay Company to the present day.

In the late 1800s, the Hudson's Bay Company developed from a
fur trader to a retailer

From Fur Traders to Takeover Kings

In 1611 Henry Hudson, his young son John, five men with scurvy and a loyal ship's carpenter were cast off the Discovery in a small open boat into the freezing waters of James Bay, never to be seen again. Victims of a mutiny, Hudson and the rest died unaware of his accomplishment. It took others, and through them the founders of the Hudson's Bay Co., to reveal the value of the English navigator's discovery of the fur trade. He had found the northern forest, the richest beaver domicile in the world, a fur trader's El Dorado.

The Hudson's Bay Co. (the common designation of "the Governor and Company of Adventurers of England trading into Hudson's Bay") was incorporated in 1670 and received a grant of "a plantation or colony" to be called Rupert's Land in honour of Prince Rupert, first governor of the company. The grant covered Hudson Strait and the drainage basins of Hudson and James Bays, and as far east as Ungava, south to the Red River Valley and west to the valleys of the north and south branches of the Saskatchewan River, some 1 486 000

squares miles, 38.7 percent of Canada's present area.

The Bay's early history paralleled frontier Canada. The company negotiated its way through Indian wars and survived decades of British battles with France, suffering the loss of forts, trading posts, ships and men. In 1821, the Bay took over the North West Co., made up of Montreal merchants and hardy wilderness men, flourishing as never before. Over the next few decades both public sympathy and political support for monopoly lessened and in 1870 the Bay sold Rupert's

Land to Canada for £300 000, retaining a claim to seven million acres of land.

While fur continued as the backbone of the Bay's business, a land department was created, a wholesale operation became a new distributing unit, a chain of large retail stores was built and cities grew around old trading posts. During the First World War the company was the shipping agent for the French government and the rest of the 20th century has seen diversification of interests into oil and gas companies, including Hudson's Bay Oil and Gas Co. Ltd.

Today, traditional trade in wild fur is less than three percent of the company's business, replaced by merchandise sales in the more than 250 urban and northern stores from Newfoundland to the Yukon. Since Donald McGiverin became president in 1972, 31 new stores have been opened, the company has entered the catalogue stores business under the name Shop-Rite with 63 stores in Ontario, and gained control of the Zeller's Ltd. chain of stores. Now, McGiverin and the Bay have added Simpsons, Ltd. to its historic shelf. It's a long way from Henry Hudson.

SOURCE: Warren Gerard, ''From Fur Traders to Takeover Kings,'' *Maclean's Magazine*, Dec. 25, 1978, p. 34. ©1978 by Maclean's Magazine; reprinted by permission.

From Fur Trading to Industrial Development

As time passed, the fur trade's dominance in Canada slowly gave way to regional interests and industries. While the West and the Pacific Coast continued to pursue the fur trade, Nova Scotia concentrated on fishing. As European demand for Canadian timber increased, the lumber industry expanded in Montreal, New Brunswick, the St. Lawrence region and the Canadian Shield. The regional specialization of industry was aided by the natural waterways of the St. Lawrence region, which facilitated transportation of these products to Europe.

Following Canada's war with the United States in 1812, there was an influx of immigrants from the United States, and the population was further boosted by massive immigration from Europe and England in the 1820s. Many immigrants settled in the St. Lawrence region and as far west as the Great Lakes. These new settlers turned their attention to producing new products and commodities, particularly potash and wheat, which could be readily exported. As a result, wheat eventually replaced timber as the dominant staple commodity.

The Need for a Transportation System

At the same time, these new settlers also demanded more manufactured goods, many of which were available only from England, Europe and the United States. To move these goods and commodities required great improvements in the transportation system, especially with the opening of the Prairies.

The impetus was thus provided in the 1840s to build the St. Lawrence canals, designed to make the system a major transportation

Halifax harbour — one of Canada's busiest ports

artery for trade between Europe and the colonies. Moreover, the promoters of this water system were convinced that it could become the major transportation artery for shipping goods from the U.S. midwest to Europe and other parts of the world.

Unfortunately for the future Canada, this hope did not materialize, since U.S. developmental policies and the completion of the Erie Canal in 1825 had preordained New York as the major North American port. Once it was realized that the canals had failed to capture their market, the colonies hastened to expand their own transportation network by building supplementary and trunk railways linking the entire St. Lawrence area with the Atlantic coast.

Thus in 1866, on the eve of Confederation, the colonies soon to be known as Canada stood alone, shouldering a huge national debt for a transportation system with unused capacity because of its failure to capture the lucrative American traffic. And looming in the west was the threat of American expansion into the thinly populated Prairies and Pacific Coast. If Canada was to survive as a continental nation, that could not be allowed to happen.

The Bank of Montreal, Canada's oldest chartered bank, took part in many developments in the nation's growth

From 1867 to 1900: The National Policy

The Reasons for Confederation

Economic considerations played a major role in the Confederation of 1867. Although the new nation would still depend primarily on the production and export of staple goods, increased production and economic expansion were among the most important benefits expected. The anticipated increase in immigration, particularly to the west, would lead to a greater internal demand for manufactured goods. The growing population in the west would likely increase production of wheat and other staple products for export to Britain and Europe. At the same time, it would reduce the threat of U.S. expansion into the prairies. As a side benefit, it was also expected that greater industrial activity and western expansion would mean better utilization of the newly built transportation system in the St. Lawrence and Great Lakes regions. This in turn would increase revenues and ensure payment of the debt incurred in building the system.[3]

There was another major benefit from economic union for the various provinces. Their complementary resources — gold and timber in British Columbia, wheat and furs in the prairies, minerals in the Lake Superior country, wheat, timber, oil and manufacturing in the existing Canada, and coal, iron, fish and forests in the Maritimes — would provide regional and national economic stability. Although regional interests led to bitter debate between the provinces, agreement was eventually reached.

Other benefits from Confederation were also envisioned. While the various provinces and regions hoped for growth in internal trade, they also anticipated increased trade with the rest of the world as Canada gained prominence and the ability to bargain for more trading privileges with other nations. Finally, Confederation was expected to improve Canada's world credit position, ensuring new loans for both public and private development.

Objectives of the National Policy

Following Confederation, the first federal government introduced a program known as the **National Policy**, which had three major objectives.

First, it was designed to help increase the export of staple commodities, especially wheat; it was also hoped that the consequent settlement of the west would thwart American invasion of the prairies. The second objective was an increase in the manufacturing of finished goods within Canada through the imposition of high tariffs. The third objective was a transportation link between east and west, to move staple commodities from the west to the east for export and ship manufactured goods to the western settlers. The link was to be accomplished through the building of the Canadian Pacific Railway, which required heavy public financing.

To make the National Policy succeed, the north-south trade relations already established between the Canadian west and the United States would have to be severed. The western settlers would have to be compelled to buy their goods from Canadian manufacturers. Thus the tariff policy of 1879 was instituted, imposing high tariffs on imported goods. The tariff for finished consumer goods, for example, was 30%. For fully manufactured industrial machinery and equipment, the tariff was 25%, while for the bulk of miscellaneous manufactured products, semi-finished goods and industrial materials it ranged between 10% and 20%. The textile industry already established in eastern Canada received high tariff protection, since large quantities of textiles were imported, and tariffs were also imposed on agricultural products, even though Canada was primarily an exporter in this area. In 1887, even higher duties were imposed and although various changes were made periodically thereafter, these tariffs remained basically unchanged until 1930.[4]

Timothy Eaton revolutionized retail trade by selling items
for cash at a fixed price

Impact of the National Policy

The National Policy, particularly the imposition of tariffs, is given
some credit for helping the growth of manufacturing industries, especially in the east. The Tory government of the time claimed that
the policy was a key factor in lessening the effects of the Great
Depression of 1873–1879. However, the intervention of other economic factors makes it difficult to assess the policy's role. What is
clear is the effect of the National Policy on the western settler. The
imposition of tariffs ensured that trade would now move in an east-
west direction, rather than north-south. Thus western settlers were
required to pay higher prices for manufactured goods, since Canadian

industries produced smaller quantities than their U.S. counterparts, for a much smaller market.

By 1870 only about one fifth of the gross national product came from manufacturing, of which sawmill and gristmill output amounted to approximately one third. New industries such as cotton factories and secondary iron and steel fabricating plants were gradually established, however, and while production was still small-scale, the new order of industrialism as evidenced in the U.S. began to become noticeable in Canada.[5]

Unfortunately this industrialization could not help Canada in the period from 1873 to 1896, which was characterized by a long recession known at that time as the Great Depression. This period represented the tail-end of the great boom era of steam and iron, which — together with a general overproduction of goods in the developed world — led to declines in prices of the primary products upon which the Canadian economy depended. And although growth in Canada's manufacturing industry increased during this period, it was not sufficient to offset the soaring rate of unemployment caused by the loss of exports of primary products.

Nevertheless, this long recession did include a boom period. The initial recessionary period from 1873 to 1879 was followed by a boom from 1879 to 1884. After 1880 the huge spending for construction of the CPR gave an additional boost to the Canadian economy. With the completion of the CPR, however, the phase of prosperity ended and a new recession set in affecting the entire economy, particularly secondary manufacturing industries, and causing heavy unemployment. During this latter period even the manufacturing output in Canada was extremely low.[6]

The Golden Age of Canadian Growth

In 1896 an overall turning point in world economic conditions brought new prosperity for Canada as exports began to rise again, first in the mining sector and later in wheat. Exports of minerals rose by 500% in the period between 1896 and 1901, compared to overall exports which rose only 162% for the same period. After 1901 exports of agricultural products rose sharply, with a marked drop in minerals and smaller declines in other products.

During this period, all sectors of the economy experienced growth in investment and capital formation. Expansion was also felt in manufacturing, although the major industrial centres were shifting between the provinces. The west experienced tremendous growth of its manufacturing sector, while the eastern provinces gave up their importance as manufacturing centres, although Ontario remained dominant. Nevertheless, by 1911 manufacturing occupations accounted for only 14% of the labour force in Canada, compared to

34% in agriculture. In contrast, manufacturing occupations in the U.S. accounted for 21% of the labour force, and agriculture for only 31%.

Although this golden era was marked by economic expansion, it did not appear to help the individual Canadian. While a demand for labour caused unemployment to drop from 1900 to 1914, the general level of wages also fell slightly. At the same time, food prices soared because the increase in agricultural production was being exported to other countries, particularly the U.S. and England.

Another factor in the higher prices for food and other products was an increase in distribution costs. The Canadian system was geared for export, not for local distribution, and the existing local branch railroad lines were inadequate. The British investors who provided the capital for railroad construction were only interested in building trunk railway lines to move Canada's staple products to the coast for export — not in providing local branch lines for Canada's own distribution needs.

Even after the major transportation system had been built, new capital was used to finance industrial mergers rather than to expand Canada's manufacturing industry. Competition was reduced as oligopolies became established, and as a consequence product prices rose further. Because there was only a limited amount of capital available for investment in manufacturing industries, production capacity for consumer goods could not be expanded as demand for products increased. The result was higher prices for consumer goods such as food, clothing and housing.

Eventually, however, the standard of living for the average Canadian improved as foreign investment flowed into Canada, primarily from the U.S., for the development of manufacturing industries. This investment was stimulated by huge population growth, which increased domestic demand for manufactured consumer goods. Between 1900 and 1910, one million immigrants poured into the west between the Lakehead and the Rockies, and although World War I reduced the flow somewhat, by the 1920s the population in this region had increased from 400 000 to 2 million. The increased demand for manufactured goods helped Canada's manufacturing industry to expand through foreign investment, and eventually the prices of consumer goods decreased.[7]

The Boom and Bust Decade

The period of the 1920s is often called the "boom and bust" decade. The rise in per capita income in Canada during the early 1920s was a direct result of the vast expansion of industrial capacity during World War I, but it was also an indirect result of general economic expansion in the United States.

For example, one major influence in Canadian industry was Ford's innovative automobile assembly line, which dramatically lowered automobile prices as it ushered in the era of mass production. At a cost of slightly over $500 the Model T, also known as the Tin Lizzie, was within reach of the common individual earning an average of $1100 in 1920. This sparked an automotive boom which intensified in 1919, when General Motors introduced annual style changes to stimulate and satisfy different consumer tastes in colours and models.

By the end of the 1920s, one in every two Canadian families owned an automobile — hence a new demand for more roads and paving. At the beginning of the decade, most roads were dirt and gravel, of little use to car owners. Ten years later, Canada had more than 125 000 kilometres of roads, of which 16 000 were paved.

Mass production of the automobile soon led to mass production of other consumer products which, together with new developments in technology, further contributed to expansion in industry. With the advent of consumer credit in the early 1920s, people clamoured for radios, automatic washing machines and refrigerators. This industrial expansion in turn created demand for the natural resources — nickel, copper, iron and steel — required for these new products.

Expansion was also felt in the west, especially in the great primary industries of wheat, pulp and paper, and cattle. In 1890, for example, entrepreneur Pat Burns settled in Calgary and established Burns Foods Limited. By the 1920s, Burns Foods had become one of the largest meat packing businesses in the world.

The bust came on October 24, 1929. On that date — also known as Black Thursday — the New York stock market collapsed. While Canadian investors fared somewhat better in the market than their U.S. counterparts, the economic consequences were deeply felt throughout the world.

From the Depression to the End of World War II

Although the stock market crash itself did not cause the depression, it did affect business confidence. Business investment dropped, and industries produced less, resulting in fewer jobs and loss of consumer purchasing power. And as fewer goods were bought, industrial output was further curtailed, resulting in more unemployment. Five years later, nearly one quarter of the population was unemployed.

Hardest hit were Canada's primary industries. the price of wheat dropped from $1.60 per bushel in 1929 to 38¢ in 1932. Exports generally fell by 25%. Fishing, mining, lumber, and pulp and paper suffered similar declines, causing a chain reaction in other industries which depended on these commodities for their own prosperity. The CPR and CNR suffered losses as transportation volume dropped drastically. Manufacturers of farm machinery closed plants and laid off workers as demand for their products fell. By the end of 1932, 600 000 of Canada's 10 million people were out of work, and in 1933, 23% of the labour force was unemployed. By 1935, 10% of the population was receiving public relief.

In the west, it was the wheat farmers who suffered the most. Many had invested everything they had in their farms, only to be wiped out as demand and prices for their product fell. And along with economic problems came natural disasters. For several years a severe drought parched the topsoil, which was then carried away by exceptionally strong prairie winds in terrible dust storms. Plagues of grasshoppers followed, destroying anything that had managed to survive the drought.[8]

Government Intervenes in the Economy

In the U.S., the government intervened in the economy to introduce a series of measures known as the "New Deal." Government financed public works and loaned money to railroads, construction companies, banks and farmers. By 1935, these policies had gradually lifted the U.S. out of the worst of the depression. In Canada, Prime Minister R.B. Bennett offered his own version of the New Deal through unemployment insurance programs, social insurance acts and other measures, including the imposition of limits on the hours of work. His programs horrified many businessmen and were often tested in court for their constitutionality. Nevertheless, the Unemployment Insurance Act was passed in 1940, helping to pave the way for the health, welfare and social security services we enjoy today.

The last half of the 1930s saw Canada's economy climb out of the depression. Government intervention, the fact that the depression had apparently run its natural course, and the beginning of World War II all contributed to the recovery. As industry readied itself to produce weapons, guns, warships and airplanes, unemployment decreased, while relief, soup kitchens and breadlines virtually disappeared.

A New Government Philosophy

What did not disappear was government intervention in the economy. The Great Depression had marked the end of the old style of capitalism and ushered in what many called the "welfare state." The principle that each individual should look after himself could no longer be accepted when the depression had caused so much suffering for people with very little influence on the system. Since the government was elected to represent all Canadians — not simply to support business and commercial interests — it had an obligation to minimize economic hardship for all.

The belief that national income should be more evenly distributed, on both an individual basis and a regional one, was gaining acceptance. Provincial governments in poorer regions of Canada received more money from federal tax revenues and various social services were established, including unemployment insurance, family allowances, pensions, veteran's allowances, hospital insurance and disability allowances.

At the same time, however, government became increasingly involved in economic management. This meant spending public funds, when necessary, to get the economy moving — a policy based on the new economic principles developed by John Maynard Keynes, to whom we will return shortly.

A Changing Industrial Structure

World War II production demands virtually eliminated unemployment in Canada, as all war industries — particularly, shipbuilding and aircraft construction — expanded dramatically. And although these industries declined after the war, others, developed as a result of war demand, continued to thrive.

By 1948 employment had fallen somewhat below the peak level reached during the war, but it was still twice what it was in the 1920s. The ten leading industries, ranked in terms of gross output, were as follows:[9]

Pulp and paper
Slaughtering and meat packing
Non-ferrous metals smelting and refining
Electrical apparatus and supplies
Sawmills
Automobiles
Petroleum products
Butter and cheese
Flour and feed mills
Primary iron and steel

Thus the first half of the 20th century showed a change in industrial dominance in Canada. Before World War I, the most important industry had been lumber, followed by various food processing industries. In the 1920s, however, pulp and paper and automobile manufacturing had grown to a point where the former outranked sawmills in total output value. Electrical apparatus also rose in importance, while non-ferrous metal, which became the second largest industry in 1933 and the largest in 1937, was not adversely affected by the depression. At the same time, automobiles and primary iron and steel production were gaining ground, and by 1939 the lumber industry had dropped to sixth place.

Canadian Tire, founded in 1922, capitalized on the growing auto trade and introduced innovative methods to provide efficient service

Foreign Investment in Canada

While the U.S. concentrated on expanding secondary industry during the latter part of the 19th century, Canada had continued to rely on the export of staple products to world markets. Both countries attempted to protect domestic industries through the imposition of tariffs, which effectively isolated Canada from the U.S. in an economic sense and increased interdependence among the different regions of Canada. However, the Canadian tariff structure gave preferential rates to British goods, and in turn Canada received preferential treatment from Britain and other members of the empire.

This policy stimulated manufacturing in Canada, but it also led to an increase in U.S. investment in Canadian industries. By establishing Canadian branch plants, U.S. industry was able to jump the tariff barriers, thus gaining entry to the British markets in empire countries, while selling American products on better terms in Canada.

While Great Britain was the main source of foreign capital investment until World War I, U.S. investment subsequently took the lead, increasing dramatically during World War II. By 1948, approximately 45% of the total assets of Canadian manufacturing corporations were foreign-owned, with the U.S. accounting for 35%, Britain for 7% and all others for 3%.

Indeed, increased foreign investment and technology in the manufacturing industry, primarily from the U.S., was precisely the aim of high tariffs, as it was believed that Canada's economic development depended on imported capital. However, tariffs and regulatory protection have also created many industrial inefficiencies and have tied the U.S. and Canada uniquely together through various corporate, institutional and government arrangements. In effect it has made Canada's manufacturing industry dependent on the pace and direction of technology development, product and market development, and investment planning of U.S. industry. The Canada-U.S. Free Trade Agreement could eventually result in even more economic integration of the two countries.[10]

KEYNES AND THE NEW ECONOMICS

Until the Great Depression of the 1930s, Adam Smith's theory of economics was generally accepted. But the world of 1930 was very different from the world of 1776. More than 150 years had passed, during which business had grown immensely, and the economic structure of many countries had changed. Businesses were no longer small but, particularly in North America, had grown into giant corporations, often with monopolistic powers. Labour unions — which did not even exist in Smith's day — had become established and presented a powerful opposing force to management. Government had been involved in the regulation of business for the past 40 years, and by the 1930s were ready to take a major role in regulating business activities and managing the economy as a whole. As the depression worsened, there was no hint that the market mechanism would lead the major world economies back to prosperity. Classical economics were not working as it should.

Why did it fail? Mainly because classical economics had always assumed full employment. According to the traditional view, depression and unemployment resulted from interference with the market mechanism that normally ensured the efficient allocation of human and material resources. That interference could come either from government or other forces, such as big business organizations and labour unions, with the power to monopolize resources. Thus, the classical economists preached that the depression could only be resolved by returning to a laissez-faire system, and by the early 20th century that was virtually impossible.

It was in 1936 that John Maynard Keynes published his *General Theory of Employment, Interest and Money*. Although the economic world held Keynes in great esteem and his book had been eagerly awaited, its revolutionary economic concepts were at first highly controversial.

The principles that Keynes expounded were not new, but he was the first to present them in logical fashion. He isolated the factors that had contributed to large-scale unemployment in the past. He strongly disagreed with the popular notion that decreasing wages would increase employment. Under this assumption, wages were considered only as production costs to the manufacturer — not as purchasing power for the consuming public that constitutes such a large part of the total demand for goods and services.

Thus in order to maintain individual purchasing power during times of heavy unemployment, Keynes recommended that government should intervene to stimulate economic activity through government spending and appropriate use of the income tax system. Proper use of these two major fiscal tools would maintain the economy in a healthy state. Government spending during times of recession and increasing unemployment would offset decreased investment on the part of the private sector and keep the sector producing capital goods alive. In addition, the progressive income tax structure would automatically ensure that the lower the consumer's income, the less tax would be taken by government, thus allowing individuals to spend as they saw fit and maintain demand for goods and services. Programs such as unemployment insurance, which both Canada and the U.S. instituted in the late 1930s, would give those who were out of work enough to purchase basic necessities — hence demand for these products would be assured.

There is no doubt that Keynes has deeply affected business thought, and government intervention in the economy may be largely attributed to him. However, perhaps government has misinterpreted Keynes. Although he supported heavy government spending during periods of depression, Keynes did not advocate socialism. Nor did he recommend excessive government spending in times of full employment, since that would contribute to inflation. Unfortunately, that is exactly what has happened. Almost half of Canada's national income originates with government, from employment, social programs, government support programs of various kinds, to business and private institutions, purchase of supplies and services, and so on. Deficit spending — where government expenditures exceed tax revenues — contributed to high inflation in the 1970s and has resulted in a great increase in the national debt to finance it. The interest payments on this debt alone take one third of government revenues. Trying to reduce the yearly deficit has become a major problem for the federal government.

Furthermore, to ensure a high rate of growth governments have continued to stimulate the economy even during times of full employment. This deficit spending — where expenditures exceed revenues — has resulted in inflation and an increase in the national debt to finance it, to the point where an ever-increasing share of taxes must go to pay the interest on this debt alone.

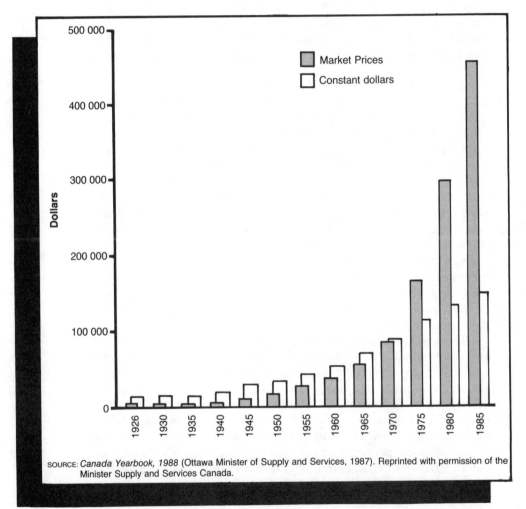

SOURCE: *Canada Yearbook, 1988* (Ottawa Minister of Supply and Services, 1987). Reprinted with permission of the Minister Supply and Services Canada.

Figure 2.4 Rise in Canada's GNP, 1926–1985, market prices vs. constant (1971) dollars

CANADA TODAY

In Canada today a relatively small number of business enterprises — less than 1% — accounts for more than one third of total sales, almost 50% of total assets, and almost the same percentage of the profits of all non-financial corporations. Table 2.2 shows some figures for 1984. In that year, 96.7% of all business enterprises were small businesses with revenues between $10 000 and $2 million; 3.9% were classed as medium size with revenues between $2 million and $20 million. Only 0.4% of businesses were classed as large, with revenues exceeding $20 million. The actual numbers of businesses in each category, along with total revenue, profits, and wages paid is also shown in Table 2.2.

The above figures do not include other economic units, such as commission sales, rental income, professionals, and farmers and fishers. If these are also included then there were approximately 2.2 million economic units in Canada in 1984, as defined by Statistics Canada.

Regardless of how we define small businesses, there is no question that they are necessary to a healthy economic environment. Small businesses often develop new goods and services, provide innovative ideas and create jobs as they expand. Unfortunately, it is not easy to start a new business and even more difficult to keep it going. Few survive, but those that do may develop into large corporations. Large firms, on the other hand, have the resources to install the newest and most productive manufacturing equipment and make production more efficient. Furthermore, costs such as executive salaries and insurance can be spread over large production volumes reducing the cost per unit and resulting in lower prices for the consumer.

Since large corporations contribute to higher productivity, and therefore profits, ultimately they pay higher wages to employees.

TABLE 2.2
Some key statistics of business enterprises in Canada, 1984

	Total	Small business	Medium business	Large business
Total number of businesses	777 100	743 400	30 400	3400
Total revenue (billions $)	782.0	146.0	157.0	478.0
Total profits (billions $)	51.2	9.7	6.3	36.2
Total wages (billions $)	104.0	29.0	24.0	51.0

SOURCE: *Small Business in Canada, A Statistical Profile 1982-1984* (Ottawa: Statistics Canada), Cat 61-231. Reproduced with permission of the Minister of Supply and Services Canada.

And since all employees are also consumers, higher wages mean a greater proportion of income for **discretionary spending** after purchasing basic necessities. The amount of money available for discretionary spending has increased steadily from 30% in the early 1960s to 40% in the mid 1980s. While increased discretionary income enhances living standards by allowing the purchase of luxury goods or services, it also provides a substantial stimulus to the economy. The increased demand for luxury products requires increased business investment for new capital goods to produce them.

Unfortunately, consumers can be fickle with discretionary income. As social values change and new fads arise, discretionary income may be channelled into different products and services. For example, the tremendous popularity of jogging has expanded the footwear industry and resulted in many new firms offering related products and services. The introduction of personal computers has also created a new industry. To satisfy their demand for these new products, consumers have probably spent less money on other products affecting the sales and health of entire industries.

The Shift to a Service Economy

In Canada, as in the United States, the rising discretionary income of the consumer has led to a great demand not only for physical goods but also for services. The **service industry** has become so dominant that both Canada and the United States are often called **service economies**. Many Canadians today are employed in such areas as teaching, business services, industrial and consumer products servicing, and food services. In fact, almost twice as many people are employed in services as in manufacturing industries. As shown in Figure 2.5, Canada's **industrial structure** has changed considerably since 1949.

In Canada there has been a shift from heavy to light manufacturing. Our economy is becoming predominantly information- and service-based, while resource development and traditional manufacturing activity is increasingly being carried out by nations just beginning to industrialize. This shift out of heavy manufacturing has led to high unemployment in Canada. It has also been responsible, however, for an explosive growth in the small business sector as many of these unemployed individuals have turned to self-employment.[11]

Canada in the 1990s

The 1980s have not been easy for Canada. From **stagflation** — a word coined to describe the condition of high inflation and stagnation,

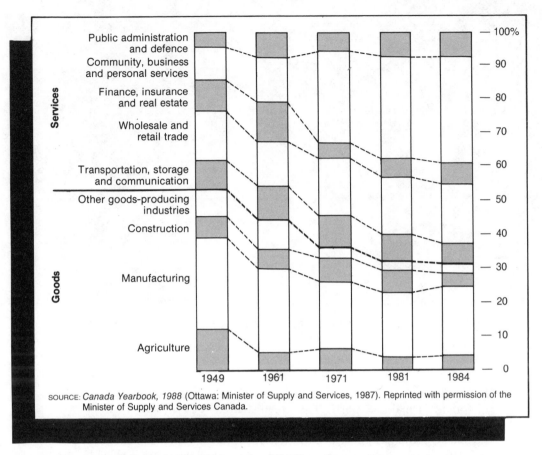

Figure 2.5 Changes in the industrial structure of the Canadian economy

sluggish economic growth — the Canadian economy went into a deep recession in 1981–1982. Although the downturn was severe, in retrospect it has made Canadian business leaner and meaner, better able to compete in world markets due to cost-cutting and productivity increases and a lower-valued Canadian dollar. The result is that Canada has risen toward the top of the industrialized nations in terms of growth. In the period from 1983 to 1987 growth averaged approximately 4.1%, outpacing Japan, the United States and Britain, and far above France, West Germany and Italy. The forecast for the 1990s is 3% real growth each year.[12]

The current situation has been particularly tough for Canada's five major resource industries. World oil prices slumped spectacu-

In recent decades, Canada has increasingly become a service economy

larly, and agriculture was also hit hard by lower prices for grain, one of Canada's major exports. The greatest impact is on the western farmer, who has to fight to retain a share of world market. Forest products, Canada's biggest exported resource, fared the best, primarily due to cost cutting and productivity improvements that turned the industry from a high-cost to a low-cost producer, and thus to a more effective competitor. In the mining sector the problem lies not in low sales, but in low prices that do not provide a reasonable profit. Perhaps one of the brightest spots is Canada's oldest industry, fishing. Canada is the world's leading fish-exporting nation in terms of value. The consumer appetite for fish throughout the world, as well as the low value of the Canadian dollar, have contributed to the success of this industry.[13]

Although Canada's economic growth is spectacular, other economic problems exist. Canada's unemployment rate in 1987 is almost 1.5% above that of 1981, with some regions in Canada faring better than others — central Canada at 6.2% and Québec at 10.7%. Canada has also not done well in terms of inflation — the highest rate of the Big Seven industrialized nations at about 4.5%. A major reason for high inflation is the federal government's huge deficit, which it continues to try to reduce with sales tax increases that directly affect the inflation rate.[14]

In the longer run Canada's revision of the tax system should help reduce the deficit. It is said to be neutral — the reduced revenue from lower income tax rates will be offset by the increased revenue from the new federal sales tax and by elimination of some of the previous income tax deductions. It should also be fairer, taxing wages and savings less and consumption more. This should encourage more people to go to work or start a business, which should lead to economic growth and ultimately higher tax revenue. Nevertheless, the deficit will not be reduced significantly unless the federal government is willing drastically to cut its spending.[15]

Then there is the Canada-U.S. Free Trade Agreement. As it comes into effect, some manufacturers — producers of leather products, textiles, rubber goods, consumer-related electrical goods, as well as grape growers, wine producers, and poultry farmers — may suffer a net loss to U.S. firms, according to a study by the Economic Council of Canada. Nevertheless, most other industries should be able to compete with their U.S. counterparts, aided by a lower value of the Canadian dollar.[16]

While the debate goes on about the effects of the free trade bill on Canada's economic and social environment, Canada remains most vulnerable to the new protectionist trade bill that was passed in the United States in 1988. Canada's dependence on U.S. markets has been increasing steadily: in 1976 only 67% of Canada's exports went to the United States. Ten years later, it had increased to 77%. While exports to the United States have increased, the lower value of the Canadian dollar has also made industrial and consumer goods more competitive on the European market. Some Canadian companies, such as CAE Industries Ltd. of Toronto (flight simulators), Litton Systems Ltd. (guidance systems), Pratt & Whitney of Longueuil, Québec (small engines), have been able to find market niches.[17]

Economic Management

What is the best way to manage the Canadian economy? There are two views. On the one hand there are those who believe in private initiative. The government would provide a climate where individuals can develop their businesses which will in turn create jobs and tax revenue. The market and competition would dictate which industries rise and which decline. On the other hand there are those who believe that the only way economies can be controlled for the benefit of all is through government taking a strong stand on long-range planning by establishing an **industrial strategy**. Government would determine which industries should be helped in their development and which industries should be phased out over a period of time. Emphasis would be placed on orderly industrial growth in order to eliminate serious fluctuations in employment (see Chapter 12).

The industrial future of Canada, and the roles to be played by business, labour and government, are difficult to predict. In any event, the Great Depression in the 1930s made it clear that business was a central part of society and, left to itself, did not look after all the needs of society. Government had to intervene to protect those who could not help themselves. Unions also had their part to play. If any one of the three sectors becomes too weak or too strong it can have serious repercussions on all citizens.

NOTES

1. Alexander Ross, *The Risk Takers* (Toronto: Maclean-Hunter Ltd. A *Financial Post*/Macmillan Book, 1975), pp. 6–11.
2. "Survey shows firm's profits up 74%," *The Globe and Mail*, May 22, 1984.
3. D.G. Creighton, "The Economic Objectives of Confederation," in John J. Deutsch *et al.*, eds. *The Canadian Economy: Selected Readings* (Toronto: Macmillan Co. of Canada Ltd., 1962), pp. 372–387.
4. *Report of the Royal Commission on Dominion-Provincial Relations*, 1954, in Deutsch *et al.*, *op. cit.* pp. 420–24.
5. See Tom Naylor, *The History of Canadian Business, 1867–1914*, Vol. I (Toronto: James Lorimer & Co., 1975), pp. 2–18.
6. *Ibid.*
7. *Ibid.*
8. For short discussions of various aspects of the depression, see articles in *Canada and the World*, Feb. 1979, pp. 12–19.
9. Gideon Rosenbluth, "The Canadian Manufacturing Industries," in Deutsch *et al.*, *op. cit.*, pp. 487–94.
10. Hugh Faulkner, "Doing better, doing more," *The Financial Post Report on the Nation*, Winter 1987–88, p. 78.
11. Robert English, "Getting in trim to face the year 2000," *The Financial Post Magazine*, Winter 1986–87, p. 32.
12. Catherine Harris, "Our economy is in better shape to take what comes." *The Financial Post Report on the Nation*, Winter 1987–88, p. 14.
13. John Soganich, "Big five remain key Canadian resources," *The Financial Post Magazine*, Winter 1986–87, p. 29.
14. See Catherine Harris, "Our economy is in better shape to take what comes." *Financial Post Report on the Nation*, Winter 1987–88, p. 15.
15. *Ibid.*,
16. James Bagnall, "Riding on our cheap dollar, bracing for free trade," *The Financial Post Magazine*, Winter 1987–88, p. 18.
17. *Ibid.*

CHAPTER SUMMARY

Among the five factors of production, capital and entrepreneurship can significantly affect the standard of living. Capital — the tools, machines and equipment used in the production of consumer goods and services — has been primarily responsible for making labour more productive in the manufacturing process. Entrepreneurship is the individual drive and risk-taking ability essential to establish new enterprises. It is the entrepreneur who combines all of the factors of production and provides the initial funds to start a business, providing jobs in the process.

Profit is a surplus of revenue over expenses. To survive in the long run, a business must make a profit. From year to year, however, profits can fluctuate and many firms experience losses for several years in a row during a recession. These losses must be recouped during better economic times.

Profit contributes to society by ensuring that firms are effective and efficient in their use of the factors of production. Profit is also necessary for the replacement of worn out capital goods and the development of new, more efficient machines and production processes. High profits thus increase productivity and tend to raise the overall standard of living. When not enough funds can be generated by the firm's operation, profit must be used to pay investors. Finally, almost half of all business profits are taken by government in the form of taxes which can be used to provide necessary services that private firms would not provide due to a lack of profit.

Competition ensures that prices are kept as low as possible, and the quality of products as high as possible. Competition must be effective and responsible to ensure maximum benefit to society. Unfortunately, many factors in the private enterprise system may interfere with competition between firms, including government and groups such as consumers and labour unions, often to the detriment of the consumer.

During the past two hundred years, Canada has developed from a relatively unexplored country dependent on the export of fur, timber and fish into a modern industrial economy. Following Confederation, the federal government took steps to make Canada an industrial nation rather than simply an exporter of raw materials. Government introduced a tariff policy designed to make imported goods more expensive than similar goods produced in Canada and to build a transportation system to move staple products from the west to the east, for domestic consumption as well as export, and to move manufactured goods from the east to the west. While this policy helped in the development of Canadian manufacturing, it also encouraged foreign investment in Canada. As a consequence, some sectors of Canadian industry are still largely foreign-owned and foreign-controlled.

Business cycles — a problem common to all capitalist business systems — have plagued Canada throughout the past century. A long period of recession which started in the 1870s finally ran its course by the mid-1890s when a new boom period began. However, the boom suddenly halted in 1929 with the crash of the stock market in the United States. Investor confidence was shaken, and the severe depression that ensued was only ended after almost a decade with the help of government intervention in the economy. Such intervention was advocated by John Maynard Keynes, the British economist, who held that government must provide spending and investment during periods when low business confidence means that private investment is not forthcoming. Keynes suggested that the classical economic principles as laid down by Adam Smith and other economists were no longer working because the nature of capitalistic economic systems had changed.

Since World War II, Canada has shifted from a manufacturing to a service economy as consumers have demanded more services. Although this shift has been responsible for high unemployment in the manufacturing and resource industries, it has also resulted in a rise in entrepreneurial activity as many individuals have taken advantage of the opportunities in the service industry.

Although Canada's economic growth in the 1980s has been spectacular, some serious economic problems persist, such as high unemployment and high inflation when compared to other industrialized countries. The federal government's high deficit has been blamed for this high inflation. It is hoped that the revised tax system and the proposed new national sales tax will raise more revenue and thus reduce the deficit.

Managing the economy is not easy. International competition can severely affect certain economic sectors, which can cause high unemployment. Government must try to reduce unemployment and keep inflation down. This is difficult, particularly in a capitalist economy where the government cannot impose its decisions on business or individuals. Various solutions have been suggested to resolve this dilemma, including the development of an industrial strategy to ensure Canada's industrial future.

KEY TERMS

Capital	Monopolistic competition
Capital formation	Oligopoly
Productivity	Monopoly
Inflation	Monopsony
Capital investment	Marketing boards
Entrepreneur	Adam Smith
Profit	National Policy
Efficiency	Great Depression
Effectiveness	New Deal
Market system	John Maynard Keynes
Equilibrium point	Discretionary spending
Demand and supply schedule	Service economy
Effective competition	Industrial structure
Responsible competition	Stagflation
Perfect or pure competition	Industrial strategy

REVIEW QUESTIONS

1. Explain how capital can help to increase worker productivity.
2. What is capital formation? How does a nation build up its capital stock?
3. How can inflation hurt a nation's productivity? How can it undermine society?
4. Why is entrepreneurship considered a factor of production?
5. What is profit? What are the benefits of profit to a business?
6. Why is profit called a regulator? Distinguish between effectiveness and efficiency?
7. How do business profits contribute to the welfare of society?
8. Why is it virtually impossible for businesses to maximize their profit?
9. What is the relationship between profit, competition, and the market?
10. Distinguish between effective and responsible competition.
11. Distinguish between the four types of competition.
12. How can competition between firms be limited?
13. Compare the market system as it existed in Adam Smith's time with the market system as Keynes saw it.
14. What were the primary reasons for Confederation?
15. What were the objectives of the National Policy? What was its impact on Canadians?
16. Why did government believe it should intervene in economic management after the Great Depression?
17. Why is there so much foreign investment and foreign ownership in Canada today?
18. What did Keynes suggest government should do to prevent another deep depression?
19. Why has Canada changed from a manufacturing to a service economy?

DISCUSSION QUESTIONS

1. Describe the consequences for Canada if the government suddenly decided to tax away all profits.
2. How might the concept of profit be applied to government and non-profit organizations, to ensure these services or products are provided effectively and efficiently?
3. Describe the competition that exists between (a) auto manufacturers and (b) airlines in Canada. Do you believe that effective competition exists in these two industries?
4. Was the National Policy necessary for Canada's economic development? Can you suggest alternative ways in which Canada might have developed its economy?
5. Is another great depression possible? Explain.

CASE 2–1 Profit and Taxation

On a recent hotline radio program, a politician expounded his views about the inequities in the Canadian income tax system. He quoted statistics on the number of individuals and corporations with high income that paid little if any income tax. He felt strongly that the tax system should be revised so that all individuals and corporations paid a minimum amount of income tax.

When the telephone lines were opened after the discussion, one caller cited a recent newspaper article which listed company profits in 1983. He claimed he was outraged to hear that some companies had increases in their profits of 75% to 200%, and asked if it was fair that they should be allowed to have these high increases. "Aren't these companies gouging the consumer when they rack up such a surplus?" he asked. Another caller offered his solution, which was to tax away all profits over a certain amount. A third caller went even further, suggesting that government tax away all corporate profits.

QUESTIONS

1. Why might companies show large profit increases in some years, particularly after a recession?
2. What problems would corporations face if all profits above a certain amount were taxed away?
3. If government taxed away all corporate profits, what potential effect might this have on our standard of living? On employment? On government revenue? On potential entrepreneurs?

CASE 2–2 Do Marketing Boards Restrict Competition?

Marketing boards were established to ensure that agricultural products would be available to Canadians at a reasonable price and in adequate supply. The boards were also to ensure that producers received a reasonable return on their investment and a reasonable income for their effort by smoothing out the severe fluctuations in earnings of farmers. However, many argue that marketing boards restrict free entry into the market and add to the cost consumers must pay for the product. Review the Issue in the chapter and then answer the following questions.

QUESTIONS

1. How might marketing boards restrict competition among producers? How do they ensure that farmers obtain a more stable income?

2. Use the demand and supply schedule in the chapter and indicate how a marketing board practising supply management will cause a rise in the price of eggs. Assume that the equilibrium point initially was established under pure competition. If the price of farm products rises, how might this affect the quantity demanded by consumers?

3. How do marketing boards infringe on the four principles of capitalism examined in Chapter 1 — private property, freedom of competition, freedom of choice, and freedom from government interference? How might marketing boards inhibit the entrepreneurial drive?

4. In your opinion, should farmers receive the kind of protection offered by marketing boards? Explain. Why or why not?

CASE 2–3 The Market System

Because we live in a market-run society, we are apt to take for granted the puzzling — indeed, almost paradoxical — nature of the market solution to the economic problem. But assume for a moment that we could act as economic advisers to a society which had not yet decided on its mode of economic organization. Suppose, for instance, that we were called on to act as consultants to one of the new nations emerging from the continent of Africa.

We could imagine the leaders of such a nation saying, "We have always experienced a highly tradition-bound way of life. Our men hunt and cultivate the fields and perform their tasks as they are brought up to do by the force of example and the instruction of their elders. We know, too, something of what can be done by economic command. We are prepared, if necessary, to sign an edict making it compulsory for many of our men to work on community projects for our national development. Tell us, is there any other way we can organize our society so that it will function successfully — or better yet, more successfully?"

Suppose we answered, "Yes, there is another way. Organize your society along the lines of a market economy."

"Very well," say the leaders. "What do we then tell people to do? How do we assign them to their various tasks?"

"That's the very point," we would answer. "In a market economy no one is assigned to any task. The very idea of a market society is that each person is allowed to decide for himself what to do."

There is consternation among the leaders. "You mean there is no assignment of some men to mining and others to cattle raising? No manner of selecting some for transportation and others for cloth weaving? You leave this to people to decide for themselves? But what happens if they do not decide correctly? What happens if no one volunteers to go into the mines, or if no one offers himself as a railway engineer?"

"You may rest assured," we tell the leaders. "None of that will happen. In a market society, all the jobs will be filled because it will be to the people's advantage to fill them."

Our respondents accept this with uncertain expressions. "Now look," one of them finally says, "let us suppose that we take your advice and let our people do as they please. Now let's talk about something important, like cloth production. Just how do we fix the right level of cloth output in this 'market society' of yours?"

"But you don't," we reply.

"We don't! Then how do we know there will be enough cloth produced?"

"There will be," we tell him. "The market will see to that."

"Then how do we know there won't be too much cloth produced?" he asks triumphantly.

"Ah, but the market will see to that too!"

"But what is this market that will do all these wonderful things? Who runs it?"

"Oh, nobody runs the market," we answer. "It runs itself. In fact there really isn't any such thing as 'the market'. It's just a word we use to describe the way people behave."

"But I thought people behaved the way they wanted to!"

"And so they do," we say. "But never fear. They will want to behave the way you want them to behave."

"I am afraid," says the chief of the delegation, "that we are wasting our time. We thought you had in mind a serious proposal. But what you suggest is madness. It is inconceivable. Good day, sir." And with great dignity the delegation takes its leave.

SOURCE: Robert L. Heilbroner, *The Making of Economic Society*, 6th ed., 1980, pp. 18–19. Reprinted by permission of Prentice-Hall Inc., Englewood Cliffs, N.J.

QUESTIONS

1. With all individuals pursuing their own interests, how does the market system ensure that mines will find miners, and factories workers? How does it guarantee that cloth will in fact be produced?

2. In a market-run nation, could each person indeed do as he wishes, yet at the same time fulfill the needs of society as a whole?

3. Could we seriously suggest to an emergent nation that it entrust its economic problems to a market solution? Explain.
4. You have been asked by the leaders of this nation to prepare a report explaining how the nation might implement a change over to a market society. Outline such a program.

Small Business and Forms of Business Ownership

Dick Hemingway

CHAPTER OUTLINE

CHAPTER PREVIEW

In Chapter 3 we look at small business, its importance to our economy, the problems faced by small business owners, the management practices and skills required to be successful in operating a small business, and the major considerations when either buying an existing business or establishing a new one. We also look at franchising, its advantages and disadvantages compared to starting your own business, and what to examine before buying a franchise. Then we look at financing a new venture, and the importance and development of a business plan.

We then survey the three major forms of private business ownership and examine the advantages and disadvantages of each. We study how a company is incorporated, and how a corporation is organized, examining the roles of shareholders, board of directors and top management. Finally, we discuss the growth of large corporations and their benefits and drawbacks, and briefly examine member-owned cooperatives.

LEARNING OBJECTIVES

After reading this chapter you should be able to explain:

1. The importance of small business to the Canadian economy;
2. The major problems faced by small business owners;
3. The management practices needed to make a small business successful;
4. The factors to consider in buying either an existing business or starting a new one;
5. The advantages and disadvantages of franchises;
6. The importance of adequate financing for the business and how to acquire it;
7. The importance of a business plan and the major items that must be addressed in it;
8. The necessity of a legal form of business ownership;
9. The basic characteristics of a sole proprietorship, partnership, and corporation;
10. Why the corporate form of business ownership has become dominant today;
11. Why most large businesses are corporations;
12. The general requirements for incorporating in Canada, both federally and provincially;
13. How a corporation is governed;
14. How businesses grow through vertical, horizontal and conglomerate mergers;
15. Why cooperatives have become increasingly important and how they differ from the other forms of private business ownership.

SMALL BUSINESS

As shown in the previous chapter, almost 97% of businesses are small, with revenues of between $10 000 and $2 million. In 1984 there were 743 400 small businesses in Canada. Figure 3.1 indicates how these businesses were distributed by industry in 1984.

Each year approximately 150 000 people go into business for themselves. Small businesses are the backbone of our economic system. People who start new businesses create new jobs, and many bring to market innovative products or services. Surveys indicate that small businesses contribute significantly to job creation and economic growth. For example, between 1971 and 1977, small firms (20 or fewer employees) accounted for 59% of overall employment growth in Canada, while representing only 30% of total Canadian employment. During those same years, firms employing 1000 or more people experienced a net loss of employment of 3%. According to the most recent statistical profile of small business in Canada, they accounted for 42% of total employment in manufacturing, construc-

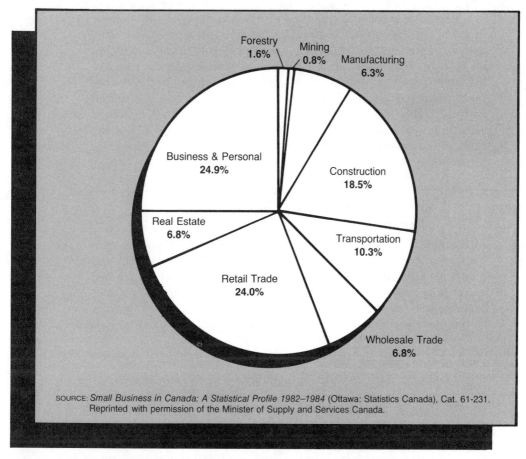

Figure 3.1 Distribution of small business by industry, Canada 1984

tion, trade and services and 47.5% of new jobs in those sectors. Furthermore, small businesses accounted for 52% of total sales in construction and 57% in services.[1]

Unfortunately, approximately 60% of those who start a business will fail in their first year of operation. According to Dun & Bradstreet, considered the source of the most precise figures on insolvency, the major reasons for business failure in 1984 are as follows: 44.9% of failures are caused by incompetence; 15.4% by lack of managerial experience; 13.3% by lack of experience in the line of business; 22.2% due to unbalanced experience (not well rounded in sales, financing, purchasing and production); 2.7% due to neglect; 1.1% due to disaster; and 0.4% due to fraud.[2] Those who make it beyond the first few years have a good chance of remaining in business providing they manage it intelligently. A few individuals even strike it rich or see their business grow into a large corporation.

A retail or service business is the easiest type of small business to start. This is evident in the many shoe, stationery, florist, drug and convenience stores that exist in shopping centres and downtown areas. Many businesses are established to provide services for large business firms or supplying parts and subassemblies for more complex products manufactured by them. Many businesses are started by individuals with expertise in an area of high technology. Some start their operation in modest quarters such as a garage, as was the case with Apple Computers, a company that today has sales approaching a billion dollars.

Problems Faced by Small Business Owners

In Chapter 2, we said that many entrepreneurs strike out on their own because they are unable to develop a new idea with their former companies. But innovative ideas or expertise in one particular area are only part of a successful business. The new entrepreneur faces several problems. Some of the most difficult are lack of management skills, inadequate finances and government regulations.

Lack of Management Skills

Many factors can account for the high failure rate of new businesses including poor sales, poor financing, problems of inventory, high operating costs, labour problems, poor location and so on. But in the final analysis, the failure often comes down to poor management or a lack of management skills. A business usually fails because of a series of mistakes made by its manager. Experience and perseverance pay off, however, Many entrepreneurs who fail in their first venture are successful the second or third time.

Inadequate Financing

Inadequate financing is often included under poor management as a major cause of small business failure. Many new entrepreneurs start a business without sufficient cash to carry them through the initial period of a year or more when sales are low and expenses high. One common source of funds is a personal loan from a family member or friend. Money can also be borrowed from one of the chartered banks or from the Federal Business Development Bank (FBDB). These sources, however, require either collateral or a personal guarantee to secure the loan as well as detailed forecasts of sales, profits and cash flow. Getting funds is therefore not always easy. One solution is to find partners who will invest money and

Small businesses begin with innovative ideas

offer complementary business experience. Another solution is to incorporate and raise money through the sale of shares and/or bring in venture capitalists. We will discuss these various options later in this chapter.

Government Regulations

Complying with government regulations costs business time and money. Large companies may have the resources to hire employees to fill out forms and supply the various levels of government with operating statistics. However, many small businesses cannot afford to hire additional employees and owners often do the paperwork after hours. Thus, many small business owners consider the time and money involved in complying with government regulations a major problem.

Mismanagement Main Cause of Failed Fledgling Ventures

As a rule, 70%-80% of all new businesses fail within their first five years.

Owner-managers with even a cursory knowledge of the small-business sector are aware of the oft-cited statistic, but they figure it only applies to the next guy.

The entrepreneur who becomes part of the statistic often enters the market with the highest of expectations, but fails to attain a good grip on his enterprise's finances. The result, of course, is disaster.

Harold Brief, an accountant and president of Toronto-based Harold Brief & Associates Ltd., trustees in bankruptcy, and Gerald Gringorten, agree that adverse business conditions beyond the ken of the entrepreneur account for only a fraction of owner-managed bankruptcies.

Gringorten notes several insolvencies he handled were Toronto retailers put out of business by subway construction that made them inaccessible to customers. Such instances are rare, though.

"The major, overall cause has to come down to mismanagement," says Gringorten.

"Without proper foresight, and proper operational decision-making, a business can't survive. But good management will bring the business through good times and bad, 99% of the time."

A common problem among small-business managers, he adds, is that they're so used to doing everything themselves, they can't delegate responsibility to subordinates.

Often as the business grows, the owner-manager can't handle all the work alone but still refuses to delegate effectively. Details fall through the cracks, the product suffers, and the enterprise slides downhill.

"The irony is that success can torpedo you as fast as anything else," says Gringorten, noting that even when responsibilities are successfully delegated, rapid growth can place owner-managers in jeopardy.

Too often the heavy borrowing to finance capital expenditures and higher operating costs far outpace revenues needed to pay creditors. The resulting cash squeeze hits when cash needs are greatest; if the gap opens too wide, the enterprise could founder.

"Even if there's just enough inflow of money to match the outflow, there could be trouble if the creditors get impatient," he adds.

"The banker who's felt perfectly comfortable extending a $50 000 line of credit gets nervous very easily and very quickly because the line is now at $250 000 and the stakes are getting uncomfortably high."

Alternately, the problem of undercapitalization could arise. This usually shows itself in an inability of the business to take off because of a shortage of operating cash. In the case of a manufacturer, all start-up capital has been invested in machinery and equipment, while with a retailer, it's tied up in leasehold improvements and inventories.

A cash shortage accompanying a growth phase leaves little room to manoeuvre. It can also jeopardize a new business if the economic climate sours, says Brief.

"With no reserves, there's nothing to fall back on during lean times. That's what happened to a lot of businesses in 1981–1982, when interest rates were in excess of 20%. That's when they were killed."

Another major cause of businesses going bust is lack of proper financial planning, Brief says. Too often, entrepreneurs discard the carefully prepared business plan (with a budget at its core) used to obtain financing as soon as the first customer walks in the door.

"The budget isn't totally inflexible," says Gringorten. "But the basic structure of it should be followed, or you could find yourself in trouble, needing the money for the next move — but not having it, and finding problems getting it."

Managing credit extended to customers is one of the biggest challenges, Brief says. Without it, the entrepreneur could turn away business, but too much generosity could mean loss of control of receivables.

"Once an outstanding account ages beyond a certain point, there should be signals sent up that it needs attention."

Instead of tracking credit accounts closely to identify the deadbeats, some businesses just keep on extending credit, with calamitous consequences.

Another common cause of small business failure is a reluctance to spend the money required to draft a proper marketing strategy and put it in place, says Gringorten.

Many entrepreneurs feel advertising is a discretionary expense and they can get by with an amateurish, low budget effort that misses the target clientele or doesn't hit hard enough.

Both Gringorten and Brief emphasize that the causes of failure they outline are found in all commercial sectors and all types of enterprises.

"You find these problems across the board," says Brief. "You can't pinpoint one sector of the economy as being more particularly vulnerable than another.

"The key is proper management and sufficient working capital. Without those, you have two strikes against you right from the start."

SOURCE: Colin Languedoc, "Mismanagement main cause of failed fledgling ventures," *The Financial Post*, May 25, 1987, p. 18.

Requirements for Business Success

Since lack of management skills appears to be the main reason for small business failure, eliminating this problem is crucial to the success of a new venture. The new entrepreneur needs to acquire the basic management skills and continue to develop management potential through business education and his own hard work, creativity and self-discipline. Successful small business management depends on the following factors.

Acquiring a Business Education

There are many stories of successful entrepreneurs who never had formal **business training** or **education**. Some appear to have an inborn talent for starting and managing a business. Others are simply fortunate to have survived. For most, starting and operating a new business is an arduous process of trial and error and learning from previous experience. The learning process can be accelerated through formal education at colleges and universities and by participation in courses. The entrepreneur needs to know about accounting, pricing, advertising, budgeting, and handling people. He cannot rely on his own particular area of expertise. A good engineer or salesperson, for example, is not necessarily a good manager. If the entrepreneur is weak in any area, partners can often supply the necessary expertise.

Careful Planning

A major function of management is **planning** for the future — establishing objectives and determining ways of achieving them. Although the future cannot be controlled and no plan can prevent future events from affecting the business, careful planning can minimize the risks by forecasting future problems and setting up contingency plans. Finding and training a reliable successor, for example, can prevent serious setbacks when an owner dies or cannot continue to manage the firm. Looking to the future can also help to identify business opportunities which might otherwise go unnoticed.

Careful Money Management

Money is the lifeblood of a business. Many profitable companies have gone bankrupt because they could not pay bills. Often, too much money is tied up in inventory or plant and equipment. Once there is a real possibility of bankruptcy, it is difficult if not impossible to secure a loan from a bank or other financial institution. **Financial planning** and **cash budgeting** can prevent serious money shortages. By projecting cash inflow and outflow for six months to a year, a business can match revenues with expenses, forecast shortages and take appropriate action. Careful money management also means control of a firm's inventory, purchases, payroll, accounts receivable, suppliers' discounts and customer services. All of these will be discussed in more detail in Chapter 9.

Keeping Accurate Records

Accurate records indicate how the firm is progressing from day to day, month to month and year to year. They can indicate trends in sales, inventory and accounts receivable, for example, allowing the owner to reverse dangerous trends early. **Business records** are required by tax department auditors and by bankers or investors if the owner needs to borrow money. Moreover, the owner has to know where he or she stands financially. An accurate record system is the cornerstone of a good control system.

Effective Marketing

Marketing essentially means getting the right product to the right customer at the right time and at the right place. Marketing includes producing a product that people need and want, and packaging, pricing and promoting it appropriately. It means launching the right sales effort in terms of advertising, merchandising and distribution, and keeping a check on the location to ensure it continues to provide good access to customers. Finally, marketing means providing customer services such as delivery, maintenance, repair and service follow-up. All of the above points must be considered before the business is started as well as during its operation. A new competitor, for example, could upset plans unless met head on with an appropriate marketing strategy.

Time Management

Any owner-manager will attest that a 70- or 80-hour workweek is common to complete necessary work. Unless the owner-manager practises **time management** by scheduling and prioritizing tasks on a daily, weekly and monthly basis, he or she will neglect work crucial to success. Time management also involves delegation. Delegation means giving responsibility and authority to others in the organization. Many new owners and inexperienced managers are unwilling to delegate because they believe they can do the job better themselves. But without delegation, an owner-manager is soon preoccupied with minor details while important problems are not given necessary attention. With careful training and supervision, employees can learn to manage their responsibilities effectively. Delegation is not abdication of responsibility on the part of the owner-manager, but the key to success and growth.

Acquiring Human Resources

Incompetent and unmotivated employees can mean financial ruin for a small business. Salaries usually represent the greatest expense for businesses and owners cannot afford employees who do not do their jobs effectively. Incompetent employees make mistakes that cost the firm money and cause poor customer relations.

Unless funds are available to employ an outside personnel agency to recruit new employees, the owner-manager has to learn the basic personnel skills of **recruiting and selecting employees**. He or she needs to know where to look for employees, how to extract critical information about the job skills and interests during the interview, how to test for necessary employee skills, and how to check on past employment habits. Once chosen, the new employee has to be properly introduced to the firm and trained for the job. Later new employees have to be critically evaluated on their performance.

To recruit and keep good employees, a firm has to pay appropriate salaries, benefits and incentives. A profit sharing plan may be an excellent way to reward effort and ensure loyalty. In addition, most people want regular evaluations of their performance so they know where they stand and have the opportunity to advance in the firm through promotions. Making employees part of a team is an important and ongoing process for the owner-manager. In Chapter 6 we discuss managing people in detail; other aspects of personnel are discussed in Chapter 10.

Growing With The Business

In the event of success, the owner-manager must decide how large the firm should become. The transition from a small to medium operation, and then to a large corporation, presents many new problems and owners often find it difficult to cope. Many prefer to remain small, particularly if they are making an adequate living and are enjoying a particular status in the community. However, if the business grows, the owner must be prepared for changes. In a large corporation, for example, he will be concerned mainly with planning and controlling products and finances.

STARTING A BUSINESS

Should you buy an existing business or start one from scratch? Each approach has its advantages and disadvantages. What you do depends on your objectives. If the product you want to produce or the service you want to offer is new, then you need to start a new business. If your main goal is to operate your own business, then you can buy an existing firm after a careful search of the available business opportunities and a subsequent in-depth analysis of the firm's operation.

Buying an Established Business

There are several advantages to buying an existing business. For example, you have an established market and clientele, a building, fixtures, and a stock of merchandise. You know who your suppliers are and need only establish credit with them to continue receiving merchandise or raw materials. You may also be able to retain the previous employees and the original owner until you know the intricacies of the business and are fully established. But be certain that the business is a sound venture. Ask yourself why the current owner wants to sell out. Remember, the present owner is not obligated to voluntarily point out any of the problems facing the business. If you ask, however, he cannot provide you with false information or you are likely to have legal recourse against him.

What should you do before actually buying an existing business? A preliminary look at the firm's financial statements, accounts receivable, accounts payable, existing assets and inventory are a must. If these prove satisfactory and there are no obvious problems, then a more thorough investigation is advisable. An accountant can provide you with a thorough analysis of the balance sheet and income statement, sales and expenses, assets and liabilities. This analysis will establish the value of plant, equipment, machinery and inventory and help in drawing up a realistic offer. A lawyer will check the legal title of the company, and find out if there are taxes owing or liens on any of the business' assets. The lawyer will also inquire into legal aspects of the existing business and identify if, for example, you are buying the shares of the company or its assets. If it is the former, you may find yourself saddled with liabilities that put a severe strain on your financial situation. The local municipal office can tell you if the business is violating any local regulations. You should also analyze the industry to see if the firm's products are viable. Statistics Canada can provide the data and the Federal Business Development Bank has counsellors who will evaluate any company and help draw up a final offer.

In terms of your total investment, you have to be sure that your new business promises a return greater than what you might earn from a bank or from investing in government bonds. Your investment should take into account that you are risking your own money and there is always a chance, no matter how thorough you are in checking out the company, that you may go bankrupt. Your potential income has to be enough to offset the risk.

Your thorough analysis may well show a firm financially sound with a good customer base and a good reputation. The owner may want to sell his business because he is retiring, for example. On the other hand, you may have uncovered chronic problems such as a shrinking market for the firm's products or an insufficient return on investment. You may also find that the firm's profitability depends on particular sales or technical skills which you do not possess. In any case, a careful investigation will make you aware of any financial or operating problems and help you to ensure your investment will be returned.

Starting a New Business

Starting a new business involves a number of steps. First you need to identify the product you want to produce or the service you want to offer and define your market. Then you need to find a location, and buy, build or lease the premises and the necessary fixtures and equipment. Next you have to find your suppliers and establish credit with them. Finally you need a marketing and an advertising plan, an accounting system and employees. Establishing a new business does involve more work than buying an existing business but it may be the only way to profit from your skills or to get a new product on the market. Furthermore you can choose the location and renovate the premises according to what you believe is best for the business. You also do not inherit problem employees, nor do you have to pay for goodwill — the payment that often has to be made to a previous owner for establishing a good business reputation.

Franchising

Since starting a new business is a big undertaking for an inexperienced individual, franchising has become extremely popular. A **fran-**

chise is a licence either to manufacture or to sell, or both, a well known product or service developed by the franchisor. The franchisee signs a contract that gives him or her the right to sell the franchisor's products or service, and use the franchisor's name, trademark, or other commercial symbols. The contract also stipulates how to operate the business based on the franchisor's established methods. The right to this franchise usually lasts for a specified period of time and is usually limited to a particular territory.

More and more new businesses are started as franchises. Some of the best known are McDonald's, Burger King and Midas Muffler. There are thousands of franchise opportunities and many of the newer ones can be purchased for as little as $5000. But beware: not all franchises mean instant riches. While some have been known to reward their owners handsomely, many others barely produce a nominal income, and some have gone bankrupt.

Franchises are particularly popular when it comes to small retail outlets, such as specialty clothing stores, shoe stores and convenience stores. They combine the advantages of large chain-store retailers, such as centralized buying of merchandise, supplies and

Mac's Convenience Stores are a major Canadian franchisor

equipment, with the advantages of the small independent retailer, such as the ability to make his or her own decisions about the operation of the business and provide the best customer service possible.

Advantages of Franchises

There are many advantages to owning a franchise. You start with a proven product or service and receive the accompanying marketing expertise and standardized operating methods. In addition, you have the benefit of the franchisor's name and good will, centralized research on the product or service, and group purchasing power. The franchisor usually helps to set up the new business and find a location. If a building is required, plans and building expertise are available; any equipment required is furnished quickly by suppliers who are aware of the necessary specifications. Help is also available to set up an advertising campaign and inventory control system. Indeed, many franchises are established as turn-key operations in which the future operator simply unlocks the door on the first day and is ready for business.

Training provided by the franchisor also avoids one of the major problems small businesses experience — failure because of lack of experience and poor management skills. Fewer than 10% of the 25 000 franchise outlets across Canada fail within the first year. Nevertheless, some franchises have failed, together with the franchisees; risk is never entirely eliminated from any business operation.

The major benefit to the franchisor is the rapid expansion of the franchisor's market without investment of great amounts of capital, and exposure of the products and/or service. The franchisees are motivated since they have a personal and often substantial investment in the business.

Disadvantages of Franchises

A franchise also has drawbacks. The initial investment may be high, especially if the franchise is well-known and successful. The franchisee is also required to adhere strictly to policies regarding hours of operation, number of staff, method of operation, and so on. The franchisee usually also pays a monthly royalty based on a percentage of sales.

The same care should be taken in buying a franchise as in buying any existing small business. Many franchises are new and have not proven themselves for any length of time. New franchises may not give the owner many advantages in starting the business and franchisors often inflate projected earnings figures and expectations in order to sell their franchises.

Buying a Franchise or Starting Your Own Business

Buying a franchise	Starting your own business
• Operational training usually provided by franchisor.	• Management ability based on your own expertise.
• Right to use a known trade name or trademark. Franchise operation completely identified with franchisor.	• Time required to establish name, but more identification of owner of business.
• Able to sell a proven product or service with established public acceptance.	• Time required to establish name, products and/or service.
• Buying a package, so ready to start full operation sooner.	• May have to start slowly. Longer time to realize full potential.
• Less working capital may be required because of tighter controls and franchisor's terms of merchandise supply.	• Risk of mistakes and longer time to start can mean greater financing needs. Terms may be difficult to get with suppliers.
• Profit and loss forecasts may be more accurate as based on proven similar operations.	• Risk of errors in estimating expenses, sales, and profits, especially for an unproven venture.
• Greater chance of initial success.	• Greater chance of failure due to time required for establishment, and possibility of mistakes, especially regarding marketing and planning.
• Sales territory defined by franchisor.	• No restrictions on expanding territory. No risk that expanded territory already has identical operation to yours.
• Benefit from standard national and local advertising of prices, products and service.	• Freedom to advertise when you want to and can afford to and to set your own specials or discounts to meet competition.
• Franchisor is often sole source for merchandise.	• Can buy from any supplier so as to get best prices and terms.

SOURCE: *Buying a Franchise*, Pamphlet #20, Management Series, Federal Business Development Bank.

Factors to Consider When Buying a Franchise

The adage "Before you invest, investigate" holds true for a franchise as well. What should you investigate? The following are some of the major points:

1. **Investigate the franchisor**. Since you are relying on the franchisor for expertise in selling or manufacturing a particular product or service, it should have an operating history. Is the franchise a large national company or a relatively unproven small company?

2. **Closely scrutinize the franchise itself**. What are you buying? Is it a product, process, or a trade name? How long has the franchise been in existence and operating? Is it well established, growing, or stable? Try to find out how many franchises are presently operating and some names and addresses of owners.

3. **How much does this franchise generate in sales and profit on the average?** You should be able to get forecasts of both sales and expenses for a number of years in the future. At the same time you should do your own market study to get an independent idea of the existing market. The franchisor might be too optimistic in his forecasts.

4. **Investigate locations and premises requirements**. Is it you who decides on the location, or the franchisor? Can you get help in this area? Do the premises have to meet certain standards, such as size or street frontage? Can you adapt existing premises or do they require new buildings?

5. **Investigate requirements for equipment, fixtures and layout**. Check if the franchise agreement requires you to purchase specific equipment and fixtures in order to maintain a uniform appearance. If so, do you have to buy them from a specific source or can you try to find the best deal? If you have to buy them from a particular source, find out if you can get comfortable repayment terms.

6. **Consider the franchise territory**. Has the territory been clearly defined? For how long is this territory exclusively yours? What protection do you have that no other franchises will be sold for a given period of time, or that you have the right to first refusal in your territory. Check to ensure that you do not have to buy more franchise operations in order to retain exclusive territory. Can the size of your territory be reduced at any time by the franchisor? Can you expand your territory? If you have a choice of location initially, examine each one carefully, preferably with an advisor, and study the potential of each location in terms of sales.

7. **The purchase costs of the franchise**. Is there a franchise fee and, if so, how much is it? What does the franchise package include? Is it just the use of a name or trademark, or are you also buying initial inventory, equipment and fixtures? Are there also service charges such as royalty fees?

8. **Training offered**. Does the franchisor provide training for you and your staff? Is it only a one-time affair or is it ongoing? Does the

training consist of management skills, product or service skills, operational skills, or a combination of all three? How much do you have to pay for this service?

9. **Prices and Sales**. Are you able to adjust prices or are they set by the franchisor? Can you offer specials on your own? Are there sales quotas and are they realistic?

10. **Products and supplies**. Does the contract specify what products you must carry? Can you stock product lines other than those of the franchisor? Are the sources for your products specified or can you shop around for the best deal? What are the payment terms? Are there minimums specified for order size?

11. **Business controls**. Does the franchisor specify how the franchisee must operate the business? Although this may seem like a curtailment of freedom, it is also the only way of ensuring that the franchises operate in a uniform manner. These controls usually include advertising policies, hours and conduct of business, accounting procedures, reports from franchisee to franchisor, and even access to the franchisee's records. It may also stipulate that the franchisee must operate the business personally and that the franchisor has the final word in any disagreements between the two parties.

12. **Understand the franchise contract**. You must understand every clause of the contract and make sure that all obligations and freedoms are specified. Especially important are clauses pertaining to termination, bankruptcy, transfer, renewal, and sale of the franchise. Under what conditions can the franchisor revoke the franchise agreement?

Many franchisors will prepare a package which includes general information about the franchise and forecasts of financial statements including cash flow and projections of future income. An accountant can help uncover potential problems which may not be easily detected by a cursory examination and which require an in-depth financial analysis. For example, you may find that the franchise will be profitable if you can capture a large market, but this may take considerable time.

Finally, check on the franchise company with all available sources including credit agencies, banks, and the Better Business Bureau. If the franchisor has had financial problems or customer complaints about the service, these sources will have the information available. Remember, the better the franchise — the longer it has proven itself in the marketplace — the higher its cost.

Financing a New Business

Getting adequate financing is a major problem faced by most individuals planning to open their own business. Initially, sales are likely to be slow, while expenses such as advertising will be high. A clear projection of the funds required for the initial year or more has to be made and reconciled with the financial resources available before you even consider going into business.

The funds to start a business usually come from the entrepreneur's own savings or from friends and relatives. However, banks, trust companies, federal or provincial agencies and venture capitalists also offer funding.

The **Federal Business Development Bank (FBDB)** can help if additional funds are required. The FBDB is a federal government institution that provides advice on the many federal and provincial loan and grant programs available to help finance small businesses. The bank also has consultants who prepare loan proposals for a reasonable fee. In addition, the bank offers long-term and operating loans to businesspeople who have been turned down by other financial institutions. That does not mean that the FBDB makes loans to poor risks, but simply that it is a last resort for businesses that look promising, but do not have the collateral or other securities that a chartered bank might want.

Venture capitalists are another source of financing. These are groups of private investors or firms that invest in new businesses which appear promising to them. There are hundreds in Canada, and they are always looking for investment possibilities. While they sometimes provide financing only, in most instances they take ownership in the firm by buying shares. Sometimes they can leave owners with little or no control over their firm. Thus, if you want 100% ownership, venture capitalists are not a source for consideration.

When applying for a loan it is important that you do not underestimate your requirements for fixed assets or for the operation. **Undercapitalization** — not having enough funds — is a common cause of failure in many small businesses. Remember that you will require money to live during the initial operating period when your business has little if any income. Unless you allow for your personal requirements, you will underestimate your financial requirements and ultimately hurt your business.

The Business Plan

A carefully drawn-up loan proposal, often called a business plan, is crucial to getting a loan from most financial institutions. Using experts such as an accountant or a financial advisor from a management consulting firm to help you look good in the eyes of potential lenders is sound advice. You have to show that your business is and will continue to be financially successful. The business plan should include the following:

Title Page: Name of company and location; telephone; date; person to contact.

Summary: A summary of the major points of the business plan.

Table of Contents

Introduction: The reason why the loan is required. A description of the product and why it is expected to be in demand.

The Company: A summary of the company. Location; reason for its establishment; number of employees if operating; principal owners or shareholders.

Management: A brief description of the principal members of the management group, along with their professional designations and expertise.

The Product: A description of the product.

The Market Place: Areas where the product will be available. The major target markets. The major stores where the product will be available.

Market Size: A discussion of the potential size of the market and its future growth.

Competition: A discussion of the major competitors; their product; their market share. Advantages and disadvantages of their products compared to yours.

Sales Plan: A discussion of your sales effort during the first year. What territory you will cover. Whom you will approach first. The number of people to be employed in sales. The advertising campaign planned.

Sales Forecast: An actual sales forecast indicating unit sales expected for a number of years in the future along with the dollar amount. If sales territories are involved they should be mentioned and a percentage breakdown given per territory.

Sources of Market Information: How the sales and market information was collected, along with sources of information.

Product Development: Is a prototype available? What ongoing research and development is required? What testing is required before product is saleable?

Production: How the product will be manufactured. Parts to be purchased from other sources. The number of people required in the production process. Special skills required, if any. Manufacturing space required.

Product Costs: A breakdown of manufacturing costs per unit.

Gross Profit: An analysis of the gross profit expected per unit. This takes into account the suggested retail price and discounts offered.

Financial Requirements: An analysis of the financial requirements; includes money invested in the venture to date. The projected first year total costs. Revenue expected during first year.

***Pro Forma* Financial Statements**: This includes *pro forma* income statements for a number of years, as well as cash-flow projections. (See Chapter 9 for a discussion of cash flow and an example of a cash-flow statement).

Financing — a Mystery to Small Business

Many small business owners shudder at the thought of taking a business loan. Many wait until it is too late; most are unprepared. Many have trouble determining how much money they need for their operation or expansion. They are usually too conservative about their costs and too optimistic about their sales. As a result they are undercapitalized.

So how can you get a loan? The following are helpful guidelines provided by George Fells, president of SB Capital Corporation Ltd.

1. Make your approach early. Most financial institutions need at least six weeks to make a decision about a loan. It might be a good idea to have a preliminary meeting with the banker to find out what the loan ceiling is and what information you should include along with your loan application.

2. Most bankers want cash flow and operating projections. While fancy presentations are not necessary, you have to be thorough and complete in the presentation of your firm's financial picture. The financial projections must present a logical picture of where the company is now and where you think it will be a year or two in the future.

3. Be sure you provide the financial information required. For example, banks put more emphasis on financial ratios (debt-equity, inventory turnover, etc.) and past performance. Long-term lenders, on the other hand, are obviously concerned with repayment of the loan and thus place more emphasis on the future profitability of the firm. Their interest lies in the collateral you can provide to secure the loan.

4. Although accountants and advisors should be used whenever needed, don't forget that you are the one that must prepare the information contained in your reports and present it to your banker. You have to be able to explain every detail.

You should provide a summary of your company and include:
— Name of the company with full address and phone number.
— Description of the company/ the date and place it was incorporated, how and where the business is conducted, and how it has developed.

— Your management background and experience.
— The amount of money required, the type of funds needed (working capital, long-term, etc.) and why. A summary of pertinent figures — sales, gross profit, selling and administrative costs, profits before taxes — for the past five years if the firm has been established that long, and projected for the next three to five years.
— Detailed financial statements/ a monthly forecast of cash flow, projected income statement and balance sheet and a statement of working capital.
— If the application is for debt capital, then you must provide an outline of the type of security available, including a recent valuation of fixed assets, and what is available as collateral for guarantees.

By doing a thorough job of providing financial details about your company you also solve another major problem — planning. While forecasting is not foolproof and does not guarantee success, it can help to limit the surprises that could force your business into bankruptcy before the first five years are up.

SOURCE: Mike Grenby, "Financing a 'Mystery' to Small Business," *Vancouver Sun*, Sept. 5, 1979.

FORMS OF PRIVATE BUSINESS OWNERSHIP

The form of business ownership you choose is simply a legal prescription indicating to the people with whom you are dealing, who will be responsible for the operation of the business, and who will reimburse them in the event of loss. For example, the government wants to know if your business profits should be taxed as part of your personal income or as part of the firm's income. If you are dealing with suppliers, they want to know who will be responsible for merchandise payment — if you were hit by a car or went bankrupt, how could they recover their money? Could they obtain it only from your business, or could they go to your private assets? Investors in large corporations want to know how their investment will be protected. How can they go about selling their ownership in the business to someone else? Finally, customers may also want to know who owns the business, in case they need recourse for defective goods or unsatisfactory performance of a service. The form of business ownership chosen is therefore very important, both to you, the owner, and to the people who will be dealing with your business.

There are three major forms of private business ownership — the sole proprietorship, the partnership and the corporation. Each form has its advantages and disadvantages, depending on the business and the nature of the product or service.

Sole Proprietorship

A sole proprietorship is still the most common legal form of business ownership in Canada, although the corporation has become dominant in industries such as manufacturing (Figure 3.2). The sole proprietorship is ideally suited for small businesses, especially those just starting out, which require flexibility in both operation and management.

A **sole proprietorship** has only one owner who is responsible for the firm's operation and takes all risks of loss. The law does not distinguish between the owner as a private individual and his business. Legally, he is the business. Anyone dealing with the firm in effect deals with the owner. Should any legal problems arise between the owner and the people dealing with the business, they can usually be resolved by the courts through the laws of contracts and sales. Sole proprietorships are generally found in small-scale retail and service businesses such as barber shops, repair shops or service stations.

Figure 3.1 Change in percentage distribution of establishments by type of organization and size, 1946-79

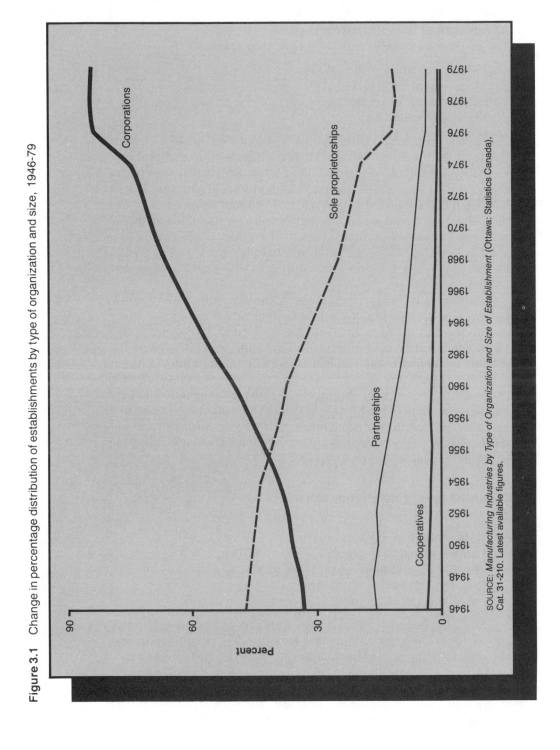

SOURCE: *Manufacturing Industries by Type of Organization and Size of Establishment* (Ottawa: Statistics Canada), Cat. 31-210. Latest available figures.

Advantages of Sole Proprietorships

The major advantages of sole proprietorship are:

Ease of formation or dissolution
Management freedom
Owner keeps all profits
Secrecy of operation

A sole proprietorship is relatively easy to establish, and faces few legal requirements. Often a business licence from the local municipality is all that is required, the cost of which will depend on the type of business, its size and the municipality in which it is located. If the owner wants to use a name other than his own, or use the words "and company," the name must be registered with the provincial Registrar of Companies. If the name is already in use, another must be chosen. In the event that the owner wants to wind up the business, a sole proprietorship is as easily dissolved as it is formed.

Management freedom is a major advantage of the sole proprietorship. In a partnership or corporation, co-owners have a say in the management of the firm. In a sole proprietorship, the owner is free to implement new operating procedures and policies, change the product or service, or move the business to another location without consulting others. Future business plans can be kept secret and, with the possible exception of employees, the owner is the only one who knows the amount of the firm's assets and debts, profits and operating expenses, or any problems the business is having. Such privacy and secrecy of operation is particularly important for a business operating in a highly competitive environment.

Disadvantages of Sole Proprietorships

The major disadvantages of sole proprietorships are:

Unlimited financial liability
Limited financial resources
Possible limited management and technical skills
Lack of permanence of the firm
Possible tax disadvantage

Since the business and the owner are legally the same, the sole proprietor is liable for all financial losses or debts that the business may incur. In the event of **bankruptcy** — when debts exceed assets — creditors can look to the owner's private assets to cover the losses. The bankrupt owner might be forced to sell his home, automobile or other belongings. **Unlimited liability** can mean financial ruin for the owner should the business fail, and is probably the major disadvantage of this form of business ownership.

A sole proprietor usually has little trouble borrowing moderate amounts of money, particularly if he has a good credit rating and if the business is reasonably successful. However, the large sums required to finance major growth or expansion are more difficult to obtain. Since most financial institutions demand some security, loans are limited by the amount of collateral available from the owner's personal assets. And — given that insufficient financial resources represent one of the major reasons for small business failure — those assets are not likely to be enough. Thus, additional financing usually depends on the owner's personal savings or business profits, together with whatever loans can be obtained from friends and relatives.

The more successful the business becomes, the easier it will be to obtain additional financing. If growth is the objective, however, it may be best to consider incorporating, so that additional funds

Canada's public markets contain many sole proprietorships

can be raised through the sale of shares to investors. Furthermore, while financial assistance is available to small businesses through various programs of both the federal and provincial governments, it is often only available to firms that have been incorporated.

In addition to financial difficulties, a sole proprietorship may also encounter management problems. The owner and manager — often the same person — may not have the business education or management experience necessary to perform the wide variety of management tasks required. The owner may simply dislike certain tasks, or neglect some essential business function such as finance or marketing. Any shortcomings in the owner's management ability or interest when the firm is small will lead to even more serious consequences as the business grows.

Another serious problem faced by the sole proprietorship is the lack of continuity of the business. When the owner dies, the business also legally terminates. The firm's assets become part of the deceased's estate and may have to be sold to pay estate taxes. However, selling the business quickly may be difficult, especially if its success has depended on the special skills of the owner. If the business is very large, on the other hand, it may be difficult to find a buyer with sufficient funds to take it over.

Finally, a successful sole proprietor may be paying more taxes than if the business were incorporated, because all profits made in the business must be included in the owner's personal income for tax purposes. Incorporation may present a tax advantage for a business owner because of certain corporate tax provisions. This topic will be discussed further when we look at corporations.

Partnership

A second major form of private business ownership, though less common than the other two, is the **partnership**. It consists of two or more people who have combined their talents and resources in a business for the purpose of earning a profit. A partnership is almost as easy to establish as a sole proprietorship, and it suffers from many of the same disadvantages. Partnerships are most common in the professions — law, medicine, dentistry and accounting — but are also found in manufacturing, wholesaling and retailing, as well as in the trades, such as carpentry, painting and plumbing.

Formation of a Partnership
A partnership may be formed either by express agreement or by implication. If the partnership is established by **express agreement**, the factors important to the partners are specified in writing, and include the following:

- the name and location of the business;
- the names of the partners;
- how profits (or losses) are to be split.
- the amount of the investment;
- the salary each partner is to receive prior to distribution of profit;
- the duties and authority of each partner;
- the life of the partnership;
- how the partnership may be dissolved.

A partnership by **implication**, on the other hand, may exist when two or more people act in a manner which a court of law deems to be a partnership, even though there is no written agreement. Often friends or co-workers may start a business but neglect to write up a formal agreement. This can cause serious problems later, should personal disagreements arise concerning the management or objectives of the firm.

Kinds of Partnership

A partnership may consist of **general partners** who own the business, work in it and share the profits or losses. However, it may also have one or more **limited partners** who are only liable for the amount they have invested in the business. Limited partners may inquire into the operation of the partnership and make suggestions about its management, but they may not take an active part in its operation. While a firm may have many limited partners, it must include at least one general partner with unlimited liability.

General partners may be actively involved in the daily operation of the business, or they may be **silent partners** who have invested in the business but who neither involve themselves in its operation nor allow their names to appear in the firm's name. However, if the silent partner's name is important to the firm, the firm might be permitted to use it for a fee. A silent partner still has unlimited liability for any debts incurred by the firm in the event of bankruptcy.

Advantages of Partnerships

The major advantages of partnerships are:

Ease of establishment
Complementary management skills of partners
Greater capacity to raise funds
Incentive for employees

A partnership is as easily formed as a sole proprietorship, and faces few if any legal or government rules and regulations. However, a written agreement specifying the terms of the partnership should be established. While this may be done by the partners themselves, they would be wise to seek legal advice. The time and money initially expended on this document may be far less than the expenses incurred later, should a serious disagreement arise as to the partners' original intentions.

Since a partnership may include a wider range of management skills than a sole proprietorship, the chances of business failure may be lessened. Two or more partners can divide the management and operating duties among themselves. Doctors, for example, may form a partnership in which each is a specialist in a different field of medicine. Or two people may establish a retail business, one being skilled in buying merchandise and in the administration of the business, and the other highly proficient in sales.

A partnership can raise funds more easily than a sole proprietorship because, collectively, the partners can provide a larger amount of money to start their business. If additional funds are required, financial institutions such as banks are more likely to make larger loans to a partnership, because the risk of business failure is lower. Even if the partnership were to fail, each partner remains financially liable for the total debts of the business.

Another major advantage of a partnership is its ability to retain valuable employees by making them partners in the business. Many accounting and law firms hire trainees with the promise of a partnership at some later date. The possibility of ownership and a share of the profits provides incentive for the trainees to work hard and contribute to the firm.

Disadvantages of Partnerships

The major disadvantages of partnerships are:

Unlimited financial liability
Management disagreements among partners
Limited ability to raise financial resources
Lack of continuity in the firm
Complexity of dissolution

As in the sole proprietorship, a major disadvantage of a partnership is the unlimited liability of each general partner in the event of bankruptcy. In addition, all partners are liable, jointly and severally, for the total debts of the business. This means that while all partners are liable for the partnership's total debts, each member is also liable for the full amount if the other partners are unable or unwilling to pay. Furthermore, any single partner can bind all the others to agreements and contracts, even without their consent.

Perhaps one of the greatest problems in partnerships is the possibility of personal disagreements regarding the firm's management or objectives. For example, while one partner might be prepared to take greater financial risks in order for the firm to grow and expand rapidly, the other might prefer that the firm remain at its present size or grow more slowly to minimize risk. If one partner lacks interest or management skills, the entire workload may fall to the remaining partners. Sometimes another person can be found to come into the business; if not, the partnership may have to be dissolved.

Depending on the size and type of business, getting adequate financing may still be a problem for a partnership. Even though more individuals are available to contribute to the business — either through their own savings or through loans — the amount raised may still be far short of that required. Even a multiple partnership, for example, may have trouble raising the large amount of capital required to establish even a small manufacturing company.

Like a sole proprietorship, a partnership is legally terminated when one member dies or is otherwise unable or unwilling to continue as a partner. Legally this is not a major problem as most partnerships specify in their written agreements how a new partner may be brought into the firm to replace another, so that operations are not seriously affected. Nevertheless, it may be difficult to find someone who is acceptable to the remaining partners and possesses the skills or funds necessary to take the place of the individual who has left.

Finally, individuals of a successful partnership may also face higher taxes, since individual tax rates may be higher than those for corporations. Again, a point will be reached when incorporation may be advantageous in terms of taxation.

The Corporation

A corporation eliminates some of the disadvantages of both the sole proprietorship and the partnership. In the eyes of the law, a **corporation** is

- an artificial person,
- with an unlimited lifespan,
- empowered by the federal or provincial government to carry on a specific line of business,
- owned by shareholders,
- who are liable only for the extent of their investment in the company.

Thus, a corporation has the same legal rights as an individual. A corporation can sign contracts, sue or be sued, and purchase, own or dispose of property as specified in its charter.

The first corporations were actually established in medieval Britain through the granting of charters to trading companies. The charter stated that no member was to be held liable for collective debts — in other words, those who owned the corporations were sheltered from being personally liable for any debts incurred by the trading company. One of the trading companies to obtain this royal protection was the Hudson's Bay Company. In a 19th-century British court case, Salomon v. Salomon, the sheltering aspect of the corporation was strengthened through the court ruling that a creditor had no right to the assets of a corporation's shareholders even if there was only a single shareholder.

Private and Public Corporations

Corporations may be either private or public. A **private corporation** may not have more than 50 shareholders. It may not offer its shares to the general public, and there are restrictions on the transfer of shares. These limitations do not apply to a **public corporation**, which may sell or transfer its shares freely on Canada's stock exchanges. However, the public corporation is subject to certain government regulations designed to protect the shareholder. These regulations include disclosing pertinent financial and operating information to its shareholders, having at least three directors and holding annual meetings for the election of board members and the appointment of an auditor.

The T. Eaton Company: A Private Corporation

The T.Eaton Co., one of Canada's major retailers, is entirely owned by the four Eaton brothers: Fred, George, Thor and John. They are the descendants of Timothy Eaton, who started in downtown Toronto in 1869 with a small dry goods store purchased for $6500. At a time when barter was the accepted method of buying, he insisted on cash and a single price to be paid by all customers. Some time later he introduced his guarantee, "Goods satisfactory or money refunded," and in 1884 he offered a merchandise catalogue for the first time, with home delivery. After only a few years, circulation of the "Wishing Book" was 200 000 copies per year.

These innovative ideas laid the foundation for a huge retailing empire consisting of 63 department stores in ten provinces, with between 40 000 and 50 000 employees. In 1977 the company's sales were estimated at $1.4 billion. There has been some speculation in the past about the possibility of Eaton's "going public." The move would depend on the company's financial standing and need for funds from public shareholders. While it may not be necessary for Eaton's to go public in order to raise capital, it has been suggested that there should be less secrecy concerning the firm's financial operations. According to a former senior executive, many Eaton's managers are not sufficiently informed of the company's financial picture to operate their departments effectively.

SOURCE: See Ian Brown, "The Empire that Timothy Built," *The Financial Post 300*, May 1978, p. 17.

Advantages of Corporations

The major advantages of corporations are:

Limited financial liability
Greater financial capability
Easy transferability of ownership
Unlimited lifespan
Greater capacity for growth and expansion
Greater ability to attract specialized management skills
Possible tax advantages

All shareholders in a corporation are limited in loss by the amount of their investment. The personal property of shareholders is not affected by a corporate business failure. Individuals dealing with a corporation are alerted to this limitation by the presence of one of the following words in the firm's name: "Limited," "Incorporated" or "Corporation" ("Ltd.," "Inc." or "Corp."). This word must be clearly displayed in the name and must appear on all invoices and stationery. Limited liability may well be the greatest advantage of incorporation.

It is important to remember, however, that incorporation cannot be used to evade creditors. For example, if a person were about to face bankruptcy and incorporated so as to safeguard his or her personal property, the Fraudulent Conveyances Act would disallow such a transfer. The Bankruptcy Act has a similar provision. The courts could also ignore the usual protection offered by a corporation if it suspected fraudulent or improper actions on the part of owners of the business. This doctrine is known as piercing the "corporate veil."

A corporation with a proven track record has the ability to acquire greater financial resources than have other forms of ownership. Since ownership in a corporation can be divided into many small parts, or shares, many small investors can purchase a part of the business. While an individual may hold as little as one share in a company, the total number of shares that may be owned is limited only by the total number of shares that the company has issued. Of course, the amount of financial capital which can be raised depends on the investors' confidence in the firm's profitability. New corporations may actually have trouble raising capital because of the limited liability of the shareholders. Lenders in such corporations want the personal guarantee of the principal shareholders that their loan will be repaid in case of bankruptcy.

Another advantage of a corporation is the easy transferability of ownership. Million of shares, representing ownership in hundreds of companies, are traded on Canada's stock exchanges every day. Since shares may change hands in hours or even minutes, investors need not worry that their investments will be tied up indefinitely should they decide to sell.

Furthermore, since the death of any one shareholder does not end the life of the corporation, it can concentrate on growth. Large corporations generally have a good credit rating and thus can borrow from financial institutions at lower rates of interest than smaller companies. Large corporations are also able to devote more money to research and development of new products and can accumulate greater stores of the capital goods necessary for production. An indefinite life span also means that large corporations can promise long-term employment and thus attract experts in many areas, including management.

Because corporations are separate legal entities they must pay both federal and provincial taxes. Dividends shareholders receive are paid out of profits remaining after all taxes have been paid. These dividends must then be included by shareholders in their personal income and are taxed a second time. To prevent shareholders from being taxed twice, the federal government allows private individuals who receive dividend income to deduct a dividend tax credit from their tax payable.

Perhaps the prime reason for incorporating is the potential tax advantage. For example, owners of corporations can pay themselves a small salary and leave excess profit in the corporation to be taxed at a more advantageous rate. Later, they can take these profits out of the corporation through the payment of dividends on which taxes are lower. Income splitting is also possible. For example, family members can be made shareholders of the corporation. They could then receive dividends which would be eligible to be taxed at a lower rate.

Being incorporated may also give a business a better image and more credibility. The effort involved in incorporation may lead potential clients to believe that a business is more serious, and thereby lead to increased business.

Another advantage of incorporation is the potential savings through the small-business tax credit. The Income Tax Act also allows qualifying corporations to pay a maximum federal tax of 15% on the first $200 000 of taxable income. Several provinces also offer lower or zero rates of provincial tax during their first years of operation. On the other hand, a person who must include business profit in personal income could pay as much as 50% in Ontario and 59% in Québec. Thus, incorporation offers a considerable tax advantage. However, even with these tax advantages there is general agreement among tax accountants and advisors that a person should not incorporate unless sales or billings exceed $60 000 to $70 000 per year. Some even suggest that $100 000 to $200 000 is a more realistic figure.[3]

TABLE 3.1
Comparison of forms of private business ownership

Form of Ownership	Advantages	Disadvantages
Sole Proprietorship	1. Retention of all profits 2. Ease of formation & dissolution 3. Freedom & flexibility of management 4. Secrecy of operation	1. Unlimited financial liability 2. Limited financial resources 3. Management deficiencies 4. Lack of continuity
Partnership	1. Ease of formation 2. Complementary management or technical skills 3. Greater financial resources 4. Employee incentive	1. Unlimited financial liability 2. Disagreements among partners 3. Lack of continuity 4. Complexity of dissolution
Corporation	1. Limited financial liability 2. Specialized management skills 3. Great financial capability 4. Unlimited life span 5. Ownership easily transferred 6. Capacity for growth	1. Difficult & costly to establish 2. Lack of personal interest by management 3. Legal restrictions and government regulations 4. Lack of secrecy in operation

Disadvantages of Corporations

The major disadvantages of corporations are:

Cost and difficulty of establishment
Lack of secrecy of operation
Legal restrictions and government regulations
Lack of personal interest by management

The major disadvantages of incorporation are the legal and accounting work required. Since a corporation is a separate legal entity, the requirements to establish it are more complicated and time-consuming. Both the federal and provincial governments require a fee for filing the necessary documents. A lawyer, if required, will probably charge about $1000 in legal fees and $300 per year to keep the books of the corporation. Owners of corporations must also fill out annual reports, hold annual meetings and file federal and provincial tax reports. Even so, accounting fees for a corporation will not necessarily be greater than those for an unincorporated business.

Another drawback, particularly for public corporations with many shareholders, is the lack of secrecy. Because corporations are owned by shareholders who must receive financial statements and other information about the company, it is difficult to keep all operations secret, and competitors may gain an advantage. This is a problem mainly for public corporations, since financial information is freely available to anyone.

In addition, both public and private corporations are subject to more legal restrictions and government regulations than sole proprietorships and partnerships. All corporations face a constant bombardment of government forms that must be filed both federally and provincially. In order to comply with these regulations and perform the required paperwork, a company may have to spend considerable time, money and effort.

Finally, large corporations are usually operated by professional managers who are not shareholders. Without an ownership interest in the company, there may be less personal incentive for management and thus less personal involvement and responsibility than in other forms of ownership.

How to Incorporate

Companies may be incorporated by special acts of either the federal or provincial governments. This method of incorporation is primarily used for establishing firms such as banks and trust companies, where specific regulations are required to protect the public. The great majority of corporations are established under either the Canada Business Corporations Act or the various provincial Business Corporations Acts. If a business will operate in only one province, it should incorporate there. However, if it intends to operate in a number of provinces from the beginning, federal incorporation may be more advantageous.

Each of the various provinces and territories uses one of two systems for the incorporation of companies. Under the **registration system**, individuals are required to register a document called a **Memorandum of Association** with the Registrar of Companies. The memorandum must be accompanied by the corporation by-laws, a Notice of Office, and the required fee. Other provinces follow the **Letters Patent system**, in which the provincial secretary, acting under the authority of the Lieutenant-Governor, issues a document called the Letters Patent after obtaining the pertinent information about the corporation from the application form.

Incorporation for private companies is generally quite simple, although procedures may vary among provinces. In British Columbia, for example, the registration system is used. Here, once the name of the corporation has been chosen and cleared by the Registrar of Companies, the next step is to complete the Memorandum of Association and the Notice of Office (Figure 3.3 and 3.4). A set of corporation by-laws specifying how the firm is to be operated can be obtained from the Registrar of Companies. The by-laws do not require alterations unless the persons so wish. All three documents are then submitted along with the required fee which is based on the number

Form 1
(Section 7)

COMPANIES ACT

MEMORANDUM

.........We...wish to be formed into a company with limited liability under the Companies Act in pursuance of this Memorandum.

1. The name of the company is AdTech Enterprises Ltd.

2. The authorized capital of the company consists of

   TEN THOUSAND (10 000) common shares without par value.

3. ....We...agree to take the number and kind of shares in the company set opposite ...our... name .

Full Name(s), Resident Address(es) and Occupation(s) of Subscriber(s)	Number and Kind of Shares taken by Subscriber(s)
John Blackstone 9499 A Street Vancouver, BC Engineer	One hundred (100) common without par value
Alfred Whiteside 7766 North Street Vancouver, BC Accountant	One hundred (100) common without par value
William Brown 1122 Central Crescent Vancouver, BC Marketing Manager	One hundred (100) common without par value
Total Shares Taken:	Three hundred (300) common without par value

Dated the ....17th... **day of** ...November............... , 19 ..90.. . .

Figure 3.3 Memorandum of association

FORM 3
(Section 10)

PROVINCE OF BRITISH COLUMBIA

Certificate of
Incorporation No. ....

COMPANIES ACT

NOTICES OF OFFICES

The offices of the undermentioned Company are located as follows:

Name of Company ....AdTech Enterprises Ltd...

....

Registered Office:

Address ....7766 North Street...

....Vancouver...

British Columbia

Records Office:

Address.......................7766 North Street...

....Vancouver...

British Columbia

Dated the   17th day of   November   , 19 90   .

(Signature) ..... *Alfred Whiteside* ....

(Relationship to Company) ..Director...................................

Figure 3.4 Notice of office

of shares the company is authorized to sell. The charter, which signifies the legal establishment of the corporation, can be expected within two to three weeks. Changes can be made at any time by informing the Registrar of Companies.

If a large firm is to be incorporated as a public company with many classes and types of shares, legal assistance is almost essential to ensure that all aspects of the organization and operation of the company are provided for.

General Information Required for Incorporation

NAME: Every corporation is required to have a name, which must not be similar to that of an existing corporation and must not misrepresent the business the firm intends to practice. The name must be followed by ''Limited,'' ''Incorporated,'' or ''Corporation,'' or the appropriate abbreviation, and it must be prominently displayed on all orders, invoices, contracts or other binding agreements, to ensure that individuals dealing with the firm are aware of its limited liability.

HEAD OFFICE: The location of the head office must be stated and readily accessible to any shareholder, director or government agency. If the firm is incorporated federally the head office may be anywhere in the country, but incorporation in a particular province requires that the head office be located there.

DIRECTORS: A company must have a certain minimum number of directors to represent the shareholders. The names and addresses of the directors, and the number of shares each owns, must be specified.

OBJECTS OF THE COMPANY: Corporations are granted the right to carry on a specific line of business — the sale of real estate, for example, or the manufacture of specific products. However, some provinces are fairly lenient regarding the restrictions of the charter, allowing a company to engage in a wide variety of activities without requiring that the charter be amended.

AUTHORIZED CAPITAL: A company is granted the right to issue a number of common and preferred shares, up to a stated maximum. (The difference between these shares will be explained later.) Certain rights may be attached to both types of shares. The number and class of shares that the company decides to issue must be clearly stated in its Articles of Incorporation.

OTHER MATTERS: The individuals incorporating the company are free to specify in the Articles of Incorporation any other matters pertaining to its organization or operation.

Organization of the Corporation

Most large corporations are operated by professional managers. The owners — **shareholders** or **stockholders** — are primarily concerned with receiving an appropriate return on their investment and, especially in large corporations, are not directly involved in the operation of the company. The board of directors is the link between the owners and managers. It is elected by the shareholders on the basis of one vote per share held and is responsible to them for the proper operation of the company. In practice, however, the board delegates the responsibility for actual operation to the firm's top managers whom it hires, appoints or elects. The governing structure of the corporation is illustrated in Figure 3.5.

The Shareholders

Shareholders are the owners of a corporation. Since many private corporations are established as family businesses, the major shareholders are usually family members and sometimes long-time employees. The ownership of many of Canada's larger public corporations is usually spread among many shareholders.

A corporation may issue two major types of shares: common and preferred. **Preferred shareholders** usually receive a specified annual dividend per share, which must be paid before common shareholders can receive any payment. In the event of the firm's bankruptcy, preferred shareholders have first claim to any assets remaining after all other creditors have been paid. **Common shareholders** have no particular right to any share of profits, nor any claims on assets, should the company go bankrupt. However, they do retain ownership of what remains after all creditors and preferred shareholders have been paid. Common shareholders have the right to attend at least one shareholders' meeting per year. They are also entitled to question the board of directors or senior management on any aspect of the company's operation. An example of a share certificate is shown in Figure 3.6.

If a shareholder is unable to attend the meeting in person, he or she may vote by proxy. A **proxy** (Figure 3.7) authorizes another individual, usually a director, to vote on the shareholder's behalf. Often proxies are solicited by company officers such as the board of directors, who are thus able to re-elect themselves to office. It would be difficult and expensive for dissident shareholders to solicit proxies from others, particularly if the corporation is a large one with many shareholders. As a consequence most corporate officers are able to perpetuate themselves in office, while shareholders are virtually powerless to challenge them regarding their method of operation or their performance. Often the only option for dissatisfied shareholders is to sell their shares — and if the company's perfor-

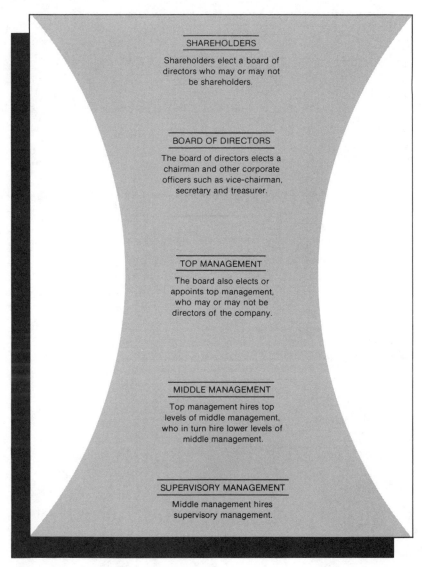

SHAREHOLDERS

Shareholders elect a board of directors who may or may not be shareholders.

BOARD OF DIRECTORS

The board of directors elects a chairman and other corporate officers such as vice-chairman, secretary and treasurer.

TOP MANAGEMENT

The board also elects or appoints top management, who may or may not be directors of the company.

MIDDLE MANAGEMENT

Top management hires top levels of middle management, who in turn hire lower levels of middle management.

SUPERVISORY MANAGEMENT

Middle management hires supervisory management.

Figure 3.5 Governing structure of the corporation

mance has been poor, its shares will not bring as high a price as the shareholders originally paid.

A company that intends to offer additional shares to the general public must prepare a prospectus for each new share offering. The **prospectus** provides information about the company, including comparative financial data for a number of past years, the movement of share prices over a period of time, the directors and their share holding, details of the company's operation, the reasons for the new share offering, and the auditors' reports.

Figure 3.6 Example of a share certificate

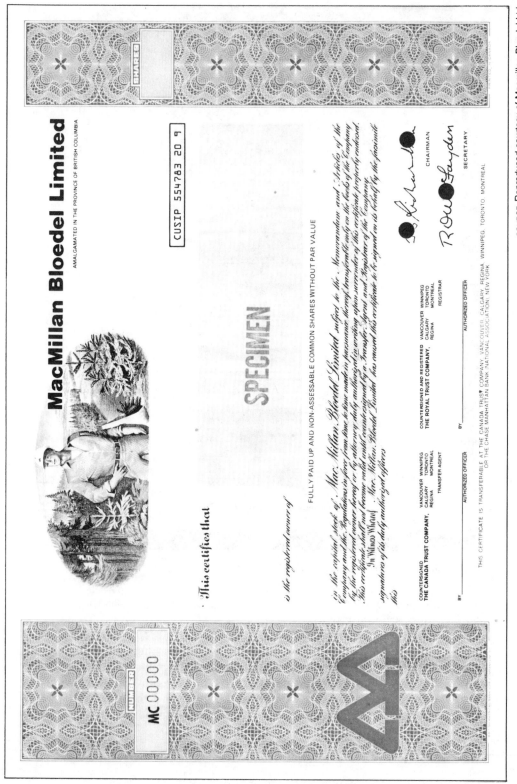

MacMillan Bloedel Limited

Proxy Solicited by the Board of Directors for the Annual General Meeting of Common Shareholders to be held at the Hotel Vancouver, Vancouver, B.C., on Thursday, March 31, 1988 at 10:00 a.m.

The undersigned hereby appoints A.H. ZIMMERMAN, or failing him, C.C. KNUDSEN, or failing him, R.V. SMITH or

G.H.D. Hobbs,   R.T. Kenny,   D.W. Kerr,   C.C. Knudsen, D.S. Macdonald,   J.A. Pattison,   A. Powis,   R.V. Smith, Jean M. Southam,   D.W. Strangway,   J.S. Walton   and A.H. Zimmerman   or to withhold authority to vote for all nominees listed above □

To withhold authority to vote for any individual nominee, write the nominee's name in the space following

2.   To vote for □ or against □ or to abstain from voting on □ the appointment of Price Waterhouse as auditors with authority to the directors to fix their remuneration.

(Continued and to be signed on other side)

to be his proxy holder to attend the Annual General Meeting on Thursday, March 31, 1988 and any adjournment thereof, and to vote and act with respect to all common shares of the Company registered in the name of the undersigned as if the undersigned were personally present, and specifically on the items of business referred to in the Information Circular for this Annual General Meeting as follows:

1.   To vote for all of the following nominees for election as directors □ except as withheld below:
D.C. Davenport,   F.J. de Wit,   J.T. Eyton,   R.E. Harrison,

(Continued from other side)

IF NO DIRECTION IS GIVEN WITH RESPECT TO THE ITEMS OF BUSINESS THE SHARES WILL BE VOTED ON A POLL FOR THE NAMED NOMINEES AND AUDITORS. HOWEVER, IF A DIRECTION IS GIVEN THE SHARES WILL BE VOTED ON A POLL IN ACCORDANCE THEREWITH. A SHAREHOLDER MAY APPOINT AS HIS PROXY ANY OTHER PERSON, WHO NEED NOT BE A MEMBER, AND IF HE WISHES TO DO SO HE MUST STRIKE OUT THE PRINTED NAMES AND SUBSTITUTE THE NAME OF HIS APPOINTEE IN THE SPACE PROVIDED.

The undersigned hereby acknowledges receipt of the notice of this Annual General Meeting and the accompanying Information Circular and ratifies all that his proxy may lawfully do by virtue hereof and revokes all former proxies.

_____ , 1988
Dated

_____
Signature

Please date, sign and mail promptly in the enclosed envelope.

Proxies must be received by the Company, Guaranty Trust Company of Canada or Shareholder Communications Corporation, at least 24 hours prior to the meeting.

SHS-21 (2-88)

SOURCE: Reproduced courtesy of Macmillan Bloedel Ltd.

Figure 3.7   Example of a proxy

The Board of Directors

The **board of directors** represents the shareholders and is elected by them on the basis of one vote per share. Shareholders who own a large number of shares have considerable influence in electing board members, and may even stand for election themselves. The number of directors on the board of a public corporation may vary, from a minimum of three to 15 or 20 in large corporations. A private corporation requires only one director, who is usually the owner. Most boards of public corporations meet on a quarterly or semi-annual basis. Once elected by the shareholders, the board elects its own chairman, vice-chairman and secretary.

Since board members are chosen for their business expertise, many are presidents or senior officers of other large companies. Individuals are not restricted in the number of directorships they may hold as long as there is no conflict of interest. Directors are not liable for the actions of either the board or company officers or agents unless the action is illegal. Their main function is to provide an outsider's point of view on major company decisions. However, there is growing public pressure for greater responsibility and liability for directors regarding company management.[4]

The board of directors has the power to manage the company, establish corporate policies and institute by-laws governing specific actions of the corporation. The board of directors seldom initiates major courses of action for the company, but is often involved in making specific decisions concerning the extent of plant expansion, the timing and nature of company expansion into other regions or countries, or the addition or deletion of particular product lines. The directors also decide on new share issues, the payment of dividends and the establishment and conduct of shareholders' meetings, including the issuance of proxies for voting.

In an effort to safeguard shareholders, the federal and provincial governments have placed restrictions on the powers of the board of directors. In addition, board members are charged to act honestly and in good faith in carrying out their duties for the company. A public corporation is required to hold annual meetings, provide financial statements about its operation and submit the company's operation to an audit, where the accuracy of the information included in the financial statements is verified by an independent accounting firm.

Top Management

The board of directors hires, appoints or elects the **chief executive officer (CEO)**, who may be the chairman of the board of directors or the corporation president, or both. The members of the board usually hire or elect the secretary and treasurer and, together with the president or CEO, hire other senior officers, usually titled vice-presidents or general managers.

The various **vice-presidents** may be in charge of the major functional areas of the company such as finance, marketing, production or personnel. The **secretary** is in possession of the corporate seal and signs all corporate documents, either alone or with another officer. The secretary also attends all board and shareholders' meetings to take minutes. The **treasurer** is in charge of the corporation's finances and in some companies is known as the **controller**.

The president and vice-presidents are responsible for the operation of the company. Their major responsibilities are for planning, both short- and long-range, policy-making and the control of operations, particularly financial control. Another major task is the development of an organization structure that will allow lower levels of management to look after the daily operations of the company. We will discuss the major management functions in later chapters.

Growth of Corporations

Virtually all businesses have their start as small companies established by entrepreneurs with a new product or idea, together with drive, incentive and the willingness to risk their own money. Although many new ventures fail, businesses that succeed in meeting their customers' needs can experience rapid growth in sales and assets.

With business growth come many advantages for the firm. As its scale of operation increases and more units of product are generated, production costs usually decrease since fixed costs pertaining to plants and equipment, management salaries, insurance, utilities and so on are spread over a greater number of units. And when costs per unit are reduced, the company can reduce the product's selling price, in turn leading to increased sales and a greater market share for the company. A successful firm has little difficulty in obtaining funds for future expansion, while the prestige that accompanies success is often an incentive for both owners and top management.

Business growth is not achieved exclusively from within. It can also occur through the outright purchase of other companies or the acquisition of a majority of the other company's shares. These **mergers** or **take-overs** may be accomplished with or without the agreement of the second company.

Vertical and Horizontal Integration

Take-overs or mergers can help a firm grow either vertically or horizontally. **Vertical integration**, for example, would occur if a manufacturing company producing kitchen appliances were to purchase a retail company primarily engaged in selling such appliances to consumers. On the other hand, a company which purchases another company in the same industry is practising **horizontal integration**. Thus the manufacturer of kitchen appliances might buy out another kitchen appliance manufacturer, while a retailer might buy other retail companies. The Hudson's Bay Company, for example, has engaged in extensive horizontal integration by purchasing a controlling interest in both Zellers and Simpsons, two large retail chains. Figure 3.8 shows the difference between vertical and horizontal integration.

Conglomerates

Sometimes one company will take over another in an entirely different field. For example, a cigarette manufacturer might purchase a food processing company or an electronics firm. In such instances the parent company may be interested in **diversification** for the sake of security in earnings. On the other hand, it may seek profitable companies to contribute to its own profit picture. The result is a **conglomerate**, control of which is exercised through some centralized top management. Examples of Canadian conglomerates include Power Corporation of Canada and Canadian Pacific Ltd. The typically diversified nature of the latter conglomerate is shown in Figure 3.9.

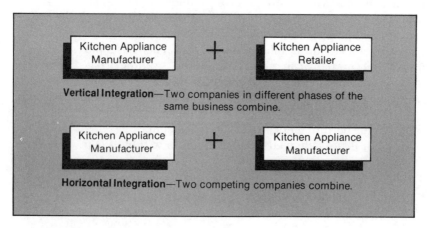

Figure 3.8 Vertical and horizontal integration

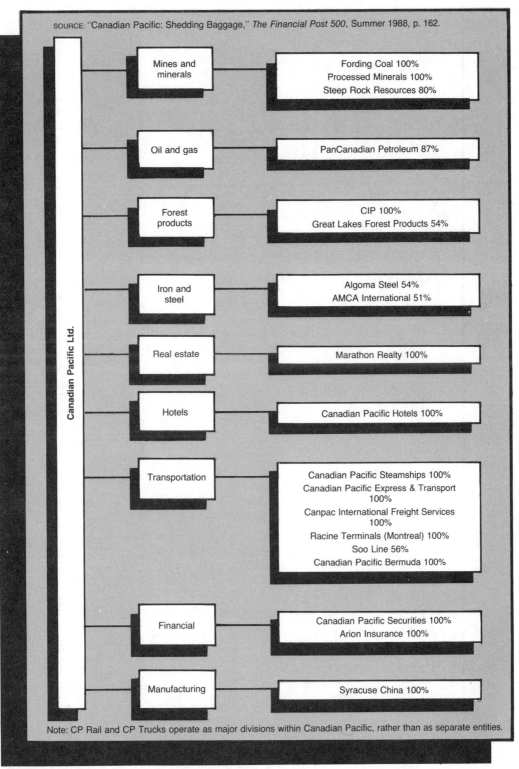

SOURCE: "Canadian Pacific: Shedding Baggage," *The Financial Post 500*, Summer 1988, p. 162.

Canadian Pacific Ltd.

Mines and minerals	Fording Coal 100% Processed Minerals 100% Steep Rock Resources 80%
Oil and gas	PanCanadian Petroleum 87%
Forest products	CIP 100% Great Lakes Forest Products 54%
Iron and steel	Algoma Steel 54% AMCA International 51%
Real estate	Marathon Realty 100%
Hotels	Canadian Pacific Hotels 100%
Transportation	Canadian Pacific Steamships 100% Canadian Pacific Express & Transport 100% Canpac International Freight Services 100% Racine Terminals (Montreal) 100% Soo Line 56% Canadian Pacific Bermuda 100%
Financial	Canadian Pacific Securities 100% Arion Insurance 100%
Manufacturing	Syracuse China 100%

Note: CP Rail and CP Trucks operate as major divisions within Canadian Pacific, rather than as separate entities.

Figure 3.9 Canadian Pacific — A Conglomerate

TABLE 3.2
Canada's 50 largest corporations.

Rank by sales 1987	Rank by sales 1986	Company (head office)	Sales or operating revenue $'000	Rank by assets	Assets $'000	Net income $'000	Employees	Foreign ownership %	Major shareholders
1	1	General Motors of Canada Ltd. (Oshawa, Ont.)	16 884 371	16	5 916 514	5 070	44 749	100	General Motors, Detroit
2	4	BCE Inc. (Montreal)[1]	14 649 000	3	26 025 000	1 087 000	117 000	8	Wide distribution
3	3	Ford Motor Co. of Canada (Oakville, Ont.)	13 976 800	30	3 622 300	123 800	27 200	97	Ford Motor, Detroit 94%
4	2	Canadian Pacific Ltd. (Montreal)	12 208 600	4	18 000 700	636 700	85 400	29	Wide distribution
5	5	George Weston Ltd. (Toronto)	11 034 800	32	3 546 100	134 100	67 300	1	Wittington Investments 58%
6	6	Alcan Aluminium Ltd. (Montreal)	9 012 822[2]	5	9 952 638	574 158	63 000	57	Wide distribution
7	8	Imperial Oil Ltd. (Toronto)	7 562 000	9	9 478 000	716 000	11 627	79	Exxon, New York 70%
8	24	Noranda Inc. (Toronto)	7 343 566	8	9 595 757	343 471	44 000		Brascade Resources 35%, Brascan 12%
9	7	Chrysler Canada Ltd. (Windsor, Ont.)	7 246 800	40	2 949 400	99 200	15 677	100	Chrysler, Detroit
10	10	Provigo Inc. (Montreal) Jan./88	6 418 100	72	1 555 000	67 200	21 000		Unigesco 21%, Sobeys 20%, Caisse de dépôt 11%
11	13	Ontario Hydro (Toronto)	5 280 000	1	32 657 000	271 000	32 147		Ontario government 100%
12	11	PetroCanada (Calgary)	5 194 000	10	8 453 000	213 000	7 204		Federal government 100%
13	16	Brascan Ltd. (Toronto)	5 178 000[3]	20	5 157 800	174 500	22	15	Brascan Holdings 49%
14	15	Hydro-Québec (Montreal)	5 095 319	2	31 659 465	509 345	18 933		Quebec government 100%
15	9	Hudson's Bay Co. (Winnipeg) Jan./88	4 845 178	31	3 614 199	(78 474)	38 000	3	Woodbridge 74%
16	14	Shell Canada Ltd. (Calgary)	4 819 000	18	5 509 000	350 000	6 913	71	Shell, Netherlands/Britain
17	17	Imasco Ltd. (Montreal)	4 814 556[4]	17	5 649 604	282 669	92 353	40	B.A.T. Industries, Britain
18	12	Canadian National Railway Co. (Montreal)	4 784 129	13	7 593 649	107 293	48 252		Federal government 100%
19	26	International Thomson Organisation Ltd. (Toronto)	4 690 062[2]	23	4 442 307	277 134	23 200	10	Woodbridge 74%
20	19	Steinberg Inc. (Montreal) July/87	4 491 355	77	1 469 353	58 469	34 000		Steinberg family 87%
21	69	Campeau Corp. (Toronto) Jan./88	4 263 646[5]	n.a.	n.a.	n.a.	38 000		R. Campeau
22	21	Sears Canada Inc. (Toronto)	4 035 098	47	2 622 452	82 074	50 000	60	Sears, Roebuck, Chicago
23	23	Canada Safeway Ltd. (Calgary) Jan./88	3 872 368[2]	103	966 176	8 539	22 000	100	Kohlberg, Kravis, Roberts, New York
24	25	Oshawa Group Ltd. (Toronto) Jan./88	3 804 015	144	672 934	49 887	19 000		Wolfe family 100%
25	29	John Labatt Ltd. (London) Apr./87	3 782 234	53	2 355 017	125 211	16 200		Brascan 37%, Caisse de dépôt 10%
26	27	Seagram Co. (Montreal) Jan./88	3 693 615[2]	7	9 616 409	687 680	14 400	46	Bronfman family 38%
27	18	TransCanada PipeLines Ltd. (Calgary)	3 355 400	14	6 669 300	160 000	2 207	3	BCE Inc. 49%
28	22	Canadian Wheat Board (Winnipeg) July/87	3 208 000	21	4 835 719	n.a.	504		Federal government 100%
29	28	Canada Packers Inc. (Toronto) Mar./87	3 205 281	143	674 968	38 587	12 500		Cedcasac Holdings 11%, company pension plan 11%
30	36	MacMillan Bloedel Ltd. (Vancouver)	3 134 500	50	2 515 800	280 600	15 226	19	Noranda Forest 50%
31	32	Air Canada (Montreal)	3 131 100	37	3 084 800	45 700	22 000		Federal government 100%
32	31	IBM Canada Ltd. (Toronto)	3 104 000	51	2 380 000	231 000	12 147	100	IBM, Armonk, N.Y.
33	30	Moore Corp. (Toronto)	3 025 260[2]	49	2 519 786	194 108	26 480	18	Royal Trustco 14%
34	•	Abitibi-Price Inc. (Toronto)	2 988 000	48	2 549 600	125 700	16 300		Olympia & York 75%
35	•	Canada Post Corp. (Ottawa) Mar./87	2 970 056	46	2 628 521	(128 981)	61 640		Federal government 100%

36	34	19	Polysar Energy & Chemical Corp. (Toronto)[6]	2 868 500	5 445 900	227 500	6 900		Nova 25%
37	33	27	Texaco Canada Inc. (Toronto)	2 649 000	3 873 000	320 000	3 288	78	Texaco, White Plains, N.Y.
38	35	271	Mitsui & Co. (Canada) (Toronto) Mar./87	2 608 542	213 465	3 796	130	100	Mitsui, Japan
39	49	62	Varity Corp. (Toronto) Jan./88	2 571 963[2]	2 069 510	66 777	16 330	70	Wide distribution
40	39	42	Domtar Inc. (Montreal)	2 567 800	2 855 000	161 200	15 871	19	Dofor 28%, Caisse de dépôt 16%
41	38	44	Stelco Inc. (Toronto)	2 546 378	2 803 650	63 393	16 960	4	Wide distribution
42	40	78	Canadian Tire Corp. (Toronto)	2 483 822	1 430 509	98 826	n.a.		Billes family 61%, C.T.C. Dealer Holdings 17%
43	46	26	Inco Ltd. (Toronto)	2 372 836[2]	3 890 599	166 070	18 706	55	Wide distribution
44	•	22	Nova Corp. (Calgary)	2 322 438	4 685 748	179 130	7 100	4	Wide distribution
45	42	86	Total Petroleum (North America) Ltd. (Calgary)	2 316 534[2]	1 317 559	(35 567)	4 800	79	Total Compagnie Française des Petroles, France 50%
46	45	54	Consolidated-Bathurst Inc. (Montreal)	2 261 430	2 264 669	181 540	15 026	15	Associated Newspapers, Britain. Power Corp. 40%
47	47	69	Ivaco Inc. (Montreal)	2 174 976	1 767 179	38 351	12 170		Ivanier family 37%, R. Klein 13%, M. Herling 12%
48	48	38	Dofasco Inc. (Hamilton, Ont.)	2 163 071	3 060 325	153 990	13 400		Ivaco 11%
49	44	145	F.W. Woolworth Co. (Toronto) Jan./88	2 025 969	665 525	33 333	26 500	100	Woolworth World Trade, New York
50	43	6	British Columbia Hydro & Power Authority (Vancouver) Mar./87	1 987 000	9 802 000	67 000	6 393		British Columbia government 100%

[1] Name changed from Bell Canada Enterprises Inc.
[2] Converted from US$
[3] Includes beneficial interest in gross revenues of consumer products, natural resources and other operations, but excludes financial services.
[4] Unaudited
[5] Estimate converted from US$
[6] Name changed from Canada Development Corp.
• Not on last year's list
n.a. Not available/not applicable

SOURCE: *The Financial Post 500*, Summer 1988. Reprinted with permission.

Issue: *Large Corporations: Are They Good for Canadians?*

Large corporations are generally beneficial to the nation. Since mass production allows them to produce goods at lower costs, their prices are able to compete with those of foreign corporations, and this helps to balance our imports and exports. Large corporations have the resources necessary for research and development and can afford to use costly technological innovations for more efficient production. They also provide numerous employment opportunities and allow for specialization in various areas, including management.

Such corporations can also be detrimental, however. They can seriously inhibit competition, to the point of becoming virtual monopolies, and the result may be higher prices and lower quality for the consumer. And since size can sometimes make a company more difficult to manage efficiently and effectively, there may be considerable waste of human, material and financial resources.

The federal government does have legislation to prevent agreements to limit competition, and prevent unfair competitive practices. Nevertheless, the Bureau of Competition Policy in a report published in 1981 found that the major oil companies attempted to entrench their market position through the use of anti-competitive practices at the expense of other firms in the industry and the consumer.[1]

With corporate size comes power. As mentioned earlier, a Royal Commission on corporate concentration was appointed in 1975 to determine how corporate power might influence Canadian society. After studying the problem, the commission concluded that:

— Corporate concentration in Canada as it existed at the time was necessary in order for Canada to remain competitive on the international scene. Moreover, any change in the future would be toward more rather than less concentration, since businesses have a natural tendency to grow. Public policy should encourage or discourage growth as necessary.

— Fears concerning the possibility of corporate influence on official public decisions and the shaping of public opinion appeared to be groundless. Nevertheless, government must provide safeguards against this potential danger, particularly in regard to the concentrated ownership of the mass media.[2]

[1] "The big oil company ruckus," *The Financial Post*, March 14, 1981, p. 20.
[2] For a summary of the general conclusions of the Royal Commission on Corporate Concentration, see "Big Business is Beautiful, Says the Royal Commission." *The Financial Post 300*, Summer 1978, pp. 33–8. For the complete report, see *Report of the Royal Commission on Corporate Concentration* (Ottawa: Supply and Services Canada, March 1978), Cat. Z1–1975–1.

FACTORS TO CONSIDER IN CHOOSING
A FORM OF BUSINESS OWNERSHIP

Now that we have examined the three major forms of private business ownership, let us review some of the prime factors to be considered in choosing among them.

The Need for Limited Liability

The first consideration has to be the need for limited liability. If you are considering a risky business which requires a large investment from creditors as well as yourself, it is imperative that you have limited financial liability; otherwise your private assets would be in jeopardy if the business should fail. You would therefore be wise to incorporate. On the other hand, if your business provides a service with relatively little investment for equipment or inventory and you therefore face little risk, a sole proprietorship or partnership might be adequate.

Availability of Financial Resources

In a sole proprietorship, your capacity to borrow funds is limited by the amount of personal assets you can offer as collateral. More funds would be available for a partnership since there are more owners who can invest. The greatest financial resources would be available to a corporation, however, since it could raise capital by issuing shares. Present shareholders would then lose some control over the company unless they purchased some of the new issue to keep their percentage of ownership the same, and they would be obliged to share profits with new shareholders. Nevertheless, the new infusion of money from the share issue could be used to enlarge the operation and thereby increase total profits, meaning more for everyone.

The Need for a Variety of Management Skills

Individuals who lack management skills or experience in certain business functions would be well-advised to seek out one or more individuals who have the complementary business skills and who may want to become partners. As an alternative specialized personnel can be hired; however, this may be expensive for a new firm with limited financial resources.

Other Considerations

Though not as important as the preceding three, there are other factors to be considered before deciding on a form of ownership. First, there is the **ease** and **cost** of starting a business. While a sole proprietorship or partnership is relatively easy to establish, a corporation is more difficult and costly and might face numerous government rules and regulations, both federal and provincial. On the other hand, the cost of incorporating may be small in comparison to the total money invested in the new business venture. Furthermore, the federal and provincial governments have special tax rules favouring small incorporated companies as opposed to sole proprietorships and partnerships. Both levels of government also provide special grants for new corporations to hire employees and for research and development.

Finally, a sole proprietorship or a partnership is always faced with the problem of **continuity**, since the death of the owner or one of the partners legally terminates the business. A corporation, on the other hand, continues regardless of what happens to its shareholders. In any case, a business established as a sole proprietorship or partnership can always be incorporated at a later date, once it has proven to be successful.

MEMBER OWNERSHIP: THE COOPERATIVE

A **cooperative** is owned and controlled by its members — not by one vote per share, as in a corporation, but by one vote per member. Its purpose is usually to supply its member-owners with products and services at a lower cost than would otherwise be possible, though sometimes a cooperative is established simply to provide a service which would otherwise not be available. Since most cooperatives today are incorporated, they have both limited liability and an unlimited lifespan. Any surplus accumulated is usually distributed among the members according to the amount of business each has done with the cooperative.

Cooperatives in Canada are doing well and their numbers are growing. This is especially true of credit unions and their Québec counterparts, the caisses populaires. With assets of more than $18 billion and eight million members across Canada, **credit unions** are actively competing with the chartered banks and have led the way in providing members with free chequing and daily interest on chequing and savings accounts. In addition, they offer residential and commercial mortgages, personal loans and other services similar to those available at chartered banks.[5]

A credit union is only one kind of financial cooperative, however. Consumer cooperatives provide members with retail goods, and marketing cooperatives are used to market products such as milk, poultry and wheat. Insurance cooperatives provide their members with life, fire and other types of insurance, while the various service cooperatives offer housing and legal services, among others.

In 1977, the provincial credit unions joined with other groups of cooperative organizations — including cooperative insurance firms,

TABLE 3.3
Canada's 10 largest cooperatives, 1987, ranked by sales

Rank 87	86	Cooperatives	Year-end	Revenue $'000	% Change	Assets $'000	Dividends Paid[1] $'000	% Change	Employees
1	1	Saskatchewan Wheat Pool	87/07/31	1 804 275	3.7	713 075	21 035	12.0	3 350
2	2	Federated Cooperatives	87/10/31	1 427 997	2.0	531 004	60 330	3.1	1 736
3	3	Coopérative Fédérée de Québec	87/10/31	1 243 656	6.2	276 398	7 225	3.2	3 147
4	4	Alberta Wheat Pool	87/07/31	1 012 517	2.8	382 640	3 000	1.3	1 620
5	5	United Grain Growers	87/07/31	905 941	-8.0	344 939	2 678	-51.5	1 641
6	6	Agropur, Coopérative agro-alimentaire	87/10/31	821 297	6.4	212 127	n.a.	n.a.	2 609
7	8	United Cooperatives of Ontario	87/09/30	503 673	-0.1	180 212	n.a.	n.a.	1 306
8	7	Manitoba Pool Elevators	87/07/31	492 307	-28.3	188 982	7 895	26.1	960
9	9	Calgary Cooperative Association	87/10/31	412 750	7.4	94 471	19 442	10.1	3 129
10	10	Co-op Atlantic	87/11/27	329 132	8.0	71 338	3 515	-17.8	732

[1]Cash, credit and/or dividends to members
n.a. Not available/not applicable

SOURCE: *Canadian Business*, June 1988, p. 170. Reprinted with permission.

In 1977, provincial credit unions joined other cooperative groups to form the Canadian Cooperative Credit Society

the Cooperative Trust Company of Canada, and the major marketing and consumer cooperatives such as the Alberta and Saskatchewan Wheat Pool — to form the Canadian Cooperative Credit Society Ltd. This body represents the cooperative movement in Ottawa and provides its members with technical advice.[6]

Nevertheless, the success of the cooperative movement has been accompanied by some problems. Many cooperatives originally started as small local organizations in which members had complete control, and any profits were returned to them. Today cooperatives have become big business and face many of the same problems as corporations — raising the capital required for expansion and operation, for example, and acquiring competent managers. At the same time, members appear to have less control over operations.

NOTES

1. Report to Constituents by Progressive Conservative MP's, Spring 1984. Information based on Statistics Canada Profile of Small Business in Canada.
2. "The Canadian Business Failure Record, 1985," Dun & Bradstreet Canada Limited, 1985.
3. "Should You Think Inc.," *The Financial Post Money Magazine*, December 1987, p. 57.
4. Murray G. Ross, *Canadian Corporate Directors on the Firing Line* (Toronto: McGraw-Hill Ryerson Ltd., 1980).
5. "Coordination creates capital for the cooperative movement," *The Financial Post 300*, Summer 1978, p. 24.
6. *Ibid.*

CHAPTER SUMMARY

Operating one's own business is a common dream. Unfortunately, many new businesses fail in the first year of operation primarily due to poor management skills and inadequate financing. Successful small business management depends on many factors, including acquiring a business education, planning, careful money management, keeping accurate records, effective marketing, organizing time, acquiring good employees and, finally, preparing to grow with the business.

An entrepreneur may buy an existing business or start a new one. Buying an existing business has several advantages, such as an established clientele and premises, together with fixtures, equipment, machines, suppliers and inventory. However, the firm should be carefully analyzed to ensure that a market exists for its product and that no hidden debts or future events will put the new owner into financial jeopardy. An entrepreneur establishing a new business must be particularly careful about the market for the product or service and that adequate financing is available to see the new owner through the initial period of low sales. In either case, professional help from accountants and lawyers should be considered.

Franchising is popular because the franchisor often assists the new owner in all aspects of starting and operating the business. Help in acquiring management skills can prevent business failure. The major disadvantages of franchises are the initial high cost of buying a successful franchise, strict adherence to policies and rules of the franchisor, and the royalty that has to be paid on gross receipts.

The three major forms of private business ownership are the sole proprietorship, partnership and corporation. The sole proprietorship, a business owned by one person, is relatively easy and inexpensive to start. The owner has complete control and can keep operations secret. Among the disadvantages are the owner's unlimited liability, the limit in the amount of capital one individual can normally raise, the need for expertise in many business activities and the fact that the life of the business is limited to the owner's lifetime.

A partnership can help to solve some of the problems faced by the sole proprietor. Two or more partners can share responsibility for the business and provide a wider range of expertise. They can probably also raise a greater amount of financial capital. However, disagreements concerning management may arise and any single individual has only partial control over the business. All partners still have unlimited liability. The partnership ceases to exist when one or more partners leave or die and partners may have difficulty selling or transferring their ownership interest. A formal agreement, although not required, is recommended to resolve some of the above problems.

The corporation has become a favoured form of ownership for a number of reasons. Legally, a corporation is an artificial person with all the rights, powers and obligations of a private individual. A business may be incorporated provincially or federally, depending on where it intends to operate.

If there are fewer than 50 shareholders, the corporation is private. The cost of incorporating is relatively low, and there are generally few rules and regulations to be followed. A public corporation, on the other hand, has more than 50 shareholders, requires at least three directors and must follow specific rules and regulations in order to keep shareholders informed of the company's financial operation.

The owners of the corporation are the shareholders who receive either common or preferred shares in return for their investment. A public corporation can also borrow money through the sale of bonds or by issuing notes to lenders. Individuals who own common shares are entitled to elect a board of directors to represent them. The board of directors in turn is responsible for the proper operation of the company and for the hiring of top management, including the president and various vice-presidents.

A major advantage of incorporation is the limited liability provided to shareholders. Once established as a profitable corporation, shares can be sold to raise additional financial capital. Ownership is easy to transfer, and the life of the corporation does not depend on individual shareholders. Among the disadvantages are the limited control that shareholders have over the company, as well as the tendency of professional managers who run large corporations to take less personal interest than the owners in the well-being of the company. In addition, large corporations particularly are subject to many government rules and regulations, and lack of secrecy in operation can be a drawback.

Another form of ownership is the member-owned cooperative, established to provide services such as product marketing, life insurance or financial services. Although many are incorporated, a basic difference between the cooperative and the corporation lies in the voting and distribution of earnings. In the cooperative, each member receives only one vote, while earnings are distributed according to the amount of business each has done with the cooperative over a period of time.

KEY TERMS

Small business	Registration system
Franchise	Letters patent system
Venture capitalists	Shareholders or stockholders
Undercapitalization	Preferred shares
Business plan	Common shares
Sole proprietorship	Proxy
Bankruptcy	Prospectus
Unlimited liability	Board of directors
Partnership	Chief executive officer
Partnership by express agreement	Secretary

Partnership by implication
General partner
Limited partner
Silent partner
Corporation
Private corporation
Public corporation
Limited liability

Treasurer
Controller
Merger or take-over
Vertical integration
Horizontal integration
Conglomerate
Cooperative

REVIEW QUESTIONS

1. Why are small businesses so important to Canada's economy?

2. What are the major problems faced by individuals operating a small business?

3. What are the seven areas of concern to which the owner-manager of a small business must pay particular attention?

4. What are the advantages of buying an existing business compared to starting a new business? What are some of the things you should check before actually making that final offer?

5. What is a franchise? What are the major advantages of purchasing a franchise? The major disadvantages?

6. What are some of the advantages of buying a franchise as opposed to starting your own business?

7. What are some of the sources of capital for starting a new business or a franchise?

8. Why do many business owners have problems in arranging financing? How can a business plan help in getting a loan?

9. Why is it necessary to choose a form of business ownership?

10. Is there any advantage in establishing a business as a sole proprietorship and incorporating if necessary at some later time?

11. What are the advantages of a partnership over a sole proprietorship? What are the disadvantages?

12. Distinguish between general partners, limited partners, and silent partners.

13. Explain joint and several liability for business debts in a partnership.

14. Distinguish between (a) a public and a private corporation and (b) preferred and common shareholders.

15. How can a company increase in size? Distinguish between (a) horizontal integration, (b) vertical integration, (c) a conglomerate.

16. What are the chief characteristics of a cooperative?

DISCUSSION QUESTIONS

1. Should the federal and provincial governments make a conscientious effort to help entrepreneurs start their small businesses? If so, how much help should the government provide?

2. What major problems might occur if one of the members in a successful partnership wanted to sell his portion of the business, assuming that no written agreement exists?

3. "Large corporations are good for Canadians!" Discuss both sides of this issue.

4. In most elections, every person eligible is allowed to cast one vote. Shareholders in a corporation, however, are entitled to cast as many votes as shares owned. Why should this be so?

CASE 3–1 Buying a Video Franchise

Two years ago Diane Letsche decided to get in on the video craze. Her reasoning was simple: no one in her neighborhood was renting out top-quality video movies. She weighed the pros and cons of going it alone or joining one of the budding video franchise companies. She chose the latter. Today the 42-year-old businesswoman believes she made the right choice. "I'm really happy with the franchise," she explains, admitting that she took a gamble when she signed the franchise agreement since the video company was so young. "I wouldn't say there haven't been frustrations because there have been," she adds, "but the benefits far outweigh them, for my money."

For Letsche, the frustrations of owning and operating a National Video franchise — one of 120 across Canada — stem from the nature of the retail sector, not the franchise itself. Running the business in Don Mills, Ont., a suburb of Toronto, requires longer hours than she had counted on. She also found the hassles some customers put her through as surprising as frustrating because she'd worked in a retail operation before.

But there were some other problems at the beginning. Because National Video was still in its infancy, it didn't have a central buying team or an advertising policy. "I think it was typical of the beginnings of a small company," says Letsche. Sometimes it was difficult to get management at the Canadian head office in Toronto to follow through on purchasing and financing because of a lack of staff. Age and experience have ironed out the wrinkles, and the company has grown substantially. Thanks to new management and the growth of the U.S.-based headquarters, problems are now few and far between.

In fact, Letsche, a former teacher who helped her husband run an audiotape manufacturing and filmstrip distribution company, is bullish on National Video and franchise operations in general. She says being part of a franchise gives an entrepreneur an added edge in the marketplace. As a franchisee, Letsche says she derives many benefits from National Video: buying power, corporate decor, information sharing and volume discounts on both movie videos and home video recorders.

But perhaps the biggest plus for Letsche and others like her is the company's advertising clout. For example, the U.S. offices of National Video are placing an ad this spring in *People* magazine, and the Toronto stores in the National Video chain cooperatively bought two months of television advertising at a cost of about $32 000. "You don't do these kinds of things if you're on your own," she says. Other local efforts have included cross-promotional advertising with a Toronto retailer of video recorders, offering consumers who bought a recorder one free movie rental for every movie they rent at National Video. Letsche says the campaign brought her store at least 200 new customers.

Still, Letsche must pay for what she receives. On top of the initial investment of a $15 000 franchise fee and $50 000 for basic inventory, she has to pay royalties for both the Canadian offices of National Video and the U.S. headquarters in Portland, Ore. These fees include 3.9% on all gross revenues (except sales of machinery) to the Canadian headquarters and 2% of all revenues to the U.S. for advertising. There's also a 4% fee that goes toward paying for advertising in Letsche's local area.

Today, a National Video franchise costs considerably more: $110 000 to $130 000, including inventory, leasehold improvements and a $25 000 franchise fee. The royalty payments have also increased to 4.9% on all gross revenues other than hardware sales — with decreasing payments as volume increases — and 3% on all sales to Portland for advertising.

Even with the royalty payments, Letsche has been able to make her business work and show a profit. In the first year of operation, rentals brought in about $150 000. Sales of video recorders brought in approximately $65 000. Letsche poured this back into the company for more movies. She also redecorated the store along the lines of National Video's red and blue corporate design for about $6 000. She came out with a profit of $20 000.

Letsche expects to do about 30% better this year and has invested another $40 000 in movies. She has also hired two full-time and four part-time employees to help ease the long hours. With these kinds of results, she's convinced that getting in on the ground floor was a smart move. "National Video," she says, "will become the McDonald's of the Video business."

SOURCE: Debra J. Black, "Buying a Video Franchise," *Canadian Business*, May 1984, p. 113. Reprinted by permission.

QUESTIONS

1. What were the advantages to Letsche of buying a video rental franchise as opposed to opening her own video rental business? What might be some of the disadvantages of buying this franchise?

2. If the owner had decided to open up her own video rental business instead of buying a franchise, what additional factors would she have had to consider?

3. Before buying this franchise what factors should Letsche have investigated?

4. Indicate how each of the seven factors of success applies to this business.

CASE 3–2 Deciding on a Form of Business Ownership

Tom Higham, a mechanical engineer, developed a windmill with a radically new design. The windmill promises to be particularly useful for farmers in the prairie regions where high winds are common. Two of these windmills, together with a storage battery system, would be capable of supplying all the normal electrical energy requirements for an average farm. With further development, Tom believes the windmills could also be used in private homes to provide at least a part of the electric power required during a normal day. However, for this market the windmills would have to be redesigned to blend with or complement the average home.

Tom attempted to interest his company in building and marketing the windmills, but management was skeptical about their commercial success. Other experts in the field, however, were convinced that through proper marketing, the windmills could be a successful product. Based on this information, Tom applied for a patent and investigated the requirements to build and sell the windmills himself.

First he visited his friend, a bank manager, to discuss the venture and inquire about the possibility of additional financing.

"Jack," he began, "I know for a fact that this windmill would be bought by farmers in the Midwest. I could sell each windmill initially for approximately $6000, but after refinement of production techniques and an increase in volume, my manufacturing costs would be reduced by at least one third. The total cost of the system to a farmer initially would be $16 000 which would include two windmills, a storage battery system and installation. Maintenance would cost between $100 and $400 a year. A farmer could expect to save enough on his electricity charges to recover the cost of the equipment within four years according to my calculations."

"How do you know farmers would buy your product, Tom," Jack inquired. "Have you done a market study or analyzed any statistics? Have you talked to some farmers to find out how they really feel about your product? Based on my experience, farmers are somewhat conservative when it comes to buying radically new products." He paused for a few moments to let what he had said sink in. "And what about running the firm, if the product did prove feasible? What would be your job? Would you work on further development or would you manage the company?"

Tom looked at Jack thoughtfully. "I don't know what you mean by a market study. I've talked to a few people who deal with farmers, and I even talked to a few farmers. They felt it was a product they would buy. As far as your second question is concerned, obviously I would be involved in further development and research. After all, that is where my expertise lies."

Tom paused and then continued. "Look, Jack, I know a little about the problems of business. I know that one can't expect to make a huge profit the first few years and that one has to put in long hours. But then, I am not concerned about that. I feel very strongly about this product and I know it would be successful once farmers knew about the savings in electricity costs. I believe that if you have a good product and if you can get a few people to buy it, and if you look after them with regards to service and warranty, then you will get other business. I believe very strongly that this is a word-of-mouth business. Once we get a few windmills sold and set up, I am convinced we would get more business than we could handle."

"Have you thought about the costs of setting up this business, Tom?" Jack responded. "I know you have put about $20 000 of your own money into this venture already by re-mortgaging your home. But you would need manufacturing facilities which are expensive even to rent. How much money would you need to set up and operate until your first revenue from sales?"

Tom appeared to do some mental calculations before answering Jack. "I think I could get another $50 000 from the bank and increase my mortgage by another $25 000. The initial equipment costs would be $45 000, and the raw material to build 10 windmills would cost $32 000. The prototype could be used for demonstrations to prospective customers. Two people have committed themselves to selling the product. One of them is a top-notch salesman who already understands the capabilities of these machines. Initially I would go with him on sales calls. Once he was fully trained I would concentrate on manufacturing. Don't forget, Jack, I would only need to hire two other people for the actual manufacturing. We could keep the firm small which would mean lower costs. The accounting end of the business would be handled by my wife."

"Tom, I have been in the business of providing loans to new businesses for quite some time," Jack said. "I think you are under some wrong impressions. You are a friend of mine and I don't want to see you lose your shirt on this venture. So I am going to be frank with you. You have some problems."

QUESTIONS

1. What are the major problems Tom Higham faces in establishing his business? Explain. Does he appear to be aware of them?
2. How could a business plan help Tom in establishing his business? What information would Tom gain from a business plan?
3. Evaluate the advantages and disadvantages of each of the three forms of business ownership, in relation to the business that Tom wants to enter. (HINT: review the section in the chapter entitled "Factors to consider before choosing a form of business ownership.")
4. What form of business ownership should Tom choose? Why?

Part Two

Business and Management

Business organizations are at the core of our economic system. They are human creations bringing together the factors of production to make useful products or services. Managers play a key role in business organizations. They are responsible for developing the goals of the organization and for planning its future course. To achieve goals and objectives, they establish an organizational structure, coordinate the efforts of all involved, and ensure that raw materials, machines and equipment are available as required. Finally, managers ensure that the organization is on the proper course by comparing plans with actual achievements.

In Chapter 4 we examine the nature of management and the specific tasks of managers. We then focus on two of the four major functions of management — planning and controlling. Finally, we look at the role of computers in business and how managers can benefit from the organized information computers provide.

In Chapter 5 we look at another essential management function — organizing, or establishing the organizational structure best suited to achieve planned objectives. This structure is established by dividing the total work to be accomplished into manageable units, and then assigning a manager to each unit. Depending on the size of the organization, several levels of management may be necessary to coordinate the various tasks.

In Chapter 6 we look at the leading function of management. Since any enterprise needs people who will perform their jobs willingly and in the best interests of the organization, managers must provide employees with motivation and leadership.

Management, Planning and Controlling

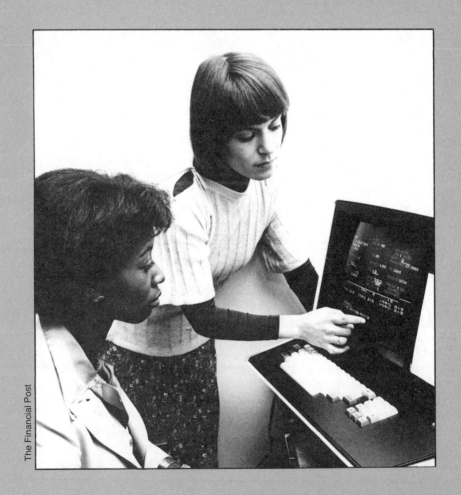

The Financial Post

CHAPTER OUTLINE

CHAPTER PREVIEW

In Chapter 4 we define management and then examine the specific duties of managers. We look at the importance of managers to organizations and focus on their role in planning objectives and the methods of achieving them. However, plans are only one step. We examine how managers must control the organization's actual performance by continually evaluating achievements in terms of projected results. We look at how an information system can provide management with the data necessary to assess actual performance. Finally, we look at computers and how they can help managers in performing their functions.

LEARNING OBJECTIVES

After reading this chapter you should be able to explain:

1. Why management is the most important ingredient for success in a business;
2. The three types of managerial skills — technical, human and conceptual — and their relative importance to each of the three levels of management;
3. The four functions of management: planning, organizing, leading and controlling;
4. The elements of planning;
5. The four steps in the planning process, and the difference between long-range and short-range plans;
6. The purpose and process of control, and why control is closely related to planning;
7. The importance of an effective management information system for proper control of operations;
8. Budgetary and non-budgetary methods of control;
9. The importance of computers to business, and how managers can use microcomputers in their operation;
10. The factors to consider in computerizing a business, including the appropriate hardware, software and vendor.
11. The human problems encountered when a computer system is installed.

Movies and television dramas often focus on giant corporations and the conflicts of top executives. We become familiar with the spacious offices and oak-panelled boardrooms of multistoried corporate buildings, but see little of management in action, nor do we learn about what a manager's job entails. In fact, we may get the impression that managers are involved only in intrigue and political maneuvres. What about the owner of the local television repair shop, or the local service station, both of whom are in business for themselves? Are they managers? What is their function? This chapter explains the functions of management and points out its importance to the successful operation of a business.

WHAT IS MANAGEMENT?

Managers achieve organizational goals by getting other people to perform necessary tasks. However, this is only a simplified definition and does not really indicate what managers do. First of all, **management** is a process — a systematic way of doing things. One of the tasks managers perform is planning, thinking about the goals and objectives they want their organization to achieve and how to go about doing so. Another task is organizing the human, material and financial resources so that all activities performed will lead the organization towards desired objectives. Managers must also influence and direct their employees to perform essential tasks. It is important to establish a proper working environment and atmosphere so that subordinates may do their best. Finally, managers must ensure that the organization is indeed moving towards its goals. If some parts of it are not doing so, it is up to managers to find out why and correct the problem.

We can now provide a more complete definition of management. Management is a process of planning, organizing, leading, and controlling the efforts of organization members in using organizational resources, so as to achieve organizational goals in the most efficient and effective manner (see Figure 4.1).

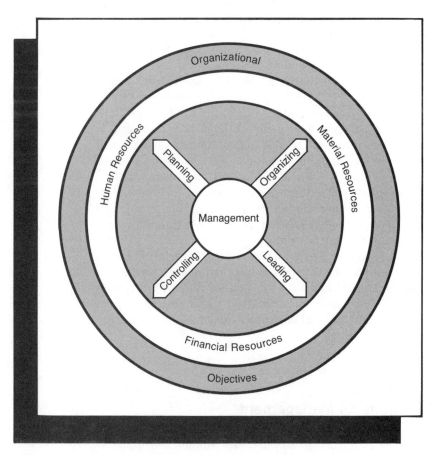

Figure 4.1 The management process within an organization

Importance of Management

In our constantly changing world, even the best-laid plans can go amiss. Since organizations are subject to many outside forces, including competitors, business cycles, government policies, and changing consumer demands, managers must constantly reassess established goals and objectives in relation to the social and economic environment. They must be aware of trends and changes so that they can direct employees toward realizable goals within the constraints of the financial, human and material resources available. Furthermore, as problems arise, the manager must make decisions to resolve them.

Unfortunately, business decisions are not always easy to make. If a manager consistently makes the wrong decisions or fails to understand all that his or her job entails; if he or she neglects planning for the future, has a loose control system and provides poor leadership; the organization is likely to show poor results. In the long run, the organization may face loss of profits or even bankruptcy. Even in organizations where bankruptcy is precluded — government organizations or hospitals, for example — poor management may be reflected in inadequate and inefficient services.

Poor management is a particular problem for small firms where the owner-manager is often required to perform all management tasks. As mentioned in the previous chapter, nine out of ten business failures can be attributed to poor management. Even if a small firm is successful, management may not be able to maintain effective control as the firm grows. In fact, growth may reveal management deficiencies that were not evident as long as the organization was small.

One of the greatest deficiencies of management in growing organizations is poor or inadequate planning. Giant corporations can go bankrupt if top management has not been able to forecast future economic conditions accurately or manage its resources effectively. One example is the Chrysler Corporation, whose financial problems were largely the result of poor economic forecasting and consequent failure to meet consumer demands for smaller, better-built, more fuel-efficient cars. New management revised plans and objectives, produced an automobile that met consumer demands, and made the company profitable again.

Functions Of Management

Managers perform somewhat similar tasks in all organizations, whether they are managing a business, government department, hospital, political party, or non-profit organization such as the Red Cross or the Salvation Army. We can classify a manager's tasks into four basic functions: **planning, organizing, leading** and **controlling**. While these functions are listed as separate and distinct activities, and even though at any given time a manager may be preoccupied with one or another, he or she is likely to engage in all of them during the course of a day.

Planning

Planning involves establishing objectives that the organization should accomplish by a future date and then determining how best to achieve those objectives with the organizational resources available. A manufacturing organization wishing to expand its operation from Ontario to western Canada, for example, must first determine the potential increase in revenue and profit that it can expect from such a venture, and assess the physical, financial, personnel and managerial resources required. Does the company have the necessary capacity in its present manufacturing facilities to produce the additional product? Does it have the necessary financial resources to open a sales office, advertise its product and hire the people for sales and support activities? Can it spread its managerial resources thinner so that the move to western Canada will not jeopardize its existing operation?

After evaluating these and many other factors, the company might decide to begin by establishing a regional sales office in one of the prairie provinces or British Columbia to test the market, and subsequently expand from there should the test prove profitable. Closely related to planning, therefore, is decision-making, or choosing a course of action from a number of available alternatives to achieve a desired result.

Organizing

Organizing follows planning and indicates how management wants to arrange its resources to accomplish the plan. The organizing function of managers involves assigning tasks, grouping tasks into departments, and then allocating resources to these departments so that the tasks can be accomplished. To ensure that the people within these departments and the departments themselves are all working toward the same goals, management must constantly communicate with their people and with other managers in the organization. This communication process is called coordination and is accomplished by establishing lines of authority so that all managers know to whom they report and the areas for which they are responsible. The result is a management pyramid, with higher levels of management containing fewer managers. At the top is the chief executive officer — the president — who has final responsibility for the performance of the entire organization. We will examine the organizing function in more detail in Chapter 5.

One of the most important organizing activities is **staffing**. Managers must place competent people in the various job positions under their authority, to ensure that set objectives can be met. However, acquiring adequate human resources is no simple task, and personnel matters are complex and time-consuming. Employees leave or retire, business conditions may dictate a reduced workforce, or the company may decide to consolidate in one area and expand in others. Therefore, virtually all large organizations and many medium-sized ones as well, include a personnel department, where specialists supervise the recruiting, selection, hiring, training, compensation and termination of employees. Nevertheless, the final choice as to who should fill a particular job is the responsibility of the manager directly in charge of that position.

Because staffing has become such an important function and requires specialized skills and knowledge, the matter of personnel is usually treated as a special business function. We discuss staffing as part of the personnel function in Chapter 10.

Leading

An organization cannot achieve its goals without people. **Leading**, or directing, involves guiding the actions and performance of people to achieve the organization's goals. It means helping to bring out the best in workers, ensuring that they are happy and satisfied with their work, and thus motivating them to work willingly toward the organization's goals. It includes assigning work to employees, explaining procedures and helping to correct errors. Managers must be able to communicate ideas and directions to others to achieve desired results. In fact, the greatest proportion of a manager's time is spent in directing employees.[1] The leading function, or "people-managing," is discussed more fully in Chapter 6.

Controlling

The fourth function of management is controlling — a term not always readily accepted as it suggests imposing restrictions on individuals. We use the term "controlling" in this book, although "evaluating" is also often used.

Controlling means ensuring that actual performance is according to plan and that organizational objectives are being met. For example, a specific level of profit is a major objective for most businesses. Hence the factors that can affect profit, such as actual sales and expenses, must be constantly checked against the plan so that corrective action can be taken if any discrepancies appear. If sales are slow, for example, management may need to promote advertising or hire more salespeople. Thus planning and controlling are closely related.

Levels of Management

Even though all managers, from the president of a large corporation to the owner of a local service station perform the same functions, their jobs differ according to the size of their organization. Large organizations have many different tasks to be performed and thus require more people than small organizations. As the number of tasks to be coordinated increases, more managers are required. Organizations therefore develop a **managerial hierarchy** and managers are classified according to the level of the hierarchy on which they operate. These levels can be divided into three categories: top management, middle management, and operating or supervisory management.

There are usually many supervisory managers on the bottom level of a large organization, but as one moves up in the hierarchy, each level includes fewer managers. At the top of the hierarchy is the president, who has total responsibility for the operation of the organization. Figure 4.2 shows an organizational or management hierarchy.

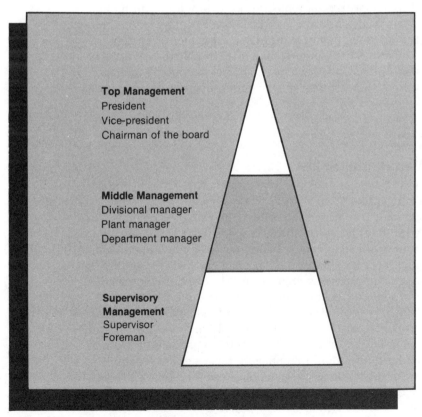

Top Management
President
Vice-president
Chairman of the board

Middle Management
Divisional manager
Plant manager
Department manager

Supervisory Management
Supervisor
Foreman

Figure 4.2 The management hierarchy

Depending on the size of the organization, **top management** may include the president, the chairman of the board, the vice-president, and in the case of very large companies, the general managers in charge of various divisions. These managers devote most of their time to long-range planning for such matters as plant expansion, international operations, major financing problems and the addition or deletion of major products or product lines. Top management is also the level directly involved with external affairs, including relations with government and the community.

Middle management, which includes division and department managers, is concerned with more specific operations. It must develop the specific plans and procedures required to implement the broader plans of top management. A middle manager might be concerned with purchasing new equipment or raw materials, establishing inventory maintenance systems and personnel policy, and determining personnel requirements.

The **operating** or **supervisory managers** are directly involved with the workers on a departmental level. Included in this group are foremen, production supervisors and hospital ward nurses. Managers on this level assign workers to specific jobs, provide training and evaluate performance. They are responsible for putting into action the detailed plans developed by middle management. As they are involved directly with the workers, they must be able to deal quickly with a constant stream of problems, major and minor. Much of a supervisor's time, therefore, is spent communicating directly with employees.

Managerial Skills

Managers at all levels should possess three basic skills: technical, human and conceptual.[2]

Technical skill is required to perform the actual mechanics of a job and may include the use of tools or specialized knowledge. For example, a supervisor in a machine shop may need to know how to operate a lathe, an accountant must know how to keep the firm's books, while a data processing manager must have some knowledge of computer programming and their general operation.

Human skill is essential to the success of managers' interaction with employees. Managers must understand employee needs and motivate them to work toward the goals of the organization. Human skill is particularly important to managers because they accomplish their job through the work of others. To perform their own jobs well, they must be able to communicate effectively in both written and oral form.

Conceptual skill refers to an individual's mental ability to perceive the organization as a whole, and see how the various parts work together to achieve long-range goals. Managers must be able to envision how their actions will affect the entire organization.

Technical skill is most important to operating and supervisory managers, who are concerned with the daily operation of the business. Supervisory managers in the plant and managers in charge of specific business areas such as accounting and advertising, for example, need technical skills to deal with specific problems as they arise. Human skills are most important to supervisory and middle managers who interact directly with employees. Conceptual skills, on the other hand, are most important to top managers involved in long-range planning and decision-making, as well as maintaining relations with outside organizations. Thus the relative importance of specific skills depends on the manager's level in the organizational hierarchy. Figure 4.3 indicates the relationship between the three management levels and the managerial skills generally required for each.

Since all managers at any given level perform similar functions, they can move from one position to another at the same level, or from one organization to another. Top levels of management probably find it easiest to move from one organization to another because at this level conceptual skills are of prime importance, while technical

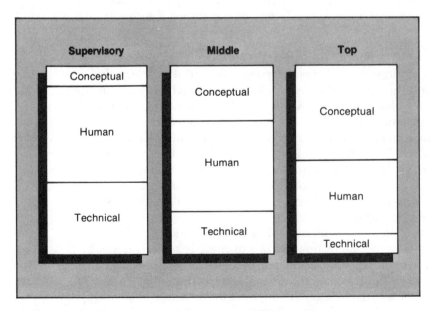

Figure 4.3 Skills required at various management levels

knowledge is virtually unnecessary. A top-level manager, for example, could move from a manufacturing organization to become a senior government official, the head of a bank or the president of a university. All of these positions involve long-range planning, communication with other organizations and responsibility for decisions on the general direction of the organization.

Technical skills are not so readily transferable between organizations. For example, a retail department store supervisor could not take over the job of a nursing supervisor because he or she would not have the necessary technical skills. However, the store manager of a large retail chain might be quite capable of taking over the position of hospital administrator, since at this level the managerial skills required are similar.

What is a Manager's Job? An Alternate View

A different method of categorizing managerial tasks was developed by Henry Mintzberg, a Harvard University researcher. In 1975 he published a study surveying the existing research on how managers spend their time and perform their work, and integrating his own research on the activities of five chief executive officers. The total survey included all kinds and levels of managers — from factory supervisors and sales managers to administrators and presidents. Mintzberg concluded that the jobs of managers at all levels are similar. According to his study, the formal authority and status of managers in the organization enables them to perform roles in three major areas — interpersonal, informational and decisional (See Figure 4.4).[3]

PLANNING AND MANAGEMENT

Managers who do not plan ahead for their organizations lack the objectives and the direction necessary in an unpredictable environment. Without clear objectives, firms may lose potential profits or produce goods and services that no longer meet consumers' needs. Furthermore, if management lacks a sense of direction, the aimlessness is certain to be carried over to other employees. Without plans, employees have no motivation to perform well. They cannot know what they are to achieve, have nothing on which to base their performance and have no one to give them direction. The result is a waste of effort and resources.

Also, since planning and control are closely related, without plans managers cannot know how the organization is actually doing. They cannot isolate specific problems and take corrective action, particularly in difficult economic times. Organizations that do not plan illustrate a familiar adage: "If you don't know where you want to go, then any road will take you there." They drift aimlessly with the hope that everything will work out in the end, rather than plan for a more successful future.

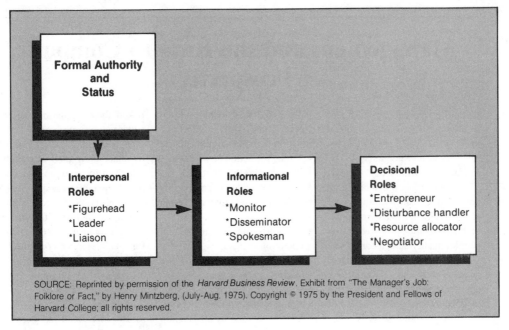

Figure 4.3 Roles of a manager

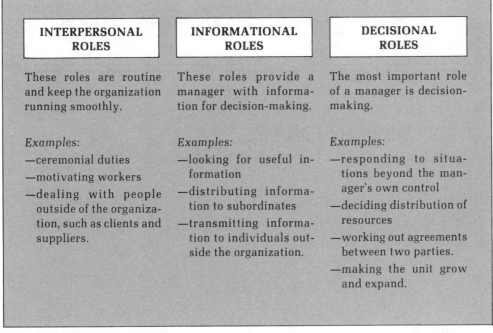

Figure 4.4 Roles of a manager

Management and the Keys to Company Prosperity

It is little wonder that the book, *In Search Of Excellence*, soared to #1 on the *New York Times* best seller list of non-fiction books. Its research confirmed that the key to prosperity for companies large and small lies in a commitment of management to such irrational, difficult-to-measure factors as people, quality and customer service. The professional managers of the 1960s and 1970s largely ignored these factors in their drive to develop computer models of the firm to predict success.

In Search Of Excellence showed that well-managed companies believe in superior quality and service and value people as individuals. Well-managed companies consistently exhibit the following qualities of excellence:
• A bias for action
• Closeness to the customer
• Autonomy and entrepreneurship
• Belief in productivity through people
• A hands-on, value-driven operation
• A tendency to stick to the knitting
• A simple form and a lean staff
• Simultaneous, loose-tight properties — autonomy at the shop floor level combined with fanatic adherence to certain ideals.

The two authors, Thomas J. Peters and Robert H. Waterman, risked their reputations as consultants with one of the world's most prestigious consulting firms by abandoning their quantitative tools and focusing on issues that many thought were best left to sociologists. They concentrated on identifying the factors that cause people to patronize firms for quality service. *In Search of Excellence* seems to confirm that business values of a half century ago are still valid today. The authors state that what they have said in their book has been said before. Unfortunately, few managers had been listening.

SOURCE: See Thomas J. Peters and Robert H. Waterman Jr., *In Search of Excellence* (New York: Warner Books, A Warner Communications Company, 1982). See also Susan Benner, ''The Secrets of Growth'' (Boston, Ma.: Inc. Publishing Corporation), July 1983, pp. 34–39.

The Need for Planning

Planning is essential to deal with changing economic and political conditions. First, planning helps to minimize uncertainty and risk. By looking to the future, management can identify both potential threats to the organization and new business opportunities to be exploited. Second, through the planning process everyone in the organization is brought to focus on goals and objectives and the means of achieving them. A clear idea of the organization's objectives helps both managers and employees to coordinate the organization's resources and use them more effectively and efficiently. Finally, planning establishes a base or standard against which future performance can be measured, to make sure that the organization is achieving its goals.

Flexibility in Planning

Although planning is essential, the plans made cannot be carved in stone. Plans must be flexible so that they can be changed as conditions change, both inside and outside the organization. Efforts must be made to forecast factors that can affect a firm's operation and plans must take these factors into account. Furthermore, alternative plans should be worked out and ready for immediate implementation should new conditions arise.

For example, now that fuel shortages are a constant threat to many businesses in Canada, a firm that relies on crude oil for production must plan for alternate sources of supply. In the case of a business whose success depends entirely on the personal characteristics of one individual, the possibility that that individual may die, retire or leave the organization must be taken into account. If risks are recognized when plans are made, alternative courses of action may be established to minimize detrimental effects.

Since the environment in which the organization operates is changing constantly, planning must also be done on a continuous basis. Managers must always be aware of changing conditions and ready to adjust organizational goals and the methods for achieving them.

Long-Range and Short-Range Planning

Any organization with long-term survival as an objective must do **long-range planning**. For example, a utility company must have long-range plans for meeting its power requirements because new hydro electric plants can take a decade or more to build. However, since the future is difficult to predict, especially when forecasts are made far into the future, long-range plans cannot be too specific. They must remain flexible so that the entire plan or parts of it can be adjusted if forecasted conditions change. Long-range planning is also known as **strategic planning** — a formalized, long-range planning process in which an organization selects long-range goals and the methods of achieving them, taking into account the available resources.

Short-range planning, also known as action planning, is usually done for a period of one year or less and covers specific objectives to be accomplished during that time. Short-range plans include advertising campaigns, employee hiring and training programs, sales incentive programs, and expenditures for specific activities such as building a warehouse or new sales offices in other regions of the country. Short-range plans outline the specific actions required in the immediate future to achieve long-range objectives. They are developed through a monthly, quarterly or semi-annual planning process which involves all levels of management. Once short-range plans are formed, a **budget** is drawn up indicating the financial resources required to carry them out and providing a guide for income and expenditures.

Planning and Decision-Making

One of the major tasks of managers is **decision-making**, the process of choosing the best course of action from among two or more alternatives. In fact, management and decision-making are so closely linked that the two are often equated.

Managers are required to make decisions, major and minor, on a daily basis. Minor decisions can be made quickly, while decisions of major consequence for the firm require deliberate thought and analysis. A manager may be able to decide quickly where to hold an emergency meeting, for example, but it is more difficult to decide on a response to a competitor's newly introduced product which threatens to take a significant share of the firm's market. To decide which alternative action to take is difficult because a manager cannot be certain of the future consequences of his decisions. He or she will likely choose the best alternative based on the risk factor associated with each decision.

Programmed and Nonprogrammed Decisions

We can distinguish between two types of decisions — programmed and nonprogrammed. **Nonprogrammed** decisions deal with unusual or unique problems, and therefore few if any guidelines exist to help a manager make these decisions. Examples of nonprogrammed decisions include planning a course of action for the future, which may involve a large part of a firm's resources, or meeting a competitor's product challenge. The ability to make nonprogrammed decisions is more important for high-level managers because they must handle these decisions more frequently.

To ensure that managers make the best possible nonprogrammed decisions, a specific process is usually followed which includes five major steps:

1. Recognizing and defining the problem
2. Collecting and gathering data
3. Analyzing data and developing alternative courses of action
4. Evaluating alternative courses of action
5. Selecting and implementing one course of action.

Occasionally the process includes a sixth step — the follow-up to the decision, to determine whether it was effective or whether it requires a change. However, the follow-up is also a step in the management function of planning and control, and therefore we will not include it in the process of decision-making itself.

Decisions of lesser importance, which managers may be required to make as part of their daily operational tasks, are known as **programmed** or **administrative decisions**. Because managers encounter these types of decisions often, organizations establish guidelines known as **policies**. As we will see later, policies are designed to limit the number of alternatives which a manager would otherwise be obliged to consider before making a decision. Although policies may appear to limit managers' freedom to act, they are established to facilitate decision-making. Customer complaints, for example, can be resolved much more quickly if policies have been established specifying what a manager should do.

Elements of Planning

During the planning process, management focuses on the specific goals of the organization, including its purpose, mission and objectives. To achieve these goals, a strategy is required, which involves both single-use plans — programs, projects and budgets — and standing plans — policies, procedures and rules. Figure 4.5 indicates the relationship between these planning elements.

Establishing Goals and Objectives

The terms "goals" and "objectives" are often used interchangeably and can be confused. We will therefore use the term **goals** as a broad category including purpose, mission and objectives.

The **purpose** of an organization is the fundamental reason for its existence. It is a broad aim which applies to all organizations engaged in a similar kind of activity. In a free enterprise economy such as Canada's, for example, the purpose of business organizations is to produce goods and services to earn a profit. The purpose of a university, on the other hand, is to pursue knowledge through research and to communicate it through formal teaching programs, while the purpose of a hospital is to provide health care.

An organization's **mission** is the particular aim that sets it apart from other organizations with the same purpose. For example, although universities in Canada may have the same purpose, the mission of one might be to specialize in engineering and technical areas; the mission of another to concentrate on medical research and training. In the same way, business organizations have many different missions. Some manufacturing firms produce cars and trucks; others make furniture or kitchen appliances.

It is essential that an organization define its mission carefully. Too narrow a definition might prevent management from taking advantage of new opportunities. Faced with changing environmental conditions, an organization may not be able to survive if it does not redefine its mission.

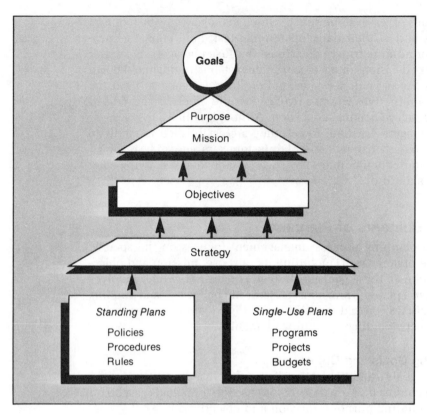

Figure 4.5 The elements of planning

In the last few decades, many railroads have experienced serious operating problems. The problems are believed to be the direct result of management's failure to adapt the missions of these organizations to changing conditions. Management continued to see the organizations' mission specifically as providing rail service, rather than defining it more broadly as providing general transportation services. The latter definition might have allowed the organizations to diversify into other areas. The Canadian Pacific Railway, on the other hand, is one organization that has redefined its mission. (See the article "Canadian Pacific Railway: A Company That Redefined Its Mission.")

Objectives are the specific ends which the organization must achieve to carry out its mission. It might be a company's objective, for example, to increase total sales by 10% over the next year, or to increase its share of the market by 3%. The various company divisions each formulate objectives which are in line with these overall

Canadian Pacific Railway:
A Company that Redefined Its Mission

A number of U.S. railroads have failed to adapt to changes in transportation, but the Canadian Pacific Railway does not appear to have fallen into this trap. Founded a hundred years ago, it was given the task of tying eastern and western Canada together. By the 1950s, however, the company realized that the highly regulated transportation business in Canada could not be relied upon for increased profitability. Thus, while it has continued to pour hundreds of millions of dollars into railway equipment and track maintenance, at the same time expanding its shipping, airline, trucking and telecommunications subsidiaries, CPR has also embarked on a program of diversification into areas not regulated by government.

It was in the late 1950s that the CPR first turned to the oil and gas industry, and in 1962 it incorporated Canadian Pacific Investments — later known as Canadian Pacific Enterprises Ltd. — as a holding company for its non-transportation investments. By 1979 the company owned or had invested in coal mining, oil and gas exploration, iron and steel, logging, pulp and paper, various manufacturing companies, hotels, and a real estate development company, among others. CPI's assets in that year totalled $5.7 billion and accounted for more than 60% of the revenues of the parent company, Canadian Pacific Ltd.

In 1985 CP president and chief executive officer Bill Stinson and his management team switched emphasis from the acquisition of companies to the prime concern of profitability — to put it more precisely, an acceptable and sustainable return on shareholder investment.

The change in strategy was to dispose of corporate holdings that did not fit in with the new CP, either because they tended to make profits volatile or simply because there was no place for them in the new hierarchy. CP sold its 52% interest in Cominco in 1986. It also sold CP Air to Pacific Western Airlines in the same year. In 1987, the company sold Maple Leaf Mills, but turned around and bought CN Hotels, as well as the outstanding 40% of Fording Coal.

CP now has five core business areas: transportation, energy, forest products, real estate and hotels, and manufacturing. The new holdings will tend to lessen the cyclical effect of economic activity, which occurs every 5 or 6 years, and had severely affected the company's profits. CP also reduced its debt load by almost $2.2 billion. The most critical change according to the president, however, has been a process of "renewal and regeneration." Right across the company, the subsidiaries have been shedding old product lines for new ones, finding new markets and increasing productivity. This has had a profound effect on profitability. CP's earnings from its remaining operations climbed 324% to $636 million, even though its revenues from those operations had changed very little. The conclusion is that most of the things CP did were significantly more profitable.

Canadian Pacific has its main subsidiaries and operating divisions set up in five main segments.

Transportation
CP Rail
Soo Line
CP Ships
CP Trucks

Energy
PanCanadian Petroleum Ltd.
Fording Coal Ltd.

Forest Products
CIP Inc.
Great Lakes Forest Products
  Ltd.

Real Estate and Hotels
Marathon Realty Co.
Canadian Pacific Hotels Corp.

Manufacturing
Algoma Steel Corp.
AMCA International Ltd.
Syracuse China Corp.
CP Telecommunications

SOURCE: See Robert Jamieson, "More Than a Railway," *The Financial Post 500*, Summer 1979, pp. 80–89, and Patrick Bloomfield, "New ethic pushing Canadian Pacific on track to profitability," *The Financial Post 500*, Summer 1988, p. 45.

objectives. In turn, departmental objectives are established in line with divisional objectives. Thus, objectives become more specific as we move down the organizational hierarchy from top management to the lower levels, as shown in Figure 4.6.

It is important that objectives be as specific as possible, so that their achievement can be measured; otherwise they may not be particularly meaningful. For example, a company objective specifying that "to provide better service to customers, the sales staff in XYZ department will be increased by five people over the next six months," is much more meaningful than an objective that states simply: "We would like to provide better service to our customers by increasing our sales in the future." It would be difficult to gauge when, if ever, the latter objective had been accomplished.

How to Achieve Goals

Once objectives in line with the organization's overall goals have been established, management must choose a strategy to achieve them. The term "strategy" derives from the military, where it signifies battle plans established in light of what the enemy may or may not do. As the enemy's actions cannot be determined precisely, a strategy must be flexible. Business managers, like generals, must take into account the actions of competitors, along with any other environmental factors that might influence the achievement of their objectives.

A **strategy** creates a unified picture of the organization's future course by ensuring that its objectives complement one another, and by specifying how resources are to be used. However, while a strategy provides the framework for the overall action of the organization, nothing could be achieved without outlining both standing and single-use plans. Standing plans include policies, procedures and rules; single-use plans include programs, projects and budgets.

Standing Plans

Many activities in the everyday operation of the organization are repetitive. A bank, for example, loans money to people for many reasons, and although each case differs in some aspects, the process used to determine the applicant's credit worthiness is identical in all instances. If an individual or a company meets certain criteria, the loan is granted. The entire credit granting function is based on **standing plans** established by middle and top management. Standing plans enable employees to carry on everyday business efficiently, without subjecting each individual case to a lengthy process of decision-making. They include policies, procedures and rules.

A **policy** is a general guide to aid managers in decision-making by placing limits on possible courses of action. Managers can make

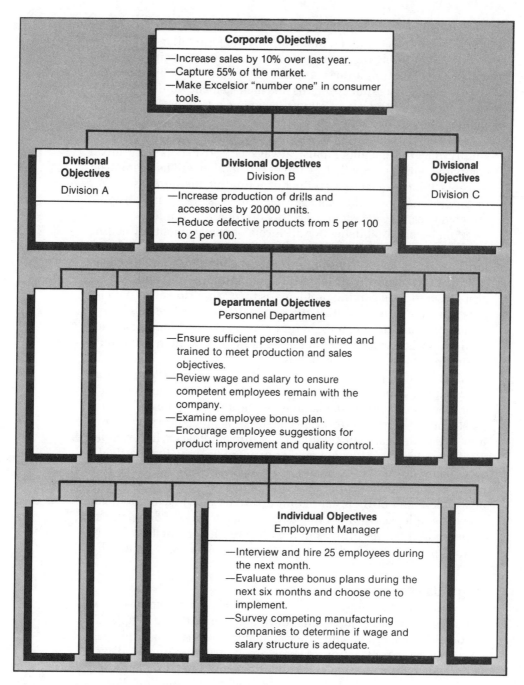

Corporate Objectives

—Increase sales by 10% over last year.
—Capture 55% of the market.
—Make Excelsior "number one" in consumer tools.

Divisional Objectives
Division A

Divisional Objectives
Division B

—Increase production of drills and accessories by 20 000 units.
—Reduce defective products from 5 per 100 to 2 per 100.

Divisional Objectives
Division C

Departmental Objectives
Personnel Department

—Ensure sufficient personnel are hired and trained to meet production and sales objectives.
—Review wage and salary to ensure competent employees remain with the company.
—Examine employee bonus plan.
—Encourage employee suggestions for product improvement and quality control.

Individual Objectives
Employment Manager

—Interview and hire 25 employees during the next month.
—Evaluate three bonus plans during the next six months and choose one to implement.
—Survey competing manufacturing companies to determine if wage and salary structure is adequate.

Figure 4.6 Hierarchy of objectives

their decisions more rapidly when they need only consider solutions that fall within set limits. For example, a major retailer may follow a policy of building regional shopping centres only in cities or areas with a population of at least 200 000. Such a policy eliminates the large number of possible locations that management would otherwise be obliged to consider and allows it to concentrate on evaluating a smaller number in greater depth.

Policies may be broad or narrow. For example, a policy stating simply that the customer must always be satisfied is very broad compared with a policy that customer satisfaction will be guaranteed by replacing the defective product or refunding the purchase price. In the first instance, the manager has wide discretion in satisfying the customer; in the second case, his discretion is limited.

Policies are established for all levels of management. By setting policies, top management may delegate decision-making to lower levels without losing control entirely. At the same time, the delegation of responsibility fosters individual initiative and allows managers discretion in solving problems as they arise. However, policies must also be revised continually as company objectives and environmental conditions change. If they are not, managers may continue to make decisions based on outdated policies and the results could be detrimental to the organization.

A **procedure** provides a detailed set of instructions for performing repetitive actions. It is a sequence of steps intended to streamline operations and control the actions of employees by describing the most efficient way to perform specific tasks. A procedure may outline how to handle customer complaints or hire employees, for example.

Rules state exactly what may or may not be done in a particular case. They do not serve as guides to decision-making, since they allow no discretion. While some rules are necessary to prevent mistakes, too many of them may limit creativity and imagination, and prevent employees from finding new and better ways of doing things. Rules should be carefully examined before implementation and reviewed periodically to determine whether they are still required.

Single-Use Plans

A **program** is a single-use plan which embodies a complex set of goals, policies, procedures and rules, together with the people, activities, raw materials, and other elements necessary to implement a desired course of action. A program is usually supported by a budget to cover operating and capital expenditures. Programs vary in scope, in cost, and in the time required for completion. For example, the federal government may establish an employment program, either for the entire country or for selected regions, to last a specified length of time. An oil company may set up an exploration

"After spending 1.6 billion dollars and ten years on this project, I've lost interest in it."

SOURCE: Cotham/*The Financial Post.* Reprinted with permission.

and drilling program for the coming year, while other businesses may initiate long-term research and development programs. A program is a single-use plan, since it is terminated once the objectives have been reached.

A **project** could be regarded as a miniature program or as part of a larger program. It might consist of the same steps as the program, but would not encompass as many activities. For example, a company program of expansion across Canada might be made up of a number of projects including the building of sales offices and plants, or the expansion of warehouse facilities. If the company were to establish a branch office in Halifax, that particular project could be independent, or it could represent a part of the general program of expansion.

A **budget** is a single-use plan specifying the financial resources that have been set aside for one particular operation and how the resources are to be allocated. Business organizations often call their budgets "profit plans," since they indicate how much of the expected revenue may be used for expenses while still providing a profit. Once budgets have been established, they can be used for control purposes, to determine how actual performance compares to the plan. In this sense, budgets are used as a standard for organizational performance.

The Planning Process

Planning is an activity that must be approached in a systematic manner. The planning process can be reduced to the four steps shown in Figure 4.7.

Step I: Establishing Goals and Objectives

Objectives must be specific. They should be clearly stated and specified in numerical terms (percentages or dollar amounts) wherever possible. Above all, objectives must be attainable. All short-term objectives must be in line with the organization's mission and long-range objectives. For example, a private business may consider market share, new products or services, or expansion into other markets to support its profit objective. Non-profit organizations will have different objectives. For example, a hospital might aim to specialize in the treatment of certain illnesses, or perform specialized operations in addition to offering regular health care.

The organization's mission is always determined by top levels of management. Even if no changes are planned, previous long-term objectives should be re-examined to ensure that they are still in line with the mission and with what has been achieved during the past year. Then the short-term objectives to be achieved during the next year must be established for the organization as a whole.

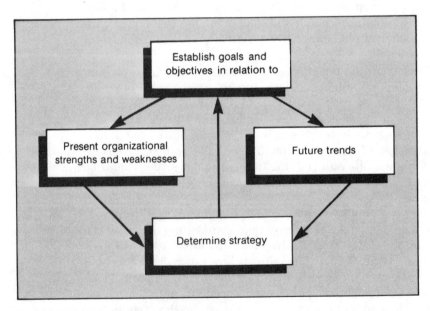

Figure 4.7 Steps in the planning process

Step II: Examination of the Organization's Present Position

Once preliminary objectives have been established, the organization must determine where it stands in relation to those objectives. It must determine whether the objectives are realistic enough to be achieved with the available financial, human, and managerial resources. Many businesses have overextended themselves because they did not realize at the outset the strain that trying to achieve unrealistic objectives would place on the organization. If resources appear adequate, then the preliminary objectives can be firmly established. Otherwise they must be revised and brought into line with what can reasonably be achieved.

Step III: Forecasting Future Trends

Once the organization has firmly established its objectives in light of its present situation, it must attempt to forecast any future changes that could affect plans once they are in operation. These forecasts might focus on possible changes in economic conditions, technology, population, lifestyles, social values and customs, or the political and legal environments, along with changes in world conditions as a whole. While some of these factors may have little impact on a company's short-range plans, their effect could be considerable in the long run.

Although management is not likely to be able to influence environmental factors, it can protect the organization by preparing alternative plans. For example, Canadian firms have little influence on the price of oil charged by the OPEC countries, but they can look at alternative sources of energy or sources of crude oil. Firms can also plan for changes in social habit. Faced with a decreasing demand for cigarettes because smoking is becoming less accepted socially, for example, many tobacco companies are diversifying into other areas.

Step IV: Determining a Strategy for Achieving Objectives

The final step in the planning process is the formulation of a strategy for achieving the organization's objectives. In fact, an organization will probably develop a number of alternative strategies based on its objectives, resources and future environmental pressures. Each alternative will be carefully evaluated and the best one chosen. In evaluating the alternative strategies, the costs and benefits associated with each must be balanced. The final choice may not be the optimum strategy, since management cannot have adequate information and knowledge of all the factors involved. Rather, decisions will be based on available information, general experience and the judgment of top management. In any event, the strategy chosen should be flexible enough that it can be changed, should future conditions make it unusable.

Action Planning and Budgeting

Once the strategy has been chosen, top management will develop a general **profit plan** for the year. The profit plan is a forecast of the total sales and total expenses, along with the profit the firm must earn. The organization is then ready to establish detailed action plans specifying how the objectives of the general profit plan will be achieved. **Action plans** are developed by individual divisions and departments. Each division sets objectives in line with organizational objectives and the general profit plan, and each department in turn establishes objectives geared to achieving divisional objectives.

After objectives have been broken down for divisions and departments, detailed **budgeting** can begin. Supervisory or operating managers become involved at this stage. Because of their intimate knowledge of specific work processes and daily operations, they can determine such matters as individual workloads, and costs for labour and raw materials. They also establish detailed monthly budgets for employee wages and salaries, including provisions for holidays and estimated sick days (see Chapter 9).

Strategic Planning And Small Business

Small business cannot ignore strategic planning. For a number of reasons, the strategic planning process is simpler for small organizations than it is for large organizations. First, a small business usually offers only a limited number of products and services with a fairly defined market. Second, there are fewer people — the owner(s) and key employees only — who have to be involved in the actual planning process. Finally, a small business has fewer resources and therefore will have a limited number of options to consider.

The strategic planning process itself can be a simple response to the following questions:

- Where are we?
- Where do we want to go?
- Can we get there?
- What do we have to do to get there?
- How can we control our performance?

Small businesses may also face problems in the planning process, however. The owner-manager may be reluctant to share his or her ideas about the future of the company with other key employees. Another problem may be the lack of resources to gather relevant information for analyzing both the strengths and weaknesses of the company, and the forces in the environment. Key employees may also shy away from systematic procedures and instead rely on their experience and intuition.

Departmental managers review these budgets with their supervisors before submitting them to their divisional managers for inclusion in the division's budget. When the division budget is complete, it is submitted to top management. If there are any discrepancies between divisional budgets and the original profit plan, they must be resolved. Depending on the nature of the discrepancy, the entire planning process may have to be repeated.

Strategic planning involves establishing long-range goals and an overall action plan for the organization. Both small and large firms require strategic plans. The article "Strategic Planning and Small Business" explains how small firms can implement strategic planning on a regular basis. "Strategic Planning for Recovery at Stelco" on the other hand, discusses how a large firm introduced a new strategy to recover from a severe recession.

Strategic Planning For Recovery At Stelco

Severe recessions force companies to undertake in-depth reviews of their corporate strategies in light of both internal and external conditions and provide management with the opportunity to take corrective actions for longstanding weaknesses. Stelco has focused its attention on developing a strategic plan and planning process that will offer clear, continuous direction for each of the corporation's divisions.

Forces in the Environment

As a first step, we [Stelco] undertook an assessment of the impact of external forces on the corporation's activities. Events of the past years indicate that developments in the external environment are increasingly important to the success and profitability of corporate organizations and that forces basically not within our control are exerting substantial pressures on us. The combination of factors at play in the economic,

political, international and social environments and in the steel marketplace will act to restrain economic and, therefore, steel consumption growth in the 1980s and will require us to think more in terms of consolidation rather than of expansion.

• First, we attempted to identify and analyze broad influences and underlying trends that are exerting new pressures not present to the same degree in previous cycles, and to determine whether their interaction will swerve our future significantly away from the past.

• Second, we carried out an in-depth study of our marketing position and developed an updated long-range forecast for each of our major product lines. From this marketing position emerged a steel-making volume trend for the corporation.

The picture that developed from the marketing and steel plan

positions suggested that our capital spending might have to be trimmed considerably over the next two or three years, but without detriment to our overall effectiveness. This led to a review of the strengths and weaknesses of our total facilities to determine where these could be shored up as best as possible and at minimum cost during the strategic period.

Elements of the New Strategy

In summary we isolated several areas of action that have been adopted as strategies by Stelco for the 1982–86 period. These are broad, but we feel that they strike at the heart of the things we have to do:

• reduce operating and administrative costs;

• improve product quality and service;

• increase market participation and search for new markets;

• build on strengths — make maximum use of existing assets;

- improve corporate liquidity and ensure financial soundness;
- reduce capital spending;
- emphasize research and development, computer, metallurgical, purchasing, and engineering capabilities; and
- optimize the use of human resources.

With financial strength having been dealt a severe blow by the recession, making recovery slow and difficult, it is essential that every aspect of the business and its operation be examined realistically and in depth. This means the scrutiny of all purchases, the reduction of inventories, the strict management of cash and receivables, the deferment of capital expenditures, the closing down of marginal activities and factory facilities, the elimination of unprofitable products and, in general, the reduction of costs in all areas.

Short-term Action with a Long-term Perspective
Short-term crisis action, however, must be carried out with the longer term perspective in mind so that future objectives of the business are not damaged. There are risks involved with survival plans, and these need to be evaluated — for example, the risks of stock depletions during inventory reduction, customer loss as a result of tough credit and collection policies, loss of skilled employees, lost opportunities resulting from manufacturing inflexibility, and diminution of research and development.

Implementing the New Strategy
It is one thing to have determined a course of strategic action, but its implementation may well be the most difficult thing to accomplish. The following guidelines are of utmost importance.

1. Clear and honest communication to managers and supervisors is the first step in such a process. The company's true situation must be made known to employees. If they understand that survival may well be at stake and are given a part to play, there will be more ready acceptance and cooperative participation. Responsibility for action should be clearly assigned. It could well be that the existing corporate organization will need to be modified to accomplish the desired ends.

2. Since a leader's visions and energy can become dissipated easily at each lower level, strategy implementation should be staffed not on a "part-time" basis, but with dedicated resources working with and through the existing corporate organization.

3. Furthermore, senior management commitment and involvement must not flag. A strategic program for recovery cannot be allowed to lose its initial momentum. The process demands strict monitoring and continual communications among all levels within the corporation.

SOURCE: John D. Allan, "Strategic Planning for Manufacturing Companies in the 1980s," *The Canadian Business Review*, Spring 1983, pp. 14–16. Reprinted by permission.

PLANNING AND CONTROLLING

There is a close relationship between planning and the other management functions of organizing, directing and, in particular, controlling. Since planning involves the uncertainties of the future, actual results are unlikely to follow precisely according to plan. Conditions can change so quickly that discrepancies could easily arise.

On the other hand, the plan might have been wrong for any number of reasons. For example, management may have planned for an unrealistically high increase in sales without taking into account sales incentive programs for their employees or the action of competitors. A new government could also affect a company's profits by introducing changes in tax rules or business incentives that the company did not anticipate. Many factors can cause actual results to differ widely from those planned.

A system of controls is therefore required to indicate when actual results deviate from plans. Although the control system may be established by anyone in the organization, in each particular case the responsibility for controlling results falls to the manager who established the plans. Managers at every level of the managerial hierarchy have the task of controlling their own part of the operation.

Issue: *What if Managers Unionize?*

A 1972 American Management Association survey of 6000 middle managers produced some startling results. Of the 1100 responses received, two thirds agreed that middle managers should be allowed to discuss working conditions in informal groups. About 18% would join a union immediately, 17% were not sure, and 65% stated they would not join. About 39% believed that managers' unions would come within the next ten years. Some 75% felt frustration and discontent were increasing among middle managers, and 52% believed that fear of reprisal would not be a major deterrent to union organization.

Although management unions have not materialized as suggested by the information in the survey, there is still evidence that managers are discontented. Managers feel they are not given the opportunity to participate in charting the direction of their companies, and that they are not adequately recognized for their work. Another major concern is job security — middle managers believe that their ranks are the first to feel the cuts. And while salaries are not the main concern for middle managers, they are concerned about the quickly narrowing gap between themselves and unionized workers.

Canadian law gives supervisory personnel the right to join a union. What if middle and supervisory managers unionized to bargain collectively with top management and the board of directors for salary increases and better working conditions? If this tendency became widespread, what problems would business encounter?

Unionization would be a sharp contrast to the situation under which managers operate today. They are considered representatives of the owners or shareholders, yet have little protection against arbitrary decisions by higher managers on salary, promotions and layoffs. And what about the supervisor? He or she is a key member in any firm. Required to answer both to superior managers and subordinate workers who, thanks to their union membership, often wield considerable power, supervisors are caught in the middle. Most often they are the ones who must deal with worker complaints about the administration of the contract, while at the same time they are under pressure from upper management to increase the productivity of the work unit.

If supervisors and middle managers were to become unionized, how would it affect their ability to function as representatives of management? What types of unions would they be? Where would supervisors' loyalties lie — with the union or with top management? How would supervisory and middle managers respond to other workers going on strike against the company? Would managers cross picket lines?

SOURCE: See John Crispo, *The Canadian Industrial Relations System* (Toronto: McGraw-Hill Ryerson Ltd., 1978), pp. 147–152.

The Process of Control

To **control**, in a business context, means to compare one thing to another. A golfer compares his score to what is par for the course, to indicate where he or she stands in relation to a good golfer playing that particular course. Similarly, in business, actual operations are compared to a plan which has been translated into a numerical dollar budget. The budget becomes the standard against which actual performance is measured. If actual performance differs from the standard, corrective action must be taken.

Many standards are used in business. Virtually all industries have established standards against which other businesses in that industry can measure themselves. Among these standards are inventory turnover, profitability and return on investment. When standards are derived from a large number of companies they can be considered as absolute standards, and usually vary little over time.

A budget is not an absolute standard, but rather an expected outcome. Nevertheless, a budget is a useful measure of performance since at the time it was established, it was believed to be achievable. If actual performance deviates from the budget, it may be because of either poor budgeting or poor performance, or both. A manager must recognize these problems and take them into account when evaluating results.

In fact, as Figure 4.8 shows, the **control process** is a continuous cycle consisting of four basic steps:

1. Establishing standards
2. Measuring actual performance
3. Comparing actual performance against standards
4. Taking action to correct deviations from standards.

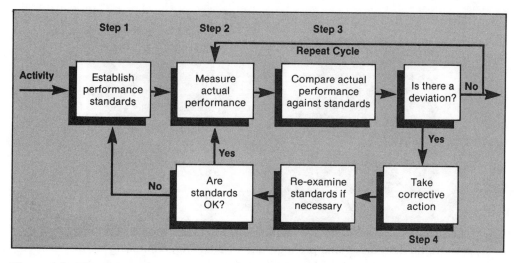

Figure 4.8 The control cycle

The control process is not complete unless corrective action is taken. Plans may have to be revised when economic conditions or other factors change, and result in year-end figures that differ substantially from plan. On the other hand, the main plan may be correct while supporting plans are wrong. If sales are down, for example, management may need to revamp the advertising campaign, increase sales commissions, or hire more salespeople. In extreme cases, the entire plan may have to be revised, even in midstream of actual operations. Re-planning gives the organization the opportunity to re-examine its objectives in light of new conditions.

Management Information Systems

To have effective control, managers require specific and accurate information. A vast data processing department with the most modern computers churning out reams of printouts may be meaningless unless managers receive the information necessary and know how to use it to correct problems. To be useful, computer information must be:

1. **Timely**. It is little help to a manager to find out in July that sales were down in May, if it is too late to correct the problem.
2. **Reliable**. Although computers can compile data into meaningful information accurately and rapidly, their output can be only as correct as the data that is fed into them. Data must be accurate, or it is of little value.
3. **Objective**. If managers are to draw effective conclusions from information, it must be objective. Figures can be presented in any number

Computers aid in interpreting data for planning, controlling
and decision-making

of ways, depending on their intended effect. Sheer numbers must not be allowed to hide a drop in quality — as in the old story of the plant manager who consistently exceeded his production quota of manhole covers because he made them thinner and slightly smaller in size.

4. **Channelled**. Information should be sent to the manager who is responsible for the operation and has the authority to make the necessary changes.

5. **Organized**. The amount of information gathered must not be so great as to make it difficult for managers to decide what is relevant. Information should be gathered only from those points in the organization where deviations from standards would cause the greatest harm. A few strategically placed controls can provide all the information required for determining harmful conditions, without necessarily using a sophisticated data processing system.

6. **Efficiently gathered and distributed**. Gathering and distributing information which is of little consequence is a waste of money. Even though computers can tabulate information quickly, someone must convert the raw data and feed it into the computer; the computer's printouts must be distributed to management before managers can even begin to interpret the data. If the control system costs the organization more to operate than it saves, it must be redesigned.

Control Techniques

There are two general types of control techniques — budgetary and non-budgetary. **Budgets** are plans that have been converted into dollar figures and that cover specific activities over a given period of time. A budget usually includes total revenues, total expenditures and expected profit. For non-profit organizations, budgets simply indicate expected expenditures for all divisions and departments. **Non-budgetary** methods of control include personal observation, reports, external and internal auditing, ratio and break-even analysis, Gantt charts, PERT (Program Evaluation and Review Technique) and CPM (Critical Path Method).

Budgetary Control Techniques

All organizations, profit or non-profit, require money to operate. A budget serves to translate all organizational activities into monetary terms, with dollars as the common denominator for a wide variety of factors. Individual budgets can be used in all departments of an organization. At every level, budgets allow an organization to compare goals and objectives with the plans to achieve them.

A budget is also a useful coordination tool. In any organization, responsibility for various expenditures rests at specific points in the managerial hierarchy, and all individuals are accountable to their superiors for the proper use of budgeted financial resources. The budget provides a check on both spending and plans, since any overexpenditure must be fully justified.

Since budgets are in numerical terms, they encourage precision in planning. If a manager wants two extra people in the sales department to help promote sales, the increase in labour costs must be weighed against the expected increase in sales. Later, a comparison can be made with the previous year to determine whether actual sales were worth the extra labour expense incurred. Thus, a budget can be a useful tool for both planning and control.

If budgets are too rigidly followed, however, they can be detrimental to the organization. Budgets are subject to errors since they deal with the future. If managers are forced to adhere to a budget that allows them no flexibility if conditions change, budgetary control may become dysfunctional. At other times, discrepancies between the budget and actual results are blamed on the manager who originally established the budget, without taking into account the reasons for the discrepancies. To protect themselves against blame and inflexibility of superiors, managers may develop unrealistic budgets. For example, they might project lower sales or plan for higher expenses to avoid problems when the final results come out.

Traditional budgeting has also tended to discourage annual reviews to determine whether particular operations are still necessary. Generally the previous year's budget is assumed to be correct, with any additions to the budget defended as necessary to cover cost increases. To guard against perpetuating unnecessary activities, a new technique known as **zero base budgeting** has been used in recent years. Under this budgeting process, a manager must justify the necessity of all activities planned for the coming year. Previous budgets, or the activities they covered, are of no consequence in the new plan.

Non-Budgetary Methods of Control

Experienced managers can often detect problems simply by inspecting a particular operation. **Personal inspection** remains a primary tool of control because some problems — such as unnecessary activities — cannot be detected by looking at the budget. Sometimes major problem areas are known, but specific causes are not. Careful study may be required and findings and solutions are then presented in a **special report**. Occasionally, personal observation of a minor problem may lead to the discovery of more serious problems. Thus, a special study can result in significant savings.

Auditing, another non-budgetary method of control, involves a detailed and systematic examination of a company's procedures. There are two types of audit, internal and external. **External auditing** is a verification of an organization's financial records performed by an outside accounting firm — usually on behalf of stockholders, or for a bank considering a loan. **Internal auditing** is conducted by an organization's own personnel. Both types of audit are designed to encourage employee honesty and safeguard the company's financial or physical resources. However, an internal audit can also bring to light outdated or inefficient procedures, and usually provides recommendations for improvements.

A third non-budgetary method of control is **ratio analysis**, used to compare current financial and sometimes non-financial results with those of previous years or with those of other organizations. For example, ratio analysis may show that an expenditure which appears exceptionally high when compared with previous years, is actually normal when compared to similar organizations for the same year. The ratios most commonly used by an organization are liquidity (ability to pay current debts), financial leverage ratios (ability to meet long-term debt), profitability (a measure of return on investment), and activity ratios (designed to evaluate and control various aspects of the organization's activities, such as inventory and accounts receivable). We discuss these ratios in detail in Chapter 9.

Break-even analysis shows graphically or algebraically, the point at which the costs of producing a service or a particular amount of product are covered by sales revenue. Managers can thus study the relationship between costs, sales volume and profits. Break-even analysis is also discussed in detail in Chapter 9.

The **Gantt chart** is a graphic presentation of the major tasks to be accomplished in the course of a particular project. It indicates the tasks that overlap and can be worked on simultaneously, and those that must be completed before work can begin on the next. It emphasizes graphically the time required for individual operations and for the completion of the project as a whole. Gantt charts are most often used in a production department. They are examined in more detail in Chapter 7.

Finally, two more control techniques to be discussed in the same chapter are **PERT** and **CPM**. The **Program Evaluation and Review Technique** was first used by the U.S. Navy in the development of the Polaris weapons system, while the **Critical Path Method** was developed by DuPont to control large, complex industrial projects. Both techniques are used to monitor the accomplishment of a series of stages, when each event requires a specific time for completion. These techniques are most useful when time is a crucial consideration and for projects that are large and unlikely to be repeated.

MANAGEMENT AND COMPUTERS

Computers have had a tremendous impact on methods of gathering and processing financial and operating data necessary for planning and controlling business operations. A computer can store huge amounts of data and process it rapidly — performing calculations, sorting or categorizing it. Computers are used for inventory management, payroll, customer billing, keeping track of accounts receivable and payable, budgeting, and many other tasks. The huge volume of daily transactions in these areas makes the computer indispensable. Even for small firms which carry on a limited number of transactions, the computer is a useful tool. It eliminates boring and repetitive jobs, and provides management with up-to-date information for decision-making.

Data Gathering and Information Processing

Businesses and scientific institutions must gather data. **Data** refers to raw, unorganized facts collected from a variety of sources. For example, a business may collect thousands of receipts from customer payments on accounts. However, the receipts tell managers nothing about overdue accounts, or whether the cash receipts are sufficient to cover the firm's expenses for the coming week or month. Not until the receipts have been organized in some manner will they become meaningful.

Information is data that has been processed and organized and can be used by management for decision-making. For example, a daily summary report of cash receipts from customer payments will tell management if enough cash is coming in to meet normal operating expenses, or if a bank loan is required. It will also show overdue accounts so that management can take action to collect outstanding debts.

Computers in Business

Because of their ability to process large amounts of raw data quickly, computers are used by most organizations. In banks, for example, they keep track of the thousands of financial transactions that occur daily. Computers have made the calculation of daily interest on savings and chequing accounts possible. In schools and universities, they keep track of student registrations and grades, and store the information as a permanent record. Factories use computers to control machines and manufacturing processes. Many facets of manufacturing have been automated. The role of computers in the production process is discussed more fully in Chapter 7.

Accessing information is essential for managers. To prepare budgets, managers need information from the past year on sales, labour costs, raw material costs and other expenses involved in the manufacture of their product. They also need factual information about competitors, customers and government policies to make accurate forecasts of sales and costs. Data can be gathered from many sources, including salespeople, trade journals and surveys, but organizing the facts into meaningful information is difficult without a computer.

A number of specialized application programs — for financial management, inventory management, payroll, general ledger, billing and sales analysis — are available to business. Computers can also be connected to control machine operations and monitor products for quality. Secretaries also use them for word processing, while managers use them for budgeting, estimating and planning.

Managers today can use computers to make their use of time more efficient

Types of Computers

There are three main types of computers used in business: the large mainframe computer, the minicomputer and the microcomputer. As technology advances, the difference between the three is becoming blurred. Minicomputers have many of the capabilities of mainframes, while new powerful microcomputers are attaining the capabilities of the minicomputer. Nevertheless, distinctions can be made. The major difference between the three computers is in their capacity and speed to handle program instructions and data. The central processing unit or CPU in a **mainframe computer** can process large chunks of instructions and data at one time, while microcomputers have to break these chunks up into small pieces and the process takes longer. Mainframe computers can therefore perform functions rapidly and have a large memory capacity to store data.

Minicomputers can perform many of the functions of mainframes but are significantly smaller as a result of technological advances in integrated circuits. Since they are less expensive than mainframes, many small and medium-size companies were able to computerize their operations. Minicomputers are available from ten to fifty thousand dollars or can be leased for a few hundred dollars per month. They are easily adapted for different uses and do not require air conditioned rooms as mainframes do. Minicomputer systems can be enlarged to meet the needs of a growing organization. Both mini- and mainframe computers are designed for multiuser systems. All users tie into the central computer through terminals — TV-type displays with keyboards. Because the computer operates at high speed, even with many users access is virtually instantaneous.

Microcomputers are small, relatively inexpensive, stand-alone computers, that are designed for a single user. Although many microcomputers on desktops today are significantly slower than either mainframe or minicomputers, the new generation of microcomputers that will be available by 1990 will have the power of minicomputers in terms of the speed at which they can handle program instructions and data and soon will rival the power of mainframe computers.

In the past, data processing needs of large companies were handled by a centralized data processing department. However, conflicts often arose between those operating the centralized data processing department and those wanting to use information in the computer. Often information was not readily available in the required form and had to be compiled. Even if the appropriate information was available as requested, the manager had no way of manipulating it or combining it with new data except to return it to the data processing department. The shuffling of information often resulted in confusion, delay and extra cost.

Mini- and microcomputers have solved this problem to a large extent. In large firms, those functions that must be centralized such as billing, general ledger and inventory management, for example, are left to the mainframe computer, while other functions such as budgeting, planning and management information gathering can be decentralized by providing these various areas with their own minicomputer. Further computing power can be given to individual managers or single departments by providing them with microcomputers or terminals that can access either a local minicomputer or mainframe. By using terminals, managers can extract data from mainframe or minicomputer files and manipulate it as required.

How Managers Can Use Microcomputers

Today, managers use microcomputers that are the size of an electric typewriter. They are many times more powerful and reliable than the earliest business mainframe computers which were large and cumbersome and required careful climate control. Together with the appropriate **software** — programs that tell the computer what to do — microcomputers can help managers in decision-making and make their use of time more efficient.

Computer **hardware** — the physical parts of the computer — and computer software are undergoing rapid technological change. Equipment is being made more compact and efficient; programs are becoming more sophisticated and easy to use. Sophisticated programs for word processing, time management, spreadsheets and data base management are helping managers to carry out their responsibilities quickly and efficiently.

Budgeting and Financial Analysis

Microcomputers are commonly used in conjunction with an **electronic spreadsheet** for budgeting and financial analysis. Prior to this innovative software tool, managers spent hours, sometimes days, putting figures on the traditional green-lined row and column paper. When a variable changed, every figure had to be laboriously recalculated by hand. With a microcomputer, pressing a few keys can provide instant recalculation of results when one or more variables are changed. Perhaps more important, it allows managers to ask "what if" questions, letting the computer recalculate complex formulas and forecasts to see the results of various courses of action. This can prevent them from making and living with a poor decision.

The computer also helps in cash budgeting by making it easy to match receipts with expenditures. Any discrepancies can be located quickly and projections can be recalculated based on the new information. To determine if the financial performance of the firm is up to par, the computer can be used in ratio analysis. Sophisticated graphs can be developed and printed out for overhead projection to a large group or to make figures more meaningful (see Figure 4.9).

Time Management

Computers can help managers use their time to optimum advantage. With the appropriate software, the microcomputer can serve as an appointment calendar reminding the manager about a meeting or the arrival of a visitor. It also provides a record of how time was used during a particular period and provides a convenient expense record for tax purposes or reimbursement from the company. Some software can calculate time spent with a client and can be used directly for billing purposes.

Word Processing

Another common use of microcomputers is **word processing**. Managers who frequently write memos and letters by hand and who write and revise long reports and documents find the microcomputer helpful. Words, sentences and paragraphs can be changed or moved around quickly without constant retyping. Once in final form, a simple command will produce a clean copy on the printer.

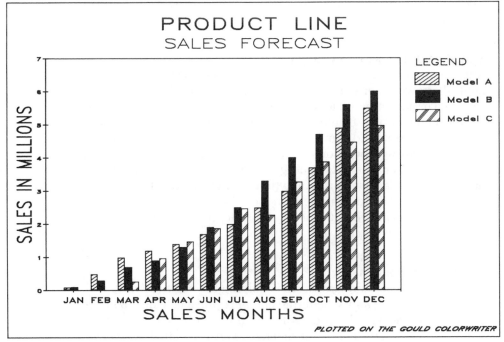

Unretouched reproduction of actual chart sample.

Figure 4.9 Bar charts developed on a plotter and used for presentations

Data Management

Data base software allows the manager to store virtually any type of information and recall it as needed, print it out, update it or analyze it. One innovation is software that combines spreadsheets, data base, graphics and word processing capabilities. A manager can use information from a data base in a spreadsheet to make sales or cost projections. The results can be shown on the screen or on paper in a variety of graphic presentations.

Inventory Management

The microcomputer can also be used for inventory management in small firms. It can keep track of items in stock and handle reorders. Inventory programs allow a manager to routinize order placements and delegate the responsibility to other employees. Furthermore, the microcomputer can project costs of carrying too much or not enough of a particular item in stock. Using an **inventory model** — the time it takes to receive an order from the supplier, the economic order quantity and the rate of consumption — allows the manager to determine the best time to place orders. He can thus minimize out-of-stock conditions, keep inventory items fresh and at the same time reduce inventory carrying costs. In addition, inventory turnover — so crucial in a retail business — can be analyzed easily once in the computer.

Statistical Analysis and Graphics

Microcomputers are particularly useful for engineers and quality controllers who can feed in data and quickly develop criteria for rejecting or accepting materials. Connected to a measuring device, a microcomputer can also automatically determine if a product is within statistical controls and provide a complete record on disk which can be printed out in reports or stored for later analysis.

Sophisticated graphics packages allow a manager to graph operating figures for analysis. Analytic graphics clearly illustrate relationships and help managers in decision-making. Presentation graphics are useful to get a point across to others about company operations, for example.

Project Management

Another area where new software is helping the engineer and manager is in planning and scheduling complex projects. Once the necessary activities have been determined along with their individual completion dates, the computer generates a critical path diagram and Gantt charts. The cost of additional human resources is also calculated and updated as required. When completion dates change, the manager can input the criteria and new dates and the computer quickly recalculates the schedules and resource costs. Without computers, the daily or weekly updating of project schedules would require a considerable amount of a manager's time.

Data Communications

One of the major advantages of microcomputers is their ability to communicate with other computers and exchange data. Using microcomputers, managers can gather relevant information for decision-making quickly and efficiently. They can access information from either their own corporate computer or from an outside data base including the growing number of data bases that store information for medical doctors, lawyers and other professionals. These information sources reduce the time and expense of searching through volumes of library material. With microcomputers, branch managers can also access data at head office from thousands of kilometres away. Furthermore, to avoid the time and expense of bringing branch managers together in one location, projections can be made and discussed using telephone conferencing.

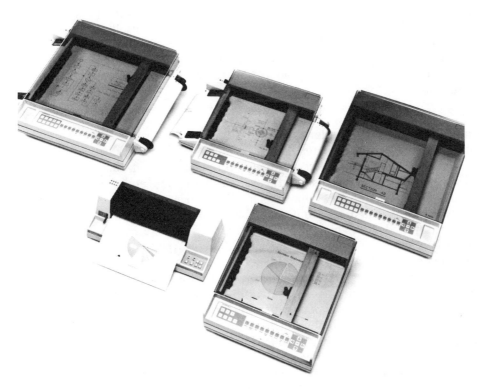

Plotters print out sophisticated graphics

Computerizing a Business

Any firm that wants to establish a computerized management information system (MIS) must deal with two major problems. First, the proper hardware, software and vendors must be determined. Second, the managers and employees in the firm — the users of the system — must become willing participants in the establishment of the computerized system.

Choosing Hardware, Software and Vendors

Once computerization of a business has been justified in terms of costs and benefits, a system has to be chosen. Most consultants advise choosing the hardware after software requirements have been determined. For example, if the accounting function is the major reason for computerizing, then the firm should first choose software that best performs those particular functions and then choose appropriate hardware.

In choosing the vendor a number of considerations should be kept in mind. Is the vendor likely to be in business in the foreseeable future? Can the vendor maintain the equipment and provide software support including possible customization of programs? Will the vendor provide assistance in converting the present operation? A final consideration should be the vendor's past performance with other clients. Often, new uses for the computer will be discovered once it is operating. It is therefore important to choose a system that can be expanded and a vendor who can adapt the system to meet future requirements.

Human Problems of Computerization

Employees may resist a computerized information system for a number of reasons. Many fear that computers will replace them in their jobs. Others may be apprehensive of a system that is new and that they do not understand. They may not realize that a computer is basically a sophisticated electronic calculator that can store information. Many will never admit that a computer can increase efficiency even once it is successfully installed. If employees continue to resist the system, it will not be efficient.

Managers may also resist computerization. In firms with a centralized data processing department, operating managers may see the computer as an instrument of power for a few privileged individuals making decisions as to who should receive particular kinds of information. As a result, conflicts arise and reduce efficiency.

The major reason for employee and manager resistance to computerization is their lack of involvement in the system's development. Small computer systems are usually set up by a single consultant, while larger systems are set up by teams of analysts and programmers. The consultants determine the objectives of the system, the type of system and the software. They design the format for data input and output. While the system may be technically excellent and work flawlessly, it often does not serve user needs. Since users were not involved in the design and implementation, they are more concerned with pointing out flaws in the system than increasing its efficiency, and see the system as a waste of money.

Overcoming Employee Resistance to Computerization

Three major premises must be clearly understood by all levels of management before a computer system is introduced in a company:

1. Everyone must realize that the system is being implemented as a resource to the users and not as a job creation scheme for data processing employees. All operating individuals have a responsibility to ensure that they make their information needs known to those implementing the system.
2. User departments must accept final responsibility for the operation of the system. Therefore, they must actively participate in the system's development and implementation. Without this participatory approach, which some senior managers consider a waste of time and resources, resistance to the system may be far more time-consuming and costly.
3. Senior management must impress on all employees that the implementation of the system is not a threat to their status or their job security within the firm.

Once employees and managers understand the above premises, an orderly process should be established to implement the computer system. First, the analysts responsible for designing the MIS system must visit the various user departments and understand their functions and requirements. Second, a permanent representative from each user area should be assigned to the design team. Third, the reaction of employees should be studied before implementing the system. If hostility exists, information sessions should be set up to explain what the computer system will mean to the company in terms of efficiency, the authority of managers and job security. If hostility cannot be overcome through these sessions, it is best to postpone the project until attitudes have changed.

The success of a computerized management information system depends on acceptance by operating department workers. The system is set up so that information can be processed for their use. They must be willing participants in the establishment of the system to ensure that the time, effort and expense incurred pays off in increased efficiency.[4]

NOTES

1. Robert L. Katz, "Skills of an Effective Administrator," *Harvard Business Review*, Sept.-Oct. 1974, pp. 90–102.
2. T.A. Mahoney, T.H. Jerdee, and S.J. Carroll, "The Job(s) of Management," *Industrial Relations*, Vol. 4, Feb. 1965, pp. 97–110.
3. Henry Mintzberg, "The Manager's Job: Folklore and Fact," *Harvard Business Review*, July-Aug. 1975, pp. 46–61.
4. "The Human Problems of Computerization," *CA Magazine*, Feb. 1976, pp. 66, 68.

CHAPTER SUMMARY

A manager achieves the goals and objectives of an organization by coordinating human, material and financial resources. Poor management has been responsible for a large majority of business failures — at the least, it can result in poor or inadequate service, with conspicuous waste.

As an organization grows, a management hierarchy develops with managers on three levels — top managers, middle managers and operating or supervisory managers. Regardless of their level, all managers perform similar functions including planning, organizing, leading and controlling. In addition, managers require three kinds of skills — technical, human and conceptual. The relative importance of these three skills depends on a manager's level in the hierarchy.

Managers plan the goals and objectives of an organization and the methods of achieving them. Without planning, resources cannot be properly utilized. The organization is also exposed to more risk if no attempt is made to forecast the future. Long-range plans apply to periods of time longer than one year, while short-range plans are made for periods of a year or less. Long-range plans or strategic plans include an organization's purpose, mission, overall objectives and broad policies. Short-range plans include budgets, procedures, rules and specific policies. All plans must be flexible, so that they can be altered should conditions change.

Once plans have been established, organizational performance must be evaluated. The control function of managers involves establishing standards, measuring performance against standards, and correcting performance if necessary. An important standard for control is the budget, which is an action plan converted into dollar terms. To control operational aspects which are not budget-based, non-budgetary control techniques are used, including personal observation, special reports, external and internal auditing, ratio and break-even analysis, Gantt charts, and PERT and CPM.

Many businesses use computers to process data and provide management with information for decision-making. The minicomputer has made computerization possible for many small and medium-sized firms and the microcomputer has become an invaluable aid to managers in their daily management function.

A firm thinking of computerizing must evaluate hardware and software requirements, and choose a vendor who will service the system after it is installed. A major problem in implementing a computerized management information system is employee and management resistance. Both groups must be assured that computerization is necessary for increased efficiency, and that it is not a threat to jobs or manager authority. Both groups should also be involved in the design and implementation of the system so that information processed will be meaningful to managers and help increase the operation's efficiency.

KEY ITEMS

Management	Strategy
Management hierarchy	Standing plans
Top management	Single-use plans
Middle management	Policy
Operating or supervisory management	Procedure
	Rules
Technical skills	Program
Human skills	Project
Conceptual skills	Budget
Functions of management	Planning process
Planning	Profit plan
Organizing	Action plan
Leading	Control process
Controlling	Management information system (MIS)
Long-range plans	External auditing
Strategic plans	Internal auditing
Short-range plans	Ratio analysis
Decision-making	Break-even analysis
Programmed decisions	Gantt chart
Nonprogrammed decisions	PERT and CPM
Goals	Mainframe computer
Objectives	Minicomputer
Purpose	Microcomputer
Mission	Computer software and hardware

REVIEW QUESTIONS

1. Explain the importance of management in an organization.
2. How do the four functions of management help organizations achieve their goals?
3. What are the three types of managerial skills? How important is each to the various management levels?
4. Why can top levels of management move to different organizations more easily than middle and supervisory levels?
5. Explain the importance of planning in an organization.

6. Why should plans be flexible?
7. Distinguish between programmed and nonprogrammed decisions.
8. What is the difference between an organization's purpose and its mission?
9. What is a strategy? How are standing and single-use plans related to strategy?
10. What are the four basic steps in the planning process?
11. Explain why planning and controlling are closely related.
12. Outline the steps in the control process.
13. Distinguish between budgetary and non-budgetary methods of control
14. Explain how various businesses use computers.
15. What is the difference between mainframe, mini- and microcomputers? Describe three major uses of microcomputers for managers.
16. What are the three major factors a firm must consider before installing a computer system?
17. How can employee and manager resistance to a computerized management information system be overcome?

DISCUSSION QUESTIONS

1. "The future is so uncertain that any long-range planning is just a waste of time — plans have to be changed anyway. I might as well wait until things really happen, and then act accordingly." Discuss this statement.
2. "To be a good manager, you have to be born for the job." Discuss this statement.
3. "Planning is the most important function of a manager." Do you agree? Explain.
4. How can business managers make sure that they have the information they need to control an organization's performance?
5. The Issue in this chapter discusses some of the reasons why managers are thinking of unionizing. Managers are representatives of the owners. If middle and lower managers were to unionize, how might this affect the daily operation of firms? How might a manager's union or association help him or her to do a better job of performing the management functions? Explain.

CASE 4–1 Why Should I Do Long-Range Planning?

The owner of ABC Press was having lunch with a friend who worked for a management consulting firm. During its three years in opera-

---

tion, ABC's revenues had increased dramatically to slightly less than $2 million.

"Why should I plan for the long run?" asked Fred Maier, ABC's owner. "I've got so much business I don't know what to do with it now. I have all the banks in town, three insurance companies, two major retailers, and a bunch of small firms all beating down my door to do their printing. I have enough problems planning how to allocate the work to my people for the next week, never mind the next six months or the next year. No, I can't see anything happening to my business — why waste my time planning for the 'long run,' as you call it?"

"That's great, Fred, but what if things should suddenly change? You're relying on these large firms for the bulk of your work. What if they decide to have their printing done at head office, or what if some other large printing company offers them a better deal? Where would that leave you?"

"No such worry, John. I've talked with them and they're happy with my work and the prices I charge. No, I don't think I have anything to worry about."

Nine months later, the largest of the three banks doing business with ABC Press entered into a long-term contract with another large national printing company. Two of the three private automobile insurance companies closed their offices in the town, and the third was to close shortly because the provincial government had taken over the automobile insurance business. Many of the other businesses told ABC that their printing requirements would in all likelihood be reduced, as they expected business to take a downturn. As a result, ABC Press received few contracts and Fred Maier began to worry about how he would pay for the recent expansion to his plant and for his two new printing presses.

QUESTIONS

1. Could strategic planning have prevented the problems Fred Maier now faces? Explain.
2. Assume that Fred Maier had two salespeople, one a part-owner in the firm. How should Fred Maier have conducted his strategic planning process?
3. Based on the information given in the case, are there any factors Fred Maier could not have foreseen even if he had engaged in strategic planning?

CASE 4–2 West Coast Steel

West Coast Steel Ltd., a family-owned firm, was the leader in the manufacture and distribution of steel shelving. Its founder, Graham Harding, developed an innovative shelving design which significantly reduced the cost of assembling warehouse shelving. The company also distributed various other products related to warehousing. Some of these products, such as dock levellers, used in the loading of trucks, were actually engineered and developed by Mr. Harding. The company was founded in the mid 1950s and its profits had been growing at an annual rate of 8–10% over the past seven years. But Graham Harding was not well and he thought it was time to turn the firm over to his oldest son, Raymond, who had been holding various management positions for the past six years. Shortly after Raymond Harding took over, Graham Harding passed away.

Graham Harding had always believed that the secret to success lay in doing one thing better than anyone else. The company's financial statements show that his philosophy paid off. The company had steadily increased its sales to almost $35 million per year. It had $3.5 million in retained earnings and no long-term debt. The secret to the company's success stemmed from an excellent product line and superior service. Indeed, the firm's success was primarily responsible for keeping a large American firm, American Racking and Shelving Corp., out of the western market. Graham Harding knew that American Racking and Shelving Corp. was well established in eastern Canada. To avoid a possible price war, which West Coast Steel had little chance of winning, he never expanded into the eastern market.

As chief executive and chairman of the board of directors, Raymond Harding had been searching for ways to diversify. With the company's cash reserves and a good credit rating, Raymond felt he had the necessary financial means to move into new markets and new industries.

For six months, he had been evaluating companies for takeover. Of all the companies he studied, a Toronto computer manufacturing company, Innovation Technologies Ltd., looked promising. The company had promises from a number of provincial governments that its computer, presently in the final design stages, would have excellent prospects of being adopted by public schools. The operating software for the computer was being developed by a Toronto software company under contract. Innovation Technologies Ltd. had provided Harding with financial statements and written documents to prove that the government pledges were indeed true. However, no contract existed between the company and any government or other large organization for the purchase of computers.

At a board meeting, Harding made his case. He concluded that by acquiring the computer company, West Coast Steel could move out of a business highly prone to recessions and into an industry that was expanding and promised to be booming during the next few decades. "The company has an excellent product with no competition in sight," said Harding. "If the government contracts come in as it seems certain they will, the company's sales should approach $5 million the first year. What the company desperately needs now is cash, which we have."

The board of directors and long-time shareholders, however, had their doubts. They did not want to expand into a new industry for several reasons:

1. The computer company was located in Toronto, while West Coast Steel was located in B.C.

2. West Coast Steel would need almost all of its financial reserves to buy out the computer company. All economic forecasts pointed to a recession which could last well into the latter half of the decade and West Coast Steel could not afford to be without financial resources.

3. The success of Innovation Technologies Ltd. was based on the contracts promised by the provincial governments. If these did not materialize, the computer company faced an uncertain future considering the rapid technological advances in the industry and stiff competition from giants such as IBM and AT&T, not to mention the many well-established smaller companies.

Raymond Harding provided various figures demonstrating the growth of the computer and software industry. He also stated that the present owners and technical staff of Innovation Technologies Ltd. had agreed to stay on indefinitely to run the company. He closed his discussion with the following statement: "It's time we got into a new line of business. The steel shelving industry is recession-prone, and high labour rates on the west coast are hindering the expansion of many companies. Companies are moving east and I can see the day when our sales will drop. We have an excellent capital position and an excellent credit rating. If that is not enough, we can take funds from our profits. Besides, our own facilities are too small and are desperately in need of upgrading. I believe we should expand into a new industry which promises high future profits."

QUESTIONS

1. Compare the philosophies of Graham and Raymond Harding.

2. What is wrong with Raymond's arguments for buying out the computer company? How valid are the objections raised by the other members of the board?

3. What types of plans should be made? What factors should be considered in the strategic planning process?

CHAPTER 5

Organizing for Management

Kim Kirk

CHAPTER OUTLINE

CHAPTER PREVIEW

In Chapter 5 we examine the organizational structure that must be established to achieve particular goals through the strategy developed and planned by management. The organizational structure has two dimensions — a horizontal division of labour called departmentation, in which all jobs are grouped together into departments and divisions, and a vertical division in which authority relationships are established to link the various departments and divisions through the hierarchical levels of management. We also consider a key aspect of the chain of command — the delegation of authority, duties and responsibilities. Finally we look at line and staff functions and the concept of centralization and decentralization of authority.

LEARNING OBJECTIVES

After reading this chapter you should be able to explain:

1. Why an organizational structure is necessary;
2. The difference between formal and informal organizations;
3. The use of organization charts;
4. The meaning of departmentation and the various methods used;
5. The necessity for distributing authority and responsibility among the various levels of management;
6. The major factors involved in the effective distribution of authority including span of control, delegation, accountability and chain of command;
7. The meaning of line and staff departments and the relationship between the two;
8. Centralized and decentralized organizations, and how to balance the two;
9. Groups and committees, and how they can be used in planning and decision-making.

Schools, universities, government, hospitals, sports teams, churches and businesses are only a few of the organizations we come into contact with every day. By combining the efforts of many individuals to achieve specific objectives, organizations can accomplish goals that would be difficult or impossible for single individuals. Organizations offer several advantages. First, they acquire information and knowledge and preserve it for future use. Second, the knowledge gained and the resources available to organizations can be used to develop and improve products. Finally they provide people with job opportunities, career development, income for basic needs and other consumer goods, and thus raise the standard of living.

THE FORMAL ORGANIZATION

An **organization** is formed whenever people join together to achieve one or more objectives. For example, the Greenpeace Foundation was established in 1971 by a group of anti-nuclear demonstrators who sailed to the Alaskan Aleutian Islands to try to stop American atmospheric nuclear tests. The group, known as the "Don't Make a Wave Committee," had a strong commitment to accomplish a specific objective. A single individual protesting against these tests may not have been noticed, but as a group, the Greenpeace demonstrators were effective in making people aware of nuclear tests and the possible consequences.

A group of homeowners who get together to protest increasing property taxes is another example of an organization. Their objective is to tell their government to hold the line on tax increases. They may show their solidarity by marching to city hall and presenting their demands to city council.

It is not unusual for individuals to get together to support a particular cause, and then disband when the task has been accomplished. But if an organization has long-term objectives, then a formal structure must be established to sustain the initial interest and effort of all involved.

To create a **formal organization** someone, usually the founders, has to develop a written description of how the organization should work. Jobs are defined along with the experience and education required to carry them out. Management positions are established along with the authority relationships which indicate who reports to whom in the organization. This formal record of organizational relationships is known as the organization chart.

Organization Charts

An **organization chart** is a graphic representation of various management positions in a formal organization. Figure 5.1 shows an organization chart. Each box represents a management position and shows a title that provides a general idea of the manager's tasks. The lines between the boxes indicate the flow of authority through the various levels from the top to the bottom of the managerial hierarchy.

The major purpose of the organization chart is to give a bird's-eye view of the formal organization structure, showing clearly what management positions exist and how they are related to one another. It can also be used to determine whether too many positions exist, or if there is an imbalance of responsibility anywhere in the organization.

An organization chart does have some shortcomings, however. It does not show the exact title and position of everyone who works in the organization, nor does it specify the responsibilities of each position. The title shown gives only a vague idea of what each manager should accomplish and does not indicate the limits to authority and actions. The major shortcoming of an organization chart, however, is that it does not show the informal organization, which often determines who has the real power. In addition, since an organization structure does not remain static, the organization chart needs to be updated periodically, as responsibilities and duties in the organization shift.

THE INFORMAL ORGANIZATION

The **informal organization** is the result of social interactions between employees and managers inside and outside the workplace. These

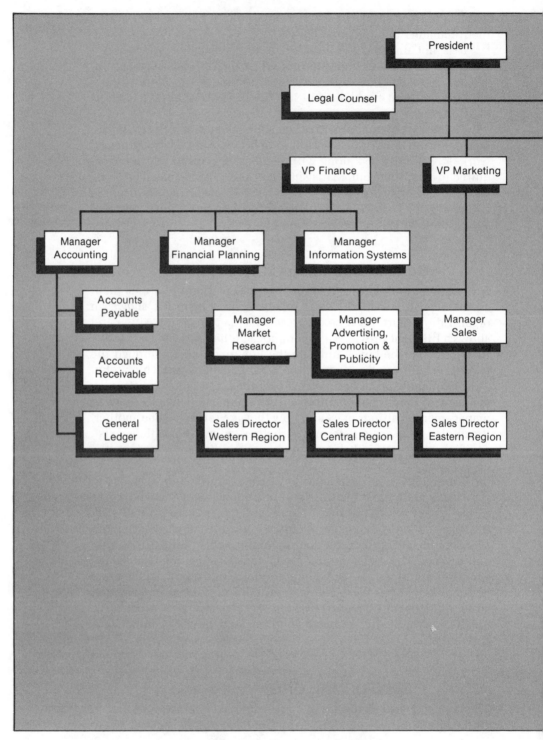

Figure 5.1 Typical organization chart for a manufacturing company

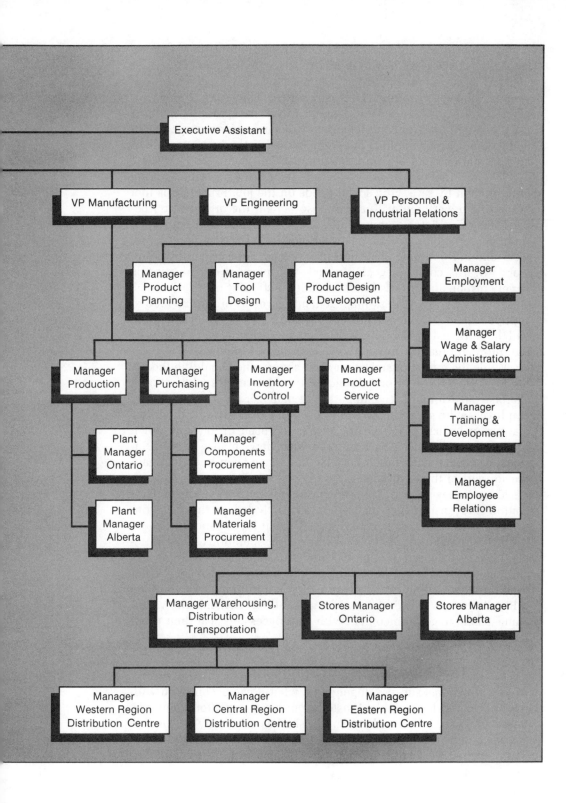

interactions create informal channels of communication. For example, a manager and a worker might belong to the same church or political organization; employees may meet regularly for coffee breaks; some employees may join a company softball team; others may simply get together because of similar educational backgrounds or skills. During this interaction, employees may discuss company operations and exchange information. The "grapevine" is the best example of an informal channel of communication.

The informal organization can help to create a pleasant working environment by satisfying social needs on the job. Friendships that cut across departmental lines can also benefit the organization because they facilitate communication between people and help solve problems. Furthermore, social relationships can encourage teamwork and build morale. Peer pressure also encourages employees to work towards common goals. In fact, the informal organization is largely responsible for the firm's smooth functioning on a daily basis. On the other hand, unless management learns to minimize its disruptive aspects — the spreading of false information, for example, and the setting of inadequate production limits by the work groups — the informal organization can have a negative influence.

While the formal organization chart shows who should, in theory, hold the power, the informal organization determines who actually exercises it. An ineffective department manager may be ignored by employees who go to the assistant for all major decisions; the informal group leader may have the power to speed up or slow down production, depending on how he or she views management decisions. Managers have failed because they have been unable to gain the support of their workers.

Thus managers must take the informal organization into consideration and ensure that its leaders are included in the decision-making process whenever possible. All employees should be encouraged to make suggestions for improving operations. The particular technique chosen to improve communication between employees and management is not important, as long as managers receive feedback on what people in the organization are thinking. A technique called "sensing" is used by some organizations. Sensing allows top management to get into contact with employees and hear their problems first-hand.

The Importance of Organizing

An organization's success depends on what it can accomplish with the limited funds available. Wasted or unnecessary effort cannot be tolerated. Every job must be accomplished as efficiently as possible and each person's effort should complement the efforts of others so that everyone works together toward the same end. Every employee

Sensing Allows Top Executives To Hear Workers' Beefs First Hand

If you're at the top management rung, how do you get ideas from your employees who are on the bottom rung of the company hierarchy? Easy, you sit down and talk with them. You sit in the hot seat and let them fire their grievances at you about the things that bother them, which could be anything from job posting to automation. This technique, called sensing, was developed in the late 1960s and several major Canadian corporations and government departments including Bell Canada, T. Eaton Co. Ltd. and the Post Office practise sensing.

The communication gap between top and lower levels in the company hierarchy is a failing of traditional management structures. Sensing bridges the gap because information is channelled from supervisors, through department heads and managers to vice-presidents and finally to the president. But there is a danger in circumventing middle-level employees. According to Ben Singer, professor of Sociology at the University of Western Ontario, sensing may generate a feeling of insecurity and perhaps even paranoia in middle management if it is done only occasionally and is thus perceived as a spot check. Sensing must be an integral part of the management process and must include follow-up on problems if it is to have any credibility.

Shell's Let's Talk program, for example, is part of an overall corporate strategy to open communications between different levels of the organization. Managers at all levels are being taught in training courses to take time away from production to listen to their employees' concerns. The company is trying to institutionalize this management style, which is already well established in its data centre. Data managers have for years sat down and listened to employee input on how to improve the working environment. While employees were suspicious of the meetings at first, changes were made at the initiative of the 600 data centre employees instituting better advancement programs for women, better training for group leaders and a better appraisal system.

At Bell Canada, sensing evolved from an attempt to determine what was troubling middle managers and to give them some insight into the decision-making process. The president or chairman spoke to groups of 30 managers who were flown in from across the country and tried to answer their questions. Topics of discussion included labour relations, technology, finance and personnel. Since these seminars were successful, similar meetings were held with the two lowest levels of management. Sessions concentrated on job-oriented issues such as office procedures.

Although sensing programs have cost the company over a million dollars for hotel accommodation and travel, the vice-president for personnel believes they are worthwhile. Top management has learned how employees perceive the company and have been able to make some changes as a result.

A less formal system exists at Eaton's, where a committee of 10 to 20 employees is selected from each store or warehouse to sit down with personnel staff and a representative from senior management once a month for six to nine months. According to the employment manager at Eaton's, the meetings identify problems and suggest solutions.

Sensing thus gives employees a feeling that they are not just a pair of hands doing a job, but rather a useful contributor to the corporation.

SOURCE: Adapted from Jennifer Grass, "Sensing allows top executives to hear worker's beefs first hand," *The Financial Times*, June 25, 1979.

needs to know what his or her job entails and how it is related to all other jobs in the organization. Thus, by establishing formal relationships, the organizing process helps to clarify the work environment for employees.

A second result of organizing is the coordination of work groups. Related activities are grouped into departments headed by a manager who is responsible for ensuring that all the people in the department work together to achieve particular objectives. In large organizations, related departments are further grouped into divisions under a divisional manager. The divisional manager thus coordinates the activities of the various department managers. In very large organizations, divisions may be further grouped under a general manager. The president at the top of the organization has ultimate responsibility for the successful performance of the entire organization. Note the pyramid-shaped structure that results (Figure 5.2).

The third result of an organization structure is the permanence and stability of relationships. Every member of the organization knows who is responsible for performing various tasks. Even if an employee leaves the organization, the position usually remains and a new person is hired to fill it. If a change in the structure is necessary because of a change in plans — as when a new department is created for producing and distributing a new product — this change is formally communicated to all employees so that everyone knows where to turn.

The Relationship Between Planning and Organizing

The purpose of strategic planning is to define the organization's mission and long-range objectives. Operating or short-range plans are then established to outline specifically methods of achieving long-range objectives. Plans in themselves, however, accomplish nothing. People move the organization toward its objectives through their efforts. An organization structure is therefore needed to group similar activities, fill the jobs with capable people and develop an effective means of communication between those who define the jobs — managers — and those who carry them out. Managers are placed in charge of various work groups to coordinate the activities of individual employees and to ensure that everyone works toward the goals and objectives outlined in the plans. When plans change, the structure must be changed, or at least examined to ensure it is still appropriate for the required task.

The Organizing Function of Managers

A structure for a large organization is seldom devised from scratch. Businesses generally start small, with an owner and a few employees. Everyone has a specific job to perform; some employees may also

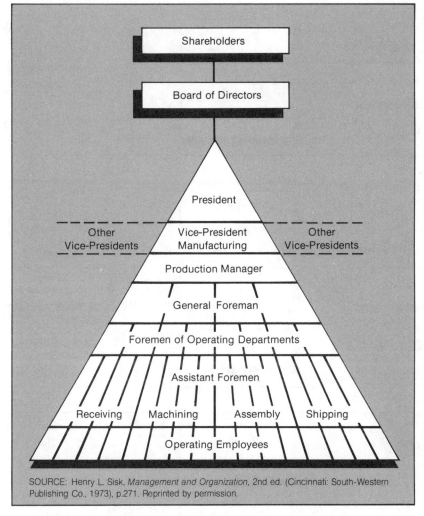

Figure 5.2 An organization has a pyramid-shaped structure

SOURCE: Henry L. Sisk, *Management and Organization*, 2nd ed. (Cincinnati: South-Western Publishing Co., 1973), p.271. Reprinted by permission.

take on supervisory duties. As the business organization grows, more employees are needed, including managers. Businesses therefore establish an organizational structure to solve specific problems arising from growth, a shift in plans, or a change in organizational strategy. While an owner may be able to oversee most aspects of an organization while it is small, as it grows he or she must bring in others to manage the sales force and the production facilities, for example (see Figure 5.3).

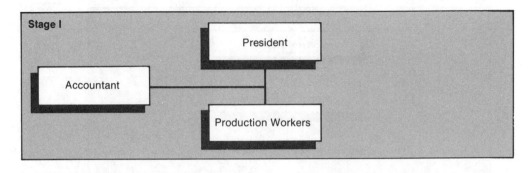

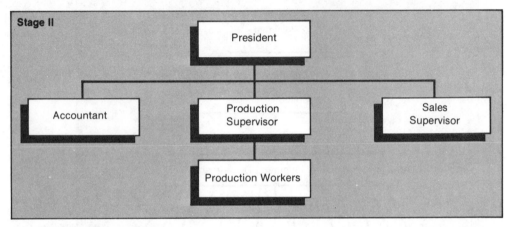

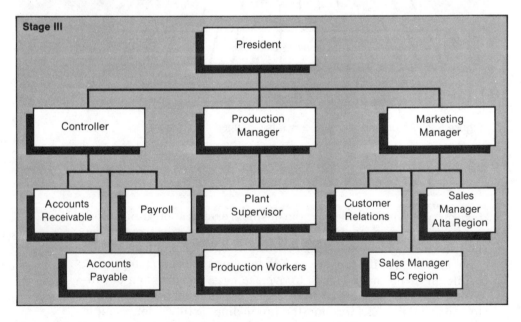

Figure 5.3 How an organization's structure changes with growth

Managers of a fast-growing organization are frequently engaged in the organizing function as new jobs are added, existing departments enlarged or combined, or new management positions created. Rather than "organizing," therefore, it may be more appropriate to use the term, **reorganizing**. When a department has become too large for one manager to coordinate effectively, for example, it may be split into two separate departments. Often the natural development of an organization leaves some departments with fewer jobs to perform. Thus management may decide to dissolve the department and merge its staff with another department that needs support. Or a company might choose to emphasize some previously neglected facet of its business by creating a new department, then assigning a manager and a group of employees. As the new department grows, more managers and staff may be added.

Thus, organizing is not a daily managerial exercise — the task arises periodically, as conditions make it necessary. Nevertheless a manager must keep the organization structure in mind whenever plans are changed, to ensure that it is adequate for the new situation.

Managers organize and reorganize as businesses grow

BUILDING AN ORGANIZATION STRUCTURE

In a small business, communication between the owner and employees is usually direct and face to face. Everyone knows the firm's objectives and problems can be resolved quickly. As the business grows, however, more people are required to perform the work, and more managers are required to coordinate the increased number of activities. Organizational growth thus tends to separate employees from top management, making it increasingly difficult for employees to identify with company objectives. Management may also find it difficult to ensure that all activities performed by employees are contributing to the company.

The **organization structure** developed by top management is therefore extremely important. While assuring the company's overall performance, the structure must allow all concerned to focus clearly on their own contributions. Broad company objectives must be broken down into divisional, departmental and individual worker objectives. Figure 4.5 in the previous chapter shows the breakdown of objectives.

The Organizing Process

Whether a new organization is established or an existing one reorganized, the **organizing process** should follow a series of logical steps:

Step I: Identify the work that must be done to accomplish the organization's goals

The first step relates to the purpose and mission of the organization and the plans that have been established in the strategic planning process. Plans and objectives must be clearly understood so that tasks required to achieve objectives can be identified. For example, equipment may have to be purchased, people hired, buildings rented or built, and relationships established with outside organizations.

Step II: Divide the total workload into individual jobs

Since organizations are established to accomplish objectives that could not be accomplished by single individuals, the total workload must be divided among the organization's members. Special care must be taken to ensure that the workload is divided evenly and that jobs are given to individuals who have the necessary expertise to carry them out. Some jobs — building plants and purchasing and installing new equipment, for example — may exist only while the organization is being established. Others, such as hiring and training employees, manufacturing, financial accounting and sales, are required on an ongoing basis.

Step III: Classify and group activities

In the third step of the organizing process, the basic organization structure is established by grouping related activities. Welding, machining and painting may be grouped under production for example, while recruiting, training and compensating employees are grouped under personnel. Activities are classified according to two basic principles: division of work and specialization of labour. **Division of work** refers to the breakdown of work activities into individual tasks. A number of these tasks are then assigned to individual employees. Division of work results in **specialization of labour** — employees may develop particular skills and become experts in carrying out specific tasks. Specialization of labour can increase productivity.

Departmentation is the grouping of logically related activities. For example, all employee matters are grouped under the personnel department. Departments in turn may be grouped into divisions, depending on the size of the organization. Departmentation gives rise to the basic organization structures based on functions — personnel, marketing, finance and production; on the products produced; or on the geographic location of the firm's operation. We return to these basic structures later in this chapter.

Step IV: Establish a coordinating mechanism to ensure all organization members work together

Once the basic divisional and departmental structure is established, managers can be assigned responsibilities and given the necessary authority to carry them out. In this step the various management levels — supervisory, middle and top — and the relationships between the various departments and divisions are thus established. These levels indicate the chain of command — who reports to whom and who can adjudicate if problems arise between departments. They also define the span of management, which refers to the number of subordinates that directly report to each manager. The formal organization structure is thus established and an organization chart can be drawn up.

Step V: Monitor and adjust the organization structure for maximum effectiveness

Since organizing is not a one-time activity but an ongoing process, each step has to be monitored as to its effectiveness in steering the organization towards its goals and objectives. As organizations grow and the environment changes, the existing organization structure must be reevaluated and reorganized as necessary.

HORIZONTAL DIVISION OF LABOUR: DEPARTMENTATION

As stated earlier, grouping related tasks into appropriate units is known as **departmentation**. Departmentation has two major advantages. First, it can increase productivity, since employees are able to specialize in performing specific, related tasks. Second, it promotes communication, since members of the same department work in close proximity and can exchange ideas or give each other support. There are three major types of departmentation: functional, product/geographic and project/matrix.

Functional Departmentation

When a business organizes itself around the major business functions of production, marketing, finance and personnel, as shown in Figure 5.4, the grouping is known as **functional departmentation**. Each of the major functions or activities may have more specialized departments on a lower level. Marketing, for example, may include lower level departments of market research, advertising and sales. A university, on the other hand, is usually departmentalized by major subject area — English, Business Administration, Physics and so on.

Functional departmentation promotes specialization in basic activities and allows an organization to build valuable expertise. However, exclusive specialization in one area should be avoided. If an employee's interest, understanding and loyalty are limited to his own department, the organization cannot benefit from the interaction between departments, and the situation will hinder the employee's opportunities for promotion to a general managerial position. Functional departmentation may also give rise to conflicts as various departments compete for financial resources.

Product Departmentation

Businesses which produce two or more major products tend to group their activities and personnel around these products. General Motors,

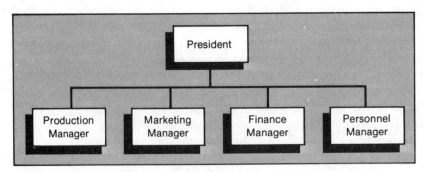

Figure 5.4 Departmentation by function

for example, practises **product departmentation**. Each of GM's five major divisions — Chevrolet, Pontiac, Oldsmobile, Buick and Cadillac — is responsible for the production and marketing of one particular make of car. As shown in Figure 5.5, each product division may then be further departmentalized on a functional basis.

Product departmentation allows a large organization to concentrate on each of its major products, to promote their growth and development. In effect, each product division becomes a separate

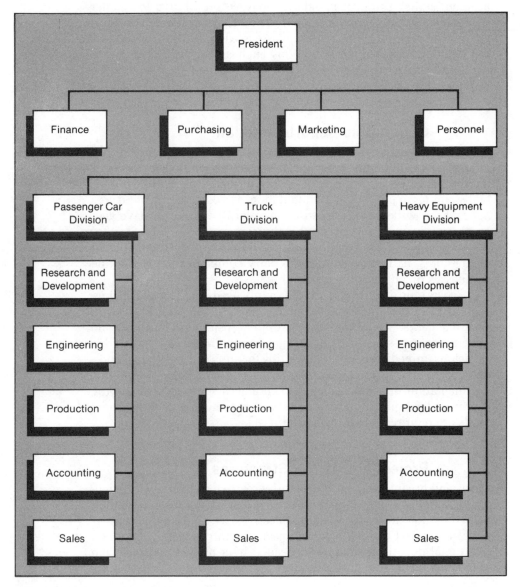

Figure 5.5 Departmentation by product

business with its own profit and product objectives. Each division competes not only with other auto manufacturers, but also with other divisions of the same company. The variety of activities that must be performed in such a division provides excellent training for general managers.

On the other hand, top management gives up considerable control when it allows divisional management levels to make major decisions. Furthermore, product departmentation requires a large number of general managers in addition to those with specific management skills. The cost in salaries may be prohibitive to smaller companies. Finally, product departmentation may mean considerable duplication of effort and expense as each division follows its semi-autonomous course. Functions such as market research, advertising, and product research and development may have to be duplicated in each division.

Geographic Departmentation

When an organization is spread over a large geographic area or has operations in different countries, **departmentation by geography** or **territory** may be appropriate. Geographic departmentation is generally similar to product departmentation, as a comparison of Figures 5.5 and 5.6 will show. Instead of product divisions we have geographic divisions. Each geographic division may however be further departmentalized by function and by product or customer. Retail chain stores, national bakeries and dairy companies are among the businesses organized on a geographic basis.

Geographic departmentation is mainly used when local decision-making is important. Regional managers can deal effectively with local concerns — such as labour supply, customers, language and governments — since they have the power to make most operating decisions immediately without waiting for approval from head office. The disadvantages are similar to those associated with product departmentation: top management experiences some loss of control, there may be duplication of services, and more managers with general skills are required, meaning higher costs.

Project and Matrix Structures

Firms and organizations, such as the aerospace industry, which regularly undertake special projects use a **project structure** — a smaller, self-contained unit with specific objectives set up by the parent organization (see Figure 5.7). The project structure is usually based on functional departmentation and headed by a project manager who is given considerable authority over the project and is free to draw

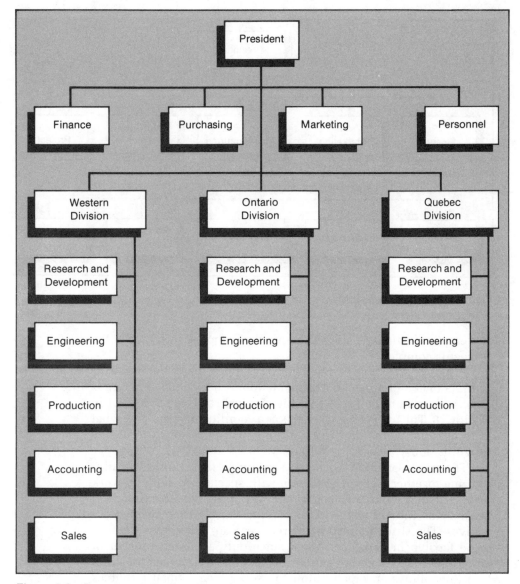

Figure 5.6 Departmentation by geography or territory

on resources from either inside or outside the parent organization. Sharing a clear purpose and objectives, employees in a project structure often become a close-knit team benefiting from informal communication and high morale.

Nevertheless, the project structure does have problems. Setting up a new structure can disturb the parent organization. For example, facilities are often duplicated and resources often used inefficiently.

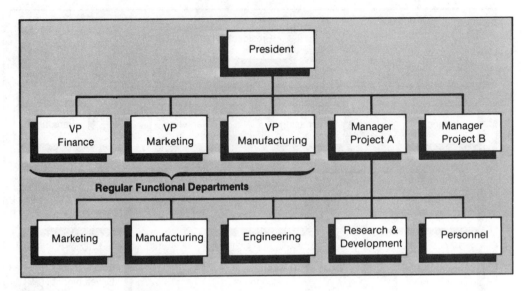

Figure 5.7 Project organization

For employees there is always the problem of job security when the project is completed.

A **matrix structure** is intended to resolve some of the problems of functional and project departmentation. A horizontal structure is superimposed on the functional hierarchical structure as shown in Figure 5.8. The project manager acts as a coordinator specifying what is to be done while allowing the functional department to decide how it is done.

The major benefit of the matrix structure is that it allows the firm to bring together a group of people with specialized skills to work on a particular project. The problems of coordination are minimized because the individuals working together have clearly defined objectives. The structure also helps reduce costs and allows the firm to be flexible in using personnel since only a limited number of employees are assigned to a project at any one time. A matrix structure thus allows an organization to use its own human resources effectively without hiring outsiders for jobs that may be of relatively short duration.

The major problem with the matrix structure is that it violates the principle of unity of command, according to which each employee should report to only one superior. If both the functional department head and the project manager request an employee at a meeting, for example, who takes priority? Conflicts can also develop between the project managers and functional department heads. Project managers may feel they have little authority over functional departments while functional department heads may feel project

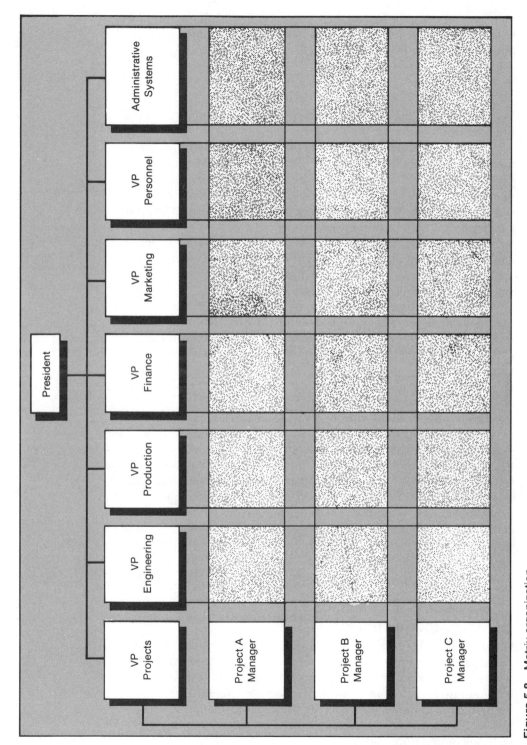

Figure 5.8 Matrix organization

managers are interfering in their territory. To minimize problems with the matrix structure, the roles, responsibilities and authority of all involved must be clearly defined.

Other Types of Departmentation

Departmentation may also be accomplished by simple number, by time, by customer or by process.

When the number of workers is the major consideration, **simple number departmentation** may be used. For example, an organization's fund drive may be launched by assigning a manager a certain number of volunteers to visit households in a given section of the city. In the same way, particular work gangs may be formed by giving a supervisor a certain number of people for a particular job.

When the workforce must be divided into shifts to cover the entire 24-hour day, then **departmentation by time** is used. An example is the police department, where most support services and activities are made available for each shift.

Departmentation by customer allows a firm to concentrate on the needs of its customers. For example, a firm that manufactures products for both industrial customers and private consumers may require two different sales forces to sell its products effectively. Retailers are another example. Products may be grouped into men's, ladies' and children's wear for the convenience of the various groups of customers.

Finally, **departmentation by process** means grouping activities around specific equipment or procedures. In many organizations, for example, data processing is a separate department which handles the information processing of all departments. Automobile manufacturers may establish special departments to manufacture parts, assemble motors, or perform service and inspection functions. The major advantage in grouping activities by process stems from specialization of labour, discussed earlier — greater efficiency is possible from both workers and machines when they perform closely related tasks.

Combining Methods of Departmentation

Often an organization will use more than one method of departmentation. For example, a major automobile manufacturer with branch plants in a number of countries may use geographical departmentation; in turn, each branch plant may use departmentation by product, while each product division may use departmentation by function. Figure 5.9 shows how a hypothetical firm might use the various methods of departmentation.

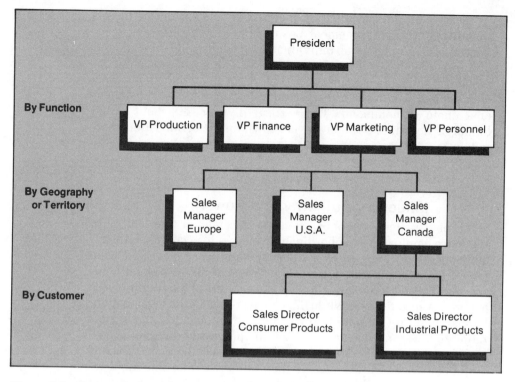

Figure 5.9   Example of a firm using several forms of departmentation

VERTICAL DIVISION OF LABOUR: ESTABLISHING AUTHORITY RELATIONSHIPS

Once the basic form of departmentation has been established, the next task is to ensure that the various departments and groups work together to achieve the organization's objectives. A **system of coordination** must be established to ensure that individual work groups accomplish the objectives of their departments, and that departments accomplish the objectives of their divisions.

Coordination is the responsibility of managers. For example, a division consists of a number of departments, with each department having its own objectives. The divisional manager acts as coordinator between the divisions, higher management and the various department managers that report to him. He ensures that there is communication flowing both ways: from the departments up to the division, and from the top of the organization down so that everyone knows what they have to accomplish and how well they are performing.

Setting up the coordination mechanism is step four of the organizing process. Management positions are established and managers placed in charge of individual work units, departments and divisions. The larger the organization, the more managers and, consequently, the more management levels. Coordination of the various management positions in the hierarchy requires the establishment of a chain of command. The vertical division of labour — the formal organization structure — is shown on the organization chart in Figure 5.1.

Influence, Authority and Power

Much of the effectiveness of managers depends on their ability to **influence** employees or subordinate managers to accomplish the required work. In most cases, a manager's influence stems from the formal authority arising out of his position in the management hierarchy. **Formal authority** allows managers to ask their employees to perform specific tasks while they are working for the organization. Formal authority is passed down from the president of the organization to lower management through the **process of delegation**. The president has been granted his authority by members of the board of directors, who in turn receive their authority from shareholders. The rights of shareholders are rooted in the laws of society, according to which private individuals may own property and do with it as they wish.

An alternate view of formal authority — the **subordinate acceptance theory** — holds that subordinates may or may not accept a superior's directives depending on how they view the order and the person giving it. Most employees will accept a manager's directives if they believe the requests are legitimate and based on the accepted job description. For example, employees would comply with a manager's request for periodic reports or for the performance of routine duties. However, if the request is illegal or against the employee's moral values, it is likely to be refused. Nevertheless, some subordinates may be so devoted to the corporation that they consider its needs above all else and carry on with activities that are against their personal convictions.

The relationship between authority, power and influence is shown in Figure 5.10. The amount of influence a manager has depends on the sources of power available to him. **Power** is the ability to exert influence. According to one study, there are five major sources of power: reward, coercive, legitimate, expert and referent power.[1]

Legitimate power is equivalent to formal authority and resides in the position occupied by the individual manager in the organizational hierarchy. Legitimate power is the most important source

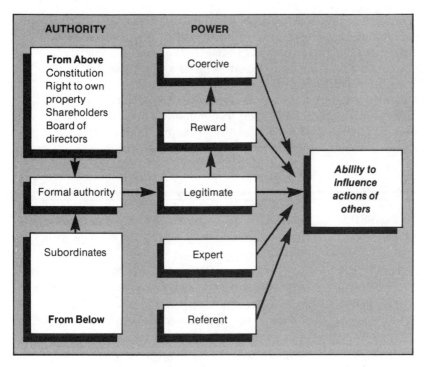

Figure 5.10 The relationship between authority, power and influence

of power as it provides the basis for operating the organization. It gives appointed managers the authority to ask their employees to perform specific tasks. It also gives managers **reward power**, since they are able to reward employees — by raising their salaries, for example, or by giving them other privileges for good performance. Legitimate power also gives managers **coercive power**, or the authority to discipline employees by withholding rewards or by firing them. In addition, all managers enjoy some degree of **expert power** as they are assumed to have considerable knowledge in their functional areas.

The only source of power that managers do not acquire as a result of their formal position in the organization is **referent power**, which depends primarily on a manager's individual personality and style. A manager with referent power or charisma can inspire a strong sense of loyalty and enthusiasm in employees.

It may be difficult for Canadians to deal with the concept of power. We have an aversion to being used to accomplish goals which are not our own goals. This fear of being manipulated, however, can be detrimental to an organization if it prevents a manager from accomplishing legitimate organizational objectives. A manager must use the sources of power available to channel the efforts of employees in the appropriate directions. A manager can thus use power positively — to encourage employees to develop the skills, competence and strengths needed to achieve organizational goals as well as their own personal goals. The Issue "Are Good Managers Motivated By Power?" brings out the difference between managers who use power for the benefit of the organization, and those who use it for self-aggrandizement and to satisfy their need to dominate others. Good managers exercise power to encourage teamwork, support their subordinates and reward their achievements — all of which raise morale.

REWARD POWER:	Some individuals have power over others because they are able to reward them for carrying out their wishes or orders.
COERCIVE POWER:	Some individuals have power over others because they can punish them for not carrying out their orders or wishes.
LEGITIMATE POWER:	Some individuals have power over others because their position in the organization allows them to issue orders and requires that others, as members of the organization, accept them.
REFERENT POWER:	Some individuals may have power over others because of the strength of their personalities; they may have personal characteristics which others would like to imitate or possess themselves.
EXPERT POWER:	Some individuals may have power over others because of expertise or knowledge in a particular field, which others lack.

Issue: *Are Good Managers Motivated by Power?*

Good managers, some might say, are the ones who get things done. Others might say they are individuals who get along well with people. According to a third theory, however, good managers are individuals who *like* power.

In a study published in 1976, David C. McClelland and David H. Burnham found that the majority of good managers were motivated by power — the desire to have impact, to be strong and influential. Such power is not the dictatorial variety used for self-aggrandizement, however, but a type known as **institutional power**.

Such managers are interested solely in achieving organizational goals and in the process creating a work climate for subordinates which motivates them also to work toward those goals. Because they give their subordinates more responsibility, they create high morale. Nevertheless, the organization will not suffer if the institutional manager leaves, since subordinates have been well trained in their jobs, and their loyalty is to the institution rather than to the individual.

Institutional managers appear to share four major characteristics:

1. They are organization-minded — primarily interested in achieving the goals of the organization;
2. They enjoy work;
3. They are willing to sacrifice self-interest for the welfare of the organization they work for;
4. They have a keen sense of justice toward their employees.

McClelland and Burnham describe institutional managers in this way:

" . . . They are more mature. Mature people can be most simply described as less egotistical. Somehow their positive self-image is not at stake in what they are doing. They are less defensive, more willing to seek advice from experts, and have a longer range view. They accumulate fewer personal possessions and seem older and wiser. It is as if they have awakened to the fact that they are not going to live forever, and have lost some of the feeling that their own personal future is all that important."

SOURCE: Adapted from "Power is the Great Motivator" by David C. McClelland and David H. Burnham, *Harvard Business Review* (March–April, 1976). Copyright © 1976 by the President and Fellows of Harvard College; all rights reserved.

Types of Authority

While all managers have formal authority, we often distinguish between line authority, staff authority and functional authority. There is debate over the validity of these distinctions; however, it is important to explain the differences between the various types of authority.

Line Authority

The authority relationship that exists between those engaged in the primary activities of the organization is known as **line authority**. The white boxes in Figure 5.11 show the line positions. Here the chain of command extends from the board of directors through the president and down to the workers and salespeople through the departments of finance, production and marketing. These three business functions are engaged in the primary activities of the firm — production and sales. In the case of a college or university, the line organization would consist of the board of governors, the president, the dean of instruction and the faculty. Since the primary activity is teaching, student services, the registrar and the business office are known as service or support departments.

Line organizations usually develop naturally as organizations grow. When a business is first started, the owner usually handles such secondary activities as public relations, personnel and legal problems in addition to personally directing employees in the primary activities of production and sales. As the business grows, however, the need for specialized assistance becomes evident. In fact, the many supporting activities once performed by the owner may become so specialized and technical, and amount to such a great workload, that one person can no longer handle them effectively. At this stage many "**assistant-to**" positions are created. Individuals in these positions have no authority over others in the organization, but handle special assignments and projects as necessary.

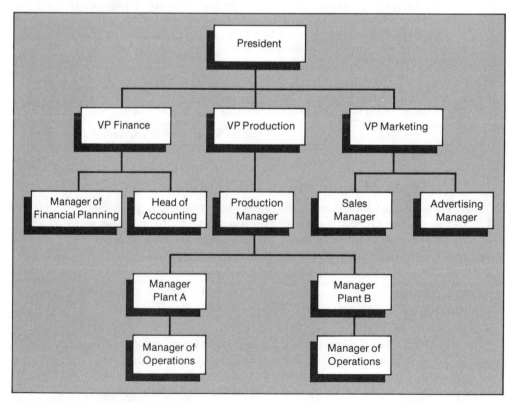

Figure 5.11 Line organization

The major advantage of a line authority organization is its simplicity. Everyone knows who is responsible for what and who reports to whom. Decisions can be made quickly because each subordinate has only one superior, and no additional advice or consent is required. The major disadvantage is that each manager must be skilled in many different areas. There are no specialists to offer advice on legal matters or personnel, for example. It may be difficult, therefore, for the various divisions and functional areas — such as sales, marketing, and finance — to coordinate tasks that require specialized knowledge and expertise. In view of these disadvantages, the pure line organization is seldom found in large organizations.

Line and Staff Authority

As organizations grow larger and the need for additional services becomes evident, **staff departments** are created to provide services in support of the line function. Staff departments may include personnel, production, planning and control, purchasing, engineering, research and development, quality control, accounting, budgeting and planning, plant maintenance, legal affairs, and public relations. Managers in charge of staff departments have only advisory authority — they have no direct authority over line managers. The dark boxes in the organization chart in Figure 5.12 show the staff departments that have been added to the original line structure.

A line and staff organization allows authority and responsibility to be clearly defined through the chain of command, but gives line managers the opportunity of obtaining expert advice. For example, the production manager who constantly requires new workers can leave most of the work involved in recruitment, selection, training and other personnel matters to the personnel department, personally interviewing only the most promising applicants. Similarly the accounting department will assist the production manager by setting up control procedures and collecting data for his evaluation.

A line and staff organization often causes conflict, however. While staff experts may believe very strongly that their advice must be taken, they lack the authority to ensure that line managers accept it. Line managers on the other hand, may resent having to seek staff advice, which they often feel obliged to accept.

Functional Authority

One way of eliminating many of the problems between line and staff positions is to extend **functional authority** to certain staff managers. With functional authority, staff managers may exercise direct authority in their specialized areas over line managers. For example, the personnel manager may have the functional authority to order salary increases for any group of employees in the company, or to insist that all personnel matters be handled through the personnel

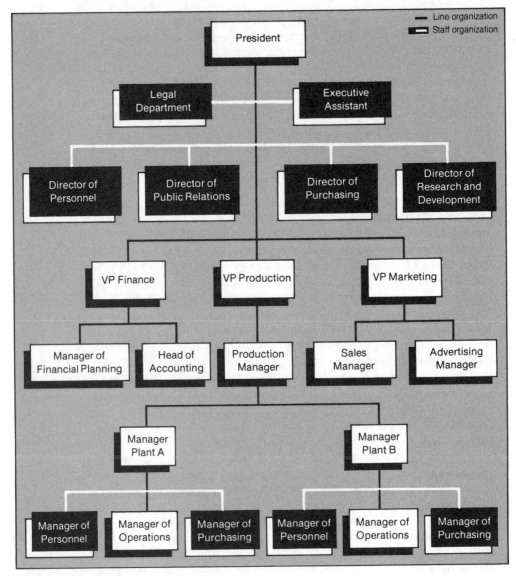

Figure 5.12 Line and staff organization

department. The accounting department may be given the authority to require that all departments and divisions follow certain reporting procedures when preparing budgets or submitting daily operating figures.

The pure functional form of organization was developed in the late 19th century by Frederick Taylor, known as the father of scientific management, to overcome the problems of the pure line organization. Instead of requiring one manager to become a generalist in many areas — which could reduce efficiency — Taylor believed

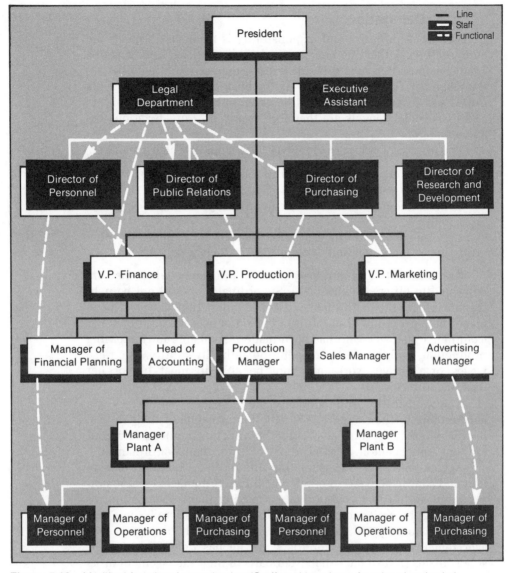

Figure 5.13   Modified functional organization (Staff positions have functional authority)

that an organization should include many specialists to whom workers would report as their jobs required.

The major disadvantage of Taylor's pure functional organization is that each worker has many superiors. As a result, conflicts of authority, shirking of responsibilities and general confusion may arise. Functional organization in its pure form is rarely found, but the modified form discussed above and shown in Figure 5.13 is common in many organizations.

Delegation

Delegation of authority and responsibility is necessary because the amount of work that one person can do is limited. Managing even a small business becomes difficult if all of the coordinating tasks are the responsibility of the owner. As the business grows, some of his duties and responsibilities must be given to others. More managers and management levels are therefore required as organizations become larger.

The process of **delegation** involves three steps in which a manager:

1. Assigns duties and responsibilities to a subordinate manager who is willing to accept them;
2. Grants the subordinate manager the necessary authority to carry them out;
3. Holds the subordinate manager accountable for fulfilling his or her duties and responsibilities properly.

Responsibility and **authority** must be in balance when they are delegated to others (Figure 5.14). Subordinates should not be held responsible for the performance of duties unless they have also been given the permission or authority to take the necessary actions. For example, a manager who has been made responsible for increasing production, without the corresponding authority to hire, fire, raise wages or reassign work, may not be able to meet his or her responsibilities.

If responsibility and authority are balanced, employees are **accountable** to their superiors for the performance of their duties. In other words, they must answer for the work that has been delegated to them and accept any criticism or credit for their performance.

Accountability is the factor that differentiates between delegation and simple abdication of responsibility. A manager cannot simply grant authority to subordinates, making them responsible for performing the assigned duties, and then blaming them if their performance causes problems for the organization. The superior manager remains responsible for the work he has delegated, even if subordinates in turn have delegated parts of their management tasks to others. A good example is the captain of a ship who is responsible for the actions of every crew member. Even though his personal performance may be impeccable, he must accept responsibility for accidents which may result directly from the neglect of one of his crew members. Therefore, although managers delegate **operating responsibility**, they cannot delegate **ultimate responsibility**.

TABLE 5.1

Comparison of line, line and staff, and modified functional organization structures

Organizational Structure	Advantages	Disadvantages
Line organization	1. Simple organization structure 2. Clear division of authority 3. Decisions can be made quickly 4. Subordinates are responsible to only one person	1. Expert advice not readily available 2. Line managers must be generalists 3. Not suitable for a large organization
Line and staff organization	1. Expert advice is readily available to line managers 2. Line managers can concentrate on their main managerial task	1. Staff managers have no direct authority over line managers and can only recommend a course of action 2. Conflicts may develop between line and staff managers
Modified functional organization	1. Expert advice is available to line managers 2. Staff managers have authority to make decisions in specified areas 3. Line managers can concentrate on their main managerial task 4. Reduces conflicts between line and staff managers	1. Employees may have more than one superior 2. Conflicts and misunderstandings may arise unless authority relationships are clearly defined

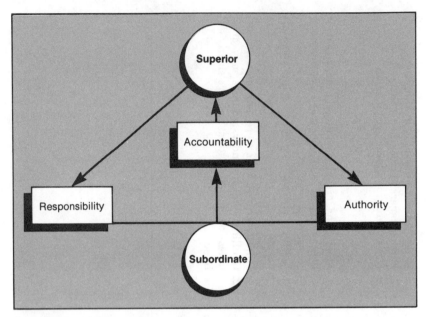

Figure 5.14   The delegation process — responsibility and authority must be balanced

Chain of Command

Delegation creates authority relationships between levels of management in the form of a hierarchy known as a chain of command. An organization chart shows the **chain of command** through the lines that connect the various management positions, indicating who can delegate to whom, and who is responsible to whom. The chain of command connects the president at the very top of the hierarchy with every worker in the organization. In effect, each worker carries out the orders of the president through the orders of managers at each of the various levels.

When problems arise between individuals or departments, the chain of command aids in the adjudication process by passing the matter up through the hierarchy until it reaches a level of management where one person with authority over both factions can make a decision to solve the problem. The decision is then passed down to the worker or department in question through the same channel. If any managers are bypassed, their authority may be undermined. If they are bypassed frequently, the balance between their responsibility and authority is upset, and it may be difficult to hold them accountable for the operation of their departments.

In practice, of course, links in the chain of command are often bypassed. Operations would quickly bog down if the complete chain of command had to be followed for every minor problem. Individual workers or managers in different departments resolve daily operating problems themselves without consulting their superiors. In an emergency situation requiring immediate action to resolve a major problem, the superior manager bypassed will be notified as soon as possible. Under normal circumstances, however, any problems out of the ordinary should be passed through the chain of command.

Span of Control

How many subordinates can a manager supervise? The answer depends on the organization and the type of people in it. Managers with many subordinates reporting to them have a wide span of control; managers with few subordinates, have a narrow span of control (Figure 5.15). The **span of control**, also known as **span of management**, determines the height of the management hierarchy and the number of management levels in it. If managers in a particular organization generally have a narrow span of control, a greater number of management levels is required than in a similar organization where each manager has a wider span of control. Many levels of management mean a **tall organization structure**, which increases costs — not only in manager's salaries, but also in support staff, office space and other facilities. Furthermore, with too many levels of management, effective communication may become impaired. The communication barriers responsible for distorting messages are discussed in Chapter 6.

A wide span of control, on the other hand, means fewer levels of management, resulting in a **flat organization structure**. However, an inadequate number of levels may not be efficient either, and could also be costly. If a manager is responsible for too many subordinates, he may not be able to make decisions quickly, consult with subordinates thoroughly, or otherwise give them sufficient support. The entire organization may suffer as opportunities slip by and necessary actions are delayed.

In practice, a common span of control covers five to nine subordinates. The span varies, however, with the particular level on which the manager operates. The number of subordinates that top management can effectively supervise is generally lower than that for middle and lower levels of management. The span of control depends on the manager's personal skill and the skill of subordinates, including how well they understand the organization's plans and objectives, and how clearly their jobs are outlined. A wider span of control is possible when the organization is operating in a stable

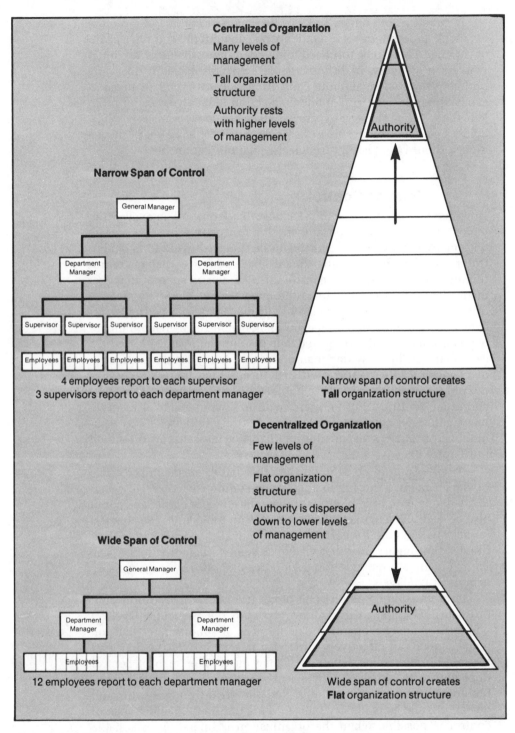

Figure 5.15   Span of control determines height of organization structure

environment, as there is less need for close communication between superior and subordinate. A manager's span of control can also be wider if employees are highly motivated and tend to work well on their own, thus requiring less supervision.

Centralization and Decentralization

The terms decentralization and delegation are often confused. While there is a definite relationship between them, the two concepts are not identical. As discussed earlier, organizational growth requires that some responsibility and authority be delegated to other individuals.

Decentralization refers to the amount of authority that has been delegated to lower levels of management, and the kinds of decisions lower level managers are allowed to make. If top management is confident of the abilities of lower level managers to make important decisions, it may delegate considerable authority to them. If top management prefers to retain responsibility for all major decision-making, keeping close control over the actions of subordinates, operations are said to be **centralized**.

The **degree of decentralization** may also depend on other factors — the environment in which the organization operates, for example, or its size and rate of growth. In an environment where markets and competitive relationships are relatively stable, decision-making can be more centralized because top management has more time to direct operations itself; the same is true of a medium-sized organization with a fairly stable rate of growth. On the other hand, in an industry where technology is changing rapidly — as in the case of computer manufacturers — decentralization is essential, if the firm is to react quickly to the moves of its competitors.

It is important that firms strike a balance between centralization and decentralization. A decentralized organization helps to train and develop managers by allowing them to make decisions and learn from their mistakes; greater freedom for creativity also increases their value to the firm. Moreover, most daily operating decisions can be made more quickly — hence effectively — when left to lower levels of management.

Decisions that may affect long-term prospects of the organization, however, should be retained by top management. These decisions include the setting of long-range objectives and goals, policy development, acquisition of financial resources, capital expenditures, new products, international expansion and organizational change. Although major decisions can sometimes be made at lower levels of management, they could prove costly unless an effective control system has been established to keep top management informed.

COMMITTEES

A **committee** is a group of people brought together to perform a particular task. An increasing number of organizations now use committees either to solve specific problems or to perform ongoing organizational activities, or simply to share information. Committees may also be used to make recommendations to upper management and to establish policy for the organization.

Committees offer a number of advantages. First, they often make better decisions than individuals can because members are able to share their knowledge. Second, committee decisions are more likely to be accepted since most of the organization's members will have been represented or at least have had some input into the final decision. Finally, committees tend to make their members more aware of how the organization functions through exposure to others and their operations. This increased familiarity with what others do may lead to better coordination between departments.

Committees also have disadvantages, however. Decision-making is often slow and may be costly in terms of the committee members' time. Moreover, many decisions tend to be compromises, due to the conflicting interests of various members. Perhaps most important, committees lack accountability. Should a decision prove to be wrong

Committees are becoming an integral part of decision-making

after it has been implemented, it is difficult to hold any one member responsible.

Nevertheless, because of the trend to more participation in decision-making, committees will likely be used even more in the future, in all types of organizations. Managers must therefore understand how committees can function efficiently. The first major step is to establish clearly the committee's goals and objectives so that members can focus on the task at hand. The authority of the committee must also be clarified so that members know whether their decisions will be implemented or simply used for advisory purposes. Finally, formal procedures should be established for meetings covering frequency, place, dates and times.

If the committee is to be permanent, a secretary must be assigned to handle all communications and correspondence. The agenda and correspondence should be distributed well before the meeting so that all members have time to study the material. Finally, all meetings should start and end on time. It is best to set a predetermined time limit for the meeting and reconvene later, if necessary, to ensure that all members can give their undivided attention to matters. If meetings are long and appear to be unproductive, members may become distracted with other business or personal matters.

The second major consideration is the committee's composition — it must not be so large as to be unmanageable. The leader, responsible for ensuring that formal procedures are followed, must be carefully chosen. Leaders must have the human skills necessary to elicit ideas and discussion from the group; they must encourage timid members to contribute, while tactfully keeping monopolizers under control. The committee members must listen carefully to evaluate all suggestions fairly; they should try to avoid illogical compromises. Most important, members should approach their task in a cooperative spirit, rather than one of competition, if they hope to arrive at solutions.

NOTE

1. John R.P. French Jr. and Bertram Raven, "The Bases of Social Power," in Darwin Cartwright and A.F. Zander, eds., *Group Dynamics: Research and Theory* (New York: Harper & Row, 1960).

CHAPTER SUMMARY

An organization is a group of people with an objective. It becomes a formal organization when management is added to direct the activities of people towards achieving the organization's objectives. Thus an organization structure is developed which ensures that employees know to whom they are responsible, and that established authority relationships are relatively stable and permanent. The formal organization structure is shown by an organization chart which indicates the different management positions, titles and authority flow.

People performing the various tasks in an organization can be grouped together into units — a process known as departmentation. The most common groupings are by function, product, geography or territory, project or matrix, customer and process. The type of structure chosen will be the one best suited to the achievement of the particular organization's objectives.

To ensure that all organization members work toward the objectives and goals of the organization, managers must be able to influence their actions. Managers base their authority on five types of power: reward, coercive, legitimate, expert and referent. Legitimate power is equivalent to formal authority and gives managers the right to act. Expert power comes from a person's knowledge and experience in a particular field, while referent power stems from an individual's personality.

We can distinguish between line authority, staff authority and functional authority of managers. The managers who are directly in charge of the organization's major activity are line managers. As organizations grow, managers require more expertise in specific areas and thus staff positions are created. When staff managers obtain authority over specific aspects of their job, they have functional authority.

Since the head of the organization cannot perform all the work himself, some duties and responsibilities must be delegated to other managers, along with the authority to carry them out. Subordinate managers in turn are accountable to their superiors for performance of their duties.

Through delegation, a managerial hierarchy known as the chain of command is established. The hierarchy can be either tall or flat depending on the number of managers in the organization and the span of control each has. A narrow span of control means that one manager is responsible for only a few subordinate managers; a wide span of control means that one manager is responsible for many subordinates. The optimum span of control refers to the number of subordinates one manager can most effectively supervise. Effectiveness depends on the abilities of both the superior and subordinate managers, the type of activities being performed and the closeness of communication required. Generally, the wider the span of control allowed to managers, the greater the degree of decentralization in decision-making within the organization.

A committee is used when representation or input from a variety of areas is required. Although the decisions made by committees are generally of superior quality, committees are costly to use. Many decisions are compromises, and they can take a long time to make. Committees also tend to lack accountability. Nevertheless, committees are now being used in the management of organizations, and managers should understand how to make them function effectively.

KEY TERMS

Organization	Power
Formal organization	Legitimate power
Reorganization	Reward power
Organization chart	Coercive power
Informal organization	Expert power
Organizational structure	Referent power
Departmentation	Chain of command
Functional departmentation	Span of control
Product departmentation	Centralization
Geographic departmentation	Decentralization
Delegation	Line organization
Accountability	Line and staff organization
Authority	Functional organization
Operating responsibility	Functional authority
Ultimate responsibility	Matrix organization
Influence	Project management
Formal authority	Committees

REVIEW QUESTIONS

1. Why are formal organizations necessary?
2. Explain the difference between the formal organization and the informal organization.
3. What is departmentation? When would a firm use product departmentation? Geographic departmentation?
4. Explain these terms: authority, responsibility, accountability. How are they related?
5. Explain one of the errors commonly made in the process of delegation.
6. Distinguish between influence, power and authority.
7. What are some of the dangers in bypassing the chain of command?
8. Why would the dean of instruction at a college or university have a wide span of control? Why would the president of a very large corporation have a narrow span of control?
9. Distinguish between centralization and decentralization. When is decentralization appropriate?

10. What is the difference between line and staff positions? Why might conflicts develop between individuals in each of these positions?

11. What is a matrix organization structure? Name some kinds of organizations that might employ a matrix structure. Describe some of the problems involved in using this structure.

12. What are the advantages and disadvantages of committees? Will the use of committees to make management decisions increase in the future? Why?

DISCUSSION QUESTIONS

1. If organizational structures are established to allow people to perform their jobs more effectively, why is it that they can also cause so much conflict and friction?

2. How can technology affect a company's organization structure? Provide some examples.

3. "The principle underlying delegation is simple, yet delegation is often a major factor of management failure." Discuss this statement.

4. "There should be a balance between centralization and decentralization in a company." Why might this balance be difficult to obtain in a rapidly growing company?

5. "More of management's work should be done through committees, since a group of people can make better decisions than one person alone." Evaluate this statement based on the information in the last two chapters.

CASE 5–1 The Greenpeace Foundation: Establishing an Organizational Structure

In 1971 a small group of activists sailed to Alaska to protest against the Amchitka nuclear tests conducted by the Americans in the Aleutian Island chain. Since then, the Greenpeace Foundation has grown to be a worldwide organization with 35 branch offices throughout the U.S., Europe, Australia and New Zealand. The head office is in Vancouver, B.C., and the president, who has a Ph.D. in ecology, is Patrick Moore.

While the organization has been criticized for being overly dramatic in its various bids for publicity, Moore says setting a symbolic example is the only way to impress on people the severity of the ecological problems facing the world today. Moore gets involved, as he did when he used his own body to shield a seal pup about to be clubbed to death, or when he and other members placed their small inflatable rafts between a Soviet whaling vessel and the pod of sperm whales it was hunting.

Greenpeace claims credit for a number of victories, from the halting of nuclear tests in the atmosphere by both the U.S. and France, to the cancellation of the gypsy moth spraying program in Vancouver's Kitsilano area.

The Greenpeace Foundation has 100 000 members worldwide, of which 20 000 belong to its head office in Vancouver. The international organization has an annual budget of $2 million, of which Vancouver handles $500 000. Nevertheless, money is still a major problem. For the whaling expedition, Greenpeace had to go into debt for $200 000. Individual members acted as co-signers for the debt in amounts of $5 000 each.

Funds are raised through the sale of T-shirts and bumper stickers, as well as through bingo games and lotteries, walk-a-thons, radio appeals, concerts and individual donations. In addition, the organization has its own newspaper with a circulation of 65 000 — unfortunately, the paper has not yet shown a profit. The organization has also received federal funding for educational programs on the subject of whales. Local Greenpeace offices retain 50% of net revenues for their own campaigns, and pass the other 50% on to the organization.

One of the greatest difficulties has always been fund-raising. But the group has also experienced organizational troubles. As Moore says, "We have grown into an organization that can't be worked on an *ad hoc* basis any longer. As we have grown, we have discovered we can no longer rely on direct relationships to ensure that our policies and financial management systems operate efficiently. We have had to develop an operational philosophy. We believe in centralism to the extent it is necessary, and decentralization to the extent that it is desirable."

SOURCE: Adapted from Jim Lyon, "Greenpeace Counts the Cost of Confrontation," *The Financial Post*, May 19, 1979.

QUESTIONS

1. What type of organizational structure would be best suited for Greenpeace? Keep in mind that the organization is largely voluntary and relies on individuals' concerns about the environment for financial support.

2. Draw an organizational chart for the Greenpeace Foundation including its head office departments and its international branches. Keep in mind that some functions need to be coordinated from head office.

3. Many of the people who work for Greenpeace are volunteers. What problems regarding authority might this cause for the chief officers of the Greenpeace organization? Explain how much they could rely

on each of the sources of power to influence the behaviour of Greenpeace members.

4. Patrick Moore says that Greenpeace is experiencing organizational problems. Outline some of the specific problems you think might be involved.

5. What kinds of activities should be centralized in this organization? Which activities should be decentralized?

CASE 5–2 Phil's Folly

Phil Bridges is the Regional Administrative Officer for a large portion of Environment Canada, the Ministry that oversees environmental protection matters. He is responsible for administrative efficiency and for budgetary procedures in a region that spends $23 000 000 yearly. The region is organized around five research laboratories and a wildlife protection service. Each facility has a junior administrative officer (A.O.). The problem is that these junior administrative officers report to a Lab Director, rather than to the Regional Administrative Officer. The Lab Directors in turn, report to Phil's boss, the Regional Director General. But Phil is still held accountable for having reports prepared and submitted on time and for general overall efficiency.

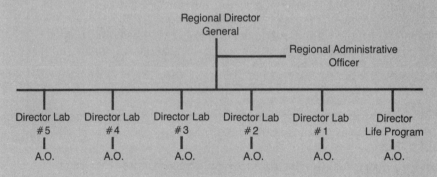

Let's listen in on a typical telephone conversation between Phil and the Administrative Office in Lab #2, located several hundred miles away:

Phil: "Listen Bob, I just have to get those final figures over the telex this afternoon. The report is due tomorrow and . . . ."

Bob: "Gee I sympathize Phil, but the Director here has given me a rush job and even if I work all night, I won't have your figures before 3:00 tomorrow at the earliest. Sorry Ole Buddy, I'll do my best, but I can't meet your deadline."

Phil:	"Can you bring in some temporary help? I'm really up against the wall here."
Bob:	"Can't do that; the Director has put a freeze on all extra hiring. You'll just have to wait!" (getting impatient)
Phil:	"Well . . . do the best you can Bob." (Hangs up the phone and says out loud) "Damn, the Region is going to be late again!"

SOURCE: Written by Dr. P. C. Wright, Business Division, Humber College, Toronto, Ontario. Reprinted by permission of the author.

QUESTIONS

1. How has the organization structure contributed to Phil's problems?
2. Would the establishment of clear lines of authority solve the problems illustrated in this case? Why or why not?
3. What should Phil do now?
4. How would you organize the Region?

CHAPTER 6

Managing People

Industrial Accident Prevention Association

CHAPTER OUTLINE

CHAPTER PREVIEW

In Chapter 6 we examine the directing function of management. Aspects of directing include motivating employees through appropriate rewards, communicating to them the organization's goals and what each individual must do to achieve them, and providing leadership. Various theories concerning motivation and leadership are discussed, along with the most common communication problems and the relationship between morale, job satisfaction and productivity. We also survey some of the techniques used to make work more interesting and meaningful for both employees and managers.

LEARNING OBJECTIVES

After reading this chapter you should be able to explain:

1. The meaning of motivation and the major theories that have been advanced to explain how people are motivated;
2. The relationship between motivation and leadership;
3. The difference between Theory X and Theory Y managers;
4. The leadership continuum, the managerial grid, Fiedler's contingency theory of leadership, the path-goal theory and the life-cycle theory;
5. The criteria that organizations should use to select leaders;
6. Japanese management techniques as compared to North American techniques;
7. The importance of good communication and ways of overcoming communication barriers;
8. The relationship between motivation, morale, job satisfaction and productivity;
9. How organizations can redesign work to make it more interesting and improve morale;
10. The meaning of management by objectives and the problems involved in implementing the MBO process in organizations.

Regardless of how well managers perform their roles of planning and controlling, and no matter how well their organizational structure is set up, goals cannot be accomplished without people. Managers need skills in human relations to obtain the willing cooperation of their employees and to draw the best from them. They must know how to direct their employees — how to motivate them, communicate with them and provide them with leadership.

MOTIVATION

Occasionally we hear of a stunt man killed while performing a dangerous stunt. Or we hear of an executive involved in an illegal activity to obtain a contract for a firm. We wonder at why someone would scale the walls of the World Trade Centre in New York or jump off the CN Tower in Toronto tethered to an elastic rope. These individuals often do not receive any tangible rewards. So why do they do it? What motivates them?

To gain a better understanding of what makes people do things, we must examine the meaning of motivation. Motivation can refer to an individual's **condition** as when we say, "Louise is highly motivated and therefore does well in her job." Managers are concerned with motivation as a **process**. What factors brought Louise to her motivated condition?

We can thus define **motivation** in general terms as that which causes, channels and sustains a person's behaviour. The cause may be a person's drives, desires, needs and wishes. A simple example is hunger, which drives us to satisfy the need for food by finding something to eat. In our example, Louise may have felt the need or desire for a reward — material, social or psychological — and believed that doing her job well would satisfy the need. Motivation thus also involves goal-oriented behaviour or the drive to satisfy a need. Figure 6.1 is a simplified representation of the motivation process.

How to Motivate People

All individuals have needs that require satisfaction. The need perceived to be strongest at any given time will dictate current behaviour. A manager can motivate employees by showing them that their needs can be best satisfied by working toward the organization's goals. He or she must convince them that they can benefit through money, status, good social relationships or some other psychological reward from doing their jobs well. But how can a manager motivate all employees to work toward the same organizational objectives, when no two individuals have the same needs at the same time? A look at some of the motivation theories that have been advanced may give us some ideas.

Classical Theory of Motivation

Proponents of the classical theory of motivation considered people as purely economic creatures with money as their prime motivator. They believed that people worked to satisfy their need for basic necessities — food, clothing, shelter — and to raise their standard of living with other material goods. To motivate people to work towards organizational goals then, a manager would only have to offer more money.

Figure 6.1 Simple motivation process

One of the chief proponents of the classical theory of motivation was Frederick W. Taylor, known as the father of scientific management. In 1898, Taylor began a series of studies on the specific tasks performed by workers in a steel company — metal cutting, handling iron and shoveling. The results of his studies were published in a series of scientific papers, and in 1911, Taylor published a book entitled *Principles of Scientific Management*. In essence, his principles stated that jobs should be scientifically studied to determine what they entail; workers should be scientifically selected and trained; there should be cooperation between workers and management to ensure that all work is done according to scientific principles; and the total work should be divided between management and workers according to what each was best able to do.

Taylor believed that if all work were divided into small activities, any person could learn the tasks easily and eventually perform them rapidly. By studying the physical movements required to perform a specific task, Taylor was able to calculate the standard production rate for the average worker. Workers who achieved the standard level of output received the standard rate of pay, but any higher level of output was rewarded with a higher rate calculated according to each additional unit produced. This was Taylor's differential **piece rate system**. He believed that since workers could double their earnings, they would be strongly motivated to increase productivity.[1]

The classical theory of motivation was most effective during the latter years of the industrial revolution when workers were relatively poor and jobs were difficult to get. By working faster employees could increase their earnings and lead a more comfortable life. However, as the workers' standard of living improved, management noticed that their productivity no longer increased as rapidly, regardless of the monetary incentives that were offered. At first, managers were puzzled by this change, but eventually they learned that the process of motivating human beings is far more complex than was believed.

Human Relations and Elton Mayo

From 1927 to 1933 Elton Mayo, a Harvard professor of industrial research, and his associates conducted motivation experiments at the Hawthorne plants of the Western Electric Company near Chicago. In one study the researchers set out to determine the relationship between physical working conditions and productivity. They divided the women workers into two groups: an experimental group and a control group. The experimental group was subjected to changes in working conditions and incentives. As rest periods were added and lighting conditions improved, for example, productivity went up. When incentives were later taken away, productivity still continued to go up. Surprisingly similar productivity increases, although not as great, were obtained with the control group which did not receive better rewards and did not experience changes in working conditions.

After rechecking their experiments and results the researchers attributed the consistent level of productivity to two factors: a feeling of importance among the women workers in both groups and a trust in the researchers and management. The women were proud to have been chosen for such an important project, and also came to believe in what management said about the state of the company. A feeling of involvement in the actual operation of the firm motivated them to work harder. Hence Mayo concluded that, regardless of working conditions, productivity tends to increase when management gives special attention to workers. This tendency has become known as the **Hawthorne effect**.

In another experiment at the same company, a different phenomenon was discovered. Researchers found that workers restricted their output to a level that could reasonably be met by all members of the group. The workers as a group established their own standards, and group pressure kept individuals from performing above or below the norm. Individuals who exceeded the group norm were called "ratebusters," while those who produced less were termed "chiselers." Since most workers adhered to the group norm, Mayo concluded that individuals have a strong need to be liked and accepted by their fellow workers, and would choose to earn less money rather than be expelled from the work group.

The results of Mayo's experiments and others have shown management that workers have needs other than money and job security. The importance of social needs must be recognized and the work environment made conducive to good social relationships. Management needs to recognize the importance of the informal work group and seek employee input when considering changes that will affect the work environment.

Maslow's Need Hierarchy

Further explorations into motivation and human needs were conducted by psychologist Abraham Maslow. In the 1940s Maslow developed a need hierarchy based on the need-satisfaction theory mentioned at the beginning of this chapter. Maslow believed that while a strong need is a motivator, once that need is satisfied the individual will no longer be motivated by it, and will then attempt to satisfy another need. Thus he arranged the major categories of needs in order of their importance to the individual. As an individual satisfied one level, at least in part, he would turn his attention to satisfying the next level. Maslow's hierarchy of needs — physiological, safety, social, esteem and self-actualization — is shown in Figure 6.2.

Physiological Needs

Physiological needs are those basic to sustaining life — food, clothing and shelter — and must be satisfied, at least to some degree, before an individual can consider higher-level needs. Since money can buy the necessities of life, it is a prime motivation at this stage. However, it loses some of its importance as the individual becomes aware of higher needs that money cannot satisfy.

Safety Needs

Once satisfaction of physiological needs is achieved, the next most important concern is to maintain the basic level of life. Workers will seek to satisfy safety needs — protect themselves from dangers on the job, ensure continued earnings and job security, and maintain a basic income required to support their life style. Today, safety needs are satisfied by programs such as workers' compensation, unemployment insurance, pension plans and various government subsidies.

Social Needs

Human beings need to be liked by others, to be needed and to have friends. Thus social needs are strong motivators and, as shown by the Hawthorne experiments, they are not readily satisfied by money. Once physiological and safety needs have been reasonably satisfied, an individual's desire to be accepted by fellow workers tends to be stronger than the desire for higher income.

Esteem or Ego Needs

Esteem needs follow social needs in Maslow's hierarchy. Individuals must feel that they and their work are important, and that they are respected and have the support of others. All of these factors are essential for an individual's self-confidence.

Sometimes esteem needs are satisfied by **status**, which refers to an individual's standing within a particular group or within society generally. Status can be acquired through wealth, education, accomplishment or occupation. Some people, for example, seek status through acquiring material possessions. Others may work long hours in a corporation to win an impressive promotion which promises an increase in prestige as well as money and power.

Self-actualization Needs

At the top of Maslow's hierarchy are self-actualization needs — the needs to achieve one's full potential, and to use talents, abilities and interests to the fullest. Self-actualization is the desire to become everything one is capable of becoming. Self-actualization needs differ from esteem needs in that a person seeking satisfaction at this level

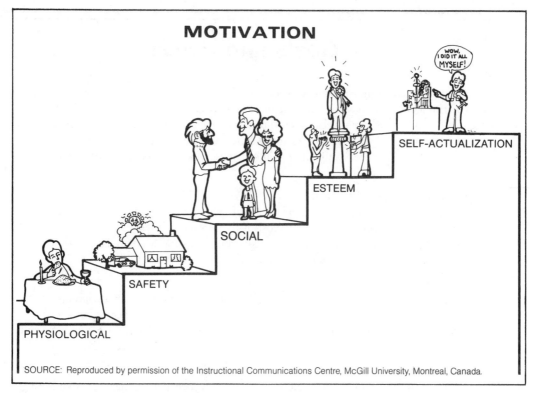

MOTIVATION

SELF-ACTUALIZATION

ESTEEM

SOCIAL

SAFETY

PHYSIOLOGICAL

WOW, I DID IT ALL MYSELF!

SOURCE: Reproduced by permission of the Instructional Communications Centre, McGill University, Montreal, Canada.

Figure 6.2 Maslow's hierarchy of needs

is not interested primarily in status or power, but rather in fulfilling an intensely personal goal. Of course, in the process of satisfying self-actualization needs, ego needs may also be satisfied.

The Individual and the Need Hierarchy

Maslow's need hierarchy is not a rigid structure applying equally to every individual. Some people require more of one kind of satisfaction than another. Some never go beyond satisfying their social needs, while others may consider safety needs all-important. Others still may strive to fulfill all five needs at the same time.

North American workers generally receive good wages, pension plans, unemployment insurance protection and other benefits to satisfy their physiological and safety needs. Many also have social needs satisfied either on or off the job by belonging to informal work groups, unions or other organizations outside the workplace. However, needs for esteem and self-actualization are not so easily fulfilled in the workplace, largely because many workers perform jobs that are boring and repetitive particularly in the service and manufacturing

Goals and Needs

Goals related to physiological needs

ON THE JOB: Money for purchase of basic goods; acceptable physical surroundings at work; vacations and personal time off from job; subsidized cafeterias.

OFF THE JOB: Availability of adequate stores of the basic necessities; adequate living space; availability of physicians; time to relax and sleep; recreational facilities.

Goals related to safety needs

ON THE JOB: Health and medical care packages; social security; safe workplace; job security; automatic cost-of-living salary increases.

OFF THE JOB: Protection against crime and fire; a savings account; an orderly family life; a freezer stocked with food.

Goals related to social needs

ON THE JOB: Association with peers; involvement with committees; group travel; staff meetings; team incentives; contacts with other departments.

OFF THE JOB: An adequate social and family life; involvement in community and social clubs; intellectual stimulation; recreation facilities.

Goals related to ego needs

ON THE JOB: Promotions based on performance; special assignments; responsibility and independence to schedule one's day; respect from one's co-workers and superiors; pay; contacts with other departments; development of unique expertise; doing better than last year.

OFF THE JOB: Gaining the respect of people one admires; being elected to the board of education; repairing the kitchen faucet; helping with homework; learning how to paint; having people laugh at one's sense of humour.

Goals related to the need for self-actualization

ON THE JOB: Setting one's own goals and standards; attending training programs; doing satisfying work; devising feedback systems to determine one's effectiveness on the job; feeling free to be open with one's peers and superiors.

OFF THE JOB: Achieving self-set standards of performance in leisure-time activities; being accepted by the family for what you are; taking night courses "just for fun"; doing volunteer work; starting one's own business; trying something new; managing time well; upgrading existing skills.

SOURCE: Reprinted by permission of the publisher, from "Motivation and Career Strategy: Giving Direction to Commitment," by Andrew H. Souerwine, MANAGEMENT REVIEW, Nov. 1977, p. 57. ©1977 by AMACOM, a division of American Management Association. All rights reserved.

industries. It is also doubtful that workers will be able to fulfill all of their needs at work in the foreseeable future. Nevertheless a manager should attempt to determine the needs of individual employees, and allow them opportunities to satisfy their upper-level needs whenever possible.

Herzberg's Motivation-Hygiene Theory

In the late 1950s psychologist Frederick Herzberg conducted a study to understand better what motivates people in their jobs. In a questionnaire, he asked a large number of engineers and accountants to indicate the factors which made them either satisfied or dissatisfied with their jobs. Herzberg found that dissatisfaction could be generally attributed to factors in the work environment. On the other hand, satisfaction could be attributed mainly to the nature of the work. On the basis of these results, Herzberg proposed his **motivation-hygiene** or **two-factor theory**.

Herzberg's study indicated a distinct difference between the work environment and the nature of the work — hence the term "two-factor." He found that individuals may be highly motivated by their work, but very dissatisfied with their organization.

The elements that caused people to feel dissatisfied with their jobs Herzberg labelled **hygiene factors**. They include quality of management, company policy, working conditions, wages and salary, status and job security. For example, hazardous working conditions and low wages would cause dissatisfaction. When these conditions were improved, workers were no longer dissatisfied, but they also did not have job satisfaction because Herzberg's hygiene factors do not act as strong motivators.

The positive satisfactions associated with the nature of the work Herzberg called **motivators**. These included responsibility, advancement, growth in the job, challenging work, recognition and achievement. These factors tended to make people satisfied with their work, but their absence did not necessarily cause dissatisfaction with the organization.

Herzberg found that, in the case of **job-satisfaction** at least, the opposite of satisfaction was not dissatisfaction, as was traditionally believed. Simply eliminating some of the dissatisfying characteristics of a person's job environment did not necessarily make that job more satisfying. Herzberg concluded that a dual continuum was involved — one for motivators and one for hygiene factors. The dotted line in Figure 6.3 indicates that motivators can be present whether hygiene factors are satisfactory or not.

What role does **money** play in job satisfaction? According to Herzberg, money is a hygiene factor. Employees who are not adequately paid may become extremely dissatisfied with the organization. They may, however, derive a high level of motivation from the job itself if it offers a feeling of importance and responsibility. On the other hand, employees who are highly motivated because of their jobs will not be motivated further by a higher salary or more fringe benefits.[2]

Figure 6.4 shows a comparison of Herzberg's two-factor theory and Maslow's hierarchy of needs. It is interesting to note that Herzberg's hygiene factors correspond to Maslow's physiological, safety and social needs, while his motivational factors correspond to Maslow's esteem and self-actualization needs.

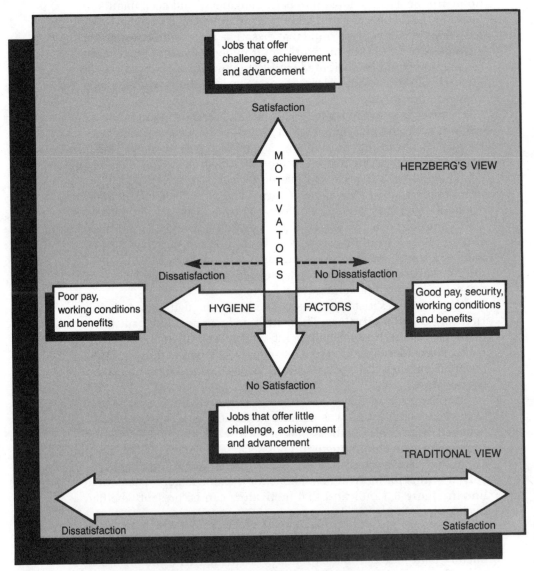

Figure 6.3 Employee job satisfaction and dissatisfaction: two views

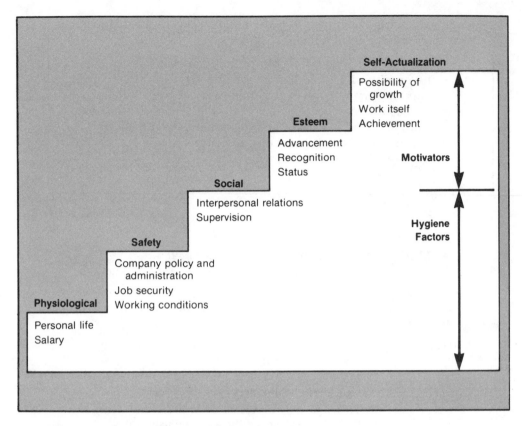

Figure 6.4 Herzberg and Maslow: A comparison

Issue: *Is KITA an Effective Motivator?*

One method of motivating employees is what Herzberg calls KITA — the kick in the ass approach. KITA can be either negative — a threat — or positive — the proverbial carrot on the stick. But the most an employer can achieve with this approach is movement, not motivation. KITA in the form of a bonus, for example, may start the employee moving, but once the bonus stops, the employee will also come to a halt. A raise is also not an effective motivator. In fact, Herzberg says, it may even become a disincentive to work — unless it is repeated every year, the employee may feel as though something has actually been taken away from him.

So what can employers do? The only real solution is to treat employees in a human way. Rather than simply making people work, employers must bring them to want to work. They must make sure that the job gives employees:

- direct feedback on the results of their performance;
- the opportunity to communicate directly with others about their jobs, without having to go through the official hierarchy;
- the chance to schedule their own work, control their own equipment and materials, and learn more about their job;
- personal accountability for their actions — supervisors should not take all responsibility.

McGregor's Theory X and Theory Y

In 1960 Douglas McGregor published a book entitled *The Human Side of Enterprise*[3] in which he proposed that the treatment of workers by managers is based on one of two sets of assumptions which he labelled Theory X and Theory Y.

THEORY X
1. The average person dislikes work and will avoid it whenever possible.
2. The average person has little ambition, shuns responsibility and prefers to be directed.
3. Therefore it is necessary to control employees through coercion and threats of punishment.

THEORY Y
1. Work is as natural as play or rest; under proper conditions, people will not only accept responsibility, but actively seek it.
2. People committed to organizational objectives will exercise self-direction and self-control, and will find satisfaction in achieving the goals.
3. Commitment to organizational objectives is a function of the rewards associated with goal attainment.
4. Many people have the capacity to use creativity, imagination and ingenuity to solve organizational problems; unfortunately the intellectual potential of the average human being is only partially utilized.

Individual leadership style and methods of motivating employees will obviously depend on the degree to which a manager subscribes to either set of assumptions. **Theory X managers** tend to be authoritarian leaders who establish tight controls to ensure that employees produce. Their motivational technique is a "carrot and stick" approach. Those employees who perform well are rewarded with more money, greater job security and other tangible rewards. Those who do not perform are threatened with the loss of these rewards, or perhaps the loss of their jobs. Theory X managers clearly believe that physiological and safety needs are the most important to their employees.

Theory Y managers focus on workers' needs. While they do not underestimate the importance of hygiene factors, they know that emphasis on lower-level needs will not motivate employees to do their best. Motivation can be accomplished only by encouraging employees to work towards satisfying their higher-level needs. Thus Theory Y managers give employees responsibility, allow them to use their creativity and ingenuity, and offer them the opportunity for advancement. Rather than establishing tight controls over their performance and subjecting them to constant supervision, Theory Y managers allow their employees to exercise as much self-control as possible.

If we asked ourselves which manager we would prefer to work for, most of us would probably choose a Theory Y manager. But it is important to keep the realities of organizational life in mind. First, not all individuals are able to control and direct themselves easily. Some employees do prefer to do only what they are told, with as little responsibility as possible. Many individuals want job security above all else. While workers might prefer more interesting jobs, many would choose to receive high wages for more mundane work, satisfying their higher-level needs off the job, in outside organizations or the pursuit of hobbies. Moreover, many jobs are by nature tedious, and there may be little management can do to make them more interesting for employees.

Thus, while managers may prefer to apply Theory Y assumptions in dealing with their people, they should keep the above factors in mind. Unfortunately, evidence suggests that many managers underrate their employees, tending toward the Theory X approach. They use minutely detailed job descriptions and work assignments, and have carried work specialization to the point where jobs are nothing more than boring, unchallenging routines. Some organizations allow employees little control over their work environment, making them passive and providing little incentive to assume responsibility for achieving organizational goals.[4]

LEADERSHIP

Theory X and Theory Y indicate two opposing views of employees. The view managers hold will influence their methods of motivation and their leadership style.

Leadership is the process of directing and influencing people to channel their efforts toward specific goals. Although this definition is straightforward, effective leadership is often difficult to achieve. Should managers be authoritarian, telling their people exactly what to do? Or should they ask employees for their opinions and suggestions? Should they maintain a forceful image and keep their distance from employees? Or should they make an effort to be part of the group? If they do, will employees lose respect for them? To understand leadership, we must examine some of the major theories that have been advanced.

Theories of Leadership

It was long believed that successful leaders possessed certain personal characteristics — intelligence, courage, leadership — that distinguished them from followers. Yet out of the many studies on leadership, no single set of specific leadership traits has emerged. Researchers have therefore concluded that specific personal traits represent only one factor in the leadership phenomenon; the situation in which the individual functions presents other factors. Situational factors include the nature of the work, the expectations, needs and attitudes of the followers, and the general environment in which all are operating.

Managerial Grid: A Behavioural Theory

Unable to isolate any specific traits contributing to effective leadership, researchers then began to wonder whether certain types of

Imperial Oil Limited

Managers work together to provide effective leadership

behaviour might be responsible for making some managers more effective leaders than others. Perhaps there was an optimum method of motivating employees, delegating tasks and communicating with subordinate managers — one method that would best achieve the goals of the organization. If so, this kind of behaviour, in contrast to traits, could be learned.

After conducting a number of studies, researchers discovered two general leadership styles, which they termed "task-oriented" and "people-oriented." A **task-oriented leader** is primarily concerned with getting the job done in the most efficient manner, and will therefore arrange working conditions to minimize interference by the human element. The **people-oriented leader**, on the other hand, pays careful attention to the human need for satisfying relationships, in the hope that a comfortable, friendly organization will achieve the best results.

These two leadership styles were used by Robert Blake and Jane Mouton to develop what they called the **managerial grid** shown in Figure 6.5.[5] The horizontal axis indicates a task-oriented style of management; the vertical axis represents the people-oriented style. Each dimension is then divided into nine parts, from low concern to high, providing a total of 81 different leadership styles. While it would be impractical to describe each of them in detail, five main styles can be readily identified.

Style 1.1 "Impoverished management" — little concern for either production or people is shown. Little is accomplished, since there is no direction and all employees can do as they please.

Style 9.1 "Task-oriented leadership" — the accomplishment of the job is the only concern, regardless of the consequences for employees.

Style 5.5 "Middle-of-the-road management" — people and production are equally important.

Style 1.9 "Country club management" — leaders are primarily interested in being liked by their followers; accomplishing the job is of secondary concern.

Style 9.9 Followers trust the leader and are committed to getting the job done because they feel they have a stake in the organization.

The managerial grid indicates how a more balanced approach between the two extremes of task- and people-oriented management can make leadership more effective. Blake and Mouton insist that a 9.9 style of management will result in improved employee performance, lower absenteeism and turnover and high employee satisfaction, regardless of the situation. However, other researchers believe that situational factors are as important as any given style of management in determining a leader's effectiveness.

The Leadership Continuum — A Situational Approach to Leadership

Two researchers, Robert Tannenbaum and Warren Schmidt, used a continuum to classify leadership according to the proportions of

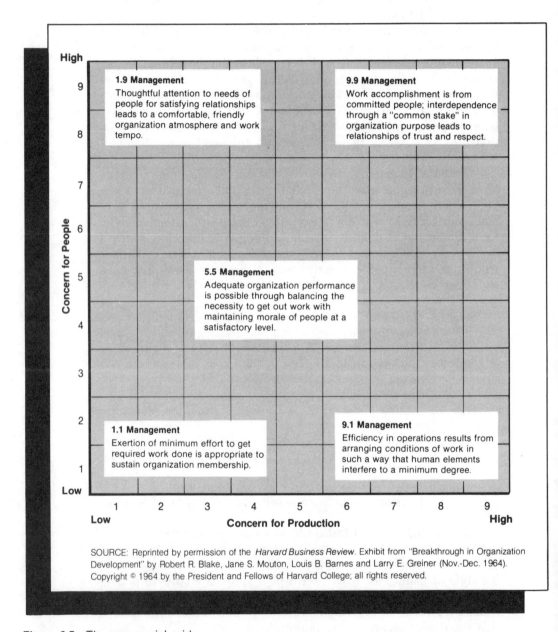

1.9 Management
Thoughtful attention to needs of people for satisfying relationships leads to a comfortable, friendly organization atmosphere and work tempo.

9.9 Management
Work accomplishment is from committed people; interdependence through a "common stake" in organization purpose leads to relationships of trust and respect.

5.5 Management
Adequate organization performance is possible through balancing the necessity to get out work with maintaining morale of people at a satisfactory level.

1.1 Management
Exertion of minimum effort to get required work done is appropriate to sustain organization membership.

9.1 Management
Efficiency in operations results from arranging conditions of work in such a way that human elements interfere to a minimum degree.

Concern for People — High 9 8 7 6 5 4 3 2 1 Low

Concern for Production — Low 1 2 3 4 5 6 7 8 9 High

Figure 6.5 The managerial grid

authority and freedom involved.[6] In effect, the classification is similar to the task- or people-oriented distinction (Figure 6.6).

Managers can choose various styles of leadership between the extremes of authority and freedom. The style ultimately chosen will depend on three sets of forces:

1. **Forces within the manager** — personal values, knowledge or experience.

2. **Forces within the subordinates** — their knowledge and experience in the job they are doing; their interest in taking responsibility and making decisions; their desire for independence and freedom of action.

3. **Forces in the situation** — the nature of the work, the pressure of time, and the clarity of goals and objectives. An important factor is the general climate within the organization, which is a reflection of how top management believes the firm should be run.

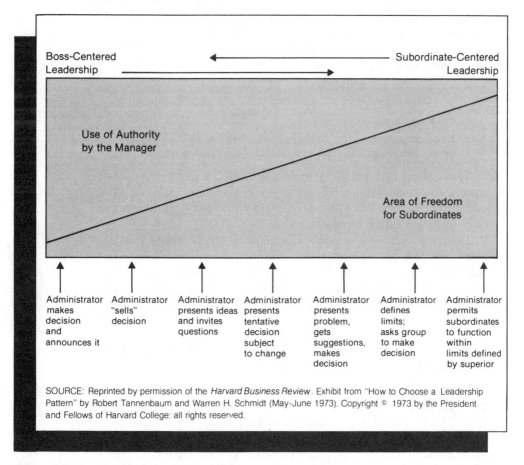

Figure 6.6 Leadership behaviour continuum

According to Tannenbaum and Schmidt, the most important factor in choosing a leadership style is that it be appropriate to the situation — there is no single optimum style. An effective leader is flexible, capable of adapting to the situation.

Fiedler's Contingency Theory

Research seems to suggest that managers adopt a leadership style appropriate to the situation. Thus managers should be trained to become both task- and people-oriented. However, one leadership researcher, Fred Fiedler, believes that it is difficult if not impossible for a manager to change his personality and leadership style to suit a situation.[7] Even if some change could be brought about, it would be a slow process, and its effectiveness could not be guaranteed. Rather, Fiedler recommends either changing the leadership situation itself or choosing the manager with the appropriate leadership style for a particular situation. In essence, he believes that any managerial leadership style can be effective in the right situation.

After examining many work situations, Fiedler identified three determining factors:

1. **Leader-member relations** — how well leaders are accepted, trusted and respected by followers.
2. **Task structure** — how specifically the followers' tasks are laid out.
3. **Position power** — the formal power that the leaders have in the organization and how they can use it to gain employees' compliance.

These three factors can be expanded into the eight possible situations shown in Figure 6.7, with leader-member relations either good or bad, tasks either structured or unstructured, and the leaders' position power either strong or weak.

Having identified the possible situations, Fiedler then surveyed the leaders of more than 800 work groups to determine whether they were task-oriented or people-oriented. He then classified their leadership situation according to the eight possibilities, and attempted to identify which type of leader was most effective in each situation. As Figure 6.7 indicates, Fiedler found that task-oriented leaders were most effective in situations where they had either great or minimal influence. People-oriented leaders were most effective in situations where they had moderate or little power.

The Path-Goal Theory

According to the path-goal theory of leadership,[8] the leader must decide on the leadership style most effective in motivating employees to achieve organizational goals. Since leaders have defined the organization's goals, they can communicate to subordinates what

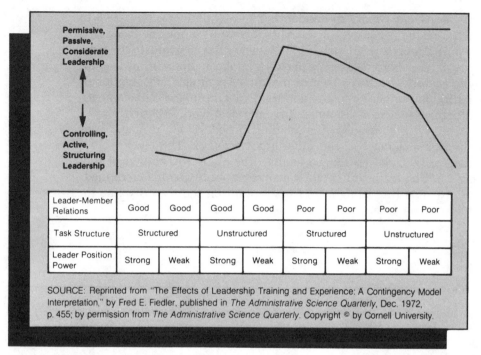

	Good	Good	Good	Good	Poor	Poor	Poor	Poor
Leader-Member Relations	Good	Good	Good	Good	Poor	Poor	Poor	Poor
Task Structure	Structured		Unstructured		Structured		Unstructured	
Leader Position Power	Strong	Weak	Strong	Weak	Strong	Weak	Strong	Weak

SOURCE: Reprinted from "The Effects of Leadership Training and Experience: A Contingency Model Interpretation," by Fred E. Fiedler, published in *The Administrative Science Quarterly*, Dec. 1972, p. 455; by permission from *The Administrative Science Quarterly*. Copyright © by Cornell University.

Figure 6.7 Effective leadership styles for various situations — Fiedler's leadership theory

must be done and then reward good performance. The path-goal theory attempts to predict how different types of rewards and leadership styles affect the motivation, performance and satisfaction of employees and subordinate managers.

A people-oriented manager, for example, offers not only pay and promotion as rewards, but also support, encouragement, security and respect. He or she is also sensitive to the fact that different individuals have different needs and desires, and therefore tailors rewards to particular individuals. In comparison, a task-oriented manager emphasizes rewards and performance by clarifying the level of performance that has to be attained to gain salary increases, bonuses and promotions. He or she offers a more limited, less individualized set of rewards.

An organization's environmental factors can also influence motivation. These factors include the type of task the subordinate has to perform, the organization's formal authority system and the subordinate's work group. Thus, a manager's leadership style should either complement or make up for the deficiencies in the work environment. For example, if a task is repetitive and the employee knows exactly what to do, then a manager who places too much emphasis on directing the employee is using an inappropriate style.

The Life-Cycle Theory of Leadership

According to the life-cycle leadership theory developed by Paul Hersey and Kenneth H. Blanchard,[9] a manager has to evaluate the maturity of his subordinate before deciding on the appropriate leadership style. Maturity in this instance does not mean age and emotional stability, but rather refers to an individual's desire for achievement, willingness to accept responsibility, and past work experience.

Figure 6.8 shows that the relationship between a manager and subordinate changes as the subordinate matures. The level of maturity is indicated by the horizontal line along the bottom of the diagram. The leadership style a manager should use is determined by drawing a line straight up from a point on the maturity line to intersect the curve.

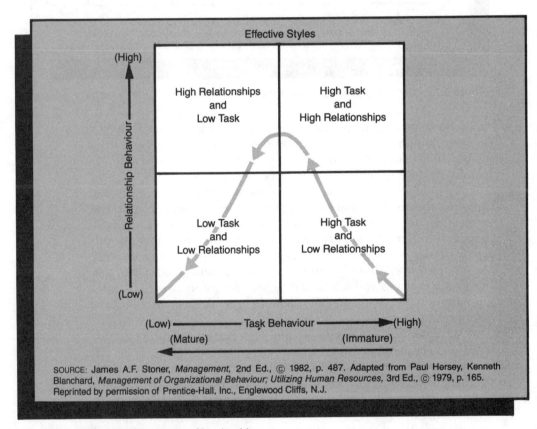

Figure 6.8 The life cycle theory of leadership

PHASE I. High task — low relationship

When employees first join an organization, they usually need direction and require specific instructions as to what they are supposed to do. They must also become familiar with the organization's policies and procedures. A task-oriented leadership approach is therefore most appropriate.

PHASE II. High task — high relationship

The task-oriented leadership style remains important even as subordinates are learning their jobs, as long as they are not willing or able to accept full responsibility for their performance. Nevertheless, as the manager becomes more familiar with subordinates and puts more trust in their performance, a more people-oriented approach should be used.

PHASE III. Low task — high relationship

As the subordinates' abilities and performance become more evident, and as experience increases and subordinates actively seek greater responsibility, the manager can relax the close direction — task-oriented style — of the previous two stages. However, the manager should continue to be supportive and encourage subordinates to take on greater responsibility.

PHASE IV. Low task — low relationship

Once subordinates have reached the point where they are self-directing, confident and experienced in their jobs, the manager can reduce the amount of support and encouragement previously provided. Subordinates are now on their own and no longer need or want a directive relationship with their manager.

Matching the Leadership Style to the Situation

What do Fiedler's leadership theory, the path-goal theory and the life-cycle theory tell us about the effectiveness of a particular leadership style? All three are contingency theories — theories that attempt to identify the appropriate leadership style based on the existing situation. They indicate that any leadership style can be effective if used in the appropriate situation. But there are differences. According to Fiedler's **contingency theory**, leadership styles are relatively fixed and that individuals have difficulty adapting to a new leadership style, if and when required. Therefore, leaders should be chosen by matching their leadership style with that required by a particular situation.

On the other hand, the **life-cycle theory** suggests that individuals can indeed change their leadership style, and should do so as their subordinates become more familiar with their job and take on greater responsibility. The **path-goal theory** links motivation and leadership style. The manager's most important task is to analyze the factors that either enhance or diminish the subordinates' level of motivation in a particular situation. Then the manager can choose the leadership style that provides the highest possible level of motivation.

Criteria for Choosing Leaders

Given the complexity of the leadership phenomenon, organizations must become more sophisticated in their selection of managers. When a management position becomes available, the leadership style required for that situation should be identified. Only those individuals who have either the appropriate leadership style or the ability to be flexible in adopting a particular leadership style should be considered. The individuals can be identified beforehand through tests and questionnaires, or observation of their reactions to various simulated leadership situations.

According to Fiedler, the organization can thus match a manager's leadership style to the situation rather than attempting to change an individual's style through leadership training. The success of the latter approach is doubtful, he says, because of the time required to change a person's attitude. While training may be beneficial in exposing managers to alternate leadership styles and making them more aware of their own leadership behaviour, research has failed to show that training leads to any significant, long-term change in leadership behaviour and effectiveness. Furthermore, training often lasts only a few days, after which managers return to their previous environment. Since there has been no change in the environment or situation, the manager is likely to revert to his original leadership style.

Promotions within an organization can also cause leadership problems. Promotions are often based on an individual's performance in a particular operating position. Thus good workers are promoted to foremen, good salespeople to sales managers, good accountants to controllers, and good teachers to principals. But good operating personnel do not necessarily make good leaders. A good "doer" is not necessarily a good manager since the tasks are different. Similarly managers who are promoted may find that their leadership styles are not appropriate to new situations. An organization may thus lose an effective worker or manager in one job, only to gain an ineffective worker in another.

Obviously, some managers will have less difficulty adjusting to situations that require different leadership styles than others. Flexibility is important for the path-goal and life-cycle theories of leadership. When necessary, managers must attempt to change their leadership style if they experience a situation in which their subordinates clearly do not perform and are uncooperative. In these instances leadership training can be helpful by making individuals aware of the meaning of leadership and giving them the ability to diagnose problems in a leadership situation. They can then alter their leadership style if and when necessary.

Japanese Management Techniques

Japanese companies have been particularly successful in marketing their products internationally. Their automobiles, cameras, stereo and video equipment have gained an excellent reputation for quality and value. The phenomenal growth of Japanese industry and Japanese technological advances have been studied extensively. A major factor contributing to the success of Japanese companies appears to be the relationship between companies and their employees.

Theory Z

What is the relationship between Japanese employees and their companies? William G. Ouchi in his book *Theory Z: How American Business Can Meet The Japanese Challenge*, explains the meaning of **Theory Z** which is in contrast to McGregor's Theory X and Theory Y examined earlier. Type Z organizations are characterized by lifetime employment, extensive training and development programs, frequent and clear performance reviews, less formal control systems and slower promotion. Instead of relying solely on modern management information systems, formal planning, management by objectives and quantitative techniques, more emphasis is placed on judgments based on experience, with decision-making taking into consideration the entire organization and the long-term view.

Individual responsibility is emphasized, with management constantly attempting to build greater trust between individual and company. Open communication is encouraged and employees participate frequently in decision-making. The company influence does not stop when the work day is finished but extends to the family and social life of individual employees.[10]

COMMUNICATION

Clearly, no organization could function without communication. Goals, objectives and plans developed at the top must be communicated to lower levels of management for implementation, and eventually to employees. The control process also depends on communication. Information must be gathered from actual operations and passed on to managers for evaluation. Thus, managers can perform their duties as coordinators only through communication with others in the organization.

Can Japanese Management Techniques Work in Canada?

Can the Japanese success be transferred to North America if companies adopt similar practices? In a recent study of 40 Japanese firms, the general consensus among the Japanese managers was that formal Japanese management techniques would not work in Canada because the cultural differences between Canada and Japan are simply too great.

Japanese management techniques rely on a special relationship between employees and the company. Employees are expected to commit themselves to the firm and, in turn, the company looks after them. A primary benefit for employees is lifetime employment. A special relationship also has to be established between management and employees. Rather than "working for" a company, as we would say in Canada, Japanese employees tend to "belong to" a company. Japanese employees willingly participate in management decision-making, will work overtime as required and patiently wait for advancement.

The Japanese managers of Canadian companies do not see this kind of relationship being established between their Canadian employees and the company. First, in Canada there is a strong tradition of mobility among skilled workers, professionals and executives. Although Canadians would like to have lifetime employment and job security, most would want these on their terms.

When opportunities present themselves elsewhere, they want the freedom to pursue them. Both Japanese and Canadian companies base the employee's future on the company's growth and success, but layoffs in Japanese companies are generally avoided by meeting reduced demand with a cutback in hours.

Canadian managers tend to be impatient when it comes to promotion. It has been difficult, therefore, for Japanese firms in Canada to attract and hold local management talent. In Japan an employee can spend years training as a generalist before moving up. Canadians simply are not that patient. Furthermore, Japanese companies in Canada do not offer the kind of career structuring that is offered by North American companies. As a result new Japanese companies in Canada have difficulty enticing Canadian managers to make a lifetime career with them. Nevertheless, Japanese firms in Canada are filling middle management positions with Canadians. Japanese managers complain, however, that Canadian managers are not willing to delegate responsibility; do not share information; and do not ensure that subordinates are trained to replace them should they retire

Does the success of Japanese companies depend on "happy" or "motivated" workers? Apparently Japanese managers don't think so. Japanese companies are successful largely because of their

working practices. Instead of focusing on short-term profit, which is often a major objective of North American firms, Japanese companies focus on obtaining customer loyalty by providing excellent service. This incidentally was also the major factor underlying success in the American firms studied by Peters and Waterman, the authors of *In Search of Excellence* (See Chapter 4). Japanese firms are very concerned about their customers and products and this attitude seems to be a major key to success.

Since excellent customer service is the primary focus of Japanese companies, it is important that all employees work toward achieving this objective. Japanese managers therefore prefer an informal, participatory style of management, involving all employees in decision-making. They like phrases such as "open communication" and "family-style work teams." They stress good communication and try to organize employees into small groups to develop a sense of closeness and identity with the company and management. However, Canadian workers seem to be uncomfortable about participating in these meetings and often remain uninterested. The level of discussion is not always high.

Nevertheless, Canadian employees are rated about equal to Japanese employees in terms of the quality of the workers, even though many Japanese managers note a fundamental difference between employees in both countries in their attitude towards work. Canadian employees are highly individualistic. Japanese managers are impressed by the aggressiveness and entrepreneurial spirit of their salespeople, for example. Canadian salespeople generally like to work alone and be evaluated individually on the number of products sold for bonuses and raises. They pay less attention to instruction or coordinating with others. Japanese managers, while uncomfortable with these work attitudes, nevertheless believe that they are appropriate for the Canadian setting.

The difference in attitude between Japanese and Canadian employees is also shown by the Canadian approach towards overtime. To Japanese workers, working overtime is considered necessary to get the job done and they do it willingly when required. The average Canadian worker, however, works overtime primarily to increase personal earnings or opportunities for advancement in his own self-interest. Japanese managers are concerned about attitude because they do not feel they can train a person who has little sense of connection between the work and the organization. They also believe that Canadian workers take an inflexible approach towards work. They want their jobs and responsibilities clearly outlined in job descriptions. Japanese managers note, for example, that blue-collar and non-managerial employees are not accustomed to the Japanese method of "bottom-up communication," which clarifies responsibilities for Japanese employees.

Other Japanese managers believe that in Canada's work environment, with rapid promotion and turnover, people cannot depend on others for training or consultation. Since many do not expect to stay long in a job, teamwork and collaboration on projects is often not possible or wanted. Job descriptions are therefore necessary for Canadians, even though Japanese managers find them constraining and unproductive.

Most small Japanese firms do not have job descriptions. Firms that do have them to avoid confusion express them in the broadest terms possible. Other companies provide employment contracts with a job flexibility clause which requires employees to perform work within their capabilities rather than confining them to narrowly prescribed duties. However, for large Japanese companies, job descriptions cannot be avoided.

If Japanese firms cannot make their management techniques work in Canada, it is unlikely that Canadian-managed companies can look to Japanese management techniques to solve their problems. The solution to the search for a new success formula may be in the findings of Peters and Waterman. They noted that successful American companies pay particular attention to customer satisfaction which in large part stems from quality products and satisfactory working relationships between employees and management.

SOURCE: Adapted from Tomoko Makabe, "How the Japanese cope," *The Financial Post*, July 28, 1984.

Problems with Communication

The communication process consists of three basic elements — a sender, a message and a receiver. A failure in any one of these elements can cause poor communication.

A model of the **communication process** is shown in Figure 6.9. The sender who initiates the communication must have the skill to translate his wishes, needs and desires into a verbal or written message that the receiver can understand and use to reconstruct the sender's ideas. If communication is face to face, the sender may use

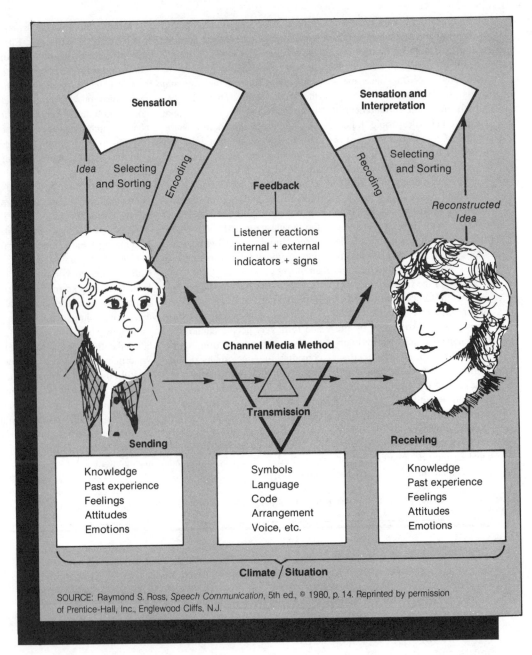

Figure 6.9 The communication process

words, actions, gestures and other body actions to transmit the message. Even so, the receiver may misinterpret the sender's actions, words or expressions and the communication may fail. If the receiver concentrates on the sender's facial expressions rather than the spoken word, for example, the message he receives may be entirely different from the one intended.

The chances of misunderstanding or misinterpretation are even greater in written communication. When the sender is not present, the receiver cannot rely on gestures or facial expressions to clarify the message, nor can he check his understanding by asking questions. With no opportunity for feedback, a message can easily be misunderstood.

Poor communication is not the fault of the sender alone; the receiver is often equally to blame. For example, one of the major reasons for poor communication is failure in listening. This is partly due to simple physical limitations in human beings — while an average person may speak at the rate of only about 150 words per minute, his listening capacity may be well over 1000 words per minute. As a result listeners may become bored and turn the speaker off, especially if they are preoccupied with other problems.

Overcoming Barriers to Effective Communication

Difficult as communication is, however, some of the barriers can be overcome. Three techniques are particularly effective — feedback, repetition of the message and the use of simple language.

As shown in Figure 6.9, **feedback** is the reaction of the listener to the sender's message. Visible reactions — a raised eyebrow, a puzzled look, anger and so on — provide the sender with signs indicating whether the intent of his original message was understood. If these reactions are contrary to what the sender feels they should be, he can restate his message and clarify any misunderstandings. Feedback can be used in both written and oral communication. Teachers, for example, receive feedback from their students through written examinations which indicate whether or not they have understood the material.

Another way of ensuring better communication is to repeat the message as often as possible, using different methods and media. Advertisers use television, radio and newspapers; teachers use lectures, films, videotapes and guest lecturers. A manager may announce a change in policy by communicating it orally to his employees, and back it up with a written memo to be read at leisure.

Finally, language must be simple and easily understood. The message should be as brief as possible, and it must be written or spoken clearly. Multisyllabic words do not impress readers, and they may have trouble understanding them. A two-page memo that could be reduced to a few sentences may be more confusing than helpful. Moreover, readers tend to shun lengthy communications — busy people may only skim a long memo, missing the important points it was intended to convey, or they may simply put it aside for another time. In either case the communication will have been ineffective.

Improving Listening Skills

As poor communication can also be due to poor listening habits on the part of the receiver, listening skills should be improved as well. One researcher, Ralph Nichols, has estimated that the average executive spends 70% of the day communicating in one way or another, and 45% of this time is spent listening. He also found that listening efficiency varies with the amount of time involved — when people listen to a ten-minute talk, they operate at only 25% efficiency. Since listening is obviously one of the most important ways of obtaining information, it is essential that this skill be developed.

In order to become a more effective listener, according to Nichols, it helps to understand the ten most common bad listening habits outlined below.[11]

1. **Assuming that the subject is uninteresting**. When listeners assume from the start that the topic will be boring, they do not listen attentively.
2. **Tuning the speaker out because of his delivery**. Listeners tend to concentrate on how the speaker delivers the message, rather than on its content.
3. **Becoming overstimulated**. When we hear something contrary to our own beliefs, we tend to become upset, which prevents us from hearing the rest of the message.
4. **Concentrating only on facts, to the exclusion of principles or generalizations**. To understand the whole picture, we must pay attention to how facts are integrated into the speaker's broader principles and generalizations.
5. **Attempting to outline everything from the beginning**. We may have difficulty outlining a speech until the presentation is well underway. Good listeners are flexible in their note-taking.
6. **Faking attentiveness**.
7. **Allowing distractions to creep in**.
8. **Tuning out difficult or technical presentations**. This is a common problem for managers listening to very detailed financial reports, for example.

9. **Letting emotional words disrupt the listening process**. Any time we hear a word which evokes emotion within us, there is a good chance that the listening process will be interrupted.

10. **Wasting thought power**. Most people speak at the rate of 125 words per minute, yet the brain is capable of handling almost five times that number. If the speaker continues for more than a few minutes, the listener is tempted to let his mind wander, returning only occasionally to the speaker to see where he is.

The article "Getting the Message: How to Make Sure You're Understood" offers suggestions for improving communication intended specifically for managers.

Getting the Message: How to Make Sure You're Understood

To do their job, managers must constantly communicate ideas, information and instructions. And be understood. For many of them, that's a daily exercise in frustration. Language and its precise use are the hurdles that trip them up.

Examine 400 common words in a dictionary and you'll discover more than 14 000 meanings — about 35 per word. Yet as a manager, you must select from this jungle of confusion words to which the receiver ascribes the exact meaning or interpretations you intended.

The odds of this happening are astronomical.

Experts define communications as: "The transmission and reception of messages." They define management communications as: "The transmission and reception of messages having the objective of achieving desired results through people." They de-

fine effective management communications as: "The transmission and reception of messages that succeed in persuading people to act as the communicator wants them to act — and like it."

Clear? Yes. Easy? No. But here are a few suggestions that'll help.

- **Think it out before you speak.**
  Decide what you want to achieve before you put your tongue in gear. Clarify the objective. It takes time, but the offspring of a pregnant silence is often comprehension.

- **Get their attention.**
  You don't need a sledgehammer. A creative approach, a stated benefit, an expression of appreciation, use of a name, a pithy question, a little excitement, a smile — they're all attention grabbers.

- **Remember Murphy's Law of communications.**
  Whenever you communicate, you automatically deal with partial information, inaccurate interpretations and inaccurate assumptions. Therefore, make it simple and specific. Use the listener's language, not your own. You don't wear your tuxedo to a barn dance; don't wear your graduation gown to the office.

- **Don't assume you are understood.**
  Get feedback. Listen to the response. Watch the reaction. Ask questions. You won't insult the receiver's intelligence — and you'll guarantee comprehension.

- **Check the communication environment.**
  If the communication is private, make it so. Is it the right

time? Are you in tune with custom and tradition? Is it the right place — should you be yelling to compete with the noise?

- **Think in terms of "you" and "your."**
Speak or write in terms of the benefits to be enjoyed by the listener or reader. Find out his wants and show how they can be obtained by what you are saying or writing. Next to one's own name, the word "reward" is the dictionary's best.

- **If you want understanding, have empathy.**
Put yourself in your listener's place — how will your message sound to him? Would **you** understand it? Accept it? Reject it? All of these are simple suggestions — but they make good common sense.

Still, if you don't have the following six skills, you're in trouble in any management function:

- **Telling:** There's a 3-C formula — clear, concise, cogent. Simple words, few of them, expressed with impact. Remember, however, this is one-way communication; it lacks feedback.

- **Asking:** This is management's responsibility. It clarifies, complements, produces ideas, advice, action and shows recognition of the receiver's importance.

- **Listening:** Study listening skills. You'll be astonished. It's 45% of the communication equation — but you'll search a long time to find a college or university that teaches it. Go to a listening-skill seminar.

- **Observing:** Observe reaction, behavior, commitment. You'll get the feedback you need to check understanding levels. Use all five senses and don't hesitate or apologize. Your career could depend on it.

- **Understanding:** Perceiving is one thing; understanding what you perceive is another. It occurs only when you correctly interpret the meaning of what you perceive. That may occur after perception, after your mind has processed the information perceived. Whether instantaneous or delayed, it simply must be present before the communication becomes effective.

- **Convincing:** Sincerity underpins conviction. It means believing in the truth of what you are saying or writing. It's aided by enthusiasm and by the action you take to prove your own conviction.

SOURCE: Gordon A. Shave, "Getting the Message: How to Make Sure You're Understood," *The Financial Post*, July 21, 1979. Reprinted by permission of the author.

MORALE

Morale is the mental attitude of employees toward their jobs and their organization. Employees will be cheerful and enthusiastic if they believe in what the organization is doing, if they think the work they are doing is contributing to those objectives, and if their jobs also contribute to their personal goals. When employees view the organization as providing them with satisfaction, results are likely to include low employee turnover and absenteeism, few grievances, improved productivity, and greater individual interest in reducing waste.

But what can managers do to ensure that their employees' morale is high? A recent study examined how managers and workers rate the various factors that can contribute to high morale (Table 6.1). The comparison indicates that managers generally view the satisfaction of employees' lower level needs as contributing to high morale, while employees tend to cite higher level needs. Despite the

TABLE 6.1
Factors in morale as ranked by managers and employees

Morale Factor	Management Ranking	Employee Ranking
Good wages	1	5
Job security	2	4
Promotion & growth with company	3	7
Good working conditions	4	9
Interesting work	5	6
Management loyalty to workers	6	8
Tactful disciplining	7	10
Full appreciation for work done	8	1
Sympathetic understanding of personal problems	9	3
Feeling "in" on things	10	2

SOURCE: Adapted from Paul Hersey, and Kenneth H. Blanchard, "What's Missing in MBO?" *Management Review*, October 1974 (AMACOM, a division of American Management Association).

discrepancy in priorities, however, many organizations are now attempting to make jobs more interesting and fulfilling for both workers and managers.

Morale, Job Satisfaction and Productivity

Clearly it is in the interest of any organization to ensure that employees' morale is high, to reduce behaviour (turnover, absenteeism, tardiness, waste) that is detrimental to the achievement of organizational goals and objectives. High morale develops when employees receive satisfaction from their total job situation. In addition to the work itself, factors involved in the total situation include pay and benefits, supervision, opportunities for promotion, and relations with co-workers. Employee satisfaction may result from any of these factors, alone or in combination.

Thus there is a definite positive correlation between job satisfaction and morale. Does the same kind of relationship exist between job satisfaction and productivity or performance? Traditionally, managers believed that rewards such as pay and benefits or good working conditions would give employees satisfaction, which in turn would improve performance and productivity. Many managers today still subscribe to this view, and indeed it seems plausible that a happy employee should also be a productive one. In the late 1960s, however, a different view was proposed — namely, that performance

What is Morale?

Morale is one of the most precious elements in a business.

In time of war, morale is the ability to endure hardship and to show courage in the face of danger. In peace time, it means willingness to serve faithfully, to get together with others in solving problems, and to work harmoniously in getting the work done.

The basic fact in morale is that it applies to a group of people who share goals in common. To attain their purpose they plan enthusiastically and work efficiently as a production team. Morale is a way of cooperative living.

No one will deny the emotional benefits of being one of a group that has high morale, but there is more to it than emotional pleasure. High morale generates thinking and planning; it stimulates initiative and enterprise; it is a most important ingredient of efficiency and only in its atmosphere are people inspired to seek the best. High morale pays off in earnings and job satisfaction, and in the effective operation of the factory or office.

Indeed, high morale spreads outward from the workshop. The workers who are happy in their jobs, with confidence in their management and cooperative relations with their working team, will spread their contentment throughout the community, and will win friends for the company. What workers say about the company is a potent force in public relations.

Consider, now, the situation when morale is low. Workers feel no great responsibility for the success of company operations; there is a big turnover of employees and there is excessive absenteeism, the workshop or office is plagued by disobedience, slowdowns, unconcern about quality, friction, abuse of privileges, and all-round tension that is bad for the health of everyone in the firm.

SOURCE: Excerpts from "About Building Morale," *The Royal Bank of Canada Monthly Letter*, Vol. 58, No. 7, July 1977. (First published 1957.) Reprinted by permission.

leads to rewards which in turn result in a certain level of employee satisfaction. These rewards can be either intrinsic or extrinsic. **Intrinsic rewards** include a sense of accomplishment from a job and increased self-esteem. In effect, they are like a pat on the back for a job well done. **Extrinsic rewards**, on the other hand, are based on the individual's performance as evaluated by superiors or group members, and may include bonuses, salary increases or promotions.

However, some research studies[12] have indicated that rewards may lead to both performance and job satisfaction; furthermore, future performance may depend on how current performance is rewarded. In other words, an employee will repeat the kind of performance that is rewarded, regardless of whether it is high or low. The implications for management are great. If managers continue to reward individuals in the aim of making them satisfied employees, then they will be likely to reward low performers and high performers more or less equally. Thus if a low performer is rewarded, he will continue to perform poorly. And as high performers will tend to see this practice as inequitable, they will eventually either reduce their own performance or seek more satisfying employment elsewhere. The various views of the relationship between job performance, rewards and job satisfaction is shown in Figure 6.10.

REDESIGNING WORK

Artists and craftsmen take great satisfaction in their work because they enjoy what they are doing, and because they have total control over their actions. Their entire effort is concentrated on producing a finished product. However, many jobs in industry allow workers neither freedom of action nor the satisfaction of creating a finished product. Most jobs, white-collar and industrial, are boring and repetitious. They only offer rewards which satisfy lower level needs — higher wages, fringe benefits and job security. Any satisfaction of higher level needs can stem only from outside the organization.

Many organizations have recognized the problem of job boredom and its associated costs, both to the employees and the organization. As the article "Can Jobs be Redesigned to Increase the Quality of Working Life?" shows, some Canadian companies are trying to do something about it.

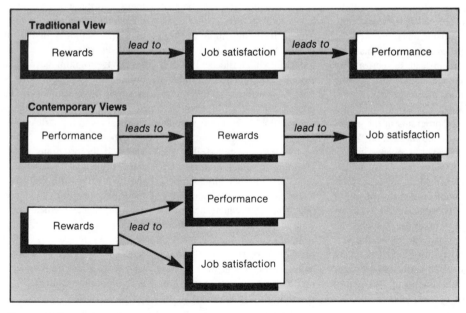

Figure 6.10 Job performance, rewards and job satisfaction

Can Jobs be Redesigned to Increase the Quality of Working Life?

Many organizations have recognized the problems of job boredom and its associated costs, both to the employees and the organization. Some Canadian companies established programs aimed at reducing the boredom of routine and repetitive work and hoped to eliminate the alienation, absenteeism and high turnover associated with such jobs. The programs are called **"quality of work life" (QWL) programs**, and are designed to shift authority, decision-making and responsibility down the management hierarchy to workers on the shop or office floor. Volvo AB in Sweden was one of the pioneers in QWL. In a series of well-publicized innovations in the 1960s, Volvo reorganized its assembly lines so that teams of workers assembled complete components on the car, instead of performing isolated and tedious tasks on the traditional assembly line.

Various Canadian companies instituted programs in the 1970s to increase job satisfaction. When Shell Canada Ltd. opened its new plant in Sarnia, Ontario, an attempt was made to peg wage rates to the number of different jobs a worker chose to master — in effect, the worker decides when he or she gets a raise. At the Canadian Industries Ltd. (CIL) plant in Carseland, Alberta, management has improved its quality control by restructuring jobs so

that the workers who make the products do the final checking as well. At Prudential and Manufacturers Life Insurance Co. in Toronto, staff turnover was reduced by restructuring work so that the people who process policies perform the whole job, including customer contact, instead of endlessly rubber-stamping pieces of paper. At the Royal Bank of Canada, some branches were set up using a "central teller system" which gave the people behind the counter more responsibility and less routine. Under this system, one central teller handles the routine transactions, such as doling out cash, while others sell services such as traveller's cheques and safe deposit boxes to customers. Other companies, including Supreme Aluminum Industries Ltd., Petrosar Ltd., MacMillan Bloedel Ltd. and British Columbia Forest Products Ltd., have a variety of QWL programs, each with different features tailored to meet specific needs.

Many firms found that the programs resulted in lower absenteeism, higher productivity, lower turnover and enhanced morale. And even where the results were not measurable, the firms were convinced that the intangible benefits, such as "people feeling better about their jobs," made the exercise more than worthwhile. In fact, so many

companies have shown interest in the job redesign concept that both the federal and Ontario governments have set up "Quality of Working Life" centres to help companies launch their own QWL programs.

Job redesign can take many forms. The most comprehensive changes in work arrangements involve autonomous or semi-autonomous work groups. Teams of people work with minimal supervision, perform a series of integrated tasks and are responsible for making decisions that affect their work. They are often paid according to the number of tasks they master. Variations of this system include **"job enrichment"** — the worker is given a greater variety of tasks, but is still under the authority of the traditional supervisor.

QWL programs have already brought improvements in a surprisingly large number of Canadian companies, but this participatory working style is still the exception, not the rule. No one knows if the programs at Shell, CIL, Prudential, Manulife and the Royal Bank are the wave of the future, or simply evidence of a shortlived management trend. If the economy gets worse, and jobs become even scarcer, will job redesign concepts be perceived as a luxury and easily shelved? Only the future can tell.

SOURCE: Adapted from Linda Rosenbaum and Barbara Diesner, "Is Job Boredom Really Necessary?," *Canadian Business*, June 1979, pp. 66–71.

MANAGEMENT BY OBJECTIVES

Dissatisfaction with their work affects managers as well as clerical and blue-collar workers. Although managers may have a better perspective than other employees on the organization's direction and objectives, they often experience conflicts between their personal goals and those of the organization. They may become frustrated when their own ideas are not implemented, or their needs are left unsatisfied.

In an attempt to reduce management dissatisfaction and raise low morale, the concept of **management by objectives (MBO)** became popular in the late 1950s. MBO allows managers and other employees to set their specific job goals in line with the overall goals and objectives of the organization.

The MBO Process

The MBO process consists of a number of stages and steps, as shown in Figure 6.11. In the first stage superior and subordinate managers discuss job descriptions together to ensure that both agree on the area of responsibility, the level of performance that will be acceptable, and the method of evaluation. Then the subordinate establishes short-term objectives in consultation with his superior — all objectives should be specific, in numerical terms whenever possible. By mutually setting these objectives, both managers may become aware of factors inside and outside the organization that could interfere with their achievement.

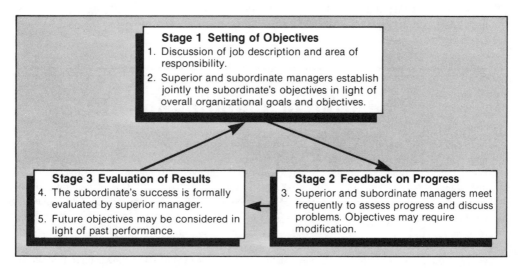

Stage 1 Setting of Objectives
1. Discussion of job description and area of responsibility.
2. Superior and subordinate managers establish jointly the subordinate's objectives in light of overall organizational goals and objectives.

Stage 3 Evaluation of Results
4. The subordinate's success is formally evaluated by superior manager.
5. Future objectives may be considered in light of past performance.

Stage 2 Feedback on Progress
3. Superior and subordinate managers meet frequently to assess progress and discuss problems. Objectives may require modification.

Figure 6.11 The MBO process

During stage two, which is the ensuing operating period, both managers should meet frequently to discuss the subordinate's progress. Actual performance should be evaluated at predetermined checkpoints, to see whether the objectives can be achieved as planned, or will require modification.

The third stage comes at the end of the operating period, when superior and subordinate jointly evaluate the results of the latter's total effort. Future objectives for a new cycle may be considered at this stage, in the light of past performance.

One of the most important activities in a successful MBO program is planning. Dale McConkey, an executive involved with MBO seminars, discusses planning in the article "The Role of Planning in MBO."

Benefits of MBO

Perhaps the greatest benefit of MBO is that it allows subordinates to participate in setting goals and objectives for their own area of responsibility. In addition, it provides them with a better understanding of how their own effort is tied in to the goals and objectives of the whole organization. Once their objectives and the methods of achieving them have been clearly identified, the subordinate managers know what is expected of them and how their performance will be evaluated. Because of this close contact between superior and subordinate managers in the MBO process, communication throughout the organization is also enhanced. Finally, the constant review of job descriptions, responsibility, and authority improves the whole process of delegation, as the accountability of subordinate managers is emphasized when their responsibility for achieving objectives is clearly specified.

The Role of Planning in MBO

Any look at the role of "planning" in the MBO system must begin by establishing a critical distinction between "running" an organization and "managing" the organization, says Dale D. McConkey.

Too often those who "run" an organization keep extremely busy — often putting in many long and dedicated hours — pursuing a wide variety of activities and **hoping** that something will happen. (Management by hopes and desires.)

Those who "manage" an organization first determine what they want to accomplish and then direct all available resources to **causing** it to happen. (Management by objectives.)

This distinction, and it is a major one, enables one to place planning in the proper perspective in the MBO system, according to McConkey. The role of planning is three-fold, he asserts:

1. It requires managers to prioritize their efforts — what is most important and what should be done first.
2. Concrete, specific objectives logically flow from, and are based on, priorities.
3. Once objectives have been established telling us WHERE we want to go, and WHEN we want to get there, it is possible for us to determine HOW we can get there. The "how" consists of planning or programming our efforts to achieve the objectives. Objectives without plans to make them come true are a myth.

Once established, the objectives and the step-by-step action necessary to achieve them serve as the cornerstone for building the preponderance of the MBO structure. For example, they serve as the basis for:

1. **Need to know communications** — we can acquaint the appropriate managers with the WHAT, WHEN and HOW of required action. Then they can determine what their role must be and how they are involved.
2. **Coordinating managerial efforts** — planning permits the coordination of the efforts of all managers into an optimized whole. Under effective planning, each manager knows his role and the roles being played by the other managers with whom he is involved; thus, the respective roles of all managers can be blended together. In the absence of planning, the individual efforts of a group of managers more often than not resemble an unassembled jigsaw puzzle. A picture is seldom clear when viewed by its pieces.

3. **Controlling** — meaningful, effective control is possible only when we are specific as to the WHAT, WHEN, and HOW. In the absence of these ingredients, control often becomes over-control and non-control. Effective control or monitoring permits closing of the loop of managerial action as it provides the input for taking corrective action or making necessary changes to objectives and plans when they become unrealistic in their original form.

Finally, says McConkey, the results of the planning process permit the effective measuring of managerial performance, the basing of rewards on results, and counselling and developing managers. Planning thus serves as the cornerstone of an effective MBO system.

SOURCE: F.D. Barrett, "MBO — Updated and Revisited," *Business Quarterly*, published by School of Business, The University of Western Ontario, Spring 1976, p. 29. Reprinted by permission.

When MBO Fails: Blame the Managers, Not the System

Let's look at the reasons for MBO rejection, listed here without order of frequency or importance:

- Ineffectual consultants, trainers or implementers who think MBO can be explained in a three-day seminar and implemented in a three-month trial.
- Stimulated managers who peek at MBO's philosophy and insist, "It should be installed at once! D'ya hear!"
- Lazy "busy-busy" executives who say, "It's good for the subordinates, but I don't need it."
- Managers who flip when asked to define an objective and break down if asked to quantify it.
- Managers who can't set objective priorities, which means they don't know what to do first, which means they don't know what to do.
- Autocratic managers who think employee participation equates to mutiny.
- Managers who work out subordinate goals, then practice delegation by abdication.

- Executives who have no time for MBO feedback meetings because they must attend crisis meetings.
- Executives who insist subordinate managers use MBO but play hide-and-seek with the information they need to use it.

- Managers who resent MBO paperwork, suffocating in the pile it would eliminate.

The error of these reasons is not that MBO is ineffective. Managers are ineffective. MBO has become a scapegoat.

MBO requires nothing more than a close and precise attention to the fundamental task of managing. To reject it because of implementation, its participative nature, demand for discipline and straight-line thinking, is to reject the fundamental task of managing.

SOURCE: Gordon Shave, "When MBO Fails: Blame the Managers, Not the System," *The Financial Post*, June 17, 1978. Reprinted with permission of the author.

Problems with MBO

The greatest drawback to the MBO process is the expense of time and money and the paperwork required. Thus, an MBO program is likely to fail unless top management encourages participation and commits the resources required to support it. In addition, authority relationships may have to be restructured to give managers sufficient authority to achieve their objectives. Control systems to measure accurately how objectives are being achieved must also be established. Finally, individual rewards may cause problems unless they are based on the achievement of predetermined objectives — many organizations reward not performance, but other factors such as good work habits, individual appearance, and the ability to get along with others. If an MBO program is to succeed, both top management and the participants must be convinced of its benefits.

The MBO system is not a solution to all of an organization's ills. Nevertheless, it does allow some integration of individual and organizational goals, and provides a better basis for evaluating and rewarding managers; many organizations today use some form of MBO.

NOTES

1. Frederick W. Taylor, *The Principles of Scientific Management* (New York: Harper and Bros., 1916).
2. Frederick Herzberg, *Work and the Nature of Man* (Cleveland: World Publishing, 1966).
3. Douglas McGregor, *The Human Side of Enterprise* (New York: McGraw-Hill Book Co., 1960), pp. 33–55.
4. See Chris Argyris, *Personality and Organization* (New York: Harper Brothers, Inc., 1957); *Interpersonal Competence and Organizational Effectiveness* (Homewood, Ill.: The Dorsey Press, 1962); *Integrating the Individual and the Organization* (New York: John Wiley and Sons, Inc., 1964).

5. Robert Blake and Jane S. Mouton, *The Managerial Grid* (Houston: Gulf Publishing Co., 1964).

6. Robert Tannenbaum and Warren H. Schmidt, "How to Choose a Leadership Pattern," *Harvard Business Review*, May-June 1973, p. 164.

7. Fred Fiedler, *A Theory of Leadership Effectiveness* (New York: McGraw-Hill, 1967).

8. See Robert J. House, "A Path-Goal Theory of Leadership Effectiveness," *Administrative Science Quarterly*, Vol. 16, No. 5 (September 1971), pp. 321–328.

9. Paul Hersey and Kenneth H. Blanchard, *Management and Organizational Behavior*, 3rd ed., p. 165.

10. William G. Ouchi, *Theory Z: How American Business Can Meet the Japanese Challenge* (Reading, Mass.: Addison-Wesley, 1981).

11. Ralph G. Nichols, "Listening: What Price Inefficiency?", *Office Executive*, April 1959, pp. 15–22. Reported in Richard M. Hodgetts, *Management: Theory, Process and Practice* (Philadelphia: W.B. Saunders Co., 1979), p. 255.

12. Charles N. Greene and Robert E. Croft, Jr. "The Satisfaction-Performance Controversy Revisited," in Richard M. Steers and Lyman W. Porter, *Motivation and Work Behavior*, 2nd ed. (New York: McGraw-Hill, 1979), pp. 270–83.

CHAPTER SUMMARY

Without people organizations could not function. However, people may not perform to their full potential unless they are motivated, and therefore their needs must be satisfied. At one time managers thought that money was the prime motivator, but the Hawthorne experiments proved that social pressure and social needs are often more important than higher wages.

Maslow proposed that there are five levels of needs which people attempt to satisfy — physiological, safety, social, esteem and self-actualization needs. Only the two lower levels of needs can be entirely satisfied with money, and only those needs which have not been satisfied will motivate people to work harder.

Herzberg discovered similar needs in workers. His "hygiene factors" correspond to Maslow's physiological and safety needs, as well as some social needs — money, job security, quality of management, company policy and adequate working conditions. His "motivators" correspond to higher level needs and include the actual work that employees do, responsibility, advancement, recognition and achievement.

McGregor's Theory X and Theory Y have implications for both motivation and leadership. A Theory X manager attempts to motivate employees through satisfaction of lower level needs. A Theory Y manager prefers to allow them the opportunity to satisfy higher level needs. Similarly, a Theory X manager will tend to be authoritarian, exercising close control and supervision, whereas a Theory Y manager allows employees considerable self-control and participation in decision-making whenever possible.

Leadership refers to the process of directing and influencing people to channel their efforts toward specific goals. Research has shown that leaders tend to be either task-oriented or people-oriented. Both the managerial grid and the leadership continuum show a range of leadership styles between the two extremes, and indicate that a balanced approach may be the most desirable. On the other hand, Fred Fiedler believes that all leadership styles can be effective provided they are used in the appropriate situations.

The path-goal theory links motivation with leadership style. A people-oriented leader would try to match rewards with the needs of individuals, while the task-oriented leader would try to create a strong link between rewards and performance with less concern about individual needs. The life-cycle theory bases a manager's leadership style on the maturity level of the subordinate. As a new employee comes to know the job and takes on more responsibility, the task-oriented leadership style should slowly give way to the people-oriented style. Ultimately the employee would need little of either style as he or she becomes intimately acquainted with the job.

Poor communication is a common problem on the part of sender and receiver alike. Communication barriers can be overcome by using clear language that is easy to understand, by repeating the message through various channels and by using feedback.

When employees have high morale they feel the organization provides them with job satisfaction. The results may include low employee turnover, low absenteeism, few grievances and less waste of resources. No clear-cut relationship has been found as yet between job satisfaction and productivity, but evidence suggests that employees who are properly rewarded for their performance and have clear-cut goals receive greater job satisfaction.

Unfortunately, many jobs are tedious, boring and monotonous. To make jobs more interesting and thereby raise morale, managers have introduced job rotation, job enrichment, flexible working hours and several other techniques. Similar steps have been taken to help managers identify more closely with the organization and see the results of their work. One major technique is management by objectives, in which managers establish goals jointly with their superiors and then participate in evaluating their progress towards these goals.

KEY TERMS

Motivation	People-oriented leader
Needs	Leadership continuum
Incentive system	Contingency theory of leadership
Hawthorne effect	Path-goal theory
Physiological needs	Life-cycle theory
Safety needs	Theory Z
Social needs	Communication process
Esteem needs	Morale
Self-actualization needs	Job satisfaction
Hygiene factors	Intrinsic rewards
Motivators	Extrinsic rewards
Theory X	Redesigning jobs
Theory Y	Job enrichment
Leadership	Quality of work life
Managerial grid	Management by objectives (MBO)
Task-oriented leader	

REVIEW QUESTIONS

1. What is motivation?
2. What is the classical theory of motivation? Why was it successful for so long?
3. How did the Hawthorne studies revolutionize theories on the motivation of workers?
4. Explain Maslow's theory of human needs.
5. Explain what Herzberg means by hygiene factors and motivators.
6. Contrast a Theory X manager with a Theory Y manager. What are some of the problems each manager might face in a modern organization?
7. Explain the trait theory of leadership.
8. Compare the effectiveness of the leadership continuum and the managerial grid in helping an individual choose a leadership style.

9. What is Fiedler's contingency theory of leadership? How does he view an individual's ability to adopt a different leadership style? How does he view leadership training?

10. Briefly explain the path-goal theory and the life-cycle theory of leadership. What is the major difference between these two theories and Fiedler's theory?

11. What is a Theory Z organization? Explain why the Japanese management approach might not be readily adaptable to North America.

12. Identify some of the major communication problems. How can they be overcome?

13. What is morale?

14. What is the relationship between morale and productivity?

15. Why are organizations today interested in redesigning work?

16. What is management by objectives? Describe what happens in each of the five steps in the MBO process.

17. Describe the benefits of MBO to an organization. Why is MBO often not successful?

DISCUSSION QUESTIONS

1. "Good managers tend to be good leaders, but good leaders are not always good managers." Discuss this statement and explain it.

2. Why does the selection of managers become more important, but also more difficult, at the upper levels of the organizational hierarchy?

3. Consider your own motivations and needs. How do they correspond to Maslow's hierarchy?

4. Identify a variety of management positions in different types of organizations, then describe the leadership style that would be most effective for each position. How should managers for these positions be selected?

5. What Japanese management techniques do you think could be adapted for Canadian companies? Explain.

CASE 6–1 Choosing a Leadership Style

After months of deliberation by the hiring committee, John Reynolds finally received word that he was to be the new director of a charitable foundation. The previous director had retired, and for 10 years had done little to promote the foundation to other agencies or groups, or to give its members a new sense of direction. By hiring Reynolds, the committee hoped to set the organization back on track and give it new purpose.

Nine months after taking the position, John Reynolds talked to one of his closest friends. He was depressed and was harbouring thoughts of leaving the organization.

"I just can't take this job any longer, Ray," John said. "Either they're going to fire me, or I'm going to quit. I can't seem to get anything done with these people."

"What's happened since you started with the foundation, John?"

"When I started, I was determined to get the organization moving. After teaching for ten years, I was itching to get back to managing. I realized that this was not a business, however, so I thought I'd start out with a survey of the members, to determine their main objectives for the organization. What I got was a mixed bag of responses. The objectives were so diverse, that it would have been difficult to embark on any course of action and get strong support. Not that they seemed that determined about what they wanted, because many didn't voice any strong preferences. Many didn't return the questionnaire, and some even seemed resentful that I had asked them."

"What have you done since the survey?"

"Actually, I have kept a pretty low profile, concentrating on normal duties. I haven't tried to implement any new programs, but have tried instead to get to know the members and talk to as many as possible on a personal basis. I am not having too much success. What is even more disconcerting is that I have the feeling I was not a unanimous choice for the job. A fairly substantial group didn't think my background in business and teaching was what was needed by this organization. The reason I got the job is that the committee was tired of searching for a director. They were having some of the same problems I am experiencing with the members. I'm reluctant to push for any change until I feel I have a consensus on the objectives for the organization. I don't know when I will get it, and I may not be here by then anyway."

QUESTIONS

1. Identify the leadership problem.
2. Which contingency theory of leadership would be best to analyze the situation in this case? Explain.
3. What leadership style should John Reynolds use? How might the leadership approach solve the lack of clear objectives and the lack of member support?

CASE 6–2 Establishing an MBO Program

The Ad-Tech Company was formed in 1967 by a Calgary petroleum engineer. Although he knew little about business, his product — a new butterfly valve for gas wells — was so necessary for the industry that the company was an immediate success. By 1977, the firm had expanded into other products, and sales approached $40 million per year; included were the sales from an oil field equipment service company purchased by the original company.

By 1983 the company's growth had slowed considerably and the rate of return had dropped from 10.5% in 1982 to 5.8% in 1983. The problems were difficult to identify and were starting to seriously affect the morale and motivation of both managers and employees and were leading to operating inefficiencies. The original founder had retired from the presidency because of ill health, and his post was filled by the former president of the oil field service company bought out by Ad-Tech.

The company finally hired a consultant early in 1984 to examine the problems and offer some solutions. After spending some time in the firm and interviewing employees and managers at all levels, the consultant requested a meeting with senior management to present his findings.

"After talking to virtually all employees in this company I have come to the conclusion that there are two major problems. The first problem is caused by your present organizational structure. When the company takes on special projects which require people from various departments, the employees affected suddenly have a new boss in addition to their regular manager, and major friction develops. The functional organization which you have set up for both organizations cannot handle the special projects — you might want to consider either a project organization, or a matrix organization.

"The other major problem is one of direction. The company has grown so rapidly, but planning seems to be relegated to something done when there is time, after everything else is accomplished. This is how many of your subordinate managers have described the problem.

"My suggestion is to implement an MBO program, to bring planning into the foreground and give the various managers and employees something to focus on."

When the president heard the words, "management by objectives," he sat up in his chair. "I've heard a lot about MBO, but it seems to me that it is another one of those schemes brought in by people who don't know what it's like to operate in the real world. They lay out these systems, regardless of how expensive they are to implement and administer. And the results are often not forthcoming. As far as I'm concerned, MBO is nothing more than proper management. A good manager doesn't need MBO."

He looked at the consultant and the other managers in the room, some of whom nodded their heads in agreement. Others, however, obviously did not agree with the president. One manager was particularly anxious to speak out.

"I think we should try some form of MBO," he said. "I've heard that our middle managers have difficulty knowing which way they should go first. We have a lot of business coming in, and some of it is not always in our field of expertise. Yet our people are often taken away from their regular jobs to spend a considerable amount of time on these new projects. I think we have to solve this problem, and define more clearly what business we are in. MBO would probably help." Most of the other managers were nodding their heads in agreement, when another manager started to speak.

"I think many of these problems will be corrected by the computerized management information system we are bringing in. As soon as we know what is going on and how the company is doing, many of the problems you have just mentioned will disappear, because our managers will know where they stand."

There was little reaction to this comment, except from the president, who had been instrumental in getting the management information system along with a new computer for the data processing department.

"Yes, I think when our new data processing system is operating, we will be able to resolve most of the problems," he agreed. "In the meantime, those of you who want to implement an MBO system in your departments are free to do so, provided it doesn't cost too much. I don't expect to see vast amounts of money go out for this exercise, which I know will not be necessary when our computerized information system is finally working."

QUESTIONS

1. Analyze the comments made by the president and the two other managers, as to their understanding of management, organizing and MBO.

2. What are the advantages and disadvantages of a project and matrix type of organizational structure, compared to a functional structure? Why might a matrix or project organizational structure solve some of the problems of this company?

3. Can the computerized management information system solve this firm's problems? Explain.

4. Do you think MBO implemented as suggested would be successful in this company? Explain.

5. How can an MBO system help managers in their planning function?

6. If you were the consultant, what would be your response to the comments of these managers? What would be your recommendations for implementing a successful MBO program?

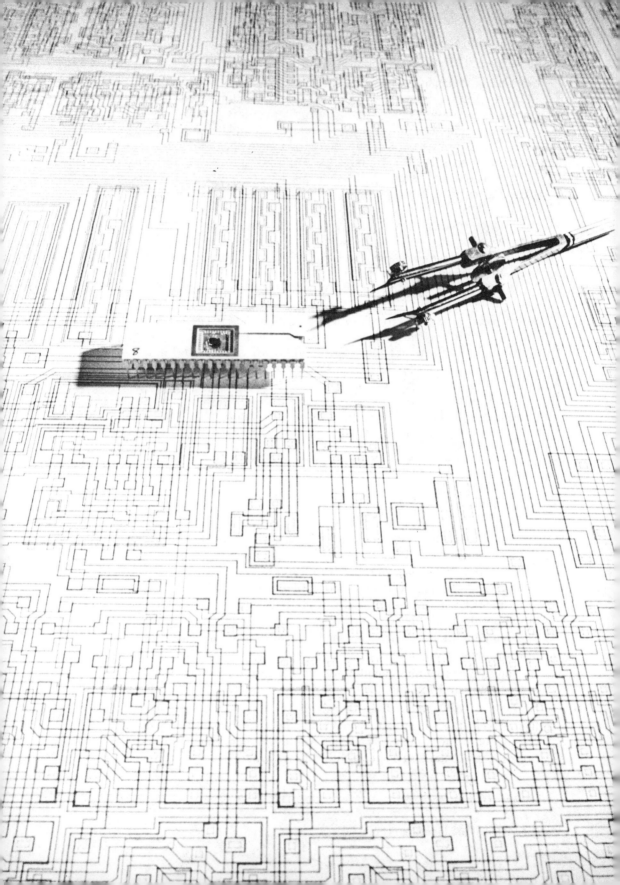

Part Three

The Business Functions

All organizations in some way perform the four major business functions — production, marketing, finance and personnel. The production function is necessary to physically produce the goods or services; the marketing function to determine what to produce and then to sell or otherwise convey the product to consumers; the finance function to provide funds required for all aspects of the operation; and the personnel function to ensure that people with all the required skills are available.

In Chapter 7 we look at the production function and its two major tasks — establishing the necessary physical facilities and managing daily production operations.

In Chapter 8 we examine the marketing function and its role as intermediary between the business organization and the consumer. We see how a business determines what products and services to produce by listening to the consumer, and we learn what the producer does to convey the product to the consumer.

In Chapter 9 we look at the finance function and the major tasks of the finance department. The finance department controls all financial operations — ensuring in particular that enough money is available for day-to-day business operations, and acquiring the necessary funds for long-term growth.

In Chapter 10 we survey the personnel function. In addition to recruiting, hiring and training employees, personnel is responsible for compensating employees for their services, and for evaluating their performance in view of continued employment, promotion, or, if necessary, termination.

CHAPTER 7

Production and Operations Management

Ganong Bros. Limited

CHAPTER OUTLINE

THE PRODUCTION FUNCTION
    Mass Production and Technology
    Custom Production
    The Job Shop
ORGANIZATION OF THE PRODUCTION
  DEPARTMENT
DESIGNING PRODUCTION/OPERATIONS SYSTEMS
    Product/Service Planning and Design
    Production Processes
    Capacity Planning
    Plant Location
    Plant Layout
    Work System Design
OPERATING PRODUCTION DECISIONS
    Demand Forecasting
    Inventory Management
    Distribution Planning
    Production Planning and Control
    Purchasing
    Quality Control
    Maintenance
    Project Management
COMPUTERS IN PRODUCTION
    Computers and Automation
    Microcomputers for the Operations Manager
COMPUTERS AND HOW THEY WORK
    History of Computers
    How Computers Work
    Elements of a Computer
    Communicating with the Computer
CASE 7–1   Planning for Production — Kwickie Kar
             Klean
CASE 7–2   Pacific Boat Works

CHAPTER PREVIEW

In Chapter 7 we will examine the production function — how goods and services are produced either for consumers or for other businesses. Particular attention is paid to mass production and the various elements on which it depends — technology, mechanization, standardization, and automation.

We will examine the production function in terms of the decisions that production/operations managers must make. Key long-term decisions involve the planning and design of production facilities. These include capacity planning, the location of manufacturing plants, plant layout, machines and equipment, and work system design. Operating production decisions, on the other hand, involve demand forecasting for the intermediate term and planning for adequate production capacity, inventory management, distribution planning, production scheduling and control, purchasing, quality control, and maintenance. Responsibility for these activities rests with the operations manager and other middle managers.

In the last part of this chapter we look at factory automation and its impact on manufacturing firms in terms of productivity, cost, and quality of product. We also examine its impact on employment. The chapter ends with a discussion of how computers work, including the hardware, the software and computer languages.

LEARNING OBJECTIVES

After reading this chapter you should be able to explain:

1. The meaning of economy of scale, mechanization, standardization, automation, and how they contribute to mass production;
2. The five major types of production processes;
3. Why capacity planning is one of the major long-term decisions;
4. The factors that must be taken into consideration when deciding on plant location;
5. When a product layout should be used and when a process layout should be used;
6. The purpose of work design;
7. Why demand forecasting is crucial to efficient production;
8. Why inventory management is important;
9. How distribution planning can minimize transportation and production costs;
10. The purpose of aggregate planning;
11. How MRP and just-in-time inventory contribute to efficient production;
12. The function of production scheduling;
13. The importance of the purchasing department in an efficient manufacturing operation;

14. The major factors to be considered in establishing optimum systems for quality control and maintenance;

15. How the automated factory works and how it can increase productivity and produce a higher quality product;

16. The elements of a computer, the meaning of computer hardware and software, and the major languages used to communicate with computers;

17. How computers process data to turn it into meaningful information for management.

Imagine for a moment that you could get virtually any product delivered to you almost instantly, personalized to your own taste, yet as inexpensive as if it were mass produced. That is what the factory of the future will be able to do.

A customer's requirements will be fed into a computer which alters an existing design and sends the information to the machines on the shop floor, which will instantly readjust themselves and begin manufacturing the product ordered. The manufacturing process will be performed by clusters or cells of multipurpose machines run by computers and served by nimble-fingered robots. Required parts will be supplied by remote-controlled vehicles.

It may seem a little far-fetched for the late 1980s, but these types of factories have already been built by companies such as General Motors, General Electric and IBM. All three companies developed highly automated plants that allowed huge increases in output, productivity, and higher quality. While the results were astonishing, the cost of building these factories was uneconomical. Nevertheless, the lessons learned were invaluable for future factory automation.

We will look further at factory automation later in the chapter. Now, let us look at the more traditional factories and how production and operations managers tackle the problems of production.

THE PRODUCTION FUNCTION

The core of activity in any business organization is the production of goods and services. As Figure 7.1 shows, **production** is the process of converting resources — raw materials, human resources, capital, technology, and information — into products and services. The conversion process, also known as the technical core, varies depending on the nature of the firm. An automobile manufacturer requires huge plants, assembly lines and specialized machines and equipment. A restaurant requires considerably less equipment to prepare its various menu items. The feedback and control function in the production process provides information about the quality of the outputs and about the efficiency of the production operation.

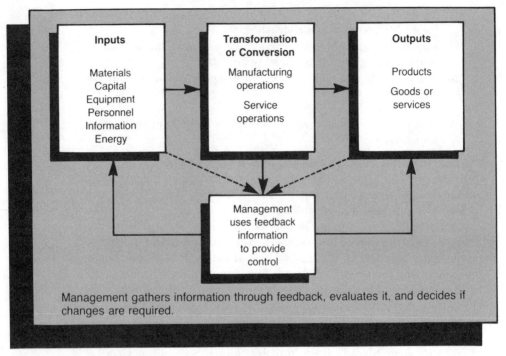

Figure 7.1 The production system

Manufacturing organizations produce automobiles and refrigerators, for example, but an increasing number of firms provide nonphysical products or services. These include medical, educational, retail and transportation services, as well as the services provided by lawyers and hairdressers.

Service businesses differ from manufacturing businesses in two major ways. First, in a service business, the customer is involved in the production process. A bus transports a person from one place to another, while a hospital treats a patient. Second, service outputs cannot be stored in inventory as can manufactured products. A lawyer cannot prepare a case for a nonexistent client, nor can a doctor diagnose a nonexistent patient.

Nevertheless, both manufacturers and service organizations are faced with common problems, for example, scheduling, whether for appointment of patients or for production workers and raw materials. Other concerns are the acquisition of materials and supplies, and quality and productivity — the output has to satisfy the customer, and it must be produced at the lowest possible cost.

Mass Production and Technology

Mass production is the manufacture of goods in large quantities. An assembly line is expensive to build, but once it is operating it can churn out vast quantities of cars, refrigerators, radios, or televisions at prices many people can afford. Mass production allows us to achieve economies of scale by matching plant capacity with required output. To understand the concept of **economies of scale** we must remember that a manufacturing plant is built to produce a specific number of units of a product based on present and anticipated sales for perhaps five or ten years in the future. Up to maximum production capacity, the costs of maintaining and operating the plant — **fixed costs** — remain fairly stable. The **variable costs**, such as wages of production workers and the costs of raw materials and parts used, vary directly with the number of units produced.

As an example, consider an ashtray manufacturer. Suppose the plant can produce 200 000 ashtrays at maximum production capacity. The plant costs $100 000 per year to operate — this figure represents fixed costs. Let us assume that variable costs are $1.00 per ashtray, including the cost of raw materials and labour. Therefore, 100 000 ashtrays would cost $200 000 to produce, and the cost per ashtray would be $2.00. However, if we produced 200 000 ashtrays which is the maximum capacity for the plant, our total production costs would be $300 000 — then the cost per ashtray would drop to $1.50. Thus, by producing more units, we have actually decreased the cost of producing one ashtray. The same principle holds for virtually all products that can be produced and sold in large quantities.

Mass production is best illustrated in the production of automobiles using an **assembly line**, a device which automatically moves the automobile along a fixed route past various workers. Each worker performs a small part in the total manufacture of the car. By introducing assembly-line techniques along with standardized interchangeable parts in 1913, Henry Ford was able to reduce the building time per car from more than twelve hours to just over one hour. He thus also reduced the price per car to the consumer by almost ten times. As a result, many more people were able to buy cars and the increased sales revenues helped to increase profit. To stem the large employee turnover caused by the monotony of assembly-line work, Ford doubled the standard daily wage rate of the industry from about $2.50 to $5.00.

The assembly line process was soon adopted by other manufacturers with a suitable product. Today the assembly line is used in countless manufacturing processes, from the bottling of soft drinks to the assembly of complex electronic products.

However, while the assembly line increases efficiency in manufacturing, it does little to enhance workers' motivation. Many as-

Henry Ford's assembly line, first used for the Model T,
revolutionized the production process

Courtesy of Ford of Canada Archives

sembly-line jobs are repetitious and boring. To relieve frustration in a tedious, unchallenging job, workers may resort to absenteeism and sometimes sabotage.

Automobile manufacturing companies have recognized the problem of boredom, however, and have instituted various schemes to make jobs more interesting. For example, workers now often perform a larger part of the assembly process and form work groups to take over supervision. Many job enrichment and job enlargement programs were pioneered by Volvo in Sweden and have since been tried in North America by manufacturers of various products.

Mechanization

Mass production depends on **mechanization**, or the use of machines to perform work previously done by human beings or animals. Without mechanization most industries in our modern industrial economy could not operate. Cranes, for example, are essential to move heavy objects and build skyscrapers, while modern earth-moving equipment makes it possible to build many kilometres of freeways in a few months — unthinkable for the pick and shovel gangs of the past. Mechanization also means that fewer people are needed to grow, harvest and process food than in the past, particularly in industrialized countries. By freeing the vast majority of people from the production of their own food requirements, mechanization allows many to work in the manufacturing or service industries, which provide for a high standard of living.

Standardization

Standardization is an important factor in reducing the cost of production of complex products. Precise control over production processes allows mass production of virtually identical parts and components. These parts and components can later be assembled into finished products or can be used to repair products that are currently in service. Think how expensive car repairs would be, for example, if each replacement part had to be built or modified by hand before it could be installed in your car.

Automation

The term **automation** refers to the process whereby one machine, usually a computer, regulates and monitors another, so that no human operator need be present. The monitoring computer can quickly analyze machine operations or production processes and command the machine either to stop a certain activity or to correct a particular process. For example, oil refineries are almost entirely automated. At each step in the refining process information is fed into a computer which analyzes it and responds with the appropriate command to keep the production process on course. Automobile manufacturers also use computers and robots to automate particular assembly operations such as welding. Computers which control machines and robots are already being used in factories to automate various processes, including the machining of parts.

Custom Production

Mass production does not mean that only identical products can be produced at any one time. Although assembly lines are ideally suited for this function, the production process can be adjusted so that items can be customized or built to order. As long as the products are not too dissimilar, **custom production** can be achieved through careful production planning and scheduling, as we will discuss later. For example, General Motors produces thousands of cars per year, but few are identical in every respect. Individual cars may vary by model, in the equipment ordered by the customer, or in outside appearance such as trim and paint. The order is scheduled into the production

Computer-controlled robot welding line

process so that the appropriate equipment arrives at the work station at the same time as the chassis arrives there, allowing a high degree of customization on an otherwise highly inflexible assembly line.

The Job Shop

By far the greatest number of manufacturing establishments are job shops that produce small quantities of a product. A customer may request one particular item from a machine shop or a small batch of identical items. To process these small quantities, **job shops** position machines in work centres so that specific operations can be performed at one time. When that operation is completed, the entire batch of semi-finished product moves to another work station. Unlike the mass production operations, which operate continuously, these small operations often have to wait until a customer order arrives. This presents particular problems in scheduling of jobs, inventory management, purchasing, and controlling other production costs.

ORGANIZATION OF THE PRODUCTION DEPARTMENT

Activities of the production department must be organized to function effectively. Small manufacturing firms usually have a line organization structure. A small firm does not have the resources to hire a variety of specialists, nor are specialists particularly necessary, as often only one product is manufactured. The owner, who most often has considerable experience in the manufacture of the product, provides as much of the necessary expertise as possible.

As the business grows and the owner must pay more attention to other areas, he or she may hire a production manager. The production manager in turn may hire an assistant production manager, who may also be known as production superintendent or general foreman. Lower-level foremen would then report to the assistant, allowing the production manager to spend more time on the general aspects of production — planning, product design, quality control, maintenance and production cost control.

As a manufacturing firm grows and enlarges its product offering, the organization structure must be changed. Large manufacturing firms require specialists, since a line operation does not allow the time or expertise required for both planning and controlling production. A large firm must spend considerable time planning for new products, for new production processes and for changes in plant and equipment. These three planning functions are known as **product engineering**, **process engineering** and **plant engineering** respectively.

Controlling the various aspects of production is also more complex in a large manufacturing firm. **Production control** is necessary to maintain production at the specific volume required for maximum utilization of resources. **Quality control** is essential to ensure that the quality of the products is satisfactory. Finally, the firm must exercise control over all production costs, a function known as **cost control**.

Thus, a large firm will have augmented its original line structure with various staff positions as shown in Figure 7.2. One drawback of the structure illustrated is the wide span of control given the production vice-president. With seven subordinates reporting to him, in addition to his responsibilities for coordinating major activities of the firm with other managers, he may have difficulty managing the production function effectively.

The line and staff organization may also encounter many of the authority problems discussed in Chapter 5. For example, if the products coming off the assembly line are found to be defective, should the quality control manager — usually a staff position — have the authority to stop the line? If the line is stopped, the number and cost of defective products would be reduced immediately, but men and

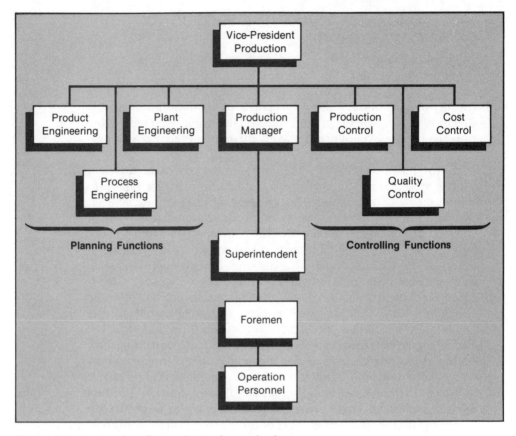

Figure 7.2 Line and staff organizaton for production

machines would be idled. The assembly-line manager, who has to answer for any cost overruns, has the actual authority to stop the line — perhaps he should be notified first. But the delay may waste precious time, during which a stream of defective parts continues to roll off the line. Thus, in a line and staff structure, it is essential that responsibility and authority be clearly specified to minimize conflicts.

DESIGNING PRODUCTION/ OPERATIONS SYSTEMS

To manufacture new products often requires new facilities which may either be added to the existing plant or built at another location. Management must make decisions about plant capacity and location, plant layout, the machines and equipment required, product and service design, and work systems design. These are all major decisions, which are costly and can have long-term effects on a firm, since they commit it to a course of action that cannot easily be changed. Since they are so significant, these decisions are generally made by top management, although production staff and management are usually heavily involved in fact-finding, analysis of information, and recommendations for building specification, the type of machines and equipment to purchase, and so on.

Product/Service Planning and Design

Products have life cycles. Depending on customer demand, products have to be changed and redesigned, or new products developed. New or changed products require detailed specifications, developed by the production division — through its research, engineering and development department — to determine the costs and physical production requirements. During this product development stage, marketing (which will be discussed in Chapter 8) and production work closely together to ensure that the product will meet the requirements of the customer and that it will be of an acceptable quality, at a price customers are prepared to pay.

Production Processes

A firm's choice of products determines the **production process** required, which in turn has a major influence on long-term production decisions. For example, a kitchen appliance manufacturer requires different facilities than a firm in the oil refining industry. The five basic production processes are as follows:

Analytic process: The analytic process divides a particular raw material into its component parts, resulting in one or more different products. For example, in oil refining, crude oil is broken down into gasoline, kerosene, lubricating oil and heating oil for homes.

Extraction: In the extraction process raw materials are taken from either the earth or water. Examples include coal mining and the recovery of salt or other minerals from sea water.

Synthetic process: In the synthetic process various raw materials are combined chemically to form a new product. For example, iron ore, coke and other materials are combined at high temperatures in the production of steel. In the production of plastics, various hydrocarbons are combined.

Fabrication: The fabrication process changes the form of a given raw material. Typical examples include making bottles from raw glass, weaving cloth, making steel beams and manufacturing paper from wood pulp. Most manufacturing involves fabrication.

Assembly: The assembly process combines a number of fabricated components to form a new product. The resulting goods are usually complex, such as automobiles, appliances and machinery. Some components may themselves require assembly; these are called sub-assemblies. For example, the automobile engine is usually assembled in a separate plant and then shipped to the main assembly line for installation into the chassis.

In some firms more than one production process is used, either on the same premises or in a different plant. For example, Sherritt-Gordon, a nickel mining and fabricating company, extracts its nickel ore in Manitoba and refines it in Alberta using the analytic process. The company also fabricates commemorative coins, as well as nickel and silver blanks for shipment to other countries where the coins are minted.

Capacity Planning

Determining the maximum production capacity of a plant is the most fundamental decision production managers must make. Management must take into account present and future demand for its products. What should the maximum capacity be and how long should the present plant last? Management must also keep in mind the swings in production volume due to seasonal variations. This means that the plant should be designed with flexibility in mind so that production volume can be increased or decreased readily, depending on customer demand.

Deciding on **maximum capacity** is a crucial decision. It costs millions of dollars to build a brewery, a hospital or an assembly plant for cars or household appliances: the initial plant size not only determines the initial construction cost but also affects the operating or overhead costs. The larger a plant, the greater will be its fixed operating cost. We discussed this cost factor earlier under mass production and economies of scale. A plant that is built to accommodate production requirements ten years in the future may be too large for today's production volume. Thus, the operating cost per unit is higher, which means that either the price to the customer must be greater or the firm earns less profit. It is probably less costly to expand an existing facility at a later date than to operate a plant at half capacity for years into the future. Ideally, demand and capacity should be matched as closely as possible to minimize operating costs.

Plant Location

Another major long-term decision is plant location. An existing firm might find it easier and less costly to relocate and build a new plant than to modernize its existing facilities. Other reasons for relocating a plant might stem from continuing labour problems at its present site, shifts in the market for its product, increased transportation costs for shipping raw materials or finished goods, or simply because it is expanding into other geographical areas. Whatever the reason, location decisions must be considered carefully — once made, they are difficult and expensive to change.

Many factors can enter into a location decision, but often one or a few factors overshadow the others. Once the most important factors have been determined, a firm will attempt to locate a suitable geographic region. Then a small number of communities will be considered where appropriate sites are available. We will first examine regional factors and then community-site factors.

Regional Factors

The major **regional factors** that must be considered in location decisions are raw materials, markets, and labour considerations. The source of raw materials and the market for its product are two of the major factors that a firm must take into consideration in locating its plant. In both cases the cost of transportation is critical.

RAW MATERIALS: Sometimes a firm finds it necessary to locate near its source of **raw materials** because a product is highly perishable or because of high transportation costs. Mines, farms, fish canning plants, cement plants and food processors are obvious examples of operations that must locate near their raw material sources for the above reasons.

Another critical factor is the cost and supply of **energy**. A ready supply of natural gas at reasonable cost is the reason Sheritt-Gordon located near Fort Saskatchewan, Alberta, even though its nickel mine is in northern Manitoba. In addition, the ammonia produced as a by-product of the natural gas is required in large amounts for nickel processing. Thus, a source of energy which included a necessary production ingredient outweighed higher transportation costs as a consideration in plant location.

LOCATION OF MARKETS: Locating near a firm's market is important if the products are perishable or bulky to ship. Firms that distribute fresh produce want to be as close to their **markets** as possible to minimize spoilage of their product on long shipping routes. Sand and gravel firms and cement processors must locate in their market areas due to the bulkiness of their products.

In the case of products such as televisions or calculators — where transportation costs are small in relation to the total cost of the product, and where the product is a manageable size and not perishable — transportation cost is a less important factor.

LABOUR FACTORS: A firm must decide whether it needs skilled or unskilled workers in its production process. If only unskilled workers are required, it may locate near a large population centre, where labour costs are low. Sometimes the existence or strength of labour unions is also a consideration. On the other hand, if access to a large pool of **skilled labour** is a major requirement, then a company's choices are more limited. Particular industries are often found clustered together in one region where skilled labour is readily available. For example, automobile manufacturers and firms that make parts for cars locate in close proximity. Another well known example is Silicon Valley, the heart of the computer industry located outside San Francisco. Many new computer hardware manufacturers have located there.

Community Factors

Many communities are anxious to attract new firms to their area because of the taxes they would pay and the jobs they would offer. However, communities as a rule do not want businesses that cause pollution or otherwise endanger the local residents or lessen the quality of life in the community. There is considerable debate, for example, over the location of nuclear power plants, chemical plants, and pulp and paper mills. On the other hand, the federal, provincial, or municipal governments may offer tax concessions to companies that locate in particular communities and thus lessen unemployment or expand industrial activity. Other considerations for a firm might include facilities for its employees in a given community, such as schools, shopping, recreation, housing, entertainment, police and fire protection, and availability of medical services.

Site-related Factors

The major considerations with respect to the site of the location are the land, transportation, and local zoning restrictions. Soil conditions and drainage ability may be critical, depending on the type of building to be erected. Other factors, such as room for future expansion, available utilities and sewer capacity, and transportation access for trucks and railroad, are often critical. For particular types of operations, such as light manufacturing or assembly work, and warehousing and customer service facilities, industrial parks are ideal locations.

Industrial Parks

The automobile, which facilitated the exodus of families from cities to the suburbs, also assisted the fledgling industrial parks that were beginning to develop in Canada in the 1950s. **Industrial parks** are

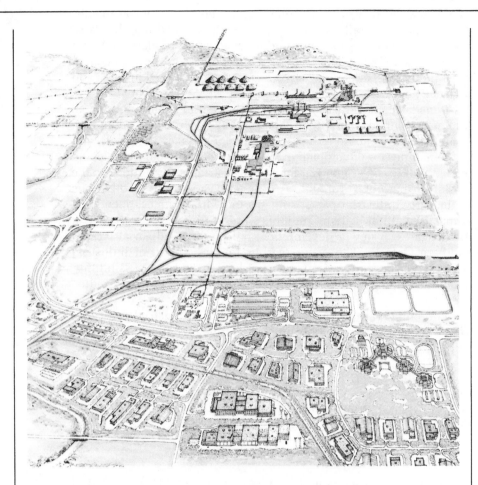

Lake Erie Industrial Park:
portrait of opportunity

This will be Lake Erie Industrial Park: a unique and significant development, destined to be the hub of an entirely new industrial area in the famous Golden Horseshoe of Southern Ontario.

Potential? Located near Nanticoke, some forty kilometres south of Hamilton, the 2400 acre (960 ha) park is ideally situated to serve key North American markets, close to major cities yet refreshingly free of their traffic congestion. It's adjacent to Stelco's massive steel plant, now in operation.

Next-door neighbours are Ontario Hydro's huge generating station and Texaco's new oil refinery. The entirely new community of Townsend is planned for the area; eventually it is expected to contain more than 40,000 people. Truly the area is poised for a bright, exciting future.

Lake Erie Industrial Park is a Stelco development that will create opportunities for a wide variety of enterprises. We'll be pleased to provide more information; write or telephone:

Lake Erie
Industrial
Park

Stelco Technical Services and Property Development Dept. Wilcox Street, Hamilton, Ontario L8N 3T1. Tel. (416) 528-2511. Ext. 4028 or 2572.

SOURCE: Reproduced courtesy of Stelco Technical Services and Property Development Dept., Hamilton, Ont.

Lake Erie Industrial Park—A Stelco Inc. Development

established by private companies and by municipal governments. Access roads and railroad spurs are provided to facilitate the transport of raw materials to plants and finished goods to markets. Water and sewers are provided, in addition to police and fire protection. Most industrial parks today strive for an agreeable working area and a visually pleasing environment.

Canada's first industrial park, Ajax Industrial Estates, located 40 kilometres outside Toronto, opened in 1953. The park had an area of 50 hectares — about a third was used for services and roads, and the remainder for development. After five years the park had leased a quarter of its sites. The 120-hectare industrial park, Malton, on the western fringes of Toronto, took only ten years to fill. Another one of the early industrial parks, Annacis Industrial Estates, opened on Annacis Island in British Columbia's Fraser River area in 1955 with 480 hectares. A newer development is Lake Erie Industrial Park in southern Ontario. The major reasons for the growth of industrial parks is the significantly lower cost of land, expansion possibilities, amenities and lower taxes as compared with sites away from industrial parks.

For municipalities and small communities, industrial parks provide a major source of tax revenue, even though many communities initially offer tax concessions to businesses as an incentive to locate there. Eventually, however, firms provide additional tax revenue and a more balanced tax base — commercial and residential — for the community. An industrial park may also attract new residents to a small community, together with retail stores and other supporting businesses.

Plant Layout

The production process to a large extent determines the layout of the plant. **Continuous processing** is used to make highly standardized products, such as televisions and video cassette recorders, in large volume. Operations are often highly repetitive, requiring low-skilled labour. Although they are expensive, specialized equipment and machines can be used because the high volume of production makes the cost per unit relatively low. **Intermittent processing**, on the other hand, involves low-volume jobs and frequent setting up of machines for new products. General purpose equipment is used to satisfy a variety of processing requirements. Semi-skilled or skilled workers are required to operate the equipment.

Plant layout involves the positioning of facilities, material storage space, machines and other equipment so that raw materials and semi-finished work flow through the plant as rapidly as possible for maximum production efficiency. Production processes that use gravity feeding systems require multistorey buildings. Heavy machines or large objects such as airplanes, on the other hand, are normally fabricated and assembled in large ground-floor buildings to facilitate the movement of materials and parts to the assembly location. For other products such as automobiles, which are best moved past the work stations on long assembly lines, the plant may be a long narrow building or large hall, with the assembly line snaking back and forth.

Since one of the main objectives in plant construction and layout is to reduce cost, it is important to choose a production process that may be adapted to various building shapes. For example, if land is inexpensive, management may prefer to build a large single-storey plant rather than a more expensive multistoried one. Other advantages of single-floor buildings include ease in moving materials, availability of natural lighting, and flexibility in modifying plant layout to future requirements. On the other hand, multistoried buildings can reduce handling costs through the use of gravity feeding systems to move raw materials.

Types of Plant Layout

The two basic types of plant layout shown in Figure 7.3 are known as process and product layout. A **process layout** is usually chosen when manufacturing depends on custom orders, and the same machines and space are used to produce a number of different products. Machines of similar type are grouped together and the raw materials and finished goods are shifted from one department to the next as required for each mechanical process. A process layout allows flexibility in plant layout since material and product movement does not have to follow a fixed route. It is also less expensive to set up because there is no need for costly assembly line equipment. However, since the semi-finished goods often have to be physically moved from one work station to another, a process layout can increase the cost of material handling.

A **product layout** is used for mass production involving continuous runs of similar products. With a product layout, which is basically an assembly line, the product moves along fixed routes, past various work stations, according to the sequence of operations to be performed. A product layout reduces material handling costs and saves space, but it is not particularly flexible, and the cost of altering a product line at a future date may be high. Furthermore, the failure of one machine may hold up an entire production process, and may be expensive if workers and machines in the rest of the product line are idled.

For some manufacturing operations it may be advantageous to combine the two types of layouts. Thus, a process layout may be used to manufacture parts of the product, which are then brought together at the beginning of a product line for further assembly.

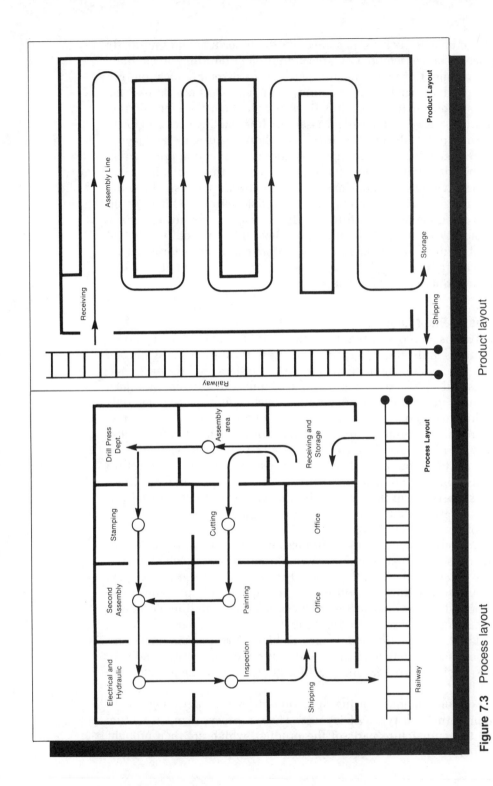

Figure 7.3 Process layout

Product layout

Machinery and Equipment

Often the type of plant layout determines the machinery required. There are basically two types of machines, general and special purpose. **General purpose machines** can perform a variety of operations, and are thus useful in process layouts, since the equipment can be adjusted as required. Metal lathes, for example, are used for a variety of machining operations. Since they are so versatile and can be sold to different manufacturing firms, general purpose machines can be produced in large quantities and costs can be kept down. However, general purpose machines are generally slower in their operation than special purpose machines. They may also require skilled labour, since they must be set up and adjusted for each new process.

In contrast, **special purpose machines** are specially designed to perform one operation. Thus they lend themselves to integration into a product layout — the speed of operation can be adjusted to coincide with the movement of the product along the assembly line. Soft drink manufacturers, for example, incorporate bottling machines that perform only one function — the filling of bottles — but they accomplish this task at high speed. Special purpose machines generally do not require skilled operators, as they seldom need resetting or complicated adjustments.

The type of machinery purchased and its cost depend largely on the product. For example, it may be possible to design a particular product so that it requires less complicated machinery but more skilled labour. If skilled labour is available at reasonable cost, a company may decide to forgo costly specialized machinery. On the other hand, a firm may find it less expensive in the long run to have machinery designed that will mechanize a production process, thus permitting the use of unskilled labour or eliminating the need for labour entirely. By eliminating labour, productivity can often be increased, and the cost of the product may be reduced.

Work System Design

An organization depends on human effort to achieve its goals. The purpose of **work system design** is to determine how to perform a given job in the most cost-efficient manner, while at the same time ensuring that the job is not so simplified that it causes boredom and worker dissatisfaction. The end result of work system design is to establish time standards for each job upon which worker compensation is based. Work system design is a complicated process, but a brief look at a few key aspects will provide some insight.

Job Design

Job design is concerned with specifying the tasks to be performed by a worker and how those tasks are to be done. The emphasis is on performing a job in the most efficient manner possible to reduce costs. Ideally, each product should be designed so that it can be produced on an assembly line with workers performing simple, repetitive tasks. However, workers who have to perform highly routine operations become bored very quickly, which leads to lapses in concentration and ultimately poor assembly of parts. Since the 1950s, emphasis has been placed on making jobs more interesting and giving workers more control over their jobs.

Job design is based on a **method analysis** of a particular operation. The operation to be performed is studied along with the machines, equipment, and materials used. The operator may be asked to provide input as to how he or she is performing the job. Each movement and action is then detailed on a process chart which can be studied later. Based on this process chart, new methods of performing an existing job may be proposed and implemented.

Motion studies are used in manufacturing companies to study how production workers perform their jobs. The objective is to eliminate any unnecessary motions, in order to make workers' efforts more productive. In motion studies a job is broken down into its elements and analyzed, either through personal observation or the use of motion pictures or video which can later be reviewed in slow motion. This allows careful study of the movements performed by workers in the course of their jobs. If workers are found to perform unnecessary motions, they are retrained in a new procedure. Sometimes unnecessary actions can be eliminated by repositioning machines and tools to reduce delays between the time that one unit leaves and another unit arrives at the worker's station.

Work Measurement

Job design, methods analysis and motion studies focus on how a job is done. **Work measurement** focuses on the length of time required to complete the job. The firm requires knowledge about job times for personnel planning, estimating labour costs, scheduling, budgeting, and for designing incentive systems. For the worker, time standards provide an idea of expected output.

Time study is used to determine how long it takes to perform a particular job. The various component activities of a certain job are timed with a stopwatch and then totalled, with an allowance made for worker fatigue and personal needs. Such studies are used to establish a time standard for the completion of a task. This standard may be used subsequently to evaluate worker performance or to determine the costs of a particular job, especially for custom orders.

OPERATING PRODUCTION DECISIONS

The daily operation of the plant is primarily the responsibility of middle and supervisory management of the production division. This includes activities such as demand forecasting, inventory management, distribution planning, production planning, scheduling of customer orders, purchasing of raw materials and parts, maintenance of machines and equipment, and control of product quality. In addition, one of the prime responsibilities of production management is the control of both fixed and variable production costs to ensure efficiency. We will now look at each of these functions in greater detail.

Demand Forecasting

Let us assume for a moment a shoe manufacturer with factories in Montreal and Winnipeg. This manufacturer also has six regional warehouses, one at each of the factories and four others located in Vancouver, Edmonton, Toronto and Halifax. These regional warehouses supply shoe stores in their region. To simplify the discussion, assume that the firm manufactures only one style of shoe. Retail shoe stores order the quantities that they think they will be able to sell and send their orders to the regional warehouses. The retailers assume that their orders will be filled promptly according to the shoe company's policy.

To meet the demand the shoe manufacturer faces several problems. First, sufficient raw materials and semi-finished components must be ordered to meet the required demand. Second, the shoes must be manufactured, which takes time. If production capacity has to be increased, additional time may be required to buy more machinery and train more production workers. Third, the shoes must be delivered to the regional warehouses from where retail orders will be shipped. If the manufacturer has not correctly anticipated the quantities ordered by the shoe stores, production will be less than demand, which means that sales and consequently profit will be lost.

To guard against this potential loss, the shoe manufacturer can do one of two things:

1. Carry a large enough inventory so that even an unusually high demand of shoes can be met if necessary;
2. Either increase or decrease production depending on whether demand is increasing or decreasing.

Either alternative poses problems. In the first case, it costs money to carry a large amount of inventory, and if sales never materialize, the manufacturer will be stuck with out-of-style shoes which may have to be scrapped. The second alternative is not very practical either. It takes time to recruit, interview, hire and train new workers. It may also take weeks or months before enough raw materials and parts can be acquired. New machines may also have to be specially ordered or reconditioned.

Fortunately, most manufacturers, including our shoe manufacturer, can get a reasonably accurate **forecast of demand**. Forecasts of expected sales are usually made for a twelve-month period. These forecasts are usually prepared using previous years' sales as a basis for determining sales in the coming year. For example, if sales have been rising steadily over the years, then the company will probably assume that sales will continue to rise in a similar manner. Each warehouse prepares a forecast using historical data, which is called a **time series analysis** (see Figure 7.4A). Then these forecasts can be examined and adjusted based on other criteria. For example, salespeople in the field will have a good idea what demand will be because they are constantly in touch with the people who are doing the ordering. Future economic conditions can also be taken into account and forecasts adjusted accordingly.

Since there is always a chance that a demand forecast may be inaccurate, and that the actual demand may be greater than the forecasted demand, a **safety stock** is incorporated into the forecast. The size of the safety stock is a policy decision of management based on its desire not to lose sales or have dissatisfied customers.

When individual warehouse forecasts are complete they are merged into a total forecast for each of the factories so that material requirements and production capacity can be determined (see Figure 7.4B). By forecasting a year in advance the firm can gear up its production schedule and order the necessary raw materials. As actual sales are realized, these new figures are used to update the forecast. With a good idea of what future sales might be, the shoe company can adjust its production capacity and inventory far enough in advance to avoid a production crisis.

Inventory Management

For production operations, **inventory management** is a complex activity. The inventory manager must ensure that enough of the raw materials and parts that are primary inputs into the production process are available as needed. At various stages, the production process yields semi-finished products that may have to be stored for use as inputs into the production process at a later stage. Finally, the amount of finished goods in inventory must be great enough to ensure that normal customer orders can be filled.

What Quantity Should the Firm Buy?

The quantity of material purchased is normally dictated by the rate at which the material is used. If raw materials or parts are used at a

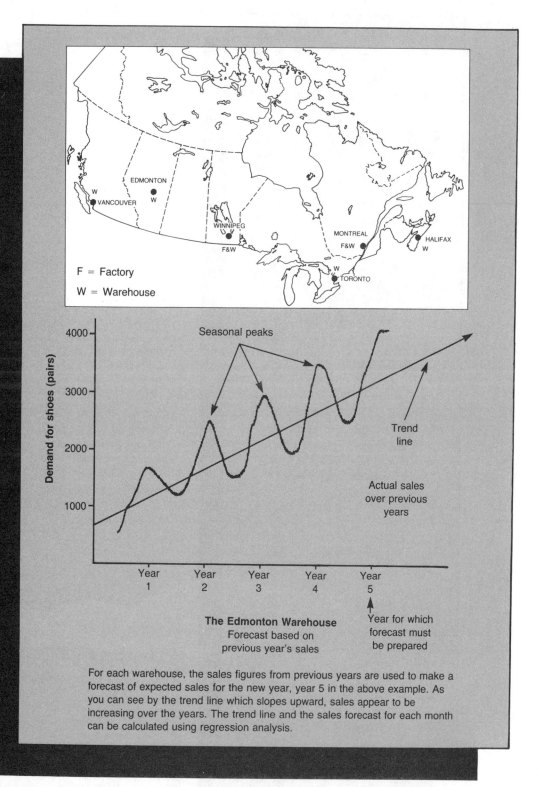

F = Factory

W = Warehouse

Seasonal peaks

Demand for shoes (pairs)

4000

3000

2000

1000

Trend line

Actual sales over previous years

Year 1 Year 2 Year 3 Year 4 Year 5

The Edmonton Warehouse
Forecast based on previous year's sales

Year for which forecast must be prepared

For each warehouse, the sales figures from previous years are used to make a forecast of expected sales for the new year, year 5 in the above example. As you can see by the trend line which slopes upward, sales appear to be increasing over the years. The trend line and the sales forecast for each month can be calculated using regression analysis.

Figure 7.4A   Demand forecast for the Edmonton warehouse

Warehouses	Jan.	Feb.	Mar.	Apr.	May	June	July	Aug.	Sept.	Oct.	Nov.	Dec.	Total
Vancouver	2 780	2 800	2 810	3 000	3 800	3 800	4 150	4 680	4 460	4 100	4 100	3 900	44 380
Edmonton	2 560	2 690	2 820	2 950	3 240	3 610	3 840	4 010	3 730	3 630	3 510	3 440	40 030
Winnipeg	2 100	2 160	1 800	1 940	2 360	2 890	3 250	3 460	3 400	3 020	2 900	2 700	31 980
Winnipeg Factory	7 440	7 650	7 430	7 890	9 400	10 300	11 240	12 150	11 590	10 750	10 510	10 040	116 390
Montreal	8 540	8 750	8 530	8 990	10 500	11 400	12 340	13 250	12 690	11 850	11 610	11 140	129 590
Toronto	13 500	13 850	13 480	14 250	16 760	18 260	19 830	21 350	20 420	10 010	18 620	17 830	198 160
Halifax	4 960	5 100	4 950	5 260	6 260	6 860	7 490	8 100	7 730	7 160	7 000	6 690	77 560
Montreal Factory	27 000	27 700	26 960	28 500	33 520	36 520	39 660	42 700	40 840	29 020	37 230	35 660	405 310
Total Production	34 440	35 350	34 390	36 390	42 920	46 820	50 900	54 850	52 430	39 770	47 740	45 700	521 700

The forecasts from each warehouse are combined to make a sales forecast for the company and what each factory must produce in the coming year to satisfy the expected sales.

Figure 7.4B Company sales forecast

constant rate, a firm may buy often and in small quantities. This strategy is known as **hand-to-mouth buying**. Buying in large quantities that will last a long time is termed **forward buying**.

Both strategies have their advantages and disadvantages. When prices are in a decline, buying in small quantities will contribute to lower material costs over time. And with less money tied up in inventory, storage costs may also be reduced. Buying in smaller quantities allows greater flexibility if a firm has to change a raw material. However, the purchaser also runs the risk that suppliers may be unable to ship the materials when necessary. Moreover, since smaller quantities are purchased, the supplier may not offer volume-price concessions.

Buying in large quantities, or forward buying, is often used during inflationary periods when prices are sure to increase over time. Forward buying also offers some protection against problems such as supplier strikes or material shortages. It may allow a firm to continue production for as long as it takes to resolve the problem. Thus, utilities and steel companies stockpile enough coal to allow production for as long as three months, in case supply is suddenly cut off.

Carrying Inventory Costs Money

A firm could guard against running out of raw materials or finished goods by always having large quantities on hand. However, carrying inventory costs money. If the firm has to borrow the money to buy the inventory, it has to pay interest on the borrowed funds. If the firm uses its own money, there is an opportunity cost — the money tied up in inventory cannot be used for other purposes which may generate income. It also costs money to store inventory and insure it against hazards such as fire and theft, and with some items there is always the possibility that it will spoil or become obsolete.

On the other hand, too little inventory can also cost the firm money. A shortage of raw materials may cause expensive delays in the production process. In the case of a retail business, potential customers will be lost, perhaps permanently, if they find that common merchandise or parts are out of stock.

Establishing an Inventory Control System

In manufacturing, some raw materials or components may be used up faster than others, while retailers may find some dress styles and sizes, for example, are sold more frequently than others. Since it is critical to carry the right amount of inventory at all times, knowing how much to order and when is crucial. A system is required to monitor how quickly inventory is moving and when a new order must be placed.

A computerized **inventory management system** may be used: sales are recorded when purchased by the customer and the item is then deducted from inventory records. When the items in inventory drop below a certain minimum level, a new order, automatically developed by the computer, is then mailed to the supplier. This minimum level, as well as the amount to reorder, must be determined for every item so as to minimize the cost of carrying inventory as well as the cost of reordering.

The Economic Order Quantity and the Reordering Process

For a better understanding of the inventory and reordering process, look at Figure 7.5. The amount of product used in manufacturing can be determined from the production order or, in the case of a retailer, from past experience or sales forecasts. In our example, it takes six weeks to use 60 units of an item and reach the reorder point when a new order is placed. The **reorder point** is chosen so that there is enough product on hand to meet sales demand or manufac-

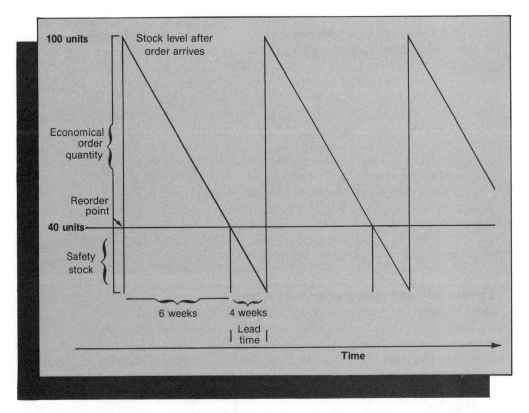

Figure 7.5 Stock movement and reordering

turing requirements until the new order arrives in stock. The **lead time** — four weeks in our example — represents the time for mailing the order to the supplier, having it filled, shipped and placed into stock. The purchasing department must know the lead times for all items since they may vary for different products and suppliers. Where inventory management and purchasing are separate departments, close cooperation between the two is required.

The **economic order quantity (EOQ)** is the lowest order size that will minimize the total annual cost of carrying inventory in stock and the reorder cost. The annual **inventory carrying cost** includes costs of insurance, storage, spoilage, obsolescence, and interest charges on the money tied up in inventory. Some of these costs are known or can be calculated while others are estimates.

The annual **ordering cost** includes the cost of issuing an order to a supplier, as well as the cost of receiving it in the warehouse. For example, the larger the order size, the greater the average inventory carried during the year and hence the greater the cost of carrying that inventory. On the other hand, the larger order size means a decrease in the number of orders that have to be issued during the year and received in stock. Therefore reorder costs decrease. Figure 7.6 shows how the EOQ is basically a tradeoff between inventory carrying cost and reorder cost.

The EOQ for the firm may or may not agree with the quantity sold by suppliers. For example, even though the economic order quantity for a particular item is five dozen, it may only be available in gross lots such as 144 dozen. In other instances, a supplier may offer **discounts** to encourage purchase of large quantities. The inventory manager must then make a decision on the quantity to order. There would be little advantage in ordering 100 units of a product simply because the supplier offers a small discount, if only 50 units are sold per year. The cost of carrying the inventory, together with the potential cost of spoilage or obsolescence, could easily outweigh the discount.

Perpetual Inventory Control

A **perpetual inventory control system** is used in manufacturing and retailing to show the inventory in stock at any given time. Additions to and withdrawals from inventory are noted on special cards or controlled through a computer, which can be programmed to reorder when the quantity drops below a minimum point. With a computerized inventory control system, the inventory is usually updated continuously as materials are withdrawn or sold, and as new stock is entered.

Perpetual inventory control is familiar to most of us through a modern department store with a computerized inventory system. All cash registers are linked to the central computer where the inventory

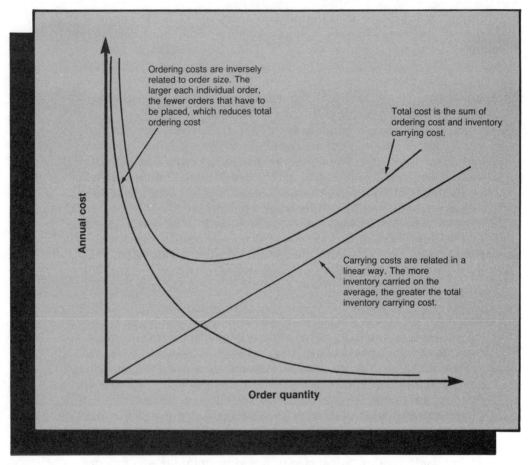

Ordering costs are inversely related to order size. The larger each individual order, the fewer orders that have to be placed, which reduces total ordering cost

Total cost is the sum of ordering cost and inventory carrying cost.

Carrying costs are related in a linear way. The more inventory carried on the average, the greater the total inventory carrying cost.

Annual cost

Order quantity

Figure 7.6 The relationship between carrying costs, ordering costs, and total cost

files are contained. As merchandise is sold, the cash register clerk enters the inventory number into the register along with the price of the item. The computer deducts this item from inventory. When the stock level drops to a predetermined reorder point, the computer automatically produces the order, which is then mailed to the supplier. Thus, the reordering process can be largely automated, provided the computer is given specific criteria as to what inventory levels are to be maintained. However, the computer cannot make judgments as to how consumer demand may be affected by future economic conditions or consumer habits. These must remain decisions of management.

The **Universal Product Code (UPC)** — the series of light and dark bars printed on many items — is designed for a computerized perpetual inventory system. An item is passed over a light in a counter

Number System Character — 0 21200 22319 8 — Check Character

Manufacturer Identification Number

Item Code

The Universal Product Code is a 12-digit, all numeric code that identifies each consumer package. The code consists of a number system character, a 5-digit manufacturer identification number, a 5-digit item code number and a check character. All 12 digits are shown in human readable form at the bottom of the bars.

Information Courtesy of Product Code

or a clerk draws a light wand across the bars signaling the computer. The computer then registers the type of product, price, and so on, and automatically reduces the inventory level. Two major advantages in computerized perpetual inventory management are the speed at which the information becomes available for management and the reduction in tedious work for clerical employees.

Physical Inventory Count

Regardless of how sophisticated an inventory system is, a physical count is still required once or twice per year. The physical count is then compared to the perpetual inventory figures. If the actual count and perpetual inventory figures do not agree, the inventory manager must find out why. Large deviations are usually the result of errors in paperwork, but they could also be caused by theft or the loss of materials in transit.

Distribution Planning

A firm with only one factory has few distribution problems as long as there are adequate transportation facilities to ship its product to market. However, if a firm has a number of factories and warehouses in various locations across the country then **distribution planning** becomes an important production decision. The objective is to minimize the total distribution costs — the costs of moving product to the various warehouses from the various factories.

For example, let us return to the shoe manufacturer with two factories and six regional warehouses. Figure 7.7A shows the location of these facilities. To make it simple, assume that each factory produces only two types of shoes, the eastern sandal and the western boot. Assume further that each factory can manufacture both styles and can ship to any of the four warehouses if necessary.

It is the task of production management to determine the lowest cost method of distributing its product, based on transportation cost and demand for the two types of shoes. It may be that both factories should produce both types of shoes and supply their own regions — the Winnipeg factory supplies shoes to the west, while the Montreal factory supplies both styles to eastern Canada. This is shown by the solid lines in Figure 7.7A. On the other hand, it might be advantageous to specialize production of the western boot in the Winnipeg factory and the eastern sandal in Montreal. Then each factory would ship its product to any of the six warehouses. The dotted lines in Figure 7.7A indicate this condition. Either of these two approaches would depend on transportation and manufacturing costs. If each factory can reduce its costs of production by manufacturing only one type of shoe, and if this reduction in manufacturing costs is greater

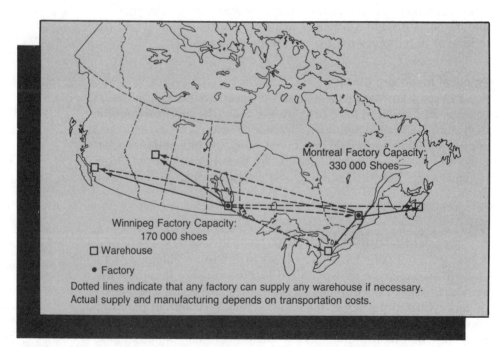

Figure 7.7A Shoe company factories, warehouses and transportation routes

than the increased cost of shipping one type of shoe to all warehouses from one factory, then it would be a viable alternative.

Distribution planning may also become important under another circumstance. Assume that Winnipeg's production facilities produce only the western boot because demand in the west for the eastern sandal is very small. In the past this demand has been supplied by the Montreal factory and shipped to the various western warehouses, even though shipping costs per pair are quite high.

For some reason, demand for the eastern sandal in western Canada increases dramatically. Montreal can gear up its production to meet the increased demand, but shipping costs from Montreal to the west are much higher compared to shipping costs from Winnipeg to the western warehouses (see Figure 7.7B). Because of the lower shipping costs, it may be advantageous for Winnipeg to begin to produce the eastern sandal even if this initially requires overtime. Figure 7.7B shows that the total cost to manufacture a pair of eastern sandals using overtime at the Winnipeg plant and shipping it to the three western warehouses is less in all instances than to have the Montreal factory supply the west with these sandals.

From (factory)	Winnipeg		Montreal		Warehouse capacity (pairs of shoes)
To (warehouse)	OT	TC	OT	TC	
Vancouver	$1.10	$0.80	$1.80	$2.30	50 000
Edmonton	$1.10	$0.50	$1.80	$1.90	50 000
Winnipeg	$1.10	$0.10	$1.80	$1.40	80 000
Toronto	$1.10	$0.70	$1.80	$0.30	110 000
Montreal	$1.10	$1.10	$1.80	$0.10	150 000
Halifax	$1.10	$1.40	$1.80	$0.70	30 000
Factory capacity (pairs of shoes)	170 000		330 000		

OT = Overtime cost to produce one pair of shoes

TC = Shipping and handling cost per pair of shoes

Figure 7.7B Cost matrix for Canadian Shoe Company, Inc.

Production Planning and Control

Planning and controlling are two important functions of managers in manufacturing firms. The production department generally incurs the greatest costs because it usually employs the largest number of people, including managers, it is responsible for virtually all purchasing requirements, and it generally has a large investment in raw materials, semi-finished or finished goods. Inefficient methods in the production process may add greatly to variable costs, and consequently increase the price to the consumer, which could affect product sales. If a few pennies can be shaved off production costs — perhaps through product redesign — it may amount to great dollar savings for a product produced in large quantities. A better designed machine to make the production process more efficient might be worth the expense in the long run.

Production planning starts with demand forecasts, usually for a period of one year, to ensure that general capacity is available for the expected demand. This aggregate plan is broken down into a master schedule for detailed production planning for specific models for the coming week or month. The master schedule is used to determine the necessary materials and parts required for production. The master schedule is also used to develop the basic production schedule, specifying which work centres will be used to produce specific orders and the time required in these work centres. We will now look at this process in more detail.

Aggregate Production Planning

Aggregate planning, also known as medium-range planning, is really the first step in the actual production planning process. Its purpose is to translate demand forecasts into planned production levels. The focus, however, is on families of products rather than individual products. Our shoe manufacturer would plan in terms of total numbers of eastern sandals and western boots, but would not be concerned at this stage with colors and sizes. Similarly, an appliance manufacturer will plan for output requirements of refrigerators, stoves and dishwashers. Later on, in the short-range planning process, when the master schedule is prepared, these broad categories are broken down into specific models such as frost-free, side-by-side or energy-efficient refrigerators.

Thus, aggregate planning is concerned with having enough production capacity to meet demand for the upcoming 12- to 18-month period. The manufacturer has a number of options available.

1. **Vary the work-force size**. If demand rises and falls, production can be increased or decreased by hiring and firing workers as required. This increases hiring and layoff costs and costs associated with finding qualified employees, interviewing, training and eventually the

costs associated with laying them off again when production levels return to normal. On the other hand, the firm reduces the cost of building up and carrying inventory to meet the increased demand.

2. **Hold the work force constant but vary its utilization**. Production can be increased with overtime work or a shortened workweek. While this strategy reduces hiring and layoff costs, it means greater payroll costs because of overtime and associated costs. Furthermore, when employees work longer hours, there is usually a drop in productivity and a greater chance of accidents because employees are more fatigued than usual. Another factor is equipment failure, or downtime of equipment, since it is used more intensively.

3. **Subcontracting**. An outside manufacturer can be used to produce component parts.

4. **Hold the work force constant and use inventories to absorb demand fluctuations**. Inventories will be built up during periods when production exceeds demand. During periods when demand increases, product will be drawn from inventory to meet the higher demand. By using this strategy the firm incurs greater inventory carrying costs. There will be higher storage costs, and money will be tied up in inventory, which is not available for other purposes.

Materials Requirement Planning

The **master schedule** is developed from the aggregate plan. It is a detailed, short-term production plan that states the quantity and types of items to be produced during a specific time period, which may be hours, days, or weeks. For example, it would specify to our appliance manufacturer detailed production rates on a daily or weekly basis of specific models of refrigerators, stoves, and so on.

The aggregate plan and master schedule will provide rough estimates of the labour, facilities and equipment that will be needed to produce the various quantities of product. However, the various raw materials and parts are not really accounted for in these plans and schedules. One approach is to ensure that enough of what a company uses is always in inventory. As already discussed, however, carrying large inventories is costly, and even large inventories do not ensure that a company will not run out of a crucial item used in the production process.

To ensure that the master schedule can be executed without huge inventory levels a company must plan to have the necessary materials, parts, and assemblies available in time for use in the production process. This requires answers to two basic questions:

1. What parts and raw materials are needed to make the end item?

2. How much of those parts and raw materials do we have on hand?

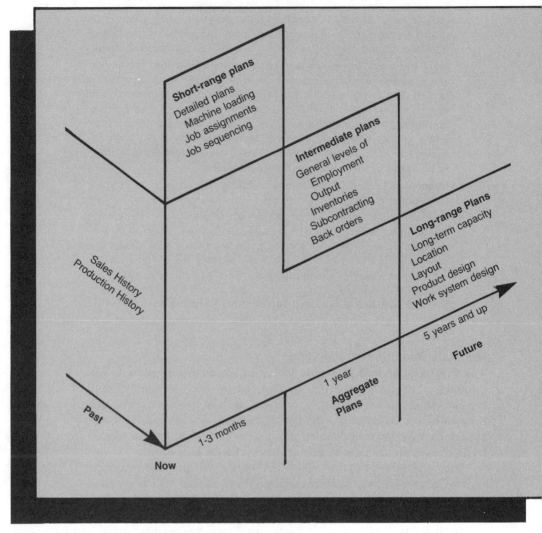

Figure 7.8 Aggregate planning and the planning cycle.

Material requirements planning (MRP) is a computerized process that requires information from the master schedule, bills of materials, and inventory records to determine when orders must be placed with suppliers to replenish inventories of parts and materials (see Figure 7.9).

Each finished product has its own **bill of materials** which lists all the assemblies, subassemblies, parts and raw materials that are needed to produce one unit of it. The **inventory records file** is used

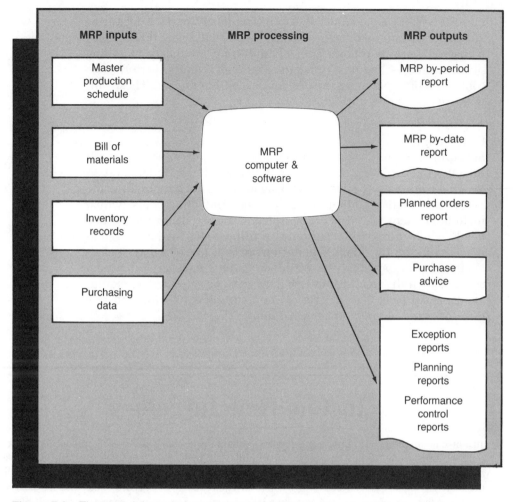

Figure 7.9 The material requirements planning (MRP) process: inputs and outputs

to store information on the status of each item by time period. Typical information stored in an inventory file are part number, on-hand quantity, on-order quantity, cost data and procurement lead time, economical order quantity, and lot size. Furthermore, information about the supplier is also usually included. The inventory records file is linked to production and purchasing so that updates can be made to orders, receipts and issues from stock.

If MRP is to be successfully implemented the firm has to have a computerized information system, since a large amount of data must be stored and processed. It is also crucial that the information fed into the system is accurate. If wrong figures are entered regarding quantities on hand and future needs, then it will break down. Once processed, various reports and schedules are produced, including planned order schedules, order releases and changes, performance control reports, planning reports, and exception reports. These outputs are also shown in Figure 7.9.

Scheduling

Scheduling is the final step in the production planning process. It involves the assigning of priorities to manufacturing orders and allocating workloads to specific work centres. Through scheduling the production manager attempts to balance conflicting goals, which include efficient use of staff, equipment, and facilities on the one hand, while minimizing customer waiting time, inventories, and process time on the other. Scheduling presents one of the most challenging day-to-day activities of the operations manager, who must adjust his production output to changes in customer orders, equipment breakdowns, late deliveries from suppliers of parts and raw materials, and various other disruptions.

Just-in-Time Inventory

Just-in-time inventory (JIT), or Kanban, stems from Japan. The idea is to have suppliers deliver raw materials and/or parts at the exact time they are needed, so as to keep inventories of the manufacturing facility at zero (or as close to it as possible). This system also keeps goods in process inventories to a minimum because goods are produced only as needed for the next production stage. Finished goods inventories are also minimized by matching production closely with sales demand.

Under the old system, also called the **batch-push system**, each work station in the production process produced at a constant rate regardless of what the next stage required. The excess was put into inventory. In contrast, with JIT, also known as the **demand-pull system**, each work station produces its product only when the next work station requires more input.

The advantage of JIT is that the financial capital not tied up in inventories can be directed toward other company uses. For example, General Motors has used JIT since 1980 and has reduced its annual inventory related costs from $8 billion to $2 billion. To make JIT work requires total coordination between all work stations of the production process. It needs precise scheduling to ensure that product arrives when needed, otherwise the next station cannot produce. It also requires motivated, cooperative employees. They must work with one another if and when problems arise. It may even mean that employees must be able to perform different jobs to help out in an area that has fallen behind. Workers experience increased job satisfaction because they have responsibility for making the system work and can influence changes and improvements in it.

Scheduling is a problem for both manufacturing and service organizations. Consider one of the more difficult scheduling problems — scheduling passengers on an airline. Each plane has only so many seats available, depending on the type of aircraft used. The airline must ensure that it doesn't overbook seats. Some customers book months in advance, while others book only a few hours before flight departure. The reservation system, essentially a scheduling system, must therefore keep track of the many flights months in advance, allowing quick updating of reservations or cancellations from anywhere in the country, sometimes even across international boundaries.

In manufacturing, scheduling depends on the nature of the production process. Different scheduling problems are experienced by high-volume production processes, a job shop, and the construction of a single large project. We will discuss project management later in the chapter.

HIGH-VOLUME SYSTEM **High-volume operations** such as assembly lines pose the fewest scheduling problems. The product follows a fixed path, produces a limited number of products, and needs little work in process inventory. The arrangement and use of highly specialized tools and equipment are designed to enhance the flow of work through the system. However, since jobs are highly specialized, worker boredom and fatigue, absenteeism, turnover, and so on, may disrupt the smooth flow of work through the system.

Another scheduling problem on high-volume systems is due to the fact that not all products are identical in model and style. An automobile manufacturer, for example, may schedule a variety of models into the assembly line, and produce two- and four-door models, with varieties of décor and optional equipment. This may mean that some work stations take longer than others to perform their task, which could hold up other work stations further down the line. The work station is thus referred to as out of balance with the regular line. Scheduling can ensure that the various models go through the line so that the workload per work station is relatively balanced. Scheduling must also take into account the different parts and materials required by each model. If the production line is to operate smoothly, the flow of these various parts and materials to the particular work station must be coordinated.

Scheduling must also take care of disruptions such as equipment failure, material shortages, accidents and absences. It is not usually possible to make up for lost production by speeding up the assembly line, which is designed to perform at a fixed rate. Thus, a firm will have to schedule overtime or subcontract. Similarly, if production has exceeded demand the line cannot be slowed down. The alternative will be to operate the line for fewer hours.

JOB SHOPS   In a **job shop**, products are made to order and orders usually differ considerably in terms of processing requirements, materials needed, processing time, and processing sequence or setup. Therefore, scheduling in job shops is usually complex. Furthermore, little can be done prior to receiving the actual job order. Thus, the major concern for job shops is to distribute the workload among work centres (loading) and determine in what sequence orders should be processed (sequencing).

Loading

Loading refers to the assignment of jobs to work centres. Problems arise for the operations manager when two or more jobs are to be processed and there are a number of work centres capable of performing the required work.

A **Gantt chart** is often used for loading and scheduling. The name derives from Henry Gantt, who pioneered the use of these charts for industrial scheduling in the early 1900s. A Gantt chart can be used to organize and clarify actual or intended use of resources over a period of time. The time scale is shown horizontally and resources to be scheduled are listed vertically. How the resources are used is indicated in the body of the chart.

A **load chart** shows when a particular machine(s) or work centre is either available or in use on a particular day or time. Some work centres may be idle for large periods of time between jobs. With a load chart a manager can reassign jobs to make better use of the work centres. For example, a new job may be inserted or the work for one particular centre can be rearranged in preparation for a large order. The load chart in Figure 7.10A shows what work centres are fully loaded and which ones are available.

In contrast to a load chart, a **schedule chart** is often used to monitor progress of jobs. The horizontal axis shows time while the vertical axis shows work in progress. The chart indicates which jobs are on schedule and which are behind or ahead. Figure 7.10B shows a schedule chart for a particular job. A major task for operations people is to update these charts continually to keep them current and thus meaningful.

Sequencing

Sequencing specifies the order in which the jobs waiting at a given work centre are to be processed. If work centres are lightly loaded and all jobs require the same amount of processing, then sequencing represents no particular difficulty. However, if work centres are heavily loaded, and there is a mix of short and long jobs that must be processed on these work centres, then sequencing becomes critical.

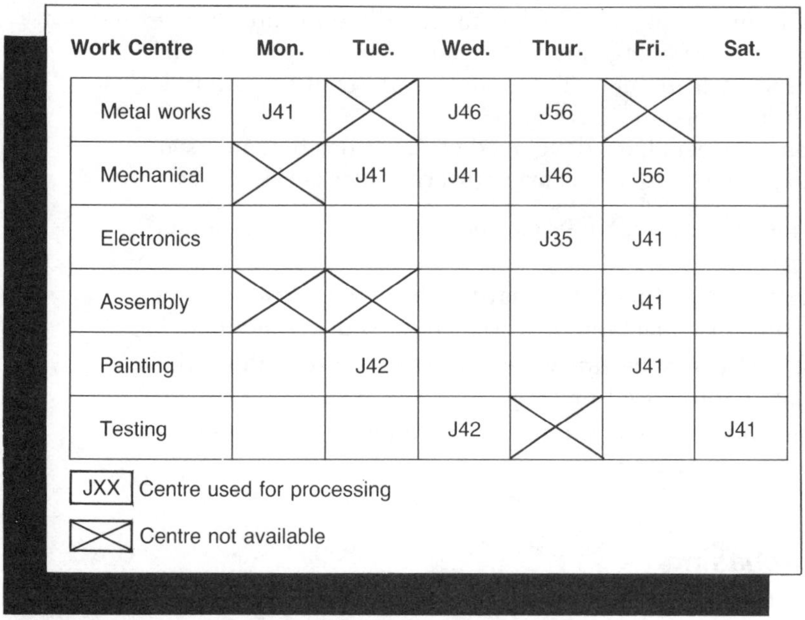

Work Centre	Mon.	Tue.	Wed.	Thur.	Fri.	Sat.
Metal works	J41	✕	J46	J56	✕	
Mechanical	✕	J41	J41	J46	J56	
Electronics				J35	J41	
Assembly	✕	✕			J41	
Painting		J42			J41	
Testing			J42	✕		J41

| JXX | Centre used for processing |

| ✕ | Centre not available |

Figure 7.10A A Gantt load chart

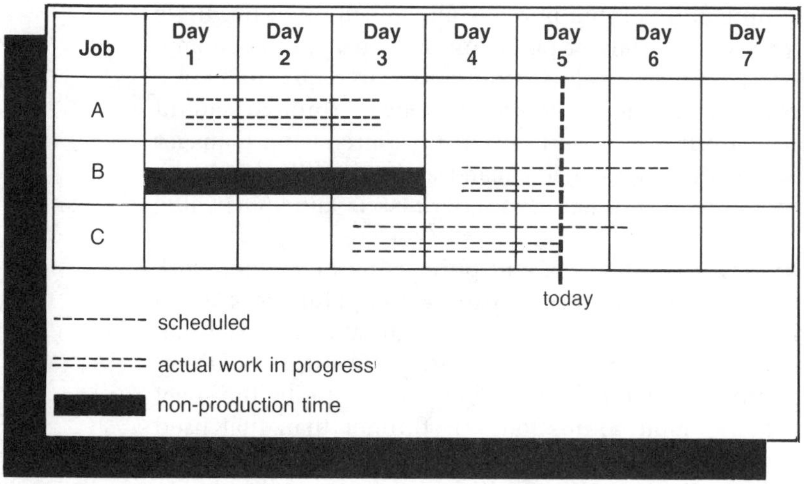

Job	Day 1	Day 2	Day 3	Day 4	Day 5	Day 6	Day 7
A							
B							
C							

today

- - - - - - - - scheduled

========= actual work in progress

▓▓▓▓ non-production time

Figure 7.10B A Gantt scheduling chart for jobs A, B, C.

For example, a number of small jobs requiring different processing setups may be ahead of a large job which should be out by a certain date if a contract is to be met. Thus, some work centres could be sitting idle while others are overworked.

Operations managers have developed certain rules that are used to decide on sequencing order. The major **priority rules** are as follows:

FCFS (first come, first served): Jobs may be processed on a first come, first served basis.

SPT (shortest processing time): Jobs may also be processed according to processing time at a machine or work centre: shortest job first.

DD (due date): Jobs may be processed in order of due date — the earliest due date is processed first.

RUSH: An emergency order or a preferred customer may get priority processing.

Purchasing

Improper attention to purchasing can mean losses for a firm. An inexperienced purchasing agent concerned only with material costs, for example, might buy low quality raw materials or components which break down in the production process causing delays and driving up production costs. If quantities purchased are too large, the firm may be faced with stockpiles of obsolescent materials. If purchases are made from new suppliers without a proper check on their ability to meet shipping dates and quantities, the production process may again be delayed.

On the other hand, an astute purchasing manager can cut costs. Through bargaining and volume purchasing, he can often negotiate a good price for raw materials or parts, and if he watches economic conditions closely he may be able to purchase large quantities of a product before a major price increase. Moreover, through careful analysis of the materials and parts used, the purchasing manager may be able to substitute less costly materials and still achieve the same quality in the final product. The latter task is known as value analysis.

In **value analysis**, engineering and purchasing personnel work together to examine materials used in the manufacture of a given product. Engineers examine the product design and proposed materials to see if less expensive materials could be substituted without affecting the quality of the finished product. For example, the sheet metal used in automobile bodies today is thinner than that used twenty years ago and reduces the cost of production for the manufacturer. Yet the metal is equally effective and because it helps to reduce the total weight of the car, it also contributes to fuel economy.

Similarly value analysis may show that a plastic gear performs as well as a more costly brass one. Any small saving in cost per individual item can amount to a large total saving on mass-produced items and result in lower prices for the consumer.

Suppliers

A major function of the purchasing department is finding suppliers for the materials required by the production firm. A supplier may be chosen on the basis of price, quality of product, ability to provide supplies as needed, speed of delivery and other services. Sometimes a firm uses only one supplier, to gain the advantages of volume purchase. Such a strategy may be risky, however, if the supplier becomes engaged in a strike, or is otherwise unable to supply the product. It may then be difficult to change to other suppliers, who may have prior commitments to steady customers.

Firms using sophisticated inventory management techniques such as MRP and JIT are placing new emphasis on long-term stable relationships with its suppliers. Since the supplier's production is so closely linked to the buyer's consumption, cost of parts and material is no longer the sole criterion for choosing a supplier. The supplier must be able to provide consistent delivery of materials. As delivery times are so crucial, local suppliers are increasingly relied on to supply all of a firm's requirements for a particular raw material or part. Needless to say, quality of product is also a major consideration.

Make-or-Buy Decisions

Manufacturing firms that use components from outside suppliers are often faced with a make-or-buy decision. If facilities are large enough and a firm has the resources, both financial and human, to make the product itself, then it might save money in the long run. Some firms have no choice, if buying parts elsewhere means giving away a secret production process, or if no other firm has the expertise or resources required to produce the parts. Other reasons for a firm's decision to manufacture its own components include control over quality, elimination of supply problems, or control over supply costs. A make-or-buy decision can be of major importance to a firm, and is usually not made without top management approval.

Quality Control

Most products today must meet stringent manufacturing standards. Otherwise they may not perform properly, wear out too quickly or break down. Producing a poor quality product can be costly if a firm must repair the product even before it is sold to customers, or if extensive warranty repairs are necessary. Sometimes the entire production run may have to be scrapped if the product cannot be repaired. Besides incurring these direct costs, a firm may lose customers, and thus revenue and profit, if it consistently produces inferior quality products.

To ensure that product quality is high, manufacturers usually inspect the products at various stages of assembly. **Quality control** can be accomplished through visual inspection to check for defects or poor workmanship. Often quality control also involves measuring various aspects of the product and comparing it with predetermined standards, which could be based on technical requirements and engineering standards, industry standards or customer expectations for operating life. For products such as appliances, quality control is performed by actually operating the product for a specified period of time. Television sets, for example, are "burned in" — turned on for a specific time period during which any defects usually become apparent. Some products, however, can be checked only by dismantling or physically destroying them. Quality control then involves taking a random sample of the manufactured product.

Regardless of how a product's quality is measured, a quality control function requires people, space and costly measuring equipment — all additional expenses for a firm. Without quality control, however, a firm could incur even greater costs since poor quality product could result in the loss of customers and reputation as well as a substantial direct loss if the defective product has to be repaired or scrapped. Thus, a firm must balance the cost of exercising quality control against these other costs.

In Figure 7.11 we show graphically the relationship between the cost of establishing a quality control function and the possible cost of producing defective products. The vertical axis represents costs in dollars while the horizontal axis represents additional units of quality control, such as quality control inspectors. The downward sloping curve represents the cost of producing poor quality product. These costs include scrap loss, repairs and loss of potential revenue from dissatisfied customers. Without a quality control function, these costs could be extremely high.

By establishing a quality control department with inspectors to check product quality and standards on the assembly line, a cost is incurred — the upward sloping diagonal line indicates that as the number of inspectors increases, so does the cost of the quality control function in terms of salary, office space and testing equipment. However, quality control costs will be offset — first because poor quality production runs are detected more readily which reduces scrap loss, and second because both customer ill will and after-sale repair costs will be reduced if fewer defective products reach the market.

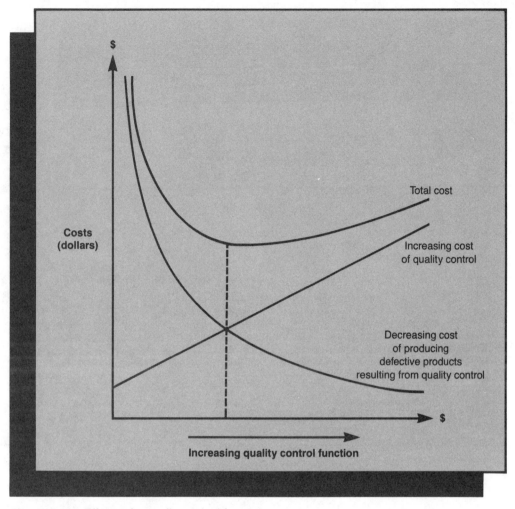

Figure 7.11 Effects of a quality control function on costs associated with defective product

However, there is a limit to the number of inspectors a firm can have in quality control. The cost of salaries and other expenses could rise to the point where they offset any additional savings from increased inspection. The firm incurs the lowest possible cost, taking both inspection and poor quality into account, at the lowest point of the U-shaped total cost curve. The curve first declines as the quality control operation reduces the costs of producing defective parts, but starts to rise again as the costs of inspection begin to outweigh the savings.

Quality control inspector monitors the manufacture of optical fibres

Maintenance

Most manufacturing processes are heavily dependent on machines. If a machine breaks down, especially one performing a crucial task, an entire production line could be shut down, costing the firm many thousands of dollars as workers stand idle while the machine is repaired. The risk of such breakdowns is minimized through **preventive maintenance**. Machines are periodically inspected and adjusted even if they are not defective. Any parts that appear defective or worn are replaced, even though the machine may still be operable. Preventive maintenance thus helps to avoid the additional expense of unexpected disruptions in a production schedule.

In preventive maintenance, as in quality control, management must strike a balance between the cost of the maintenance function and the potential cost of unexpected machine failure and its effect on the production process. A chart similar to Figure 7.3 could be used to determine the optimum amount of preventive maintenance. The optimum amount would again be at the lowest point on the total cost curve, where the decreasing costs of machine failure are offset by the increasing costs of the maintenance function.

Project Management

Building large, complex projects — power dams, high rise office complexes, a new airplane, ship, or space vehicle — presents a particular problem for the production manager. Few of these projects are ever alike, and unforeseen problems could arise at any time, delaying completion of the project and costing the firm considerable sums of money when contract deadlines are not met. Other firms involved in the project could also be affected.

Any major project can be broken down into specific tasks that have to be completed over a period of time with the resources available. Some tasks can be started only after others are completed. Other tasks can be worked on simultaneously. A project manager establishes a **project schedule**, or **network**, that specifies the tasks that have to be completed, the time required for each task, and the sequence in which the tasks have to be completed. In addition, the resources available for completing each task — people, equipment, space, and so on, are also specified.

One technique in common use for planning major production projects and for controlling their completion time is **PERT (Program Evaluation and Review Technique)**. First used in the production of guided missiles for the Polaris submarine, PERT was quickly adapted for use in industry. A second technique, **CPM** or **Critical Path Method**, was developed by DuPont for the planning and control of complex industrial projects.

The two techniques, PERT and CPM, are essentially similar, except for their method of establishing the time required for the completion of the various segments of the project. PERT is used when the completion times for various project tasks are unknown or difficult to estimate. Statistical methods are then used to determine the longest, most likely, and shortest probable time for completing that task. CPM, on the other hand, is used in projects where the completion times for various tasks are reasonably well known.

To illustrate, a CPM network for the construction of a custom-designed automobile is shown in Figure 7.12. The completion of each task is shown by a separate path, and the time required to complete each task, in days, is indicated. The sequence of tasks that will require the longest time to complete is indicated by the thick

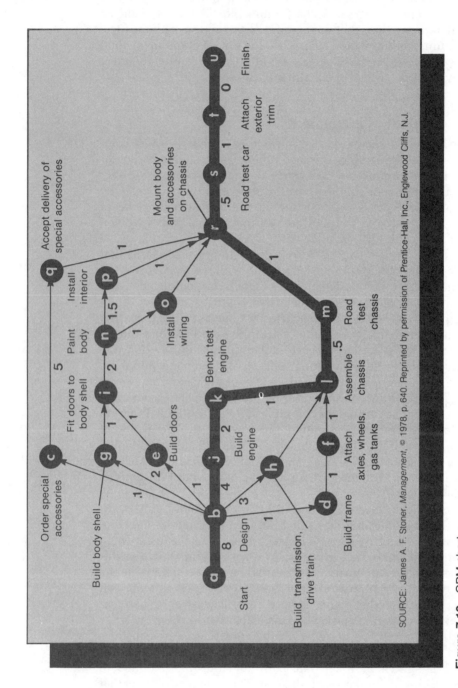

Figure 7.12 CPM chart

SOURCE: James A. F. Stoner, *Management*, © 1978, p. 640. Reprinted by permission of Prentice-Hall, Inc., Englewood Cliffs, N.J.

arrows, and is known as the **critical path**. Any delay in the critical path will mean that the project completion date will also be delayed. Delay in non-critical paths, however, may not cause a delay in the total time required to finish the project.

CPM and PERT networks are complex and difficult to establish. Before computers, they had to be drawn by hand and updated manually, which was extremely time-consuming and subject to errors in calculations. Since updating was such a difficult chore, it was done only infrequently. Eventually, mainframe computers were used for the planning and control of major projects where the expensive computer time could be justified. However, managers of smaller projects had difficulty accessing the expensive mainframe computers.

With the great computing power and memory of today's microcomputers, project management programs for micros are now available to help production managers schedule and coordinate projects of virtually any size. The project manager can readily develop complicated project networks. The computer prompts the manager for the required information — tasks, time for completion, sequence, resources to be used and their cost (see the task input form, Figure 7.13A). Once the information is entered in the computer, it establishes the network and calculates the critical path. Figure 7.13B shows the tasks and the time required for completion arranged in the form of a Gantt chart. Based on this chart a variety of reports can be prepared including Gantt, PERT, status, task, resource and cost reports.

Once it is established, the manager can quickly update the network schedule hourly, daily or weekly, as completion times and resource requirements change. Updated reports can also be prepared quickly for analysis or distribution, or both, to other managers.

COMPUTERS IN PRODUCTION

The first computer dedicated to business data processing applications was UNIVAC I and its first major use was in the U.S. Census Bureau. Even though business data processing was possible, the first-generation computers were still oriented primarily toward scientific applications. They were suitable for number crunching — having tremendous mathematical capabilities — but were not very efficient at business data processing, which requires the input of large volumes of data on which simple calculations are performed.

The importance of computers to business was nevertheless soon realized. The first major uses were in production planning and scheduling, and in inventory management. Today, computers are a major part of a firm's management information system: accounting, planning and budgeting are largely computerized. In production departments computers are an integral part of the entire system. They are

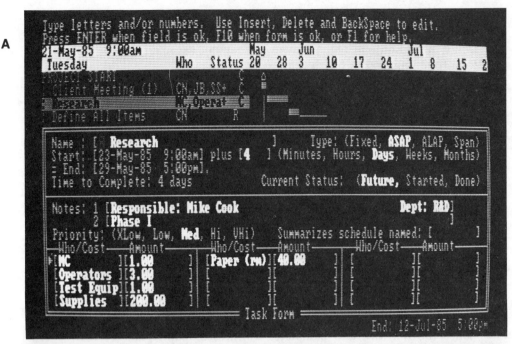

A

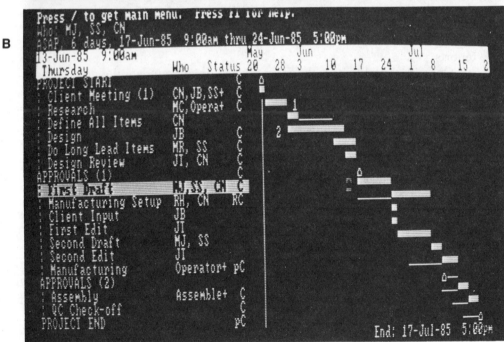

B

Picture A shows the input screen used by Timeline, a project management software package. The information from this section is used to develop the chart in picture B, which shows the time required to complete each portion of the project, as well as the total project. The program can also show a PERT chart on screen, which can also be printed out.

Figure 7.13 Establishing a project management schedule

used for production and distribution planning, MRP and inventory management, production scheduling, and the keeping of central data bases.

On the shop floor, many machines are already controlled by computers. There are computer-controlled stacker cranes, automatic materials-handling equipment, direct computer-controlled machine tools, automatic inspection and test equipment including computerized quality control. Due to high costs and lack of technology, only a few large corporations have integrated all of these machines and computers into a highly automated manufacturing facility. Nevertheless, giant strides are being made to make the automated factory more prolific.

Computers and Automation

Automating the production process has several advantages. One major advantage is the reduction in manufacturing costs because of the efficient use of machine tools and other capital equipment. For example, analysis of the manufacturing process indicates that the average product spends only 5% of its time in the machine; 95% of the time is spent moving between work stations and waiting for further processing. As a result, the cost of processing inventory rises and may be as high as 22% of annual sales. If the product spends less time in the actual manufacturing process, inventory carrying costs would be reduced and the final product would reach the customer in less time.[1]

Computers are also used in many areas other than manufacturing. For example, sawmills use computer-controlled saws, while miners underground use computers to analyze rock structures and robots to perform particularly dangerous operations. In retailing, computerized laser scanners read prices at checkouts and automatically update inventory levels. Some supermarkets use cash registers that call out the items individually as they are rung up. The completely automated gas station, prevalent in Europe and in the U.S., will probably appear in Canada as soon as provincial laws allow gas stations to operate without attendants.

CAD/CAM, Robots and the Automated Factory

What will the automated factory of the future look like and how will it work? The basic machine will be the **CNC (computerized numerical control)** machine tool. Hooked to a computer, this machine allows a manufacturer to make as many different types of components as there are computer programs that can tell the machine what to do. CNCs can be simple and perform only a few related activities, or highly complex and perform a variety of tasks such as drilling,

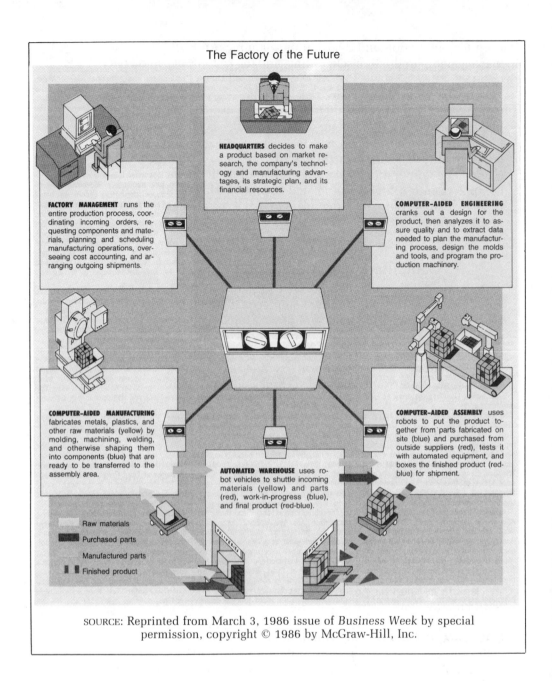

The Factory of the Future

HEADQUARTERS decides to make a product based on market research, the company's technology and manufacturing advantages, its strategic plan, and its financial resources.

FACTORY MANAGEMENT runs the entire production process, coordinating incoming orders, requesting components and materials, planning and scheduling manufacturing operations, overseeing cost accounting, and arranging outgoing shipments.

COMPUTER-AIDED ENGINEERING cranks out a design for the product, then analyzes it to assure quality and to extract data needed to plan the manufacturing process, design the molds and tools, and program the production machinery.

COMPUTER-AIDED MANUFACTURING fabricates metals, plastics, and other raw materials (yellow) by molding, machining, welding, and otherwise shaping them into components (blue) that are ready to be transferred to the assembly area.

COMPUTER-AIDED ASSEMBLY uses robots to put the product together from parts fabricated on site (blue) and purchased from outside suppliers (red), tests it with automated equipment, and boxes the finished product (red-blue) for shipment.

AUTOMATED WAREHOUSE uses robot vehicles to shuttle incoming materials (yellow) and parts (red), work-in-progress (blue), and final product (red-blue).

Raw materials
Purchased parts
Manufactured parts
Finished product

SOURCE: Reprinted from March 3, 1986 issue of *Business Week* by special permission, copyright © 1986 by McGraw-Hill, Inc.

boring, milling, tapping and threading without having to change its grip on the piece being machined.

The factory becomes further automated when smart robots and AGVs join the CNCs on the shop floor. **AGVs (automated guided vehicle)** are used primarily to ferry parts and components between work centres or fetch them from inventory. **Robots** would provide the arms and movement often required in manufacturing products. The movements can be precisely controlled by a computer so that processing time is reduced as much as possible.

The first industrial robot joined the production line at General Motors in 1961 and since then some 20 000 robots have been put to use in U.S. industrial plants. In Japan, more than 80 000 industrial

The Financial Post

Using CAD/CAM in machine design

robots are being used. The second generation robots that are now being used are equipped with sensors that allow them to pick up parts from a bin and adjust their grip to different objects.[2]

Automating the manufacturing process is one thing; developing the product design in the first place is another. This task was and often still is performed today by designers using drawing boards and developing the design on paper. However, more than a decade ago, CAD/CAM (a term used to indicate the relationship between computers and manufacturing) began. **CAD** stands for **computer-assisted design**; **CAM** refers to **computer-assisted manufacturing**, sometimes also called **CIM** (**computer-integrated manufacturing**).

CAD provides a technological advance that increases the productivity of designers and engineers dramatically. The designer makes sketches on a computer screen using either a light pen or a "mouse." The wiggly lines thus produced are straightened automatically by the computer. The software program contains hundreds of preprogrammed standard shapes that can be called up by the designer. If necessary, any of these shapes can be easily changed. A new rectangle can be drawn by simply specifying three corners, and a new circle can be drawn by specifying the centre and radius. Figure 7.14 shows a machine part designed with CAD.[3]

For example, an architect can design a house in three dimensions, then view it from the front as a simple line drawing with all lines exposed. Then the architect can remove view lines that would not be seen if the house were solid; he or she can shade the roof with crosshatching, mark off the chimney and make it smaller if required, color the garage door blue, rotate the house to view it from a corner, in perspective, add new windows, and even pull a drainpipe from a library of symbols and install it under the eaves.

CAD can be used to design many items, from auto parts to blue jeans to paper mills. Since one designer in front of a computer screen can do the work of 3.8 designers on the drawing boards, CAD will certainly have an impact, perhaps even spell the end for manual drafting skills in a few years.[4]

Canadian General Electric's Cobourg plant was the first in North America to use CAD/CAM to make molds for producers of plastic parts. The first step in the CAD/CAM mold-making process is to draw a design, — for instance, for a circuit breaker mold on the computer screen. This design is then fed into the computer operating the milling machines (computer numerical control) which in turn produce the mold, based on the computer's commands, at high speed. The operator simply loads the machine, monitors its operation and unloads it when the job is done. A similar process is used to control robots for welding or spray painting.[5]

What is still required before our automated factory is complete is a method of tying the design process, the computer, the robots,

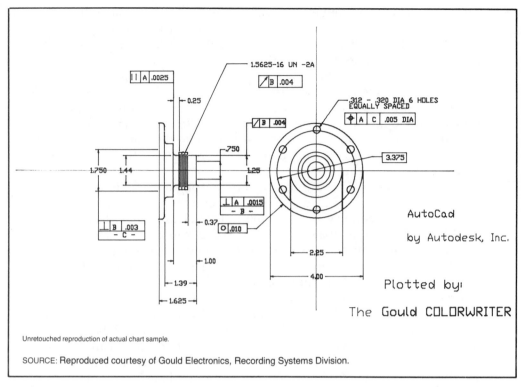

SOURCE: Reproduced courtesy of Gould Electronics, Recording Systems Division.

Figure 7.14 Machine part designed using an Autocad program and reproduced on a plotter

AGVs and CNCs together so that they can all communicate with one another. The resulting communication network is called a **manufacturing automation protocol**, or **MAP** for short. It is a set of rules that governs how, in an ideal world, machines of any make would communicate with one another. MAP was pioneered by General Motors and has since been embraced by firms producing industrial computers and communications, as well as major users of machine tools in other industries. More than 1000 manufacturers worldwide now adhere to the MAP standard.

The Problems of Automation

While computers and robots make production processes more efficient, they also alter many people's jobs and contribute to the unemployment problem. In addition, automation has made the marketplace more competitive — many firms must either automate or face bankruptcy.

The forest industry in B.C. faces severe financial difficulties because its outmoded plants and equipment are raising production costs and making its products uncompetitive. In response, one mill has introduced computers to measure logs electronically and direct saws to cut them to yield the greatest amount of lumber. The computer is more accurate than a human sawyer and reduces waste by 10%. In addition, the mill can be reprogrammed quickly to produce various types of lumber, depending on customers and their needs. The mill can produce as much with 350 employees as an unautomated mill employing 500. Some argue that automation has thus caused the loss of 150 jobs in the forest industry; others argue that 350 jobs are saved, because without increased productivity the entire mill would have to shut down.

The Canadian manufacturing industry is using more and more robots. According to a study done by the Ontario Ministry of Industry, Trade and Technology, some 1100 industrial robots had been installed in Canada by 1985. These robots were "reprogrammable, multifunctional manipulator[s] designed to move objects through variable programmed motions for the performance of a variety of tasks."[7] According to the study, 95% of the robots were used in Ontario, the automotive sector installing 70% of all units. All four major automobile manufacturers use robots: General Motors in its Ontario facilities alone is expected to use 2300 robots by 1991. Robots can significantly increase productivity for automotive manufacturers. Japanese automakers using many robots can produce a car in about 57 hours as compared to an average of 100 hours in North America. Of course, robots will affect employment. It is estimated that manufacturing jobs in Canada will become as rare as farming jobs. They will drop from employing 17% of the work force to less than 10% within a decade.[8]

There are no easy solutions to the automation dilemma. Those displaced from their jobs require retraining. It is not likely that they will be employed in building robots, since Canada imports most industrial robots from Japan and other countries. Even in those countries, there are indications that even robot production will be automated.

How will automation affect managers and professionals? The computer is not likely to replace managers in the near future. Computers are not capable of making the intuitive judgments that managers often must make; instead, they are valuable tools managers can use to evaluate data and make better decisions. Because computers reduce the drudgery of many tasks, they may help managers become more creative as well as more productive.

Professionals such as lawyers, accountants and doctors soon will all have to use computers. Lawyers are already using on-line commercial data base information services to increase their productivity in researching cases. Doctors will resort to using the computer as a diagnostic tool. By feeding in data about a patient's symptoms, the computer can quickly search its data base for health problems related to those symptoms. Architects and draftspeople already use computer-aided drafting — drawings are produced by a computer at high speed and true accuracy. If changes are required the computer does the recalculations and reproduces the new plan quickly. Unless these professionals and business managers in particular learn to use the computer, they could seriously inhibit their future possibilities for advancement and their incomes.

Microcomputers for the Operations Manager

Microcomputers are particularly useful to managers in the operations division. Besides **budgeting**, **word processing** and the storing of information in **data bases**, operations managers are involved in a considerable amount of **mathematical data analysis** in forecasting demand and production requirements, quality control, inventory management simulations, waiting line theory, and scheduling, to name only a few. The microcomputer is also essential in developing bids for projects, and for performing **break-even analysis** to indicate if and when a new product or project will be profitable. Business software is becoming much more sophisticated; what once required mainframe computers can now in most instances be handled by powerful microcomputers.

For example, a microcomputer and a spreadsheet program can be used in quality control. A manager can develop a **spreadsheet quality control template** and enter data from periodic measurements of samples of the product into one section of the template (see Figure 7.15). Then with a few keystrokes the manager can activate the graphics portion of the spreadsheet, which will show a statistical control chart with the upper and lower control limits. All of the sample measurements are plotted on the chart. If they fall within the upper and lower control limits, the production process is in control and no adjustments to the machinery is required.

For more sophisticated quality control, the computer can be connected to calipers that automatically measure the diameter of a steel rod as it comes from the milling machine. This measurement is compared to the data in the computer's memory and the computer program keeps track of all individual measurements and provides printouts and graphics showing how the particular process is operating. The quality control manager has a continuous stream of information about the product's quality. When deviations from specific standards become evident, the computer is instructed to stop the process for adjustment. In some instances the computer performs this adjustment automatically.

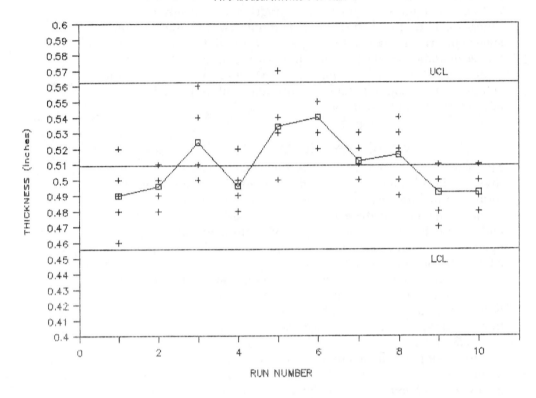

Figure 7.15 Statistical control chart created with a spreadsheet program showing upper and lower statistical control limits.

As discussed earlier, another major application of the microcomputer is in **planning and scheduling of major projects**. Time is critical in the building of a large project and there are often penalties if particular steps are not completed on time. A PERT or CPM network can help managers keep close control over time and resources.

COMPUTERS AND HOW THEY WORK

Computers have been used in business and science for several decades. They are useful because they perform complicated tasks in a short time. To understand how computers work and how they are used, it is helpful to examine their historical development.

History of Computers

The first electronic calculator, **ENIAC (Electronic Numerical Integrator And Calculator)** was developed in 1946 at the University of Pennsylvania by J.P. Eckert and John Mauchly. ENIAC could perform a calculation in three-thousandths of a second, compared with the Mark I developed two years earlier, which required three seconds for the same calculation. ENIAC, however, had no memory and had to be instructed using a series of switches. The further development of computers can be broken down into generations. In each generation, there were significant technological developments in size, reliability, memory availability and computational power.

IBM Corporation

ENIAC, developed in 1946, was the first electronic calculator

First-Generation Computers (1951–1958)

First-generation computers were extremely large and had poor reliability. Vacuum tubes used in the computers generated tremendous heat and were prone to failure. Computer rooms had to be air-conditioned to eliminate the heat so that systems would operate properly. Data and instructions were entered into the computer using punched cards. Holes in the cards represented a code for the various numbers, letters and special characters used in data processing. A card reader read the cards and translated the data into machine language that the computer could understand. The data was stored on magnetic drums which rotated at high speeds below read/write heads that interpreted the magnetized spots on the drum. The data was manipulated according to a program or set of instructions. The results of the operation were punched on blank cards which could be read by other machines and printed out.

First generation computers were used primarily for scientific applications that required tremendous mathematical calculation capability. But when **UNIVAC I** was developed by the same people who developed ENIAC, businesspeople became aware for the first time that computers could be used for data processing — the manipulation of raw data into meaningful business information. Business data processing requires large volumes of data input and output, but relatively simple calculations.

However, communicating with the computer was still a major problem. **Program instructions** had to be coded using the **binary system** — a series of 1's and 0's which is the only language computers understand. This coding process was cumbersome, tedious and time-consuming. To remedy the problem, symbolic languages were developed that allowed programmers to write instructions in mnemonics (memory aids) rather than long strings of 1's and 0's. A program consisted of a series of mnemonics which the computer could translate into its own binary language, also known as **machine language**.

Second-Generation Computers (1959–1964)

In second-generation computers, transistors replaced vacuum tubes. Since transistors are smaller and generate less heat than vacuum tubes, second generation computers were smaller, more reliable, processed data more quickly and had an increased storage capacity.

Punched cards were still used to enter information into the computer, but information was now stored on magnetic tape. Once on tape, programs and data could be loaded into the computer's memory more quickly than with punched cards. Programming techniques were also refined and new **"higher level" languages**, which resembled English more than symbolic languages did, were developed. **FORTRAN (FORmula TRANslator)** was developed in the mid-1950s by IBM, and FORTRAN IV became a standard still used today for scientific applications. However, FORTRAN was not suitable for processing large volumes of business transactions. Thus a new language, **COBOL (COmmon Business Oriented Language)** was developed in the early 1960s.

Third-Generation Computers (1965–1971)

In third-generation computers, transistors were replaced by **integrated circuits (ICs)**. Hundreds of electronic components could be put on a small silicon chip less than two millimetres square. Thus, computers were again made smaller, more reliable and with increased processing speed.

The first third-generation computers were the IBM System/360 **mainframe computers**. This computer series was designed to provide all types of data processing and consisted of six different computers, each offering different main storage capacities. Competitors such as RCA, Honeywell, Univac and Burroughs soon developed similar models.

Along with the third-generation computers came two innovations: the minicomputer and the remote terminal. **Minicomputers** were smaller and less expensive than mainframe computers and had relatively sophisticated data processing capabilities. They filled the needs of many small businesses while large companies extended their data processing capabilities by adding minicomputers to branch offices and tying them in to the central computer system. The **remote terminal** — a keyboard and screen — allowed users from various locations to connect to the central computer and communicate with it. Users were also able to run separate programs simultaneously, a process known as **time-sharing**. Because the computer processes data so quickly, it appears to users that they have exclusive access to the central processor. Terminals are on-line and results are available instantaneously.

The Fourth Generation (1972–present)

The fourth generation, although not as clearly definable as the first three, began in 1972 when electronic components were further miniaturized through **large-scale integrated circuits (LSI)**. Thousands of transistors could be placed on a single silicon chip, which replaced magnetic cores as the primary storage medium inside computers. Processing speed was significantly increased.

LSI made possible the development of **microprocessors** — the heart of a computer, which performs all calculations and data manipulation. With microprocessors, microcomputers could be used in homes and businesses as well as in microwave ovens, automobiles, and thermostats, for example.

The Fifth Generation

Fifth generation computers are presently being developed. There is a race between the U.S. and Japan to develop an intelligent computer that will be able to converse with humans in natural language and understand speech and pictures. Computers with **artificial intelligence** will be able to learn, associate, and make inferences and decisions, coming closer to the human ability to reason.

How Computers Work

Most microcomputers are housed in a rectangular metal box with one or two disk drives accessible from the front, a small panel of lights and, on some, a reset switch. The monitor, or CRT screen, usually sits on top of the computer and a keyboard is used to input data and instructions. If you were to open the box you would see

Computer software includes operating systems and application programs

the power supply in one corner, the drives in another corner, and a number of vertical "boards" plugged into a mother board lying across the bottom of the box. These so-called boards actually contain circuits and computer chips that perform a wide variety of computer functions.

Computer Hardware and Software
The hardware of a computer consists of the physical elements and its related parts. These elements include the keyboard, monitor, disk drives, printer and the metal box that houses the central processing unit (CPU) and internal memory. The software includes application programs and operating systems that tell the computer what to do.

Bringing the Computer to Life
Computer hardware cannot do much by itself. What makes a computer function and become useful to us is the software that goes along with it. To make the hardware come to life we need an operating system. It consists of a series of programs that provide an

IBM Corporation

Software packages are programs; they perform particular tasks, such as word processing, spreadsheet analysis and accounting functions

interface between the hardware and the operator. When you first turn the computer on, a small program is loaded from one of the chips in the computer called a prom (programmable read only memory). Its sole purpose is to check the hardware to make sure everything is functioning and then go to the diskette in Drive A and look for the "boot" sector on the first track of the diskette, which must be previously inserted. The boot sector contains information about the other operating systems programs and where they are located on the disk. These are then read into the computer's memory and executed.

Now the stage is set for us to use the computer. When the operating system is loaded and ready to perform for us, we see the system prompt (Figure 7.16), a little open-ended triangle on the left side of the screen. We can now either do some file management, such as copying files from one diskette to another, erasing files from the diskette, or renaming files, or we can go ahead and type the name of a program which the operating system will locate for us on the disk and load into memory. This is the application program. If we load a word processing program, for example, we can type letters or reports; with a spreadsheet program we can develop budgets and have the program perform a variety of calculations. A data-base program is used to enter information that we want to keep track of and recall at a later date.

Computers are very effective in helping us organize raw data. A series of temperatures, for example, may be meaningless until the figures are sorted showing highs and lows for particular months and how they compare to previous years. The sorted or processed data then become meaningful information that can be used in making decisions.

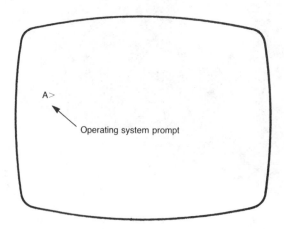

Figure 7.16 System prompt

Elements of a Computer

To use a computer we require a method of entering data, or an input device. The most common input device today is a keyboard, but other input devices include disk drives, scanners, light pens, digitizers, punched paper tape, or magnetic tape. The input device converts the data into a form the computer understands. Figure 7.17 shows the various input and output devices. Data typed on the keyboard shows up on the screen of the monitor as it enters the computer memory, where it is either processed immediately or stored for later processing. Once processed, the data must be routed to an output device — a printer, for example, or a storage unit such as magnetic tape or a disk drive. The latter two output devices allow the information to be stored for later use.

A computer operates according to the instructions contained in a program. A simple BASIC program that multiplies two numbers together is shown in Figure 7.18. Today software programs are complex, sometimes containing millions of lines of program instructions.

Technician assembles the elements of a computer

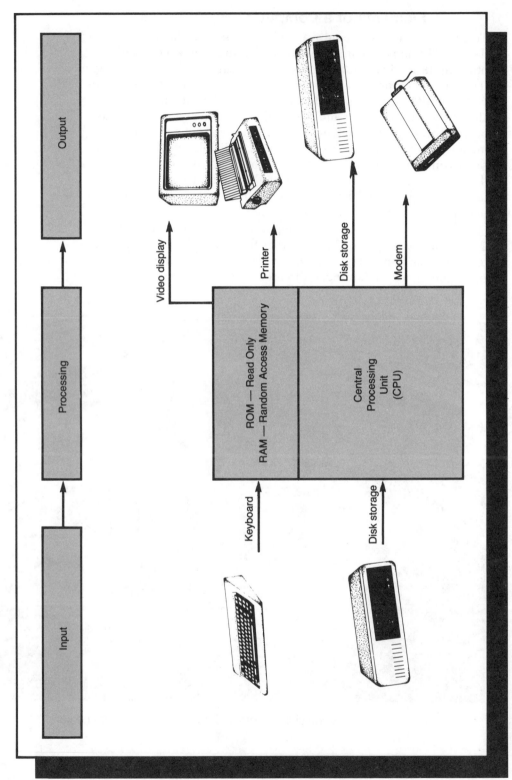

Figure 7.17 How computer hardware is related to the input-processing-output cycle

Regardless of how complicated the program is, the entire program or parts of it must be read into the computer's memory so that it can be accessed by the **central processing unit (CPU)**, as shown in Figure 7.19. The CPU consists of three parts: the control unit, the arithmetic/logic unit, and the primary storage unit, also called the registers. All three components are connected by what is called a bus, so that data bits can be shuttled to and from the components and the computer's main memory very quickly.

The **control unit** maintains order and controls the activity of the CPU. It interprets the instructions of a program in storage and issues commands to execute them. The control unit also communicates with the input device, such as a terminal, and with the output device, such as a printer or disk drive. The control unit also gives commands to send data into storage and to retrieve it.

The **arithmetic logic unit (ALU)** performs arithmetic computations and logical operations. It might, for example, compare two customer account numbers to determine which is less and then put them into a particular order. Or the computer program might specify that two pieces of data be compared to each other and, if they are the same, the computer is instructed to perform a particular command. Most internal processing of data involves calculations and/or comparisons.

The **registers** provide a temporary storage location within the CPU. They accept, and transfer data and instructions that will be used very shortly for further processing. When this data has been processed it is sent to main memory for later use. For example, a program instruction that is to be executed must be retrieved from

```
10 REM     THIS PROGRAM PRINTS OUT THE RESULTS OF          ⌉ Program
20 REM     A MULTIPLICATION OF 10 AND 20
30 PRINT
40 LET X = 10
50 LET Y = 20
60 LET Z = X*Y
70 PRINT "THE PRODUCT OF "; X; " TIMES "; Y; " = "; Z
80 PRINT "THIS IS THE END"
90 END

RUN                                                        ⌟

THE PRODUCT OF 10 TIMES 20 = 200                           ⌉ Printed
THIS IS THE END                                            ⌟ Output
```

Figure 7.18 A BASIC program and its printed output

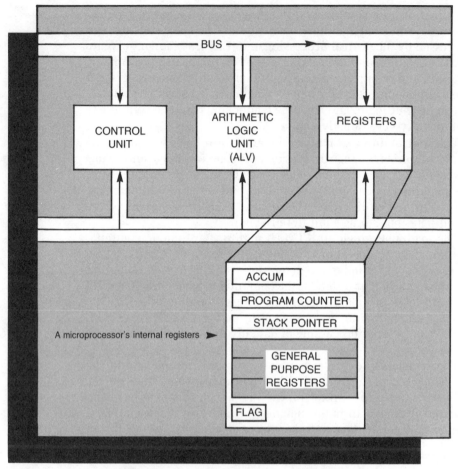

Figure 7.19 A microprocessor, its internal structure, and how the three components are connected

main memory and placed in a register. The control unit then interprets the instruction and fetches the data required to carry out the requested operation. The data is then placed in general purpose registers that can be accessed by the ALU.

In general, the more registers available for processing, and the greater the capacity of the registers to hold data, the greater the processing power of the microcomputer. Some personal computers have microprocessors that have a capacity to hold only 8 bits of data at a time. Others can hold 16 bits and the newer ones have 32 bit registers. These latter microprocessors can process data in chunks four times as large as 8-bit processors, making operation considerably faster.

Communicating with the Computer

A computer can only understand whether or not a current is flowing in its circuits. We depict these two states by using a 1 when the current is flowing and a 0 when it is not. This system is known as **binary representation**. The binary number system (base 2) is used in the same way as the decimal system, which is built on the base of 10. Instead of using numbers between 0 and 9, however, we can use only 0 and 1. Whatever we want to communicate to the computer has to be coded using these two numbers. Since binary representation is difficult for us to read, we use a shorter form called **hexadecimal notation** (base 16). Binary, decimal and hexadecimal notations are shown in Figure 7.20.

Each digit position in a binary number is called a **bit**. Since we are using binary notation to represent numbers, letters and special characters, we have to have enough positions to be able to represent them all. With an 8-bit code — known as **Extended Binary Coded Decimal Interchange Code (EBCDIC)** — we can represent upper and lower case letters, numbers and special characters such as percents, dollar signs and quotation marks (see Figure 7.21).

Binary 8	4	2	1	Hexadecimal	Decimal
0	0	0	0	0	0
0	0	0	1	1	1
0	0	1	0	2	2
0	0	1	1	3	3
0	1	0	0	4	4
0	1	0	1	5	5
0	1	1	0	6	6
0	1	1	1	7	7
1	0	0	0	8	8
1	0	0	1	9	9
1	0	1	0	A	10
1	0	1	1	B	11
1	1	0	0	C	12
1	1	0	1	D	13
1	1	1	0	E	14
1	1	1	1	F	15

Figure 7.20   The binary, hexadecimal and decimal number systems

Character	ASCII Bit Configuration	EBCDIC Bit Configuration	
A	1000001	1100	0001
B	1000010	1100	0010
C	1000011	1100	0011
D	1000100	1100	0100
E	1000101	1100	0101
F	1000110	1100	0110
G	1000111	1100	0111
H	1001000	1100	1000
I	1001001	1100	1001
J	1001010	1101	0001
K	1001011	1101	0010
L	1001100	1101	0011
M	1001101	1101	0100
N	1001110	1101	0101
O	1001111	1101	0110
P	1010000	1101	0111
Q	1010001	1101	1000
R	1010010	1101	1001

Figure 7.21   ASCII and EBCDIC code for representing characters and numbers

In an attempt to develop a standard code for all computers, a 7-bit code — **American Standard Code for Information Interchange (ASCII)** — was developed with the cooperation of several computer manufacturers. However, since most computers accept 8-bit rather than 7-bit patterns, an 8-bit version of ASCII was created. ASCII and EBCDIC are similar except for the bit patterns used to represent certain characters. Figure 7.21 compares the bit patterns of the two codes.

The smallest unit of data that is useful to us is a character, and since 8-bits are sufficient to represent any letter, number or special character we may need, it is logical to operate on data in 8-bit groupings. An 8-bit grouping of data is known as a **byte**. The symbol 'K' represents 1024 bytes. Thus an 8-bit computer with 65536 8-bit storage areas in its main memory is commonly called a 64 K computer.

The Program
A **program** is a set of instructions written in a computer language that tells the computer what to do (see Figure 7.18). The **programmer**

is the specialist who develops the application program. He or she must understand the task the computer is to accomplish, then break the task down into its component parts. Programmers develop **flowcharts** to provide a clear, visual framework of all the steps that the computer must perform. The various symbols on the flowchart represent the type of processing that is performed by the program (see Figure 7.22).

Programming Languages
Once the flowchart has been developed, the programmer begins to program or code instructions according to the flowchart using the

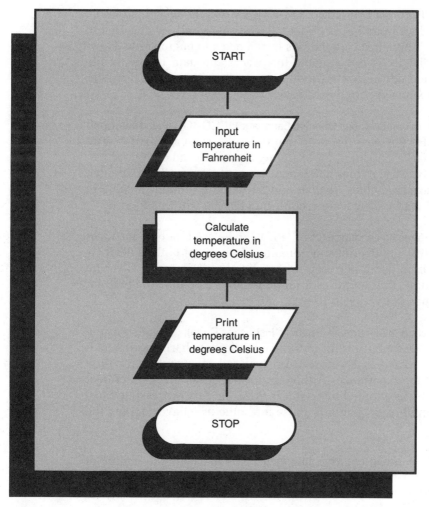

Figure 7.22 A simple flowchart showing major computer operations

most suitable computer languages. The following are a few of the common languages developed for computers. Each language has its advantages and disadvantages.

ASSEMBLY LANGUAGE: It is difficult to develop a complex application program in binary language using 1's and 0's. Assembly language uses **mnemonics** which are English-like abbreviations for various computer commands. The computer translates the mnemonics into binary or machine language and then stores the translated program. The computer can then execute instructions quickly at any given time. Speed is the primary consideration in assembly language programming.

FORTRAN (FORmula TRANslator): **FORTRAN** was the first "high level" language, developed in the mid-1950s. It is especially well suited to complex arithmetical calculations in science and engineering. However, FORTRAN is not suitable for processing data involving file maintenance, editing or the production of documents and is therefore not used extensively by businesses.

COBOL (COmmon Business Oriented Language): **COBOL** was developed primarily for business use — to maintain files such as payrolls or to compile market research, for example. It can be used on almost any computer because it does not depend on a particular CPU. Although the language resembles English and is therefore understandable to the casual reader, this feature contributes to its wordiness.

PL/1: (Programming Language One): PL/1 can be used for both business and scientific applications. It combines features of both FORTRAN and COBOL in that it performs arithmetic calculations as well as file manipulation. PL/1 requires a large memory for storage, however, and thus has not yet been used on microcomputers.

BASIC (Beginner's All-purpose Symbolic Instruction Code): BASIC was developed at Dartmouth College for use with time-sharing systems. It is relatively easy to learn and can be used by people with little programming experience. Although developed as an instructional language it was adopted by business firms for data processing. Most microcomputers, particularly those for home use, have adopted the language.

BASIC is an interactive language, which means the computer prompts the user for input and responds directly to each instruction. Most BASIC programs therefore need an **interpreter** — a program that translates one instruction after another of the application program into machine language and then executes the instruction. With BASIC, programs can be tested easily and any errors can be corrected quickly. However, BASIC is many times slower than a compiled program in which a compiler translates all BASIC instructions of the program into machine language and stores them on disk as a machine language program. When needed, the program can be read from disk into the computer's memory and, because it is in machine language, it is executed quickly, since the slow interpretation stage is eliminated.

IBM Corporation

Personal computers were introduced in the fourth generation of computer development

Software Packages

Whatever language is used, the ultimate result is a **software package** — a program or series of programs that performs a particular task such as word processing, spreadsheet analysis, data-base management and accounting functions. There are, however, thousands of programs available for different computers, some that perform highly specialized tasks. Many software packages are similar in their function, but each may have a variety of different features.

To purchase the appropriate software package for your business or for private use, you should first clearly establish your needs. In addition, you should be sure you have a clearly written reference manual and instructions on how to use the program. Other important considerations are after-sale service, program customization and updates when new features are developed or errors corrected. For example, if you are buying a U.S. payroll or tax package, will the supplier customize it for use in Canada? Or if there are errors in the program, can you call the developer for help to solve the problem? Finally, since software is undergoing such rapid change, new features are constantly added to existing programs. Will the company advise you when the new programs are available and can you purchase the update for a reduced price?

NOTES

1. Canada. CAD/CAM Technology Advancement Council, *Strategy for Survival: The Canadian CAD/CAM Option.* Ottawa: Technology Branch, Department of Industry, Trade and Commerce, September 1980, pp. 1.4–1.9.
2. "Factory of the Future," *The Economist, A Survey,* May 30, 1987.
3. *Ibid.*
4. Daniel Stoffman, "Arm in Arm: The alliance of workers, robots and CAD/CAM," *Canadian Business,* p. 40.
5. *Ibid.*
6. *Ibid.*
7. Renate Lerch, "Robotmakers face cooler times for hot technology of early '80s." *The Financial Post, Special Report,* September 7, 1987. p. C8.
8. *Ibid.*

CHAPTER SUMMARY

The material well-being of many Canadians is largely a result of high productivity through mass production. Mass production of goods is made possible through mechanization, the assembly line, standardization and automation.

Production management is faced with two major types of decisions: production system design and operating production decisions. Production system design decisions include product planning and design, capacity planning, plant location and layout, and work system design. These long-term decisions always involve top management: they are major decisions and, once made, are difficult and costly to change. Marketing and production, particularly the research and development department, work closely together to determine what to produce, on the basis of customer demand. The product determines to a large extent the type of manufacturing process to use. Determining plant capacity is a critical decision because it affects operating costs and ultimately the price of the final product. Plant location requires careful analysis of the firm's markets, the availability of labour, energy and transportation, proximity to raw materials, as well as community and site factors. The type of production operation will also determine plant layout and machines and work system design.

The major operating production decisions are medium- and short-range production planning, distribution planning, inventory management, aggregate planning, materials requirement planning, and production scheduling. Demand forecasting provides production management with information for planning production requirements for the coming year. Based on this demand forecast, inventory requirements and distribution plans for finished goods are made. This in turn provides information for aggregate production plans to ensure that sufficient raw materials and adequate plant capacity, labour and machinery will be available for production. The aggregate plan is the basis for developing the master schedule for material requirements planning, as well as daily production scheduling.

Since the production department is the major purchaser of raw materials and may have large inventories of semi-finished and finished products, the purchasing and inventory functions are particularly important. The purchasing department must buy the right material and components at the right price for fabrication or assembly. This occasionally involves a decision as to whether to make a component part or buy it. Inventory management must ensure that sufficient raw materials and finished goods are available at all times, while minimizing the cost of carrying the inventory and ordering. To keep track of inventory and orders placed, an inventory control system is required. The more sophisticated production facilities have a highly computerized inventory management system (MRP) to ensure that raw materials, parts and components are available for production as required. To reduce inventory carrying costs, just-in-time inventory systems are increasingly being used.

Production scheduling is the attempt to coordinate labour, materials, and machinery for maximum production efficiency. Production scheduling is critical because it makes the optimal use of machines and equipment and ensures that customers receive orders on time. A Gantt chart can be used to organize and clarify actual or intended use of resources over a period of time and can be used for loading and scheduling. A load chart shows the loading and idle times of a group of machines. It can show that a particular machine or work centre is either available or in use on a particular day or time. A schedule chart is often used to monitor progress of jobs. The charts indicate which jobs are on schedule and which are behind or ahead.

Quality control is another major concern for production management. Waste due to the production of defective products, extensive after-sales repair costs, and a loss of reputation which can hurt product sales, can be reduced through quality control. Another critical function is preventive maintenance — the periodic inspection and replacement of parts in crucial machines to prevent machine breakdown and avoid costly delays in normal production.

Computers have automated many functions in the manufacturing firm. CAD (computer-assisted design) makes the design process more efficient while CAM (computer-assisted manufacturing) uses computers to control machines previously controlled by people. Robots are also increasingly being used on production lines. In addition to automating the production process, computers are used to check quality control, maintain inventory, and reorder automatically when necessary. Managers use microcomputers to aid in budgeting, data management and break-even analysis. Computers also figure prominently in project management — the planning and controlling of large projects. Project management software for microcomputers can handle large projects, allowing easy updating if there is a change in task completion time or in resources used, and allows the manager to prepare a large variety of reports for analysis.

Understanding how they function can reduce fear of computers in some people, and may persuade others to use computers to increase efficiency. A computer uses the instructions given in a program to process data — organize, categorize, compare — so that it becomes meaningful information. Computers can be programmed in a variety of languages, with some languages more suitable to specific tasks than others.

Microcomputers are very common in offices today and thousands of software packages (programs) are available, including word processing, spreadsheet, data base, graphics, statistics, project management, and communications, to mention only a few categories. Managers will have to become knowledgeable about computers: they will be an indispensable tool for decision-making and data analysis.

KEY TERMS

Production

Service business

Mass production

Economy of scale

Assembly line

Mechanization

Standardization

Automation

Custom production

Job shops

Production process

Analytic process

Extraction

Synthetic process

Fabrication

Assembly

Industrial parks

Plant layout

Product layout

Process layout

General-purpose machine

Special-purpose machine

Work systems design

Job design

Methods analysis

Motion study

Time study

Work measurement

Demand forecasting

Inventory management

Reorder point

Lead time

Economic order quantity

Inventory carrying costs

Ordering costs

Safety stock

Perpetual inventory control

Universal product code

Distribution planning

Aggregate planning

Master schedule

Material requirements planning

Bill of materials

Inventory records file

Just-in-time inventory system (JIT)

Scheduling

Loading

Gantt chart

Sequencing

Purchasing

Value analysis

Make or buy

Quality control

Preventive maintenance

Project management

Project schedule or network

PERT and CPM

Critical path

CAD/CAM

Robots

Manufacturing automation protocol

Computer

Input device

Output device

Central processing unit

Arithmetic/logic unit

Program

Flowchart

Bit

Byte

ASCII and EBCDIC codes

Machine language

Assembly language

Mnemonics

Application software

REVIEW QUESTIONS

1. How do service businesses differ from manufacturing businesses?
2. How can mass production contribute to an increase in the standard of living?
3. Briefly define mass production, mechanization, standardization and automation.
4. Why is capacity planning a critical decision in the design of production systems?
5. What are some of the reasons for relocating a plant? What are the major factors to be considered in plant location?
6. Distinguish between product and process layout.
7. What is work system design? How might motion study be used in job design?
8. Why is demand forecasting important for a manufacturer? How could a manufacturer react to uncertain demand?
9. Distinguish between hand-to-mouth buying and forward buying. What are the advantages and disadvantages of each?
10. What is perpetual inventory control? What role can a computer play in this system?
11. What are the consequences of carrying too much or too little inventory? Explain why the economic order quantity is the order size that will minimize the sum of the annual costs of holding inventory and the annual costs of ordering inventory.
12. When is distribution planning an important consideration for manufacturing companies?
13. What is aggregate planning? What four major strategies can the production manager use to meet the requirements of the aggregate plan?
14. What is material requirements planning? What information is required by MRP?
15. Explain why scheduling can be viewed as both a planning function and a control function? Why is scheduling for high-volume systems relatively easy compared to the job shop?
16. Discuss the difference between loading and sequencing?
17. What is the significance of the purchasing function in a manufacturing firm?
18. Explain how a make-or-buy decision can resemble a plant location decision.
19. Why is quality control necessary? What are the factors to be balanced in practising quality control?
20. Explain how the process of finding an optimum level of preventive maintenance resembles determining optimum quality control.

21. What is project management? How is a project schedule created? How can a computer help managers both in creating a project schedule and in updating it as the project advances?

22. How does CAD relate to CAM? How are computers used in automating the manufacturing process? What are its implications for unemployment and productivity?

23. What are the major elements of a computer? Describe briefly how computers process raw data.

24. How does the computer hardware interact with the software? What is an operating system used for? What is an application program and how does it interact with the operating system?

DISCUSSION QUESTIONS

1. How will continued automation affect production management?

2. Name five factories located in close proximity to your community. Identify and explain the factors likely to have led to the location of each.

3. If technological change, for example, CAD/CAM, can make production more efficient and thereby raise our standard of living, why are labour unions generally opposed to such change, particularly automation?

4. Discuss the following statement. "A firm should make sure that its products are of the highest quality possible."

CASE 7-1 Planning for Production — Kwickie Kar Klean

Tim Jones, owner-manager of Kwickie Kar Klean, sat in his office mulling over the results of his first year's operations. Before entering the automatic car wash business, Tim had investigated carefully the claims of several manufacturers of automatic car wash equipment and found considerable variation in what was considered the optimum amount of automatic equipment necessary for a successful business. One manufacturer suggested an installation costing over $200 000 exclusive of land and buildings, and pointed out that the savings in labour would soon pay for the equipment. At the other extreme, there was a unit for $56 000 but it required almost twice as much labour on high volume days. Tim chose the latter course; however, the equipment was designed to permit adding fully automatic units later.

He considered himself fortunate in being able to rent a building for $1400 a month on a busy through street in the centre of a large residential area. Thus, his only capital outlay was for equipment capable of washing at least 600 cars a week. A summary statement of average monthly expenses for Kwickie Kar Klean during its first year of operations appears below.

Tim regarded most of these expenses as fixed since there was little he could do to control the first five items. Therefore, he decided to direct his attention to controlling the amount of money spent for labour and improving output per man-hour.

Expense	Average per month
Heat, light and power	$ 550
Water	420
Supplies (towels, detergents etc.)	250
Depreciation and repairs	500
Building and land rent	1400
Labour	7280
Total expenses	**$10 440**

The conveyor that pulls the cars through the washing process is 27 metres long. At the front of this line there is a portable vacuum cleaner used in cleaning the interior of the car. Next, there is a steam cleaning unit used to steam the wheels, bumpers and grill; and following this is the mitting area where one man on each side washes the entire car with detergent as it is pulled through the conveyor. The next three operations are automatic; a side and top brush unit (including automatic pre-rinse) washes the top and sides of the car; an automatic rinsing unit removes detergent and loosened dirt left by the washing unit; a drying unit completes the automatic process. The car is moved forward to the front of the building to be wiped and finished manually.

Tim carefully studied the time required for each operation and concluded that the bottleneck was at the end of the line where the cars are manually wiped. He discovered that two workers could wipe one car in three minutes and concluded that his total daily production should be 20 cars per hour, or a total of 200 cars per day since the auto laundry remained open ten hours each day. However, such was not the case because customers did not appear on a regular schedule. He decided to record the total number of cars washed during a 10-hour day for varying crew sizes. Here is a summary of the production records:

Workers	Cars washed		Workers	Cars washed
3	90			
4	120		8	230
5	155		10	270
6	180		12	350

When using three workers, one worker at the front of the line operated the vacuum cleaner and the steam cleaner, while the other two men worked in the mitting area, one on each side of the car. Then, as the car moved through the automatic units of the line — the side and top brush, the rinsing unit and the drying station — the two mitters moved to the end of the line and served as wipers after Tim drove the car from the conveyor to the front of the building. When the crew consisted of four men, the additional man was placed at the end of the line to help the mitters in wiping the car. The addition of a fifth man meant that there was still one man at the front of the line, two mitters now remaining in the mitting area, and two men functioning solely as wipers. Though this arrangement of manning yielded the highest average per man for a 10-hour day, it was found that there were times during the day, for example, during the lunch period, when the effective crew was actually four men. Also, if one of the men was absent, the result was a definite undermanning, and if it was a good day for business, Tim felt that he lost customers when they drove by and saw a line of cars waiting to be washed. Consequently, he decided that for the weekdays, Monday through Friday, he would man the crew regularly with six men, which almost always assured him of an effective crew of five, thus allowing him to handle peak periods on these days with ease. With a crew of six, one man vacuumed, one operated the steam cleaner, two were in the mitting area and two wiped.

During the first year Kwickie Kar Klean washed, on the average, 500 cars a week, but the number washed was not distributed evenly throughout the six working days. Usually by Friday evening only 40 to 60% of the week's total had been completed, which meant that in order to reach the weekly average of 500, it was necessary sometimes to wash as many as 350 cars on Saturday. The addition of two more wipers, making eight, could handle 250 cars, but this was not enough for the busy days. And increasing the total crew to 10 men, with six of them wiping, enabled Tim to turn out only 20 more cars per man in a 10-hour day. After analyzing the production of a 10-man crew, Tim decided that the cars were not being prepared fast enough for the conveyor line, so he decided to put two men on the vacuum cleaning, two on the steam cleaning, and of course, two in the mitting area. These six on the front of the line seemed to be able to keep the six wipers supplied with cars even during rush periods.

SOURCE: Henry L. Sisk, *Management and Organization* 2nd ed. (Cincinnati, Ohio: South-Western Publishing Co., 1973). Reprinted by permission.

QUESTIONS

1. Explain why a five-person crew is the optimum crew size according to Tim's figures. Why did Tim decide to have a six-person crew during weekdays?

2. If the price charged for washing a car is $6.00, how many cars must be washed during a month in order for Kwickie Kar Klean to break even (revenues = expenses)?

3. There were many weeks during the year when the total output, Monday through Friday, was 300 cars with the standard crew of six persons. It is possible for these six persons to wash approximately 200 cars on Saturday, thus bringing the weekly total to 500. Yet, Tim called in six additional persons on Saturday to raise the possible output to 350, or 650 for the week. How much is it costing Tim to be prepared for the additional 150 cars? Would you recommend that this practice be continued? Why?

4. Tim is considering making his car wash fully automatic. The cost of the new equipment is $200 000 less the cost of the original equipment. In addition there is an installation charge, which amounts to $20 000. The purchase of new equipment would eliminate four workers — the two in the mitting area and the two in the steam cleaning area. Perform the necessary calculations to show whether or not he should go ahead with the purchase of this equipment, assuming that he has to have a payback period of less than five years. Briefly discuss the other costs he has to take into account before making his final decision. What costs or problems might this decision eliminate or help to decrease, if any? What might be the impact of fully automatic equipment on his business?

CASE 7-2 Pacific Boat Works

Pacific Boat Works was started in 1958 on the Fraser River south of New Westminster, B.C., to manufacture small aluminum boats for large fishing vessels. By 1979 its major business was to build seiners and gillnetters, boats up to 30 metres in length.

The plant and offices are housed in a steel shed, and company personnel numbers approximately 40 people, depending on the amount of work to be done. Orders for the large boats are handled by Jack Gilbert, the owner and president, together with a marine engineer, who is a major shareholder. After the price and plans for a new boat have been finalized with the customer, the supervisor orders materials and schedules production.

The supervisor has been with the company since the beginning and owns about 10% of the shares in the company. He is 56 years old, and prides himself in being from the old management school. He carries a heavy workload and is one of the most knowledgeable people in the boat building business. When the work has to get out, he drives his workers, who on more than one occasion have charged him with unfair treatment. While Mr. Gilbert had to reprimand him a number of times for driving his workers, no one has been found to replace him and there is no assistant supervisor.

In 1979 the company's fortunes improved when it received a number of orders for large fishing vessels. With additional employees and the crowded plant, Gilbert noticed that costs started to soar. He knew that few records were kept. The workers' time slips were used only to calculate wages. Since the workers belong to unions, their wages are negotiated on an industry-wide basis. However, there is no way of comparing productivity among them, and although the supervisor claims he knows who the top performers are, there is no way of comparing productivity. No attempt has been made to specialize the workers and most perform whatever jobs are required.

As long as the firm was producing only small aluminum boats, the lack of a production system was not a problem. Material requirements were generally consistent and ordering was handled by the foreman, who knew what was required. When the firm began to produce large boats, however, large volumes of parts and raw materials were required. The lack of an inventory system often resulted in all workers on a large boat shifted to various other jobs because raw materials and parts had not arrived or had not been ordered.

The major problem remained production control. For example, the firm knew how many hours it took to build a large fishing vessel, but no one knew if any of the hundreds of jobs could be done more efficiently. Since there was no specialization, the same tasks were regularly done by different workers. Thus, no one person acquired expertise in a particular operation. In addition, a number of profitable projects had to be turned away because they could not be handled under the present production control system.

Although management had received advice on establishing a production control system, it was reluctant to install the system. Mr. Gilbert and the board of directors did not want to hire the additional staff and add to overhead costs. The supervisor was adamant that such a system was simply not necessary. He stated that he works as hard as is humanly possible and does not have the time to fool around with more details. Management also felt that since the company is so small, the existing informal system might actually be the most efficient way to operate, even if it meant turning away a few orders. Although Mr. Gilbert had contemplated expansion, he had some doubt as to whether the present organizations could be expanded without a complete reorganization. He also wondered whether a change in management methods should be made before or after expansion.

QUESTIONS

1. What is wrong with management's and the supervisor's arguments against implementing a production control system? What would the advantages of such a system be?

2. The company has three choices on how to devise and install a production control system: a) assign the task to the supervisor; b) employ a qualified worker from another company; c) use a firm of consulting engineers. What are the merits of each alternative?

3. If you were asked to outline a production control system for Pacific Boat Works, what major factors would you take into consideration? (Keep in mind the future expansion of the firm.)

4. How would you answer Mr. Gilbert's question of whether the production control system should be changed now or after expansion?

5. How might a computerized production control and inventory system help the company? How would you go about implementing the system?

CHAPTER 8

Marketing

West Edmonton Mall

CHAPTER OUTLINE

CHAPTER PREVIEW

In Chapter 8 we examine marketing, the business function responsible for getting a product from the producer to the customer. After
considering marketing as a concept that focuses on satisfying the
needs of consumers and achieving long-term profits, we look at the
specific elements of marketing research, marketing strategy and marketing mix. Four components of the marketing mix are particularly
important: product, price, promotion and place. Each of these "four
P's of marketing" is examined in detail.

LEARNING OBJECTIVES

After reading this chapter you should be able to explain:

1. The functions of marketing;
2. The marketing concept and how marketing research is used to select a target market;
3. The four basic components that make up the marketing mix;
4. The difference between consumer and industrial markets and the types of goods appropriate for each market;
5. The concept of product life cycles and their effect on a firm;
6. How a firm actually sets the price for a new product, and the two major pricing strategies that may be used to introduce a new product;
7. The four major types of promotion;
8. When to use mass advertising as a major promotional tool, and when to use personal selling;
9. How goods get from the producer to the consumer or industrial customer;
10. The function performed for manufacturers and retailers by wholesalers;
11. The major types of retail outlets;
12. The problems involved in the physical distribution of goods.

We have all seen television commercials — some insult our intelligence; others are witty and appropriate. The objective of a commercial is to have us take notice of a product. An advertisement may stimulate a desire for the product, or it may simply remind us of the product as we pass the supermarket shelf. Either way, if we are influenced to buy the product, the commercial — whether we like it or not — has been successful.

THE IMPORTANCE OF MARKETING

Advertising is the aspect of marketing that makes consumers aware of existing products. But marketing encompasses many more activities. It involves contacting consumers and businesses to identify products that are needed and in demand. Marketing is also responsible for pricing, advertising and sales promotion, and for getting the product to the customer through one or more channels of distribution, including wholesalers and retailers.

Marketing products and services is costly for a business, and often accounts for more than half the cost of a product. Therefore, we might ask, why not reduce marketing activities, and thereby reduce the price of the product to the consumer? Surely lower prices would give a producer an edge over the competition. In fact, some firms do reduce the marketing function to a bare minimum. An example is the mail-order house, which allows the customer to shop conveniently at home by ordering through a catalogue.

However, many of us want to look at products, feel them, try them on and compare prices when we shop. Before we buy a best-selling novel, for example, we read the back cover. Before we invest in a new car, we test drive it and compare various makes. Thus, some marketing functions are essential and could not be eliminated, regardless of how much a producer may wish to cut product costs. Marketing is as basic a business function as production, finance and personnel.

THE FUNCTIONS OF MARKETING

Marketing is "the performance of business activities that direct the flow of goods and services from producer to consumer or user."[1] To ensure that these activities are carried out, specific functions must be performed, each of which adds value to the product for the consumer. This value, or **utility**, represents the ability of goods and services to satisfy a human want or need. The marketing function adds three types of utility — time, place and ownership utility. To add time utility, marketers determine what products the customers want available at particular times. Having the product available at a convenient location for purchase adds place utility. Ownership utility is created by facilitating the transfer of title for the product from seller to buyer. A fourth type of utility, known as form utility, is created by the production function, which converts raw materials into useful products for consumers or businesses.

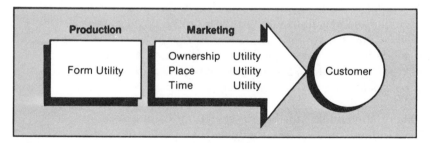

Figure 8.1 Marketing adds utility to products

There are eight marketing functions:

Buying	Risk-taking
Selling	Financing
Transporting	Standardizing and grading
Storing	Information gathering

BUYING: Before a business can produce or resell products, it must buy raw materials, parts or finished goods. It must seek out suppliers and purchase the right product in the right quantity. Retail buyers, for example, take a number of factors into consideration including style, size, colour, quantity, quality and brand. Buying entails risk, and mistakes can be costly if products remain on the seller's shelf because they do not appeal to customers.

SELLING: Before a business can make a profit it must sell the products it has bought or produced. Thus, potential buyers must be made aware of the product's existence, usefulness and price. Sellers may therefore offer various services to make the product more attractive. A producer, for example, may provide the retailer or wholesaler with advertising allowances, demonstrate use of the product to customers and maintain inventory. Both the producer and retailer may provide warranties, credit, delivery and servicing facilities to the consumer.

TRANSPORTING: A product must be transported from the place where it is produced to a location convenient for the customer. The gasoline in an Alberta refinery, for example, is of no use to the motorist in Toronto unless it is made readily available through service stations.

STORING: Retailers and wholesalers as well as specific marketing institutions such as warehouses and transportation agencies store goods to ensure they are available when customers are ready to buy. Thus, goods as diverse as fresh fruit and books or furniture are readily available almost anywhere in Canada.

RISK-TAKING: Buying, selling, transporting and storing all entail some risk. Some stocked items may not sell, goods in transport may be damaged and goods in storage may spoil. The producer, wholesaler or retailer must then bear the loss. Businesses can protect themselves against specific risks by purchasing insurance.

FINANCING: Many consumers and businesses either cannot or do not wish to pay immediately for the products they purchase. The seller therefore provides the buyer with credit for a specified period of time following receipt of the goods. A retailer buying a product from a manufacturer, for example, may be able to resell it and make a profit before he is required to pay for it.

STANDARDIZING AND GRADING: Many products are priced according to standards of quality, size and colour. When the manufacturer or producer standardizes and grades goods, the seller need not inspect each unit he receives. Turkeys, eggs and fruits are graded according to size, quality or condition, and many other goods are manufactured according to standards established either by the industry or by government. For example, all products with the stamp "CSA Approved" are manufactured to meet certain minimum standards laid down by the Canadian Standards Association.

INFORMATION GATHERING: Information on products and consumer needs is essential, since a firm may prosper or go bankrupt depending on its ability to adjust to market demands. The marketing department is responsible for gathering information on consumer needs and product acceptance. Sales generally give an accurate indication of product acceptance, while other product information can be gathered from retailers and wholesalers who are in close contact with customers. Marketing executives also gather information about products, markets and consumers from trade journals and marketing magazines. In addition, firms regularly conduct market studies and research to obtain information not otherwise available.

THE MARKETING CONCEPT

In the past, business firms were not as concerned with consumer needs as they are today. The early phase of marketing, now known as **production marketing**, lasted until the late 1930s. During this phase, the marketing function was of minor importance, as indicated by Henry Ford's famous statement: "They can have their Model T in any colour, as long as it's black." Consumers had few alternative products to choose from, but the demand for goods was enormous. More goods gradually came on the market, however, and prices began to drop because of mass production. Advertising media were developed to inform the public of available goods. Hence the sales function of marketing became increasingly important as competition for the consumers' dollar increased. Producers concentrated on selling products using sophisticated sales techniques, and the **sales-oriented marketing** era began, lasting through World War II.

After World War II, however, something akin to a marketing revolution occurred. Once consumer goods could be produced on a mass scale, new products became available at relatively low prices.

Market shelves display a variety of products competing for the consumer dollar

Competitors could take an existing product, improve on it and offer it to the consumer, often at a lower price than the original product. With many products to choose from and a better educated consumer market, old-style sales techniques were no longer successful. Companies that ignored consumer needs and wants found themselves out of business, while firms that listened to consumers prospered. Thus the **marketing era** began. Salespeople and marketing executives studied customers to determine their needs and wants, and once these were known a firm could channel all of its resources into producing the most suitable product or service.

Marketing Research

If a firm intends to gear its entire activity toward producing goods and services for its customers, it must find out specifically what those customers want — what forms, colours, packaging, prices and retailers the consumer frequents; what types of advertising, public relations and selling practices appeal to the consumer. **Marketing research** is the systematic gathering, recording and analyzing of data related to the marketing of goods and services.

Comprehensive market research consists of five basic steps:

1. **Defining the problem**: The first step — defining the problem — is the most important and often the most difficult job of the marketing researcher. It is easy to mistake symptoms for the problem. Defining the problem may take time, but if the wrong problem is examined, money and effort are wasted. Consequences may be serious if a solution to a wrong or non-existent problem is implemented. For example, a drop in sales could result from a variety of problems including inadequate advertising, poor quality product, or a lack of salespeople. Sometimes market research is also used to determine if a problem exists. For example, a sales analysis may indicate increased sales over previous years, but after further market analysis the firm may find that it is actually losing market share.

2. **Gathering secondary data**: The next step is to gather secondary data from company records, trade magazines, government and private information sources, library sources or similar market studies. If a problem can be resolved at this stage it will cost far less than gathering primary data.

3. **Gathering primary data**: If secondary data does not provide the answer, or if more data is required, then primary data must be gathered. Primary data is gathered through observing people; through experiments such as test marketing a product in a particular area to see how consumers react; or through surveys in which individuals are questioned by telephone, mail or in personal interviews.

4. **Compiling data**: The fourth step consists of compiling the data that has been gathered. At this stage the marketing department clarifies relationships between various factors. For example, researchers may try to establish a relationship between income and the type of product purchased. Extensive correlations are facilitated by the use of computers.

5. **Interpreting the information**: The final and most important step is the interpretation of the data. A mistaken interpretation may prompt management to take the wrong action. For example, it may reject a potentially successful product or decide to produce a product consumers will not buy.

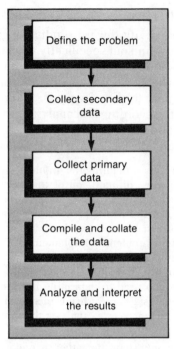

Figure 8.2 Steps in marketing research

Marketing Strategy

As noted earlier, a business cannot simply produce a good product and hope for the best — it must satisfy the needs of the customer. The marketing manager thus establishes a plan or **marketing strategy** which consists of two parts:

1. **Identifying the target market**. Since not all consumers will be interested in a particular product or service, the group most likely to buy a product because it fits its needs or wants must be identified.

2. **Developing a marketing mix**. The marketing mix is the assortment of variables that the marketing manager can adjust to suit the specific target market. It involves making a product with specific features that customers want, choosing a price or range of prices they are prepared to pay, choosing an effective method of promotion to reach the customers, and distributing the product in the most appropriate way. The marketing mix is often referred to as the four P's of marketing: product, price, promotion and place.

Identifying the Target Market

All individuals have needs and wants for particular goods and services. Marketers classify groups of consumers with similar demands and firms can thus develop variations of a given product to satisfy the particular demands of each group. For example, a television manufacturer may produce a variety of models including both expensive, high-quality sets with many features, and simpler, lower-priced models. Each model is designed to appeal to particular groups of people or target markets. Some consumers prefer a low-priced black and white set, while others want a colour set with a large screen and ornate cabinet.

Dividing the total market into a number of target markets based on specific criteria is known as **market segmentation**. Among the criteria identifying a given target market are income, cultural background, interests, education, life style and occupation. Each target market or market segment may require a different marketing mix.

The consumers who make up the target market for one product may be entirely different from those in a target market for another product. For example, people in the target market group for a feature-laden colour television, may or may not belong to the target market for an instant breakfast designed to appeal to the single working person.

In Canada, marketers for certain products may be concerned with the various ethnic markets, particularly the French- and English-Canadian markets. One or the other of these two major target markets may prefer some products over others. For example, Québec leads all provinces in expenditures for clothing and cosmetics, and has the highest per capita sales of sweets in Canada. When these markets are segmented, particular attention is paid to cultural and language criteria because there are significant differences in consumer attitudes and behaviour.

Developing the Marketing Mix

Once the characteristics of the target market are known, the next step in the development of a marketing strategy is the creation of the marketing mix. The marketing department determines the best possible combination of product, price, promotion and place to satisfy the particular target market. Of course, the marketing mix must also take into account management's objectives for the firm, competition, social values and customs, and legal restraints.

The marketing mix is illustrated in Figure 8.3, which shows the four P's focusing on the target market. It is important to note that the initial combination of the four P's is not necessarily the best and may need adjustment over time. For example, a dress manufacturing firm may find that its line is so well received by customers, that the original advertising strategy can be altered and advertising costs reduced. It may also find that it can reduce the number of styles and colours offered, if only a few styles sell well.

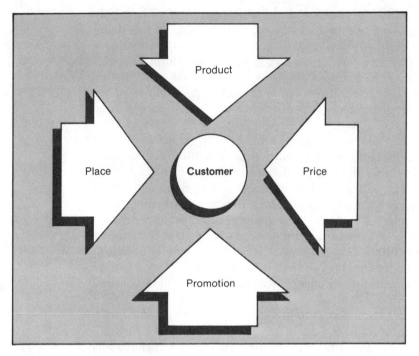

Figure 8.3 The four P's of marketing

The Four P's of Marketing

Product: In addition to the basic characteristics appropriate for the target market, the product also includes the proper packaging, branding and labelling, colour, size, delivery, and any warranty or service that may be required.

Price: The product must be priced so as to appeal to the target market while providing a reasonable profit for the firm.

Promotion: The promotion campaign must be geared to the specific target market, and may mean either mass advertising or personal selling, or some combination of the two. A firm might also use other sales promotion techniques, and attempt to stir up publicity for its product through newspaper or television reporting.

Place: A channel of distribution must be determined to make the product available to the consumer or business customer. The producer may choose to sell directly to the retailer, or he may hire the services of a wholesaler to distribute the product to retail stores. Often both methods are used.

Segmenting the market for a video disc player

When a new home entertainment product such as a video disc player or giant screen television is made available for purchase, who will actually buy it? That is a big question for manufacturers. One common method marketers use to segment the population to determine the various target markets is to consider income and family life-cycle stage. Because of its development and marketing costs, a new product is usually high priced when it first comes on the market. However, as demand for the product picks up over a few months or years, the price slowly drops. This makes income a key criterion — someone in a high income bracket is better able to afford an expensive new entertainment product.

In conjunction with income, another set of criteria used is family cycle-stage. These are classed as follows:

1. Bachelor stage (young single people);
2. Young married couples with no children;
3. Young married couples with children;
4. Older married couples with dependent children living with them;
5. Older married couples with no children;
6. Older single people either still working or retired.

This classification obviously lacks one group quite common today: the young single mother with children. Depending on the product, marketers may or may not include this group in their market analysis. High priced electronic entertainment systems will probably not be purchased by this group to any great extent.

Figure 8.4 shows the market grid for the disc player. Across the top are various family life-cycle stages, while down the left side are the various income groups. Each family life-cycle stage can now be surveyed as to their desire to want such a product and also their willingness to pay the price to own it. If the marketer already believes that only certain segments will be interested in the product, then only those segments will be surveyed.

High income families or individuals, for example, are quite likely to be interested in a video disc player. This target market may want a feature laden product and have little concern about price. On the other hand, this product may also appeal to lower income groups, for example, young married couples with children, who now may be able to enjoy many more movies at home without the expense of babysitters and the other costs associated with going out to a movie. This target market may be very concerned with the price and thus prefer a basic unit with few frills but good performance. In fact, these two groups might represent the two primary target markets.

There may also be smaller target markets that the company can satisfy by changing the product mix slightly. For example, the manufacturers of colour televisions produce a large variety of types and styles to suit every conceivable target market.

Once the actual product and the price have been determined, an appropriate promotional plan will be developed that is geared to each target market. This may include advertising on television, in selected magazines, newspapers, radio, and other media, depending on which target market they want to reach.

Making the product readily available for purchase is the final concern for the marketer. In the case of an entertainment product, department stores and specialty retail stores are the most likely places where this product would be sold initially. As the product becomes more accepted and sought out, discount stores may also carry it. Since manufacturers of entertainment equipment are usually large companies, they have their own distribution centres and sales force and sell the product directly to the various retail outlets. They seldom use wholesalers or other middlemen. This puts them closer to the customer and provides a much better idea of how the product is selling.

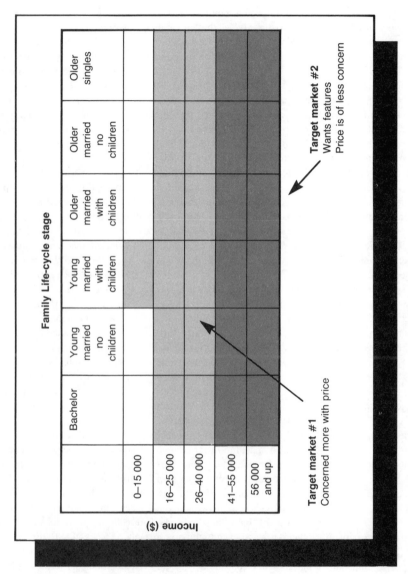

Figure 8.4 Segmenting the market for videodisc players

Consumer and Industrial Markets

The total market for goods can be divided into two categories — consumer and business or industrial markets.

Although many products are used by both sectors, business products are put to more strenuous use and must be more durable; hence they are usually more expensive than consumer products. A typewriter, for example, is used almost continuously by a secretary, while a student may use it only occasionally.

Since many businesses make products for both consumer and business use, it is important that the marketing department understand the difference between the two markets. When sales in both categories are substantial, the marketing activities of a firm may be divided into separate consumer and industrial departments. The firm can thus gear its marketing effort specifically to each group of buyers.

Consumer Goods

The market for consumer goods is generally large and geographically widespread. **Consumer goods** directly satisfy the needs and wants of the purchaser. Thus consumers often buy goods on the basis of emotional or psychological factors such as fear or the desire for prestige. Many consumer purchases are made on the spur of the moment, a practice known as impulse buying. Consumer goods can be classified into three categories: convenience, shopping and specialty goods.

CONVENIENCE GOODS: Convenience goods include products which are needed often and are bought without much deliberation — bread, cigarettes and razor blades, for example. No one wants to hunt for these products, and they are expected to be widely available.

SHOPPING GOODS: Since shopping goods are usually expensive, the consumer is prepared to spend considerable time comparing quality, price and, when necessary, after-sale warranties. Shopping goods include automobiles, furniture and television sets.

SPECIALTY GOODS: Specialty goods include products that the consumer is prepared to make a special effort to buy. Brand names are often important, and the consumer may not be willing to accept a substitute. High-priced and imported cars usually fall into this category — a person wishing to buy a Mercedes, for example, may go to great lengths to locate a dealer. And for people who favour a particular brand — clothing by Pierre Cardin, or a Nikon camera — there may be no substitute.

Two factors must be kept in mind in the classification of consumer goods. First, what is a specialty good to one person may be a shopping or convenience good to another. For example, the affluent household may regularly buy T-bone steak at the local market regardless of price, while the college student may be able to afford this luxury only occasionally and only after carefully comparing prices at a number of stores. Second, what was considered a shopping or specialty good in the past may be considered a convenience good today. Many non-food items such as children's toys or low-priced cameras and film are now found on supermarket shelves because consumers expect them to be readily available.

Industrial Goods

Industrial goods are those purchased by businesses for their own production purposes. Most industrial products are relatively expensive compared with consumer goods, and many are extremely complex and technical in nature. Thus industrial products are often bought by purchasing agents; engineers and other personnel, well informed about the technical aspects of available products, may also be involved. Professional purchasing decisions are based largely on economic considerations, rather than on emotional or convenience factors. Since industrial products are complex and since there are fewer industrial customers than consumers, the marketing approach for industrial goods is different from that for consumer goods. Industrial goods can be classified into six major categories: installations, raw materials, parts, accessory equipment, supplies and services.

INSTALLATIONS: Installations include large and costly capital goods such as heavy machinery, airliners, freighters, blast furnaces and turbine generators. Since these items are purchased infrequently and are expensive, their suitability is carefully examined prior to purchase, and they are often built to specifications.

RAW MATERIALS: Raw materials may include grains, minerals, timber or cotton. Because they are used constantly and in large quantities, these materials must be readily available, and even small variations in price can be significant. Other considerations important to the buyer include grading, storage and transportation.

PARTS: Firms that assemble products such as automobiles often buy subassemblies, or parts, from other businesses. Some parts may be manufactured according to the buyer's specifications, while others are of standard design. For example, in the automobile industry, manufacturers buy parts from thousands of different suppliers. Each major manufacturer, however, may buy the same part from one supplier and the part may be standard or designed for a specific automobile.

ACCESSORY EQUIPMENT: Accessory equipment includes the tools and equipment needed in manufacturing, along with items such as typewriters, computers and copiers. Accessory equipment is often bought by individual department heads through the purchasing department. Expensive equipment may require careful analysis in terms of price and capability for the job.

SUPPLIES: Supplies are items not used in the actual manufacturing process, and include maintenance and office supplies such as paper, typewriter ribbons and labels.

SERVICES: In order to function, a firm requires many additional services provided by people who are not employees. Included are legal services, maintenance or repair services, consultants and advertising agencies.

CREATING THE PRODUCT

When we hear the word "product," the first thing that comes to mind is probably some physical object — a bicycle, a book, a typewriter. To marketing managers, however, the word has a broader meaning. They keep in mind that the consumer buys a product to derive a particular benefit from it. Thus a student buying a typewriter may look forward to better grades on term papers, while a person buying a bicycle may be thinking of benefits such as recreation, physical exercise, or status, as well as transportation. The marketing manager can therefore make a product more attractive by emphasizing benefits such as quality, packaging, detailed instructions on use, brand name, product guarantees and credit, delivery or after-sale service.

In discussing the concept of the **total product** then, we will no longer distinguish between a physical object and a service. For example, the product of a medical doctor is a service — patients often receive nothing more tangible from a doctor than advice. Similarly, the product of a lawyer or an accountant is a service. And an automobile would be less desirable as a product if service were not readily available, or if the car came without a warranty to protect the consumer against premature breakdowns.

Product Mix and Product Line

Some firms produce and sell only one consumer or industrial product, but many firms manufacture or sell a **product line**. A product line may consist of products that are similar in design, in use, or intended for a similar market. A kitchen appliance manufacturer, for example, may produce toasters, steam irons and electric kettles as part of its product line. A product line can be expanded with additional related products or services.

In deciding whether to offer more products or product lines, a firm's resources obviously play a major role. For example, a firm may specialize in one product to make production more efficient or because financial resources are limited. On the other hand, a broader **product mix** might be prudent for a company whose sales depend on consumer tastes and economic conditions. For example, a firm that handles only one product could be severely hurt by a sales slump in that product. On the other hand, if this firm handled a broader product mix, a sales slump in one product or product line might not seriously affect this company's financial position if other products continued to sell well.

Product Planning and Development

A firm must constantly ensure that all of its products contribute to the goal of profitability. Therefore management engages in **product planning** to determine whether new products could be produced or existing ones improved. The ideas for new products can come from customers, retailers and wholesalers, or from market research.

Once the product planning function is established, **product development** becomes an ongoing activity in six stages — generating new product ideas, screening, concept testing, business analysis, test marketing and commercialization.

New product ideas can be generated in a variety of ways, from soliciting information from retailers and wholesalers to primary market research. All new product ideas are subjected to **screening**, which assesses a product's general usefulness to the consumer and decides whether it should be considered for further study. **Concept testing** is then conducted. Ideas on how the product may be used and an estimated price are presented to a small group of potential consumers who are asked to comment. Even a negative response from the sample group is likely to be followed up with further study.

After concept testing, a thorough **business analysis** is undertaken to determine whether the product could be commercially successful. The analysis focuses on product features, estimated sales and profitability, competitive strength and potential for growth. The firm's current resources for producing and distributing the product are also examined.

Following the business analysis, the product is produced in limited quantity and tested for quality and performance. Often the prod-

Large companies, such as Procter & Gamble, market a wide
variety of product lines

uct is tested by having consumers use it or compare it with an existing
product. **Test marketing** may or may not be conducted depending
on the results of the product tests. In test marketing, the company
introduces the product for sale to consumers in selected geographical
areas and studies responses. During this stage any design, production
or distribution problems can be corrected.

Once test marketing has been completed, **commercialization** —
launching the product in the general market — must follow quickly,
or competitors could gain the upper hand in sales and profit since

they have been spared the cost of testing a similar product. Management may therefore bypass test marketing if it is confident that the product will be profitable. However, the gamble could be expensive; studies have shown that only two of every hundred product ideas result in successful commercial products. By omitting the test marketing stage, a company may spend millions of dollars introducing a product, only to see it fail on the market.

Product Life Cycles

Since products have a limited life span, product planning and development are ongoing activities. A new product spawned by a fad may last only a few months on the market. On the other hand, the demand for a product such as the automobile may continue indefinitely. Nevertheless a product may change radically over time with changes in technology, competition, economic conditions and consumer tastes. Hence, even products in constant demand require ongoing product planning and development. A firm that ignores this function could lose customers. The Chrysler Corporation, for example, did not adapt its product to economic conditions and customer needs until bankruptcy was imminent. It continued to produce large cars when consumers were demanding smaller, more fuel-efficient vehicles.

The product life cycle shown in Figure 8.5 consists of four stages — product introduction, market growth, market maturity and sales decline. During the **product introduction stage** the firm's primary objective is to make potential customers aware of the product's existence. Managers therefore develop an appropriate promotional campaign, which may include mass advertising, personal selling and various methods of sales promotion. At first promotion costs are high in relation to product sales and profits. Home computers and digital audio-disc players, for example, are products now in the introduction stage.

If the product survives the introductory stage and customers accept it as useful, sales will increase. The product is then in the **market growth stage**, when the firm that introduced the product must recover its development costs and make a profit. As product prices tend to remain high, competitors are drawn into the market, each claiming a better product design. By the end of this stage a wide variety of products are available and total product sales are still increasing. However, the profit for the original company is now reaching its peak, which marks the beginning of the end for the product.

In the **market maturity stage** competition among manufacturers becomes more intense, as many similar products compete for the

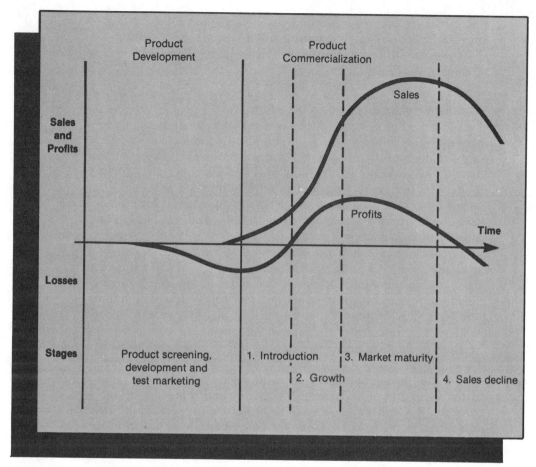

Figure 8.5 Product life cycle

consumers' dollar. As each firm tries to obtain a greater market share
through increased advertising, price cutting and product differen-
tiation, profits begin to decline. Some manufacturers may drop out
of the market altogether, as their sales and profits decrease. Most
firms will concentrate on developing new products to replace the
old. At the end of the market maturity stage the market is saturated
and total product sales begin to decline slowly — colour television
reached this stage in the late 1970s.

In the final stage of **sales decline**, new products introduced to
the market cut into sales of established products. Nevertheless, through
vigorous price competition, a few firms may continue selling an
established product which may remain profitable for many years

before it is withdrawn from the market. Consumer loyalty and specific need often account for continued sales. Even today, for example, slide rules are still available, often at higher prices than sophisticated calculators.

Effect of Product Life Cycles on a Firm

The concept of product life cycles means that a company cannot rely on a successful product for long periods. Technological advances, for example, rapidly make many products obsolete and shorten product life cycles. Competitors may also make a successful product obsolete by introducing a simple modification such as a change in flavouring or a new package design. Competitors who seize the opportunity to improve a product can hasten the decline of profits and sales for the pioneering firm.

Thus, companies must continually develop new products and adjust the marketing mix to take advantage of high profits in the early stages of a product's life cycle. A firm must introduce its product quickly and see it to the market growth stage before competitors introduce their version. Otherwise a firm may not recover its investment in product planning and development.

Finally, the firm must be acutely aware of consumer needs, and translate these needs into products. It must also plan for the decline of a product in the latter part of its life cycle — rather than simply withdrawing the product from the market and replacing it with a new one, the firm might be able to improve or repackage it. Thus product life cycles are an essential consideration in a firm's marketing strategy.

Branding, Packaging and Labelling

Branding, packaging and labelling are included in the total product concept. These three factors are important throughout the product life cycle.

Branding

A brand serves to identify a firm's products; it can be a name, sign, symbol or any combination which differentiates one firm's products from those of its competitors. Virtually everyone recognizes McDonald's golden arches, for example, or the brand names "Ford" and "Coca-Cola." When symbols and names are registered with the federal government, the original firm retains sole and exclusive use. Without such protection competitors could exploit an established brand name with no regard for the product, and the brand name would lose its recognition value to the original firm.

A successful brand name can also contribute to a firm's future marketing success. Subsequent product introductions by the same company may be more readily accepted by customers if previous brands proved satisfactory. Customers naturally assume that a new product with a reputable brand name will meet similar standards of quality and service. A brand name can also help a firm in its introduction of a competitive product, even if it did not introduce the original product. For example, if an unknown firm develops and markets a successful product which is then copied by a firm already well-known for similar products, customers may well choose the product of the well-known firm.

Packaging

Consumers have come a long way from buying sugar and flour by scooping it out of a sack. Today, most products come neatly packaged in various shapes and sizes, including blister packs for thumbtacks and individually packaged dinners.

Packing can be a significant product characteristic if it offers the consumer additional benefits. A package designed to be resealed can protect products from becoming stale or spoiling, and one that can be used as a container makes storage easy. Packaging may also be a boon to the retailer. A well packaged product is easy to handle, can be displayed in a small space, and attracts customers' attention.

SOURCE: Trevor Hutchings—*Marketing Magazine*. Reproduced courtesy of the artist.

"The name's Fred Wilson, not Pierre Cardin or Yves Saint Laurent—now show me a shirt with a fancy FW on it and you've got yourself a sale."

If a change in packaging improves the total product, it can be as effective as a new product in increasing sales. A new package may appeal to a new target market without losing the previous market — for instance, food packaged in smaller quantities may attract the growing single-person market while continuing to appeal to the original family market.

Labelling

A label provides information about the product or its manufacturer. Information may include instructions for use, especially important in the case of drugs, or a list of the product's ingredients.

With the consumer movement came charges of misleading, false and deceptive labelling. Mouthwash could no longer be advertised as preventing or curing sore throats once it was found to be ineffective, and today all mouthwash advertising and labelling can only claim that the product kills germs which cause bad breath. Federal legislation such as the **Food and Drug Act** and the **Consumer Packaging and Labelling Act** protects the consumer by requiring that manufacturers provide accurate information on labels.

PRICING THE PRODUCT

In Chapter 2 we stated that a product's price is determined by the interaction of supply and demand in the marketplace, and theoretically that statement is true. But firms require more concrete methods of setting prices for their products — they cannot simply place the product in stores and set the price based on the number of people who buy the product. The producer or manufacturer must know the price of a product to plan for production and profit. Wholesalers and retailers must also know product prices to plan their resale prices and to determine their profits.

Product pricing directly affects a company's profit and therefore requires careful analysis. The marketing manager must know the costs of manufacturing, sales and overhead as well as the profit objectives of the firm. He must also have a pricing strategy for each product. We now examine pricing strategies and how specific prices can be set.

Pricing Strategies

A pricing strategy depends on the specific objectives of a firm but may follow two general trends — skimming the market and penetration pricing.

A **skimming the market** pricing strategy is used when a new technological product, such as video recorders and home computers, is introduced to the consumer market. Due to initially high research, development and production costs and a low anticipated sales volume, the price of this product will be relatively high when it is first introduced. This strategy is based on the assumption that some people, perhaps with relatively high incomes, want the latest that technology has to offer and are willing to pay the high price for ownership of a new product. By "skimming" these customers off the top of the market, a company can maximize profits on new products. As demand increases for the product and more is produced, manufacturing costs drop and prices to consumers also drop. Prices may also be affected as competitors introduce similar products at a lower price hoping to gain a share of the market.

A skimming strategy may also be dictated by the existing level of technology to mass produce the product. Sometimes new products require considerable labour in their manufacture, which raises costs. Nevertheless, a company may want to be first on the market with a new product regardless of the initial price. Subsequently it can improve production techniques, and thus reduce production costs and lower consumer prices.

A second strategy is **penetration pricing**, in which a company introduces a product at a low price to gain a large portion of the market quickly. If customers accept the product, then the company can benefit from economies of scale in production and lower its costs. If the firm can establish the new product on the market in this manner, profits could be high. At a later date the firm could introduce one or more similar products at higher prices and gain greater profits. At the same time, the low price of the initial product and the strong market position may discourage competitors from entering the market since they would likely be faced with low profit per unit.

Pricing Methods

It is a difficult task to price products so that they will both attract consumers and provide a profit. There are four specific pricing methods:

1. Full-cost
2. Flexible
3. Gross margin
4. Suggested and going rate

A firm should use a combination of all four methods in its pricing strategy. The firm must cover its regular production costs, its selling costs, and general administrative expenses, as well as provide for a profit. However, the initial pricing structure must also take into account the costs of research and development and the cost of introducing the product to the market, including extensive advertising and promotional schemes.

Full-Cost Method

With the full-cost approach all costs — fixed and variable — are taken into consideration and then a profit figure is added to calculate an appropriate return for the company. The full-cost method is a formula approach. Many of the prices are based on the **break-even analysis**.

Break-even analysis shows the minimum sales volume required at a particular price in order to cover all costs. Total costs are made up of both fixed and variable costs. **Fixed costs**, up to a point, remain unchanged regardless of production volume. They include costs such as insurance, utilities, managerial salaries and a variety of overhead costs. **Total variable costs**, on the other hand, increase directly with the volume produced. Included are items such as direct labour and raw materials required to produce each unit. Total revenue is determined by multiplying price by the number of units sold.

Figure 8.6 shows a break-even calculation and the **break-even point**. If the volume of product sold is above the break-even point, the firm will make a profit. Once a schedule has been established, the marketer can compare various profit results with various prices for the product, then choose the price most compatible with the target market and develop a pricing strategy.

The full-cost approach is relatively simple but the resultant price may turn out to be too high for consumers. Competitors selling a similar product also have to be taken into account and the price adjusted accordingly. On the other hand, if this method produces a price lower than what customers are prepared to pay, the firm may lose potential revenue.

Flexible Pricing Approach

With the flexible pricing approach a careful analysis is made of potential sales based on different prices. If the price is lowered, for example, total revenue from increased sales could more than offset the drop in the price per unit. On the other hand, raising the price of the product may have little or no effect on sales revenue.

Since most firms sell a variety of products, one product may be used as a **loss leader**. The objective of a loss leader is to attract consumers to the product in the hope that they will eventually buy a higher-priced model. Thus, sales of other products increase and profits rise. Even though we are using the flexible pricing approach, full-cost pricing may be used to determine the initial price that the firm needs to cover its production, distribution, research and development costs, as well as make a profit. Once this price is established as a floor price or reference point, the actual price will be determined by customers in the marketplace.

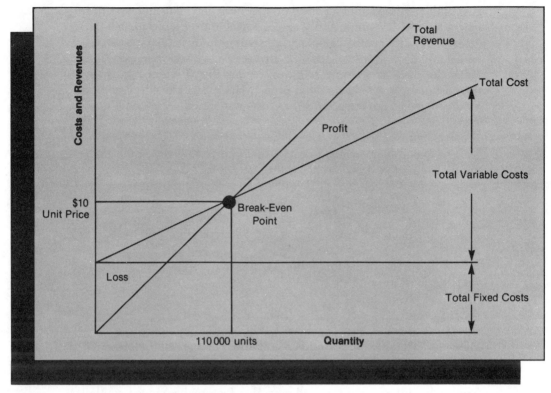

Figure 8.6 Break-even method for pricing products

Mark-up and Gross Margin Pricing

Mark-up pricing is often used to ensure that planned gross margins exceed expenses incurred by the firm in its operation and provide the necessary profit. First we must determine the gross margin percent for a firm, department or class of merchandise. The **gross margin percent** is obtained by subtracting the cost of goods sold from gross sales, and dividing the resulting figure by the sales dollar volume and then multiplying it by 100.

$$\text{Gross margin percent} = \frac{\text{(gross margin dollars)}}{\text{(sales in dollars)}} \times 100$$

The difference between mark-up and the gross margin is that mark-up is the initially planned margin, while the gross margin is what is actually realized after a period of operation and takes into account mark-downs, discounts, shrinkage of goods and pilferage. Once the gross margin percent is calculated, then an appropriate mark-up can be established to ensure that the firm can cover its expenses and make the necessary profit. Mark-up means the difference between the cost of an item and its retail price. Mark-up can be expressed as a percentage of the retail price or of the cost price.

$$\text{Mark-up at cost} = (\text{Selling price} - \text{cost})/\text{cost}$$

For example, if an item costs $1.00 and is sold for $2.00, then the mark-up at cost represents 100%.

$$\frac{\$1.00}{\$1.00} \times 100 = 100\%$$

$$\text{Mark-up at retail} = (\text{Selling price} - \text{cost})/\text{Selling price}$$

Using the same example, but calculating the mark-up at retail, we get a mark-up of 50%.

$$\frac{\$1.00}{\$2.00} \times 100 = 50\%$$

Mark-up at retail or **mark-on** is also known as the retail method of pricing.

Gross margin pricing takes into account all internal costs, customer demand, competitors and any other factors that may affect the sales volume. Therefore the percentage for mark-up or mark-on varies depending on individual products or groups of products. For example, cameras are generally discounted items and the mark-on may be only 12% to 15%. A retailer may not be able to cover the costs of operating the camera department and may rely on photofinishing and camera accessories for higher gross margins to cover some of the losses of selling cameras. On the other hand, a department selling imported wood carvings, which may be in great demand, can sell these items for many times their cost, achieving a high mark-on of perhaps 200% or more. Thus, a department store can simplify its pricing task by using the gross margins for each of its merchandise categories to establish prices for all or most merchandise sold under that category.

Once the price has been determined using the gross margin approach, it can be analyzed in terms of its appeal to customers. Will the high price prevent people from buying the product? Will there be seasonal mark-downs? How is the competition pricing a similar product? The past sales performance of similar merchandise should also be considered when prices are established in this manner.

Suggested and Going-Rate Pricing

Suggested and going-rate pricing are relatively simple, but both are subject to problems. With suggested pricing, also known as **list pricing**, the seller uses the manufacturer's recommended price. Often the list price is then used as a base for discounts, a method often used to sell stereo and video equipment. Consumers seldom pay list price for these items.

Going-rate pricing places emphasis on the competition and the prices that people appear willing to pay. For example, when there is a bumper crop of apples, prices are low to entice people to buy more apples. At a public market, prices vary constantly based on demand. The alternative is to transport the product home again and risk spoilage.

Under either suggested or going-rate pricing, the risks are high for the producer, if there is strong competition or if there are forces beyond the sellers' control that determine demand for the product. For example, most manufacturers attempt to keep their list prices reasonable; nevertheless, an important consideration for the individual store owner is that his or her expenses are in line with those of the industry. If they are not, then list prices may yield a low profit.

Other Pricing Considerations

Consumers tend to believe that price and quality are related — the higher the price of a product, the better the quality. Marketers must keep this **price-quality relationship** in mind when pricing a product. If an item is priced too low, a large segment of the target market may assume that quality is also low and may not purchase the product.

Another factor often considered is **psychological pricing**. In pricing products at 79¢, $9.95 or $29.95, instead of 80¢, $10 or $30, marketers hope that the customer will unconsciously view $9.95 as significantly less than $10.

Psychological factors have not been proven conclusively, but odd pricing also functions as a control factor. For example, if an item costs an even $10, a sales clerk could pocket the money without ringing it into the till. Firms therefore set odd prices since the clerk is usually obliged to make change.

PROMOTING THE PRODUCT

We are bombarded from all directions by various kinds of promotions. Products are promoted on billboards, on television, in newspapers and magazines, and through displays and demonstrations. Promotion is not restricted to products, however; it also extends to ideas. Institutions use various methods of promotion to tell us what they do; political parties use promotion to persuade us to vote for a particular candidate; government uses promotion to publicize its services.

One major criticism of promotion comes from consumers who believe that producers spend an excessive amount of money to sell their products. The advertising techniques used to influence consumers in their buying behaviour are also frequently questioned.

Promotional Mix

The promotional mix available to marketing managers includes four basic techniques:

1. **Mass advertising**. Marketers may use various media such as radio, television and newspapers to reach a large group of consumers.
2. **Personal selling**. In personal selling, salespeople use a one-on-one approach and deal directly with customers.
3. **Sales promotion techniques** other than advertising. Marketers may arrange attractive displays in retail stores or offer contests or rebates to either the customer or the retailer.
4. **Publicity or non-paid advertising**. Since publicity is non-paid, marketing managers may have little influence on what is said about the product, and sometimes publicity is adverse. Nevertheless, the media can generate interest in a product or service through newspaper, radio or television reports.

The promotional methods chosen by the marketing manager will depend primarily on the target market and the product offered. Industrial customers almost always require personal selling because of the technical aspects of the product and because the target market is relatively small. For consumer products, on the other hand, advertising is often the most effective means since the objective is to reach a large number of people and to tell them about a product which is usually simple to use and relatively inexpensive.

Often, of course, both techniques are combined. Automobile manufacturers use all four methods, for example. They rely on mass advertising to tell consumers about the new cars available, and use personal selling once the customer enters a dealer's showroom. At that point, various sales promotion techniques may come into play, including rebates, extended warranties, attractive displays, contests and give-aways.

Automobile manufacturers also receive frequent publicity for their advances in technology and new model changes and gadgets, even though the publicity is sometimes adverse. When consumers heard about the financial difficulties of Chrysler, for example, many may have refrained from buying Chrysler cars for fear that the company might be forced to close down its operation. Similarly, people may have hesitated to purchase a Ford Pinto after hearing reports that the gas tank had exploded in a number of car accidents.

Advertising

The most important feature of advertising is its ability to reach large numbers of people through the use of **mass media** such as television, newspapers, radio and magazines. Advertising can also reach particular segments of the population by selective use of media. Thus Mercedes-Benz might use the National Geographic magazine and financial newspapers to advertise its cars, while Ford will use television and newspapers to advertise its lower-priced models which appeal to a larger segment of the population.

Mass advertising is not as expensive as it may appear. A colour newspaper supplement may cost a retailer hundreds of thousands of dollars, but considering that it reaches the majority of households in Canada, the cost per household is very small. Similarly, the high cost of sponsoring a major television production or movie may turn out to be small on a per capita basis. Furthermore, by advertising during a particular television program, a company may gain exposure to a large portion of its specific target market. Table 8.1 shows the amount of money some Canadian companies and institutions spend on advertising.

Advertising Media

Advertising can be analyzed in terms of the media used to reach particular target markets. Each medium has advantages and disadvantages, depending on the product and its market. The popularity of the various media is best illustrated by the percentage of total advertising dollars spent on each, as illustrated in Figure 8.7.

Among the factors to be considered in choosing an advertising medium are cost, flexibility, length of life, quality of reproduction, and the amount and type of creative services and assistance provided. Levels of geographic and qualitative selectivity may also be important factors. An advertising medium that reaches most of the people in a particular geographic region is said to be high in **geographic selectivity**. **Qualitative selectivity** means that the medium is successful in reaching specific types of people such as doctors, lawyers or homemakers. Table 8.2 lists the major types of advertising media together with the various characteristics that the advertising manager must consider in choosing among them.

TABLE 8.1
Top 100 national advertisers, 1987

Rank	Company	Total Dollars ($'000)	Rank	Company	Total Dollars ($'000)
1	Government of Canada	66 416.2	35	Nestlé Enterprises	10 847.3
2	Procter & Gamble	53 142.9	36	Hyundai Auto Canada	10 679.5
3	General Motors of Canada	39 739.0	37	Nissan Automobile Co. of Canada	10 602.8
4	The Thomson Group	38 283.0	38	CKR	10 525.4
5	John Labatt	36 036.0	39	Mazda Canada	10 202.8
6	Unilever	31 706.4	40	Honda Canada	10 051.9
7	Chrysler Canada	29 692.0	41	Gillette Canada	9 883.4
8	RJR	29 031.2	42	Ralston Purina Canada	9 719.1
9	The Molson Companies	28 792.2	43	Provigo	9 655.6
10	Ontario Government	27 907.5	44	Brick Warehouse	9 537.3
11	Bell Enterprises Canada	27 635.5	45	Quaker Oats Co. of Canada	9 121.7
12	Pepsico	26 869.5	46	Trilon Financial Corporation	9 100.1
13	Carling O'Keefe Canada	26 827.5	47	General Mills Canada	8 985.9
14	McDonald's Restaurants of Canada	25 093.6	48	Sears Canada	8 644.3
15	Kraft	22 290.4	49	H.J. Heinz Co. of Canada	8 468.8
16	Imasco Holdings Canada	21 732.3	50	McCain Foods	8 145.4
17	Ford Motor Co. of Canada	18 871.7	51	Shell Canada	7 996.8
18	Warner Lambert Canada	18 727.8	52	Rowntree Mackintosh Canada	7 870.2
19	Coca-Cola	18 649.7	53	Intertan Canada	7 724.9
20	General Foods	18 398.6	54	Royal Bank of Canada	7 665.5
21	American Home Products	18 322.3	55	Kimberly-Clark of Canada	7 602.7
22	Kellogg Salada Canada	18 155.2	56	American Express Canada	7 277.7
23	Toyota Canada	15 765.7	57	Sandoz Canada	7 227.8
24	George Weston	15 307.3	58	Wardair International	6 975.8
25	Canadian Tire Corporation	14 850.0	59	Pillsbury Canada	6 939.2
26	Rothmans, Benson & Hedges	14 406.2	60	Campbell Soup	6 838.9
27	Effem Foods	14 206.3	61	Kodak Canada	6 710.7
28	Imperial Oil	13 533.7	62	Leon's Furniture	6 704.3
29	Canadian Airlines International	12 879.0	63	Cara Operations	6 616.0
30	Quebec Government	12 618.0	64	Volkswagen Canada	6 513.9
31	Johnson & Johnson	11 883.0	65	Wrigley Canada	6 462.1
32	Dairy Bureau of Canada	11 310.8	66	Government of Alberta	6 247.6
33	The T. Eaton Co.	11 052.5	67	The Seagram Co.	6 237.9
34	Bristol-Myers Canada	10 956.3			

Rank	Company	Total Dollars ($'000)
68	S.C. Johnson & Son	6 212.1
69	Hershey Canada	6 085.1
70	Goodyear Canada	6 053.7
71	Texaco Canada	5 849.4
72	Canada Packers	5 842.4
73	Beatrice International Canada	5 734.5
74	Chrysler Dealers Association	5 050.1
75	Government of British Columbia	5 041.0
76	Desjardins Groupe	5 028.1
77	Beecham Canada	5 021.4
78	IBM Canada	4 972.1
79	Metropolitan Life Insurance	4 953.8
80	Noxell Canada	4 890.5
81	Bank of Nova Scotia	4 843.1
82	Corby Distilleries	4 817.4
83	Cadbury Schweppes	4 507.2
84	Quality Records	4 499.4
85	Atlantic Promotions/Feature Products	4 467.3
86	Dow Chemical Canada	4 463.6
87	Scott Paper	4 357.2
88	Midas Canada	4 338.7
89	Suzuki Canada	4 318.3
90	Granada TV Rental	4 296.6
91	Tambrands Canada	4 284.7
92	Home Hardware Stores	4 279.1
93	Warner Communications Canada	4 233.6
94	Scot's Hospitality	4 172.7
95	Maclean Hunter	4 169.2
96	Gilbey Canada	4 114.1
97	Steinbergs	4 112.9
98	Shears Marketing	4 030.5
99	Dairy Queen Canada	3 884.3
100	Power Corporation	3 873.8

SOURCE: Media Measurement Services, Inc., Toronto, Canada.

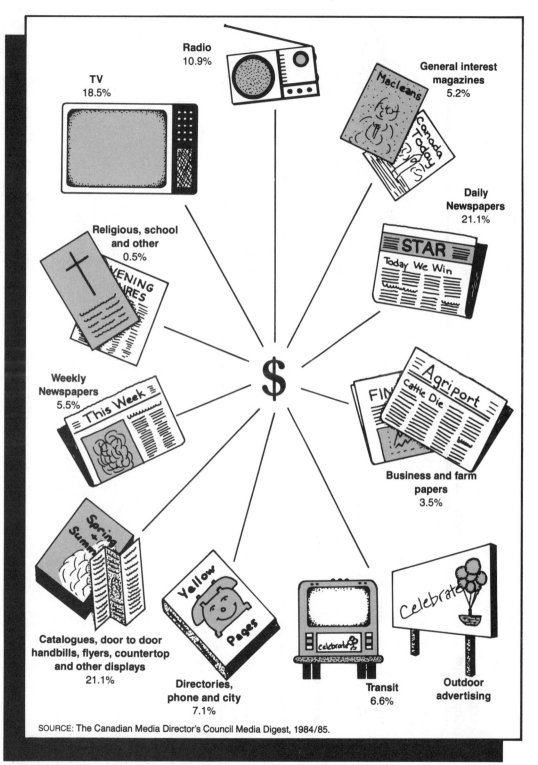

Figure 8.7 Percentage of advertising dollars spent on various media

TABLE 8.2
Characteristics of various advertising media

Media Characteristics	Newspapers	TV	Radio	Direct Mail	Magazines	Outdoor
Geographic selectivity	High	Good	Good	High	High	High
Qualitative selectivity	Low	Moderate	Moderate	High	Moderate	Relatively low
Cost	Relatively low	High	Relatively low	High	High	Relatively low
Flexibility	Good	Poor	Good	Good	Poor	Poor
Length of life	Short	Short	Short	Generally short	Relatively long	Long
Quality of reproduction	Poor	High	No visual stimuli	Advertiser has choice	High	High
Creative services and assistance	Generally provided	Not generally provided	Some services provided	Left to advertiser	Left to advertiser	Usually provided

Personal Selling

The main advantage of personal selling is face-to-face contact with the potential buyer, in contrast to the impersonal nature of mass advertising. In personal selling the sales approach can be tailored to fit different situations; the salesperson can answer questions about the product, handle customer objections and, above all, gain a great deal of information about the customer's requirements. A salesperson can establish a relationship of trust with the customer, persuading him that his personal satisfaction and welfare are uppermost in the seller's mind. The major disadvantage of personal selling is its high cost — each salesperson commands a fairly high salary, but can only call on a limited number of customers. Personal selling is therefore generally restricted to industrial, wholesale and large retail customers, whose potential purchases amount to a substantial dollar value.

The Sales Process

Personal selling may bring to mind the travelling salesman with his practised pitch persuading customers to buy. While the sales approach still follows a basic process, the salesperson must identify the particular sales situation and make necessary adjustments to the basic presentation. The sales approach follows seven basic steps:

1. **Prospecting and qualifying**. Potential sales depend on the number of new prospective customers a salesperson can identify. The customers must have a potential interest in the product and be financially qualified to purchase.

2. **Approach**. Information about the prospects must be gathered and analyzed, so that the salesperson can prepare for the first meeting with the potential customer.

3. **Presentation**. When making the presentation, the salesperson must stimulate the customer's interest in the product. Information is provided concerning the main features of the product, its advantages to the customer, and evidence of other consumers' satisfaction.

4. **Demonstration**. A demonstration allows the customer to see the product or service in actual operation. The benefits of the item may also be explained with the aid of graphs, charts or pamphlets.

5. **Handling objections**. Experienced salespeople welcome customer objections, since they provide an opportunity to set the customer's mind at ease through detailed explanation of the product's use.

6. **Closing**. Unless a sale is closed, even the most knowledgeable salesperson and the best sales approach may come to nothing. Once the five previous steps have been completed, the salesperson must adopt the positive attitude that the customer will indeed purchase the merchandise. Walking to the cash register or starting to write up the order can help to remind a hesitant customer of his decision to buy.

7. **Follow-up**. Follow-up is the link between the first sale and future sales. The salesperson must ensure that the order is processed quickly and that all terms of the sale — delivery dates, installation and service — are carried out.

Sales Management

Large or small, a sales force must be coordinated by a manager. The sales manager performs all management functions, including planning for future sales personnel needs and recruiting and hiring salespeople. The training and development of salespeople and the evaluation of their work are particularly important. **Leadership** and **motivation** also play a major role — since salespeople generally enjoy their freedom and do not like close supervision, a good sales manager must be able to exert control without stifling initiative.

Sales Promotion

In addition to personal selling and advertising, various types of sales promotions can help stimulate consumer buying through specific one-time sales efforts. The most common technique is "**point of purchase**" **advertising**, which includes displays and demonstrations of a product, usually close to where it can be purchased. Another common promotional technique is **specialty advertising**, which involves giving away inexpensive articles — pens, calendars or ashtrays — with an imprint of the firm's name. Some companies may also use **training seminars** and **trade shows**. While these are usually geared to retailers and wholesalers, the general public may be invited to view the firm's products and services. The fashion industry often uses this kind of promotion. Contests for cash or merchandise prizes are also often offered. Other techniques designed to build customer loyalty for a product or service include merchandise samples, coupons, premium merchandise and trading stamps.

Publicity

New products, particularly when they are the result of breakthroughs in technology, are newsworthy. Thus the various news media provide publicity, which is in effect free advertising. While publicity can increase product sales when the news is favourable, adverse reports can result in decreased sales. Many trade magazines also provide publicity through articles about specific products and thus may attract consumer interest. Manufacturing firms often go out of their way to make products available for testing in the hope that articles written about them will be beneficial.

DISTRIBUTING THE PRODUCT

Would you order a can of peaches or a tube of toothpaste through a catalogue? We usually need these items quickly, and are not prepared to wait a week or more for delivery. Thus many small retail stores exist alongside larger retailers, and all are interested in attracting the customer with a variety of merchandise readily available for sale.

To get the merchandise to the consumer, producers can choose between various channels of distribution as shown in Figure 8.8. They can sell their product to the consumer through door-to-door sales, through catalogues, or through intermediaries such as agents, wholesalers and retailers.

Channels of Distribution for Consumer Goods

PRODUCER-CONSUMER: Obviously the most direct route is to sell to the consumer without the use of intermediaries. Some producers establish retail outlets or catalogue stores and supply them directly. Others such as Avon and Fuller Brush use door-to-door salespeople. Artists, craftsmen and artisans often sell their wares through their own stores, as do fruit and large produce growers. While direct distribution can mean lower prices for the consumer, it is usually more

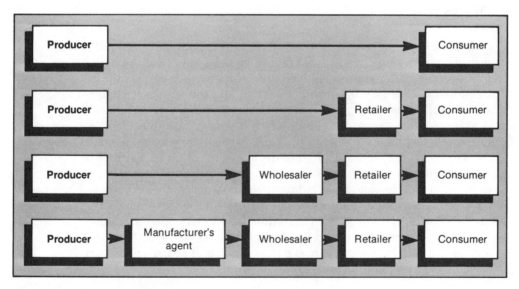

Figure 8.8 Channels of distribution: consumer goods

expensive for the producer, who must perform many of the marketing functions normally handled by intermediaries. Moreover, the producer may not have the expertise or capital required to establish the retail outlets or sales forces necessary for adequate distribution. Most producers, therefore, choose to leave the distribution function to intermediaries.

PRODUCER-RETAILER-CONSUMER: Rather than selling directly to consumers, many manufacturers prefer to deal only with retailers. The producer may have a sales force to sell directly to retail stores, particularly large chain stores, and he thus has more control over the selling situation. For example, if a retailer wants special concessions in return for a large order, the salesperson can communicate directly with head office to get approval for the sale under the specified conditions. Most large chain stores — particularly furniture and appliance stores — also have their own buyers who visit the manufacturer's premises to negotiate purchases.

PRODUCER-WHOLESALER-RETAILER-CONSUMER: Most consumer products are distributed through this chain, particularly low-priced items such as toiletries and cigarettes. The producer may employ a sales force to sell to wholesalers, who generally buy in bulk. The wholesaler in turn employs a sales force to sell to the thousands of smaller retailers in a given geographical area. Because the wholesaler distributes a wide variety of products, the cost per item of the additional sales force is relatively low.

PRODUCER-AGENT-WHOLESALER-RETAILER-CONSUMER: Small manufacturers who cannot afford their own sales forces yet sell their products over a large geographical area, often use a manufacturer's agent as intermediary between themselves and the wholesaler. The agents employ sales forces to sell to wholesalers and large retailers. A manufacturer's agent may represent a number of producers with non-competing products, receiving a commission from each producer.

Producers may use any or all of the above channels to distribute their product. The choice will depend on the target market they want to reach. The Firestone and Goodyear tire companies, for example, have established retail outlets to sell directly to the consumer, and use wholesalers to sell to service stations and independent tire outlets. They also have sales forces to sell to automobile manufacturers and institutional markets such as government, and in particular the armed forces and taxi or car-rental companies.

Channels of Distribution for Industrial Goods

Producers of industrial products may sell their products to industrial customers directly, through manufacturer's agents, or through wholesalers. They may also use a manufacturer's agent to sell to wholesalers who then distribute the product to various industrial customers. Figure 8.9 shows these channels.

The direct channel accounts for the greatest dollar volume in sales of industrial goods. Large installations such as nuclear power plants, turbine generating stations and locomotives are always sold directly to the user. On the other hand, office equipment and supplies and building materials are usually sold through industrial distributors. A producer without a marketing department may use agents to sell directly to industrial users or industrial distributors.

Wholesalers

Wholesalers reduce manufacturers' distribution costs by providing a sales force to sell a large variety of products to several retailers. In addition, many wholesalers store and deliver the merchandise, relieving the producer of responsibilities for warehousing and transportation. Retailers can thus also keep lower inventory levels and

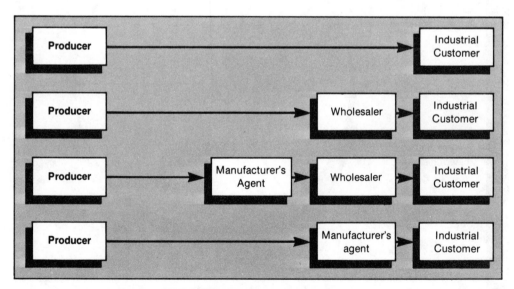

Figure 8.9 Channels of distribution: industrial goods

reduce their inventory costs. The wholesaler also provides retailers with trade credit and other merchandising assistance. Wholesalers can be classified into two general categories — merchant wholesalers and agents.

Merchant wholesalers take title to the products they buy from producers or manufacturers. They therefore own the merchandise outright. As temporary owners they offer a full service to both producers and retailers, paying the producer for the product, storing it until it is sold to retailers, shipping it to retailers and providing them with trade credit and, when necessary, grading and sorting. Because of the risks they take and the services they perform, merchant wholesalers may charge a fee amounting to 25% of the retail price.

Agents do not take title to the goods they distribute, and seldom take possession of the goods. Their major function is to provide the producer with a marketing service by employing a sales force to cover

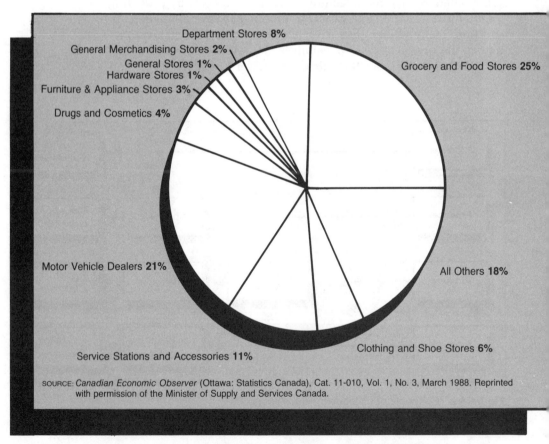

Figure 8.10 Retail trade in Canada, 1987 (total retail sales in 1987: $153.727 billion)

a particular territory. Often, manufacturer's agents handle the products of various non-competing producers. Because the service they provide is limited, agents charge a lower fee or commission, perhaps 5% of sales.

The producer must determine the need for either or both of these channels of distribution. When a producer does not have his own sales force, he is likely to use both kinds of distributors.

Retailers

The retailer is the intermediary who meets the consumer face-to-face; as such, he is the most important link between producer and consumer. Retailers buy their merchandise from the producer or wholesaler, and then resell the goods to the consumer. Since they are so close to the consumer, they can provide the producer with information about both the product and the changing needs and wants of consumers.

Retailing is a competitive business. Small retail stores can be established with little capital, and educational and legal requirements are few. Moreover, retailing requires virtually no previous experience. While these factors attract many people into retailing, the rate of failure is high. Retailers must have a keen ability to forecast consumers' demands. In addition, successful retailers must be imaginative; they must be astute buyers, efficient in their operation and able to provide good service to customers.

Retailing is an important aspect of the Canadian economy. The approximately 152 000 retail stores in Canada employ over 700 000 people. Total retail trade amounts to approximately $150 billion. An average of $5900 for every man, woman and child in Canada is spent in retail stores — over half the average per capita family income.[2]

Retail Chain Stores

Many retail stores have grown into large chain stores with branches in the shopping centres of virtually all major cities. In 1956 independent stores handled 81.8% of total retail sales in terms of dollars; the remaining 18.2% was handled by chain stores. By 1985 chain stores had increased their share of total retail sales to 42%.[3] Table 8.3 lists the top 20 retailers in Canada in 1987, ranked by sales volume.

One major advantage that chain stores have over the independent small retailer is their buying power. Almost all chain stores use some form of **centralized buying**. With a central buying office receiving orders from all of the chain's branches, specialized buyers can comb domestic and world markets and buy merchandise in large quantities. Volume purchases in turn allow these retailers to receive quantity discounts, and the saving can be passed on to the consumer.

TABLE 8.3
Top 20 retailers in Canada, 1987, ranked by sales

Rank by Net Income		Retailers	Net Income		500 Rank
				%	
87	*86*		*$'000*	*Change*	
1	1	Canadian Tire	98 800	12.5	36
2	2	Sears Canada	82 074	4.8	21
3	3	Steinberg	46 066	4.5	19
4	4	F.W. Woolworth	33 333	−19.1	45
5	9	Gendis	22 412	−0.5	153
6	6	K mart Canada	21 466	−25.1	58
7	10	InterTAN Canada	20 090	15.8	243
8	12	Kinney Canada	14 159	7.6	207
9	13	Leon's Furniture	12 402	8.1	324
10	14	Sobeys Stores	10 535	10.3	95
11	11	Reitmans (Canada)	9 400	−36.9	230
12	8	Grafton Group	8 400	−62.8	149
13	25	Henry Birks & Sons	8 298	330.8	225
14	17	Computer Innovations Dist.	6 020	55.7	262
15	16	OE	5 893	19.6	360
16	15	Becker Milk	4 948	−10.9	236
17	18	Trans Canada Glass	4 868	32.5	311
18	23	Silcorp	4 254	84.6	145
19	30	Val Royal Group	3 280	166.2	476
20	19	Carpita	3 130	28.3	448

SOURCE: *Canadian Business, Special 1988 Annual*, June 1988, p. 143.
Reprinted with permission.

Another advantage of chain stores is their capacity for large-scale advertising, often nation-wide. Large-scale advertising reduces costs of television commercials, newspaper advertisements, catalogues and special promotions. Although costly, these advertisements amount to little per dollar of sales when spread over many stores and a large total sales volume.

Retail chains are also able to hire professional managers to specialize in the merchandising of specific products — carpets and rugs, housewares or men's clothing. Department managers know their merchandise well; they can watch for subtle changes in consumer preferences and quickly pass them on to the central buying office.

While chain stores have a number of advantages because of their size, independent retailers are able to concentrate on the areas in which chain stores are deficient — close customer relationships, personal service and specialized merchandise. For example, small cloth-

Retail chain stores may have branches in shopping centres
throughout Canada

ing retailers can be attuned to their customers' needs and wants, call
them when specific clothing items appear in the store, and ensure a
proper fit. Chain stores are not particularly adept in providing personal service, nor do they generally handle merchandise which does
not appeal to a mass consumer market.

The Retail Franchise

In an attempt to combine the advantages of large chain store retailers
with those of the small independent retailer, retail franchising has
become popular. A retail franchise allows centralized buying of merchandise, supplies and equipment, while retaining the virtues of
independent ownership. For an initial investment, which may range
up to $200 000 or more, the franchisee or independent owner can
take part in the success of a well-known firm with a well-known
product. In addition, he or she can benefit from centralized buying,
training, and management services, as well as assistance in locating
advertising and inventory control. If a building is required, plans

and building expertise are available; any equipment required is furnished by suppliers who are aware of the specifications. Retail franchises are discussed in more detail in Chapter 3.

Types of Retail Operations

There are several types of retail operations, each with advantages and disadvantages.

GENERAL STORES: The earliest retailers, general stores offer a wide variety of merchandise and are still common today.

DEPARTMENT STORES: Department stores are, in effect, large general stores with merchandise grouped in departments, each headed by a manager responsible for buying and selling the department's merchandise. Department stores may be either large independent stores, or parts of a chain.

SUPERMARKETS: Supermarkets are large retailers offering a variety of food and other merchandise, self selection, and lower prices than most independent markets.

DISCOUNT STORES: Discount outlets usually offer a variety of merchandise at substantially lower prices than regular stores. There are generally few services such as credit or delivery, and little in the way of elaborate displays or wrappings.

CONVENIENCE STORES: Convenience retailers offer a limited selection of food and some non-food items and are established in convenient locations to save people time and travel. Convenience stores remain open for long hours and may charge relatively high prices for their merchandise.

SPECIALTY STORES: Specialty stores carry only one particular kind of merchandise such as sporting goods, high-priced suits or cameras. By narrowing their total merchandise offering, they can provide a more thorough selection, together with technical expertise and service.

VENDING MACHINES: Merchandise such as soft drinks, sandwiches and candy bars can be sold in vending machines at a low operating cost. Entertainment can also be provided in the form of pinball machines, various electronic games and video cassette rentals.

HYPERMARKETS: Hypermarkets are huge discount stores offering food and general merchandise. Particularly popular in Europe, the idea has spread to both the United States and Canada.

MAIL ORDER: A wide variety of merchandise is available through catalogues and is shipped to the consumer by mail. Mail orders offer convenient shopping from virtually anywhere, and delivery is usually rapid.

Changing Retail Concepts

The classification of retail operations is becoming difficult to apply, since modern retailers are in a continual state of transition. Many outlets start by offering relatively low prices and a minimum of service. As they mature they tend to add services to satisfy their customers and then become vulnerable to undercutting by newer outlets offering lower prices and fewer services. These outlets in turn eventually reach the same maturity stage and are also faced with new competition. This retail cycle is called the **wheel of retailing**.

A second factor that confuses retail classifications is the concept of **scrambled merchandising** — the addition of different types of merchandise to the retailers' original product mix in order to attract more customers. Thus drugstores come to resemble small department stores as they add cameras, stereo equipment, toys, kitchen wares, small appliances, books and records to their basic stock. Supermarkets too have begun to expand into non-food items such as T-shirts, running shoes and stationery. Service stations are also beginning to offer a variety of merchandise and services in addition to gasoline sales and car repairs.

Physical Distribution

So far in our discussion we have considered only the channels of distribution and their members, without focusing on the actual task of transporting products. **Physical distribution** is the aspect of marketing that encompasses all the activities necessary to move products efficiently from producer to consumer. In addition to the transportation of goods, physical distribution involves warehousing, physical handling, packaging for shipment, inventory control, order processing and customer services.

Physical distribution must be considered from an overall point of view. Transportation is often the most costly aspect of the total physical distribution cycle, but the least expensive method is not necessarily the best. The product and the customer must also be considered. Thus while railroads may be the most efficient means of handling large, bulky items such as household appliances, they are not ideal for shipping the latest fashion goods, which must get to the market quickly. Air freight may be more cost-effective. A comparison of the major types of transport is shown in Table 8.4.

TABLE 8.4
The four major forms of transportation ranked by characteristics

	Best	Second	Third	Worst
Speed	Plane	Truck	Train	Ship
Availability	Truck	Train	Plane	Ship
Delivery flexibility	Truck	Train	Plane	Ship
Bulk transportation capability	Ship	Train	Truck	Plane
Cost	Ship	Train	Truck	Plane
Frequency	Truck	Plane	Train	Ship
Dependability	Truck	Train	Ship	Plane

Storage is another major concern, particularly for producers who supply a large area. Railroads can ship large quantities of goods but they must then be stored in regional warehouses. In contrast, trucks can ship smaller quantities and thus reduce the cost of storage and inventory, but transportation costs are higher.

NOTES

1. *Marketing Definitions* (Chicago: American Marketing Association, 1960), p. 15.
2. Statistics Canada, *Canada Year Book, 1988* (Ottawa: Minister of Supply and Services, 1987).
3. *Ibid.*

CHAPTER SUMMARY

Marketing concerns the movement of goods and services from the producer to the consumer. It consists of eight specific functions — buying, selling, storing, transporting, standardizing and grading, financing, risk-taking and information gathering. Most firms today that cater to the consumer are marketing-oriented or geared towards producing the goods and services wanted by consumers.

Since success depends on satisfying the customer's needs, marketing managers must determine the characteristics of the market, whether consumer or industrial, through market research. They then select a target market and determine the particular combination of product features, price, promotion and distribution channel best suited to satisfy it. This combination is known as the marketing mix.

Inevitably, the life cycle of any product is limited. Therefore a firm must constantly plan for the development and introduction of new products. It must also determine the particular product mix that it wishes to sell. The product mix may consist of a single product line or a number of product lines, each made up of products with similar physical characteristics or uses. Other important marketing considerations include branding, packaging and labelling, all of which are significant product characteristics.

Another key marketing decision involves pricing. A firm may choose two general strategies — skimming the market and penetration pricing. To determine specific product prices, a firm may use the full-cost, flexible, gross margin or suggested pricing method. Other considerations in pricing include price-quality relationships and the effects of psychological pricing.

The third element of the marketing mix is promotion, which includes advertising, personal selling, sales promotion and publicity. Advertising takes the largest chunk of the promotion budget, but because it reaches the largest number of customers, it can mean a relatively low cost per person or household reached. The largest amount of advertising money goes to newspapers, with television next, followed by the various other media. Personal selling includes retail sales, door-to-door selling, and sales to industrial customers. Sales promotion is intended to increase sales by supplementing a firm's basic sales effort through displays, demonstrations, specialty advertising, trade shows, samples, coupons, premiums or promotional contests. Publicity is non-paid advertising for a company or its products in trade publications and consumer media; although reports are often favourable, adverse news can be detrimental.

Placing the product means getting it from the manufacturer to the consumer or industrial customer. The manufacturer can choose one or all of the channels available — manufacturer's agents, wholesalers and retailers. Wholesalers are the intermediaries who store products, take credit risks and provide market information. The wholesaler makes it more convenient for retailers and industrial customers to get products as required. Retailers buy goods from manufacturers or wholesalers for resale to consumers.

Most retail stores are small, but a few chain stores in Canada account for a substantial proportion of total retail sales. There are many types of retail operations including department stores, discount stores, supermarkets, convenience stores, mail-order and automatic vendors.

The most common means of transporting products are trucks, railroads, planes and ships. The cost of transportation is important, but other factors such as warehousing, selling and financing must also be taken into consideration.

KEY TERMS

Four P's of marketing
Utility
Buying
Selling
Transporting
Storing
Risk-taking
Standardizing
Grading
Production marketing
Sales-oriented marketing
Marketing era
Marketing research
Marketing concept
Marketing strategy
Target market
Marketing mix
Market segmentation
Consumer goods
Industrial goods
Convenience goods
Shopping goods
Specialty goods
Installations
Total product concept
Product mix
Product line
Product life cycle

Brand
Label
Promotional mix
Advertising
Personal selling
Sales process
Publicity
Sales promotion
Skimming the market
Penetration pricing
Full-cost pricing
Break-even analysis
Flexible pricing
Gross margin pricing
Suggested pricing
Mark-up
Psychological pricing
Channel of distribution
Retailer
Wholesaler
Manufacturing agent
Centralized buying
Chain store
Retail franchising
Wheel of retailing
Scrambled merchandising
Physical distribution

REVIEW QUESTIONS

1. What functions does the marketing department perform?
2. Distinguish between production marketing and sales-oriented marketing. How did the marketing era develop?
3. How can market research be used to select target markets?
4. What is involved in establishing a marketing strategy?

5. Why may each target market require a different marketing mix?

6. Distinguish between consumer and industrial markets.

7. Define each of the three categories of consumer goods.

8. What is meant by the total product concept? Distinguish between product mix and product line.

9. How important is the concept of product life cycles to a firm? Describe each of the four stages in the product life cycle.

10. Why should a salesperson follow the basic sales approach? Explain the importance of each step in the basic sales process.

11. Distinguish between the two pricing strategies — skimming the market and penetration pricing.

12. What is meant by promotional mix? Identify some product examples and indicate the best promotional mix for each.

13. What is a channel of distribution? Define the three channel members.

14. What advantages do retail chains have over small independent retailers? How can franchising provide these advantages to the small retailer?

15. Describe two pricing techniques. What factors must the marketing manager keep in mind when determining a product price?

DISCUSSION QUESTIONS

1. Evaluate the statement: "Marketing costs too much."

2. What are the pros and cons for the consumer of allowing present large Canadian retailers to become even larger through mergers with smaller retail chains?

3. In what aspects of marketing do you favour more government regulation?

4. Is marketing a more important function than production? Debate this issue.

CASE 8-1 Big Screen Television

Television is nothing new to Canadians, except when it comes to 31″ and 35″ direct view sets. The first 35″ direct view set came on the market in 1986 and while it was initially regarded as a high end product it soon gained great popularity.

Large TV pictures are not really new, because projection TVs have been on the market for some years. While they are cheaper to manufacture they are plagued by poor picture resolution, and brightness problems. While projection sets have made substantial advances over the years, they are basically reflected and enlarged images from a set of cathode-ray tubes. Direct view TVs, on the other hand, have large picture tubes which eliminate the problems of projection sets. The main reason why direct view TVs are so popular is that they have a large, crisp, sharp image. After only two years on the market, direct view TVs pose a real challenge to the projection TVs and at this moment it is a tight race between the two types.

Direct view sets are the real thing, but designing these large tubes presented a real challenge to the engineers and research into improving them hasn't stopped. The cost of research and development have also been staggering.

The main problem is implosion. A CRT is basically a vacuum tube. The bigger it is, the stronger it has to be to withstand the atmospheric pressure that wants to cause it to collapse. But this is basically a mathematical problem that was solved with CAD/CAM computer systems to develop the correct thickness and shape of the tube. Now it is every manufacturers' concern to make the big picture better. As the screen gets bigger, the more visible will be the flaws in the picture. For example, the manufacturers had to improve the focussing of the picture in the corners, and improve overall brightness and resolution of the picture. The technical problems that had to be overcome were immense, and as they were resolved, the manufacturers set their sights on making even bigger sets. Forty-one-inch sets are already available for professional and commercial use. But the high cost of producing these sets makes buying one almost impossible for the average consumer. Then again the manufacturers already have designs in the works for 45″ screens and in the not too distant future consumer versions of these sets will be available at affordable prices.

SOURCE: Eric Blare and Glenn Kenny, "Breaking the size barrier," *Video Review*, June 1988, p. 27.

QUESTIONS

1. If you were the marketing manager at SONY, RCA, Mitsubishi, or Hitachi, what criteria would you use to determine the various target markets for large screen TVs?

2. Considering the rapid changes in technology, identify the major concerns of any manufacturer of a new home entertainment product such as a large-screen direct view TV, VCR or videodisc player?

3. What general pricing strategy are the manufacturers using when marketing new home entertainment products? Why are they using this strategy?

4. Which of the pricing methods would a manufacturer of the large direct view TV screen use to price the sets to consumers?

5. Explain how one of the above manufacturers might use the four promotional techniques to promote the direct view television sets.

CASE 8-2 A&W Restaurants: The New Image

In the 1950s and 1960s people were attached to their cars and preferred to stay in them if at all possible. A whole host of services, from drive-in banking to drive-in church services, was developed to cater to the car-bound customer. When it came to drive-in restaurants, A&W was the pioneer.

The 1970s brought intense competition. McDonald's vaulted to the top, with 45% of today's fast-food burger market. Burger King is in the number two spot, while Wendy's, Harvey's and others are trying to overtake Burger King. A&W is part of this group. Its mission is to become the number two fast-food outlet in Canada, and its strategy is to press the pack and look for niches it can fill with speciality foods. According to market research A&W is considered to have the best-tasting food in the adult market. Research further indicates that both the 18–35 prime target age group and the 35-plus age group are becoming more health conscious. With this in mind, A&W is trying to appeal to consumers who want to watch what they eat.

The transformation has been quiet. A&W started with a new management team, the rebuilding of its restaurants, and the refining of its menus. Currently it has 340 restaurants in Canada, with 110 of these corporately owned. The rest are franchise operations mainly operating in suburban or smaller towns. A&W also owns the western Canada franchise rights for Cultures Restaurants, which focus on food for the health conscious. A subsidiary company controls six outlets: two each in Vancouver and Winnipeg, and one each in Edmonton and Calgary. Another newly opened chain in Victoria, B.C., is Frisco Jacks, a restaurant that offers sourdough bread products with a variety of toppings including sweet dessert fillings and chicken a la king. This restaurant caters to the lunchtime crowd that wants a nutritious meal. Financial results seem to indicate that A&W is successful in its new form. A&W projects revenues of $200 million in 1988, up from $145 million in 1986 and $170 million in 1987. There has been an eight-fold improvement in return on investment.

SOURCE: Adapted from Jean Sorensen, "The Burger Team," *BC Business*, September 1988, p. 30.

QUESTIONS

1. Identify the target market and describe the marketing mix of some of the major fast-food restaurants that you know, such as McDonald's and Burger King.
2. What can A&W do to achieve its mission of becoming the number two fast-food restaurant chain?

CHAPTER 9

Finance

Dick Hemingway

CHAPTER OUTLINE

CHAPTER PREVIEW

In Chapter 9 we examine the finance function of a business. First, the finance manager must ensure that the business always has enough cash on hand to pay its bills as they come due; occasionally he or she must secure short-term loans. Second, the business requires a system of accounts detailing all financial transactions that occur. An accounting system is necessary to prepare the financial statements required by management for decision-making, as well as by government bankers and investors. Accurate financial information is also necessary to compare business performance with the past and with the performance of other businesses in the same industry. A third major task of the financial manager is to ensure that funds are available to expand the business and to replace plant, equipment and machines. This task is known as long-term financing, since plant, equipment and machines are expected to last for many years, and the funds borrowed to purchase them are usually repaid over a long period of time.

LEARNING OBJECTIVES

After reading this chapter you should be able to explain:

1. The three major functions of the finance manager;
2. The meaning of cash flow, and how a finance manager ensures enough cash is always on hand to meet expenses;
3. The major sources of short-term financing;
4. The purpose of an accounting system, and why it is essential to any organization;
5. The necessity for each of the three major accounting statements — balance sheet, income statement and statement of changes in financial position;
6. The most common financial ratios, and how they are used for control purposes;
7. The differences between debt financing and equity financing;
8. The advantages and disadvantages of stocks and bonds;
9. The difference between common and preferred shares;
10. The major factors that a financial manager must consider before deciding between stocks and bonds as a means of raising long-term funds;
11. The basic operation of the stock and bond market.

How can a corporation raise $800 million to build a new automobile assembly plant? How does a small business raise the funds required to build a new plant or purchase an expensive machine? Few companies would have sufficient funds readily available in a bank account. Companies, like individuals, must either save or borrow for major ventures and the availability of loans depends on the applicant's credit rating. The credit rating in turn depends on how well a company is managed — usually indicated by the profit the firm has made in the past — and the likelihood that it will continue to be profitable in the future.

A healthy cash flow from their operation and a good credit rating are therefore as important to business firms as they are to individuals. Manufacturing firms must purchase the raw materials required for production, while wholesalers and retailers must buy finished goods for resale to consumers. Businesses must pay salaries to their employees, in addition to rent and utilities, while worn out buildings and equipment must be replaced. And as businesses grow, they require funds to expand. The finance manager must therefore control the inflow and outflow of funds carefully, and plan for additional funds to meet future needs.

THE FUNCTION OF THE FINANCE DEPARTMENT

Finances are a major concern of every business. In a small business the owner is personally responsible for ensuring that funds are used efficiently, and for borrowing as necessary. In a large corporation the finance function is usually a separate department, headed by a vice president and including a number of lower-level managers to perform specialized functions. The finance department performs three major functions:

1. **Acquiring operating funds**. A business must have cash available at all times to handle expenditures incurred in normal operations. Employees expect to be paid for the work they do, and suppliers expect to be paid for the raw materials or finished products they provide. In addition to these payments, the firm has various other financial obligations such as rent, utilities and services provided by other firms, not to mention provincial, federal and municipal taxes. If the firm is unable to meet these payments, it could face bankruptcy.

2. **Analyzing operations**. The finance department performs a regular analysis of the firm's operation to ensure that it is functioning efficiently. This analysis requires an accounting system and the collection of financial data. At the end of a specific time period the information is summarized in a number of accounting statements. The three major accounting statements used in financial analysis are the income statement, the balance sheet, and a statement showing the source and use of funds. Management uses the statements to determine how the firm is doing and to compare performance with previous years, or with other businesses in a similar industry. Except in small businesses, the accounting function is usually a separate department, although the accounting manager usually reports to the firm's top financial executive, often the vice-president of finance.

3. **Acquiring long-term funds**. Even gradual growth may require large amounts of money that the firm can repay only over a long period of time. A new plant in another province, for example, may require a few million dollars more than the regular operation can supply. The finance manager must raise the required funds either by borrowing or by selling shares of ownership in the company to investors.

ENSURING FINANCIAL SOLVENCY

Even a profitable company can become bankrupt. Profits shown on financial statements do not mean that a firm has managed its funds efficiently. A firm may not be able to pay current debts if too much money is tied up in accounts receivable and inventory, or if money was invested in additional plant capacity, equipment and machinery. If a firm has no cash to pay its operating debts, creditors could petition the courts to have the firm declared bankrupt. Thus, the most important function of the finance department is to ensure that the business can pay its bills as they come due.

Working Capital and the Cash Budget

Cash is basic to the operation of any business. As Figure 9.1 indicates, cash is used to purchase the capital goods — buildings, machines, equipment and furniture — necessary for the firm to operate. This is **fixed capital**. But cash is also required in current operations, to generate sales revenue through either the manufacture of goods or the provision of a service. Cash used for these purposes is known as **working capital**. In a retail business, for example, cash is used to buy inventory, pay for wages and salaries and the many other expenses incurred in its regular operation. When merchandise is sold, the firm once again receives cash, either at the point of sale or somewhat later if the sale is on credit. Thus **cash flows** in a circular pattern, and it generates not only sales revenue but also the firm's profit.

Although management has little control over sales since it cannot force people to buy, it does have control over the amount of inventory purchased, the number of people on the payroll, the collection of accounts receivable, and other expenses. Planning and sales forecasting are therefore important. The firm's operation must be geared to anticipated sales. If planned sales revenue does not provide sufficient funds to meet expected expenses and debts that must be paid, the firm can plan to borrow money to continue operating during slow periods.

Expected inflows and outflows of funds over six months to a year are summarized in a **cash budget**, as shown in Figure 9.2. Starting with the cash balance at the beginning of the period, the estimated receipts for each month are added up and the estimated expenditures deducted to arrive at a month-end cash balance.

With a cash budget, finance managers can determine periods when they may expect a shortage of cash, and how much the shortage might be. Thus they are able to make arrangements to borrow money when necessary and repay loans during the months when there is a surplus.

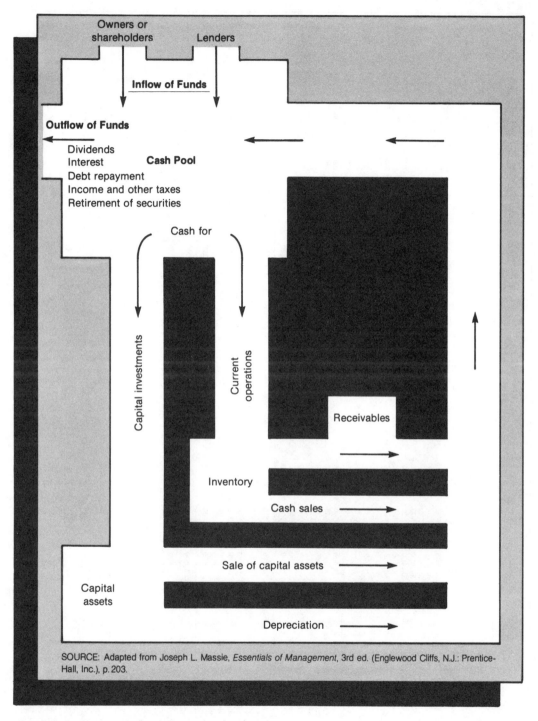

Owners or shareholders

Lenders

Inflow of Funds

Outflow of Funds

Dividends
Interest
Debt repayment
Income and other taxes
Retirement of securities

Cash Pool

Cash for

Capital investments

Current operations

Receivables

Inventory

Cash sales

Sale of capital assets

Capital assets

Depreciation

SOURCE: Adapted from Joseph L. Massie, *Essentials of Management*, 3rd ed. (Englewood Cliffs, N.J.: Prentice-Hall, Inc.), p. 203.

Figure 9.1 How cash flows through a business

Figure 9.2 Wombat Ski Equipment Co. Inc.—Cash Budget for the year 1990

	JAN	FEB	MAR	APR	MAY	JUN	JUL	AUG	SEP	OCT	NOV	DEC	TOTAL
Sales													
Ski equipment cat 150	67,000	57,000	51,000	36,000	22,000	14,000	14,000	22,000	64,000	92,000	126,000	136,000	701,000
Equipment rentals cat 250	13,000	9,000	7,000	3,000	3,000	3,000	3,000	5,000	10,000	14,000	25,000	31,000	123,000
Travel packages cat 300	8,000	8,000	4,000	4,000	4,000	4,000	3,000	6,000	12,000	18,000	22,000	25,000	118,000
Other income	2,000	2,000	2,000	3,000	3,000	3,000	3,000	3,000	3,000	3,000	3,000	3,000	33,000
Total sales	90,000	76,000	64,000	46,000	32,000	24,000	20,000	36,000	89,000	127,000	176,000	195,000	975,000
Collections													
During month	54,000	45,600	38,400	27,600	19,200	14,400	12,000	21,600	53,400	76,200	105,600	117,000	585,000
One month lag	33,000	27,000	22,800	19,200	13,800	9,600	7,200	6,000	10,800	26,700	38,100	52,800	267,000
Two month lag	9,600	11,000	9,000	7,600	6,400	4,600	3,200	2,400	2,000	3,600	8,900	12,700	81,000
Total collections	96,600	83,600	70,200	54,400	39,400	28,600	22,400	30,000	66,200	106,500	152,600	182,500	933,000
Expenditures													
General & administrative:													
Rent	2,000	2,000	2,000	2,000	2,000	2,000	2,000	2,000	2,000	2,000	2,000	2,000	24,000
Management salaries	3,000	3,000	3,000	3,000	3,000	3,000	3,000	3,000	3,000	3,000	3,000	3,000	36,000
Clerical salaries	1,500	1,500	1,500	1,500	1,500	1,500	1,500	1,500	1,500	1,500	1,500	1,500	18,000
Utilities	520	520	520	520	520	520	520	520	520	520	520	520	6,240
Office supplies	300	300	300	300	300	300	300	300	300	300	300	300	3,600
Legal & accounting	350	350	350	350	350	350	350	350	350	350	350	350	4,200
Miscellaneous	500	500	500	500	500	500	500	500	500	500	500	500	6,000
Total gen. & admin. expenses	8,170	8,170	8,170	8,170	8,170	8,170	8,170	8,170	8,170	8,170	8,170	8,170	98,040
Selling:													
Wages	5,200	4,500	3,000	3,000	3,000	3,000	3,000	3,000	5,000	8,000	12,000	12,000	64,700
Advertising	4,500	2,000	500	500	500	500	500	800	2,000	2,500	3,500	4,000	21,800
Supplies	1,000	1,000	700	700	400	400	400	400	700	900	1,300	1,400	9,300
Delivery	1,000	800	700	500	300	200	200	600	900	1,200	1,700	1,900	10,000
Miscellaneous	800	800	500	500	500	200	200	200	200	300	600	1,200	6,000
Total selling expenses	12,500	9,100	5,400	5,200	4,700	4,300	4,300	5,000	8,800	12,900	19,100	20,500	111,800
Total expenses	20,670	17,270	13,570	13,370	12,870	12,470	12,470	13,170	16,970	21,070	27,270	28,670	209,840
Cash inflow from operation	96,600	83,600	70,200	54,400	39,400	28,600	22,400	30,000	66,200	106,500	152,600	182,500	933,000
Less:													
Total expenses	20,670	17,270	13,570	13,370	12,870	12,470	12,470	13,170	16,970	21,070	27,270	28,670	209,840
Purchases (net)	44,000	37,000	36,000	21,000	15,000	15,000	24,000	104,000	136,000	116,000	135,000	96,000	809,000
Net cash flow	31,930	29,330	20,630	20,030	11,530	1,130	(14,070)	(87,170)	(86,770)	(60,570)	9,670	57,830	(85,840)
Balance beginning of month	23,140	55,070	84,400	105,030	125,060	136,590	137,720	123,650	36,480	55,290	10,280	4,390	
Cumulative cash end of month	55,070	84,400	105,030	125,060	136,590	137,720	123,650	36,480	(50,290)	(5,280)	610	62,220	
Minimum cash balance required	5,000	5,000	5,000	5,000	5,000	5,000	5,000	5,000	5,000	5,000	5,000	5,000	
Surplus or (deficit)	50,070	79,400	100,030	120,060	131,590	132,720	118,650	31,480	(55,290)	(10,280)	(4,390)	57,220	
Bank loan required									55,290	10,280	4,390		69,960
Bank loan repayment												57,220	57,220

Short-Term Borrowing

As the cash budget for Wombat Ski Equipment Company Inc. shows, receipts and expenditures are not always in line. In fact, while expenses are fairly constant throughout the year, sales revenue fluctuates widely. Since Wombat sells only ski equipment, sales are very low for the months of May through October. Nevertheless, the firm must continue to pay rent, utilities, salaries and a host of other expenses. Once the ski season is in full swing, sales revenue will quickly exceed expenditures. To cover expenses in the off-season, however, Wombat has to borrow money, which is repaid during periods when sales revenue is high. Many businesses, large and small, resort to short-term borrowing when revenues are low to avoid bankruptcy.

A business that borrows money to operate is not necessarily inefficiently run or on the verge of bankruptcy. Many businesses regularly borrow money to tide themselves over slow periods when expenses may be greater than the cash inflow from sales. Alternatively a company may need short-term financing to purchase inventory for anticipated sales increases due either to growth or to a sudden economic upswing. A firm may also need short-term financing to meet expenses during a strike, or to take advantage of a new business opportunity.

Borrowing money when necessary is a common business practice. Keeping a large surplus of cash in the bank is not always advantageous. Money in a chequing account usually does not earn interest. A limited amount of cash can be kept in the bank to pay bills as they come due, while any surplus can be used either in the operation of the business or it can be invested in securities that will earn interest. Should a shortage of funds occur, the firm can then convert the securities into cash. A firm that does not have a cash reserve in the form of securities must borrow money as required.

Sources of Short-Term Funds

The major sources of short-term funds are trade creditors, commercial banks, factor companies, sales finance companies and other businesses and investors. We now examine how each source can serve a business.

Trade Creditors

An established business that has built a reputation for sound operation and has a good credit rating, can buy inventory, raw materials or other supplies on credit. The supplier ships the goods ordered and allows the buyer a certain length of time to pay for them. This period of time may vary from one week, as is customary for meat and produce, to three months or more for some raw materials. Generally, however, thirty days are allowed. Credit, however, represents a cost to the supplier. To induce the buyer to pay sooner, the seller often grants a discount shown as "2/10 net 30" on the invoice — the buyer can deduct 2% from the total amount of the invoice if he pays within ten days of the billing date. Otherwise he must pay the full invoice amount within thirty days.

Advantage of Cash Discounts

If you can take advantage of cash discounts, you in effect obtain a reduction from the supplier on the price of the product. If you were offered 2/10 net 30 on a $1000 invoice, for example, you would save $20 by paying within ten days. While you would lose the use of the $1000 for twenty days, the discount means more than a 36% return per annum since there are slightly more than eighteen twenty-day periods in a year. Thus it is to your advantage to borrow $1000 from the bank at 10% in order to earn 36% from supplier discounts.

Types of Trade Credit

OPEN BOOK CREDIT: Most trade credit is given on the so-called "**open book account**" which allows a purchaser to obtain goods from the supplier and pay for them after a specific period of time. The buyer phones or mails in an order, which the seller fills and ships together with an invoice for the goods. The seller then enters the amount of the purchase in a sales ledger and waits for the buyer to send the payment according to the terms and conditions established at the outset of their business dealings. However, this form of trade credit is usually extended only to firms with a good credit rating.

The procedures for setting up an open book account may be stringent or easy, depending on the supplier. For example, a supplier might find that liberal credit policies mean sales increases proportionately greater than the potential losses from firms that do not pay their debts. Thus it may be in the seller's interest to be relatively lenient in granting credit.

CONSIGNMENT: When goods are purchased on consignment, the seller retains ownership since the buyer does not pay for the goods until they are sold to customers. The seller also absorbs the cost of credit and any losses that may be incurred, unless otherwise specified.

PROMISSORY NOTES: A promissory note is a business "I.O.U." Some sellers prefer to have a written agreement made out and signed by the customer. The customer pledges to pay the seller a certain sum of money at a specified date. A promissory note also states the rate of interest payable until the principal is paid. It is generally used for sales of valuable goods or when the customer has been slow in paying for merchandise on the open book account.

TRADE DRAFTS AND TRADE ACCEPTANCE: A trade draft combines the advantages of allowing customers to order merchandise on the open book account with the relative security provided by a promissory note. Upon receiving the order, the seller, or **drawer**, originates a draft and sends it along with the merchandise to the customer, or **drawee**. If the drawee accepts the draft, he or she writes his or her name across the face of it. In the case of a **time draft**, the customer has a specified period of time to pay for the merchandise. When the document is signed, it becomes a **trade acceptance**. On the other hand, a **sight draft**, as shown in Figure 9.3, requires the customer to pay on presentation.

Trade or **commercial drafts** are commonly used when goods are sold to customers, often foreign, whose credit rating is either poor or unknown. The seller then sends a sight draft to the customer together with an **order bill of lading** — a receipt from the shipping company. When the customer presents the order bill of lading to the shipping company, he or she can take possession of the goods provided the sight draft has been paid.

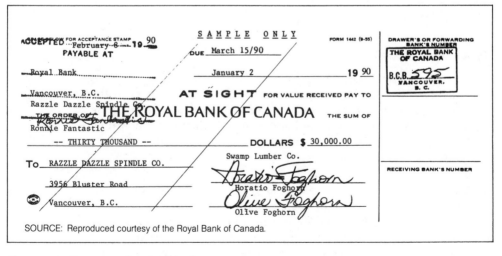

SOURCE: Reproduced courtesy of the Royal Bank of Canada.

Figure 9.3 Example of a sight draft

Loans from Chartered Banks

Although trade credit is the most common source of short-term credit, businesses often need money to make an outright purchase, to pay debts or to buy additional materials for manufacturing or merchandise for sale. If the money is needed for a period of less than one year, a business is likely to turn to a chartered bank for a short-term loan. Repayment terms are usually flexible and are often geared to cash flow. There are fourteen chartered banks in Canada; some are regional, but the "big five" — the Royal Bank of Canada, the Canadian Imperial Bank of Commerce, the Bank of Montreal, the Bank of Nova Scotia and the Toronto Dominion Bank — have branches across the country.

Secured Bank Loans

When you approach a bank manager for a business loan, he will want to know something about your business. For example, is the firm new, or is it an established operation? Do you manufacture a product, or provide a service? Are you in a rapidly growing industry? What are your qualifications for operating the business — your business experience and past successes? In addition the bank will usually want some security, known as **collateral**. Collateral refers to items of specific value which may be signed over to the bank for as long as the loan is outstanding, and can be seized and sold if the borrower is unable to repay the loan. In some instances, particularly when the business is incorporated, the borrower may be asked to provide a **personal guarantee** to repay the loan. Alternatively, the borrower may be asked to pledge personal assets as security, apart from the assets of the business.

Types of Collateral

ACCOUNTS RECEIVABLE: Accounts receivable are monies owed to the business — monies it expects to collect from customers in the near future. A firm's representative signs a statement promising the lender the receivables until the loan is repaid. Customers continue to send their payments to the business and the business in turn forwards them to the bank.

INVENTORIES: A company with a large inventory of products that are not required for sale immediately may use the inventory as collateral for a short-term loan. The inventory is stored in an independent warehouse which gives the company a trust receipt. The receipt is then signed over by the borrowing company to the lender. Before the borrowing firm can recover its inventory for sale, it must pay off the loan to the bank, which will then return the trust receipt to the borrower. Should the borrower default, the bank may sell the inventory to cover the loan.

OTHER PROPERTY: Any valuable property can be used as collateral — buildings, automobiles, trucks or farm machinery. However, for this kind of collateral the bank may require that the business sign a chattel mortgage agreement in addition to the normal loan agreement. With the chattel mortgage, the borrower has the use of the equipment and is responsible for it, but the lender has the legal right to seize it if the borrower does not repay the loan as specified in the agreement.

Types of Loans

The most common business bank loan is the **demand loan**, for which the borrower signs a **demand note**. Under this arrangement, the bank may demand payment at any time — for example, if it loses confidence in the firm's financial situation.

Often a demand loan is combined with a **line of credit** which allows the business to borrow up to a pre-arranged maximum over a fixed period of time. The advantage of the line of credit is that the business can borrow only what is required, and the remainder is available at any time during the life of the agreement. Interest rates may therefore be reduced, even though the bank charges a stand-by fee since it must have the financial resources available should the business ask for further loans under the agreement. In some instances, the bank may require that the business maintain a **compensating balance** — a fixed percentage of the line of credit — in an

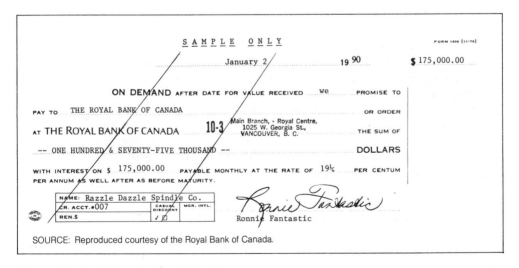

SOURCE: Reproduced courtesy of the Royal Bank of Canada.

Figure 9.4 Example of a demand note

interest-free account. The compensating balance in effect raises the cost of borrowing for the firm, since the funds are not available for use in the business. Meanwhile, the bank is free to use the funds, without having to pay interest on them.

Unsecured Bank Loans

If the bank manager is willing to give the business an unsecured loan, no collateral is required. The bank manager is satisfied that the borrower will repay the loan according to the agreement, usually because the firm has a good credit rating. However, the bank will also consider factors such as the firm's future profitability and the amount of the owner's equity in the business. If the equity is substantial, the bank's risk is reduced.

Acquiring Funds Through Factoring

A business may also raise money by selling its accounts receivable directly to a **factor company**, which buys the receivables from the business at a discount and then collects the money from the firm's customers. The factor company makes its profit by buying the receivables at a discount. If the factor company has no recourse — in other words, if it cannot return uncollectable accounts to the business from which it bought them — the discount may be substantially greater than if the original firm is prepared to accept bad debts.

Although factoring may be costly for the firm, it is one method of freeing funds which would otherwise be tied up in accounts receivable. It does, however, leave the firm less flexibility with its customers, and may be detrimental to customer relations since clients are required to deal with the factor company when paying their accounts.

The principle of factoring also underlies bank-sponsored credit cards such as Master Card and Visa, which allow customers to purchase merchandise from a wide variety of retailers. When these retailers deposit their credit card receipts with their bank, their account is credited with the amount of the customer's purchase less a handling charge of up to 6%. The charge may appear high; however, the credit cards provide merchants with a large number of customers and do not tie up their funds in accounts receivable, as would be the case if they were to extend credit themselves.

Finance Companies

Finance companies serve both private individuals who purchase material goods, and businesses that require short-term funds. The interest rates charged by finance companies tend to be higher than those charged by banks, because finance companies will lend money in higher risk situations, for example, to companies that do not have good collateral. Several of the finance companies operating in Canada today are owned in part by chartered banks.

Loans by finance companies are most often made against collateral such as accounts receivable, inventories or the equipment to be purchased with the borrowed funds. Finance companies also provide outright financing for machinery and equipment through **conditional sales contracts**. If a business can make only partial payment for an item, the finance company will draw up an agreement specifying the number of installments required to repay the loan, the interest rate charged and where ownership of the machinery or equipment will lie for the term. Similar conditional sales contracts are used when a consumer purchases a car, for example.

Finance companies can also provide money to businesses by **discounting trade drafts** and **promissory notes**. Both of these financial instruments represent money owed to the firm by customers or other debtors, to be paid at a future date. A business that needs the funds immediately may sell the financial papers to a finance company in return for the face value of the note, less a discount. When the note comes due, the finance company collects the full amount owed from the original issuer.

Loans from Investors and Other Businesses

Large companies requiring short-term funds may borrow in the short-term money market by issuing promissory notes, also known as **commercial** or **corporate papers**. Investment dealers play a large part in these transactions because they bring borrowers and lenders together. For example, a large company with a cash surplus may be prepared to lend to other firms for 30, 60 or 90 days or more. Both the lender and the borrower benefit — the lending company earns interest on its surplus funds, while the borrower can usually obtain the funds at an interest rate lower than that offered by financial institutions, and often free from many of their restrictions.

Sources of Funds from the Federal Government

The federal government has established a number of agencies and organizations to provide direct loans or loan guarantees to businesses. Loans may be for business improvements; to help specific industries threatened by international competition; to help manufacturing and processing industries located in regions with particularly high unemployment; and to support businesses dealing with foreign purchasers of Canadian goods and services. The **Federal Business Development Bank** (FBDB), for example, provides loans to businesses that cannot obtain financing from conventional sources.

As noted earlier, borrowing money for business operations is an important, often necessary requirement for almost all businesses, regardless of size. Nevertheless, many small businesses find it difficult to raise money, primarily because they are ill-prepared for presentations when they approach financial institutions. The article "Financing — A Mystery to Small Business" (in Chapter 3) points out the problems small businesses face and suggests solutions.

CONTROLLING FINANCIAL OPERATIONS

Ensuring that sufficient cash is available to meet debts as they arise is the most important control requirement of any business. However, a business also must know how well it is operating — how profitable it is, and whether its assets are increasing or decreasing. For this purpose the firm must establish an accounting system. **Accounting** is the process of recording, gathering, organizing, reporting and interpreting data and information to describe the operation of the firm and help in the decision-making process.

Accounting can be broken down into two major functions — financial and management accounting. **Financial accounting** keeps track of the firm's resources in dollar terms and prepares financial reports, which can be shown to anyone interested in the performance of the firm, such as owners, potential investors, the tax department, lenders and managers.

Management accounting provides information used primarily by internal managers in decision-making. For example, it involves overall budgeting, forecasting and break-even analysis, and the evaluation of investments to determine those that are profitable. It can help management isolate problems — in production, sales, finance or inventory, for example — and aid in resolving them.

Accounting and Bookkeeping

Accounting is often mistaken for bookkeeping. **Bookkeeping** is the clerical task of recording daily the firm's financial transactions. **Accounting** is the task of summarizing the recorded data into meaningful information and reporting on the firm's operation. Accountants may specialize in particular aspects of accounting such as cost accounting, auditing or taxation. They acquire expertise relative to their business or industry and help in financial decision-making.

Financial Accounting

The accounting system provides financial information essential for managers in decision-making. Financial statements show where the firm stands in terms of profit and loss at a particular time, and can indicate future directions. Owners and shareholders can see how much profit the firm has made during a particular month or year. Financial statements are also required by government for tax purposes, by lenders to ensure their loan is secure and by suppliers before they grant trade credit. Last, but certainly not least, financial information is needed to substantiate the firm's tax liability to Revenue Canada.

The Accounting Process

In the first part of this chapter we emphasized the inflow and outflow of cash resulting from business transactions. A day's sales in a department store, for example, may consist of thousands of transactions between the firm and its customers. A method must be developed to record the individual sales made in various departments. Records must also be kept on payments made to employees and suppliers, and on the hundreds of merchandise shipments received by the firm.

Specific accounts are set up to record individual transactions. The transactions are usually summarized monthly and reports are made to management. Management, for example, must know the total sales and expenses of each department. It must also know whether inventories and customer credit accounts have increased or decreased during the month so that appropriate action can be taken. For example, if sales have decreased from the previous month while inventories increased, then too much money may be tied up in merchandise and management must make sure that the firm does not face a cash shortage. Financial statements for outside parties such as shareholders and investors are usually prepared quarterly, semi-annually or annually.

Accounting Statements

Although every business prepares a variety of financial statements, three statements are standard. The first is the **balance sheet**, which shows the firm's financial standing at a particular point in time. Second is the **income statement**, which summarizes business transactions over a period of time, showing sales, expenses and the profit or loss that has been realized during that period. The third, known as a **statement of changes in financial position**, shows how the firm obtained and spent the cash received during a particular period of time. Figure 9.5 shows the relationship between the income statement and two balance sheets, one for the beginning and one for the end of the year.

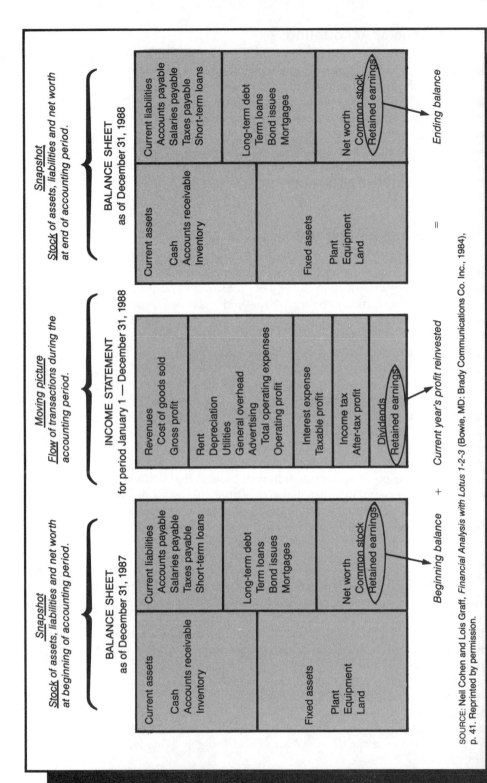

Figure 9.5 Accounting model of a business

The Balance Sheet

The balance sheets in Figure 9.6 show the financial condition of Wombat Ski Equipment Company Inc. at the beginning and end of the year. Each balance sheet shows the firm's total assets in dollars and indicates how much of the total belongs to owners of the business and how much to creditors. **Total assets** include all property that belongs to the business — cash, accounts receivable, inventory, buildings, furniture and fixtures. Since our example is a retail business, assets such as plant, equipment and machinery, which would be included in the balance sheet of a manufacturing firm, do not appear.

The **liabilities** or debts owed by the business include money the firm owes to suppliers and employees, rent to the landlord, and taxes to the tax department. The section known as **shareholders' equity** represents the book value or equity that the owners or stockholders have in the business. The book value of a business is based on cost data and may differ substantially from the market value of its assets.

The total dollar value of the assets must always be equal to the total dollar value of liabilities, plus the equity of the shareholders, as shown in the following equation:

$$\text{Assets} = \text{Liabilities} + \text{Shareholders' equity}$$

The two sides must always balance, as all the firm's assets must belong to someone, whether to owners or to creditors such as suppliers, banks or mortgage companies.

Current and Fixed Assets

The assets section of the balance sheet contains two major categories — current and fixed assets. **Current assets** consist primarily of cash, accounts receivable, inventory and other prepaid expenses which make up the working capital used in the firm's regular business operations.

Accounts receivable represent money owed to the firm by customers who have made their purchases on credit. Usually accounts are paid monthly. If an account is not paid within the time allotted, then the firm must take immediate action to recover its money. A lax policy of collecting outstanding accounts could lead the firm into bankruptcy since it may not have enough cash to meet its debts.

Inventories represent merchandise, raw materials or parts that have not as yet been sold. As discussed in Chapter 7, proper inventory management is important because excess inventory ties up a firm's cash and money may not be available to take advantage of other business opportunities or to pay debts. **Prepaid expenses** represent cash outlays usually for services that have not as yet been used, such as insurance, rent or utilities.

Fixed assets include items such as plant, equipment and machinery, trucks, and office equipment used in daily business oper-

WOMBAT SKI EQUIPMENT CO. INC.

Balance Sheet As at December 31, 1989		Balance Sheet As at December 31, 1990	

ASSETS

CURRENT ASSETS		CURRENT ASSETS	
Cash	8,894	Cash	23,140
Marketable Securities	40,000	Marketable Securities	45,000
Accounts receivable	93,240	Accounts receivable	137,340
Inventory	187,450	Inventory	127,030
Prepaid expenses	8,900	Prepaid expenses	13,500
Total current assets	338,484	Total current assets	346,010
FIXED ASSETS		**FIXED ASSETS**	
Land	0	Land	0
Buildings	0	Buildings	187,000
Less:Accum Dep	0	Less:Accum Dep	18,700
Equipment & Fixtures	76,600	Equipment & Fixtures	86,450
Less:Accum Dep	15,320	Less:Accum Dep	29,546
Total Fixed assets	61,280	Total Fixed assets	225,204
TOTAL ASSETS	399,764	TOTAL ASSETS	571,214

LIABILITIES

CURRENT LIABILITIES		CURRENT LIABILITIES	
Accounts payable	115,948	Accounts payable	122,530
Loans payable	23,000	Loans payable	35,000
Accrued liabilities	19,934	Accrued liabilities	23,450
Total current liabilities	158,882	Total current liabilities	180,980
LONG-TERM LIABILITIES		**LONG-TERM LIABILITIES**	
Long term loan on equip	85,300	Long term loan on equip	72,000
		Mortgage on buildings	98,653
Total liabilities	244,182	Total liabilities	351,633
SHAREHOLDER'S EQUITY		**SHAREHOLDER'S EQUITY**	
Common stock	100,000	Common stock	100,000
Retained earnings	55,582	Retained earnings	119,581
Total shareholders equity	155,582	Total shareholders equity	219,581
TOTAL LIABILITIES & EQUITY	399,764	TOTAL LIABILITIES & EQUITY	571,214

Figure 9.6 Comparative balance sheets at two different time periods

ations to produce goods or services for sale. Fixed assets are always valued at their initial cost to the firm. As they are used and wear out, they depreciate in value.

Depreciation is a regular operating expense and appears on the firm's income statement. The total depreciation of each fixed asset as of a particular date is shown on the balance sheet.

The federal tax department states how much a firm may depreciate a fixed asset for tax purposes, which is known as the **capital cost allowance (CCA)**. Methods of depreciation allowed by the tax department may or may not be identical to methods the firm uses for its own purposes. For example, the tax department may allow a firm to take CCA on an automobile at 30% per year on a decreasing balance basis. The firm could claim the 30% CCA as an expense against its income to calculate income subject to taxes. However, for its own statements, the firm may believe that a straight line depreciation will better indicate to shareholders the worth of the firm and the income for the year. In straight line depreciation the total cost of an asset minus expected salvage value is divided by its expected life in years, and the resulting amount is then charged off as depreciation. A $10 000 truck expected to last for five years, for example, would be depreciated at the rate of $2000 per year. Under these circumstances the firm would maintain two sets of records, one for the tax department and one for its own shareholders.

Once the truck is fully depreciated on the firm's books it will no longer represent any dollar value as an asset, even though it may still be useful. When the truck is eventually sold, the proceeds, if any, must be shown as income — an extraordinary gain from the sale of fixed assets. Fixed assets are not ordinarily turned into cash except when equipment or a building is no longer required for regular business operations, or when a firm experiences a severe cash shortage with little chance for borrowing the money.

Current and Long-Term Liabilities

The liabilities section of the balance sheet is also broken into two main categories — current and long-term liabilities. **Current liabilities** represent the debts that the business has incurred in the regular course of operations. They include accounts payable — amounts owed to suppliers for raw materials and merchandise purchased — wages to be paid to employees, and taxes payable to the government based on current operation. They may also include rent or billings for advertising, and any other debts to be paid during the coming year. Liabilities are current if they are expected to be paid off within the year.

Long-term liabilities are debts such as bank loans, mortgages on buildings, or payment for trucks or other equipment. The payments will be made over a number of years. Only the current year's payments are included as current liabilities.

Shareholders' Equity

The category known as shareholders' equity shows the amount of money that the owners — shareholders — have invested in the business. The amount listed opposite common stock in Figure 9.6 is the total money raised from the initial sale of shares to the owners. **Retained earnings** represent profits not taken out of the company.

Shareholders' equity can also be regarded as the amount of money that would remain for the owners if they were to sell their assets at book value and pay off all liabilities. For a firm that is not incorporated — a sole proprietorship or partnership — the term **owners' equity** or **partnership equity** is used.

The Income Statement

The income statement shows the net profit or loss resulting from the operation of the firm over a period of time. Figure 9.7 shows a typical income statement for a one-year period.

Gross sales represent the dollar value of all sales made to customers during a particular period. **Net sales** represent actual sales after all returns and customer allowances have been deducted from gross sales.

The **cost of goods sold** — the cost of the actual merchandise sold to customers — is deducted from net sales, leaving an amount called the **gross profit**. The cost of goods sold figure may be calculated by adding net purchases for the period to the value of the initial inventory and then subtracting the value of the final inventory. Both inventory figures are usually arrived at by physically counting the value of the stock.

Expenses incurred in the course of regular business operations are then deducted from the gross profit, to give the **net profit before taxes**. Expenses may be broken down into **operating expenses** and **general** and **administrative expenses**. The distinction is generally not important in a small business, but in a large firm with many departments, general and administrative expenses are those that pertain to the firm as a whole, and may include salaries and office expenses for support personnel, head office personnel, including the president, and research and development. These expenses are distributed among departments based on some method such as the percentage each department has sold of total sales.

If the business is a corporation, it is a separate legal entity and will be taxed as such. The **net profit** is the amount that remains after corporate income taxes have been deducted. This profit belongs to the owners or stockholders of the business. Dividends, for example, are paid from the net profit. In a sole proprietorship or a partnership, on the other hand, the business profit is not taxed. The net profit

```
                    WOMBAT SKI EQUIPMENT CO. INC.

                         Income Statement
                    Year ended December 31, 1990
--------------------------------------------------------------------

Net Sales                                   889,560        100.0
    Cost of Goods Sold                      516,145         58.0
------------------------
Gross Profit                                373,415         42.0

Operating Expenses

        Selling Expenses        96,345                      10.8
        Advertising             11,190                       1.3
        Supplies                 7,810                        .9
        Insurance                6,940                        .8
        Rent                    36,000                       4.0
        Utilities                5,470                        .6
        Administrative Expenses 35,330                       4.0
        Depreciation            32,926                       3.7
        Bad Debts                2,700                        .3
        Miscellaneous            6,230                        .7

Total Operating Expenses                    240,941         27.1

Operating Income                            132,474         14.9
- Expenses                                   30,725          3.5
----------------------

Taxable Income                              101,749         11.4
- Income Tax                                 37,750          4.2
----------------------

Net Income                                   63,999          7.2
- Dividends                                       0           .0
----------------------

Increase in Retained Earnings                63,999          7.2
                                            =========      =======
```

Figure 9.7 Income statement

becomes the personal income of the owner(s), and is taxed on the basis of individual income tax rates.

The net income is arrived at through the following calculations:

$$
\begin{array}{l}
\quad\text{Sales} \\
-\ \text{Cost of goods sold} \\
\hline
=\ \text{Gross profit} \\
-\ \text{Operating expenses} \\
\hline
=\ \text{Net profit before taxes} \\
-\ \text{Income taxes} \\
\hline
=\ \text{Net profit} \\
-\ \text{Dividends} \\
\hline
=\ \text{Retained earnings}
\end{array}
$$

The net profit shown on the income statement is not necessarily cash. As stated earlier, a profitable company can become bankrupt if it is unable to meet its expenses because too much cash has been tied up in fixed assets. The cash dividend paid to shareholders, for example, would depend on the amount of cash available — the cash not required for operations — rather than on the net profit shown on the income statement. In Figure 9.7, no dividends were paid so that the net profit is an addition to retained earnings as shown in the retained earnings section of the balance sheet.

Statement of Changes in Financial Position

The statement of changes in financial position shows management how cash was obtained during a given period of time and how it was used in the operation of the business. The information is obtained by comparing the dollar amounts of various categories of assets and liabilities of two consecutive balance sheets, and from the income statement and statement of retained earnings for the same period. The statement of changes in financial position explains the change in cash (or cash equivalent) from one balance sheet statement to the next. "Cash" is considered to be actual cash, plus short-term investments, minus short-term loans.

It is easier to understand what categories of these two statements to consider when determining changes in financial position if you remember the following. Net income and depreciation both represent a source of funds from the income statement, while dividends paid represents a use of funds. When considering the balance sheet, the following rules exist:

1. An increase in an asset account means a use of funds has occurred;
2. A decrease in an asset account means a source of funds has occurred;
3. An increase in liability and net worth accounts means a source of funds has occurred;
4. A decrease in liability and net worth accounts means a use of funds has occurred.

A reconciliation of the change in cash, and a statement of changes in financial position for Wombat Ski Equipment Company Inc. is shown in Figure 9.8. We see that the net change in cash to be reconciled in the statement of change in financial position arose from an increase in cash and marketable securities (short-term investments) and decrease in loans payable (short-term loans).

Cash provided by operations results from an adjustment of net income for non-cash items such as depreciation, and an adjustment

```
                    WOMBAT SKI EQUIPMENT CO. INC.
                         Changes in Cash

                                             1989        1990

Cash                                         8,894      23,140
Marketable Securities                       40,000      45,000
Loans Payable                          (    23,000) (   35,000)
                                          ---------   ---------
                                            25,894      33,140

            Increase in Cash                 7,246
            in 1990                        ---------
                                            33,140
```

```
                    WOMBAT SKI EQUIPMENT CO. INC.
                 Statement of Changes in Financial Position
                   For the Year Ended December 31, 1990


Net Income from Operations                              $63,999


Add:
    Depreciation                           32,926
    Increase in Accounts Payable            6,582
    Decrease in Inventory                  60,420
    Increase in Accrued Liabilities         3,516       103,444

                                        ------------

Deduct:
    Increase in Accounts Receivable     (   44,100)
    Increase in Prepaid Expenses        (    4,600) (    48,700)

                                        ------------   -----------

    Cash Provided by Operation                          118,743



Investing Activities
--------------------------
    Purchase of Buildings               (  187,000)
    Purchase of Fixtures & Equipment    (    9,850)
                                        ------------
    Use of Cash in Inventory Activities              (  196,850)


Financing Activities
--------------------------
    Payment on equipment Loan           (   13,300)
    Mortgage on Building                    98,653
                                        ------------
    Cash provided by financing activity                 85,353
                                                     ------------
    Increase in Cash                                    $7,246
                                                     ============
```

Figure 9.8 Statement of changes in financial position

of all accruals arising in the current asset and liability accounts. Increases in asset accounts represent a use of cash, whereas an increase in liabilities are a source of cash to the firm because that firm has in effect borrowed on a short-term basis.

We can see from the statement of changes in financial position that operations and financing provided cash in the amounts of $118 743 and $85 353 respectively, whereas cash was used in investing activities — purchasing more fixtures, equipment and buildings.

The financial data in a statement of changes in financial position thus summarizes data present in other statements. The summary gives managers a clear idea of how funds were used in the past and allows them to plan for future requirements. A statement of changes in financial position can also be used to establish a cash budget, as discussed earlier in this chapter.

Financial Analysis

Once the financial statements have been prepared, what do they actually tell us about the business? The income statement will tell us whether or not we have made a profit and how much, but is this profit adequate for the investment in the business? Another question is the operating efficiency of management. Are they using the funds to the best advantage? Analysis of financial statements can provide valuable information on a firm's profitability and financial strength.

There are two main methods of analyzing a company's financial statements. We can calculate a variety of ratios and compare these ratios to standard ratios for the industry and to the company's previous financial data. A second method is to analyze a company's operation by turning its key figures into percentages, which allows easy comparison of income statement and balance sheet figures to previous years and to industry standards. To illustrate financial analysis, we will use the balance sheets and the income statement for Wombat Ski Equipment Company.

Ratio Analysis

A ratio is used to compare two quantities against a predetermined standard. If the ratio is above or below the standard, it provides a general idea of the current status of the business. There is a book available that lists 429 different ratios, but to apply them all might leave little time for running the business. A few key ratios, however, can give an owner or financial manager a reasonable indication of the firm's financial health. Most ratios mean little in isolation, but are used to follow the trend within a business, and to compare an individual firm's performance with other firms in the same industry. To help us in our ratio analysis we will use the following figures showing information for all industries, as well as for the retail and wholesale industries in Canada.

Industry	Current ratio	Total debt to equity	Collection period (days)	Sales to inventory	Gross margin %	Profits on sales %	Profits on equity %
All firms	1.1	3.0	52	5.9	31.6	5.6	11.9
Retail trade	1.3	2.2	11	6.4	26.7	3.3	28.8
Wholesale trade	1.2	2.4	37	6.4	16.8	1.6	12.5

The ratios can be classified into four groups. The ratios in each group provide information about a particular aspect of the firm's financial operation. Some key ratios in each group are as follows:

Liquidity ratios
1. Current ratio
2. Quick or acid-test ratio

Activity ratios
1. Inventory turnover ratio
2. Average collection period

Financial leverage ratios
1. Debt ratio
2. Debt-to-equity ratio

Profitability ratios
1. Gross profit margin ratio
2. Net profit margin ratio
3. Return on investment
4. Return on stockholder's equity

Liquidity Ratios

A firm's ability to meet its short-term financial obligations is often a critical concern to management and lenders. The cash budget we already discussed provides the best picture of a firm's ability to pay; however, liquidity ratios are a quick measure of a firm's ability to provide sufficient cash to carry on business in the immediate future.

CURRENT RATIO: The current ratio indicates the firm's ability to pay its short-term debts.

$$\text{Current ratio} = \frac{\text{Current assets}}{\text{Current liabilities}} = \frac{\$338\ 484}{\$158\ 882} = 2.13$$

A rule of thumb often cited is that this ratio should be 2, implying that the firm could meet its short-term obligations through its current assets. This ratio is important to creditors, who would not want a firm in a short-term financial crisis having to sell its fixed assets to meet its current liabilities.

Wombat's current ratio of 2.13 in 1989 is well above the industry average of 1.1. For every dollar of current liabilities there are slightly more than two dollars of current assets which, if necessary, could be used to pay off the firm's liabilities. At the end of 1990 this ratio dropped to 1.91 — not a serious drop but it certainly needs some investigation. A current ratio much below two could signify that the company will have difficulty meeting its short-term debts through its current assets. However, it is important to examine the current assets that make up the ratio. If a large portion of the assets represent inventory, which may be difficult to turn into cash quickly, even a large current ratio may not be meaningful. In such cases the acid-test ratio is often used.

QUICK OR ACID-TEST RATIO: The acid-test ratio provides a more stringent test of a firm's ability to meet its current liabilities, since it excludes prepaid expenses and inventory from current assets, which may be difficult or impossible to convert into cash quickly when necessary. The remaining resources — cash, accounts receivable and marketable securities — are known as quick assets.

$$\begin{matrix} \text{Quick} \\ \text{(acid-test)} \\ \text{ratio} \end{matrix} = \frac{\text{Current assets} - \text{(Inventories} + \text{Prepaid expenses)}}{\text{Current liabilities}} = \frac{\$142\ 134}{\$158\ 882} = 0.89$$

A common standard is one dollar of quick assets to cover each dollar of current liability. Wombat was just slightly below that standard in 1989, with quick assets of 89 cents to cover every dollar of current liabilities. By the end of 1990, this ratio went up to 1.14 which means that the firm could quite easily pay off most of its current liabilities with its liquid assets.

Activity Ratios

Activity ratios indicate how efficiently a firm is using its assets to generate sales. By comparing activity ratios for the various asset accounts of a firm with established industry standards, a person can determine how efficiently the firm is allocating its resources. The two ratios we will examine are inventory turnover and average collection period. In both instances cash is tied up either as inventory or receivables.

INVENTORY TURNOVER RATIO: The inventory turnover ratio measures the number of times the average dollar value of inventory carried during the year is sold or replaced in that period. An adequate inventory ratio is particularly important since inventory is generally a sizable investment; poor management may result in high costs of carrying — storing and handling — the inventory. Moreover, merchandise that does not sell may become shopworn or obsolete.

$$\text{Inventory turnover} = \frac{\text{Cost of goods sold}}{\text{Average inventory}} = \frac{\$516\ 145}{\$73\ 787} = 6.99$$

The average inventory carried during the year or during each month of the year must be calculated from the figures in the beginning and ending balance sheets for the period. Generally, the higher the inventory turnover, the more profit the firm makes, since inventory is converted to cash rapidly. However, it could also mean that the firm is frequently running out of stock and losing sales to competitors. The inventory turnover ratio varies for different types of businesses. For example, a grocery store with a small profit margin on each item may turn over its inventory 20 times per year; in a furniture store, where the profit margin on each item is significantly greater, inventory may turn over only three times per year.

Due to the seasonal nature of the ski business, the inventory turnover ratio for Wombat may not be meaningful — the average inventory was calculated over a twelve-month period, even though for five of these months the inventory carried was low. Hence, the average monthly inventory is reduced, resulting in a relatively high inventory turnover ratio. The turnover ratio would be more meaningful if it were calculated only for the seven-month ski season. In Wombat's case then, the inventory turnover ratio is significant only if it is compared with ratios of previous years and of other firms in the industry.

AVERAGE COLLECTION PERIOD: A business that provides credit to its customers must carefully control the length of time the accounts are outstanding, or it may find a high rate of non-payment on the outstanding accounts. If the customary credit period is 30 days, any accounts not paid within that period require notification. If no response is received, collection procedures must be implemented quickly.

The average collection period is the average number of days an account receivable remains outstanding. We can calculate it by dividing the year-end receivables balance by the average daily credit sales which is based on a 360-day year.

Receivables can be controlled by determining the number of days' sales that total accounts outstanding represent — a usual and realistic time period is 30 days. If this period of time increases, the firm may face losses because money is tied up in unpaid accounts. Individual accounts can also be analyzed as to the length of time each has been outstanding.

To determine the number of days' sales represented by accounts receivable, the net sales figure from the income statement is divided by the value of the outstanding accounts receivable to give a turnover rate for the receivables per year or month. The following example uses Wombat's net sales for 1990 and the amount of receivables outstanding at the end of 1990.

$$\text{Average collection period} = \frac{\text{Accounts receivable}}{\text{Annual credit sales}/360} = \frac{\$137\ 340}{\$889\ 560/360} = 55.8 \text{ days}$$

On the average, therefore, Wombat's accounts receivable represent 56 days of sales. Here too, however, the seasonal nature of the ski business means that the ratio should be based on only seven months rather than twelve, since the firm does virtually no business during the five summer months. The receivables outstanding would thus be reduced to 32 days' sales, which is below the industry average for wholesalers. Wombat considers its accounts receivable well managed. Only its wholesale customers — other ski shops — are granted credit, and no account has required more than 35 days to pay for purchases.

Financial Leverage Ratios

Whenever a firm borrows money to finance its fixed assets through stocks, bonds, or leases, it is using financial leverage. In other words, management is using someone else's money to carry on business in an attempt to increase the firm's profit. Financial leverage ratios measure the degree to which the firm is using financial leverage. These ratios are important to creditors and owners or shareholders. We will discuss financial leverage in more detail later in this chapter.

DEBT RATIO: This ratio measures the proportion of a firm's assets that is financed with borrowed funds. In these instances, debt includes all short-term and long-term borrowing.

$$\text{Debt} = \frac{\text{Total debt}}{\text{Total assets}} = \frac{351\ 633}{\$571\ 214} = 0.615$$

A debt ratio is stated as a percent. In Wombat's case, the debt ratio at the end of 1990 is 61.5%. This means that Wombat's creditors are financing 61.5% of Wombat's total assets while the owners or shareholders only have an equity of 38.5%. As the equity base declines, investors are more hesitant to put money into the firm because they are simply acquiring more debt. The only way such a company might be able to continue borrowing money is if it can show that it is capable of high growth and will have relatively stable future earnings.

DEBT/EQUITY RATIO: The debt/equity ratio indicates the relationship between the amount of a firm's debt financing to the amount of owner financing.

$$\text{Debt-to-equity ratio} = \frac{\text{Total debt}}{\text{Total equity}} = \frac{\$351\ 633}{\$219\ 581} = 1.60$$

The debt-to-equity ratio is similar to the debt ratio and is also stated as a percentage. Wombat's debt to equity at the end of 1990 is 160%. This means that Wombat has raised nearly $1.60 from creditors for each dollar invested by owners. When compared to industry ratios,

Wombat is considerably lower than all firms where this ratio is 3, and for retailers and wholesalers where it is 2.2 and 2.4 respectively.

Profitability Ratios

Profitability ratios measure how effectively a firm's management is generating profits on sales, on total assets, and on stockholders' investment. This in turn is important to investors who are expecting long-run adequate returns in the form of dividends and share appreciation.

GROSS PROFIT MARGIN RATIOS: This ratio measures the relative profitability of a firm's sales after the cost of goods sold has been deducted. The gross profit must be enough to cover expenses and provide a reasonable profit for the firm after payment of taxes. The ratio is calculated by dividing gross profit by net sales, and multiplying the result by 100. This ratio reveals management's effectiveness in making decisions regarding pricing and the control of production costs. The ratio may be calculated monthly, quarterly, or yearly.

To calculate this ratio we use income statement figures. The ratio is defined as follows:

$$\text{Gross profit margin} = \frac{\text{Sales} - \text{Cost of goods sold}}{\text{Sales}} = \frac{\$373\ 415}{\$889\ 560} = 0.419$$

An increase in the gross profit ratio over time indicates that the spread between net sales and the cost of buying the goods is increasing. It means that the business is buying at lower prices, or selling at higher prices, or both. In contrast, a decreasing gross profit ratio indicates a decreasing spread — the business is either selling at prices that are too low, or paying too much for the merchandise, or both. Figure 9.9 shows in percentage terms the income statements for the past three years for Wombat as well as a comparison to the industry.

NET PROFIT MARGIN RATIO: The net profit margin ratio uses figures from the income statement to measure the amount of profit in each sales dollar. It measures how profitable a firm's sales are after all expenses, including taxes and interest, have been deducted.

$$\text{Net profit margin} = \frac{\text{Net profit}}{\text{Sales}} = \frac{\$63\ 999}{\$889\ 560} = 7.19\%$$

The ratio is directly influenced by the firm's gross profit and operating expenses, which should be analyzed if the net profit ratio declines. The net profit ratio is most useful when compared with previous years or with other firms in the same industry. This ratio should be compared to the industry standard. Wombat has a net profit margin of 7.19%, which is good compared to industry standards.

RETURN ON INVESTMENT: The return on investment ratio measures the firm's net income after taxes compared to total assets invested.

$$\text{Return on investment} = \frac{\text{Earnings (after taxes)}}{\text{Total assets}} = \frac{\$63\ 999}{\$571\ 214} \times 100\% = 11.2\%$$

While this ratio measures the return on total assets, return on investment can also be measured in terms of the stockholder's investment. For Wombat in 1990, this would be $63 999/219 581 = 29.1%.

Investors can then compare the resulting percentage with returns on other types of investments available to them, such as the interest rate paid on bank savings accounts. If a bank would pay 10%, while their investment in the business is only 7%, it might be advantageous for them to withdraw their money from the business and put it into a savings account or buy Canada Savings Bonds. Another consideration for investors is the return compared to the risk involved. Money earning 10% at the bank is relatively safe, but a 10% return from a business is not as secure. Because of this risk factor, investors may require a return of 18% to 20% on their investment.

In Wombat's case it should be remembered that the firm is a new enterprise in a relatively new recreation area. It is unlikely that the 29% rate of return on stockholder's equity will persist once competitors have become established. Even if Wombat remains the only ski equipment business in the area, the return on investment ratio could decline over the coming years as expenses and investments rise.

Comparative Analysis of Accounting Statements

All dollar figures on balance sheets and income statements can be turned into percentages for comparison with previous years. Many companies provide this information so that investors can see how the firm has progressed over a period of time. A percentage comparison can be revealing if sales are designated as 100% and all other items — cost of goods sold, all expenses, taxes and net profit — are shown as percentages of sales.

In Figure 9.9, for example, the comparative income statements for Wombat show that gross profit in 1990 was down from the previous year, but still higher than in 1989. However, Wombat's gross profit has never approached that of the industry, which is 45%. Expenses have followed a similar path as gross profit and have risen and declined along with gross profit. In terms of expense as a percentage of sales, Wombat looks good compared to the industry as a

```
                    WOMBAT SKI EQUIPMENT CO. LTD.
                    Comparative Income Statements
--------------------------------------------------------------------------------

                        1987      1988      1989   Industry  Deviation
                                                    Average  Ind-1988
--------------------------------------------------------------------------------

Sales                  100.0%    100.0%    100.0%   100.0%    100.0%

Cost of goods sold      63.3%     56.9%     58.0%    55.0%      3.0%

Gross profit            39.9%     43.1%     41.9%    45.0%     -3.0%

Operating expenses      25.7%     28.3%     27.1%    31.0%     -2.8%

Net income before taxes 14.2%     14.8%     11.4%    14.0%      -.2%

Net income after taxes   7.4%      7.7%      7.2%     6.3%       .9%
```

Figure 9.9 Comparing Wombat's current income statement with previous two years and with industry standards

whole. Another important point is that net income after taxes has remained fairly steady for Wombat and is significantly higher than it is for the industry.

Forecasting and Budgeting

A business cannot wait for the future to happen — it must make an active attempt to reduce future uncertainty by forecasting possible developments during the planning process described in Chapter 4. Once plans have been made, the cost of carrying them out can be determined and set out in a budget. A budget states in financial terms the course of action planned for the coming year. **Budgets** show all expected cash inflows from sales, borrowings and owner investments, as well as all outflows, such as expenses, withdrawals (dividends) and loan repayments. Even though budgets are made for the entire year, they are often broken down into three- or six-month segments. Budgets are considered firm commitments and are not meant to be altered except for unforeseen changes in the level of operations or in the economic environment.

The budget forecast provides financial data for a projected income statement and a projected balance sheet for the year. These projected financial statements, together with detailed budgets, are used during the operating period as standards in the control process. Thus, actual results can be compared against planned results and any discrepancies between the two can be corrected.

The Budgeting Process

Budgeting usually starts three months before the end of the **fiscal year** — the business' operating period — to ensure that the budgeting process can be completed before the new operating period begins. As Figure 9.10 shows, the budgeting process begins with the sales department making its forecast for the year. All other budgets are developed from the **sales forecast** and culminate in *pro-forma* financi l statements. The budgeting process varies somewhat from business to business, depending on whether the firm is manufacturing, retail, or service. We now look at the budgeting process in more detail.

Sales Forecasting

Since the entire operating plan of an organization depends on planned sales, accurate forecasting of future sales is critical. The finance department, usually in charge of the budgeting process, provides both planned and actual sales figures for the previous and current year. In large companies the marketing department also spends considerable time in economic forecasting, taking into account governmental policies, the general economic outlook, the industry and the competition. The result is a **market-based forecast** not only for the current year, but also for future years, since market factors may also influence plans for expansion and thus affect the capital budget. The firm also develops a **sales-based forecast** for the coming year. The sales forecast is based on the total expected sales of each salesperson for each product on a monthly basis. Many small firms may use only a sales-based forecast for budgeting.

Once the sales budget has been established, other budgets are developed, including the selling and administrative expense budget, the capital budget and the production or manufacturing budgets.

Manufacturing Budgets

Marketing and sales must work closely together, particularly if the product is subject to spoilage or rapid obsolescence. Production must then be geared directly to sales to keep inventory low. On the other hand, if the product can be stored, the volume of production can be more uniform, which tends to lower production costs because plant facilities are not overworked at some periods and idle at others. Costs of hiring and laying off employees are also reduced and productivity often increases because hiring and training costs are reduced and workers have higher morale because of greater job security.

The **manufacturing budget** is based on the inventory required according to the sales forecast, taking into account spoilage, and storage and productive capacity. Once the number of units to be

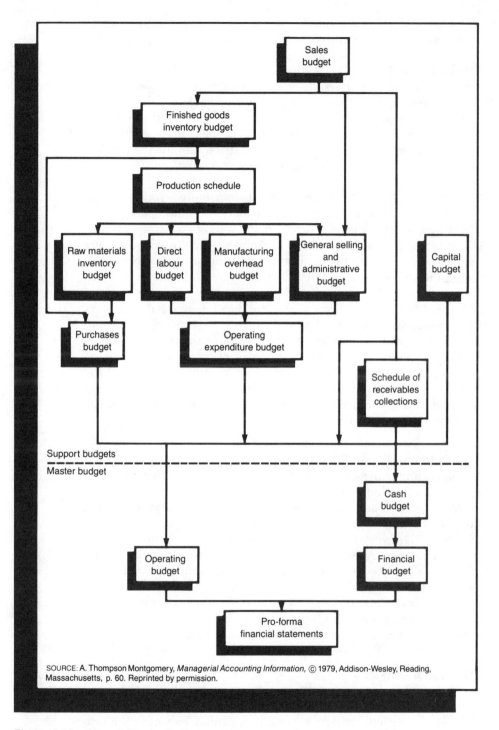

SOURCE: A. Thompson Montgomery, *Managerial Accounting Information,* © 1979, Addison-Wesley, Reading, Massachusetts, p. 60. Reprinted by permission.

Figure 9.10 Steps in the budgeting process

produced has been determined, the budgets for raw materials, direct labour and factory overhead can be drawn up.

RAW MATERIALS BUDGET: With the level of production established, the quantities of raw materials or parts required can be determined. A **purchases budget** is thus developed by the purchasing department, which is in close touch with suppliers and has a good idea of the costs of materials and parts. Again, if materials can be stored, the purchasing department does not have to strictly follow the production cycle and may take advantage of seasonal or volume discounts.

DIRECT LABOUR BUDGET: The direct labour budget projects manpower requirements based on the sales and production plan. As the various production times to produce one unit are generally known, labour costs can be determined by multiplying the person-hours required per unit with the total number of units to be produced and then multiplying the result by the rate of pay for labour.

FACTORY OVERHEAD: Direct labour and direct materials do not cover all expenses associated with manufacturing. Expenses such as rent, insurance, repair and maintenance, supervisory salaries and utilities would be incurred regardless of the level of production. These expenses are known as **factory overhead**. Sometimes freight and the costs of purchasing, receiving, handling and storing materials are also included in factory overhead since it may be difficult to break these costs down per unit.

The Operating Expenditures Budget

The **operating expenditures budget** includes all sales revenues and all expenses, including direct labour costs, manufacturing overhead, selling expenses, and general and administrative expenses. **Selling expenses** include the costs of promoting, selling and distributing the products. They are usually broken down by product lines, sales regions, customers, salespersons or some other method. **General** and **administrative expenses** are the costs of maintaining a head office, and the associated salaries and expenses. These costs are charged against various departments or products depending on the type of business. Nevertheless, individual budgets are prepared for comparison with previous years and for control purposes.

The Capital Budget

An operating budget does not take into account that the assets used in the firm's operation — plant, equipment and machinery — wear out and must eventually be replaced. A **capital budget** is thus established, indicating management's estimate of when plant and equipment will need to be replaced and how the necessary funds will be raised. For example, if the firm knows it must replace five trucks in three years' time, it can set aside a certain amount each year from profits to cover the purchase.

The capital budget is somewhat outside the main budgeting process. It includes detailed plans for the acquisition or disposal of major capital assets either through purchase, lease or construction. Although the capital budget pertains only to the current year, capital investment and planning will extend beyond one year depending on the long-term plans of the firm. For example, a firm that intends to expand its plant 10 years hence can detail its plans to raise the money in a capital budget. Thus, the year prior to expansion, the capital budget will indicate the amount of money the company plans to take from earnings for the expansion and the amount to be obtained through loans or through the direct sale to investors of bonds or shares.

The Cash Budget

With the completion of the capital budget, all the necessary schedules are available to develop the cash budget. A **cash budget** is a forecast of all expected cash receipts and expenditures for the year. If sales are made on credit, a separate schedule of receivables may be prepared based on the firm's history of collections. This schedule compares dates at which cash from sales is received with dates at which the product was originally sold. Thus, management can control overdue accounts and cash flow, and ensure that adequate cash is always available to pay bills as they come due.

The Master Operating Budget and the Financial Budget

The **master operating budget** combines the various operating components of the total company — manufacturing, purchasing, sales, administration, personnel — and shows the anticipated revenues and expenditures for the coming year. If the master operating budget calls for capital expenditures — for example, if sales are expected to increase dramatically over the next few years — then a **financing budget** will be established to indicate how money will be raised for the additional financial outlays required. The financing budget lists the capital expenditures from the capital budget, as well as the total expected cash inflows and outflows from the cash budget. These cash outflows would take into account expected payments of dividends to shareholders. The financing budget will then indicate how any cash shortfalls will be met, most likely through borrowing, but also possibly through an additional share offering. The financing budget can take the form of a projected statement of changes in financial position, which is similar to the statement of sources and uses of funds discussed earlier.

Pro-Forma Financial Statements

Large companies will develop the master operating budget into **pro-forma financial statements** — a forecasted income statement and a balance sheet that represent the final step in the budgeting process. The **projected income statement** consists of the sales forecast with some adjustments for sales returns and the forecasted costs-of-goods-sold statement. The difference between net sales and cost of goods sold is the gross margin, which will have to cover all expenses and provide the before-tax income for the firm. Then the various operating expenses — sales and administrative — are deducted to arrive at the operating income figure. Net income is, of course, the income after taxes. The **projected balance sheet** indicates the firm's financial position at the end of the coming year. Together, the projected income statement, projected balance sheet, cash budget and financial budget, are known as the firm's master budget. Medium and small companies often do not have a master budget and develop only the pro-forma financial statements.

How Budgeting Benefits the Organization

Since it forces all levels of management to forecast possible future developments and their effect on the firm's sales and revenue, the operating budget is a valuable planning tool. Once established, it serves to coordinate the activities of the various departments and divisions, since the planned dollar figures provide the limits within which each must operate. At the same time, the budgeting process itself gives the various managers involved a better idea of the firm's purpose and direction.

Finally, the operating budget serves as a standard in the control process. Although it is generally drawn up for six months or a year at a time, the operating budget is usually broken down into monthly budgets. Thus, actual sales and expenses for each month can be compared with planned sales and expenses. In the event of discrepancies between the two sets of figures, management can decide whether corrective action is necessary. In some cases, unforeseen events may make it necessary to rework the total company operating budget. However, if only certain areas are affected, the required over-expenditure in one department or division can be offset by reducing expenses in other areas.

Break-even Analysis

An important tool in sales forecasting and budgeting is **break-even analysis**, which indicates the amount of sales needed to make a profit and gives management some idea of the relationship between sales, costs and profits. The relationship between these three factors can be demonstrated graphically or algebraically, depending on the manager's requirements. The use of microcomputers has made break-even analysis simple. The figures can be entered into a spreadsheet model and the relevant calculations are instantly available.

Break-even analysis is based on the fact that all costs can be divided into fixed and variable costs. **Fixed costs**, often called **overhead**, are those that are relatively constant regardless of the volume of goods produced. Even if the plant were forced to shut down completely and could produce nothing, costs would still be incurred for minimal heat and light, interest charges on plant and equipment, rent, insurance and management salaries. **Variable costs**, on the other hand, vary directly with the level of production and/or sales. Included are wages of workers involved in producing goods or services and the cost of raw materials, power and fuel.

To illustrate break-even analysis, let us assume that the owner of Wombat Ski Equipment Co. Ltd. intends to establish a new business renting skis from the Snow Valley Ski Lodge. Given that his main concern is the profitability of the operation, he would have to determine how many ski packages, including skis, bindings, boots and poles, he would be required to rent per day or week to make a profit.

He would start by designating all costs as either fixed or variable, as follows:

Fixed Costs	
Annual depreciation expense on skis	$3 780
Rent in ski lodge	3 400
Advertising	1 500
Liability insurance	1 750
Manager's salary	9 350
Other fixed labour	730
Miscellaneous	1 750
Total fixed costs	**$22 260**

Variable Costs	
For every 10 sets of skis rented:	
Repairs, per day	$30
Additional labour costs, per day	20
Total variable costs	**$50**

Wombat's owner anticipated that he could rent skis for seven months of the year, from October to May, although business in the first and last months would probably be light. He would thus have 210 days in which to rent skis. Daily fixed costs would therefore be $106, while total variable costs would be $50 per day for every ten sets of skis rented. The rental charge to the customer for each set of skis would be $9.

How many units would have to be rented per day to break even on this operation? The break-even point can be computed by the following formula:

$$\text{Break-even point} = \frac{\text{Fixed costs}}{\text{Selling price} - \text{Variable cost per unit}}$$

$$\text{BEP} = \frac{\$106}{\$9 - \$5} = \frac{\$106}{\$4} = 26.5 \text{ or } 27 \text{ sets/day}$$

The above calculation shows that each set of skis rented contributes $4 towards the fixed costs, or to profit.

If, on the average, the owner can rent more than 27 sets of skis per day during the seven months, he would make a profit. Knowing this break-even figure, he can now look at the market more closely. If he finds that the demand for rentals is much greater than that required to break even, then he should proceed as quickly as possible. If, on the other hand, initial demand may not be sufficient, he could either try to reduce some of his fixed costs, or consider increasing the charge for each rental. Or he could simply accept the low revenues until demand improves. In any case, break-even analysis is a useful tool for assessing new ventures.

Break-even analysis can also be done graphically, as shown in Figure 9.11A. Revenue and costs are shown along the vertical axis and the number of units of skis rented, in sets of ten, along the horizontal axis. Variable costs are then plotted on top of fixed costs at the rate of $50 per ten sets of skis rented. The diagonal line originating at "0" indicates revenue and varies directly with the number of sets of skis rented.

At the **break-even point**, total fixed plus total variable costs are equal to the total revenue and Wombat makes no profit. If the number of rentals per day is below the break-even point, the firm suffers a loss. Rentals above the break-even point bring a profit which increases with the number of sets of skis rented.

Another way to calculate the break-even point is to use a computer and an electronic spreadsheet or a simple BASIC program. Figure 9.11B shows the calculation of the break-even point for the ski rental proposal. The program asks for input of the various costs and parameters for calculation. Then it provides a printout showing the cost, revenue, profit/loss and unit cost along with the break-even point.

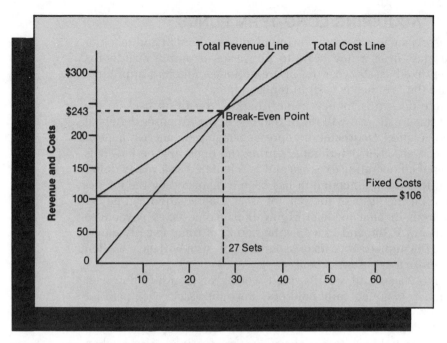

Figure 9.11A   Break-even chart for Wombat Ski Equipment Company Inc.

```
                        COST/REVENUE SCHEDULE
         Enter the following information:


         Fixed costs ?                           106
         Variable costs per unit ?                 5
         Unit price ?                              9
         Beginning quantity for computations ?    15
         Ending quantity for computations ?       35
         Step increments to be printed ?           1

         ......................................................

         QUANTITY     COST    REVENUE    PROFIT/LOSS    UNIT COST

            15         181      135          -46          12.07
            16         186      144          -42          11.63
            17         191      153          -38          11.24
            18         196      162          -34          10.89
            19         201      171          -30          10.58
            20         206      180          -26          10.30
            21         211      189          -22          10.05
            22         216      198          -18           9.82
            23         221      207          -14           9.61
            24         226      216          -10           9.42
            25         231      225           -6           9.24
            26         236      234           -2           9.08
         ------------------------------------------------------
           26.5       238.5    238.5        BREAKEVEN
         ------------------------------------------------------
            27         241      243            2            8.93
            28         246      252            6            8.79
            29         251      261           10            8.66
            30         256      270           14            8.53
            31         261      279           18            8.42
            32         266      288           22            8.31
            33         271      297           26            8.21
            34         276      306           30            8.12
            35         281      315           34            8.03
         ......................................................
```

Figure 9.11 B   Calculating the break-even point using a computer and a basic program

ACQUIRING LONG-TERM FUNDS

Fixed assets such as manufacturing plants, equipment and machinery may last from a few years to fifty years or more. Eventually, however, fixed assets wear out or are no longer efficient in production, and the firm needs cash to replace them.

Where does this money come from? If you think back to the income statement, you will recall that one of the expenses deducted was depreciation. **Depreciation** represents management's estimate of how much an asset deteriorates during the operating period. It is considered an operating expense and is calculated as a yearly dollar amount, for which a maximum has been established by the tax department on the basis of the type of asset. Depreciation can be deducted from income in determining the income taxes payable to government. At the end of a specific period of time, usually an estimate of the number of years of useful life, the firm will have written off the entire asset as an expense.

Unlike wages and salaries paid weekly or monthly, however, depreciation is not actually paid out, since the assets were paid for when they were initially purchased. A firm can therefore set aside the yearly depreciation amount and use it, together with profits not paid to shareholders, to purchase or replace fixed assets when necessary.

If these internally generated funds are not enough to replace worn-out assets or expand operations, the firm will need to borrow money from other sources. A large, financially strong company can raise long-term funds by selling its own corporate securities — either bonds, known as **debt capital**, or common and preferred stock known as **equity capital**.

Types of Corporate Securities

The two major types of corporate securities are bonds, which represent debt for the company, and common or preferred stocks which represent ownership in the company. A comparison of stocks and bonds is shown in Table 9.1.

Bonds

A **bond** is a certificate issued by a company and traded to another company or to private individuals in return for an amount of money known as the **principal**. A **bond certificate**, as shown in Figure 9.12, states the **maturity date** when the company must repay the face value of the bond. A bond may reach maturity in five to fifty years, although the usual time period is ten to thirty years. The certificate also states the amount of interest the company must pay to the bondholder each

TABLE 9.1
Comparison of stocks and bonds

Stocks	Bonds
1. Represent ownership	1. Represent debt
2. No principal is repaid	2. Principal is repaid upon maturity
3. May pay dividends	3. Must pay interest
4. Any dividends are paid after taxes	4. Interest is paid before taxes
5. Stockholders usually have some say in management	5. Bondholders have no say in management

year. Most corporate bonds are sold in $1000 denominations, but a portion of each issue may be in denominations of $5000, $10 000, $50 000 and $100 000. The latter amounts are usually purchased by other large corporations, or by insurance companies and pension funds.

Bonds may be in either registered or bearer form. When a company issues a **registered bond**, it knows the owner's name, and mails interest cheques directly to the bondholder when they are due. A **bearer bond**, on the other hand, has dated coupons attached to it, which the bondholder uses on the specified dates to collect the interest owing. The interest is not usually paid directly by the issuer, but by the institution that acted as a distributor for the bonds, often a trust company. This process of "clipping coupons" is a common feature of federal government bonds.

What Backs a Bond?

When you borrow money to purchase a car, the bank or finance company will usually require the car as collateral. Thus the lending institution can seize the car in the event that you are unable to make your payments. Similarly, a company that borrows money by issuing bonds must usually provide the lender with some backing. Bonds backed in this manner are called **secured bonds**, which indicate that the company has pledged specific property or fixed assets which could be seized by the bondholder if the company is unable to repay the principal on the date specified in the bond issue. The security may be a piece of real estate, or specific equipment or machinery.

On the other hand, a company may issue **unsecured bonds**, backed not by specific collateral, but rather by the name and financial strength of the firm. Should the company fail, the bondholders still have claims on its assets prior to any stockholders. However, lenders with claims to specific assets will be repaid before unsecured bondholders.

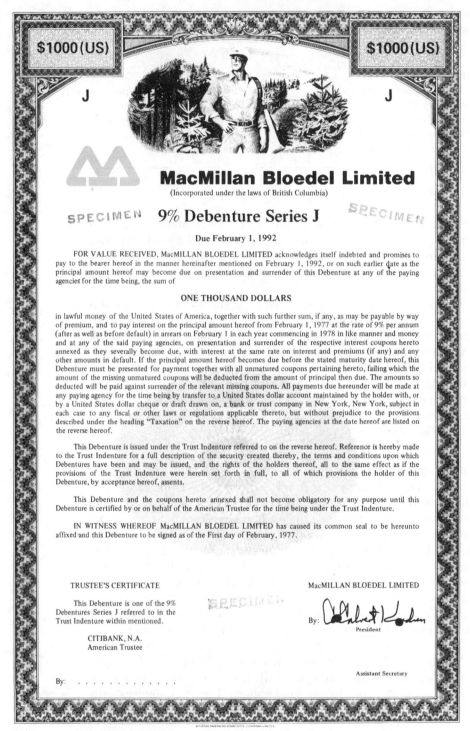

Figure 9.12 Bond certificate (specimen)

Unsecured bonds are also called **debentures**. Debentures are usually issued by financially strong companies, whose credit rating is judged to be exceptionally good by a firm such as Dun and Bradstreet — which specializes in analyzing and rating the financial condition of various companies.

How Are Interest Rates Set on Bonds?

The interest rate that the issuer must pay on a bond issue is determined by the firm's financial strength, and whether the bond is secured or unsecured. It also depends on the general level of interest rates in the country at a particular period — when interest rates are rising, the company will have to pay a higher rate of interest to make the issue attractive to investors. However, the final decision on what rate to pay is made by the board of directors.

Calling and Converting

Calling and converting are two features occasionally included in a bond issue. By making a bond **callable** (redeemable), a company has the option of recalling it before the maturity date, which may be done in the event that interest rates drop. For example, let us suppose that a callable bond was issued to pay 10% over a period of twenty years, but after three years interest rates dropped to 7%. The company could then recall the bond as specified on the bond certificate, pay off the bondholders, and issue new bonds at a lower interest rate.

The company then gains a substantial saving in interest payments. Suppose that the interest rate dropped from 10% to 7% within a five-year period, and the company had issued $100 million worth of bonds at 10%. If the firm called the bonds after five years and issued new ones for the remaining fifteen years — thus saving three percentage points per year — the annual saving would amount to $3 million, or $45 million for the remaining fifteen years. The call value of a bond is usually above face value because the issuer pays a premium to bondholders for the privilege of recalling the bonds before maturity date.

Convertibility is another feature that may benefit both the investor and the corporation. It allows the holder to convert the bonds to common stock. If all investors took advantage of convertibility, the company would not be required to repay the funds originally borrowed. Furthermore, the investor is assured of a continuing income from the bond, and at some time has the option to participate in the company's financial success by sharing in any profits and capital appreciation of shares. Convertible bonds are thus considered a good investment, and companies that issue them can usually do so at interest rates lower than those for regular bonds.

How Are Bonds Converted?

Let us suppose that a company issues a $1000 bond convertible to 50 shares of common stock when its shares are worth $15 each. At the time of issue it would not be worthwhile for the investor to convert the bond to stocks, because their value would only be $750. If, however, over a period of five years, the stock rises to $25 per share — perhaps because the company promises to be profitable — the investor could convert the bond to common stock. The $1000 bond would then be worth $1250 — a $250 appreciation for the investor in addition to the interest received on the bond for the previous five years. If the company's financial outlook continues to be good, the shares could continue to appreciate in value.

Common Stock

Stocks are shares of ownership in a company. When a business incorporates, it can specify the number of **authorized shares** that it intends to offer. But the number of shares the firm is authorized to sell is often different from the number of **issued shares**, or shares sold to shareholders. Any shares not sold initially are available to future investors. For example, a small company that has recently incorporated with three equal shareholders might issue 100 shares of common stock to each individual. Since the minimum number of authorized shares is usually 10 000, 9700 shares of stock would be left for sale to other investors.

An investor who purchases common stock gives money to the company in return for a **stock certificate**, which represents shares of ownership in the company and indicates the number of shares bought, the name of the shareholder and the special characteristics of the stock. A sample share certificate is shown in Chapter 3. Common shareholders almost always hold voting rights and may vote for directors at the annual meeting. However, common shareholders have no special rights or privileges for dividends, and they are the last to be considered in the event that the company goes bankrupt. Furthermore, common shareholders have only last claim to undistributed profits, should any ever remain.

Given these disadvantages, why do people buy common stock? The major reason for purchasing common stock is its potential for appreciation. When a company is profitable and its earnings outlook is good, common stock can appreciate rapidly — prices have been known to double and triple in a matter of weeks.

Many companies also pay good dividends which is another reason for investing in common stocks. If a company has had an exceptionally profitable year, common shareholders may also receive an additional special dividend from the surplus of funds. However, it is important to note that a company is not obligated to pay dividends to its shareholders.

The common shareholder may also benefit from a stock split, a procedure that companies often use to reduce the price of stock which has risen over a period of time. Splitting makes the stock more accessible to the small investor. For example, a stock which has risen from $30 to $100 may be attractive to more investors if it is split into four shares, each worth $25. Thus all previous common shareholders also receive four times the number of their original shares. A stock split often causes another rapid rise in the new share price, since many more investors are now able to buy the stock.

Finally, an investor may benefit from appreciation of his or her stock when another firm attempts to gain control of the company, either through the purchase of shares on the open market or through a direct offer to existing shareholders. Usually the company attempting the take-over will offer a high premium over the current selling price of the stock, giving shareholders the opportunity to sell their stock for substantial capital gains.

Common shareholders also enjoy what is known as residual right to a company's earnings. When all interest has been paid to holders of bonds and other long-term debt certificates, and all payments have been made to preferred stockholders, the remaining earnings are available to common shareholders.

However, while common shareholders can sometimes gain substantial rewards from their stock, they are also prone to sudden and equally large losses. When a company becomes bankrupt, the common shareholder is not protected. If the firm has outstanding mortgages, or if it has many bondholders or preferred shareholders — all of whom have first claim to assets — there may be no funds left for common shareholders, and they may lose their entire investment. Stock prices may also fall drastically during periods of economic recession or when there are poor economic forecasts that may affect a company's profit outlook. Since low profits may also mean a restriction on the payment of dividends, stock prices could drop further still.

Thus common stock may be a sound investment when the company and the economy are doing well, but during difficult economic times shareholders may receive little income, and the value of their shares may drop substantially. In extreme instances, they may lose their entire investment.

What Is a Dividend Tax Credit?

When a shareholder receives a dividend from a Canadian corporation, the amount reported as taxable income is greater than the actual dividend. This grossed-up amount represents a portion of the income taxes paid by the corporation, since dividends are a distribution of profit after tax. In turn, the investor can then claim a dividend tax credit against federal tax payable, which also reduces provincial income tax payable. The effective rate of tax thus paid is less than the rate paid on other income. Under the new tax system, the dividend tax credit has been reduced from 22% to 16 2/3% of the actual dividend. That means that the top personal income tax rate on dividends will be about 30% compared with the top rate on other income of about 45%. These rates vary from province to province because of the different provincial income tax rates.

The reason for the dividend tax credit is mainly to do away with double taxation — once when the corporation is taxed on its net income and then again when the investor has to report his or her income from all sources including dividends. However, it is also an incentive to invest in Canadian corporations that pay dividends because income earned through dividends is taxed at a lower rate than income earned through employment or interest earned in savings accounts, term deposits or bonds.

Preferred Stock

To provide greater security and a steadier income for investors, yet still allow them some appreciation of their investment if the company is doing well, preferred shares were developed. **Preferred shares** pay a dividend to shareholders, the amount being specified on the stock certificate. The dividend is either a fixed dollar amount or a percentage based on the issued price of the stock. For example, a preferred share may be issued at $25 with a $2.50 dividend, which represents a 10% return. Each share receives the specified dividend each year, usually paid quarterly, regardless of whether the value of the stock has gone up or down. Preferred shares may be issued in any denomination.

Preferred shares, along with the common stock, tend to rise and fall depending on the financial fortunes of the company or the industry. However, the fluctuations are considerably less on preferred shares, primarily because of the fixed dividend that is paid. To some extent, the fixed dividend resembles a rate of interest. Preferred shares tend to fluctuate in their value as interest rates fluctuate. For example, if bank interest rates go up, then the price of preferred shares must go down in order to keep their relative return vis à vis interest paid at the bank. Similarly, the price of preferred shares goes up if bank interest rates go down. Preferred shares and common shares, however, are eligible for the **federal tax dividend credit** which reduces the tax on dividends from Canadian corporations and thus effectively raises the return on dividends compared to interest received from bonds or bank savings accounts. Above all, preferred shares pay a fixed dividend which is often considerably higher than dividends paid to common stockholders.

To make preferred shares even more attractive, particular features may be added. For example, **cumulative preferred shares** guarantee that even if a dividend is omitted for one or more years, the company must first pay the dividends in arrears owed to preferred shareholders before paying common shareholders. **Participating preferred shares** entitle the holder to receive a further share of the company's earnings once common shareholders have received dividends equal to preferred dividends. The amount of this additional dividend is either specified on the share certificate or left to the discretion of the board of directors.

A company may also issue **convertible preferred shares**, which allow the holder to convert preferred stock into common stock prior to a specified date. If the price of the common stock rises to a specified price before the expiry date, then conversion will usually take place although by that time the preferred stock will have risen to an equivalent price. Convertibility may make a preferred stock issue more attractive to investors because there is great potential for capital appreciation while still receiving a good dividend.

Preferred shareholders have claim to dividends and assets before common shareholders, particularly in the event of company bankruptcy. Whatever remains after bondholders and other creditors have been paid goes to preferred shareholders. Any remaining funds may then be paid to common shareholders. Preferred shareholders usually do not have the voting rights that common shareholders do, although some issues may include voting rights on matters which concern preferred shareholders, such as the sale of a major part of the corporation, mergers or takeovers. However, this type of voting right must be specifically stated in the prospectus for the preferred share issue or in the articles or bylaws of the corporation

Choosing the Type of Security to Issue

When financial managers need to raise long-term funds, they must consider the three major types of securities — bonds, preferred stocks and common stocks — and choose between additional debt or equity. Choosing additional debt through a bond issue creates another fixed annual cost for the business, since interest must be paid to the bondholders each year. Moreover, the face value of the bonds must be repaid on the maturity date. On the other hand, if a new stock issue is chosen, the firm is not obligated to pay any dividends or to repay the principal. However, the existing shareholders must share the company's profits with the new shareholders. All these factors must be considered in long-term financial decisions — the wrong decision could have severe consequences for both the firm and the common shareholders, whose interests are the financial manager's main concern.

Another factor in financial decision-making is the concept of **financial leverage**, also known as **trading on the equity**. Common shareholders can gain through financial leverage if the firm is able to borrow at a rate of interest lower than the rate of return from the firm's operation. For example, if a company can issue bonds at an interest rate of 10% and earn 16% by using these borrowed funds in its operation, then the difference of 6% goes into the company earnings from which common shareholders benefit. Table 9.2 shows in more detail how financial leverage works. Both Company A and Company B plan to expand their operation by acquiring an additional $100 000, which would bring their total assets to $200 000. Company A will raise the funds through the issue of additional common stock, while Company B will issue bonds at an interest rate of 10%. If we assume that the earnings of both companies after the expansion will remain at 20% of investment, then Company B, which issued bonds, will earn a greater return on the total investment before tax.

Company B makes the greater return because money was borrowed at 10% and used by the company to earn 20%. Thus the shareholders of Company B have increased their potential share of profits by 10% without any additional investment on their part. However, financial leverage can also work against common shareholders when company earnings drop. For example, if the earnings of both

TABLE 9.2
Comparative rates of return using debt and equity financing

	Company A	Company B
Initial investment	$100 000	$100 000
Additional investment		
Common Stock	$100 000	0
Bonds (10%)	0	100 000
Total investment	**$200 000**	**$200 000**
Earnings (20%)	40 000	40 000
Less: bond interest	0	10 000
Net profit before tax	**40 000**	**30 000**
Return on shareholders' equity (before tax)	$\frac{40\ 000}{200\ 000} = 20\%$	$\frac{30\ 000}{100\ 000} = 30\%$

companies dropped to 10%, both companies would still show a 10% return on shareholders' investment. But the drop in return would have been twice as high for Company B, which financed its expansion by issuing bonds. If earnings dropped to zero, Company A would break even, but Company B would suffer a $10 000 loss because it had to pay that amount in bond interest.

Thus, financial leverage must be used with caution, particularly by companies that face considerable fluctuations in earnings. The increased return on investment from financial leverage could become a financial nightmare for a company with a fixed high interest payment, if its earnings were suddenly to drop. With the concept of financial leverage in mind, we can now briefly examine some of the factors the financial manager must consider before deciding on a method of raising long-term funds. These factors are:

1. Cost of financing
2. Taxation
3. Voting control
4. Risk
5. Ease of raising capital

Cost of Financing

As we have just seen, one of the foremost considerations for the financial manager is the rate of interest to be paid on a bond issue. If annual interest rates are high, a bond issue could become a liability if earnings take a sudden drop and the company still has to meet high interest payments each year. Thus a company, particularly one with irregular earnings, may decide against issuing bonds and look to raising long-term funds through stock issues instead.

Taxation

Bonds offer an advantage to a corporation because bond interest is considered a business expense and can be deducted from corporate income before the calculation of income taxes. Dividends paid to shareholders, however, cannot be deducted since they are not considered an expense but a distribution of profits after taxes. The tax advantage of bonds compared to stocks is illustrated in Table 9.3. Although both companies had the same before-tax earnings, in the end Company B has retained earnings which are 50% greater than those of Company A. Company B raised funds through a bond issue, for which the interest payable is considered a before-tax expense. In contrast, Company A raised funds through a stock issue and, instead of interest, had to pay dividends, which come out of after-tax earnings. The treatment of bond interest as an expense is a major reason for the popularity of bond issues as a means of long-term financing.

TABLE 9.3
Effect of corporate income taxes on equity and debt capital

	Company A	Company B
Earnings	$40 000	$40 000
Less: bond interest	0	10 000
Profit before tax	40 000	30 000
Less: tax at 50%	20 000	15 000
Net profit	20 000	15 000
Less: dividends	10 000	0
Retained earnings	**$10 000**	**$15 000**

Voting Control

Raising funds through a bond issue does not mean that existing shareholders lose control of the company, since bondholders have no voting rights. However, the original shareholders do lose some control of the company when additional shares are sold and the number of shareholders increases, unless they maintain their original proportion of outstanding shares by purchasing more of the new issue.

Risk

Businesses assured of steady earnings year after year, such as government-regulated public utilities, prefer bond issues since they have no difficulty meeting fixed interest payments or repaying the principal of the bonds at maturity. However, steel, construction or manufacturing companies, whose earnings may fluctuate considerably with business cycles, must be careful when issuing bonds. They may have difficulty meeting their fixed interest charges in years when earnings are low. Financial managers in these companies must pay particular attention to financial leverage and the debt/equity ratio.

Ease of Raising Capital

Decisions on long-term financing through debt or equity issues may be influenced by the existing market conditions for the sale of stocks and bonds. During buoyant economic periods when stock prices are rising and investors feel positive about the stock market and the economy, a corporation may have no problem selling new stock issues. When the economic outlook is poor and stock prices are falling, however, new stock issues may be more difficult to sell, as investors trying to protect their investment will look for a more secure income. A corporation may then prefer to sell bonds, even though it may mean paying a higher rate of interest.

Marketing Corporate Securities

Once the best type of corporate security to raise the required financial capital has been chosen, the stock or bond issue is sold to potential investors. The finance manager then enlists the aid of a **securities underwriter**, whose job it is to market the new securities to the general public, to insurance companies or to other financial institutions such as those dealing in pensions and mutual funds.

For example, suppose a company has decided to raise $10 million through a new share issue. The underwriter's first step is to investigate the firm's operation, particularly its financial condition, with the assistance of accountants, financial analysts and various individuals with expertise in the business. If the analysis shows that all is in order, the underwriter then negotiates details of the share issue with the firm. Once negotiations are complete, the underwriter usually purchases the share issue, either alone or in partnership with other investment companies.

One critical task of the underwriter is pegging the stock at the right price for sale. Accurate forecasting is essential, as the stock could easily rise or fall between the time the price is determined and the time the shares are actually put onto the market. The underwriter also assists in obtaining approval for the share issue from the various government agencies concerned and from the securities commission. In addition, the underwriter aids in the preparation of the **prospectus**, which is a detailed description of the company and the new share issue. A prospectus must be issued to each potential buyer of the new shares, to provide the investor with all the necessary information about the company. The underwriter's fee, also known as the **spread**, is the difference between the price for which he sells the issue in the market and the price at which he bought it from the firm. The spread will, of course, depend on how difficult it is to sell the stock.

The Securities Markets

Stocks and bonds are popular investments because they can be converted into cash quickly. However, an investor who has purchased shares or bonds issued by a company cannot get his money back from the firm, since in the meantime it will have purchased fixed assets or otherwise used the funds in its operation. Therefore, the holder sells his shares through a **securities** or **stock market** to others who are willing to purchase them. A stock market provides a means for buyers and sellers to meet and exchange securities at mutually agreeable prices.

The world's oldest stock exchange, in Amsterdam, began operations in 1611 when the Dutch East India Company first sold its

Private Placement

A relatively unknown way of raising capital in Canada and in the U.S. is **private placement**. Although brokerage houses are involved in bringing together borrowers and lenders, securities are sold privately to a small group of investors, usually insurance companies and wealthy individuals. Since these securities are not sold to the general public, lengthy prospectuses are not needed and the cost of issuing securities is significantly reduced. Furthermore, companies can issue their stocks and bonds quickly and confidentially. However, because of the lack of a public market for resale of these securities, interest rates are higher in private deals. In Canada, the domestic market for private placements grew from only 45 issues amounting to $1.1 billion in 1976, to 198 issues worth $5.4 billion in 1981. With the recession the total declined to approximately $3.4 billion in 1982. Considering the advantages of private placement, this method of raising capital is likely to grow in the future.[1]

shares to the general public. In London, stockbrokers met in various coffee houses to sell stocks until 1773, when they moved to Sweeting Alley, which became known as the Stock Exchange Coffee House. Since the "Big Bang" in October 1987, this exchange has been known as the International Stock Exchange of the United Kingdom. Other cities with well-known stock exchanges are Paris, Tokyo, Zurich, Frankfurt, Melbourne, Copenhagen, Hong Kong, New York, Chicago, Montreal and Toronto. The network of securities markets as a whole consists of stock exchanges, over-the-counter markets and a variety of financial institutions including chartered banks, brokerage firms, investment companies and security dealers.

Stock Exchanges
A stock exchange is essentially a marketplace for corporate securities — members of the exchange purchase or sell securities, either for themselves or for clients.

Canada has five stock exchanges, in Toronto, Montreal, Vancouver, Winnipeg and Calgary. The Toronto Stock Exchange, started in 1852, is by far the largest, accounting for almost three-quarters of the total value of shares traded in Canada. In order to sit on the stock exchange a seat must be purchased, which entitles the holder to four traders, plus himself, on the floor of the exchange. These floor traders are the only ones permitted to transact business on the floor of the exchange. In 1980 the Toronto Stock Exchange had approximately 80 members.

The trading floor of the Montreal Exchange

Computerized Trading

Many Canadian exchanges are preparing for the day when global securities trading by computer becomes a reality. It will not be long before investors will be able to use their computers to trade on the world's stock exchanges 24 hours a day. While it is already technically feasible, it probably is still a few years off. The prime reason for the delay is not technical but cultural, and concerned with accounting practices, trading rules and exchange rates. But when these problems have been solved, any investor or broker with a personal computer will be able to access stock quotations on a 24-hour basis, and program their machines to pick the best price of stocks that are interlisted on several stock exchanges. A recent deal signed between Telerate, an electronic quote vendor, and Lotus Corp., will allow investors to download stock quotations into their spreadsheet for analysis.

Meanwhile, the computer is being increasingly used by stockbrokers and traders. The Toronto Stock Exchange (TSE) has CATS (computer-assisted trading) system, which allows buyers and sellers to make deals through their own computers. The Vancouver Stock Exchange installed its computerized trading system in 1988. This will allow traders to trade anywhere in the world, 24 hours a day. The computers do not have to be in a particular brokerage office or on the stock exchange floor. Ultimately this will work against the trading floor, which will no longer be required. Instead the trading floor will be wherever the central computer is located.[2]

How Securities are Bought and Sold

Suppose you received a gift of $2000 and decided to try your hand at investing in the stock market. How would you go about it? Obviously you would have to determine which stock to buy, either by reading about various companies in financial newspapers, or by asking individuals who are informed. You might also evaluate firms by researching their products, financial condition and future profit outlook.

Another source of information is a **stockbroker**; listings can be readily found in the yellow pages of the telephone book. In addition to buying stocks or bonds for you, the broker can serve as an advisor and counsellor, suggesting stocks that may be appropriate and providing other current information about securities and the operations of various companies. Stockbrokers, sometimes known as account executives, can also make stock purchases for their clients once accounts have been opened with them. As in opening an account with a department store, some personal information will be required.

Let us assume that after establishing an account with a local brokerage firm, you have decided to purchase 200 shares of stock — known as a **boardlot**—in Canadian Pacific. The shares are trading at a price of $24 1/8 per share (Figure 9.13). Amounts other than board-lots can also be purchased, but they usually cost slightly more per share. Your broker will teletype your order to the stock exchange that trades the stock of the company you wish to purchase. When the order is received in the exchange, it is relayed to a floor trader who shouts out your order to other traders. If another trader has a client who wishes to sell 200 shares of the stock at your price of $24 1/8 per share, the transaction will be completed. Once the **floor trader** working for your broker has teletyped the confirmed transaction back to the brokerage house, the purchase is recorded on your account.

On the **settlement day** — usually three days later — you must make payment to your broker. Since the total cost of the stock you have purchased is $4825 plus the broker's commission, but you have only $2000, you will need to **margin**, or borrow, the remainder from your broker at a monthly interest charge. The commission, normally 3% of the value of the total stock transaction, is the payment for the work the brokerage house and the account executive have done for you in purchasing the stock. Investors who purchase large blocks of shares are usually able to negotiate the commission and receive a lower rate.

The Over-the-Counter Market

Only approximately 10% of Canadian companies have their stocks listed on any of the country's five exchanges. A listed stock must be

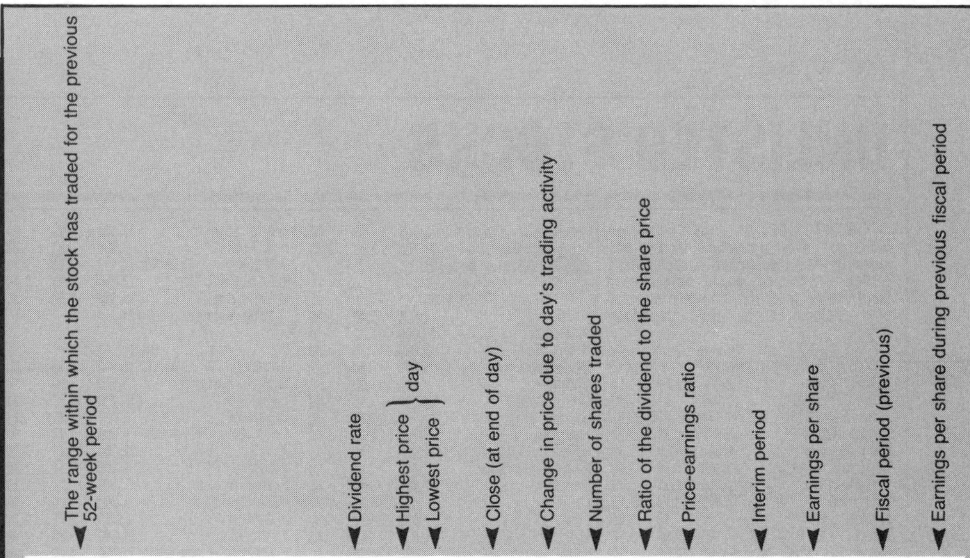

Annotations (left to right, pointing to columns):

- The range within which the stock has traded for the previous 52-week period
- Dividend rate
- Highest price } day
- Lowest price
- Close (at end of day)
- Change in price due to day's trading activity
- Number of shares traded
- Ratio of the dividend to the share price
- Price-earnings ratio
- Interim period
- Earnings per share
- Fiscal period (previous)
- Earnings per share during previous fiscal period

52 Week High	Low	Stock	Div Rate	High	Low	Cls or Latest	Net Chge	Vol 100s	Yield %	P/E Ratio	Interim Period	Eps	Fiscal Period	Eps
20	9	Cdn Media Arts...............	....	L	15Apr88	9	....	nil V	....	....	......	.....	......	....
83	20	Cdn Microcool ★..............	....	42	40	40	—1	60 V	....	....	......	.....	......	....
$22	14	Cdn Occidental Pete........	0.40	$20⅛	19⅜	19⅜	—⅝	181 T	2.1	22.3	1987 Dec	.87	1986 Dec	.62
$30¼	17¾	Cdn Pacific Ltd..............	0.60	$24⅛	23¼	23⅜	unch	16083 T	2.6	11.0	1987 Dec	2.12	1986 Dec	.50
145	95	Cdn Pacific C$ pf...........	0.04	L	18Apr88	110	....	nil	3.6	....	1987 Dec x1273.40		1986 Dec x281.64	
140	95	Cdn Pac sterling pf.........	0.0234	92	92	95	unch	z8 T	2.5	....	1987 Dec x1273.40		1986 Dec x281.64	
$16⅜	16⅜	Cdn Pacific $US.............	....	L	4Jan88	16⅜	....	nil			......	.....	......	....
$17½	9¼	Cdn Satellite ☆................	....	$12	11½	12	+⅛	108 T	....	63.2	Feb 6m	.09	1987 Aug	.16
$55	27	Cdn Tire......................	0.24	$37½	36	37	—1	4 T	0.6	33.6	1987 Dec	1.10	1986 Dec	1.01
$16⅛	8½	◊Cdn Tire A..................	0.24	$16	15⅝	15¾	—⅛	4250 T	1.5	14.3	1987 Dec	1.10	1986 Dec	1.01
$54	50	Cdn Util 4.25 pf..............	4.25	L	9Feb88	54	....	nil	7.9	....	1986 Dec	x2.23	1985 Dec	x2.34
$62	55	Cdn Util 5.00 pf..............	5.00	L	6Apr88	61	....	nil	8.2	....	1986 Dec	x2.23	1985 Dec	x2.34
$25	22	Cdn Util 7.30 pf..............	1.8250	$24¾	24¾	24¾	—¼	4 T	7.4	....	1986 Dec	x2.23	1985 Dec	x2.34
$21⅝	15	◊Cdn Utilities A..............	1.32	$19⅞	19⅜	19⅞	+⅝	442 T	6.6	11.2	1987 Dec	1.78	1986 Dec	2.16
$21	16	Cdn Utilities B...............	1.32	$20	19¾	19¾	—⅜	78 T	6.7	11.1	1987 Dec	1.78	1986 Dec	2.16
$27⅜	25⅛	Cdn Util 2nd pf I...........	2.18½	$26	25⅝	25¾	—⅛	107 M	8.5	....	1986 Dec	x2.23	1985 Dec	x2.34
$26⅜	24¾	Cdn Util 2nd pf K..........	1.95	$25½	25⅛	25⅜	+¼	72 T	7.7	....	1986 Dec	x2.23	1985 Dec	x2.34
$26½	24¼	Cdn Util 2nd pf L...........	1.92½	$25½	25⅜	25½	unch	33 T	7.5	....	1986 Dec	x2.23	1985 Dec	x2.34
$25⅞	23¾	Cdn Util 2nd pf M..........	1.77	$24⅞	24⅞	24⅞	—⅛	2 T	7.1	....	1986 Dec	x2.23	1985 Dec	x2.34
$25½	23⅝	Cdn Util 2nd pf N..........	1.77½	$24¼	24¼	24¼	—⅛	7 T	7.3	....	......		......	
$74½	64	Cdn Util 6.00 pf..............	6.00	$69	69	69	—2	1 T	8.7	....	1986 Dec	x2.23	1985 Dec	x2.34
$10¼	8¾	Cdn W NatGas 4 pf...........	0.80	$9½	9	9	—½	11 T	8.9	....	►1987 Dec	x4.11	►1986 Dec	x4.41

Figure 9.13 Typical stock quotations

approved by the provincial **securities commission** and the exchange itself must approve it for trading. To obtain approval the corporation must meet the exchange's minimum financial standards and show a reasonable management performance. Prices for stocks listed on the stock exchanges are available at all times; most major newspapers list the high, low and closing prices of every stock as it is traded during the day. Also, many television cable companies broadcast stock trades as they happen and provide a summary listing similar to that in newspapers.

UNLISTED STOCKS

TORONTO (CP) - June 14 transactions in over-the-counter stocks provided by the Investment Dealers' Association of Canada under authority of the Ontario Securities Commission. Volume includes client and inter-dealer trades.

INDUSTRIALS

	Volume	High	Low
A.H.A. Auto.	2,000	1.55	1.50
Action Traders	12,000	.41	.39
Alta En. 7.75cv pf	11,685	26.625	25.425
Autocrown	30,000	.22	.22
Cons Branly	10,000	.30	.30
Contrans A	65,500	10.75	10.00
Eclipse Cap.	2,000	.72	.70
Longford	45,000	2.75	2.75
Nelma Inform.	7,000	.50	.50
North. Tel 5½A pf	100	10.00	9.50
North.Tel 5½C pf	100	10.00	9.50
z-Oakville Wood	20	1.25	1.25
O'Tooles Fd	29,000	.75	.67
Polycom	500	5.75	5.75
Polycom Sys. pf A	3,000	5.50	5.50
Westcoast 8.25cv pf	94,350	27.625	25.00
z-Cdn Util. A wts	78	3.90	3.90
Cdn Util. B wts	195	3.90	3.90

Longford Equip.wts	16,000	.06	.06
National Bk wts	11,700	3.00	2.25
Total Volume: 340,178.			

MINES

Ansil	1,000	.80	.80
Argentex	55,000	.65	.52
Biron Bay	5,000	.30	.30
Blythwood	4,000	.20	.20
Chance	4,500	.60	.58
Cindy Mae	6,100	.90	.40
Golden Hope	2,000	.70	.70
Hedman	3,700	2.10	2.00
Holmer Gold	2,000	.75	.75
Isaac's Harbour	2,000	.10	.10
Keezic	17,500	.45	.40
Launay	550	1.70	1.70
Loki	7,000	.30	.30
Milner Cons	6,000	.45	.40
New Athona	1,400	.08	.08
New Dimension	8,800	3.125	3.05
Orrwell	25,500	.57	.50
Pelangio	5,000	.31	.28
Perrex	34,000	.475	.37
Puissance	5,000	.70	.60
Redaurum R L	1,000	.65	.65
Sandy Cay	2,000	.30	.30

White Star	10,000	.23	.23
Loki wts	5,000	.03	.03
y-Mountain Frontier	2,500	2.70	2.70
y-Pan East	3,250	2.05	2.00
y-McAdam	31,380	1.50	1.50
Total Volume: 251,180.			

OILS

Asamera 8cv pf C	16,900	25.00	10.00
B.Y.G. Natural	1,000	.50	.50
Canterra	19,250	12.875	12.05
Cessland	5,000	.23	.23
Cons Grandview	9,000	.90	.90
H.W.I.	22,100	1.35	1.20
Jupiter	1,500	.50	.50
z-New Realm	300	.15	.15
Petrolantic	3,000	.40	.40
y-Dewey	750	2.75	2.75
y-Interfirst	15,850	1.40	1.40
y-Balfour Channel	13,750	1.70	1.70
y-Fairfax Bay	20,450	1.10	1.10
y-Falcon Point	17,350	1.60	1.60
y-Sussex Ex.	11,000	1.85	1.85
Total Volume: 157,200.			

y - Stock issue in primary distribution.

z - Odd lots traded.

MINES AND OILS BID AND ASKED

TORONTO (CP) - Quotations Monday on unlisted mines and oils supplied by Dominion Securities Pitfield Ltd.

	Bid	Ask
Aik Rus	10	15
Accord	25	35
Argentx	53	58
Aubet	13	18
Augdom	13	18
BironBay	30	33

	Bid	Ask
Blythwood	16	20
Cane Cor	30	40
Canper	35	40
Carling	10	15
Cast B	7	10
Chance	58	63
Cleyo	130	140

	Bid	Ask
Cleyo wts	-	10
Concopper	22	27
Craibe	50	60
East Bay	5	10
Edda Res	35	40
Edomar	6	9
Elmwd	30	35
Errington	24	26
F Cdn Gd	5	-
Gldn Eth	7	12
Gold Hr	18	22

	Bid	Ask
Gold Hope	75	85
Grandad	50	70
Hedman	190	210
Init	40	60
Key Lk	13	18
Langis	9	12
Loki Res	30	35
Lori R	5	15
Lyndx	20	30
Mextor	25	- -
Milner	35	45

	Bid	Ask
Nahani pf	10	20
N Texmt	8	13
Nwthona	8	13
Ontex	17	20
Perrex	45	50
Pinetree	50	60
Puisnce	50	60
Punters	13	17
Redaur	60	65
Richg	75	80
Sharpe	26	30

	Bid	Ask
Sheldon	18	23
SlvUrke	100	125
Sunvall	100	125
Swansea	10	-
Track Rs	5	10
Urban Rs	3	6
Wabgn	3	6
Yellorex	7	12
Yng Dav	35	40
OILS		
Petrintc	40	50

INDUSTRIAL BID AND ASKED

TORONTO (CP) - Over-the-counter industrials bid and ask quotations supplied Monday to the Investment dealers Association of Canada by Dominion Securities Pitfield Co. Ltd.:

	Bid	Ask
A.H.A. Auto	1.50	1.65
Abstainers 10 pfd	8.75	10.00
Action Traders	.38	.43
ARC International	3.00	3.25
Autocrown Corp.	.23	.28
Belgium Standard	2.75	3.00
Benvan Holdings	1.35	1.50
Candy Investments Ltd.	.20	.25
Cdn Gas Egy B wts	28.00	30.00

	Bid	Ask
Carvern	.75	.85
Commercial Finance	4.00	5.00
Consolidated Branly	.40	.60
Continental R and D	.50	.60
Eclipse Capital	.65	.70
Gemini Food	1.15	1.25
Global Communications com	37.00	
Global Shelter	.30	.40
Goderich Elevator	27.50	29.00
H.O. Financial	1.20	1.30
Highland Queen	1.25	1.75
Levy Ind	15.00	16.00
Longford Equip	2.50	2.88
Longford pfd	2.50	2.75

	Bid	Ask
Longford wts	- -	.15
Memotec Data	4.87	5.13
Nelma Info	.48	.53
O'Toole's Food	.63	.68
Paramount Funding Corp	1.25	1.75
Polycom cmn	5.50	6.00
Polycom pfd.	5.50	6.00
Pony Sporting Goods	.05	.10
Real Time Data Pro	2.00	2.50
Russell Holdings	.35	.45
Seel Mortgage	9.25	9.75
Superpack Corp	3.25	3.75
TEC Syn Intl	9.50	10.00
York Centre B	4.00	5.00

Figure 9.14 Listing of industrial and other stocks trading over-the-counter

For the other 90% of Canadian corporations whose stock is not listed on the stock exchanges, there is another method of trading known as the **over-the-counter market** where large volumes of stocks and bonds are traded. In the past, information on a small number of these stocks was available only to investors from day-old newspapers or from brokers who had to telephone other traders for the latest prices. However, since the fall of 1985 the over-the-counter market became automated. Brokers can now publicly display quotes on all over-the-counter stocks and report and store information. This system has the ability to be upgraded to a regular trading system.[3] Figure 9.14 shows some of the unlisted over-the-counter stocks before the system was automated.

Why Buy Stocks and Bonds?

Although the stock market is sometimes used by speculators who hope to make large gains quickly, it is primarily intended to raise money for business investment. Companies offer shares of ownership to the public, and potential investors hope to receive dividends from their investment as well as appreciation of their shares if the firm is profitable. The businesses in turn use the money raised from the sale of stock to improve and expand their operation to increase production and profits. Prospective investors have a wide choice of securities available to them, including common shares, preferred shares and bonds, each offering a variety of features.

Investment in the stock and bond market is risky. Since stock prices are determined by supply and demand in the market, sudden fluctuations can occur because of company misfortunes or because of economic or political events that might affect the company's profits. Nevertheless, there are companies that promise to return to investors more than the interest received from the bank on a similar deposit in a bank savings account. Proper investment provides a greater return but the risk is also higher. Preferred shares and bonds can reduce this risk considerably. Some stock investments have rewarded their investors handsomely over the years, while others have been a disaster. Common and preferred stocks do offer the investor some protection against inflation. Companies can increase the prices for their products to ensure that their profits increase relative to inflation.

An important consideration for many investors is the **liquidity** of their investment — the ease with which it can be turned into cash. Because of the network of stock exchanges, most stocks and bonds can be sold within hours if the investor requires cash quickly. For investments in real estate or other assets, on the other hand, buyers are not as readily available.

NOTES

1. Martin Mittelstaedt, "Private Placement Canada is a leader in this quiet market," *The Globe and Mail*, July 9, 1984.
2. Bruce Gates, "Around-the-clock trading not much more than a keystroke away," *The Financial Post Special Report*, April 25, 1988, p. 43.
3. "Unlisted stocks to go electronic," *The Financial Post*, May 11, 1985, p. 38.

CHAPTER SUMMARY

In general, the most important function of the financial manager is to ensure that the firm survives. Even a well-managed company occasionally has to borrow to meet its financial obligations. The financial manager must examine the future cash flow of the business and establish a cash budget to indicate when the business will need to borrow money to survive, such as during periods when cash outflow exceeds inflow. The principal sources of short-term funds are banks, various financial institutions, and other businesses. These sources may provide funds on a secured or unsecured basis — security can be provided by accounts receivable, inventories or other property. Another important source of short-term funds is trade credit, which is often extended on an open book basis, though sometimes promissory notes or trade drafts are required.

The financial manager must also keep track of the performance of the business. An accounting system is thus established, providing information that is used to compare current performance with that of previous years and other businesses. Methods of financial analysis include ratio analysis and comparisons of income statements and balance sheets. Management also uses information from these analyses and from break-even analysis in decision-making.

The two most basic financial statements are a balance sheet and an income statement. A balance sheet gives an indication of the firm's financial position at a particular point in time. An income statement shows the results of business transactions between two particular periods of time, and shows the income earned through the firm's operation. However, neither the income statement nor the balance sheet specifies where cash came from, or where it went. This information is provided by a statement of changes in financial position, which is used by management to plan for future cash requirements. The financial manager is also responsible for establishing operating and capital budgets and comparing actual performance with budgetary plans.

For the long-term funds required to purchase fixed assets, a firm can raise either debt or equity capital. A bond signifies that the company issuing it has borrowed money from investors, while stocks or shares represent equity capital and indicate ownership in the company. Shares can be either preferred or common. Preferred shareholders receive dividend payments before common shareholders, but they usually do not have the voting rights that common shareholders have.

In deciding how to raise long-term capital, the financial manager must consider current interest rates, the respective advantages of bonds and stocks in terms of taxation, future earnings of the company, the voting control exercised by common shareholders, as well as general economic conditions, which may favour either stocks or bonds at any particular time.

Investors purchase stocks and bonds to obtain a return that is potentially higher than bank interest rates because of the potential capital appreciation of the shares, and because of the speed with which stocks and bonds can be turned into cash if necessary.

KEY TERMS

Financial solvency
Short-term borrowing
Cash budget
Cash flow
Trade creditors
Cash discounts
Open book credit
Consignment
Promissory note
Time draft and trade acceptance
Secured loan
Unsecured loan
Collateral
Factoring
Commercial paper
Accounting
Financial accounting
Management accounting
Balance sheet
Income statement
Statement of changes in financial position
Current assets
Current liabilities
Fixed assets
Long-term liabilities
Equity
Retained earnings
Gross profit

Net profit
Ratio analysis
Current ratio
Quick or acid-test ratio
Forecasting
Break-even analysis
Fixed costs
Variable costs
Operating budget
Capital budget
Depreciation
Debt capital
Equity capital
Bonds
Common stock
Preferred stock
Maturity date
Principal
Interest
Registered bond
Bearer bond
Debenture
Financial leverage
Securities underwriter
Stock market
Stock exchanges
Brokerage firm
Over-the-counter market

REVIEW QUESTIONS

1. Describe the three major functions of the finance department.
2. What is meant by financial solvency? Why must a business borrow money on occasion?
3. Explain the meaning of cash flow. Why is a cash budget necessary for a business?
4. Why is trade credit included as a source of short-term funds? What are the various types of trade credit?

5. What is a factor company? When would a business use the services of such a company?

6. Why do small businesses have difficulty arranging financing?

7. What is accounting? What is the difference between financial and management accounting? Why does a business, regardless of size, need an accounting system?

8. Explain the importance of a balance sheet and an income statement. What is the purpose of a statement of changes in financial position?

9. What is the purpose of ratio analysis? Identify five common ratios. How are they useful in analyzing a firm's operation?

10. Why is break-even analysis a useful tool for business forecasting and analysis?

11. Why does a business distinguish between short- and long-term financing?

12. Distinguish between equity capital and debt capital. Under what circumstances would a company prefer equity to debt capital?

13. Explain how depreciation can be a source of long-term funds.

14. Distinguish between common and preferred stock.

15. Explain the concept of financial leverage. Why is financial leverage an important consideration for the finance manager who must choose between debt and equity financing?

16. How are corporate securities marketed? What is the function of the securities underwriter?

17. What is the purpose of a stock exchange? Of a brokerage firm?

DISCUSSION QUESTIONS

1. Which financial statement do you think would be more useful to banks and other institutions considering a loan to a business: the balance sheet or the income statement? Explain.

2. "It is more important to have firm control over cash flow, than to have an accurate picture of profits." Do you agree or disagree with this statement? Explain your answer.

3. One way of getting around the problem of choosing between debt and equity financing for a new plant, office building, or warehouse is to let someone else build it and then lease the facilities from them for a fixed number of years at a regular monthly charge. Explain how leasing might be advantageous for a company.

4. After studying both the management and the finance function of a business, can you explain why these two areas represent the major reasons for business failure?

CASE 9-1 Raising Money for Publishing

Rita Foster and Keith Andrews had known each other since university. For the past eight years Rita had been working as a market research analyst particularly involved in life-style research. Keith had been teaching a college business communication course; for the past four years he had also been editor of a publication called "Business Communication Today." The two decided to produce a new magazine together called "Lifestyles Today." Since the topic was of considerable current interest, they thought the project could make money; they were both also keenly interested in the venture, and they looked forward to considerable job satisfaction.

Although magazine publishing is not an easy venture, Rita and Keith had heard that subscriptions usually cover publication costs after six months, while advertising revenues provide the profit for the business.

"Lifestyles Today" would have one feature article per month solicited from freelance writers for which Rita and Keith would pay $3000. They also wanted up to six shorter supplementary articles for which they would pay $600 each. Additional costs for pictures and copyrights were estimated at approximately $2000 per issue. Rita and Keith expected to do the monthly layout themselves, which would cost approximately $450 for the cover and $1600 for the magazine. After receiving estimates for printing costs from a number of printers they settled on one who charged $870 per 1000 copies for the first 10 000 and $690 per 1000 for the next 20 000 copies. These costs were fixed for at least one year. Thus they were reasonably certain about their printing and production costs.

During the first month they expected to sell 4000 copies on the newstand and these sales were expected to increase by 600 copies per month for the first year. Thereafter they expected sales to level off. In addition to newstand sales Rita and Keith expected the following subscription sales:

Month	Subscriptions	Month	Subscriptions
1	0	7	400
2	400	8	300
3	600	9	200
4	800	10	100
5	800	11	100
6	700	12	100

The costs of distributing the magazine to newstands and through the mail averaged 40¢ per copy. From an advertising agency they learned that they could expect net advertising revenues of approximately $6000 per month after the first year. During the first year they expected advertising revenues to increase by $500 per month.

Rita and Keith studied the magazines that were similar to their own and felt that initially a price of $2 per issue would be satisfactory. Based on this price they decided to sell a yearly subscription for $20 for twelve issues. They rented an office for $300 per month, and hired a part-time secretary for $600 per month. Telephone, power and miscellaneous costs were estimated at about $150 per month. They also hit upon a novel advertising idea. The print run during each of the first three months would be 15 000 copies. Any copies not sold on the newsstand or through subscriptions would be distributed free of charge to selected households in and around the city during the following month. They hoped this tactic would encourage subscriptions.

All in all, Rita and Keith felt they had a good idea of what was involved in the venture. They had talked to a number of acquaintances with some knowledge of the business, and they had done considerable research on publishing. They each had $8000 to contribute to the venture and they were confident that any chartered bank would be happy to give them a loan if and when necessary. They were also confident that they could raise money by selling shares to investors.

Both were full of confidence in their future success. Rita left her job to devote her time to the publishing venture. She would take $600 per month to cover her expenses. Keith felt he could continue to teach and edit the magazine at the same time. He did not expect to take any money out of the business for at least the first year.

However, after two and a half weeks of operation, they realized they would have financial problems. The sale of advertising space in the magazine was extremely slow; they had difficulty both in deciding on the kinds of material to put into the magazine, and in attracting suitable articles from freelance writers. They needed more money and so they got busy drawing up a cash budget and putting together a proposal to establish a line of credit at the bank.

QUESTIONS

1. What did Foster and Andrews overlook before starting into this venture?
2. If Foster and Andrews approach a lending institution to borrow money, what kind of information would they be required to provide before they could receive a loan? Before they could expect an investor to buy shares in the company, what would they have to do?
3. Prepare a break-even analysis for this operation, and explain how break-even analysis can be used in financial planning for the company.

4. Prepare a cash budget for the first year of this publishing venture. Indicate if and when Foster and Andrews need to borrow money and when the loans might be repaid. Assume for this exercise that they always want to have a minimum balance of $2000 in their account. Assume that all subscriptions begin the month following receipt of the order, and that all print runs have to be in thousands of copies.

CASE 9-2 Prairie Industrial Corporation

The following pertains to the Prairie Industrial Corporation, a manufacturing company.

	December 31 1989	December 31 1990
Accounts payable	$ 60 030	
Plant and buildings	320 000	
Equipment	95 300	
Inventory finished goods	115 430	
Accounts receivable	35 470	
Prepaid expenses	7 600	
Notes payable	110 000	
Accumulated depreciation on plant	128 000	
Accumulated depreciation on equipment	23 600	
Accrued liabilities	32 260	
Current portion of long term notes payable	20 000	
Common stock (issued at 10 initially)	80 000	
Retained earnings	187 450	
Cash	43 540	
Marketable securities	24 000	
Revenue from manufacturing	764 350	
Other income from operations	47 250	
Interest income	2 900	

The following additional information is provided to help establish financial statements for Prairie Industrial Corporation.

1. Accounts payable increased by $14 400 during the year.

2. There were additions to the plant of $65 000, which can be depreciated by 5% in 1990.

3. There were additions to equipment of $33 000, which can be depreciated by 7.5% in 1990.

4. The current portion of long-term notes payable was paid; in addition, the remaining long-term notes payable was completely repaid.

5. During 1990, $20 000 of the long-term notes were repaid.

6. During 1990, 10 000 additional shares of stock were issued at $16 per share.

7. The existing plant annual depreciation rate is 10% per annum (straight line).

8. The existing equipment annual depreciation rate is 15% per annum (straight line).

9. Inventory of finished goods increased by $8000 in 1990.

10. Accounts receivable decreased by $9500.

11. Prepaid expenses increased by $2300.

12. Accrued liabilities pertaining to 1990 amounted to $53 600.

13. Cost of manufactured goods amounts to 61% of revenue from manufacturing.

14. Taxes payable amount to 20% of net income under special federal tax rules.

15. Provincial taxes amount to 11% of net income.

16. Operating expenses amounted to $146 430 (excluding depreciation).

17. General and administrative expenses amount to $32 720.

18. Securities decreased by $14 000.

QUESTIONS

1. Develop a comparative balance sheet for Dec. 31, 1989 and for Dec. 31, 1990.

2. Develop an income statement for fiscal year 1990

3. Develop a statement of changes in financial position for the fiscal year 1990.

4. Compute the following ratios:
   a. current ratio — for beginning and end of period;
   b. acid-test ratio — for beginning and end of period;
   c. inventory turnover ratio;
   d. average collection period;
   e. debt ratio;
   f. debt-to-equity ratio;
   g. gross profit margin ratio;
   h. net profit margin ratio;
   i. return on investment.

CHAPTER 10

Personnel

Kim Kirk

CHAPTER OUTLINE

CHAPTER PREVIEW

In Chapter 10, we examine the personnel department. One of the personnel manager's major responsibilities is to plan for future personnel requirements, both managerial and non-managerial; he or she must also analyze all jobs in the organization and identify the skills required and the duties to be performed in each case. It is personnel's function to recruit, select, hire, and train people for employment in the organization; once good employees have been found, the firm must provide competitive salaries and various benefits. Finally, the performance of all employees must be evaluated in view of salary increases, future promotions and transfers or, in some cases, termination of employment. An effective evaluation system should identify both the employees who are experiencing problems in doing their jobs and the nature of the problems so that performance can be improved.

LEARNING OBJECTIVES

After reading this chapter you should be able to explain:

1. The major activities of the personnel department;
2. How personnel managers plan for future employee requirements;
3. The process of recruiting employees, from the initial job analysis to the final interview;
4. Hiring, orientation, training and development procedures, and programs for employees;
5. The meaning of wage and salary administration, and the various methods of compensation;
6. The importance of fringe benefits and health and safety programs for both the employee and the organization;
7. The necessity for staff evaluation and the problems involved.

Sometimes we forget that organizations are successful because of their people. A champion hockey or football team cannot be bought; it has to be developed. You start with a coach who has the technical skill, the leadership qualities to inspire the players, and the conceptual ability to plan game strategies. Then the players who have the skills required to win games and bring home the cup are selected. The same principles apply to a business, a university or a factory. The organization's success depends on people. Even if we distinguish between the jobs of managers and those of regular employees, both groups are dependent on one another.

PERSONNEL MANAGEMENT AND THE STAFFING FUNCTION

As mentioned briefly in Chapter 4, staffing — or placing people in the various positions that must be filled to achieve organizational objectives — is an essential task for any manager. Many, however, lack expertise in personnel functions, which have become increasingly specialized. In many small firms, for example, managers have the technical expertise to produce goods or services, but lack the specific skills required for personnel management. Their only recourse, then, is to rely on outside agencies who will recruit and hire staff.

Personnel management is the recruitment, selection, development and motivation of human resources. Because people are important to the success of an organization, personnel management has become a specialized business function, particularly in large organizations. Large firms must continually plan for future personnel needs, meet the requirements of government legislation and deal with the increasing demands of unions. Large firms therefore usually employ various personnel specialists or human resource professionals such as employment managers, training managers, wage and salary administration managers, and labour relations specialists.

Personnel: A Staff Department

While production, marketing and finance are considered line departments, the personnel department is a **staff department**. It performs a support function in relation to the line departments. As a staff department, it has four main functions:

POLICY INITIATION: The personnel manager establishes new policies to cover recurring problems or to prevent anticipated problems. These policies are designed to aid other managers in making decisions about employee matters such as working hours or performance standards.

ADVICE: Personnel specialists counsel line managers on matters such as how to handle grievances or how to discipline an employee.

SERVICE: Service responsibilities include recruitment, hiring, training and wage and salary administration. For example, the personnel department plans and sets up training programs and maintains all employee records.

CONTROL: The personnel department carries out control functions, such as monitoring other departments to ensure that they are following established personnel policies, procedures and practices.

It is important to remember that while the personnel department provides support for line managers, it does not take over the staffing responsibility. Staffing is a management function. Managers make the final decision on who will work for them, and it is their responsibility to ensure that employees are productive and are working toward established goals.

Personnel Planning

When a firm develops long-range corporate objectives it must keep its human resources in mind. Employees must possess the skills and education necessary to achieve the firm's objectives. Thus, the personnel manager must analyze future personnel requirements, taking into account current and past employee performance and any special recruitment problems that may be encountered. This analysis is particularly important for new firms starting up or for firms in industries

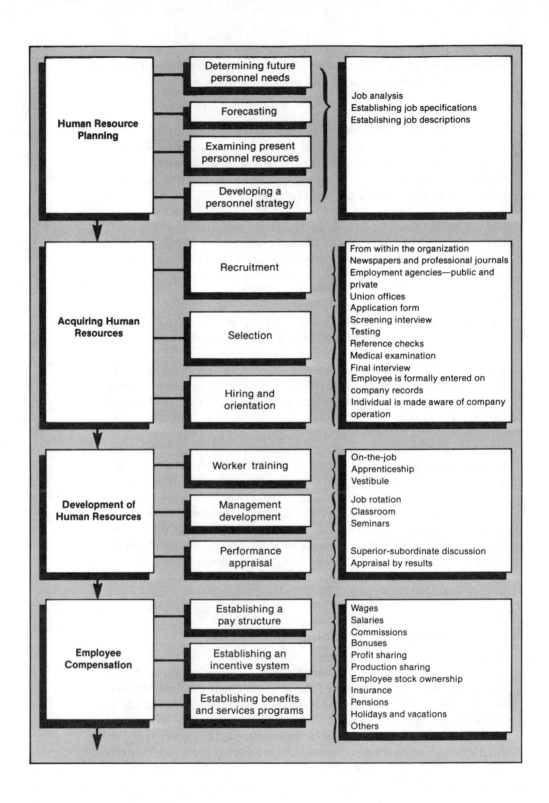

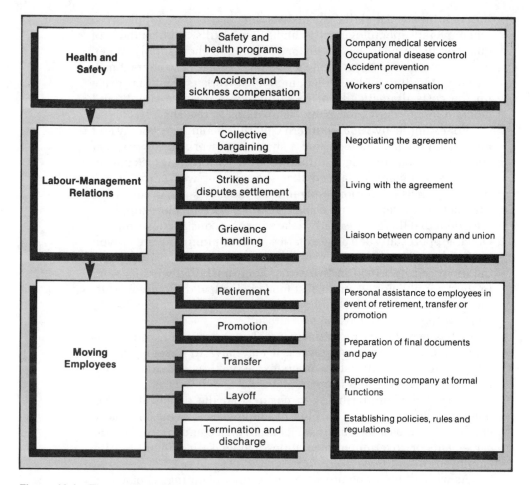

Figure 10.1 The personnel function

that require special skills. Specialists may be in short supply even when overall unemployment is high. Some skills, such as those of qualified machinists, have a history of being in short supply. When booming economic times create a general shortage of workers it may also be difficult to find qualified, motivated workers. This may drive up the costs dramatically of recruiting employees as supply and demand force salaries for many occupations to rise sharply.

For example, by 1988, southern Ontario's booming economy and low unemployment rate created a shortage of workers so great that companies were finding it difficult to fill job openings. Some recruitment companies claimed that shortages of workers were approaching crisis proportions, spanning all industries and occupations. Bricklayers, carpenters and cement masons were in short supply to the extent that there were costly delays in some construction projects. Office support staff such as secretaries and receptionists were in even greater demand, with entry-level salaries for secretary positions having increased by $3000 in two years. Even unskilled workers were in short supply. For example, fast food chains had difficulty recruiting part-time workers for kitchen and counter staff, and they had to increase their hourly pay rates as a result.[1]

A business facing recruitment problems must plan well in advance to get necessary employees. It may have to develop special training and apprenticeship programs, as well as provide various incentives to attract and keep employees.

Personnel planning helps to ensure that the organization has neither a shortage nor a surplus of employees. Having too many employees can be a serious financial drain on a company, and union agreements or government regulations may make it difficult to trim employees from the payroll.

As with all planning processes, personnel planning is not a one-time exercise. As long-range corporate objectives change or are adjusted on the basis of short-range results, long-range personnel plans must also be revised.

The personnel planning process consists of four steps:

1. **Determining future personnel needs**. Future needs will be based on the organization's objectives, taking into account plans to expand or reduce operations. The nature and number of new positions required should become evident during this first step.
2. **Evaluating current personnel resources**. The personnel manager evaluates the skills and productivity of current employees to determine the organization's human resources. The turnover rate, the ages of employees and the potential impact on the company of any impending retirements are also considered.
3. **Forecasting**. Having determined both future company objectives and current human resources, the personnel manager can estimate how

much current employees can contribute to future plans, and the number of new employees and skills that will be required.

4. **Establishing a personnel strategy**. The information acquired in the forecast can be used to establish specific programs for recruiting and training new employees and for retraining present employees to meet future objectives.

Job Analysis, Job Specification and Job Description

Before an individual is hired for a new position, a **job analysis** is made to determine the nature of the job and the work to be performed. From the job analysis the personnel manager develops a **job description** outlining the job and listing the employee's duties and responsibilities. The personnel manager will also develop a **job specification** detailing the special qualifications — education, experience and personality — required to perform the job satisfactorily. The job description and specification may be combined in one document, but both are invaluable for hiring. Figure 10.2 shows the relationship between job analysis, job description and job specification and outlines generally what each contains.

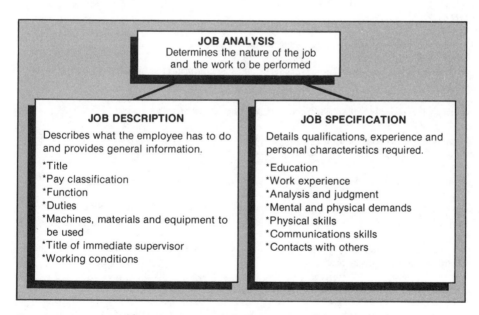

Figure 10.2 Job analysis leads to job description and job specification

JOB DESCRIPTION

Job Title	Number
BUYER	B-8

Department	Division	Date Classified
PURCHASING & FACILITIES SERVICES	BUSINESS SERVICES	1988 03 18

Title of Immediate Supervisor
DIRECTOR OF PURCHASING & FACILITIES SERVICES

Positions Supervised
Provides direction to and oversees the work of Shipper/Receiver and Purchasing Clerk

Purpose
Under the general direction of the Director of Purchasing and Facilities Services, ensures that the material, supply and equipment requirements are adequately met through the application of established purchasing policies and procedures.

==

DUTIES AND RESPONSIBILITIES

- Communicates with personnel in other departments as required to determine the nature, quality and quantities of a wide variety of items to be purchased.

- Prepares and processes purchase requisitions for goods to be purchased.

- Issues purchase orders for stationery, supplies, books, equipment, and for some capital expenditures.

- Investigates and researches products and sources of supply.

- Prepares tender calls, reviews quotations and makes recommendations regarding goods to be purchased.

- Resolves any discrepancies that may occur on packing slips and invoices.

- Corresponds with suppliers, dealers, manufacturers and others as required on any matter related to the supply, shipment, status or condition of any commodity.

- Reconciles outstanding purchase commitments records, using EDP equipment.

- Sets up payment schedules of monthly leases and equipment contracts and forwards necessary documentation to Accounting.

- Maintains contact with customs brokers and supplies necessary documentation to ensure that goods can be cleared through customs.

- Maintains equipment inventory records for all capital goods purchased.

- Organizes and directs annual capital inventory count, using EDP equipment.

- Maintains contact with tax officials, interprets and applies regulations as they apply to the tax status of the company; reviews and applies for payback of taxes.

Figure 10.3 A Job description

RATING

Dgr.	Pts.	Factor

| 3 | 75 | PROBLEM SOLVING | Incumbent is required to evaluate supplies, material quality and prices to ensure the best materials are purchased at the lowest possible cost. Must also have the ability to judge whether materials of lower quality can be substituted if there is a substantial savings in cost. For complex materials, this substitution must be done in consultation with various technical departments. |

Considerable responsibility for loss from incomplete shipments, poor quality products, out-of-stock conditions because of late shipments from suppliers. Loss can also occur from incomplete knowledge of products and prices.

Incumbent provides direction to and oversees the work of two junior employees.

| 3 | 60 | QUALIFICATIONS | Education/Training: |

High School Graduation, supplemented by relevant course(s) in purchasing. Some data processing skills required.
Experience:
Minimum three years' related purchasing experience, preferably in institutional buying.

| 1 | 15 | EFFORT | Considerable mental demand to evaluate supply orders and compare supplier price quotations. |

| 1 | 10 | CONTACTS | Incumbent must have the ability to communicate with suppliers and various company executives. Must seek out new sources of supply, and constantly evaluate materials and prices. |

| 1 | 5 | WORKING CONDITIONS | Normal office conditions; no hazards or probable injury. |

Score Range: 155 – 185   Grade: C

RATING	P	Q	E	C	W	Total
Degree	3	3	1	1	1	--
Points	75	60	15	10	5	165

==

APPROVED: _____   _____   _____
          Department Head   Divisional Manager   Industrial Relations Mgr.

==

Figure 10.3 B Job specification

Shortcomings of Traditional Job Descriptions

Traditional job descriptions such as the one shown in Figure 10.3 are generally vague, provide few clues as to working conditions, and do not set standards for minimally acceptable employee performance. They thus provide managers with little useful information for recruitment, orientation, MBO goal-setting or performance evaluations. Employees also find job descriptions of little help for orientation or performance improvement. Duties are only briefly described, and employees must wait until they are actually on the job to find out about working conditions and standards. The failure to provide a clear performance expectation from the beginning may cause unrest between organizations and their employees.

A more effective approach is what is known as results-oriented job descriptions (ROD) which should contain the following:

1. **Tasks**: What behaviour, duties or functions are important to the job?
2. **Conditions**: How often is a particular task done? What conditions make the task easy or hard to complete? What written or supervisory instructions are available to aid the employee in performing a task?
3. **Standards**: What objectives and performance expectations are attached to each task? Standards of quantity, quality and timeliness should be clearly related to organizational objectives.
4. **SKAs**: What skills, knowledge and abilities are required to perform each task at the minimally acceptable level?
5. **Qualifications**: What education and/or experience (length, level and type) are needed to ensure that employees will have the SKAs required for optimum performance?

ACQUIRING HUMAN RESOURCES

Consider this scenario. You have just finished reading your secretary's letter of resignation. Surprised and dismayed, you urge this indispensable employee to reconsider, even offer an increase in salary, but to no avail. Eventually you resign yourself to the fact that you will simply have to find and train someone else. After all, there must be many qualified secretaries looking for a job.

Since your firm has no personnel department, you will have to place the job ad in the various newspapers, review the applications as they come in and interview the most promising candidates yourself before making the final choice. While this process will add extra work to your already busy schedule, you are not overly concerned, because you do not expect many problems. So you write the ad next morning and have it placed in the local newspaper; as a precaution, you also contact the Canada Employment office.

A few days later the applications start to come in, and you arrange to spend an evening going through them to pick out the most promising applicants. You soon realize that few have the qualifications

```
┌─────────────────────────────────────────────────────────────────────────┐
│                           TYPIST / RECEPTIONIST                           │
│                                                                           │
│    Tasks            Conditions                    Standards               │
│                                                                           │
│    Type             When asked to by supervisor,  All letters error-free; │
│    letters          using an IBM Selectric type-  completed by 5 p.m. if  │
│                     writer; according to the      assigned before 3 p.m.  │
│                     office style manual.                                  │
│                                                                           │
│    Greet            As they arrive, referring     No complaints from visitors │
│    visitors         them to five executives       referred to the wrong office, │
│                     with whom they have scheduled or waiting before being │
│                     appointments.                 referred.               │
│                                                                           │
│    Skills, knowledge and abilities required                               │
│                                                                           │
│    *  Ability to type 40 wpm                                              │
│    *  Ability to use Selectric typewriter                                 │
│    *  Knowledge of office style manual                                    │
│    *  Courtesy                                                            │
│                                                                           │
│    Minimum qualifications                                                 │
│                                                                           │
│    *  High school degree or equivalent                                    │
│    *  Six months' experience as a typist, or equivalent performance test  │
│                                                                           │
│    SOURCE:  Donald E. Klinger, "When the Traditional Job Description is Not Enough." Reproduced with permission │
│             from Personnel Journal, copyright April, 1979.                │
└─────────────────────────────────────────────────────────────────────────┘
```

Figure 10.4 Results-oriented job description

specified, and at the end of the evening you are left with only a few barely qualified candidates. You begin to realize that you may not find anyone suitable this time and that the entire process may have to be repeated. Even if you do find someone, there is no guarantee that the person chosen will be good at the job, or will stay for any length of time.

Finding qualified people who are prepared to stay with a firm is a difficult task for any company, large or small, with or without a personnel department and trained personnel specialists. We now examine some of the methods used to recruit and select employees in more detail.

Recruiting Job Candidates

No organization can expect to find qualified employees without an active search. Some jobs require people with specific skills and qualifications, and these people are often difficult to find. Where, then, does a firm search for employees?

Before actively searching outside the organization, the firm often first considers its **own employees**. There are many advantages to having people currently working in the business fill positions of responsibility and higher pay. The appointments often raise morale and reduce employee turnover. Training costs are also reduced because employees are knowledgeable about the firm and its policies. However, the organization may be a relatively limited source of new employees and promotions may create additional work because lower level positions become vacant. However, even if present employees are not suitable for the new position, they may know other qualified people who would be interested in working for the firm.

The most common method of recruiting employees outside the organization is through **advertising**. Local newspapers reach a large number of people, and advertising in them increases the firm's chances of finding qualified candidates. On the other hand, the large number of applications received as a result of newspaper advertising may mean that much more time is required to weed out the unqualified applicants.

Canada or **Québec Employment Centres** and **private employment agencies** offer a list of potential candidates already screened and classified according to their skills and qualifications. These centres send the employer only those candidates with the specific qualifications requested. One disadvantage of private employment agencies is that employers often pay a high fee, although occasionally the employee pays the fee.

How do RODs Affect Organizations?

Advantages of RODs

Results-oriented job descriptions focus on performance standards, the conditions that differentiate jobs and the linkages between standards, SKAs and qualifications. In so doing, they resolve many of the problems attributed to traditional job descriptions.

- They give the program planner a means of relating personnel inputs to organizational outputs.
- They give managers a means of orienting new employees to performance expectations, set-

ting MBO goals and evaluating employee performance objectively.

- They give employees a clearer idea of organizational performance improvement expectations and of the minimum qualifications for promotion and reassignment.
- They increase the impact of personnel managers on organization and employee productivity, rather than merely on position management and control.

Disadvantages of RODs

While they are useful for these purposes, RODs appear to have some serious disadvantages: 1) changes in conditions and standards require constant rewriting of RODs; 2) each position requires a different ROD; 3) some positions do not have measurable performance standards; and 4) RODs cannot be used to classify jobs for human resources planning purposes or to evaluate them for pay comparability purposes.

SOURCE: "When the Traditional Job Description is not Enough." Donald E. Klinger. Reprinted with permission, *Personnel Journal*, copyright April, 1979.

For unionized firms, the main source of skilled workers is the local **union headquarters**. However, the company may have a limited choice of employees because the candidates with priority for the job, and who are highest on the union seniority list, may not have the specific skills required. Nevertheless, except under a closed-shop situation, the employer may hire whom he or she pleases, whether the candidate belongs to the union or not.

Schools, colleges and **universities** are also sources of employees, although recent graduates usually have little experience and may require costly training. It is also difficult to predict how long they will stay with the firm after they have been trained.

Firms may also recruit employees from other organizations or businesses. Enticing skilled personnel away from other firms is known as **pirating**. Firms in "Silicon Valley" outside San Francisco that develop microchips and other computer products are legendary for using this tactic. Technicians and scientists often leave one firm in the evening, and the next morning start at another firm which may be just across the street. These people are enticed away from their employer by higher salaries, better working conditions and fringe benefits. Thus, qualified candidates may be easily obtained by pirating at a relatively low recruitment cost, but the possibility naturally remains that another company will entice them away again by offering greater rewards or opportunities. Thus, pirating is not always advantageous.

Selecting the New Employee

When selecting a new employee, it is essential to match an individual's skills with the tasks to be performed. As discussed earlier, the job analysis identifies the duties and responsibilities of a position and the skills required to perform them well. The job specification describes the person best suited for the job in terms of skills, education and previous experience. Unless some attempt is made to match the person with the job, problems may develop. Individuals who are too highly qualified, for example, may become bored with the job and leave soon after being hired. Those without the necessary skills and education may not be able to perform the job adequately, and the firm may be forced to let them go. In either case, the costly and time-consuming process of recruitment must then be repeated.

Human Rights Legislation

Personnel managers must ensure that any rejection of candidates is based on lack of qualifications rather than on any discrimination, which could result in charges and a hearing before the **Human Rights Commission**. According to the **Human Rights Act** of 1977, an individual cannot be discriminated against because of race, national or ethnic origin, colour, religion, age, sex, marital status, conviction for an offence that has been pardoned, or physical handicaps. The Human Rights Commission was established to oversee employment practices for employees who come under federal jurisdiction, although most provinces have similar agencies.

Most company executives are sincere when they say that their companies do not discriminate in their hiring practices; nevertheless, there is evidence indicating the opposite. Discrimination was shown in almost three quarters of all cases that came before a board of inquiry between 1975 and 1980. In fact, the situation may be worse because the bulk of the cases do not go to the board, but are settled by conciliation and persuasion.[2]

Increasingly, Canadian employers are examining their employment and hiring practices. Some companies openly state they are equal opportunity employers, and they are replacing the traditional résumés with employment and education histories. Many companies are also looking at their job descriptions to ensure they do not contain discriminatory requirements. In the recruitment and selection process, managers must ensure that candidates are screened out only for job-related reasons. Interviews should be highly structured and only questions of direct relevance to the job should be asked. Special training and entry requirements have to be shown necessary. Performance evaluations and compensation plans must reward performance and not other characteristics that may preclude certain individuals.

Some large companies have established programs through which employees can voice complaints and concerns when normal channels to management are not adequate. The Royal Bank, for example, employs an outside consultant to conduct a yearly attitude survey among employees. The survey is designed to bring cases of real or perceived discrimination to the attention of management so they can be investigated and resolved. Nevertheless, many executives agree that if equal opportunity employment is to be firmly established, management must be committed to the concept.[3]

Most companies publicize their equal employment opportunity practices. However, companies often do not include affirmative-action programs which would give preference to disadvantaged and minority groups. The Canadian Human Rights Act encourages affirmative-action programs to improve opportunities for groups that have been at a disadvantage in the past.

The Selection Process
The process for selecting new employees varies among organizations, but it usually includes the following steps:

1. **Application**. The application form or letter of application is usually the first step; it provides the company with background information including the applicant's education, skills and experience. When selecting management personnel, however, the application step may be preceded by a pre-screening interview, which reduces the number of candidates to a manageable level by selecting only those who are most suitable for the job. The pre-screening interview is often based on the candidate's résumé, which may be used in lieu of an application form.

2. **Testing**. After the number of applicants has been reduced to a manageable level, the next step usually involves testing. Intelligence, personality, aptitude and skills tests are all commonly used to assess the candidates and their skills.

3. **Reference Checks**. Once testing has further narrowed the field of applicants, reference checks are usually conducted, in which previous employers are questioned about the candidate's job performance.

4. **Final Interview**. The final interview is the last stage in the selection process. By this time specific information about each candidate is available, and a skilled interviewer can ask questions that will reveal a candidate's aptitudes and abilities, including speaking ability and personal goals. The interviewer then has an indication of how each individual might fit into the job and the organization.

It is important to remember that this selection process may vary among organizations; additional steps may be included depending on the type of position to be filled. For example, a candidate for a high-level management position may be asked to three or more interviews before the final selection is made. Figure 10.5 shows a comprehensive selection process.

Hiring and Orientation

Once an applicant has been chosen for the job, he or she must be introduced to both the organization as a whole and the people in the immediate work environment. The employee's name must also be formally entered on all company records to establish his or her right to benefits such as unemployment insurance, the Canada Pension Plan, company pensions, special bonus and profit sharing plans and, of course, the payroll.

Then the new employee must be given time to become familiar with the company. Many large firms include a formal orientation program. While some last only a few hours, longer programs may offer an introduction to the firm's operating philosophy, internal procedures, compensation and fringe benefit programs, and methods of promotion. In addition, new employees may be required to become familiar with company procedures and policies outside of their immediate area of concern, to acquire a better understanding of how the company operates as a whole.

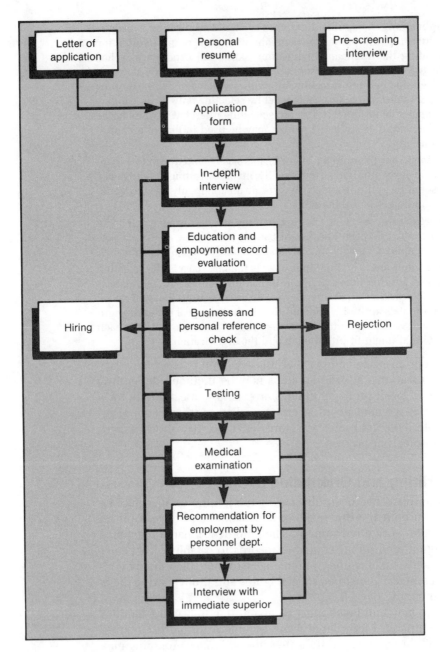

Figure 10.5 The selection process

Do's and Don'ts at the Job Interview

Do's:

- Be punctual. The first five minutes are critical. No matter how legitimate your excuse, a busy interviewer will not feel charitable if kept waiting.
- Pay careful attention to your appearance. Get your clothes pressed and your shoes shined; get a haircut. Don't drink beforehand. Go early, find the washroom, and check yourself in a mirror. A tie askew on the outside of the collar may be a small point, but can look sloppy.
- Dress conservatively. If in doubt, pick up a copy of John T. Molloy's *Dress for Success* or *The Woman's Dress for Success Book*, the sartorial bibles of upwardly mobile executives. Don't show up in a T-shirt and Bermuda shorts, as one senior executive did in Miami; he took the advice to "dress comfortably" too literally. No matter how hot the weather, wear a suit (for women Molloy suggests a skirted suit). And make sure it's appropriate to your role. One highly qualified applicant for a financial controller's job was turned down because he wore a dark shirt with a light-colored suit and tie. The prospective employer thought he looked like Al Capone.
- Know your strengths and be sure to communicate them. Don't rely on the interviewer to draw this information out; he or she may not have good interviewing skills.
- Be enthusiastic. Tell the employer you want the position. One executive was turned down because he just didn't seem interested. He was — but he hadn't let it show. He was crushed when he didn't get the job.
- Answer all questions in a business-like manner. Never volunteer negative information about yourself, but never lie when asked. It's a good idea to think of the worst possible questions you can be asked, and have your answers — **positive** ones — ready. And be prepared when the interviewer asks you what questions you have for him. If you've done your research you won't appear uninformed or uninterested in the company.
- At the end of the meeting, tell the interviewer that you can handle the job and that it interests you. Confirm it in a brief bread-and-butter thank-you letter. If the job doesn't interest you but the company does, send a note as well.

Don'ts:

- Don't talk too much. That may seem obvious, but stress plays peculiar games with perfectly normal people. One applicant for a vice-president's job with a major multinational talked nonstop for an hour and a quarter answering a single question.
- Watch your language. Vulgarity and colloquialisms show a lack of professionalism in communicating.
- Don't smoke unless you're invited. In fact, it's best to refrain even if you are invited. Fumbling around with packages and matches reveals nervousness and stress.
- Don't ignore the person who takes you into the interview. Many senior people ask their secretary or receptionist what they thought of the applicant.
- Don't raise the question of money. Many applicants price themselves out of the market. Wait until you get the job offer, and negotiate from strength. If you're asked how much you want, give a range rather than an absolute figure.
- Don't lose interest if the job isn't what it appeared to be. If the company is sufficiently impressed with you, it may change the position to suit you, or it may make something else available later.
- Don't talk about what the company can do for you, talk about what you can do for the company. One Toronto tax manager was more interested in the benefits than the job. He wanted a $60 000 salary, stock options, a company car, a month's vacation and a five-year employment contract. Needless to say, he not only didn't get the perks, he didn't even get considered for the job.
- Don't criticize your previous employers. No matter how sour the grapes, don't make the in-

terview an exercise in self-justification. The new employer will only think you'll bad-mouth him someday. And don't reveal confidential information about previous employers, such as sales trends, financial situation or office immoralities. There's no need to give specific information, even if you're selling yourself. You can say, "I was responsible for a $2- million turnaround," without revealing how much your former company was earning.

- Finally, if you're applying through an executive search firm, remember that it's paid to be safe. You'll have to convince them that you're indisputably what they want. And if you're seeing the person who may someday be your boss, remember that although he may be a superb executive, he may be a lousy interviewer. He might even be more nervous than you are. If that's the case, take a few minutes to relax him before launching into an account of your exploits or a barrage of questions. Being interviewed can be as much an art as interviewing.

SOURCE: Mike MacBeth, "The Job Interview: How Not to Blow It," *Canadian Business Magazine*, Nov. 1979.

Training and Development

Employees who have been well-trained are generally more productive and satisfied because they know how to perform their jobs effectively. Some companies therefore set up elaborate training programs. Many firms also encourage employees to take courses and develop new skills and knowledge outside their areas. Both specific training in management skills and general education courses can help to make employees eligible for future management openings.

The various levels of government often institute job training programs. For example, in 1985, the federal government announced the Canadian Jobs Strategy, a $2 billion program aimed at specific unemployed groups, including the young, native peoples, women, the unskilled and the elderly. Under some of these programs, companies receive funds to take on unskilled workers and provide training.

The Canadian Labour Congress has called this a "wage subsidy program dressed up as a training program." The CLC believes that companies should contribute money to a common fund and then receive a grant for any training conducted. The Canadian Federation of Independent Business, on the other hand, is strongly opposed to a grant-levy system. They do, however, agree that small businesses often train new workers, who are then lost to other, often larger companies.[4]

Employee Training

Job training programs are established to make new employees as productive as possible in the shortest period of time. For relatively simple jobs, **on-the-job training** may be all that is required. The new

employee is placed on the job under the direct supervision of an experienced employee or the department supervisor, who provides guidance, advice and assistance as required until the trainee has gained sufficient experience to perform the job without supervision.

In the case of trades, on-the-job training may be combined with **classroom instruction** in an **apprenticeship program** designed to give the inexperienced worker both practical and theoretical knowledge. These programs may range from two to four years in length, and are generally used to teach skilled trades such as carpentry, welding, electrical work and plumbing. Apprenticeship programs are often established jointly with a union, to ensure that skills and training are uniform.

If on-the-job training is not possible, too costly or too dangerous, a technique known as **vestibule training** is often employed. In simple vestibule training, workers learn to perform their jobs outside the regular work process. They thus gain the necessary skills while the cost of mistakes is reduced. For example, airline pilots are trained in a simulator where they can perform the actual operations of flying an airplane, encountering realistic flight conditions and problems to test their reactions, without the dangers and risks of a real flight. Vestibule training may also be employed in conjunction with classroom training. The employee then learns the theoretical aspects of a particular operation and gains some degree of competence before performing the actual job.

Management Development

The problems involved in management training and development are different from those encountered in training employees to perform specific jobs. While it may be relatively simple for colleges and universities to establish management programs to teach the functions of management — planning, directing people, organizing and controlling performance — it is difficult to teach logical thinking and decision-making, human relations skills, the ability to analyze the future, and good business sense. Yet these are precisely the skills required in management positions.

The objective of management development is to improve the skills and advancement potential of employees and improve their future contribution to the organization. Candidates for development fall into two groups, and each presents different training problems. The first group consists of new management recruits who may have the necessary theoretical background, but lack practical experience. In addition to gaining actual management experience, they must learn how the company operates. The second group consists of experienced managers who have been in their positions for a number of years, but may require development of particular management skills. They may also lack basic theoretical knowledge in new management principles and practices.

Large companies usually operate **in-house training** programs. The new manager spends a few days or weeks in a variety of departments to gain an understanding of how the company operates as a whole. The trainee may then receive on-the-job training by assisting an experienced manager, while continuing classroom instruction in company procedures, policies and management skills. At the end of the training period, which may last from six months to two years, the trainee should have gained sufficient practical experience to take over a regular management position when the opportunity arises.

Development of the experienced manager presents a different problem. While these individuals are usually enthusiastic about learning new theoretical concepts of management, it is not easy to change habits. It may be difficult to persuade a manager to use a new leadership approach, or take a less authoritarian stance with employees. While short **seminars** may alert managers to some of their managerial problems, their regular work environments will not have changed, and when they return they may find it difficult not to revert to their previous managerial styles. Nevertheless, management development programs point out problems and new concepts.

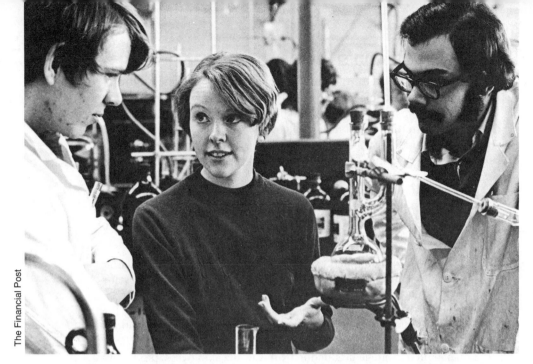

Many companies provide on-the-job training for new employees

Training Supervisors — On and Off the Job

Whether or not a person has had formal education in business and management, most practical training takes place on the job. On-the-job training provides direct, practical experience, but a new supervisor may also learn faulty methods from the training. A carefully designed plan will ensure that the right information is acquired.

On-the-job: On-the-job programs require extensive development and include stated objectives, experienced trainers, scheduled performance reviews and a schedule of specific experiences that the employee should acquire. The programs may involve grievance handling, training workers and reviewing employee performance.

Observation and guided practice are other key methods for learning on the job. In addition to observing other department heads and supervisors, the trainee may be given a temporary assignment as assistant supervisor during a regular manager's absence.

Off-the-job: The classroom lends itself to a more structured learning process, in that information can be presented in a logical sequence. Various training devices including visual aids can be used to clarify difficult concepts and situations. Role-playing and business games can simulate real world experiences and provide practice in handling such situations. Other areas covered in the classroom include leadership skills, employee motivation, management principles, and company policies and practices.[5]

WAGE AND SALARY ADMINISTRATION

Compensation administration, also known as wage and salary administration, is concerned with the establishment and implementation of sound policies and methods of employee compensation. It includes job evaluation to establish wage and salary rates; development and maintenance of wage structures, surveys, incentives, changes, supplementary payments and profit sharing plans; and control of compensation costs.

Employees must be paid competitive wages and salaries that adequately compensate them for their skills, experience and education, or they will go elsewhere. A compensation plan should achieve the following three objectives:

1. It should attract qualified workers to the firm with wages and salaries that are at least equal to those paid by similar firms in the same industry or area.
2. It should be fair to all workers, and should take into account the difficulty of the job as well as the education, special qualifications and experience required.
3. It should encourage production by rewarding employees' productivity through wage incentives, stock options and profit sharing plans.

Establishing Wages and Salaries

Wages and salaries are based on the following factors:

FEDERAL AND PROVINCIAL LAWS: Almost all employees are covered by minimum wage laws established by either the federal or provincial governments. There are also laws which prohibit discrimination in pay based on sex, age, race, etc.

ABILITY TO PAY: The financial health of the firm may also determine the wages paid. Profitable firms tend to pay higher wages than firms that make only marginal profits.

PREVAILING WAGES: Wages are often based on rates other firms are paying for the same class of work in the same labour market or industry. This prevailing wage rate may rise or fall as supply and demand for particular skills fluctuates.

JOB REQUIREMENTS: Pay rates for jobs are based on the difficulty of the job, the amount of skill and effort required and the responsibilities involved in relation to other jobs in the organization.

COST OF LIVING: Wages tend to rise as the cost of living rises so that purchasing power remains constant. Many union agreements now contain a cost-of-living adjustment clause specifying that wage rates rise according to the consumer price index.

PRODUCTIVITY: Increased productivity leads to a rise in the standard of living. Increased productivity is generally measured in increased output of goods and services, which may be the result of technological improvements, greater capital investment, more efficient methods of production, better education and job skills, and more effective management. Generally, a productive firm can pay higher wages than other less productive firms.

BARGAINING POWER: Unionized workers have the power to bargain for higher wages. On the other hand, non-unionized workers do not have that power and must accept what the employer is willing to pay. During times of inflation the wages of unionized workers are more likely to keep up with the rate of inflation than the wages of non-unionized workers.

Setting Wage Rates — A Problem for Small Businesses

Without the resources to hire personnel specialists, the owner-manager of a small business may find it difficult to establish wages and salaries for employees and to compensate them for their performance. The three primary factors to keep in mind when setting or revising wages and salaries are federal and provincial legislation regarding minimum pay, vacation pay and termination pay, the firm's ability to pay, and prevailing wages in the industry.

Wage Legislation
Provincial and federal legislation specifies minimum wages, and vacation and termination pay rates for all employees. Labour Canada periodically publishes minimum pay rates for all provinces and territories and notes any changes.

Ability to Pay
The financial health of the firm is an important consideration in setting pay scales. A profitable company can pay relatively high wages and thereby attract good employees. A firm with financial problems may lose employees to competitors who can provide better pay and benefits.

Prevailing Wages
Most firms pay their employees according to prevailing wages and salaries in the community and/or industry. Wage rates can be determined by conducting a wage survey. The local board of trade, provincial Department of Industry and other local employers can usually supply average wage rates and ranges for similar jobs. The survey has to be based on job descriptions and specifications, so that accurate comparisons can be made.

Once wage rates for employees have been established, then an ongoing system of performance appraisal must be set up. Appraisals should be done once a year and should include a written review. The larger the firm, the more formalized the appraisal process will be. The main concern is the objectivity of the owner or manager doing the performance appraisal. An employee has to feel that the appraisal is objective so that a meaningful discussion can take place to point out what the employee is doing well, where improvement is required and how it can be accomplished. Once the performance appraisal is complete, a wage revision can be implemented.

Equal Pay for Equal Work vs. Equal Pay for Work of Equal Value

For some time employers have had to ensure that compensation plans do not discriminate against people or groups doing similar jobs. The concept of **equal pay for equal work** — all people who perform similar jobs should be paid equally — is firmly entrenched in Canadian employment legislation. Generally, jobs are compared according to four categories — skill, effort, responsibility and working conditions. If the jobs are shown to be equal in each category, then they require equal pay.

Another concept — **equal pay for work of equal value** — requires that the relative worth of two different jobs be determined, as for example a receptionist and junior accountant. Once the relationship between the jobs is established, pay scales are adjusted accordingly. The drive behind pay equity is the current difference between the average earnings of men and women. In Ontario, for example, the two million women who work outside the home earn, on average, 36% less than men.[6] While on the surface it may appear that **pay equity** will address this problem, it may also result in greater unemployment for women, as proposed in the article later in this chapter, "Women Will Foot Bill for Equal-Value Pay."

Pay equity has been in force in the federal public service and in Québec for several years, and is included in the human rights code. As of January 1, 1988, all Ontario employers in the public and private sector with ten or more workers have to pay the same wages to women performing jobs judged to be equal in value to those performed by men in the same workplace.

The business community has argued that equal pay for work of equal value would be difficult and costly to implement; any measurement of relative worth would be difficult to make and basically a value judgment. Another argument against the concept is that market forces could be severely hampered in their allocation of labour based on supply and demand.[7]

Implementing pay equity will not be easy. First, it will probably be costly. According to an Ontario government report in 1983, it could cost the private sector as much as $8 billion dollars. Another major problem, particularly for smaller firms, is the lack of people qualified to perform job analysis. Only 5% of firms with 100 people or fewer have personnel managers, only 25% have job descriptions, and even fewer have a formal job evaluation procedure. Whatever the problems, personnel consultants and human resource managers are advising firms in the private sector to set a pay equity classification system as quickly as possible so as to avoid government intervention and potential fines for noncompliance. The sooner firms address the pay equity issue, the sooner they will discover potential problems with their existing pay classification system, which may require extensive restructuring.

Methods of Compensation

There are three main methods of compensating people for their work. Some receive a monthly salary, others are paid for the specific number of hours they have worked, or for actual production — for the number of units produced or the amount sold. Each method has its advantages and disadvantages, but the one chosen must be appropriate to the particular situation.

Wages

The most common method of compensation is payment for the number of hours worked. Sometimes hourly workers can increase their earnings by working overtime — working more hours per day or week than what provincial legislation specifies as a normal work day. Overtime usually means that a person gets paid either 1 1/2 times the normal hourly rate or twice the hourly rate.

Piecework and Incentive Pay

A straight hourly wage does not provide incentives to produce more than the basic minimum for an average working day. To entice employees to work faster and therefore earn more money, some companies offer a direct incentive by paying more when more items are produced. This is called **piecework**. A sewing machine operator, for example, may receive a basic hourly wage rate of $5.00 per hour, based on the fact that a person can sew on average five pairs of jeans in that time. Thus, each unit is worth $1.00. If output is greater, then the employee earns more money, but in any case the person earns no less than the standard rate of pay which is $5.00 per hour.

Salary

The other major method of payment is salary — a fixed sum paid weekly, biweekly or monthly. This system is used primarily in jobs where output cannot be easily measured. Salaried employees usually do not receive overtime pay, but they are also seldom penalized for absences due to illness or other reasons. Salaried employees may also have some flexibility in their work hours; most are paid their full salary for statutory holidays and exceptional occasions when the firm may be closed due to a strike or major equipment breakdown.

Bonus Plans

To provide extra incentive for both hourly and salaried employees, many companies have instituted bonus plans. A **bonus** is a sum paid to employees in addition to their regular wages or salaries and may be based on seniority, production or various other factors. Bonus plans can be an effective incentive, provided employees believe their effort will have some effect on the size of the bonus. However, if the bonus is based on arbitrary criteria — for example, how employees fit in with the organization — it may provide little incentive, since an increase in actual productivity will not necessarily increase the bonus.

The most common bonuses are production sharing, commissions, profit sharing and employee stock ownership plans.

Production Sharing: The most direct method of distributing a bonus is production sharing, which rewards employees on the basis of cost savings rather than on an overall profit increase. If employees work harder and produce more, or reduce the production costs per item, then a portion of the savings is returned to them.

Commissions: A commission plan may operate in conjunction with a guaranteed monthly salary or it may be the sole method of compensation; sometimes salespeople are paid straight commission according to a percentage based on their total sales volume. Commissions for salespeople are similar to piecework incentive systems for production workers — the salesperson is usually required to achieve a basic dollar volume of sales, and receives a commission either for all sales made, or for any sales above the basic amount.

Profit Sharing: Profit sharing encourages employees to work harder in the hope that their increased productivity will result in greater profits for the company at the end of a specified period. A portion of the increase in total profit then flows directly back to the employees. Profit sharing may take the form of a direct cash payment or as shares in the company. The major problem with a profit sharing plan is that factors over which employees have no control could interfere with achieving an increase.

Employee Stock Ownership Plans (ESOPs): Making employees owners in the company is a relatively new method of encouraging higher productivity. The company usually offers its shares to employees at a discount from their market value. Employees usually do not have to pay commissions and they can pay for their share purchases in monthly installments. In some instances the company may even guarantee that for a specific time period any drop in share prices will be absorbed by the company. Having some ownership in the company, employees feel as if they are working for themselves and are motivated to perform better and need less supervision. Share ownership also creates a better climate for relations between workers and management and promotes the sharing of results, knowledge and problems.

The major problem with stock purchase plans is that only a few people in a company have a direct impact on the price of the firm's stock. Lower level managers and regular employees have no control over management decisions that affect corporate performance, or over market forces. Furthermore, in a multiple division firm, the problems of one division may be so overwhelming that it affects the stock of the total company and thus employees in other divisions. Then there are general economic problems that can affect the stock market and reduce share prices even though the company is performing well.

For example, managers and employees at Vancouver-based MacMillan Bloedel Ltd. increased their share purchases of the company's stock in August 1987, shortly before the stock market crash, through monthly payroll deductions. They paid between $24–$29 per share, but after the 1987 stock market crash their shares were worth approximately $16. While stock prices generally increase in the long run, which makes ESOPs a good investment, a sudden significant drop in share values can be a demoralizing experience for many employees, particularly if they have to continue to make monthly payments for devalued shares.[8]

Nevertheless, many employees are benefiting from stock ownership plans. The article "Sharing at Canadian Tire" explains how ESOPs have benefited these employees, while the article "Profit sharing plan must be tailor-made to work properly" outlines some of the problems and solutions involved in establishing profit sharing plans. Profit sharing is further examined in Case 10-2 at the end of the chapter.

Sharing at Canadian Tire

Canadian Tire Corp. is the most legendary stock ownership success story of all. In the gravy years between 1944 (when shares were first offered to some employees) and 1971, the company's value increased 225 times. So, even though broad-coverage profit sharing was not introduced at the parent company until 1957, an office clerk was able to retire with $324 000 after 14 years' service, and a floor sweeper pocketed $300 000.

Lately, Canadian Tire shares have dipped and those windfall gains are stale news to many of today's employees. The more interesting experiment these days is the one under way at Canadian Tire's 319 independently owned dealerships, which function much like small businesses. More than 200 of the dealers now offer stock ownership and profit-sharing plans to their employees, who benefit according to the performance of individual stores.

Arch Brown is president of A.J. Brown (Barrie) Ltd., a large Canadian Tire dealership in Barrie, Ont. Brown was the first dealer to introduce employee stock ownership and profit sharing in the early 1960s, and was founding chairman of Canadian Tire's profit-sharing committee. "Some of the dealers are involved in employee ownership because they believe in the concept, and some are in it for motherhood reasons," he admits. "I don't believe a dealer should go into profit sharing unless he believes in the philosophy."

The dealers' plans are somewhat different from those of the parent corporation in that they hedge against the possibility of stock depreciation. Approximately half the profit-sharing award is paid into an employee savings plan rather than into stock; the parent plan is all invested in stock. "Generally speaking," says Brown, "a portfolio is less spectacular but not as dangerous. We don't want to have all the employees' eggs in one basket."

Brown believes that small businesses in particular have the most to gain by selling shares and sharing profits with employees. "Small businesses should be given tax incentives to allow their employees to buy into the company," he says. "The typical independent hardware store, for example, is not that marketable at the time the owner retires. But if he gets into profit sharing, employees can be buying shares. Then, when he wants to retire, he can get his money out by allowing employees to go to the bank and use the shares as collateral to pay him off. Employee ownership offers a tremendous potential for the perpetuation of small businesses."

SOURCE: Mark Witten, "Employees can be partners too," *Canadian Business*, Nov. 1979, p. 86. Reprinted with permission of the author.

Profit Sharing Plan Must be Tailor-made to Work Properly

If management fails to properly design and implement a profit sharing plan, the plan won't do what it is supposed to — improve productivity and labour-management relations.

The first step is to determine whether a profit sharing plan is consistent with the overall compensation strategy of the organization and if it is attractive to employees. For example, a relatively older group of employees may be more interested in improved pensions or job security than cash. And if the company pays wages and salaries lower than the industry average, employees will probably want the security of wage increases, rather than taking their chances on fluctuating profits.

Second, the company should determine how many plans to have. The closer the payout relates to employees' actions, the more likely they are to be motivated. In addition, the smaller the group is, the better. The purpose of the profit sharing plan must be defined next, and it will be reflected in the form of the payout — either cash or company shares. Cash has a higher short-term motivational impact, while shares tend to encourage long-term commitment to the organization. If the plan is also supposed to encourage employee involvement, it should include mechanisms to open lines of communication and encourage employee suggestions.

Third, the company must define what profits are to be shared. This involves two closely related questions: determining the profit pool and deciding the proportion of that pool to be distributed. A company might decide to distribute, say, 25% of profits in excess of previous years' levels; 50% of divisional operating profits before head office expenses and interest costs; or 15% of pre-tax profits. The definition of profit decided upon must encourage behaviour that supports corporate goals and strategy. If profit growth is the goal, then the pool should be a portion of increased profit over the last year or years. If the target is a certain return on investment, then profits would be available for sharing only after the specified level was reached.

The next major question is how to allocate the profits among plan participants. This may be done in proportion to employees' earnings, hours worked during the year, job level, individual performance, or a combination of these variables.

Once the above decisions are made, a prototype should be tested using actual historical and projected operating results. Of utmost importance is that management explain the plan to employees before the start of the fiscal year.

The essential purpose of profit sharing is to motivate employees to increase productivity, by working harder and smarter. They cannot be motivated by something they don't know about or understand. At the end of each year, the plan should be reviewed to ensure that it's achieving the objectives set out at the start of the process.

SOURCE: Adapted from David Tyson, "Profit sharing plan must be tailor-made to work properly," *The Financial Post*, March 3, 1984, p. 12.

Employee Benefits

Financial and non-monetary benefits may include life, health and accident insurance plans, unemployment benefits, medical and dental plans, pensions, paid holidays and sick pay. Specific benefits and the ways in which they are administered vary among companies. Basically, all benefit plans are designed to protect employees from loss of income due to factors beyond their control. However, they are also used as incentives to attract qualified people and encourage current employees to be more productive. **Fringe benefits** are expensive for employers, amounting to approximately one-third of total Canadian wage and salary costs.

Insurance Plans

Insurance plans — life, health and accident — are usually established on a group basis and cover all the firm's employees. Sometimes the premium is paid by the employer, and sometimes it is shared with employees. Life insurance coverage is usually 2 or 2 $\frac{1}{2}$ times the employee's gross annual salary, with varying benefits for those unable to work because of serious health problems or accidents.

Often medical and dental plans are also established on a group basis, with the premium paid either entirely by the employer or split on a percentage basis with employees.

Pension Plans

All individuals between the ages of 18 and 70 employed in Canada are covered under the **Canada Pension Plan**, established in 1965.

The benefits to be paid on retirement are based on an individual's earnings during his or her working life, and contribution to the plan is compulsory. Both employer and employee contribute equally; self-employed individuals must pay the entire amount themselves.

In addition to the Canada Pension Plan, many large companies offer private pension plans. Usually both the employer and the employee contribute to the plan over the employee's working life with the firm. The money is invested in securities of various kinds. This is usually done by an outside pension fund manager who chooses the particular investments, which may be common stock, preferred stock, bonds or other investments. The return on these investments provides a large part of the pension that an individual eventually receives. Depending on the type of pension plan, the management of the fund, and conditions that affect the securities market, it could have a big impact on the pension a person receives at retirement.

There are two basic kinds of pension plans:

1. The **defined benefit plan** guarantees a pension at retirement, based on salary and years of service. If there is not enough money in the fund to cover the promised pension, the employer must make up the shortfall.

2. The **defined contribution plan** specifies how much the employer and/or employee will contribute each year. The amount of pension remains a mystery until retirement date, when accumulated funds are used to buy an annuity. (Annuities are purchased from an insurance company which guarantees the owner a certain payment per month over a stated number of years. The amount paid out per month depends on the principal and the existing rate of interest.)

Workers who are members of defined benefit plans have virtually nothing to fear because their pension is guaranteed. While only a small percentage of workers in Canada (6%) belong to the defined contributions plan, they could be either better or worse off than if they belonged to a defined benefit plan, depending on the performance of the investments in the pension fund. For example, the stock market crash in 1987 severely reduced stock prices, which affected pension funds as well. Workers who retire shortly after such a major drop in value of the fund could have their pension payment drastically reduced.[9]

For many years the federal and provincial governments have discussed **pension reform**. One major problem is the lack of portability between private pension plans. One recommendation is to have a person's private pension vested after five years. If they subsequently leave that employer, they should be able to carry the pension with them or transform it into a Registered Retirement Savings Plan (RRSP). Another major concern is the single pensioner who is often unable to cope with living expenses on current pension rates. A large proportion of single pensioners are women whose benefits were curtailed when their spouses died. To end this inequitable treatment of women in pension arrangements, it is proposed that a pension be treated as a family asset, to be shared equally either on retirement or in the event of marital breakdown.

A final controversial proposal is the indexing of pension plans. Employers have generally opposed this move because the cost of indexing cannot be precisely computed. Workers who belong to pulp and paper, automobile and airlines unions have won indexed pensions in their negotiations in 1987, but these contracts will eventually expire. However, in 1988 a three-person task force issued a report that appears to be workable and may make Ontario the first province in Canada to require all pensions to be indexed. The indexing factor is based on the consumer price index and would not apply to pensions accrued to date or to existing pensioners.[10]

Pensions come under provincial jurisdiction, and while rules are essentially similar there are variations. Generally, pension reform has improved coverage for part-timers and women and has ensured that the employer's contribution becomes the property of the employee much sooner.

Unemployment Benefits

While the **Unemployment Insurance Commission (UIC)**, established in 1940, has insured most workers against loss of wages from unemployment, the new **Unemployment Insurance Act** of 1971 made contributions to the fund compulsory for all workers. To cover benefits paid to the unemployed, all employees and employers must contribute equally, and any shortages of funds are covered by general revenue.

To receive unemployment insurance benefits an individual must have worked a minimum number of weeks and must be available for work. Benefits vary from the maximum weekly amount according to the employee's contribution. All benefits are subject to regular income tax depending on the individual's annual earnings.

Other Benefits

Along with the benefits directly related to salary and income protection, companies also offer their employees paid annual vacations and statutory holidays in excess of what is required by law, sick pay, premiums for overtime and for unusual hours, legal aid, training and development at educational institutions, low interest loans and maternity leave. The list is long, and new benefits and services are constantly being introduced — often at the request of unions. In the future, benefits may become as important as wages and salaries.

The Cost of Fringe Benefits

The cost of employee fringe benefits is approximately 33% of gross payroll, which is more than double the percentage 30 years ago. The most costly benefits are vacations, holidays, rest periods, group plans and pension plans. Other common benefits include severance pay and service awards, dental insurance, home-buying aid, cafeteria subsidies, bonuses, profit-sharing plans and recreation and company discounts. Benefits currently losing favour with employees include recreation, free meals and savings plans.[11]

The cost of major employee benefits as a percentage of total payroll cost is shown in Table 10.1. Many employers have found that a large percentage of their employees do not realize how high their benefit costs are. In one survey of a Toronto firm, out of 850 employees surveyed only 5% knew their benefit costs. Other surveys have shown that the larger the company, the better employees understood their benefits because larger companies had the resources to provide information sessions and printed brochures.

Keeping employees informed of benefits and their cost to the company is important to counteract employee dissatisfaction. A more flexible approach in distributing benefits is also effective. Allowing employees to choose the types of benefits they want — cafeteria style — and adding them to a core program is popular in the U.S. for example. Employees choose benefits up to a particular cost. U.S.

TABLE 10.1
Employee benefit costs in Canada, 1982

Benefit	Percentage of total payroll
Vacations	6.4
Holidays	3.5
Coffee breaks and rest periods	4.8
Compassionate and other paid time off	0.8
Unemployment insurance	1.6
Workers' compensation	1.2
CPP/QPP	1.1
Company pensions	4.9
Group plans (life and health, long-term disability, etc.)	5.0
Severance pay and savings plans (group RRSPs etc.)	0.6
Bonus and profit-sharing plans	1.8
Other: company car, parking, perks	1.8

SOURCE: Thorne Stevenson and Kellogg. Reprinted in *The Financial Post.* Dec. 3, 1983, p. 26.

employers tend to offer a lump sum which is most appropriate for this type of plan. Thus, two individuals could have widely different benefits for the same cost. Younger workers and women would have lower costs for pension benefits and life insurance coverage, for example.[12]

In the past, companies added individual benefits based on popularity, union demands, or the personal interest of the benefits manager. As a result, there were gaps in some benefits and duplications in others. Managers did not consider a total package, flexible enough to appeal to employees of different ages. Today, employees are more concerned about benefits; they want plans that meet their needs.[13]

Health and Safety

In 1886 the Ontario Factories Act came into effect in response to the growing opposition to child labour, the unsanitary conditions that existed in the factories and the dangerous working conditions that caused disease and injuries. This act, which underwent several changes and revisions over the past 100 years, was the forerunner of the Ontario Occupational Health and Safety Act.

Occupational safety and health is a major concern because standards are quickly outdated as technology advances. Accidental deaths may decline as automation eliminates dangerous jobs, but new hazards from nuclear devices, radioactive materials and chemicals may cause industrial diseases. Today there are approximately 56 000 chemicals that are currently approved for use, of which 6000 have the potential to be either deadly or harmful from long-term overexposure. Office workers are concerned about poorly ventilated office buildings and the potential hazards from computer video screens. Some dangers may not become evident for many years. For example, the long-term health hazards of asbestos were unknown when U.S. and Canadian workers first began mining the substance. It is now estimated that 20 000 asbestos workers will die each year until the turn of the century because of past exposure to the substance, with almost three times that number being affected in at least some way.[14]

Federal and provincial regulations aim to prevent accidents and occupational diseases. Regulations are concerned with noise, lighting, dangerous substances, the handling of materials and personal protective equipment. In 1982 a federal government task force established the Workplace Hazardous Materials Information System (WHMIS), a joint federal-provincial project which includes representation from industry, organized labour and the federal and provincial governments. Its aim was to determine criteria to evaluate and classify hazardous materials and distribute this information to all concerned while still protecting trade secrets. The committee's

As technology advances, there must be continued attention to occupational health and safety

work resulted in the amendment of the Hazardous Products Act in 1987, which represents significant progress in informing workers about the hazards of the products they are working with. Provincial legislation is also being brought in line with federal regulations.

Organizations Concerned with Safety and Health

There are two major organizations concerned with safety and health. The **Canadian Centre for Occupational Health and Safety** was established in 1978 and reports to Parliament through the Minister of Labour. Its tasks are to advise on occupational and safety matters; collect data to develop codes of practice and standards; provide technical advisory services; deal with hazardous substances; and maintain contact with national and international organizations.

The **Industrial Accident Prevention Association (IAPA)** is a federation of ten safety associations including approximately 65 000 firms and more than $1^1/_2$ million workers. It is funded by the Ontario manufacturing and retailing industry, and its staff provides consulting and educational services throughout Ontario. The association also studies company safety programs and the cause of accidents. Based on its findings it often suggests training courses and preventive measures.[15]

When employees are injured at work they receive the major portion of their salary from the **Workers' Compensation Board** until they are able to return to work. Contributions for this benefit are made entirely by employers, and companies are concerned with preventing accidents in their plants. Hence many firms mount extensive health and safety programs designed to prevent accidents.

Women Will Foot Bill for Equal-value Pay

As recent developments in Ontario have shown, there is growing political support for the concept of equal pay for work of equal value.

Many women favour the idea because they clearly think it is in their best economic interests. It probably is not.

Economics is about costs as well as benefits, and while some women will certainly benefit from equal pay for work of equal value, it's likely that others will bear even greater offsetting costs.

Equal pay for work of equal value, also called comparative worth or pay equity, is a straightforward concept. Jobs would be rated according to their underlying intrinsic value and incumbents paid accordingly.

Arbitrary judgments

Right now, what people are paid is determined in large part by supply/demand conditions in the labour markets. Equal pay for work of equal value would replace those labour market judgments with the arbitrary judgments of bureaucrats and administrators taking into account things such as education, skill level, danger, responsibility, accountability and risks.

(Equal pay for work of equal value should not be confused with the eminently reasonable equal pay for equal work, which means that people with the same capabilities doing the same job should get the same wage regardless of sex, age or whatever.)

On the practical level, where does one find someone with the wisdom to achieve a consensus on the relative values of, say, an enforcing goon in the National Hockey League, a corporate takeover specialist, a roughneck on an oil rig, a *Financial Post* editor and a lobbyist for equal-pay-for-work-of-equal-value legislation?

Moreover, once one does away with market-determined wages, how does one assure that there will be a sufficient number of people with a given skill to meet the public's demand for that skill? Someone with an acute appendectomy will not be impressed, for example, with the observation that while a doctor is not available to meet his needs, a university professor, weighted at an equal number of job points, is.

What obviously appeals to many who support the equal pay concept is the prospect of an immediate and substantial pay increase based on an anticipated upward reclassification of their work. Since women, on average, are paid less than men, and since women dominate in many lower paying jobs, such as sales, clerical, and service, it's hardly surprising that the concept has become something of a rallying cry for the women's movement.

But we should make no mistake that the idea would involve costs, too. Someone will have to pay for the increases that people get with the stroke of the job-judge's pen. No supporter of equal pay for work of equal value should be under any illusion that a substantial increase in wage without a corresponding increase in productivity can occur without someone, somewhere, bearing the cost.

Confronted with an imposed increase in their wage costs of the type implied by equal pay for work of equal value, employers are likely to do a number of things.

First, they would try to pass the wage increase on to the consumers of their goods and services by raising product prices. It's unlikely, however, that the public would come close to accepting this very real increase in its cost of living, given the sluggish nature of our economy and the availability of many foreign products whose prices are based on wages that are substantially below ours — even without equal pay for work of equal value.

Employers would, therefore, have to look to other than the consuming public to bear the brunt of the increase in their costs.

This is where women would get hurt. As the costs for a particular class of employee increased without offsetting productivity increases, employers would respond as they always do. They would use fewer of the employees in question by doing things such as mechanizing, substituting part-time workers for full-time workers, and shifting production to jurisdictions where wage legislation is more to their liking.

To the extent that some women were the major beneficiaries of higher wages because of equal pay for work of equal value, it stands to reason that other women would bear the brunt of the accompanying layoffs and other adjustments.

Downward adjustments

It might be argued that as some wages went up because of equal pay for work of equal value, others would come down, providing the needed offset. This may happen, but downward adjustments in nominal wages are certainly few and far between in our history.

Women should note the experience Australia has had with its version of equal pay for work of equal value. Obviously, other factors are involved, but it is probably more than coincidence that five years after the enactment in 1972 of equal pay legislation, Australia found a higher rate of female unemployment, more women working part time and a slowdown in the female work force participation growth rate.

The likelihood is that those women who benefit from equal pay for work of equal value will do so in large part at the expense of other women. What is for sure is that whatever benefits accrue will have to be paid for with a cost imposed on someone.

Milton Friedman is fond of saying there is no free lunch — it's only a matter of getting someone else to pay for it. Before women eat the equal pay for work of equal value lunch, they would be wise to figure out who will really pick up the tab.

SOURCE: John C. McCallum, "Women will foot bill for equal-value pay," *The Financial Post*, June 22, 1985, p. 9. Reprinted by permission.

STAFF EVALUATION

Periodic staff evaluations are essential both to companies and their employees. For the company they provide proof of job performance or non-performance; staff evaluations are necessary both to terminate employment and to identify candidates for promotion. For employees, staff evaluations are important factors in motivation and morale — all employees like to know how they are doing, and whether they are meeting the expectations of the job and of their superiors.

Choosing the proper method of evaluation, however, can be a problem. While productivity and performance can be evaluated on the basis of an objective standard, such as the number of units produced, objective evaluation of a worker's relationship with other employees and of his or her contribution to company morale is more difficult. A salesperson, for example, can be judged directly on the number of sales made, but it is not easy to evaluate his or her contribution to future sales or customer goodwill.

There are many other jobs for which objective standards cannot be established, despite constant efforts to quantify information that is essentially qualitative. How can a manager's job be evaluated? Can a teacher's contribution to student learning be measured objectively?

One method of evaluating employees is to judge their performance on the basis of the objectives established in a results-oriented job description. Objectives set by employees together with their immediate superiors can also serve as a standard. This variation of management by objectives (MBO) is known as **appraisal by results**.

Once an employee's job performance has been evaluated, the manager discusses the results with the employee who then signs the evaluation to indicate awareness of the comments. Thus the employee has the opportunity to read and discuss the evaluation. If the assessment seems unjust, the employee may go to higher levels of management for recourse; union members may file a grievance.

Promotion, Transfer and Separation

Virtually all firms experience some employee turnover. Some employees leave the company; others are promoted to higher positions; others still are transferred laterally to positions where responsibility and duties, though similar, pertain to a different area of the firm's activities. As positions become vacant new employees must be recruited, hired and trained to fill them.

Promotion usually refers to upward movement within a particular organization, into a position with greater responsibility, increased authority and, usually, higher pay. As managers move up in the company hierarchy, positions in the lower levels are often filled through promotion of operating personnel. Thus individuals who started at the lowest level have been known to rise to the position of president.

Promotions for management are almost always based on **merit**, which refers to employees' performance and the quality of their work in previous positions. However, when a worker is promoted to supervisor in a unionized firm, problems may develop if the union insists that seniority be used as the basis for the promotion decision. **Seniority** refers to the length of the employee's service with the company. Promotion based on seniority alone does not always provide the company with the best qualified supervisor. To resolve the problem of merit versus seniority, a compromise is usually reached whereby length of service is used as a basis for promotion only when there are two or more candidates with equal qualifications.

The horizontal movement of workers or managers from one position to another of equal responsibility or authority is known as a **transfer**. Generally transfers are used to give individuals a wider range of experience within the company, but they can also provide an employee with new challenges and interests. Often transfers require movements between geographical regions; many companies have established various compensation plans to cover the expenses incurred in transfers. In some instances, a transfer also means an increase in salary.

Separation occurs when employees either resign, retire, are fired or are laid off. Some workers find new jobs and leave; others who cannot perform to the required standard must be terminated. When economic conditions require decreased production and a reduction in the firm's expenses, workers must be laid off. Finally, workers leave the company upon retirement. While the retirement age is usually 65, compulsory retirement no longer exists.

NOTES

1. John DeMont, "Ontario finds workers in short supply," *The Financial Post*, January 25, 1988, p. 7.
2. Marilyn Goneau, "Discrimination is still part of the workplace," *The Financial Post*, Nov. 21, 1981.
3. *Ibid.*
4. Madelaine Drohan, "CLC says business should fund training," *The Financial Post*, January 25, 1988, p. 5.
5. See Dr. Margaret Bahniuk, "Training and Education," *Office Administration and Automation*, April 1984, p. 84.
6. Shona McKay, "Getting Even," *Canadian Business*, May 1988, pp. 48–54.
7. Christopher Waddel, "Equal pay for work of equal value still has hurdles to beat," *The Financial Post*, Oct. 29, 1983.
8. Tessa Wilmott, "Crash sparks review of employee share plans," *The Financial Post*, November 2, 1987, p. 41.
9. Robin Schiele, "Crash spotlights pension debate," *The Financial Post*, November 9, 1987, p. 32.
10. Robin Schiele, "Ontario may pick up pensions gauntlet," *The Financial Post*, January 25, 1988, p. 5.
11. Brent King, "Many employees don't know what their firm's benefits are worth," *The Financial Post*, Dec. 3, 1983, p. 26.
12. "Flexible benefit package could become standard," *The Financial Post*, March 19, 1983, p. 29.
13. *Ibid.*
14. See "What we need in a new Federal Law," *Canadian Labour*, Vol. 26, No. 8, Oct. 1981, pp. 18–19.
15. Robert W. Sexty, *Issues in Canadian Business* (Scarborough, Ont.: Prentice-Hall Canada, Inc., 1983), p. 119.

CHAPTER SUMMARY

Every manager is responsible for staffing his or her department with qualified people, training and motivating them. However, as organizations grow, personnel matters become increasingly time-consuming and complex; thus, large firms hire specialists in personnel planning, recruiting, hiring, training, compensation and evaluation. With the growth of unions, personnel specialists have also become involved in contract negotiations and liaison activities between the parties involved.

Personnel planning is an attempt to forecast future personnel needs in conjunction with long- and short-range organizational plans, while it keeps present personnel resources in mind. Planning also involves job analysis, from which job descriptions and job specifications can be developed.

One major task of the personnel department is the hiring of competent employees. Employees can be recruited through advertising, government and private employment agencies, union headquarters and schools. Whenever possible, however, firms fill job vacancies from within by promoting employees.

The selection process involves obtaining information on suitable employment candidates, screening, testing, in-depth interviews and reference checks. Once hired, workers usually undergo a formal orientation program to introduce them to the company.

With the passage of the Canadian Human Rights Act in 1977, personnel managers have become particularly concerned about discrimination against employees. Many companies have reviewed their recruitment, screening and hiring processes to ensure that they comply with the legislation. Companies are also voluntarily establishing committees through which employees can voice concerns about discrimination. Management can then investigate and resolve problems.

When the training required for a new employee is minimal, it is usually done on the job. When potential dangers and costs make on-the-job training impractical, vestibule training or a combination of the two may be used, sometimes including classroom instruction. When the training required is extensive, apprenticeship programs are common. Managers, both new and practising, may also require further training and education.

Compensation is also of prime importance to employees, and it can be a strong motivator. A compensation plan should attract qualified employees, treat them fairly and encourage increased production. Wages and salaries are based on minimum wage legislation, the firm's ability to pay, the prevailing wages paid in the community and/or industry, cost of living clauses and union bargaining power. Direct monetary compensation may take the form of wages and salaries, bonuses, profit sharing or commissions. Indirect forms of compensation, or fringe benefits, include life insurance, pension plans, medical and health insurance, holiday, vacation and sick pay.

Profit sharing and employee stock ownership plans are becoming popular among companies and employees. Some plans have provided employees with large payouts at retirement. Companies that have instituted these plans have found that they decrease labour strife and increase productivity. Nevertheless, the programs must be properly administered and employees must be educated to understand how profit works and what they can expect if profits for the company should increase or decrease. The programs should not be used in lieu of adequate compensation, however.

The most difficult task faced by managers is employee evaluation. The personnel manager can help by developing evaluation systems. The evaluation system chosen must be as objective as possible and should be based on criteria established with the employee at the beginning of the evaluation period. Evaluation is particularly important for employees who are to be fired for poor performance and for those who are in line for promotion. Deciding whether promotion should be based on seniority or merit can be a major problem.

KEY TERMS

Personnel management
Personnel planning
Job analysis
Job specifications
Job descriptions
Results-oriented job descriptions
Recruiting
Employee selection process
Human Rights Legislation
Hiring
Orientation
On-the-job training
Apprenticeship program
Vestibule training
Management development
Compensation system
Equal pay for equal work
Equal pay for work of equal value
Wages
Salary

Bonus
Incentive
Profit sharing
Production sharing
Commission
Employee stock ownership
Fringe benefits
Industrial Accident Prevention
  Association (IAPA)
Workers' Compensation Board
Unemployment Insurance
  Commission (UIC)
Staff evaluation
Promotion
Transfer
Termination
Layoff
Seniority
Merit

REVIEW QUESTIONS

1. What are the functions of the personnel department?
2. Outline the steps in the personnel planning process.
3. What is job analysis? Distinguish between a job description and a job specification.
4. What are the sources of job candidates available to the personnel manager?

5. What are the major steps undertaken by personnel departments to ensure they are not discriminatory in their hiring practices?

6. Outline the steps in the employee selection process.

7. Describe the various types of worker training programs.

8. What are the three major objectives of a good compensation program?

9. What are the major factors that determine wages and salaries? What are the most important factors for the owner-manager of a small business to consider in setting wages and salaries?

10. Distinguish between pay for equal work and pay for work of equal value.

11. Give an example of jobs for which each of the following would be an appropriate method of payment: (a) hourly wages; (b) monthly salary; (c) straight commission; (d) piecework.

12. What are the major considerations for companies in establishing a profit sharing plan? What potential benefits does a firm get from a profit sharing plan?

13. What are some of the major fringe benefits offered by a large company?

14. Why should employees undergo periodic formal evaluations by their managers?

15. Distinguish between promotion and transfer. When do companies promote based on seniority? When do they promote based on merit?

DISCUSSION QUESTIONS

1. Should employers be responsible for providing unemployment benefits? What is their responsibility for employees' health and safety?

2. Should retirement age be compulsory? Why or why not?

3. How can one reconcile the problem of discrimination in employment versus freedom of a business owner to hire whomever he or she wants?

4. What is your view of affirmative action and equal pay for work of equal value?

5. Do you think employee stock ownership plans will become more important in the future as an incentive for employees? Explain your answer.

CASE 10-1 The Printable Dilemma

The printing plant was the heart of *The Daily Post*, a mass circulation newspaper in an urban market of over two million. It was so important that about five years ago, the paper invested nearly $40 000 000 in new computer controlled printing presses and finishing machines. Now the

Post not only prints the paper, but acts as a jobber, with salesmen aggressively searching for printing jobs throughout the community.

While the paper may have benefited from the investment, the pressmen who actually run the machines are not at all happy. Before computers arrived, pressmen were skilled professionals, proud of their craft and their traditions. Now their role is basically that of computer operators. Although no one has lost a job and retraining has been massive, morale is low. This is especially true on the dayshift, where because of the job security agreement negotiated by the union, there are too many hands for too few jobs.

An additional problem is that management would like to retrain more of the pressmen to be press mechanics (who, of course, will be called technicians) and electronic trouble shooters. Even though a great deal of time and effort will be spent on this activity, the union is resisting because of the tradition that says a "pressman" runs a press, he doesn't fix it.

The present foreman, who has come up through the ranks of pressmen, is well-liked and capable in old-style press operations. However, he is due to retire in three months and management is searching for a successor. At present, the candidates are:

Avril Kennedy: age 30, has no direct press experience, but is a community college graduate in mechanical technology. Since graduating from college she has completed a night school diploma in computer programming and graphics. At present, she is lead hand in the finishing plant, a separate facility owned by the *Post*, but not directly connected with printing the paper. She is very good at her job. Turnover in her section is low.

Bently Steeves: age 49, an experienced pressman, active in the union but not a militant. Bently knows little about computers, but is the "favourite" candidate among the pressmen. It is said, "the man is a mechanical genius; he can fix anything." Bently has 22 years of seniority with the company.

George Reeves: age 45, an outsider, George is a mechanical engineer who works for a company that installs presses. George wants to stop roaming the world with the installation crews and settle down. Although his technical expertise is unquestioned, George is an unknown quantity in the supervisory area, as he has never held a management position.

SOURCE: Written by Dr. P.C. Wright, Business Division, Humber College, Toronto, Ontario. Reprinted by permission of the author.

QUESTIONS

1. Outline the strengths and the weaknesses of Avril, Bently and George.

2. Without referring to personalities (about which you know nothing) choose the best candidate for the job. Support your answer.

3. Study each candidate in turn and predict the problems that each would have if selected foreman.

CASE 10-2 Union-Free Workplace

On a Sunday afternoon last December more than 30 000 people filled Number 3 Galvanizing Line Building of Hamilton-based steelmaker Dofasco Inc. Inside, ornaments sparkled on a 36-foot-high Christmas tree and booths displayed teddy bears, record albums and other free children's gifts. It was Dofasco's 50th annual Christmas party, one of many bonuses that the company provides for its employees. It does so in part because Dofasco — like Markham, Ont.-based car parts manufacturer Magna International Inc. and McCain Foods Ltd. in Florenceville, N.B. — is a notable exception in a widely organized industry: it operates successfully without a union. But officials of those companies say that the benefits they provide for their workers are not designed simply to keep unions out. Said Dofasco spokesman Peter Earle: "It has been part of Dofasco's culture since the company was founded to ensure a stable work environment so that individuals can pursue worthwhile careers and have security in their retirement."

Earle and officials of the other two firms say that their companies and their employees are better off without unions. Dofasco, for one, has consistently maintained its lead as North America's most profitable integrated steelmaker, earning $136 million last year. By contrast, Stelco Inc. — Canada's largest steel manufacturer — earned less than half that amount, and during the past six years it has reduced the 12 000-member unionized workforce at its Hamilton-based Hilton Works by one third. But Dofasco's 11 500-member workforce has remained unchanged, and Dofasco continues to pay slightly above Stelco's rates — offering an average hourly wage of $16.54. For its part, McCain — an expanding multinational corporation with 2500 employees in a province with a 13.2-per cent unemployment rate — improves its employees' salary and benefit package every year, according to chairman Harrison McCain.

Still, some critics claim that those companies are simply paternalistic operations in which the workers have no real say in determining wages. Said Cecil Taylor, president of Stelco Local 1005 of the United Steelworkers of America from 1979 to 1985: "Stelco workers are bitter because Dofasco workers don't pay union dues, and they say that's freeloading." But labor analyst Noah Meltz, a professor of economics and industrial relations at the University of Toronto, says nonunionized employees who are treated fairly — and paid union-level wages — have no incentive to organize.

Both Magna and Dofasco emphasize profit-sharing, benefits and incentives. To that end, Magna chairman Frank Stronach introduced a corporate policy in 1985 that guarantees the allocation of 10 per cent of the company's pretax profits to his 9000 employees. Stronach describes his business philosophy as "fair enterprise."

Dofasco channels 11 per cent of its pretax steelmaking profits to its 50-year-old Employees Savings and Profit-Sharing Fund, with the result that a worker with 40 years of service could retire this year with as much as $400 000. And it rewards employees who make workable cost-cutting suggestions with cheques for as much as $50 000. Employees are encouraged to take their grievances to president Paul Phoenix if they cannot get them settled elsewhere. Said Earle: "What we try to do is treat everybody like an individual. It sounds corny, but we do abide by the golden rule — treat other people the way you would like to be treated yourself."

At McCain's, where benefits include life insurance and pension plans, there is no formal grievance procedure, but McCain told *Maclean's* that employees "are confident they can speak out with impunity." But critics such as New Brunswick labor organizer Robert Davidson say that McCain's wages and working conditions do not compare favorably with similar unionized operations. Added Davidson: "If anyone tries organizing up there — and some have — they're blacklisted in the community and pretty soon they're out of a job." But McCain says that the company's salaries and benefits are very good by local standards — paying up to $9 per hour. In addition, he says that his workers are a close-knit group. Said McCain: "For a supervisor, that lady on the line is his aunt, that guy on the loading dock is his brother and that guy at the freezer is his drinking buddy. They have a community of interest."

Still, large companies that operate without labor problems are relatively rare. Said Meltz: "It's not that easy. Co-operation and teamwork really do pay off, but to be consistent and fair you really have to work at it." Some Canadian employers have worked hard to achieve that goal — and they are now enjoying the benefits.

SOURCE: Anne Steacy, with Chris Wood and Kathryn Harley, "Union-free workplace," *Maclean's*, July 13, 1987, p. 35.

QUESTIONS

1. How do these three companies ensure that their workers are treated well?

2. Respond to the charge by some critics that these three firms are simply being paternalistic.

3. How can profit sharing contribute to higher productivity and better employee relations?

4. Suppose that a large company such as one discussed in the case wanted to establish a profit sharing program. How should the company go about implementing the plan?

5. Do you think the unions are justified in their opposition to profit sharing plans? What might be the underlying cause for their opposition to such plans?

Part Four

Business and Its Environment

Businesses today operate not in isolation, but in constant interaction with consumers and labour unions, with government on the federal, provincial and municipal levels and, increasingly, with other countries. Part IV examines these relationships in detail.

In Chapter 11 we look at labour unions — their goals and aims — and describe the collective bargaining process between management and labour. We also briefly examine the history of unions before focusing on some current problems between management and labour and how they might be resolved in the future.

In Chapter 12 we examine the relationship between business and government — how government on one hand promotes business for increased economic growth and prosperity, but on the other hand attempts to control it, sometimes stringently, through legislation, rules and regulations.

In Chapter 13 we look at international trade and its benefits for all countries. We discuss both the factors that hinder trade between nations and the steps that have been taken to remove international trade barriers. We also look at international finance and the multinational corporation.

In Chapter 14 we examine the relationship between business and society. The specific ethics of business behaviour and the broader question of business' responsibility toward society are both issues of major concern today.

CHAPTER 11

Business and Labour

Canadian Auto Workers Union

CHAPTER OUTLINE

CHAPTER PREVIEW

In Chapter 11 we examine the relationship between business and labour. Before workers were organized and joined together in unions, they had difficulty voicing their concerns and negotiating for changes in working conditions. Management had the upper hand; however, the situation has changed over the past one hundred years. Today, once a union is certified, management is obliged to bargain to establish a contract. If no agreement is reached, the government arranges for mediation or arbitration. If government intervention does not produce an agreement, the union may take strike action or management may resort to a lockout. Collective agreements — the contracts between unions and management — generally address a wide range of specific issues, but union security, wages and salaries, hours of work and job security are of prime importance. In the latter part of the chapter we examine the history of the union movement, including major labour legislation enacted by government. We also discuss some of the problems faced by unions today, and how labour-management relations could be improved in the future.

LEARNING OBJECTIVES

After reading this chapter you should be able to explain:

1. Why workers join unions;
2. What a union is;
3. Why management is often reluctant to deal with unions;
4. The process required for certification of a union as the sole bargaining agent for a group of workers;
5. The major issues at stake in negotiations between labour and management, and how the collective bargaining process works;
6. The weapons at the disposal of both labour and management to back up their demands;
7. The roles of mediation, conciliation and arbitration when the negotiation process does not lead to an agreement;
8. The history of the labour movement in Canada and the problems facing it today;
9. How current labour-management relations may be modified in the future.

Imagine for a moment that you are the owner of a manufacturing company. For the past 10 years you have struggled to make it successful through tireless effort, taking extraordinary risks, and often spending sleepless nights worrying about your financial obligations. One day your employees announce that they now belong to a union and present you with a list of demands for their first contract. As you look at the proposal you realize that the company cannot meet the demands. You are both outraged and hurt — you have always treated them well, paid good wages and endeavoured to build a good relationship with them. "Why are they doing this to me?" you ask. A strike begins and you see your revenues dwindle as your customers, whom you have worked so hard to win over, take their business elsewhere. If you were this owner, how would you feel about labour unions?

Now put yourself in the position of the worker. You do not feel that you are participating in the success of the business. Although you have been treated reasonably well and have received regular wage increases, your raises have not kept pace with inflation. When you talk to your friends who are unionized, they appear to have fared much better. In addition to large wage increases, often tied to the cost of living, they have also received many other benefits, including job security and shorter working hours. Obviously there appear to be advantages in belonging to a union, and so you decide to join.

This general scenario has been repeated many times in the past. In Canada today many small and medium-sized businesses deal with unionized workers. In addition, public employees on all levels — federal, provincial and municipal — have been eligible to join unions and have held the right to strike since 1967.

AIMS OF MANAGEMENT AND LABOUR

The foregoing example serves to indicate why management and labour are at odds. Both the owner (management) and the workers have different goals which influence their philosophy and their actions. Management and owners generally believe that only a profitable firm can offer competitive wages and benefits. If workers demand wages beyond what the firm can afford, its financial stability is jeopardized and the result could be bankruptcy. Workers on the other hand often believe that firms make large profits at their expense and that they do not receive enough of the firm's profits in return for their efforts. These opposing views cause conflicts between labour and management.

The conflict, however, is not always noticeable. Today, workers of many small and medium-sized firms and public employees on all levels are unionized, but for the most part, workers and management appear to work well together. We hear of strikes, but almost 90% of collective agreements are concluded without a strike. Clearly, then, while there are differences between management and labour, they share a common aim — to ensure that the business provides income for both the workers and its owners. We now examine the aims of management and labour more closely.

Aims of Management

Management represents the owners or stockholders of the business, who want both a reasonable return on their investment and some assurance that it will be protected in the future. It is management's responsibility to ensure that the firm survives. Ideally, management would like to maintain high revenues while keeping the costs of operating the firm as low as possible. Since labour is a major cost factor in most businesses, keeping wages down is a central concern. At the same time, however, it is in management's interest that workers are productive, skilled, educated and above all, loyal to management and the firm.

Aims of Labour

In general, the major aim of labour is to improve its material well-being through increased wages and salaries, improved fringe benefits, better working conditions, and job security. Workers realize that, without a union, they have little bargaining power with management — they can either accept what management is prepared to give them, or do without work. As an organized group, however, workers have more power — if they withhold their services they may bring a giant corporation to a standstill. Although some companies use management to fill in for striking workers, the output in goods and services is usually reduced and the firm's action often merely delays the inevitable shutdown.

Labour's aims are not limited to economic benefits, however. Traditionally organized labour has played a major role in furthering social issues through political action. In Great Britain, for example, one of the two major political parties specifically represents labour, and periodically forms the government. Although it has not established a political party in the United States, labour there has a history of lobbying for its interests. In Canada, labour has generally not been directly involved in politics. However, with the rise of the New Democratic Party, formerly the CCF, which has made a significant effort to represent labour's interests, labour and politics have become much closer. In fact, the Canadian Labour Congress has in the past endorsed the NDP, and local unions often support the party financially.[1]

WHAT IS A LABOUR UNION?

A **labour union** is a group of workers who have joined forces to achieve common goals. **Craft unions** consist of workers with a particular skill or trade, such as carpenters, painters or printers. **Industrial unions**, on the other hand, include all workers in a particular industry regardless of their skills or trades — the Canadian Auto Workers, for example, or the United Steel Workers. The unions with more than 50 000 members in Canada in 1987 are shown in Figure 11.1, while Figure 11.2 shows the percentage distribution of union membership throughout Canadian industry.

THE UNION PROCESS

It is important to understand that the entire union process, indeed Canada's entire industrial relations system, is bound by federal and provincial government regulations. The government specifies what a union must do to become the bargaining agent for a group of workers, how both sides must conduct themselves during negotiations, and what both sides must do before a strike or lockout can be called. Within this legal framework both union and management are free to bargain for as much as each can obtain from the other.

Before workers can bargain as a group with management, however, they must become a legally recognized body; otherwise, any contract negotiated would not be binding on management. Union certification alone does not ensure that negotiations will result in a contract. Even after exhaustive bargaining, management and unions may remain far apart on many issues, in which case conciliation, mediation and arbitration may be used to arrive at a contract. For workers who are engaged in essential services and are therefore forbidden to strike, compulsory arbitration is required. In compulsory arbitration, an outside party imposes a settlement. Should problems arise during the term of a contract, they can be resolved through a grievance procedure established during negotiations.

We now examine each of the steps in the negotiation process in more detail.

Certification

Union **certification** ensures that a particular group of employees is legally recognized as a bargaining unit, so that a collective agreement concerning wages and working conditions can be negotiated and later enforced. Certification also indicates to the employer that a sufficiently large number of workers wish to belong to the union.

The **certification process** begins when a group of workers either approach a union or are invited by a union to become members. Those wishing to join fill out an application and pay an initial fee to indicate their commitment.

Federal and provincial labour laws specify that a union must acquire a minimum membership before it is certified. Once this minimum has been obtained, an application is made to the appropriate

Figure 11.1 Unions with 50 000 or more members (January 1, 1987)

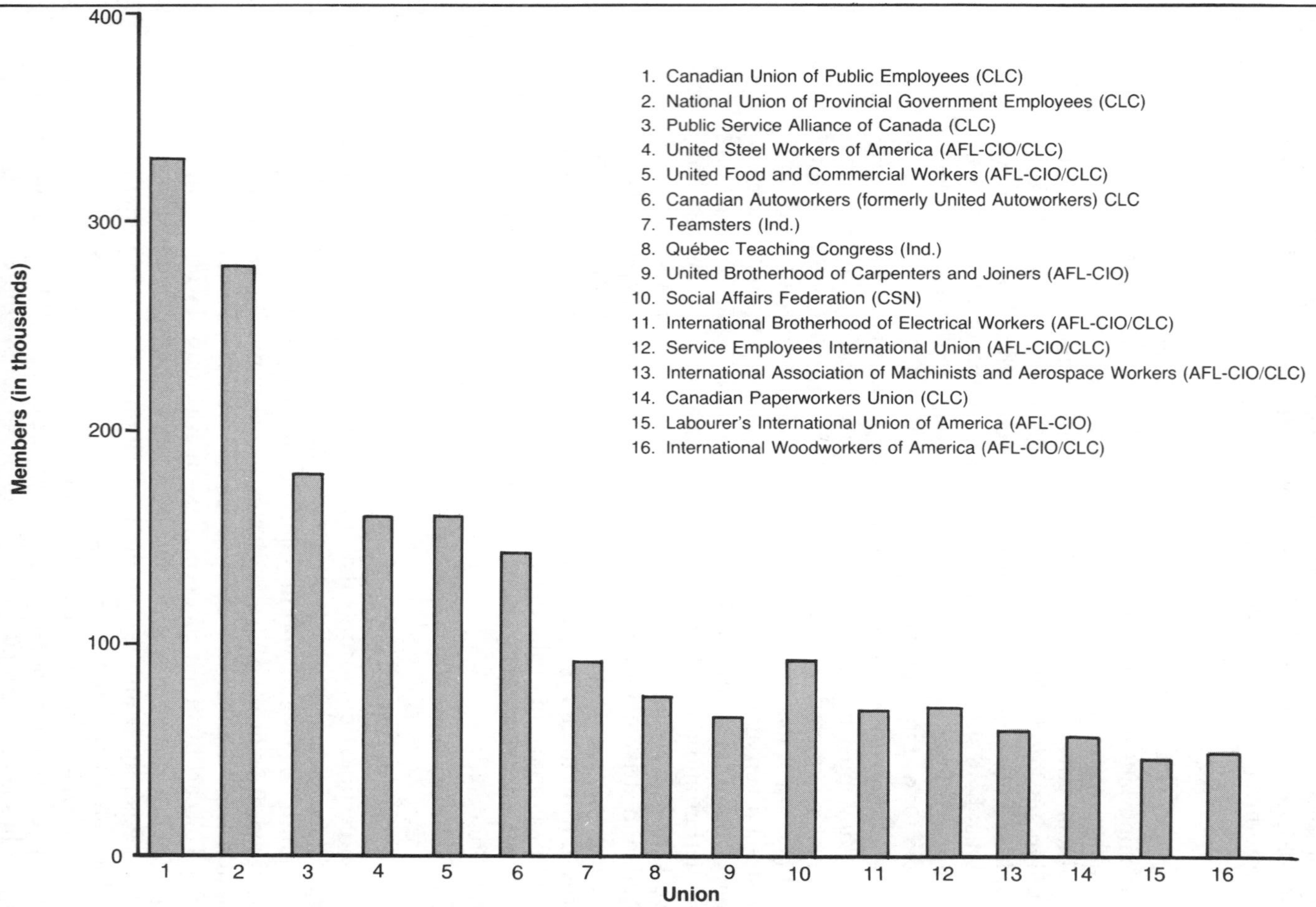

Members (in thousands)
400
300
200
100
0
1 2 3 4 5 6 7 8 9 10 11 12 13 14 15 16
Union
1. Canadian Union of Public Employees (CLC)
2. National Union of Provincial Government Employees (CLC)
3. Public Service Alliance of Canada (CLC)
4. United Steel Workers of America (AFL-CIO/CLC)
5. United Food and Commercial Workers (AFL-CIO/CLC)
6. Canadian Autoworkers (formerly United Autoworkers) CLC
7. Teamsters (Ind.)
8. Québec Teaching Congress (Ind.)
9. United Brotherhood of Carpenters and Joiners (AFL-CIO)
10. Social Affairs Federation (CSN)
11. International Brotherhood of Electrical Workers (AFL-CIO/CLC)
12. Service Employees International Union (AFL-CIO/CLC)
13. International Association of Machinists and Aerospace Workers (AFL-CIO/CLC)
14. Canadian Paperworkers Union (CLC)
15. Labourer's International Union of America (AFL-CIO)
16. International Woodworkers of America (AFL-CIO/CLC)

SOURCE: Bureau of Labour Information (Ottawa: Labour Canada, 1987).

Labour Relations Board for certification. The **Canada Labour Relations Board**, which we discuss in more detail later, is responsible for the certification of bargaining units for employees that fall under federal jurisdiction. In addition, each province has a Labour Relations Board to perform a similar function for workers under provincial jurisdiction. These boards ensure that voting for certification is properly conducted, that the proposed **bargaining unit** is appropriate for both the workers and the firm, and that the trade union in question is legally constituted and recognized.

The members of a new **local union** elect their own officers — president, vice president, secretary, treasurer — to look after the local's affairs. Part of the dues paid by the members remain in the local union; the remainder goes to the national and/or international union. In return, the local receives a wide variety of services and

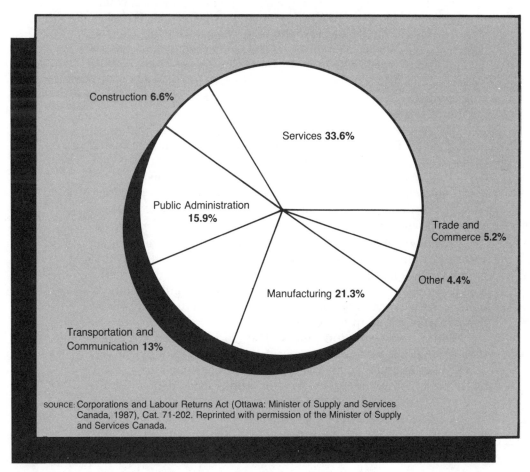

SOURCE: Corporations and Labour Returns Act (Ottawa: Minister of Supply and Services Canada, 1987), Cat. 71-202. Reprinted with permission of the Minister of Supply and Services Canada.

Figure 11.2 Percentage distribution of union membership, 1985

assistance to help in negotiations with employers, including research, education and publications.

The local union for its part must maintain the support of a majority of the workers. Otherwise the members or the firm's management may apply for **decertification**. In practice, however, management generally does not seek decertification when members are dissatisfied, since this action might lead to the formation of a new and stronger union and would not be in management's interest.

Negotiation — Collective Bargaining

Once a union has been certified as the bargaining agent for a group of workers, **negotiations** between the union and management may begin for the purpose of establishing a contract. Each side is obliged to bargain with the other in "**good faith**," which means that both parties must make every reasonable effort to come up with a **collective agreement**. However, the two sides often differ on what is reasonable. Attempts to reach a precise definition of "good faith" in collective bargaining have so far been unsuccessful, and except when one side or the other shows a clear unwillingness to negotiate, there is little recourse other than a strike or lockout. British Columbia and Québec are exceptions, in that their laws allow either party to have outstanding issues in a first contract settled by an outside party.

The process of **collective bargaining** begins when the local union holds a series of meetings to discuss management's proposals and to select members who will act as the bargaining committee. The committee may also ask an affiliated union to provide experienced negotiators who can help with technical subjects such as pensions.

The contract proposals may address a wide variety of issues — some of the most common are listed in Table 11.1.

In collective bargaining, management and union are often adversaries. Proposals advanced by the union are met with counter-proposals by management. Sometimes proposals are discussed at length and amended, or concessions are made by either side. Periodically the bargaining committee reports to the union members; the management group to its superiors.

While the negotiation process may be lengthy, minor issues such as job posting and hiring procedures are often settled relatively quickly. Major issues such as wages and job security may also eventually be settled voluntarily. The concessions made depend on the relative strength of each group. Management is in a strong position during a recession or when the company is performing poorly since it may threaten to lay off employees or even shut down. On the other hand, when the company is doing well and is profitable, the union

TABLE 11.1
Items usually included in a union contract

Union rights and management rights

Union activities and responsibilities
      Collection of union dues
      Union officers and shop stewards
      Union bulletin boards
      Wildcat strikes and slowdowns

Wages and salaries
      Wage structure
      General wage adjustments
      Job evaluation
      Wage incentives
      Time studies
      Pay for reporting and call-in
      Shift differentials, bonuses, profit sharing

Hours of work and time off
      Regular hours of work
      Holidays
      Vacations
      Overtime pay regulations
      Leaves of absence and sick pay
      Rest periods and lunch periods

Job rights and seniority
      Seniority regulations
      Transfers
      Promotions
      Layoffs and recalls
      Job posting and hiring procedures

Insurance and benefit programs
      Group life insurance
      Medical insurance
      Pension program
      Supplemental unemployment benefits

Health and safety

Discipline, suspension and discharge

Grievance handling and arbitration

has the advantage since management does not want to jeopardize its operation with a lengthy strike. But regardless of how much power either side has at any given time, both sides have a common interest — to see that the organization survives and continues to provide income for all concerned. In most instances, this common interest is incentive enough for both sides to reach an agreement and sign a contract.

When an agreement has been reached, union members must **ratify** — vote to accept — the contract. If the contract is accepted by the union membership, it becomes a legal agreement binding on both sides for the duration of the period specified. If problems arise in the interpretation of the contract at a future date, a grievance procedure can be used to resolve them, whether they involve a particular individual or the entire union.

If the contract is rejected, bargaining may be resumed by both parties. If further bargaining is not possible, federal and provincial labour laws provide other methods to help reach an agreement.

Conciliation and Mediation

When contract negotiations reach an impasse, relations between union and management can become strained and deteriorate. Both sides hold to their views and neither may be willing to concede on any issue lest concession be interpreted as weakness. A government mediator is then appointed to help reach a settlement and avoid a strike or lockout. The process is known as **mediation**. The first stage in the mediation process is **conciliation**, in which the mediator tries to persuade both union and management to return to the bargaining table for further discussion of their differences.

Conciliation is a requirement for both parties before a legal strike or lockout can occur. Both the federal and provincial governments employ full-time mediators to help settle disputes. Alternatively, judges, lawyers, priests, university professors, or people from other occupations may be appointed as mediators.

The mediator's first task is to bring both parties back to discussions. He or she meets with both sides to determine whether they are serious about reaching a settlement, or whether they are simply going through the process of mediation as a legal requirement before calling a strike or lockout. Mediators explain their role in the mediation process and indicate how they expect to help in reaching an agreement, whether by recommending a possible settlement or by acting as spokesperson for each side. Since mediators hold no special powers, the success of their efforts depends entirely on the trust and respect the two parties have for them.

"Another setback — the mediators just went out on strike."

SOURCE: Artist—Al Kaufman. Reproduced by permission of the Masters Agency, Capitola, California.

If the mediator finds the parties want a settlement, he or she determines the issues to be resolved and the positions of both parties. The mediator then meets with each side separately to determine what concessions each may be prepared to make in coming to a settlement. At this point, the mediator's skill and experience is important — he or she must convey to each side how far the other is prepared to come toward a settlement. The mediator then tries to lead the two parties toward an agreement without letting either side feel it has capitulated.

If the mediator is able to bring the two parties to an agreement, then a contract is signed. Otherwise the union may call a strike or management may resort to a lockout. A union may not strike until members have voted on the strike by secret ballot. Sometimes a strike vote is held early in the bargaining process to impress upon management that the workers are prepared to back up union demands. A number of other conditions have to be met before a strike can be called. The requirements vary somewhat among the provinces. In all provinces, however, the parties may move to another step called arbitration.

Arbitration

Both sides may agree to the establishment of an **arbitration board** which is composed of three people — one nominated by the company, one by the union, and the third, the chairman, selected by the two board members. If there is a disagreement over the selection of the chairman, the Minister of Labour may make the appointment.

The board listens to both sides and includes its findings and recommendations in a report. The findings of the board are not binding on either side, but may influence both to come to a voluntary agreement. By agreeing to **voluntary arbitration** both sides take some risks, since they may be obliged to concede more than they would have in the event of a strike. If an agreement is reached, then a contract is signed. If no agreement is reached, however, then after a period specified in the federal and provincial labour laws, workers may strike or management may institute a lockout. The decision to strike depends on the outcome of the strike vote.

For employees in essential services — hospital workers or police, for example — legislation may prohibit strikes and lockouts, and thus **compulsory arbitration** is required. Under compulsory arbitration both management and union are compelled to submit unresolved issues to the arbitration board, and its decision is binding on both parties. Compulsory arbitration has been criticized and is often not considered as effective as strike action, but it can prevent the loss of income and profits that might result from a prolonged strike or lockout. Arbitration thus maintains union-management relations since both parties are interested in securing their incomes. Arbitration may also save face for both sides, as neither is seen to concede to the other and both may claim that the settlement was imposed on them by an outside party.

Grievances

Even when a contract exists between management and the union, problems may arise in the interpretation of its terms. For example, a worker may believe that she is not receiving the rate specified in the contract for the job she is doing. In another instance a worker who has been laid off may claim seniority over another worker who has not been laid off. Workers who believe they have been unfairly treated according to the terms of the contract may file a **grievance** which will then be processed according to the procedure established during collective bargaining.

When a grievance is filed, management and the union first try to resolve it within the worker's department. If the problem cannot be solved at that stage, progressively higher levels of union and management personnel become involved. If still no settlement results, the grievance may be submitted to an impartial third party known as an arbitrator, or to an arbitration board, whose decision will be final and binding on both the union and the company.

Occasionally a grievance may lead to a **wildcat strike** — an illegal and unauthorized strike by workers to show that they are not satisfied with the handling of the grievance by either management or the union or both.

WHEN ALL ELSE FAILS

Though management and union are often adversaries, the collective bargaining process is generally successful in resolving differences and usually results in a contract. Occasionally, however, one side may resort to the use of certain "weapons" to force the other to an agreement. Table 11.2 lists the weapons commonly available to each side.

TABLE 11.2
Weapons of labour and management

	Weapon	*Effect*
L A B O U R	Strike	Union members refuse to work.
	Picketing	Discourages customers and suppliers from dealing with the firm; spreads information about the strike.
	Boycott	Members of other unions and/or the public refuse to do business with the firm.
M A N A G E M E N T	Lockout	Workers are prevented from entering the firm's premises to work.
	Injunction	Legal means are used to stop union activities such as strikes or picketing. Though used primarily by management, an injunction may also be requested by the union to stop illegal actions on the part of management.
	Employers' association	A number of firms make a cooperative effort to deal with unions, particularly in contract negotiations.

Weapons of Labour

A union's most effective weapon is **strike** action — the total withdrawal of labour's services in order to halt production. A strike is
costly to the union since it does not receive regular dues from members while they are on strike, but instead pays them a token amount
each week from the union strike fund. Unless it has adequate funds,
therefore, the union will not usually resort to a strike. Nor are workers
generally willing to forgo regular wages in a protracted strike, since
the loss is seldom recovered. Hence, when a union decides on strike
action it usually means that the issues at stake are important.

On the other hand, the mere **threat of a strike** is often equally
effective in achieving a settlement with management, particularly if

Strike action by union members

a strike would disrupt an otherwise profitable operation. Unions thus often ask their members for a strike vote early in the bargaining sessions, to show management that its members are prepared to strike to back up their demands.

The strike is usually the last act a union considers after all avenues of negotiation have been exhausted and after the mediation step has been concluded. Sometimes, however, a union's members may go on an **illegal strike**. Case 11–2, "Ending a bitter strike," indicates why the Alberta nurses took this drastic action and how the strike was finally settled. "Issue: Should Government Employees be Allowed to Strike?" examines some of the factors involved in public-services strikes and whether or not such strikes should be outlawed.

Picketing during a strike serves two major purposes. First, the signs and placards carried by union members outside the firm's premises let the public know that a labour dispute exists, and often provide information about it. Second, picketing attempts to discourage other firms from dealing with the firm engaged in the strike. Strikers attempt to persuade employees of other firms not to cross the picket line. While this action is often successful, on occasion it has caused violence and property damage.

A **boycott** is an appeal to customers not to buy the firm's products, especially if the company has been able to operate using managerial staff. A primary boycott attempts to prevent other union members from dealing with the firm. A **secondary boycott** is an attempt to discourage other unionized businesses from patronizing the firm by threatening that their own employees may resort to a work stoppage. For example, if a steel mill which is engaged in a strike is able to continue selling the products in its inventory to manufacturing firms, employees of those firms could threaten work stoppages if the firms continue to purchase from the mill.

Issue: *Should Government Employees be Allowed to Strike?*

The **right to strike** was given to public-service workers in the federal government and in Québec and New Brunswick in the late 1960s, and in British Columbia and Newfoundland in the early 1970s. However, this right was soon circumscribed by the ordering of employees back to work by many governments. In 1978, Acts of Parliament ended the walkout of 375 marine engineers who worked on Canada's Great Lakes fleet, and by 23 000 inside postal workers whose service was considered essential to the public. In October 1987, the same

23 000 postal workers were ordered back to work by the federal government, which two months previously had passed legislation to end a national rail strike. Public service employees in both Québec and Saskatchewan, and the nurses in Alberta, were also forced back to work by government-imposed contracts.

The right to strike by public service employees has never been popular with the Canadian public. In April 1987 the Supreme Court of Canada ruled that unions do not have a sacrosanct right to strike simply on the grounds that the 1982 Constitution guarantees freedom of association.

The federal government, along with the governments of New-foundland and Québec, has recently limited the number of union members in a bargaining unit who are eligible to strike by designating a greater number of workers as essential for ensuring public safety and health. In British Columbia, the 1987 new industrial labour reforms even give independent commissioners the right to order a 40-day cooling-off period whenever they think the public interest is not being served.

But would outlawing public service strikes put an end to them? Organized labour argues that to take away the right legally does not end strikes but results in defiance of the law. This was true in the 1978 postal walkout as employees continued to maintain picket lines even after the legislation was passed. The legislation was also defied in 1988 by the Alberta nurses who continued to strike, preferring to accept a court-imposed fine for each day that they remained on strike. Furthermore, if the strike right is denied, unions ask, what guarantee do employees have that their rights will be upheld? It is the option to strike that gives negotiators bargaining power. Without it, the power of the employer would be increased. Obviously, if the right to strike is to be denied, adequate compensation would have to be made for the loss of that right.

Denying the right to strike to public sector employees is an argument based on the fact that differences exist between collective bargaining in the private, profit-oriented sector, and in the public sector, which is directly supported by taxes.

A strike or lockout is supposed to hurt both sides in a dispute, and thus bring about the motivation for a settlement. If a strike occurs in the private sector, the public can usually obtain the goods from other sources, therefore suffering minimal inconvenience. When a strike occurs in the public sector — the post office or hospitals, for example — the public is directly affected because alternative services are not readily available. Instead of hurting the employer, the strike is actually hurting the public at large.

There is also the argument that private employers have more incentive to hold out against high wage demands because they would affect the company's prices and hence its ability to compete. Governments, on the other hand, are likely to settle a strike more quickly and be more generous in their settlement because they can raise taxes to cover the higher costs.

Another consideration is the value of public services. The public becomes accustomed to certain services and expects them to continue. When they are suddenly discontinued because of a strike, it reminds people dramatically of the worth of such services. It brings to the forefront the fact that public services must be paid for, and the public payroll is part of the cost. It is something the taxpayer generally does not like to hear, and contributes to the unpopularity of public-service strikes.

Columnist Don McGillivray, in the October 23 edition of the Montreal *Gazette*, termed specific back-to-work laws as a "confession of failure." "They [specific-back-to-work laws] mean, in essence, that a legal strike is transformed into an illegal one," he wrote. "The right to give or withhold labour, which is taken for granted by most of us, is removed from a specific group of citizens. They are told by Parliament that they must work, under penalty of law, whether or not they are satisfied with the pay and conditions. Such suspensions of rights — similar to those possible under the War Measures Act — are justified in a democracy only by a national emergency."

The present Progressive Conservative government has made it plain that it will not hesitate to end future strikes by legislative order, particularly for those federal unions that have the greater capacity to inflict public damage than others. This could include postal workers, air traffic controllers, highway maintenance workers, and others providing high-profile public services. Historically, strikers ordered back to work have often come out ahead of the disputed employer under terms set out in the legislation or arbitrated later.

What effect will the new tough labour policies have on future negotiations? One official with the Canadian Union of Postal Workers said that Canada Post stopped negotiating the moment the labour minister started talking about back to work legislation. The best collective agreements are those agreed upon jointly by workers and management, the two parties that have to live with a labour contract. If a stalemate develops, a mutually agreeable settlement usually results because the threat of a strike or lockout produces movement at the bargaining table. When governments threaten legislation, however, what incentive is there for management to continue to bargain in good faith?

SOURCES: *The Labour Gazette*, Nov.-Dec. 1978, pp. 492–3. See also, James Bagnall, "Tough new era faces public-sector unions," *The Financial Post*, October 19, 1987, p.3.

Weapons of Management

The **lockout** is one of management's chief tools to force labour to accept its demands. The employer closes his plant, thus cutting employees off from their source of income. Management seldom initiates a work stoppage since it would reduce the firm's production. However, a lockout might be used if, for example, production has been curtailed because one union is on strike, while other employees belonging to non-striking unions are still working. A lockout of all employees would then reduce costs and possibly put pressure on the striking union for a settlement.

An **injunction** is a court order prohibiting an illegal practice on the part of either the union or management. For example, if a union has too many picketers in front of the employer's place of business, management or customers may be prevented from entering the premises — this practice is illegal, and management may apply for a court injunction to have it stopped. Similarly if management is engaged in an illegal practice with respect to the union, the union may apply for an injunction. While today the injunction can be used by both parties, in the past poor legislation allowed employers to use the injunction to prohibit strikes. This practice is no longer permitted, and today the injunction is used mainly to prevent excessive picketing and to restrain violence and damage to company property.

The formation of **employers' associations** is another tool of management in dealing with labour. Employers may join together as a group to lobby government and bargain with unions for an industry-wide settlement. Examples are the Canadian Manufacturers' Association, the Forest Industrial Relations Bureau in British Columbia, and the Ontario Trucking Association. In the past, employers were reluctant to join together and bargain with labour because of their traditional concern about competition for customers. However, when there are many small firms in an industry and only one or a few large unions, employers have found it advantageous to be represented by a single bargaining group, so that all firms face the same labour costs.

BASIC ISSUES IN COLLECTIVE BARGAINING

As Table 11.1 indicated, a typical union contract may include a wide range of issues to be negotiated. Some issues are of major importance in any agreement, however. These include union security, wages and fringe benefits, hours of work, job security and promotion.

Union Security

It is not easy for a union to gain legal recognition as the sole bargaining agent for a group of workers in a given firm or industry. Certification is costly and requires considerable effort on the part of the organizers. Certification also does not guarantee security. If union members become dissatisfied with their present organization, they may ask for decertification in order to have another union represent them. And if a rival union, or even management, senses dissatisfaction among members of a union, they too may seek decertification. Thus security is usually one of the first issues negotiated in any new contract.

Security, to a union, means members. The more members it has, the stronger it is, both financially and in the eyes of management. The ideal situation for a union is a **closed shop** — only union members are permitted to work in a particular firm or industry. If a closed shop cannot be negotiated, the next best alternative is the **union shop** — employers are free to hire as they please, but the new workers are required to join the union after a probationary period, usually thirty days. A modified version of the latter, the **union shop with preferential hiring**, means that employers are obliged to hire union members if any are available; if there are none, and non-union workers are hired, they must subsequently become union members.

Under simple **preferential hiring** rules, employers must hire union members if available, but no one need become or remain a union member unless he or she so wishes. Another situation, known as the **Rand Formula** or **agency shop**, leaves the worker the choice of joining or not joining the union; however, all workers must pay union dues. Finally, the **open shop** allows workers to join a union if they wish, but non-union workers are not required to pay dues. In any of the last three situations, the union is not particularly secure.

By maintaining its membership, a union also strengthens its financial security through members' dues. The union will usually negotiate to have the employer deduct union dues from the workers' paycheques, a practice known as **dues check-off**.

Wages and Fringe Benefits

Wages are always a key issue in any contract. The union attempts to obtain an increase in real income for its members, which means an increase over and above the rate of inflation. Since this may be difficult to obtain — especially when inflation is high — unions often negotiate for a **cost of living allowance clause (COLA)**, which allows wages to rise automatically in direct proportion to the consumer price index. COLA arrangements were popular in Canada while inflation was high. In 1977, more than one fifth of Canadian workers were covered by a cost of living allowance clause in their contracts. However, this trend peaked in 1980 when 42.6% of workers were covered by new contracts with COLA clauses. By 1986 only 12.7% of new contracts were so covered.

The cost of fringe benefits is also rising and management is becoming increasingly concerned. As noted in the preceding chapter, typical non-wage benefits include holidays, paid medical and dental plans, and pensions. However, the list is becoming longer as unions continue to seek new benefits such as paid legal services, day-care cost sharing for working mothers, and subsidies for cafeteria lunches. Fringe benefits amount to approximately one third of the average Canadian worker's total wages.[2]

Hours of Work

A hundred and fifty years ago, standard working hours stretched from dawn till dusk, six days a week. Even at the turn of the century, 60- to 72-hour weeks were not uncommon. Today the legal workweek is 40 hours, and many people work only 30 or 35 hours per week. This reduction in the length of the workday was accomplished primarily by unions in the early part of the 20th century, and was aided by government legislation.

In addition to regulating the length of the workweek, unions negotiate for **overtime** and **shift differential pay** if their members are required to work hours that differ from the norm. Workers usually receive time and one half or double time if they are required to work longer than the regular quota of hours per day or week, or on weekends or holidays.

Job Security and Promotion

People generally want to be assured of a job and a steady income. Sudden loss of employment can cause tremendous hardship for individuals and their families. Unions are therefore often forceful in their attempts to gain job security for their members. For example, they have insisted that if layoffs are necessary, they should be done on the basis of seniority. Certainly, from the union's point of view, letting the last person hired be the first to leave is a fair method of solving the problem. However, employers would naturally prefer to retain the most productive workers, laying off those who are not performing as well. Management claims that a layoff system based on seniority tends to lower the productivity of workers who have been with the firm for a long period, as their jobs are virtually assured regardless of performance.

In protecting their members' jobs, unions sometimes contribute to inefficiency through the practice known as **featherbedding**, wherein they attempt to keep workers in jobs that are no longer necessary. Railway unions, for example, insisted that engine firemen be retained, even though they were no longer required once all railroads had converted to diesel engines. Nevertheless it took thirteen years to resolve the issue. Job security was also at the heart of the eight-month newspaper strike in Vancouver during 1978–79, when computer typesetting threatened to make the jobs of some workers obsolete. The question became a major strike issue when the union insisted the jobs be retained. To resolve such issues management generally resorts either to early retirement of workers whose jobs have become obsolete, or to payment of a healthy separation allowance.

When workers are to be promoted to better paid jobs or supervisory positions, unions also insist that management proceed according to seniority. Employers, however, generally do not readily accept the seniority rule, since not everyone is capable of performing all jobs equally well, or of being a good manager or supervisor. Management therefore often compromises, taking both merit and seniority into consideration. If two employees with equivalent qualifications are considered suitable for promotion, the one with the longer service record is promoted first.

HISTORY OF LABOUR UNIONS IN CANADA

Unions were first organized in Canada in the early decades of the 19th century, though various economic downturns meant that most were relatively short-lived. While some of these unions originated locally, most were international, with British unions dominating in the 1840s and 1850s and American unions from the 1860s on.

In 1871 five Toronto craft unions established the **Toronto Trades Assembly**, and similar trades councils were subsequently formed in other major Ontario cities. In 1873 the Toronto group called a convention of unions and a national central organization called the **Canadian Labour Union** emerged. This body held meetings for four consecutive years starting in 1874, but ceased meeting thereafter because of the depression of 1878–82.

In the last two decades of the 19th century union membership increased, particularly in the West, and mainly as a result of the construction of the CPR and the growth of Canadian industry encouraged by federal government tariff protection. The first industrial union was established in 1878 by the Nova Scotia coal miners and included all workers in that industry. In 1881 an industrial organization called the **Knights of Labour** entered Canada from the United

States. In all, more than 100 new locals were established during the 1880s, almost half of them in Ontario, with 21 in the Maritimes, 19 in Quebec and 18 in the West.

Labour councils and assemblies were also revived in the 1880s following the depression. In 1883 delegates from various Ontario unions and the Knights of Labour assemblies in that province formed the **Canadian Labour Union Congress**. This body underwent various name changes at subsequent meetings until 1892, when it became the **Trades and Labour Congress of Canada**. Although the Knights of Labour initially had the majority of delegates in the congress, membership declined rapidly after 1894 because of internal organizational disputes, and the group was eventually expelled from the congress.

The early decades of the 20th century were characterized by upheavals in the labour movement, as unions broke away from existing congresses and formed new groups. In 1902 various unions expelled from the Trades and Labour Congress formed the National Trades and Labour Congress, which became the **Canadian Federation of Labour** in 1908. In 1919 the **One Big Union** was established by western unions that had broken away from the Trades and Labour Congress. In 1921 a number of local unions in Québec formed the **Canadian Catholic Confederation of Labour** and in 1927 the **All-Canadian Congress of Labour**, made up of the Canadian Federation of Labour and other national unions, was established.

In the United States, the **American Federation of Labour (AFL)** expelled the industrial unions because of continuing conflict over the right of member unions to organize on an industrial basis rather than on a craft basis alone. These expelled unions then established the **Congress of Industrial Organizations (CIO)** in 1935. The AFL demanded that the Trades and Labour Congress in Canada also expel the affiliated CIO unions. Although the TLC initially refused the request, eventually it did comply, expelling a total of 11 international unions representing 22 000 members.

In 1940 the expelled CIO unions joined the All-Canadian Congress of Labour, which up to this time had been a relatively insignificant rival to the TLC. At a convention held that year, however, the constitution of the All-Canadian Congress was revised and the organization's name changed to the **Canadian Congress of Labour**; it thus became the Canadian counterpart to the CIO. The CCL thereafter experienced tremendous growth and became the second largest labour organization in Canada, next to the TLC.

Following the merger of the AFL and CIO in the United States in 1955, the two major Canadian labour federations — the TLC and the CCL — also merged to form the **Canadian Labour Congress (CLC)**.

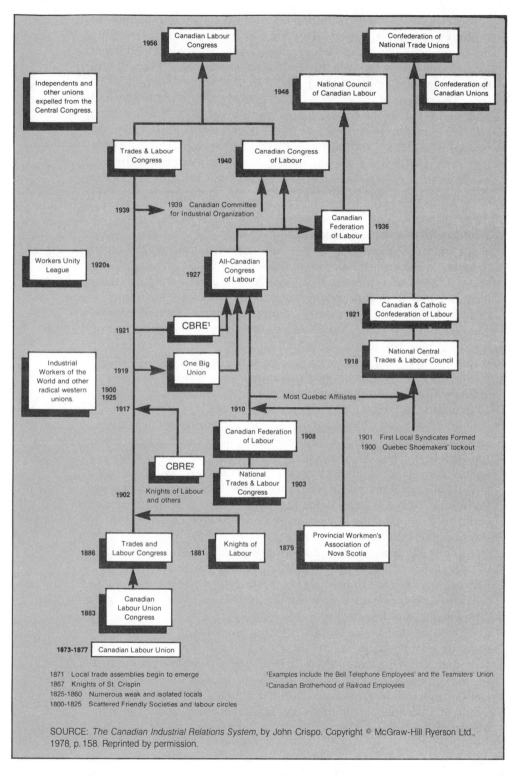

Figure 11.3 History and development of the Canadian labour movement

Altogether, these mergers united 111 international unions and 32 million members. Approximately 300 000 workers remained outside the Congress; of these, 200 000 belonged to independent, non-affiliated locals, and the remainder to the **Confederation des Travailleurs Catholiques du Canada (CTCC)**, which in 1956 voted to join the CLC.

The merger of the various congresses in Canada and the United States brought peace to the labour movement in North America. Unions were able to concentrate their efforts on the improvement of wages and working conditions for their members until the late 1960s and early 1970s when the movement once again became active in its drive to organize white collar workers, government employees and professional groups.[3]

The Canadian Labour Congress

The Canadian Labour Congress is the major labour organization in Canada, uniting national, international and local unions, labour councils and other union federations. The purpose of the CLC, aside from acting as a liaison among the various labour organizations, is primarily political. It presents a common front to the federal and provincial governments for all organized labour in Canada. From a founding membership of about one million, the CLC had grown to 2 150 000 by 1986, representing 57% of the country's 3.7 million union members. CLC membership increased significantly in the early 1970s with the addition of many public service unions. By 1985, 10 of Canada's 16 largest unions belonged to the CLC.

In 1988 the CLC started negotiations to bring the Teamsters back into the CLC after they rejoined the American labour congress, the AFL-CIO. The CLC expelled the Teamsters in 1960 because of its tendency to get members by raiding other unions. Although there is still considerable opposition from other member unions to having them back in the CLC, the Teamsters with its 90 000 members would certainly strengthen the federation and provide an increase in annual dues of $500 000.

The CLC is also attempting to bring the Canadian Federation of Labour back into their ranks. This rival of the CLC left in 1982 because of a jurisdictional dispute. CFL unions consist of 290 000 workers who would also be welcome additions to the CLC in both membership and finances.

Perhaps the major problem facing the CLC is to diffuse the growing antagonism between Canadian- and U.S.-controlled unions. Canadian unions generally feel that they are being treated unfairly by the American-controlled international unions. For this reason, the Canadian Auto Workers pulled out of the United Auto Workers union and became an independent Canadian union under the leadership of Bob White. This same union is now attempting to recruit

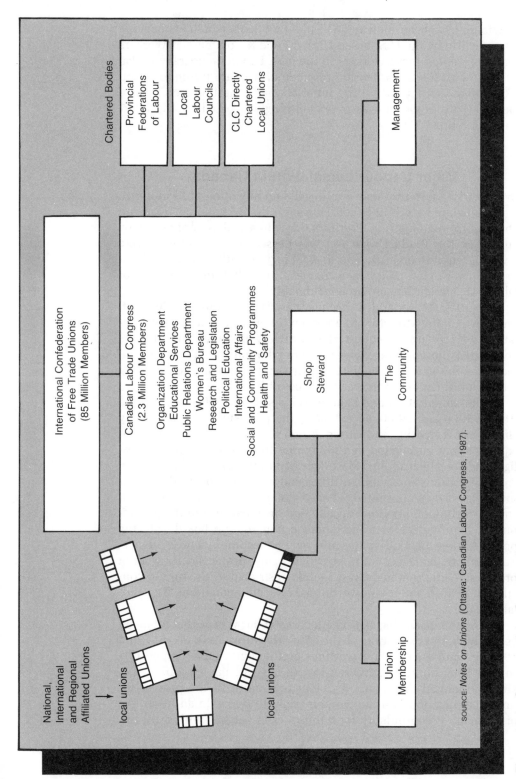

Figure 11.4 Structure of the Canadian labour movement.

Chartered Bodies

Provincial Federations of Labour

Local Labour Councils

CLC Directly Chartered Local Unions

Management

International Confederation of Free Trade Unions (85 Million Members)

Canadian Labour Congress (2.3 Million Members)

Organization Department
Educational Services
Public Relations Department
Women's Bureau
Research and Legislation
Political Education
International Affairs
Social and Community Programmes
Health and Safety

Shop Steward

The Community

National, International and Regional Affiliated Unions

local unions

local unions

Union Membership

SOURCE: *Notes on Unions* (Ottawa: Canadian Labour Congress, 1987).

Newfoundland fishermen and fish-plant workers, which is not being taken lightly by the U.S.-based United Food & Commercial Workers that represented these workers in the past. Union democracy is also at issue with the Canadian longshoremen, who are trying to set up a Canadian district within the International Longshoremen's Association. This proposal was overwhelmingly rejected by the international union.[4]

Major Labour Legislation in Canada

In the early 1800s unions were illegal, and any attempt to unionize was considered a criminal act. However, the designation was soon changed from a violation of criminal law to a violation of civil law, and when the **Trade Union Act** was passed in 1872, unions were given the right to organize and to exist legally without being subject to criminal or civil conspiracy charges. Since that time, the body of labour legislation has grown considerably.[5]

In 1900 the federal government passed the **Conciliation Act**, under which the Minister of Labour could provide voluntary conciliation services upon request. The **Railway Disputes Act** of 1903 eliminated the voluntary aspect of conciliation for CPR trackmen, requiring the use of a mediation board and voluntary non-binding arbitration if conciliation was unsuccessful.

The **Conciliation and Labour Act** passed in 1906 combined the Acts of 1900 and 1903 and extended the provisions of the Railway Disputes Act to other industries. When this Act proved to be inadequate, it was succeeded in 1907 by the **Industrial Disputes Investigations Act** which applied to workers in the areas of mining, transport, communications and public utilities, but could also be used by other industries if they consented. The act was passed because a series of strikes during the previous decade had been harmful to the general public. It provided for a three-person conciliation board with the power to investigate disputes and request testimony and evidence. Furthermore, no strike could be called while these hearings were in progress. While the board was mainly restricted to the role of conciliator, it did have the power to make recommendations if conciliation failed.

No other major legislation affecting labour was passed for many years, with the exception of the **War Measures Acts** of 1914 and 1939, intended to ensure wartime production would not be disrupted. Then in 1944 an Order-in-Council was passed which specifically defined the rights of unions and outlined the process for union certification and the workers' right to strike. In addition, the order made it compulsory for employers to bargain with duly certified unions, prevented employers from interfering with any union activity, and required unions to expose their activities to union members and to the general public. It also required compulsory conciliation, designed as a "cooling-off" period when negotiations broke down, before a strike could be called.

Finally, in 1948, the passing of the **Industrial Disputes Investigations Act** incorporated the 1907 Act and the Order-in-Council of 1944 and rescinded the War Measures Act. In 1971, previous federal legislation governing employment practices and labour standards was consolidated in the Canada Labour Code. Since then there have been no major changes in the federal labour legislation.

Federal Labour Legislation

Most Canadian labour legislation is provincial, since it is considered law in relations to property and civil rights over which provincial legislatures have authority. The federal government has authority only over industries under its jurisdiction, federal government employees, and those matters delegated to the federal government by the provinces. These laws are embodied in the Canada Labour Code which came into force in 1971.

The federal Department of Labour (Labour Canada) was established in 1900. The Minister of Labour is responsible for the **Canada Labour Code**. It sets out employment standards such as hours of work, minimum wages, and annual vacations; it also provides for fair employment practices, equal pay for women, and employee safety and industrial relations.

Matters delegated to the federal government by the provinces include the payment of unemployment insurance benefits and pensions. Under the new Unemployment Insurance Act of 1971, all employees and employers are required to contribute toward insurance protecting all employees against loss of wages caused by unemployment. The Canada Pension Plan, which came into effect in 1965, also requires contributions from both employer and employee to provide retirement pensions for all employees.

The administration of labour legislation rests primarily with the **Labour Relations Boards**, which are quasi-judicial tribunals composed of representatives from labour, management and the public. There are eleven such boards in Canada, one under the jurisdiction of the federal government and one for each of the ten provinces. The boards are an alternative to the courts of law, which may not be able to respond adequately to labour problems. Although the boards are a subject of ongoing debate, they do offer a number of advantages. Their small size allows them to handle disputes more quickly than the courts. They are informal and cost relatively little to operate.

Moreover, because they are specialized, members can develop expertise in labour matters. The boards' mixed composition — labour, management and the public — means that their decisions are more readily accepted by both sides. They also have flexibility in settling disputes as they are not constrained by common-law precedents.[6]

Provincial Labour Legislation

All provinces have legislation designed to establish harmonious relations between employers and employees and to facilitate settlement of industrial disputes. These laws guarantee freedom of association and the right to organize. They also provide for labour relations boards or other bodies to certify trade unions as bargaining agents, and require that employers bargain with the certified union representing its employees. Other legislation establishes minimum wages, working hours, general holidays, vacations with pay, minimum age restrictions, fair employment practices, equal pay for men and women, apprenticeship legislation, termination, and workers' compensation. All provinces have passed labour relations acts to provide a framework for conciliation, mediation and arbitration services as required. However, the 1980s have been characterized by new labour legislation, passed in many provinces, which has curbed the power of unions. In B.C., for example, under the new labour law passed in 1987 an Industrial Relations Council can recommend an end to strikes that are against "the public interest."

LABOUR UNIONS IN CANADA TODAY

With the 1982 recession, labour's woes began. The federal government introduced a wage restraint bill, followed by British Columbia, that in effect suspended collective bargaining rights for two years. Similar curbs were later adopted by most provinces. Both the federal and provincial governments have been especially tough on public-service unions: they have legislated them back to work more often and declared many public-service employees essential to public health and safety, effectively removing their right to strike. (See the issue in this chapter, "Should Government Employees Be Allowed to Strike?")

Labour's ability to fight back depends on the economy. When the economy slows down and unemployment rises, job security and working conditions are at the top of a union's bargaining list. Wage increases are only possible when the economy improves and companies declare profits. Wage increases have trailed the consumer price index in eight of the 10 years up to and including 1987. Average wage gains amounted to about 4% while the consumer price index rose 4.4%.[7]

Labour won a major victory, however, by concluding a landmark agreement with Chrysler Canada in early 1988, that linked pension increases with the inflation rate. With this agreement, indexing will be a major new issue in Canadian industrial relations.[8]

Although the labour movement is experiencing problems mainly because of the poor economic climate in the 1980s, it is unlikely that it will decline in importance. Nevertheless, there will be a constant struggle for labour to maintain its membership. Some of the problems facing it in this area are technological advances for automating factories, the expected free trade agreement between Canada and the United States, federal and provincial government cutbacks to reduce their deficits, and the trend towards self-employment as communication and computerization continue to expand. Unions have been especially frustrated and continue to lose ground in their efforts to unionize the white-collar sector in financial institutions and retail stores. The number of unionized bank branch workers, for instance, has slipped by one third during the past decade. As shown in Figure 11.5, the percentage of the labour force affiliated with the union movement has not grown appreciably in the past few decades.

Another reason perhaps for the slowdown in the growth of union membership is the lack of a clear-cut cause. In the past, low wages and poor working conditions provided workers with ample reason for joining a union. Today, the gains already achieved in these areas make organization less of a necessity. Moreover, it is unlikely that current economic conditions will allow either substantial reductions in hours of work or large increases in wages.

Hence unions are now turning to other concerns such as social reform, environmental problems and politics. This shift is due partly to the retirement of older workers and the influx of many young workers who grew up during a period of affluence. With over half of their members today under 35 years of age, and their basic concerns largely taken care of, unions can turn their attention to a wider range of issues.

One major problem the labour movement faces today is a poor public image. This image is based largely on public employee strikes and what are perceived as substantial wage increases. Generally the public sees unions as strike-happy, with little concern for the economy as a whole and for those who are not unionized. Unions are seen to be right behind business as the villains in the economy. There is also evidence that even a union's own members often do not support it.[9]

However, unions are attempting to communicate with the public and show their involvement in the advancement of the welfare

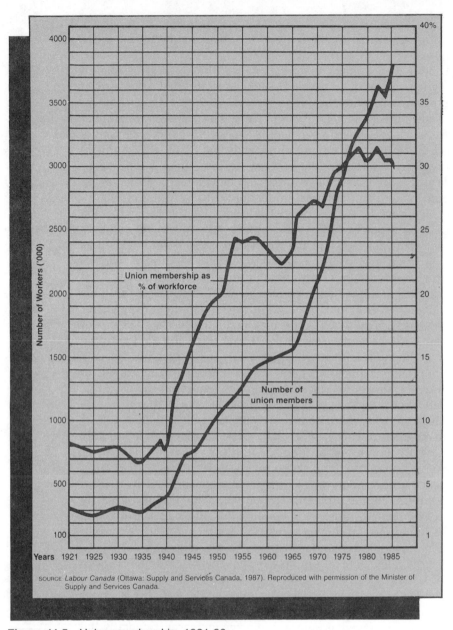

Figure 11.5 Union membership, 1921-86

of all Canadians through a commitment to social causes such as medicare, unemployment insurance and better housing for low-income workers. Efforts have also been made to explain the history of the labour movement and its present role to school children. A 30-minute film commissioned by the Canadian Labour Congress shows the human side of unions and their members.[10]

LABOUR-MANAGEMENT RELATIONS — SOME CRITICAL ISSUES

Labour unions came into existence to strengthen the bargaining power of workers and improve working conditions. To improve the worker's plight over the years and the constant need to maintain workers' economic position relative to other groups in society has kept the labour movement in the spotlight. It has not been easy to get owners/management to accept collective bargaining. Even when it is finally accepted, management still often holds the upper hand because it ultimately controls the union members' jobs. Often the unions are forced to accept lower settlements, or even to lose benefits when the economy is performing poorly and the company is not earning a profit.

Labour-management relations in North America have at times been stormy. This is particularly true of times when many agreements come up for renewal during a particular year and strikes occur more frequently than normal. The general public also takes notice when public-service unions go on strike and cause major disruption in services. During such times, the effectiveness of the whole process of collective bargaining is questioned with cries of "there must be a better way," particularly when long strikes affect many innocent people. Let us look at some of the major issues in labour-management relations.

The Adversary Nature of Collective Bargaining

Collective bargaining between labour and management is still considered the best method of sharing the surplus produced by the firm. The strike or threat of it is the weapon to back up the union's demands, while the lockout or loss of jobs is the weapon behind management's attempts to keep the union demands in line. Most labour agreements are settled peacefully. When we look at the period 1967 to 1975, considered a stormy time in Canada's labour scene, almost 80% of all major collective agreements covering 500 or more persons in the private sector, and nearly 90% in the public sector, were concluded without any disruption; half of these did not even require third-party intervention. If smaller bargaining units were included, the percentage of peaceful settlements would be even higher.[11]

Nevertheless, collective bargaining is an adversary process. Unions make their demands and management tries its best to minimize those demands: thus, conflict develops. During good economic times, management will give in to union demands more readily because it does not want to risk a strike. On the other hand, when times are bad, management has the upper hand because it can threaten the union with layoffs or, in extreme cases, with plant closure. Some times both sides simply dig in their heels, particularly on issues that involve basic rights to management or survival for the union. If mediation cannot resolve the issues, a strike or a lockout is the final step.

The Effectiveness of the Strike

An increasing number of people are now convinced that a strike is not the way to resolve issues that cannot be settled in the normal collective bargaining process. Halting production reduces the total amount of wealth available for distribution to both parties. More significantly, it seems that the strike or threat of strikes no longer effectively generates pressure for a settlement. The economic impact of the open-ended strike is lessening because in many instances, the employer can continue to operate; at the same time, alternative economic benefits such as strike pay or benefits, working spouses or employment elsewhere for the duration of the strike, all make settlement less urgent for striking employees.[12]

If the strike is out of date from an economic point of view, it is used by workers for other reasons. Some employees take strike action for ideological reasons; others regard it simply as a break in routine. Some experts believe that considerable study and research should be done to learn more about the modern strike before considering any alternatives.[13]

Labour Disputes in Canada

Canadians have been accused in the past of having an unsettled labour scene. For example, in 1977 Canada shared first place with Italy with the greatest total number of workdays lost among the reporting industrialized countries.[14] One reason the number of working days lost in Canada is high is that when strikes occur in North America, on average they last much longer than those in most other industrialized countries. In Italy, for example, general strikes involving many workers occur much more frequently than in North America.

Compulsory Arbitration

Regardless of the cost of a strike, it is really the main weapon available to labour to back up its demands. While compulsory arbitration has been cited as an alternative to strike action, it is often an unacceptable alternative for both unions and management. In many cases it compromises on what labour and management have been unable to resolve themselves. Both sides may entrench themselves in extreme positions, knowing that compulsory arbitration is likely to bring a settlement in the middle. And some of the pressure to resolve disputes is relieved when an outside party works out a solution. While some argue that compulsory arbitration has a place in labour-management relations, other methods must also be found.

Labour in the Boardroom

A possible solution to present problems in labour-management relations is to allow labour more involvement in industrial development by granting workers a larger part in major management decisions, particularly those that affect their jobs and working conditions. The practice known as **mitbestimmung** — roughly translated, "joint decision-making" — has been successfully tried in West Germany. However, a fundamental change in management's attitude toward labour would be necessary, as management has traditionally claimed the sole right to make decisions. Labour in both the United States and Canada has also been reluctant to become more involved in management decision-making. Since unions would be required to show more restraint in their contract demands and more responsibility for the successful operation of the firm, leaders believe such a move would prevent unions from bargaining effectively for their members.

The first step was taken in 1980, when Douglas A. Fraser, President of the United Auto Workers union, joined the Chrysler board of directors as part of the deal in which workers were to assist the ailing company by deferring wages and other benefits. Chrysler was thus the first major U.S. corporation to allow a labour representative to sit on the board of directors. In 1983, Douglas Fraser was elected to his third one-year term, but there is considerable doubt that the seat would be extended to his successor when Fraser retires, primarily because the new president is viewed as "unwilling to hold hands with management." Some say, therefore, that the bold Swedish-style experiment in labour-management relations may not as yet be generally accepted in the U.S.

According to Fraser, workers have benefited from his position on the board by knowing about plant closings and economic dislocations beforehand so that they can be prepared. In another instance Fraser was able to prevent 119 Chrysler workers in the tank division from losing their seniority rights. From management's point of view, communications between union and management have improved considerably. Nevertheless, the future of the arrangement remains in doubt, as does its long-term benefit for the labour movement. According to another labour leader, this practice has not won widespread acceptance, since one executive on the board cannot change a corporation. If Fraser is the last union executive to sit on the board of directors, even small gains made will not be repeated.[15] However, it may be too early to call the experiment a failure — in the future it may be more accepted and if other countries are any example, the benefits for industrial relations and labour peace could be tremendous.

Sharing Information and Management Credibility

Another potential method of resolving conflicts between labour and management is increased sharing of information between the two factions regarding the firm's financial condition and future plans, especially as they affect the worker.

A survey, conducted by Hay Management Consultants Ltd. of Toronto, questioned employees of about 1900 organizations each year for the past ten years. The results indicated that most employees of better-performing companies feel that senior management is open and frank with them. In general, the survey found that most workers considered their managers credible, even though the believability rate has slipped a little over the past ten years.[16]

Data drawn from the survey compared employees' opinions and corporate performances of 500 firms over the past four years. Employees at all levels in companies that were performing well viewed information from executives as more credible than did those in poorly-performing firms. They were satisfied with the amount of information the company provided to them. On questions about satisfaction with pay, opportunities to learn new skills, how the company is perceived as a place to work, and so on, in each case senior management in the better-performing companies received high marks from their employees.[17]

In contrast, poorly performing companies generally keep their employees in the dark about what is happening with the company. Companies who fail to involve their workers will quickly see the results show up on their financial statements.

The article "Good Credibility is Good Management" seems to underscore the results of the survey. Employees generally feel that they are not involved in decisions that affect their jobs and that management does not communicate with them about the plight of the company. Strikes are not primarily caused by money disputes, as many executives seem to believe, but more by poor communication and the poor credibility thus generated.

Good Credibility is Good Management

Canada's desire to improve its competitive position in world markets will go nowhere if management and labour fail to end the confrontations that have given Canada one of the industrial world's worst records for time lost to strikes. A way for management to bring these confrontations to an end is to improve communications with employees, says Woodruff Imberman, president of Chicago-based industrial relations consultants Imberman & DeForest, which has clients in the U.S. and Canada.

Many executives believe strikes are primarily caused by money disputes. Not so. Every employee wants more money — just as every executive does. Wages and benefits are negotiable. What isn't negotiable is the employee's desire to punish the company for reasons not always apparent to management.

The road to a strike is usually paved with top management's inadequate, and often late, efforts to establish effective two-way communications and the credibility that such programs generate.

Managers must learn early to uncover employee concerns and how to handle them without incurring resentment. If this isn't done, then management credibility will be nonexistent and employee cooperation on quality, productivity and cost containment will be minimal.

Employees typically complain that, "Nobody in management asks us anything or listens.

They just tell us. Why should we accept *their* say-so?"

Most employees want a say in the issues that affect their working lives. They will not take seriously management's concerns about competitiveness in the market, productivity, financial structure, budget, staff costs, research — unless management takes employee problems seriously.

If management is to build credibility so that employees do accept the data and logic proposed by executives and do feel that their future lies with a healthy, prosperous company, it must find out directly from the employees how they feel about their company, their jobs, their working environment, their management and their future — and why.

The only way to do this is through effective and consistent two-way communications over time. This requires management to sit down in face-to-face interviews with groups of employees.

A starting program of two-way communications is modest. It may require some training of interviewers and some training in evaluating employee reactions and comments. These meetings, if handled honestly and adroitly, will provide all the clues to the issues that may be causing employee discontent — and may help avoid a strike, because the employees will have a chance to see things from management's side.

The results will be a big improvement in employee accep-

tance of management's position and acceptance of concession bargaining without labour upheavals.

Managers who use this strategy often gain enormously in credibility — which is the secret of harmonious labour-management relations.

For example, Timken Co., the world's largest tapered roller bearings manufacturer with plants in St. Thomas, Ont., the U.S., Europe and South America, started "Our War on Competition" in 1982. It was a worldwide two-way communications effort designed to obtain comment and generate Timken employee cooperation to meet the challenge of the changing nature of competition.

The company held face-to-face group meetings with employees and obtained thousands of comments, complaints, ideas and suggestions for lowering costs and improving efficiencies.

Timken did this 18 months before contract negotiations were due, so, when steelworker negotiations concluded in late 1983, Timken members in U.S. plants overwhelmingly approved a deeply concessionary contract without a strike, and without rancor. Timken has continued its two-way communications policy since the contract settlement, inviting employee ideas during group meetings with management. The company has put many of these ideas into effect. The result has been a 10% cost reduction.

There are other successful international companies with plants in Canada practicing such methods. Among them: aircraft and auto parts maker Rockwell International of Canada Ltd., processed food maker Kraft Ltd., camera equipment maker Bell & Howell Ltd., Canadian General Electric Co., and Johnson & Johnson Inc.

Two-way communication works, although the strategy may be new to some Canadian companies. However, as David Culver, president of Alcan Aluminium Ltd., says, ''We are prepared to accept that some new methods of managing our economic affairs are urgently needed.''

SOURCE: Woodruff Imberman, ''Good credibility is good management,'' *The Financial Post*, June 27, 1985, p. 37. Reprinted by permission.

NOTES

1. See John Crispo, *The Canadian Industrial Relations System* (Toronto: McGraw-Hill Ryerson Ltd., 1978), pp. 220–29.
2. Brent King, ''Many employees don't know what their firm's benefits are worth,'' *The Financial Post*, Dec. 3, 1983, p.26.
3. See David A. Peach and David Kuechle, *The Practice of Industrial Relations* (Toronto: McGraw-Hill Ryerson Ltd., 1975), Chapter 2. See also Eugene Forsey, ''History of the Labour Movement in Canada,'' in Deutsch et al, eds., *The Canadian Economy: Selected Readings* (Toronto: Macmillan Co. of Canada Ltd., 1962), pp. 106–119.
4. John DeMont, ''CLC seeking peace with Teamsters,'' *The Financial Post*, January 18, 1988, p. 3.
5. See Peach and Kuechle, *op. cit.*, Chapter 3.
6. Crispo, *op. cit.*, pp. 52–5.
7. John DeMont, ''Unions face toughness and dissent,'' *The Financial Post*, December 28, 1987, p. 10.
8. John DeMont, ''Employers hold cards for '88 labor talks,'' *The Financial Post*, January 4, 1988, p. 3.
9. Wilfred List, ''Labour movement unsure about its public image,'' *The Globe and Mail*, Nov. 5, 1979, p. B5.
10. *Ibid.*
11. Roy La Berge, ''Work Stoppages and the Problems of Conflict Duration,'' *The Labour Gazette*, Nov.-Dec. 1978, pp. 498–500.
12. Dave Stockand, ''What does a strike mean?'' *The Vancouver Sun*, Sept. 5, 1979.
13. *Ibid.*
14. ''Canada and Italy head strike table,'' *International Labour Organization (ILO) News*, Dec. 12, 1977.
15. ''A Union Boss on the Board,'' *Maclean's*, May 16, 1983, p. 34.
16. Colin Languedoc, ''Informed workers linked to success,'' *The Financial Post*.
17. *Ibid.*

CHAPTER SUMMARY

Early in the 19th century, workers first attempted to increase their bargaining power with employers by joining together into labour unions aimed at improving their income and working conditions. However, unions could not legally organize until the Trade Union Act was passed in 1872. Thereafter, the union movement experienced tremendous growth, even though economic conditions and internal union disagreements caused periodic disruptions.

A major upheaval occurred in 1935 when the industrial unions in the United States split away from the craft unions to form the Congress of Industrial Organizations; a similar split followed shortly in Canada. Thereafter, the industrial unions in both countries grew rapidly until 1955, when the CIO in the U.S. merged again with the craft unions represented by the American Federation of Labour. Again, a similar merger followed in Canada between the Trades and Labour Congress, acting for the craft unions, and the Canadian Congress of Labour which represented the industrial unions. The merger brought peace to the labour movement and enabled it to concentrate once again on union growth and improving wages and working conditions for members.

Before a union can become the legal bargaining agent for a group of workers it must be certified by the appropriate Labour Relations Board. For certification a majority of the workers must indicate their desire to belong to that particular union. Once certified, the union can begin negotiations with management on issues affecting the workers, such as wages and fringe benefits, working conditions, hours of work, job security and promotion.

If management and the union cannot reach agreement on these issues and establish a contract, then both must go through a process of conciliation and mediation. If this step still does not produce a settlement, the two parties may voluntarily put the unresolved issues to an arbitration board for settlement. If the union and management cannot agree to voluntary arbitration, then the union is free to strike, or management to lockout employees. In some instances, particularly if essential services are involved, a strike or lockout is illegal — all issues are then subject to binding arbitration. The entire collective bargaining process must be carried out according to federal or provincial government labour legislation.

In addition to the strike, unions may resort to picketing and boycotts; they are also making increasing use of their financial influence to gain concessions. Management for its part is turning to employer associations for industry-wide bargaining.

With the unionization of public employees, union growth has once again stabilized and future growth will come from organizing agricultural and white-collar workers. Unions today are often accused of having too much power and of using it unwisely; calls for limiting union power and curtailing their ability to strike are not uncommon.

Although collective bargaining is still considered an effective method of distributing a firm's surplus between owners and labour, there is concern that the strike is becoming outmoded, and that alternative methods must be found to settle union-management differences. Perhaps more sharing of information between management and labour will improve the relationship: labour would then have a better understanding of the financial situation of the firm and the problems facing it.

KEY TERMS

Labour union	Lockout
Craft union	Injunction
Industrial union	Employers' association
Certification	Closed shop
Collective bargaining	Union shop
Bargaining in good faith	Agency shop
Conciliation	Preferential hiring
Mediation	Dues check-off
Voluntary arbitration	Cost of living allowance (COLA)
Binding arbitration	Featherbedding
Grievance	Canadian Labour Congress (CLC)
Strike	Labour Relations Boards
Wildcat strike	Canada Labour Code
Picketing	*Mitbestimmung* (Co-determination)
Boycott	

REVIEW QUESTIONS

1. Describe the aims of labour and those of management.
2. What is a labour union? Explain the difference between a craft union and an industrial union.
3. Explain the steps in the union process: certification, collective bargaining, conciliation, mediation, arbitration and grievance.
4. List and describe the weapons at the disposal of labour and management, respectively, to back up their demands.
5. Why is the strike weapon important to unions?
6. Briefly describe the four major issues in collective bargaining. Why are they important?
7. Briefly outline the history of the labour movement in Canada.
8. What is the purpose of the CLC?
9. Briefly outline the major federal labour legislation.
10. What are the advantages of labour relations boards compared to labour courts?

11. Why is collective bargaining described as an adversary process?

12. Why is the strike no longer considered to be an effective weapon in settling disputes?

13. How could a union representative on the board help in union-management relations? Why has management in North America not accepted union representation on the board of directors?

14. How can better sharing of information between management and labour improve relations? What does the article "Good credibility is good management" suggest that management has to do to increase its credibility with its employees?

DISCUSSION QUESTIONS

1. Discuss the following issue: "Should government employees be allowed to strike?".

2. What would be the repercussions if lower and middle managers belonged to unions?

3. Discuss both sides of the issue: "Unions have become too powerful."

4. Will labour unions always be necessary? Explain.

5. Is the collective bargaining process the best method available for labour to ensure its share of the economic pie? Explain.

CASE 11–1 What Do I Give? — What Do I Keep?

"Oh the sad lot of the independent businessman," thought Jean Festinger. "Sure the money was good, but dealing with employees on a day-to-day basis could sure be a pain."

Jean owned and managed a mid-sized custom printing operation. Life had been good to Jean, and the business had grown and prospered. Jean knew that he had to keep hustling for contracts, however, because the larger he grew, the higher his overhead and the greater his responsibilities. Now 75 employees and their families depended upon him for their livelihood — and you'd think he was Attila the Hun by the way they acted sometimes!

Take last Monday, for example. Jean had returned to the plant in an upbeat mood, as he was almost certain of getting the *Rare Earth* magazine contract. He had been greeted at the door by a delegation of employees demanding that Charley Greene be fired. Now Charley was one of Jean's original employees, who had been promoted to shop foreman. Sure he threw his weight around a bit and yelled a lot, but Jean

---

owed him a great deal. What was he to do? Finally, a compromise had been reached and Charley was banished to the shipping and receiving area, still with the foreman's title and salary, but with little real authority.

And yesterday. . . . Yesterday another group had come to him and demanded changes in working hours and in vacation time. You can guess which they wanted to shorten and which they wanted to lengthen. Hell! He hadn't taken a holiday in five years! By the way they talked, you would think he was the worst employer in the world! Jean had "put his foot down" this time. "No way," he declared. "You get as good or better as any other print shop around here. I can't remain competitive if I start giving the business away!"

Now there were mutterings about joining a union. Some employees were saying that he was insensitive to their grievances — that he wouldn't listen. What was he to do? How far do you give in to employee demands? Should he put the entire business at risk? He couldn't afford to raise his costs any further, yet he couldn't afford labour unrest either, especially with the *Rare Earth* contract so close!

SOURCE: Written by Dr. P.C. Wright, Business Division, Humber College, Toronto, Ontario. Reprinted by permission of the author.

QUESTIONS

1. How should Jean handle his employees' threats to join a union?
2. If Jean really can't afford to spend more on vacations and other benefits, what should he do?
3. How far should a businessman like Jean bend when faced with employee demands?
4. Was Jean really insensitive? Discuss.
5. What approach should Jean take if a union really did attempt to organize his company?

CASE 11–2 Ending a Bitter Strike

During the 18-day illegal nurses' strike in Alberta, a committee met each morning at the Calgary Foothills Hospital to make life-and-death decisions. The strike, which began on Jan. 25, forced the 1000-bed hospital to reduce surgery to 13 operations each day from roughly 100. The hospital performed emergency operations as usual but it postponed urgent surgery for more than 200 patients. "These are war conditions," said Dr. Robert McMurtry, Foothills' head of surgery, during the walk-out. By the time the nurses reached an agreement with the Alberta Hospitals Association and voted 5237 to 1118 on Feb. 12 to return to work, one hospital had transferred patients to another province because it could not care for them, and another was investigating whether or not certain deaths occurred because patients did not receive proper treatment. The strike had quickly reduced hospitals to providing only emergency care. But by this week, with the Olympic Winter Games in full swing, fully staffed hospitals were expected to be treating the backlog of surgery and readmitting patients.

The walkout by nurses was, they said, as much an angry statement against Alberta's restrictive labor laws as it was a bargaining tool for better wages and increased benefits. Nurses — like firefighters, police and almost all public servants — are prohibited by Alberta law from striking. But on Jan. 25, after three months of negotiations, the 11 400-member United Nurses of Alberta braved −30°C weather and criminal charges as they began to picket hospitals, claiming that not having the right to strike had prevented them from reaching an agreement. As the strike dragged on, critics warned that the government should re-examine the labor laws. Said Donald Macgregor, president of the Alberta Hospital Association: "When a law results in this much frustration developing in a particular group, the legislature should consider some changes. I think the law worked against the interests of everybody involved."

Clearly, the strike had its gravest repercussions for seriously ill people in Alberta. Just hours before the tentative agreement was reached on Thursday evening, the Calgary General Hospital flew three critically ill patients to two hospitals in British Columbia after the union refused to staff the intensive-care unit. The president of Foothills Hospital, Ralph Coombs, is investigating seven deaths "which, under normal circumstances, may have been preventable."

Ultimately, pressure from the provincial government, eager to host the Olympics without an unsettling labor dispute clouding the event, helped bring about the settlement. Premier Don Getty intervened on Thursday when he learned that all the issues had been settled except for one: the hospital association was demanding the right to halt automatic union dues deductions from nurses' paychecks for six months, which is possible under the Labour Relations Act — a move that could have bankrupted the union. Getty asked Hospitals Minister Marvin Moore to instruct the association — which negotiates on behalf of the hospitals, which are funded by the government — to expedite an agreement. That evening the two sides reached a tentative settlement, which gave the nurses wage increases of up to 10.9 per cent over 27 months and improved some benefits. The average nurse's salary would move to $30 000 per year.

At the last moment the association withdrew an amnesty clause that would have allowed more than 80 nurses, who had been fired for walking out, to return to work. Civil contempt charges against 62 individual nurses resulted in fines ranging from $250 to $500 for disobeying back-to-work legislation. The union paid a $250 000 fine for a criminal contempt conviction and is fighting a second charge. But it said that it wanted the amnesty clause back before a ratification vote this week.

While the nurses claimed the settlement was a victory, many were also bitter that they had had to stage an illegal walkout to win a contract. In turn, government members complained that the nurses had not spoken out about their problems with the health care system. "We weren't as politically active as we should have been," said Kathy James, president of the union local at Foothills Hospital. She said that many locals were already planning committees that would report nurses' concerns. "We still have empty hospitals; they're still misspending the money in the health care system," said James. "From now on we aren't going to wait for negotiations to come around before we talk about these things." While Olympic officials — who had feared a health crisis would spoil their Games — applauded the nurses' return last week, some health professionals predicted that the labor peace might not outlast the goodwill engineered by the Games.

SOURCE: Cindy Barrett, with Mary Nemeth, "Ending a bitter strike," *Maclean's*, February 22, 1988, p. 26.

QUESTIONS

1. Do you think that government employees, or people working in essential services, such as nurses, should have the right to strike? Why or why not?

2. If the right to strike is taken away from essential-service workers, what power do these unions have to force employers to bargain in good faith?

3. If essential-service workers are not allowed to strike, how can they ensure that their members have proper wage settlements, working conditions, and job security?

4. Some of the nurses were bitter that they had to stage an illegal strike to win a contract, while the government members complained that the nurses had not spoken out earlier about their problems with the health care system? This implies that workers have a responsibility to make their complaints known. Do you agree?

5. What do you suggest could prevent these types of strikes from occurring in the future?

CASE 11–3 Nationalism Takes Off in De Havilland Dispute

To understand the current strike-bound circumstances of de Havilland Aircraft Company of Canada, the best place to start is not the boardroom, or the union hall, but the parking lot.

It is truly an atrocious parking lot. When the assembly workers' day shift leaves the northwest Toronto plant at 4:15 p.m., the brotherhood of labor crumbles in a pellmell rush. Drivers shun the inadequate exits and spill out over the curbs several cars abreast. The exit and nonexit users convene in unimaginable bottlenecks, with no quarter given.

The parking lot is to be changed to suit the work force better. Meanwhile, the 76% of the work force that is unionized is manning the picket lines because management wants to change them to suit the business better.

Among management's many proposals is that overtime be made compulsory, not optional. It wants to combine job classifications to reduce specialization, which the company says frustrates smooth production. A single employee, de Havilland says, should be able to tackle a final assembly chore alone without having to call in a different skill classification to perform one simple aspect. The ability of afternoon shift workers to compress their work week into four days, giving themselves perpetual three-day weekends through 10-hour days, would be eliminated. In exchange the company has offered a $3000 ratification bonus, improved benefits, and 3%-3.5% raises in years two and three of the contract.

The Canadian Auto Workers Union fears if the company gets its way, there will be fewer cars trying to get out of the parking lot. It has called the company's proposal an assault on Canadian nationalism by U.S. labor relation standards. The parent firm, Boeing Co. of Seattle, Wash., calls it simply building airplanes.

"Nationalism has nothing to do with it," says Boeing spokesman Craig Martin, who has taken up residence in a Toronto hotel. "And nationalism has nothing to do with selling aircraft in an international market. The changes are not being imported from Seattle. They have been suggested by de Havilland. By Canadian supervisors in a Canadian plant."

There isn't anything precedent-setting in the company's proposals, says Martin, echoing de Havilland spokesman Colin Fisher's assertion that management's demands for less restrictive work rules can be found in existing CAW contracts elsewhere in the Canadian aerospace industry.

The high-flying world of airplane sales is free trade at its most visceral. Parts subcontractors, consortiums and clients span continents, oceans, languages and labor codes. When you're flogging aircraft to buyers in Bonn and Burundi to whom production costs are irrelevant, management argues, the union concept of job security has to go. "We think job security is gained when a plane competes in the marketplace," says Fisher. "The CAW believes that job security lies in rigid work rules."

The labor concern is that, without those rules, it will be all too easy for de Havilland to slash employment and use the savings to build cheaper planes.

De Havilland's bread-and-butter product, the twin-prop Dash 8 commuter plane, is a market success under competitive pressures from such international rivals as the SS-340 from Sweden's Saab-Scania and the ATR 42 from the French-Italian consortium Aerospatiale.

Since acquiring de Havilland from the federal government in early 1986, Boeing has made no secret of its displeasure with the performance of its new subsidiary. De Havilland has built more than 70 Dash 8s, and has a backlog of 62 orders. However, says Martin, "they're not delivering on time and they're not delivering at a cost that allows competitive pricing."

De Havilland employs 5400 people. Its 4100 striking union employees are divided into two CAW locals — local 112, which represents 3500 plant workers, and local 673, which represents 600 office workers and clerical staff. Given that 98% of the plant workers voted to strike; given that this stand-off represents the first test of wills between the de Havilland work force and the new owner; and given that in 1978 de Havilland workers, who have never shied from walking out, stayed off the job for four crippling months, Boeing and de Havilland could be in for a long summer.

SOURCE: Doug Hunter, "Nationalism takes off in de Havilland dispute," *The Financial Post*, June 29, 1987, p. 1.

QUESTIONS

1. Is there in fact a relationship between "nationalism," as the union claims, and the action of the company? Explain.
2. What does the union want to achieve? What does the company want to achieve?
3. What might be a possible solution to this union-management confrontation?
4. Which side is more correct: The company that believes that job security is gained when a plane competes in the marketplace; or the union that believes that job security lies in establishing rigid work rules that the company must follow? Discuss.

CHAPTER 12

Business and and Government

Air Canada

CHAPTER OUTLINE

CHAPTER PREVIEW

In Chapter 12 we consider the relationship between government and business. We examine how the federal government has influenced Canadian economic development by promoting business, while it has at the same time established legislation, rules and regulations to control business. How government finances its operation through taxation, the types of taxes used, and fiscal and monetary policy, are also discussed. We close by examining the growth of government, including its financial deficits and its effect on the national debt and on individuals, and speculate about the future relationship between business and government. We also introduce the concept of industrial strategy and consider whether Canada should develop such a strategy.

LEARNING OBJECTIVES

After reading this chapter you should be able to explain:

1. Why government believes it should help to promote business and economic activity in Canada;
2. How tariff and non-tariff barriers to international trade help to promote business;
3. Why the various levels of government provide incentives for both industrial and natural resource development;
4. Some of the major services provided by government to assist business;
5. The reasons for competition legislation and some of the provisions of the Competition Act of 1986;
6. Some of the controls imposed on retailers and the consumer protection provided;
7. The provisions in the National Transportation Act of 1988 that will help to deregulate the transportation industry;
8. Why deregulation has become such an important objective of federal and provincial governments;
9. Why communications are under government control, and what the CRTC controls;
10. Why and how public utilities are controlled;
11. Why Crown corporations are established, and why there is now a determined move to privatize government-owned business and Crown corporations;
12. Why foreign investment was controlled in the past and how the mandate has changed for Investment Canada;
13. Some of the major taxes levied by government to finance its operation;
14. The meaning of fiscal policy and how it can be used to stabilize economic activity;
15. The role of the Bank of Canada, the meaning of monetary policy and how it can be used to stabilize economic activity;
16. How government has grown, and the effect of its growth on business and private individuals;

17. The meaning of industrial strategy and how it might help Canada in its industrial development.

Two hundred years ago, Adam Smith described the capitalist business system in his book *The Wealth of Nations*. As noted in Chapter 2, a key force in the system as Smith saw it was the individual. Individuals have a number of basic needs and desires they strive to satisfy. According to Smith, this satisfaction of individual needs does not result in chaos, as might be expected, but enhances the welfare of society through the invisible action of the "market." By the force of competition, the market ensures the orderly distribution and allocation of resources among individuals.

In a market system, the role of government is limited to one of support. It should provide a system of currency, law and order, and protect the country from foreign attack. Any other government involvement, according to Smith, would result in a breakdown of the system because it would disrupt the orderly workings of the market.

Smith's concept of the market system and advocacy of nonintervention by government received wide support, because the system worked well, especially in North America. Here, businesses were relatively small and communities were isolated; large business corporations and big labour unions did not exist. Thus, no single person or group could significantly influence wages, the supply of labour or the prices of goods produced.

However, as business firms became giant corporations and labour unions grew powerful, government was forced to reassess its role. Gradually it became more involved in the economy, providing legislation to regulate business conduct and protect individuals in society. Since the Great Depression of the 1930s, the governments of most capitalistic countries have taken an active role in the general management of the economy by controlling business cycles and managing the money supply. Government has also paid particular attention to the welfare of individuals by providing benefits for people who are ill, out of work, or unable to care for themselves.

It is the relationship between government and business in Canada that we want to examine more closely in this chapter, taking particular note of how government promotes business while simultaneously controlling and regulating it.

GOVERNMENT INVOLVEMENT IN THE CANADIAN ECONOMY: A HISTORICAL PERSPECTIVE

As we saw in Chapter 2, cooperation between business and government began early in Canada's history with the building of the Canadian Pacific Railway. The railroad, which was to link western Canada to the east, was made a virtual condition of Confederation by many provinces. Improved transportation was required to provide Canada's widely distributed population with necessary manufactured goods, and to move natural resources from the interior of the country to the seaports for export. Another major reason for the building of the railroad was the fear that without it U.S. settlers might eventually take over the sparsely populated west.

The building of the railroad required capital, which was not readily available in Canada. Financing came from English and American investors for the most part, with the Canadian government guaranteeing many of the loans. The government also granted the CPR approximately 10 million hectares of land and $25 million, as well as those sections of railroad in the east-west link that it had already built.

Although the building of the CPR created a massive national debt, many believed that it would strengthen east-west ties within Canada and thus counteract the strong social and economic link between Canada and the United States. In an effort to strengthen the east-west bond further, in the 1870s the government imposed tariffs on American goods, forcing Canadians to buy goods manufactured in eastern Canada, where industry was starting to become established. The prices of manufactured goods for western Canadians thus increased significantly because of the smaller market available to Canadian industry and the monopolistic freight rates established by railroads that transported goods west from Ontario.

Since Confederation the Canadian government has sought to even out regional economic differences with subsidies to the poorer provinces and regions. In the last half-century it has established various agencies to foster economic development, and has provided grants and loans to finance businesses that might otherwise have difficulty raising capital. The federal government has also invested in commercial enterprises and joint ventures to provide services that private firms might be hesitant to provide because of the widely distributed population and the poor prospects for profit.

Thus the federal government has been heavily involved in business and economic development throughout Canada's history. We now consider the various ways in which government has promoted and controlled business in Canada.

GOVERNMENT PROMOTION OF BUSINESS

Initially, the federal government promoted business by protecting it from foreign competition through tariff and non-tariff barriers. Incentives for industrial and resource development have also played a major role, together with services including business loans, statistical information, and the granting of copyrights, patents and trademarks.

Protection from Foreign Competition

Throughout Canada's history the federal government has protected businesses by imposing tariff and non-tariff barriers on goods imported from other countries. These measures were designed to ease pressure on domestic producers by making goods from other countries as expensive to Canadians as those produced domestically. In some instances, however, imports have been severely restricted in quantity and some have been completely banned. The various tariff and non-tariff barriers are examined below.

Tariff Barriers to Trade

A **tariff** is a special tax on imported goods, designed to make their prices equal to those charged for similar domestic goods. However, the use of tariffs is controversial. While some believe that the government has a duty to protect newly established industries within the country from foreign competition, others point out that tariffs tend to remain long after the business or industry is established, while the lack of foreign competition may result in either high prices or poor quality — or both — for domestic goods.

Others, following 19th-century economist David Ricardo, believe that tariffs create industries or manufacturing activities that would not be established if foreign goods were allowed into the country tariff-free. In other words, the artificially high prices charged for some foreign goods because of tariffs lead some entrepreneurs to seek easy profits by producing these goods domestically — in the process using financial and other resources that might be better used to produce goods that cannot be imported.

Nevertheless, tariffs have been widely used by most countries in the past and are in use today. Most of Canada's industrial development can be attributed to protectionism through the tariffs imposed in 1879 by Sir John A. Macdonald's **National Policy**. For 60 years afterwards, the use of tariffs was frequently debated in Parliament. Free trade was often proposed, especially with the U.S., yet no substantial reductions in tariffs were made during that period. In fact, the protection of industry through tariffs increased after 1930, as a worldwide trend to protectionism spread even though most countries realized that in the end they gained no advantage from this action. As one country raised tariff barriers, so did another, and countries such as Canada were particularly hurt since they relied on world markets to sell their raw materials.

Today, significant moves have been made to reduce tariffs on a worldwide basis, primarily through the **General Agreement on Tariffs and Trade (GATT)** signed by a large number of countries in 1947. We discuss GATT in more detail in the next chapter.

Non-Tariff Barriers to Trade

Tariffs are not the only means used by the federal government to protect domestic industry from foreign competition. A variety of **non-tariff barriers** are also employed, including quantity restrictions on imports, selective use of government purchasing power, and subsidies to Canadian manufacturers for producing goods that might otherwise be imported.[1]

Quantity restrictions on imports, or **import quotas**, are a favourite tool of government for two reasons. First, their effect is immediate, as only a limited quantity of products is allowed into the country. Tariffs, on the other hand, only raise the price of the product, and anyone who prefers the imported product to a similar domestic product may continue to buy the former even at the higher price. Second, it is easier to apply import quotas selectively, against particular exporting countries; they are therefore more flexible than tariffs from an administrative point of view.

Import quotas have been applied on textiles, shoes, Japanese automobiles and some agricultural products. The quotas, however, may cause shortages since the supply of imports is limited and domestic manufacturers often cannot expand their productive capacity quickly enough to meet the increased demand. As a result, prices rise and consumers suffer both from higher prices and a shortage of the product they want to buy. Even if domestic manufacturers increase production, they may not provide the product, quality or style that consumers want.

Another method of protecting specific industries is through the **selective use of government suppliers**. As the largest single purchaser of goods and services from the private sector, the federal government can give its business to Canadian firms rather than foreign-owned or controlled companies, or to particular regions and businesses that may require economic stimulus. When the government uses this method to aid businesses or industries, the prices it pays for the products or services are not a prime consideration.

A third method of protection is **direct aid**. The federal government may provide **production subsidies** to domestic industries that have difficulty competing with imported goods. It may also provide **temporary employment support programs** to industries facing decreased sales when foreign countries impose tariffs on their products. Finally, the government may provide **temporary adjustment assistance** to domestic industries that face lower sales following the elimination of tariffs on competing imports.

Industrial Development Incentives

The objective of the **Department of Regional Industrial Expansion (DRIE)** is to increase overall industrial, commercial and tourism activity in all parts of Canada, and thus also reduce economic disparity across the country. The core program of DRIE is the Industrial and Regional Development Program (IRDP) designed to promote industrial and regional development. IRDP provides a range of financial support to businesses based on four basic elements:

1. innovation
2. establishment
3. modernization/expansion
4. marketing

Because IRDP is flexible, assistance can be tailored to the nature of the project, the need for support, and the particular circumstances of the applicant. Assistance is based on particular targeted areas across Canada that are economically depressed. The department has a development index based on census data and an objective and equitable statistical method of determining which regions of Canada are most in need of support.

There are four tiers of assistance. Tier I represents a basic national-level support. Tiers II, III and IV provide progressively more assistance. To address special short-term economic downturns in a Tier I region, the program provides for one year of Tier II assistance for the modernization/expansion elements. Special criteria exist to determine when a special Tier I can come into effect. Figure 12.1 shows the various eligible projects and the tier support provided for the first element listed above, innovation.

DRIE is the result of a 1983 merger with the Department of Industry, Trade and Commerce (IT&C) and the Department of Regional Economic Expansion (DREE). The merger has resulted in a highly decentralized department with a strong core of knowledge and expertise in manufacturing, processing and service sectors of the Canadian economy. DRIE also offers many other programs, a few of which are listed below:

Business Improvement Loans program under the Small Business Loans Act assists new and existing small business enterprises to obtain intermediate-term loans to help finance specified fixed asset needs.

Business Opportunities Sourcing System (BOSS) is an authoritative data base on Canadian companies, their products and the markets they serve.

Cape Breton Development Corporation (DEVCO) aims to promote and assist the financing and development of industry on Cape Breton Island; to provide employment outside the coal-producing industry and broaden the base of the economy of the Island; and to contribute to the rehabilitation and modernization of mines in the Sydney coal field.

Defence Industry Productivity Program (DIPP) is designed to enhance economic growth through the promotion of viable defence or defence related exports; to provide a defence industrial base; and to maintain a defence technological capability.

Native Economic Development Program assists native people in the development of economic self-reliance.

Small Business Office provides general information and help with problems relating to government regulations, paperburden, and red tape. A call to the "Hotline" will get information or help in overcoming a particular difficulty. The office also provides help in how to establish a business and provides information on programs and services offered by provincial and municipal governments, associations, small business groups, etc.

Special ARDA (Agricultural and Rural Development Act) is designed to assist residents of remote and northern areas (in particular those of native ancestry) to improve their economic circumstances.

Tourism Canada: Information provides a number of useful services that help to ensure the continued success of Canada's tourism industry.

SOURCE: Adapted from *ABC Assistance to Business in Canada*, Federal Business Development Bank, 1987. Ottawa: The Minister of Supply and Services Canada.

Provincial and municipal governments are also active in their efforts to create new employment opportunities by offering incentives for industry to locate in their areas. Municipal governments may provide property tax incentives or establish low-cost industrial parks in order to attract industry to their jurisdictions. To encourage the establishment of large-scale industry, a provincial government may provide either special tax incentives or outright grants.

Every province has some government agency or ministry to foster economic development. Nova Scotia, for example, established Industrial Estates Ltd. (IEL) in 1957 to encourage expansion in the private sector by providing loans for new ventures, and even taking part-ownership in new or expanding companies. Similarly, the British Columbia government has established a number of programs to assist businesses establishing in B.C. For example, the B.C. Enterprise Corporation provides financial assistance to manufacturing and processing businesses wishing to expand existing operations or create new economic activity within the province. The Ministry of Economic Development provides a host of programs to facilitate the expansion and diversification of the province's industrial base and support the development of independently owned businesses. Other

Element: *Innovation*

To encourage the development of new products, new processes and to increase industrial productivity and international competitiveness through support of research and development projects which show promise of economic success or strategic importance to a region and which would not be undertaken without support.

Eligible Projects	*Tier I and Special Tier I*	*Maximum Level of Assistance*		
		Tier II	*Tier III*	*Tier IV*
a) **Studies** — Assistance may be made available toward the cost of hiring qualified consultants for studies on project feasibility, technology transfer, market research and venture capital search associated with prospective innovation projects.	33.3%	40%	50%	50%
b) **Developing New Products or Processes** — Assistance may be provided for projects to develop or demonstrate new or improved products or processes including pollution control. These must be scientifically feasible, entail significant technical risk and represent attractive prospects for commercial exploitation.	33.3%	40%	50%	50%
c) **Developing Technological Capability** — Projects for the improvement or expansion of technological capability which do not lead directly to identifiable sales may be supported if the technological capability is of strategic importance to the firm and the regional industrial development priorities of the government.	33.3%	40%	50%	50%
d) **Development and Demonstration** — Projects to develop or demonstrate new products or processes, but which *do not* entail significant technological risk may be supported in a way similar to those in section b) above. However, this assistance will be repayable upon successful commercial exploitation of the resulting product or process.	33.3%	40%	50%	50%
e) **Design** — Assistance may be made available for the design of a new, durable product, capable of being mass produced, that offers good prospects for commercial exploitation.	33.3%	40%	50%	50%

SOURCE: *Industrial and Regional Development Program* (Ottawa: Government of Canada, Regional Industrial Expansion, Nov. 1984).

Figure 12.1   Industrial and regional development program assistance for innovation

provinces have departments and agencies that provide similar services. These are the Ontario Ministry of Industry, Trade and Technology, the Prince Edward Island Development Agency, Société de développement industriel, the Manitoba Department of Business Development and Tourism, the Saskatchewan Economic Development and Trade Department, and the Alberta Opportunity Co., a Crown agency.

Agriculture and Natural Resource Development Incentives

The importance of natural resources to Canada's economy makes agriculture and natural resource development prime candidates for government aid programs. Programs to help agriculture range from support for 4-H clubs to agricultural product marketing, from financial assistance to farmers to race track supervision and the promotion and financing of farm fairs.

The mining industry has also received incentives through specific tax provisions, depletion allowances, and the opportunity to write off exploration and development costs rapidly. In the past the government has protected the petroleum and natural gas industry from foreign competition and helped to open the U.S. market to domestic producers, in addition to providing various tax incentives. To meet the objectives of the now defunct **NEP (National Energy Program**) the federal government gave grants under the **Petroleum Incentive Program (PIP)** to Canadian-owned oil companies to help defray costs in drilling for oil in hostile environments such as the arctic and offshore regions.

To focus on natural resources, the federal government has established the Department of Energy, Mines and Resources, which has two main programs. The Energy program recommends, coordinates and implements energy policies and programs for the development, production, transportation and processing of resources, as well as their conservation and use. The second program, called the Minerals and Earth Sciences program, develops mineral policies and strategies, assesses the structure and properties of Canada's land mass, and is involved in surveying and mapping.

Other Federal Government Assistance

The federal government has a number of departments and many agencies that provide a wide variety of services to consumers and businesses. A good source of the programs and services available is the *Handbook of Business Assistance Programs* (*ABC* for short), published by the Federal Business Development Bank. Let us look at a few of the federal departments for a brief overview of their services and assistance.

The Department of Consumer and Corporate Affairs

When the Department of Consumer and Corporate Affairs was created in 1967 its purpose was to bring together a number of related laws designed to help consumers and business function better in the Canadian marketplace. Its primary mandate was to promote competition in Canada's market system and protect the interest of consumers. Through legislation and regulation, it attempts to balance the interests of consumers and business.

The Department consists of four bureaus:

1. **The Bureau of Competition Policy** enforces rules that govern and promote policies that improve the efficiency and fairness of a competitive and dynamic Canadian marketplace. This is accomplished primarily through Canada's competition legislation.

2. **The Bureau of Consumer Affairs** attempts to provide a fair, orderly and safe marketplace for both traders and consumers. In consultation with various other departments and private agencies its voluntary programs attempt to protect the consumer by ensuring that goods are identified accurately, and measured fairly. It also ensures that inherently dangerous products are identified and those that can cause injury or death are under certain circumstances removed from the marketplace.

3. **The Bureau of Corporate Affairs** provides a regulatory framework for the business community in Canada. It helps to ensure the orderly conduct of business in Canada, encourages economic development and promotes creativity, innovation and the exploitation of new technology. The Bureau consists of the Bankruptcy Branch, the Corporations Branch, and the Intellectual Property Directorate, which comprises the Patent Office, the Trade Marks Office, and the Copyright and Industrial Designs Office. There are several key pieces of legislation administered by the bureau. For example, the Canada Business Corporations Act governs all federal business corporations and provides a format for good corporate administration and for protecting the investor.

4. The activities of the **Bureau of Policy Coordination** include legislative review and reform, research, policy analysis and proposals, strategic and corporate planning, interdepartmental, federal-provincial and international relations, program evaluation, and communication.

Industrial designs allow the manufacturer to register the outward appearance of an article of manufacture. This registration gives the owner sole rights to use the design in Canada for a period of five years, further renewable for another five-year period.

Copyrights give the creator of literary, artistic, musical and other intellectual works exclusive rights to sell, copy or otherwise dispose of their works during their lifetime and for fifty years thereafter. Copyright in Canada is automatic, but should be formalized as soon as possible. The copyright sign, ©, should appear on the work.

Trademarks refer to words, names or symbols which distinguish the product or service of one manufacturer from another. If trademarks are properly registered and renewed periodically, they belong to the original owner forever.

Patents are issued to protect individuals or companies that have discovered new processes, or developed new machines or substantially improved existing ones, often accomplished only after investing large amounts of time or money or both. Patents are designed to reward the discoverers or inventors by granting them a time period of seventeen years to use, sell or collect royalties from the invention. After that period, however, other firms or individuals may use the invention as they desire.

SOURCE: Consumer and Corporate Affairs, *Annual Report 1987*. Minister of Supply and Services Canada. Reproduced by permission of the Minister of Supply and Services Canada.

Statistics Canada

Statistics Canada, under the Department of Supply and Services, gathers information and statistics on all aspects of Canada's population and economic life, and makes the data available to businesses free of charge or at a nominal cost. It has advisory services staff in centres across Canada who offer statistical consultative services and business-oriented seminars.

Canada Employment and Immigration Commission

The Canada Employment and Immigration Commission provides a variety of programs to encourage the unemployed to find work. It provides public works projects for temporary employment, helps employers hire people who have faced severe difficulties in finding work, encourages and assists foreign entrepreneurs to establish businesses in Canada, operates a host of training programs for workers, and also provides counselling services for employees experiencing problems because of technological change.

Labour Canada

Labour Canada provides mediation and conciliation services for unions and employers engaged in collective bargaining. The department also collects, processes and analyzes data on labour-related matters for use by both business and the public and provides financial assistance for labour education. In addition, it handles the **Women's Bureau, Occupational Health and Safety Program**, and **Employment Relations and Conditions of Work**.

The Federal Business Development Bank

Established in 1944, the Industrial Development Bank became the **Federal Business Development Bank (FBDB)** in 1975. FBDB is a Crown corporation set up to promote and assist most types of businesses in Canada at various stages in their development. It pays particular attention to small and medium-size businesses.

FBDB offers three principal services to Canada's business community: **financial services** (loans, loan guarantees and financial planning), **investment banking**, and **management services** such as counselling, training and information. It complements the services offered by private financial institutions by providing worthwhile projects with funding that might not be available elsewhere on reasonable terms and conditions.

FBDB is also prepared to provide equity financing by purchasing shares if that is required by the nature of the business. However, the Bank's policy is to remain a minority shareholder. Its prime goal in this situation is to increase the amount of risk capital available to small and medium-size businesses by using its own capital or serving as a catalyst to attract more equity financing from the private sector. Equity investment might be necessary for companies with high growth potential but little access to capital markets.

The function of FBDB's management services is to provide the most complete source of business counselling, training and information for small and medium-size businesses in Canada. Through **CASE — Counselling Assistance to Small Enterprises** — some 1500 retired businesspeople counsel firms in all areas of business management, including bookkeeping, marketing, production and personnel. Case counsellors have helped over 70 000 businesses avoid difficulty and improve profitability. Other services provided include business management seminars, individualized clinics on business problems, owner-manager courses, information services, and special publications such as the *Minding Your Own Business* series.

The Bank has been a prime source of business information since its beginning. At first it was provided informally. In the mid-1970s the **Small Business Information Service (SBIS)** began to provide information or advice about federal, provincial and municipal programs and services. Anyone could obtain the information — MPs, industrialists, company officials, investors, foreign business persons, the general public and even other civil servants. Today, an information database known as **AIM (Automated Information for Management)** is maintained by the FBDB to meet the needs of small and medium-sized businesses. It contains information on federal, provincial and municipal government assistance programs for business, information sources and business opportunities. The information is stored in microcomputers and is easily retrieved through software developed by the Bank.

GOVERNMENT CONTROL OF BUSINESS

The concept of government control and regulation of business appears to be at odds with a private enterprise economy such as Canada's. According to the traditional theory, the force of competition alone should ensure that quality goods are available at the lowest possible price and in adequate supply. Competition generally works well when a number of firms produce a similar product or service. When that is not the case, however, some businesses could restrict output, charge higher prices or let the quality of the products and services deteriorate, in order to make a higher profit.

For example, services such as transportation, utilities and telephones in Canada are often provided by only a single firm — first, because of the tremendous capital investment required, and second, because inconvenience and cost to the customer would both increase if these services were provided by a number of competing firms. Under these circumstances, nothing would prevent a private firm from charging excessive rates or allowing its service to deteriorate if government did not exercise some control over service and rates.

The alternative is for government to establish and operate a firm that provides a required service or product. When this happens a Crown corporation is usually established, such as Ontario Hydro or Alberta Government Telephones. If the government believes there is not enough competition, or some areas are not served as they should be, it can establish a competing service. For example, Canadian National Railway competes with Canadian Pacific Railway, and Air Canada competes with Canadian Airlines. Sometimes, government is required to be a partner with one or more private firms because of the cost of the venture and the expectation of low profit. For example, various provincial governments and private firms created Syncrude Canada Ltd., a joint venture to develop Alberta's tar sands. In the following section we will discuss government control of business in more detail.

Regulation of Competition

Without competition, businesses have little incentive to produce goods and services at the lowest possible cost. When there is no other seller, a company is free to charge whatever price the public is prepared to pay, often with little concern for the quality of the product. Thus, in a monopoly situation the consumer is at the mercy of the producer, especially if the product or service is a necessity. To protect the consumer, government can enact legislation designed to promote and maintain competition among business firms.

Anti-Combines Legislation: A Historical Perspective

As late as the 1880s, businesspeople were relatively free to conduct their activities as they saw fit. Monopolies and cartels took advantage of consumers with little interference and fraudulent practices, swindles and misleading advertising were common. Through such practices some individuals built huge business empires — and personal fortunes. Consumers had little recourse when products were unsatisfactory, and could rely only on the Roman principle of **caveat emptor** — "let the buyer beware."

For example, to curb the discrimination in rates and services perpetrated by the railroads in the United States — which eventually resulted in public outcry — the U.S. government introduced the Interstate Commerce Act in 1887. Soon afterwards, the Canadian government appointed a House of Commons Committee to examine similar practices in Canada, as well as monopoly situations, combinations and trusts.

In 1889 the Committee's findings resulted in the passage of an act under the Criminal Code that made it a misdemeanor to conspire, combine, agree or arrange unlawfully so as to restrict competition and fix prices in various activities, including transportation, production and storage of commodities. Although some convictions were made, the act was vague and difficult to enforce; it was subsequently revised a number of times to facilitate prosecution of individuals and companies that persisted in undermining competition.

Finally, in 1923 the **Combines Investigations Act** was passed, which clarified the procedure for administering the legislation and specified the penalties for knowingly assisting in the formation of, or being party to, a combine. Further changes were made to the legislation in 1952 and 1960. In 1966 the federal government asked the Economic Council of Canada to study the whole field of combines, mergers, monopolies, and restraint of trade, together with the system of granting patents, trademarks, copyrights and industrial designs. Later, the Council was also asked to include in its study the need for consumer legislation, and to recommend appropriate government action in this area. As a result of this study, the government hoped to enact comprehensive legislation regarding competition and consumer protection.

The Combines Investigation Act (1975)

Stage I of the new Combines Investigations Act, dealing with deceptive selling practices, became law in 1975. The act made it illegal to restrain trade in any manner, and outlawed monopolies of both consumers and producers — neither could combine to restrain competition. Discriminatory pricing, other than for quantity discounts, was made illegal, and differences in prices to customers had to be accounted for. Advertising and display allowances were regulated, and misleading advertising was outlawed — as were selling practices misleading to the consumer — such as "bait and switch," referral selling and selling at prices higher than those advertised. Specific conditions were established for performance and other tests used in advertising, and for testimonials, games and lotteries. Finally, suppliers could recommend minimum prices — they could not set them.

The second part of the act dealing with mergers and monopolies was prepared by the federal Liberal government in the early 1980s. Through close collaboration and consultation with the business community, the government put together legislation which at the time appeared to be workable. It provided precise definitions of what constitutes an illegal merger, or illegal anti-competitive behaviour.

With clearer rules the government could improve its ability to identify and prosecute those engaged in illegal business practices. A civil court rather than a criminal court would judge the implications of a merger and a civil court could be more flexible in assessing the impact of a merger or dominant position on the economy. A merger that resulted in substantial net savings for the economy, for example, would not be prohibited. Where a merger was considered detrimental, however, instead of a fine the offending corporation could be forced to undo the merger or sell some of its assets. Finally, the new act also specified that large companies with assets in excess of $500 million would have to give advance warning to anti-combines officials before a deal could be completed.

The second part of the act dealing with mergers and monopolies was, however, never passed. When the Conservative government came to power business lobbied to have the proposed act reviewed. First, business people were not happy with the merger provisions, which were considered to be too harsh and might interfere with international competitiveness. Second, business also did not like the proposed National Economic Tribunal, which was to adjudicate mergers, abuse of dominant position and other related offences, such as specialization agreements. Instead, business wanted civil courts to do that. Third, major business groups wanted the government to soften the definition of illegal behaviour by a firm with a dominant position in the market. The old bill had eight examples of anti-competitive behaviour, including price squeezing, or use of fighting brands. Business claimed that this list should be eliminated as many of these practices constitute normal competitive behaviour and if not, at least that it should be rewritten so that there is clear reference to anti-competitive intent. Finally, business suggested that the search and seizure powers of the government should be sharply curtailed.[2]

Competition Act (1986)

The new **Competition Act** was finally passed in 1986 along with the **Competition Tribunal Act (CTA)**, which created the Competition Tribunal. It consists of four judicial members appointed from among the judges of the Federal Court, and not more than eight non-judicial members, with a judicial member acting as chairman. The Director of Investigation and Research who enforces the Act has significant powers of investigation. He can enter premises and seize evidence, subpoena witnesses to give evidence, produce documents and provide information under oath about any matter under investigation.

The tribunal has jurisdiction over matters that were previously reviewed by the Restrictive Trade Practices Commission, abolished under the new Act. It also has exclusive jurisdiction to hear and determine applications concerning non-criminal matters such as refusal to deal, exclusive dealing, tied selling, market restriction, abuse of dominant position in the market, specialization agreements and mergers. Over non-criminal matters the Tribunal has broad remedial powers including prohibition orders, interim injunctions, dissolution of a merger transaction, and divestiture of assets.

Offences falling under criminal jurisdiction include agreements made to restrain trade, discriminatory and predatory practices such as price discrimination, predatory pricing and promotional allowances, price maintenance and refusal to supply, and misleading advertising and deceptive practices. To commit a criminal offence is cause for severe penalties — a fine, imprisonment, or both.

Control of Retailing and Consumer Protection

Although retailing in Canada is of major importance to the Canadian economy, no overall policy to regulate or control the retail sector has been advanced by either the federal or provincial governments. Nevertheless, retailers are affected by other government legislation, regulations and controls. Excise taxes and tariffs affect their product mix of imported and domestic products.

Consumer legislation on both the federal and provincial levels specifies the types of products retailers may sell, the warranties they must give and the information they must provide to credit customers. Provincial legislation regulates working hours for employees, minimum wages and fringe benefits such as holidays and workers' compensation. At the municipal level retailers are subject to zoning laws specifying where they may locate, the size and shape of their buildings, and the facilities they must provide. The municipal government also regulates store hours and days when businesses must be closed such as Sundays and holidays. In addition, federal inspectors ensure that product quality meets acceptable standards. Finally, retailers are required to comply with the following acts passed by the federal government and administered by the Department of Consumer and Corporate Affairs:

Consumer Packaging and Labelling Act
  Consumer Packaging and Labelling Regulations

Textile Labelling Act
  Textile Labelling and Advertising Regulations

National Trademark and True Labelling Act
  Garment Sizing Regulations
  Fur Garment and Labelling Regulations
  Watch Jewels Marking Regulations

Precious Metals Marking Act
  Precious Metals Marking Regulations

Hazardous Products Act, 1969
  Hazardous Products Regulations

Weights and Measures Act, 1974
  Weights and Measures Regulations

Canada Agricultural Products Standards Act
  Egg Regulations
  Processed Poultry Regulations
  Honey Regulations
  Fresh Fruit and Vegetables Regulations
  Processed Products Regulations
  Beef Carcass Grading Regulations
  Veal Carcass Grading Regulations
  Lamb and Mutton Carcass Grading Regulations
  Maple Products Regulations
  Dairy Products Regulations

Food and Drug Act
  Food and Drug Regulations

Fish Inspection Act
  Regulations Respecting the Inspection of Processed Fish and Processing Establishments

Broadcasting Act
  Radio Broadcasting Regulations
  Television Broadcasting Regulations

Control of Transportation

Government control over transportation began in 1895 with the historic deal made between the Canadian Pacific Railway and the prime minister, Sir Wilfrid Laurier. The government promised the CPR the money it needed to build a transcontinental line if the CPR would promise to carry the wheat produced by western farmers to the sea or lake ports forever at the rate then negotiated. The Crow rate as it has become known was finally revised in 1982 after much debate. In 1970, the National Transportation Act established the Canadian Transport Commission (CTC) to regulate and control the various modes of transportation in Canada. Included were motor, air and water transport, railways, and transport of commodities other than oil and gas through pipelines.

The National Transportation Act, 1988

The CTC era officially ended on January 1, 1988, when the new **National Transportation Act** came into force and officially ushered in a new era of deregulation of transportation. The new legislation contains a revised, comprehensive declaration of National Transportation Policy, a statement that establishes the focus of transportation in the future. These key elements are:

1. The safety of the transportation system is the top priority.
2. The transportation system exists to serve shippers and travellers.
3. Competition and market forces are to be the prime agents in providing economic, efficient and adequate transportation services at lowest total cost.
4. In order to encourage competition both within and among the transportation modes, economic regulation of carriers will be minimized.
5. Carriers should, so far as practical, bear a fair share of the costs of facilities and services provided at public expense and to be compensated for publicly-imposed duties.
6. Transportation is a key to regional development.
7. Undue obstacles to the mobility of all, including disabled persons, should not be created by carriers.[3]

The National Transportation Agency

With the passage of the new National Transportation Act, the Canadian Transport Commission was replaced by the National Transportation Agency, which was created at the same time but with different authority and a different structure. The agency has authority to grant transportation licences, review public complaints and help resolve disputes between shippers and transportation firms. In most cases it will not initiate action on perceived problems, but act only on request. It will be guided by the need to encourage competition and efficiency within the transportation industry while protecting the public interest in a safe, adequate transportation system.

One of the most important functions of the new agency is to resolve public disputes affecting the transportation industry. It offers

Many regulations were done away with in the airline industry in 1984. Under the new act, it is easier to start an airline, and existing air carriers can begin services anywhere as long as they can show that they are fit to operate safe air service. They can also drop unprofitable routes or reduce service simply by giving 120 days' notice. They can increase or cut fares if they wish without regulatory approval. Furthermore, they can negotiate confidential contracts with their customers. However, air carriers in northern and remote areas may not have the same freedom as the rest of Canada if essential air services to these areas remain necessary. The government hopes that the removal of previously restrictive economic regulatory controls will produce a more competitive, market-oriented industry that is more cost-conscious, more productive and more flexible.

 For railways and their customers, regulatory reform has been even more dramatic. The CNR and CP Rail can no longer jointly set freight rates, which reduced competition, as they had since 1967. Shippers can now negotiate confidential contracts and shop for the rates and conditions that best suit their needs. All rates must cover the variable cost of carrying the particular shipment, which rules out railways adopting predatory rates designed to drive competitors out of the market. The new legislation also makes it easier to sell a rail line to an independent operator who will run it as a smaller, short-line service. This is necessary because these short, sparsely used branch lines are costly to operate. If a rail line has economic potential, the Agency may order the railway to operate it on a subsidized basis. Otherwise, it may be abandoned, with or without a delay of up to two years to allow a smooth transition to an alternative service. Although the railways do not expect severe freight rate cutting, they are nevertheless moving quickly to make their operations as lean as possible. While the railways will be allowed to compete fairly with American carriers, the concern is that U.S. transportation companies will have equal access to about $2 billion in Canadian shipments. Both CN and CP are stating that if competition dramatically cuts revenues, the companies may have to delay investments in new equipment, facilities and new technology. This could mean that the railway will not be able to provide adequate levels of service to customers.

 In marine shipping, competition has been boosted with changes in the Shipping Conferences Exemptions Act, the legislation that controls the price-fixing shipping cartels known as "conferences." Although conferences are still exempt from federal competition regulations, the conference members can offer rates lower than those set by the conference as a whole. Customers can now negotiate confidential service contracts, and it is illegal for conferences to force customers to ship all their goods with one carrier.

 In the trucking sector, deregulation is designed to make it easier for new firms to enter the interprovincial or international market, and for existing firms to expand operations. Applicants must show that they can conduct operations safely and have proper insurance coverage. The new law allows confidential contracts to be negotiated between truckers and their customers instead of the standard rates that existed in the past. Shippers hope the private deal-making will drive prices down.

 Regulations affecting short-distance commodity pipelines will focus exclusively on safety and environmental protection.[4]

Figure 12.2 How the new National Transportation Act affects the carriers

voluntary mediation services to resolve differences over rates and conditions of service quickly. If voluntary mediation will not resolve the dispute then an arbitrator will be appointed to choose between the final offer of both parties and choose one of them.[5]

The Motor Vehicle Transportation Act

The passage of the new National Transportation Act also brought the passage of the new **Motor Vehicle Transportation Act**. Truckers no longer need to obtain approval for extra-provincial rates. This will save them time and costs. Shippers will benefit from more competitive rates and a wider choice of trucking services. In the north, the new legislation will provide remote communities with the same benefits of increased competition and improved productivity, while allowing a greater degree of economic regulation than in other areas of Canada, recognizing that transportation needs and conditions are quite different from those in the more populated areas of the country.

Increased competition among existing trucking firms, as well as the opening of the Canadian market to U.S. shippers, is the major concern of Canadian truckers. Truckers feel that the new pricing will drive prices down and truckers out of the business because there are many more trucking firms in the industry than there is freight to go around. With such intense competition, some companies could price themselves out of the market. However, some trucking companies believe there is ample opportunity to integrate service with American carriers since most American carriers probably do not want to adhere to the Canadian regulations. Thus, Canadian trucking firms could take shipments from American truckers at the border and ship them to the Canadian destinations. After the dust settles, it is hoped that there will be greater stability in the market and a better return for the survivors.

Nevertheless, the winners will be shippers and consumers who will benefit from lower freight prices. But in the long run, some critics contend, Canadians will pay a much higher price. With increased competition, drivers will have to work longer hours. Routine maintenance and major repairs may be compromised to keep trucks on the road, jeopardizing safety, as evidenced by U.S. trucking deregulation in 1980. To counteract that, the federal and provincial governments are planning to implement a national highway safety code by 1989. This will mean regular safety checks for trucks and equipment and regulated working hours for drivers. Heavy penalties and strict enforcement is expected to make it work.

The Move to Deregulation

The objective of government regulation is to "protect the public interest." The railroads were the first to have controls applied since it was believed that "the public convenience and necessity" could not be served by the free market. As trucking and airlines became more important, control over these carriers was also exercised. Truckers, for example, were prevented from attracting off-peak loads or filling up empty vehicles for back hauls, which in effect has restricted them from optimizing their economic productivity. In a U.S. study in 1976, estimated costs of regulations amounted to US$66 billion, $63 billion of which should have been borne by business, but were naturally passed on to consumers. This amounted to a hidden tax for every man, woman and child in the United States of US$307. By 1980 the costs of regulations were more than US$100 billion.[6]

The deregulation of the airline industry in the United States in 1978 ushered in bargain air fares because of competition from new, low-cost carriers. Some airlines went bankrupt, while other established carriers suffered heavy losses. Unions suffered a beating as the industry laid off personnel

to cut costs and stay alive. Similarly, the trucking industry was deregulated in 1980, which meant complete abandonment of route and rate regulation.

Deregulation of the airline industry in Canada began in 1984, and with the passage of the new National Transportation Act, airlines can fly the routes they want, with the airplanes they want, as often as they wish. The distinction between national and regional carriers is eliminated. Any airline is able to offer any combination of scheduled and charter services on their current routes and is not restricted in offering discounts. Canadian Airlines, for example, was created to challenge Air Canada nationally through the amalgamation of Pacific Western, Canadian Pacific, Eastern Provincial, and Nordair, and it established links with regional feeder carriers. Air Canada also boosted its feeder network while Wardair has added scheduled service and new airplanes to its charter runs.

Those arguing against deregulation of air fares in Canada claim that the population is spread too thin to support the kind of competition that would bring significantly lower fares. Airline

unions have predicted that deregulation will bring labour chaos, threaten service to many smaller communities and endanger safety.

The Consumer Association, the federal Department of Consumer and Corporate Affairs and other groups fully support the move but want the chance to go back if the results are unsatisfactory. They believe that deregulation would work in Canada as it did in the United States. The government made the move toward **deregulation** because it feels that Canadian carriers have to learn how to compete internationally and not seal off the borders. One of the major forces behind this move was the large number of Canadians taking advantage of the low airfares in the United States.

Whenever an established system is changed, people will suffer in the turmoil created. New competitors will enter the market and provide services not available before at lower prices. Existing carriers react by cutting costs, which in all likelihood means a loss of jobs. Although this is unfortunate, the public should ultimately benefit from a decrease in prices of fares and shipping costs.

Control of Communications

The federal government established the **Department of Communications** in 1969 to provide Canada with the best possible communication services and to control international broadcasting, particularly from the United States. In 1976 the **Canadian Radio-Television and Telecommunications Act** was passed, and the **Canadian Radio-Television and Telecommunications Commission (CRTC)** was established to regulate broadcast operations. This body is responsible for licensing all radio stations and television broadcasting stations, including cable companies, in addition to regulating types of broadcasts and the amount of Canadian content. The CRTC also oversees the rates charged by federally incorporated telephone and telegraph companies. In addition to the federal government regulations, the provinces have control over some telecommunications companies that operate within their borders. This creates an exceedingly complex regulatory patchwork and red tape that many feel hinders competition. Furthermore, it ties up the telecommunications industry in federal and provincial politics more than any sector of Canadian business.

The Supreme Court of Canada is expected to clarify the regulatory problem when it hands down its decision in the case involving Alberta Government Telephones, a provincial utility, that is trying to keep CNCP Telecommunications from interconnecting with its telephone network. It is expected that the Court will favour CNCP which would give increased authority to the federal government in regulating telecommunications.

Unfortunately, the Court's decision will not remove the red tape, regulatory nitpicking and political involvement in the industry. For example, a small Toronto company, Call-Net Telecommunications Ltd. leases phone lines from Bell Canada and then rents them to clients. This company wants to offer its clients a service that keeps track of the details of long distance phone calls. The federal cabinet is trying to decide if this company should be allowed to provide this service. The decision hinges on whether Call-Net is enhancing the service that Bell Canada would otherwise provide, or is simply re-selling a basic Bell service. The latter is not acceptable.

Many in the industry hope that the forces of deregulation will affect this sector in the coming years and remove some of the red tape and regulatory problems for the industry. In the immediate future, some of the companies would simply like to see a little more order in who is responsible for regulations.

In spite of the politics and regulations involving this industry, Canada is a leader in telecommunications expertise with companies such as Northern Telecom Ltd., Mitel Corp., Microtel Pacific Research Ltd., and CNCP Telecommunications. Canada has excellent satellite and land-based business communications systems, and Canadians enjoy relatively inexpensive telephone service — including cellular telephone service and state-of-the-art products such as electronic mail, voice mail, facsimile, and video conferencing.[7]

Control of Public Utilities

In some cases it is in the public interest that certain services be provided by one firm, giving it a monopoly on a particular service. These are generally services for which competition would be impractical, expensive or inconvenient for the consumer. For example, the capital investment required to provide telephone service is so great that costs can be lowered only by distributing them over as many customers as possible. If there were two phone companies, each would have to provide service for every neighbourhood, yet each would receive payment from only a portion of the total number of subscribers. The duplication of service would be expensive, while the inconvenience of making connections through two different companies for one call would be a major drawback. Services that fall into this category include telephones, cable, gas, electricity, water, as well as railroad, bus, subway, pipeline, air, water and motor transport companies.

Regulation of Service and Rates

Most public utilities are operated by either the municipality or the province. When a private firm provides the service, however, the rates it may charge are government-controlled. Rates are generally based on the level of service required of the company, while allowing for a fair rate of return. The latter is determined by the value of the utility company's property, the calculation of which may be based either on the original cost, or on replacement cost.

Hence, a regulatory agency must make two critical decisions — establishing a fair rate of return, and determining the value of the company's property. Both of these decisions are particularly difficult during inflationary periods when costs increase rapidly. For example, to renew or upgrade their plants and equipment, public utilities require increasingly larger investments, which must come from company earnings or from outside borrowings. In either case, the companies require greater returns on investments — therefore rates must increase.

The regulatory process was demonstrated in 1984 when the CRTC, which regulates the communications industry in Canada, rejected a rate increase sought by Bell Canada. The company wanted to increase monthly residential and business telephone rates and long-distance rates for its more than six million subscribers in Ontario, Quebec and the Northwest Territories. The rate increases would have provided additional revenue of $45 million in 1984 and $140 million in 1985. The Commission said that it could find no reason for allowing Bell to raise its rates and suggested the company could earn more by cutting its expenses. The Commission, however, did say that it was prepared to schedule a public hearing in the fall of 1985 for a new review. The company stated that it may have to reduce its work force if its financial performance suffered in the next year.

In 1987 another major hearing between the CRTC and Bell Canada got under way. About 30 interest groups were invited to present their briefs at a public hearing. The issue was the lowering of long-distance charges in order to remain more competitive with those in the United States and to prevent Canadian companies from bypassing the Canadian network by routing calls south of the border. This rate rebalancing is expected ultimately to affect the residential subscriber by increasing residential rates.

However, the Consumers Association of Canada (CAC) and the National Anti-Poverty Organization say that increases in residential phone rates would force some low-income subscribers to give up their phones. The CAC director suggests that new technology will reduce operating costs for Bell and that lower long-distance rates will increase use by customers. Both factors will increase revenues and profit without the necessity of higher rates for residential subscribers.[8]

A regulatory agency is always placed in a difficult position. The utility must be allowed to increase its rates to finance future capital investment and ensure that it can operate effectively, while the consumer, who is subject to a monopoly situation in an essential service, must be protected.

Government Ownership

Instead of regulating the operation of a private business in a monopoly situation, a government can establish Crown corporations to compete with private companies. As noted earlier, there are a number of instances in Canada where public and private companies compete with one another. When government competes with private companies, however, a fundamental question must be answered — should a public company be concerned primarily with providing service to the public, or should it compete with private companies in all respects, including the making of profit?

If service is of primary concern, the government must be prepared to make up operating deficits incurred by the public company. A private company receives no such assistance, and losses are borne by the shareholders. In effect, shareholders pay twice — first, when they absorb their own losses, and again when they pay taxes, some of which go to support public corporations. If service to the public comes before profits, how can we tell if a public company is effective and efficient in its operation? How can we compare the operations of public and private companies? Valid arguments can be made on all sides, and the issue is far from resolution.

Crown Corporations

Crown corporations are owned by federal, provincial, and municipal governments and are generally used to provide special functions for the public. The Bank of Canada, for example, has the responsibility for regulating credit and currency, while the Central Mortgage and Housing Corporation provides financial capital for private housing. In some cases federal or provincial governments may create a Crown corporation to take over a private firm that has decided to close its operation, if this closure threatened significantly to harm the region economically.

Two examples are the formerly privately-owned companies, Canadair and de Havilland Aircraft of Canada Ltd. Both were about to close their doors because they were not profitable when the federal government bought them out and turned them into Crown corporations to continue operations. This move provided direct employment to approximately 45 000 people, not including the jobs provided by subcontractors for this industry, and gave Canada an aerospace industry. On the negative side, both firms cost the Canadian taxpayer approximately $2 billion dollars as of the end of 1983. In 1986 the federal government sold these two Crown corporations to private companies (Canadair to Bombardier Inc. of Montreal for $120 million, and de Havilland Aircraft of Canada Ltd. to Boeing Co., Seattle, Washington, for $90 million).

Crown corporations may also be established to assist in the economic development of particular regions of the country, to undertake basic research, to prevent a Canadian company from being taken over by a foreign firm, to ensure competition, or to provide a service that otherwise might not be available. Table 12.1 shows the twenty largest federal and provincial Crown corporations in 1987, ranked in terms of assets.

Since Crown corporations are often established for activities too risky for the private investor, they do not always make a profit; indeed, they may not break even. A Crown corporation that loses money on its operation relies on the government that owns it to make up the loss. Government assistance often extends to the financing of fixed assets, if the Crown corporation cannot raise the money on its own in the private money market. The following article taken from *INFOMAT*, published weekly by Statistics Canada, provides some idea of the profits or losses associated with Crown corporations.

TABLE 12.1
The 20 largest Crown corporations ranked by amount of assets

Rank 87	Rank 86	Crown Corporations	Year-end	Assets $'000	Revenue $'000	Net Income $'000	Employees
1	1	Ontario Hydro	87/12/31	32 657 000	5 280 000	271 000	31 817
2	2	Hydro-Québec	87/12/31	31 659 465	5 095 319	509 345	18 933
3	3	Caisse de dépôt et placement du Québec	87/12/31	28 914 000	n.a.	2 868 000	195
4	4	Bank of Canada	87/12/31	23 023 199	2 007 604	1 843 897	2 246
5	5	Alberta Heritage Savings Trust Fund[1]	87/03/31	12 745 531	1 445 944	1 444 906	n.a.
6	6	British Columbia Hydro and Power Authority	87/03/31	9 802 000	1 987 000	25 000	6 393
7	7	Canada Mortgage and Housing	87/12/31	9 540 117	n.a.	35 036	3 029
8	8	Petro-Canada	87/12/31	8 453 000	5 079 000	172 000	7 204
9	9	Canadian National Railway	87/12/31	7 594 000	4 784 000	120 600	50 862
10	10	Export Development	87/12/31	6 900 000	665 000	1 400	498
11	n.a.	Alberta Treasury Branches	87/03/31	5 519 593	523 329	(32 455)	3 100
12	12	Farm Credit	87/03/31	4 914 084	482 992	(132 490)	573
13	11	Canadian Wheat Board	87/07/31	4 835 719	3 208 000	n.a.	462
14	13	Alberta Mortgage and Housing	87/03/31	3 974 387	292 137	(356 249)	490
15	n.a.	Régie de l'assurance automobile du Québec	86/12/31[2]	3 392 557	825 144	128 387[3]	n.a.
16	14	Manitoba Hydro	87/03/31	3 240 128	569 688	13 448	3 886
17	17	Air Canada	87/12/31	3 084 800	3 131 100	45 700	22 200
18	16	Saskatchewan Power	87/12/31	2 939 000	859 000	36 000	2 881
19	15	New Brunswick Electric Power Commission	87/03/31	2 829 712	825 230	29 305	2 402
20	18	Canada Post	87/03/31	2 628 521	2 970 056	(128 981)	52 760

n.a. Not available/not applicable
1. A regulated fund, not a corporation
2. Figures for fiscal year-end 1987 not available
3. Surplus revenue over expenditure

SOURCE: *Canadian Business*, June 1988, p. 163. Reprinted by permission.

Over the past 35 years the Republic of Korea has developed into a strong industrial nation with a world-class technology base. To supply some of the growing energy requirements of the nation, the Korea Electric Power Corporation chose a 600 Mw CANDU reactor development by Atomic Energy of Canada Limited. The Wolsung-1 CANDU Nuclear Power Plant began operation in 1982.

Crown Corporation Financial Statistics

In 1986, federal government business enterprises showed a total after-tax net loss of $757 million, down sharply from $1.2 billion a year earlier. The privatization of a number of firms has resulted in a substantial reduction in total losses, due primarily to the elimination of non-profitable manufacturing and wholesale trade enterprises. De Havilland Aircraft of Canada, Pêcheries Cartier, Canadair, Transport Route Canada and several other Crown corporations were sold in 1986 and their financial activities are no longer the responsibility of the federal government. Overall, Crown corporations have shown net losses since 1981, with a record loss of $1.8 billion in 1982.

The significant turnaround for Crown corporations in the mining sector reflected the improved financial results of Petro-Canada. Streamlining, integration of operations of previously independent firms and the partial recovery of international oil prices contributed to the improvement at Petro-Canada. In addition, the 1985 figures incorporated a writedown of Petro-Canada's frontier oil and gas properties ($865 million).

The sale of Canadair and De Havilland of Canada reduced the losses previously associated with the manufacturing group. The net loss posted in 1986 was $51 million, down from $311 million in the previous year.

Continuing economic difficulties in the agricultural sector forced the Farm Credit Corporation to increase its allowance for loan losses by $219 million and the resulting charge to operations was a major factor in the corporation's loss of $132 million. Cash payments under loan guarantees for the troubled Bank of British Columbia and the Northwest Trust Company resulted in greater losses for the Canada Deposit Insurance Corporation. In total, net losses for the finance, insurance and real estate group were $293 million, up from $89 million in 1985.

Enterprises in the wholesale trade industry recorded a net loss of $98 million, versus a profit of $364 million in 1985. A major factor in this change was the loss of $159 million by the Canadian Wheat Board, one of the largest in its 50-year history. Price-depressing stocks of wheat and course grains, and large export subsidies offered by the U.S. and the E.E.C. depressed earnings in 1986.

SOURCE: *INFOMAT*, February 12, 1988 (Ottawa: Statistics Canada), Cat. 11–002E, weekly. Reproduced by permission of the Minister of Supply and Services Canada.

Privatization

For years, the federal and provincial governments purchased private companies and turned them into Crown corporations, until the late 1970s when a turning point occurred. In 1979, Premier Bill Bennett of British Columbia returned a number of government-owned companies to private ownership by establishing the B.C. Resources Investment Corporation, and giving each B.C. resident five free shares in the company. Prime Minister Joe Clark wanted similarly to sell a part of Petro-Canada, and also give away five free shares to every adult Canadian. It never happened because his government fell.

Spurred by Britain's drive to revitalize a stagnant economy, privatization of government-owned enterprises took on a new meaning as the British government sold off numerous Crown companies, some at fire-sale prices. Government-owned housing was sold to its renters, and the sale of well known companies, including British Airways PLC, Jaguar PLC, British Telecommunications PLC and Rolls-Royce, has shifted more than 600 000 workers into the private sector.

Privatization means selling Crown corporations either in whole or in part to the private sector. It is based on the belief that under private ownership these enterprises would be managed more efficiently because they have to show a profit and compete with other firms.

In 1984, the Progressive Conservative government that came to power made plans to sell off some of its $60 billion of government enterprises. De Havilland Aircraft of Canada Ltd. and Canadair Ltd. were both sold in 1986. In early 1988 the government sold Teleglobe Canada Inc., which handles overseas satellite calls for the telephone and telecommunications companies, for $488 million to Memotec Data Inc., a small Montreal firm. By 1988, Ottawa had sold $2.1 billion of assets to the private sector. The federal government had divested itself of 13 companies and announced the sale of five others, including a share issue for Air Canada and Eldorado Nuclear Ltd.

The 45% sale of Air Canada through a treasury share issue was expected to provide from $200 million to $500 million for the airline. While the government would hold 55% it pledged that it would not interfere in the airline's operation. Air Canada's president predicted that the privatized company, free from government control and with the injection of new equity, would take advantage of new opportunities more quickly in the deregulated and competitive environment. In the past the budget of the airline had to be approved by the Minister of Transport, the Department of Finance, and the Treasury Board. These departments were not market driven, which resulted in delays before funds were approved for the airline. Air Canada's president stated further that in the future the market would decide if the company should receive new funds through equity issues; they would not have to depend on government whims or priorities. Being government-owned was also damaging psychologically to its employees, who were perceived by the public as inefficient government employees. Now employees will get the chance to demonstrate their worth.

The province of Québec, which in 1968 owned 79 Crown corporations, including subsidiaries, with a net value of close to $60 billion, had more Crown corporations than any other province. In 1986 the Québec government began to sell off its Crown corporations. SOQUEM, a Crown corporation holding various Québec mines, and Raffinerie de sucre du Québec, a sugar refinery, were sold in 1985. The money-losing Québecair Ltd. was sold in 1986, ultimately giving the province $5 million, after it had paid $21 million for the company in 1981. The Québec government is continuing its privatization program, although at a slower rate.

A very successful privatization plan was the 1983 share offering of Pacific Western Airlines, which raised a large amount of money for PWA and allowed it to take over CP Air three years later to form Canadian Airlines International Ltd. The Alberta government bought PWA for $38 million in 1973 to prevent its head office from moving to British Columbia.

In 1986, the Ontario government sold 85% of UTDC Inc., a company that manufactures trains, for $30 million to Lavalin Industries Inc. of Montreal. The new UTDC has since become a significant federal defence contractor, and has overcome the loss of a $380 million Via Rail contract it expected to get. According to a spokesman for the old company, privatization has made UTDC much more dynamic than its predecessor. It has reduced a bureaucratic management structure from 33 vice-presidents to six and is operating in a much more business-like manner.

Saskatchewan has also privatized a significant number of companies, worth approximately $430 million. British Columbia is also very active, having sold $1.1 billion of Crown assets as of 1988. It sold B.C. Hydro's gas distribution division to Inland Natural Gas Co. of Vancouver for $741 million.

Not everyone is happy with the privatization drive, especially unions. Case 2–1 at the end of this chapter looks further at why unions are worried about privatization.

SOURCES: Robert Sheppard, "$4.6 Billion Later, Privatization Gets Tough," *The Globe and Mail*, August 15, 1988, p. B1. Richard Blackwell, "Air Canada Welcomes Freer Hand at Throttle," *The Financial Post*, April 16–18, 1988, p. 1. Mathew Horsman, "Innovation Marks Province's Privatization Spree," *The Financial Post*, June 22, 1987, p. S4.

Control of Foreign Investment

Foreign capital has played a major role in Canada's industrial development. **Foreign investment** has been beneficial to Canadians by providing jobs, capital, technology and access to foreign markets. Initially, much of it came from England, but after World War II most came from the United States, which has remained the major foreign investor in Canada.

In 1985, U.S.-controlled companies continued to hold a dominant position. They represented 71.5% of the assets, 75.6% of the sales and 85.9% of the profits of all foreign-controlled firms. Nevertheless, the foreign-controlled share of assets declined by 0.8 percentage points to 23.4%. This compares to a peak of 37% in 1971; since that time, foreign ownership has decreased steadily, with the majority of the decline originating in the mining and petroleum industry. Within manufacturing, the petroleum and coal industry has seen the sharpest drop in the share of foreign-controlled assets, which has declined over the past 21 years from 99.7% to 42.1%. Since 1965, U.S.-controlled firms have accounted for 96% of the overall decline in the share of foreign-controlled assets.[9]

There is little evidence that the behaviour of foreign companies in Canada is different from that of domestic companies, and generally the advantages of foreign investment outweigh the costs.[10] Nevertheless, there is concern that the increased foreign ownership of Canadian companies and assets could affect Canada in a number of ways. First, there is the fear about preserving the Canadian culture, particularly with the United States having such a dominant investment position. Can the Canadian identity be maintained in the face of the powerful social, economic, and political influence from the United States? Second, there is the fear about the economic influence of foreign firms on Canada. A financially-troubled company is more likely to close a Canadian subsidiary plant than one in its home country. This could affect the jobs of Canadians. When it comes to increased spending on research and development, will the money be spent in the home country or in Canada? Foreign firms could also affect the Canadian balance of payments by taking profits and other fees out of Canada. Finally, when foreign governments impose controls on their corporations, these controls would also apply to Canadian subsidiaries: Canada could thereby lose some control over national affairs. We will discuss foreign ownership and its associated problems in greater detail in Chapter 13.

The Foreign Investment Review Agency

To retain some control over foreign ownership and investment in Canada, the federal government established the **Foreign Investment Review Agency (FIRA)**, (now known as Investment Canada), to screen takeovers and the establishment of new businesses in Canada by foreign-controlled corporations, or foreign individuals or governments. The first part of the FIR Act was instituted in 1974 to investigate all foreign takeovers of Canadian businesses by non-Canadians. The second part came into effect in 1975 and covered the establishment of new businesses in Canada by foreigners.

When assessing foreign takeovers or the establishment of new companies in Canada by foreign investors, the review commission was primarily interested in the benefits that would accrue to Canada.

However, FIRA quickly came under criticism by foreign investors. While few objected to an agency to screen foreign investment to ensure that it met the needs of Canadians, many objected to its tactics and procedures. They claimed that FIRA's policies were often arbitrary and poorly communicated; foreign investors were unable to determine in advance what kinds of investments might be approved, and the screening process was conducted in total secrecy with no right of appeal. They also stated that foreign investors had no way of knowing what FIRA might do in the future.

Investment Canada

The Progressive Conservative government elected in 1984 moved quickly to change FIRA's mandate. In 1985 FIRA was renamed **Investment Canada**, and its new function was to act as a monitoring device to uncover abuses by outside investors, particularly in areas where some measure of domestic ownership is considered essential to Canada. Since that time, Investment Canada has not turned down a single foreign takeover. As part of the Free Trade Agreement with the United States, the federal government has relaxed the rules for American takeovers of Canadian companies. Under the present rules, only foreign takeovers of Canadian firms with less than $5 million in annual sales or assets escape the screening process. By 1993 this limit will have risen to $150 million. By 1992 indirect takeovers involving U.S. companies, which are now reviewed if the Canadian company has assets in excess of $50 million, will no longer be subject to review. However, even under the new rules, Investment Canada can still require a U.S. company to retain research and development in Canada or to transfer technology to Canada as a condition for approval of a takeover that falls within the reviewable category.

HOW GOVERNMENT IS FINANCED

While it might be difficult for some individuals to state accurately their gross earnings each month, most know what their net pay is: the amount of money they receive when they cash their paycheques. The difference between net and gross pay is often quite substantial, and most of it goes directly to the government tax department. Approximately 20% of the average Canadian's gross pay goes for income taxes. But taxes affect more than the amount of money that individuals or businesses have left to spend — they also affect the overall economy in various ways. In the remainder of this chapter we examine the means by which government raises revenue for its operation, and how it can influence business cycles and economic growth through fiscal and monetary policy. Finally, we look at the growth of government and its effects on Canada.

Types of Taxes

With three levels of government and a relatively small population, Canadians are sometimes referred to as the most overgoverned people in the world. Electing representatives on the federal, provincial and municipal levels, the citizens of Canada also pay the cost of operating all three levels of government through taxes. According to a study by the Vancouver-based Fraser Institute, a family with an average income of $31 000 in 1983 paid $15 688 or 52% of its income in taxes. In comparison, in 1961, taxes amounted to only 33% of income. The study also found that the average family income rose by 620% between 1961 and 1983, but the average tax bill increased by 837% in the same period.[11] Table 12.2 shows the share of revenue each government received from specific taxes in 1986.

Revenue Taxes

Revenue taxes include individual and corporate income taxes, property taxes and sales taxes; together they provide most of the revenue for the three levels of government.

Individual income taxes are the largest source of revenue for both the federal and the provincial governments. Table 12.2 shows the revenue the federal and provincial governments received from personal income taxes. Personal income taxes are levied on the incomes of private individuals and on the net profits of proprietorships and partnerships. The amount of income tax that individuals pay depends on their level of income. Under the new tax system there are only three brackets, 17%, 26% and 29%, as compared to the 10 brackets that existed under the system in effect until 1987. In all provinces, with the exception of Québec, the federal government collects provincial income taxes along with the federal tax, and then distributes the appropriate amount to the provinces.

Corporate income taxes represent the second largest source of revenue for the federal government, though not for the provinces, where they rank after natural resource, general sales and health and social insurance levies. Corporations are taxed on their net profit at a combined federal-provincial rate which can vary from 45% to 55%, depending on the province. These rates are subject to change according to government policy, which may use taxation to stimulate corporate investment or raise additional revenue. In 1985, for example, the federal government imposed a corporation surtax of 5% for one year.

Unlike individual income taxes, corporate taxes are not progressive — a corporation does not have to pay a proportionately greater amount of tax the higher its income. Corporations operating in a foreign country must, of course, pay corporation taxes in that country. The federal government thus allows the company a tax

TABLE 12.2
Revenue of federal, provincial and local governments (fiscal year ended March 31, 1986)

Source of revenue	All governments consolidated $'000	Federal government Amount $'000	Federal government Share of total revenue %	Provincial governments Amount $'000	Provincial governments Share of total revenue %	Local governments Amount $'000	Local governments Share of total revenue %
Taxes							
Personal income taxes	54 491 666	34 764 101	38.5	19 727 565	20.8	—	—
Corporation income taxes	12 855 706	9 210 106	10.2	3 645 600	3.8	—	—
Real property taxes	14 924 940	—	—	—	—	14 924 940	37.1
General sales taxes	19 577 570	9 382 695	10.4	10 194 875	10.7	—	—
Motive fuel taxes	3 949 678	769 723	.9	3 179 955	3.3	—	—
Customs duties	3 974 955	3 974 955	4.4	—	—	—	—
Health insurance premiums	7 557 840	—	—	7 557 840	8.0	—	—
Unemployment Insurance Contribution	8 782 602	8 782 602	9.7	—	—	—	—
Universal pension plan levies	5 622 284	4 384 208	4.9	1 238 076	—	—	—
Natural resources	11 261 355	3 172 567	3.5	8 088 788	8.5	—	—
Other taxes	9 469 936	5 165 913	5.7	4 304 023	—	—	—
Sub-total—taxes	152 468 532	79 606 870	88.2	57 936 722	61.0	14 924 940	37.1
Privileges, licences and permits	2 517 795	152 835	.2	2 131 575	2.2	233 385	.6
Sales of goods and services	8 349 818	2 185 762	2.4	2 011 529	2.1	4 152 527	10.3
Return on investments	18 628 776	6 247 944	6.9	11 492 016	—	888 816	2.2
Other revenue from own sources	4 297 559	2 035 622	2.3	1 414 004	1.5	847 933	2.1
Transfers from other levels of government							
For general purposes	8 758 700	—	—	6 460 230	6.8	2 298 470	5.7
For specific purposes	30 442 148	—	—	13 590 643	14.3	16 851 505	41.9
Sub-total—transfers	39 200 848	—	—	20 050 873	21.1	19 149 975	47.6
Total gross revenue	225 527 701	90 229 033	100.0	95 036 719	100.0	40 261 949	100.0

— = Not applicable

SOURCE: Statistics Canada, Cat. Nos. 68-204, 68-207, 68-211. Reproduced with permission of the Minister of Supply and Services Canada.

credit deductible from the taxes it would normally be required to pay in Canada if all its income had been earned here.

Sales taxes are levied on the retail price of goods when they are sold to consumers. A sales tax is known as selective if only certain items are taxed, and general if most items are taxed. As Table 12.2 shows, sales taxes provide revenue for both the federal government and for all provincial governments. For the provinces, sales taxes are a major source of revenue. The rate varies from 5% to 10% among provinces, and some provinces allow exemptions for various types of goods. Alberta is the only province that does not levy a retail sales tax. It has been able to cover its expenditures with the royalty revenues from its huge oil and natural gas reserves.

Property taxes provide no revenue to either the federal or provincial governments, but as shown in Table 12.2, they are the largest source of revenue for municipal governments — counties, cities, villages and municipalities. In some provinces the tax rate is based on an appraisal of the current market value of real property; in others the rate is based on the historical cost of the property. The tax rate, often termed the mill rate, is then set at a given number of dollars per thousand of the appraised value of real property. The revenue derived from property taxes is intended to cover the operating costs of the municipal government and the services that it provides.

Estate and **gift taxes** were levied by the federal government until 1971. An estate tax is a tax on the wealth of a deceased person. Since 1971, only the provinces have levied succession duties and gift taxes. A succession duty is levied on the deceased's property located in the province and on the value of property passing to inheritors. By 1977 only Québec, Ontario and Manitoba continued to levy and collect succession duties. Individuals can easily circumvent the payment of such taxes by transferring their holdings to provinces with no succession duties, or to countries such as Bermuda where there are no taxes of any kind. Another alternative is to transfer, while still living, part of one's wealth to other people; however, such transfers may be subject to gift taxes. By 1977 gift taxes were also levied only in Québec, Ontario and Manitoba, where rates range from 15% to 50% depending on the value of the gift.

Regulatory Taxes

Although regulatory taxes produce some revenue for the governments that levy them, they are primarily designed to curb the use of certain commodities or services that are potentially harmful to the individual or to the economy of the country. The two major types of regulatory taxes are excise taxes and customs duties.

Excise taxes, also known as **selective sales taxes**, curb potentially harmful practices by making products such as tobacco and liquor much more expensive than would otherwise be the case. Excise taxes are also levied on non-essential or luxury goods and services such as gasoline, airline travel, movie tickets, telephone calls, fine furs and jewellery. The gasoline tax, for example, is used by provincial governments to finance the building and maintenance of highways. As a conservation measure, however, in 1976 the federal government levied an additional tax on gasoline to discourage excessive use. Taxes on cigarettes and liquor, on the other hand, are strictly regulatory.

Customs duties or **tariffs** are levied on many goods imported from other countries to make them more expensive than similar domestically produced goods. As discussed earlier in this chapter, customs and tariffs are intended to protect Canadian industry, and therefore jobs, from foreign competition. The customs duties imposed vary according to the product and the country of origin.

Fiscal Policy

Many years ago, when the federal government budget represented only 6% or 8% of national income, relatively large changes in the various budget balances of revenues or expenditures had relatively little impact on the economy. However, as the federal budget began to increase to 20%, 30% and, as is the case today, approach 50% of national income, changes in either the revenue or expenditure side of the budget had significant impact on the levels of economic activity. Government leaders soon realized this and the budget became a powerful tool for creating economic stability. By carefully choosing how revenue is raised, and how this revenue is dispersed, can affect various economic sectors. A **fiscal program** constitutes a carefully chosen plan for raising revenue through various tax measures together with a carefully chosen program of expenditures to combat a specific economic problem, such as a recession. **Fiscal policy** is the choice of a fiscal program.

For example, when a business recession threatens the existing level of economic activity, taking less money from individuals and business in income taxes and leaving it in their hands to spend as they see fit, may be enough to stimulate consumer and business demand and neutralize the recession. A more serious recession may require additional government expenditures — new roads or public building construction, or specific job creation programs — to augment private investment and thereby ensure that employment is kept as close to pre-recession levels as possible. If fiscal policy is applied at the appropriate time, there should be little fluctuation in the level of economic activity because employment and the demand for goods and services will remain fairly steady.

Timing is a major problem with fiscal policy. It is difficult for the government to react quickly when economic activity is threatened by a recession. Thus, a fiscal program is often applied either too early or too late. For example, if tax reductions are provided while the economy is still strong, then the extra money injected may simply fuel inflation; on the other hand, if the recession has already started before action is taken, then the recession will continue on its course, although it will probably not be as severe as it might otherwise have been.

Fiscal policy can also be used to curb spending during inflationary periods. Inflation — a general rise in prices of all goods — stems from excessive demand on the producing sector of the economy. By raising taxes the government can siphon off the excess money available to individuals, which may reduce consumer demand sufficiently to ease inflationary pressure.

Fiscal policy can be shaped so that it affects different sectors in society. For example, federal tax policies can be designed to influence a firm's investment decisions. If businesses are allowed to depreciate new investments in plant and equipment more rapidly, they will be able to write off a greater part of their investments against current profits and thus reduce the amount of current taxes payable. The reduction in taxes may be enough to entice firms into making new business investments which will help employment.

Fiscal policy is not limited to the federal government; it is also practised by provincial and local governments, since both of these levels collect taxes and spend money for various projects. Tax incentives from all levels of government can induce companies to locate in specific regions where unemployment may be high. Federal, provincial and municipal governments alike may be prepared to offer tax concessions now to create jobs, hoping for future higher tax revenue from these businesses and from the jobs created. Provinces and municipalities can spend money to upgrade highways and public projects during recessions or when employment drops.

A stable economic climate is good for everyone. Since uncertainty about the future and risk of loss from a deep recession is reduced, businesses are better able to plan for inventory levels, hiring and training of people, and for investing in new ventures. It also allows them to concentrate on production efficiency and expansion. For individuals, less worry about losing their employment allows them to spend more on discretionary goods and services, as well as plan for major expenditures in the future — cars, furniture, housing, vacations, and so on.

Can Tax Reform Help Canada's Economy?

Canadians generally agree that a tax system is necessary to finance the operation and expenditures of government, but many do not believe they get their money's worth. In a 1979 poll only 14% of Canadians thought they received good value for the money they pay in taxes. A larger proportion — 44% — said they get an adequate return, while 37% said they get poor value for their money.

Income tax was seen as the fairest form of taxation by 43% of Canadians, followed by sales tax (23%) and property tax (18%). The proportion of people who thought taxes were too high and much too high was 38% and 33% respectively. Only 23% thought taxes were about right; 1% thought they were somewhat low. There were even some, 0.2%, who thought taxes were much too low.[12] It is unlikely that Canadians' attitudes have changed significantly since the poll was taken.

There is widespread belief that the present progressive tax system intended to shift income from the rich to the poor is not very effective. In fact, studies have shown that a progressive tax system with marginal tax rates above 30% probably results in net losses to the economy because it reduces the incentive to produce and increases the incentive to avoid paying taxes through methods both legal and illegal. For example, a burgeoning underground econ-omy exists, generating billions of dollars of economic activity, but no transactions are documented and thus no tax revenue is produced. In the United States, underground activity is believed to amount to $100 billion in lost tax revenues, while in Canada the loss is estimated at $18 billion. However, some estimates range as high as 25% of gross domestic product, which would amount to $100 billion. If this tax revenue could be collected it would wipe out the deficit.[13]

Some individuals suggest abolishing income tax altogether and replacing it with a consumption tax. If income were not taxed, there would be no incentive to go underground. There are a number of problems with such a tax, however. First, a consumption tax is regressive, meaning that on a percentage basis low income earners pay a higher rate than higher income earners. Second, according to studies done in Britain, underground activity may not be influenced by the tax system at all. When someone employs an underground carpenter or plumber they may do so because they are getting a better job done, or pay lower prices. Further evidence comes from the United States, where a series of federal tax cuts began in 1981. The IRS found no clear improvement in what it expected it should get in tax revenue and what it actually received.[14]

Some economists think tax re-form will have similar effects in Canada. Some Canadians will begin reporting their income because the risks of being caught become greater as tax rates drop. Others, however, may feel that having operated in the underground in the past, they may risk detection if they start reporting this income. Then there is always a small group of persons who never report their income. Revenue Canada officials hope that the more stringent reporting requirements and higher penalties for not reporting income will reduce the tax gap.

The New Tax System

Tax reform was necessary in Canada to reduce the amount of tax taken from income and make the system fairer to those who work and produce. Individuals have more incentive to work hard, and invest their money in new ventures. The result is increased individual effort, and entrepreneurial risk-taking, which are necessary to adapt to rapidly changing economic conditions. Tax reform will also fuel economic growth and raise the standard of living in Canada. It is hoped also that, despite the evidence collected to the contrary, it will reduce underground economic activity and thus increase government revenues and reduce deficits.

The new tax system that came into effect in 1988 will have only three tax brackets; 17% under $27 500; 26% from $27 501 to $55 000; and 29% on income over $55 000. The old system had 10 brackets ranging from 6% on the first $1320 to 34% on taxable income over $63 347. What used to be exemptions that would be deducted from income before tax was calculated are now tax credits. Many tax shelters have been eliminated and some deductible business expenses cut altogether, while others have been substantially reduced. The new tax system is expected to take some 850 000 people off the tax rolls while reducing the tax paid by top earners. The result is a fairer income tax system, but one that will also reduce total federal tax revenue significantly.

To recoup this revenue, the federal government must also implement the other part of tax reform, the new national sales tax, which at the time of writing has not been accomplished. The ex-isting 12% manufacturers' sales tax is applied only to selected goods and not to services. The tax was criticized as inefficient and it was claimed that it distorted trade. The proposed national sales tax would provide the same revenue at a lower rate and allow the government to get rid of some existing surtaxes.[15]

The best way to implement the national sales tax is to integrate it with the various provincial sales taxes. This would provide obvious benefits since only one body would administer the tax. The provinces could lower their tax rates, but since the new tax would cover a much broader range of goods and services, revenue would remain the same. Conversely, a slight increase in the rate would increase their revenue significantly. On the other hand, the old system allowed the provinces considerable flexibility in setting their sales tax levies which would no longer be the case with the integrated national sales tax. Even though there are benefits for the provinces it is still necessary to convince them to give up this flexibility.

Another problem is to determine what goods and services, if any, should be exempt from the tax. If too many are exempted, the tax base would be too narrow and the provincial sales tax rates would have to be too high. The breadth of items subject to tax is directly related to the sales tax credits that low income families should receive to lessen the impact of the natural sales tax on them. The more goods and services that are covered, the greater the credit will have to be, especially if the tax covers food. In 1987 the federal government and the provinces tentatively agreed to exempt basic groceries, drugs and municipal services, but other items may yet be excluded. (See Case 12–2 for more information on the proposed federal sales tax.)

Monetary Policy and its Effect on the Economy

Fiscal policy — the judicious use of government tax revenues and expenditures to affect economic activity — is one tool government can use to alleviate the severe effects of business cycles. **Monetary policy** — controlling the money supply to affect specific economic results — is another. In Chapter 9, we discussed how businesses acquire loans from banks and other financial institutions when necessary so they can carry on their operations. We now look at how the government can use the banking system and the Bank of Canada to regulate the economy.

Chartered banks and most of the other financial institutions in Canada are privately owned. They take deposits from private individuals and businesses in the form of chequing and savings accounts

The Bank of Canada regulates Canadian money operations and acts as a control agent for the chartered banks

and in turn loan this money to individuals and businesses requiring it. The borrowers pay interest, while the lenders receive interest from the bank. The bank's income is derived primarily from the difference between what they receive from borrowers and what they pay out to lenders. They also offer other services for which they charge various fees.

Prior to the Great Depression, banks and other financial institutions could easily become bankrupt. To ensure that private individuals could be confident in the banking system, Parliament passed the Bank of Canada Act, creating a central bank — the **Bank of Canada**. The Bank has two major purposes. First, it acts as a control agent for the chartered banks. It requires them to provide regular reports about their operations, and to deposit reserves with it. Second, it has the responsibility of formulating monetary policy and regulating monetary operations in Canada.

Although the government in power has ultimate control over the Bank and its actions, it generally does not intervene, leaving the governors of the Bank relative independence in setting monetary policy. Nevertheless, there is close consultation between the minister of finance and the governor of the Bank. In the event that the Bank's policy is in serious disagreement with the government's economic policy, the actions of the latter prevail.

Controlling the Money Supply

Monetary policy is primarily concerned with regulating the money supply to best serve the needs of the economy. The major tools used to control the money supply are cash reserves, open market operations and the bank rate. Monetary policy is most effective in combatting inflation because raising interest rates and restricting the money supply is an effective way of reducing demand. During a recession, the Bank of Canada can strengthen bank reserves, reduce interest rates and establish an attractive climate for borrowing, but it cannot directly affect the will of individuals to borrow. As long as the business outlook is poor, borrowers will hold off and the desired increase in loans and spending will not happen.

Cash Reserves

Each chartered bank is required to hold primary and secondary **reserves** in the form of deposits and notes with the Bank of Canada. These reserves in effect limit the amount the banks can loan out to individuals or businesses. For example, if a 10% reserve is required, then for every $1000 of deposits a chartered bank can loan out $9000. Changing this reserve requirement would have an immediate effect on how much the chartered banks could lend out. If the reserve requirement were to increase, for example, the banks would have to curtail the amount of money lent out or attempt to get more deposits from customers. (In actual practice, changing the reserve requirements is never used as an instrument of monetary policy.)

The Bank of Canada exerts its influence by managing the cash reserves of the banking system. For example, a chartered bank can borrow money from the Bank of Canada if its lending needs for customers become greater. The cost of the loan to the chartered bank is called the bank rate, which we will discuss shortly. If the Bank of Canada wants to reduce the amount of money in circulation, it raises the bank rate and the chartered banks in turn raise the interest rate they charge their clients. Conversely, a lower bank rate would act to expand the amount of money in the economy because the price of borrowing money — the interest rate — would go down. This drop might encourage business investment which creates jobs and stimulates economic activity.

Open Market Operations

The Bank of Canada can also control the money supply by buying or selling government securities — treasury bills — in the money market. If the Bank sells its government securities on the open market, the increased supply of securities would lower their price, just as the price of any commodity is reduced if its supply increases. As the price of a fixed security falls, its **yield** — return to investors — rises. The market would probably interpret the sale of a large amount of securities to mean that the Bank of Canada is considering higher interest rates.

The sale of securities changes the reserves of the chartered banks and hence the money supply. To understand how this works, remember that when individuals and institutions buy securities from the Bank of Canada, they issue cheques on their accounts with the chartered banks. Since the amount of money these banks have available as deposits is reduced, they must increase their cash reserves with the Bank of Canada. To bring their reserves into line, the chartered banks can either borrow from the Bank of Canada at the existing bank rate or reduce the amount of money they loan out. In either case, the result could be higher interest rates for borrowers, which in turn would reduce the demand for loans. Similarly, if the Bank buys securities in the open market, the money supply would be expanded, which would also tend to increase economic activity.

The Bank Rate

Every Thursday afternoon the Bank of Canada auctions off **91-day treasury bills**. The funds are used by the federal government to finance its operation. The bank notifies the market — the chartered banks and investment dealers — of the total amount it has for sale a week in advance. The Bank of Canada can also bid for treasury bills and always puts in a reserve bid in case the total of all bids by the other banks and investment dealers falls short of what is available. All bids have to be lodged with the Bank before noon on Thursday, and two hours later, the total amount of all bids is known, along with the high, low and average price paid at the auction. (Treasury bills are given to the highest bidder first, then the next highest until all the bills are disposed of.)

The Bank's bid for a part of the total amount of the treasury bills affects the average yield. It also provides the market with an indication of the Bank's intentions for interest rates. For example, if the market expects interest rates to rise, the Bank can enter with a high bid — meaning a low yield — and acquire a substantial portion of the treasury bills. This action tells the market that the Bank resists higher interest rates.

The **average yield** on the 91-day treasury bills is a key short-term rate from which other rates including the bank rate, are derived. For example, the short-term rate plus one quarter of a percentage point becomes the **bank rate** for the week. The **prime rate** — the rate of interest charged to a bank's best customers — is usually one percentage point above the bank rate. **Consumer interest rates** are derived from the prime rate which varies among institutions depending on the competition between them for deposits and loans.

How the Bank of Canada Can Affect the Economy

The Bank of Canada has significant influence on the money supply. If it wants to stimulate the economy it can reduce the bank rate and make more money available. A lower bank rate means lower interest rates for businesses and consumers. Businesses are more liable to invest in new ventures because there is a better chance of a return on the investment. This leads to job creation. Borrowing for consumers also becomes less expensive, encouraging demand for goods and services. The overall effect of an increased money supply thus means more employment, increased production and consequently more income for both businesses and consumers. For the government it means higher tax revenues.

Should the Bank decide that the economy is being subjected to inflationary pressure because the demand for goods is becoming too great for the existing productive capacity, then it can attempt to reduce the money supply. The reduction would raise interest rates and make borrowing money more expensive, eventually reducing economic activity. Obviously, monetary control is a delicate process because there is always a lag between the time action is taken by the Bank and the time results are achieved. Often events outside the Bank's power also influence economic activity — such as government fiscal policy and the actions of other nations, particularly the United States.

GROWTH OF GOVERNMENT

The Canadian government has always played a major part in developing Canada's economy. However, government's main entry into the direct management of the Canadian economy was largely in response to the tremendous unemployment caused by the Great Depression. Government saw the hardship inflicted on people who had no responsibility for causing the depression. Its first major task was to check the high level of unemployment and provide relief to those in dire need. Thereafter, it instituted programs that were designed to prevent the recurrence of another serious depression. World

War II, along with some hastily developed economic and social programs, brought Canada and the United States out of the Great Depression. After the war, the work of John Maynard Keynes found many followers and government began to apply his revolutionary economic teachings. Fiscal and monetary programs were employed to maintain full employment. Thus government came to accept the responsibility of creating jobs and maintaining full employment. Soon everyone looked to government if unemployment increased; of course, government was also quick to take credit for any decrease in unemployment.

To achieve full employment, there had to be constant economic growth, which in turn required high investment by business and high consumption by consumers. Whenever demand for goods and services appeared to slacken, threatening a recession, government intervened with fiscal and monetary programs to ensure that the level of economic activity remained high. As Canadians became more affluent, they also demanded more government services and most came to believe that government could cure all economic ills.

However, government was not satisfied with only economic management. There was a strong push, particularly during the Liberal governments from 1968 to 1984, to mold Canada into a more social democratic society with power centralized in Ottawa. To recognize the French-speaking minority in Canada, bilingualism was promoted. There were also efforts to make Canada more self-sufficient in energy and to reduce foreign ownership of Canada's manufacturing, petroleum, and mining industries. There was a fear that too many decisions affecting Canada were being made abroad, particularly in the boardrooms of American companies.

Although some of the social and economic programs and policies were good for Canada, the appropriateness and cost of others were greatly disputed. Not only did the programs cost money to implement, but their administration required an increase in the number of civil servants, which required new layers of management, support services, office space, and so on. Furthermore, new programs require rules and regulations which must be written and enforced. Needless to say, the expanding government sector became more expensive to operate, but the major problem was to finance the economic and social programs the government developed and the policies that it embraced.

Financing Government Programs

Government can finance its operation, and the programs and services by either increasing taxes, or by borrowing, either from its citizens or from other countries. If new programs are financed through tax increases, the spending power of the private sector is reduced, leaving less money in the hands of individuals to spend as they see fit. It also draws attention to the fact that government cannot provide services without cost. This would in all likelihood drastically curtail new government programs and services. On the other hand, if government chooses to finance its spending by borrowing, it is considerably easier to implement new services and programs since it does not affect the pocket book of Canadians directly. Unfortunately, a greater debt means higher interest payments on that debt requiring a greater amount of tax revenue. As long as the debt remains within Canada, that is, the government borrows from its people, then at least the interest paid remains in the country. If money is borrowed from other countries, however, the interest paid flows out of Canada and is not available to the Canadian economy.

A country with a large debt also faces other problems. For investors and entrepreneurs a high debt often represents economic mismanagement, which creates a bad business climate and fear that the government in the future will have to take drastic action to combat the debt. This could mean large tax increases, affect the strength of the dollar internationally, and lead to unemployment and a drop in the standard of living.

Much of the maintenance of Canada's economy, the various programs and services offered, and most of the social programs established have had to be financed through borrowing, owing to a shortfall of tax revenue because the government decided against increasing taxes to pay for these expenditures. The result has been a huge increase in the national debt. By 1988 the **net public debt**, which represents the accumulated deficit since Confederation, approached $300 billion. Interest on this debt amounted to approximately $25 billion or 35 cents out of every tax dollar received by the federal government in 1986. Table 12.3 shows government deficits from 1968 to 1986 along with the national debt, the interest paid on the debt, the debt per capita and the interest paid per capita. The **Consumer Price Index (CPI)** is also shown, as well as the percentage of GNP represented by debt. (The CPI measures the increase in prices of a selected number of consumer goods over a period of time.)

Result of Government Growth

This uncontrolled spending of unearned money was the major factor leading to the high rate of inflation in the late 1970s and early 1980s. As this "unearned" money flowed into the economy and was used to purchase goods and services, prices rose because total national income on aggregate was greater than total national production. Other factors that contributed to high inflation were the increases in the

TABLE 12.3
Federal expenditures (surplus or deficit), public debt, interest charges on public debt, and consumer price index (CPI)

Year	Federal Revenues-Expenditures (surplus or deficit) ($'000 000)	Gross Public Debt ($'000 000)	Net Debt ($'000 000)	Net Debt per capita	Interest paid on Debt (gross) ($'000 000)	Dollars (per capita)	CPI	Net Debt as % of GNP
1968	− 11	32 924	16 760	809	1 270	62	38	25
1969	+ 1 021	35 919	17 336	825	1 442	69	39	24
1970	+ 266	38 150	16 943	792	1 676	79	41	21
1971	− 145	42 976	17 322	810	1 877	83	42	20
1972	− 566	47 687	17 936	824	2 091	90	44	19
1973	+ 387	51 716	17 455	792	2 274	96	48	17
1974	+ 1 109	55 557	18 128	812	2 548	115	53	15
1975	− 3 805	62 699	19 276	851	3 164	139	58	13
1976	− 3 356	59 802	23 296	1 051	3 908	170	63	14
1977	− 7 693	67 075	29 586	1 274	4 662	200	68	15
1978	− 11 357	79 893	39 622	1 690	5 473	273	74	19
1979	− 9 131	98 481	55 807	2 360	6 856	341	81	24
1980	− 10 393	103 626	68 595	2 865	8 492	355	89	23
1981	− 7 366	118 461	85 681	3 520	10 657	438	100	24
1982	− 18 904	134 107	100 553	4 082	15 114	615	111	27
1983	− 27 816	159 470	128 369	5 158	16 903	680	117	33
1984	− 32 399	—	160 768	6 399	18 077	720	122	38
1985	− 38 324	—	199 092	7 850	22 445	885	127	44
1986	− 34 404	—	233 496	9 297	25 441	1 013	132	63

NOTE: Gross Public Debt includes total liabilities of the federal government.
Net Debt is the Gross Public Debt minus recorded assets but excluding physical assets such as public buildings. The Net Debt represents the accumulated overall deficit since Confederation.
Recorded Assets represent cash, investments, sinking funds, advances to exchange fund account, securities held in trust, deferred charges, miscellaneous loans, and sundry expense accounts.
All physical assets such as public buildings are not recorded on the balance sheet but charged as expenditures when acquired.

SOURCE: *National Finances, 1979-1980* (Toronto: Canadian Tax Foundation). Also *National Income and Expenditure Accounts,* Cat. 68-211 annual, and *Canadian Statistical Review,* Cat. 11-003E monthly.

price of oil due to OPEC, as well as structural changes in the economy. In any case, once started, inflation can quickly spiral out of control unless drastic action is taken. Among the effects of inflation are the devaluation of money, high unemployment and, eventually, a drop in the standard of living. At its extreme it may have severe social consequences, leading to internal disorder throughout the country. For example, inflation contributed to the rise of totalitarianism and dictatorship in Germany following World War I.

The federal government's financial policies have been the subject of considerable debate and critics, including politicians, economists and business leaders, have charged that the growth of government expenditures is out of control. Government expenditures increased from $10.5 billion in 1967 to $55 billion in 1980. At the same time the size of government bureaucracy went from 369 000 employees in 1967 to 494 000 in 1980.[16] Thus, federal spending increased five-fold in thirteen years, while the civil service increased by one third. The increase in federal government employees was even more pronounced from the end of World War II to 1975. Over these 30 years the number of federal civil servants multiplied seven times, while the Canadian population only doubled.[17] Fortunately, in the early 1980s the federal government realized that its policies were responsible for inflation. It capped wage increases at 6% and put a hiring freeze on the federal civil service. This resulted in a drop in inflation from a high of 12.5% in 1981 to 5.8% in 1983. From there it decreased further to approximately the 4% level. The number of civil servants also decreased and by 1986 had declined to 223 000. Unfortunately, the federal deficit and the national debt have not decreased and are still cause for great concern.

Government Rules and Regulations

Another major issue is the increasing government control over private individuals and businesses. In order to provide more services, government is constantly seeking to learn more about people — their wants and needs — and in the process it requires more information about people's private lives. Similarly, businesses must be prepared to disclose their operations to government representatives and adhere to the ever-increasing number of regulations, the need for which is often questionable.

Coping with the rules and regulations of federal, provincial and municipal governments may be one of the greatest difficulties faced by business. In 1977 the government began to compile a list of all existing regulations. In all, 12 000 computer printout sheets were used; when bound, they made up 15 volumes of 800 pages each. And these are only federal regulations — they do not include the regulations issued by provincial and municipal governments.[18]

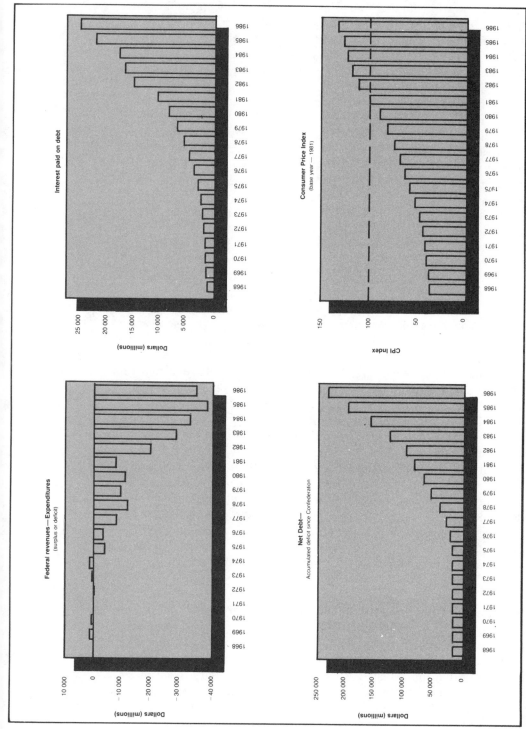

Figure 12.3 Graphs for federal expenditures (surplus or deficit), public debt, interest charges on public debt, and consumer price index (CPI)

Surveys indicate that Canadian business people spend 35% of their time complying with government regulations. Although no study has been done in Canada as to how much it costs to comply with these regulations, it was estimated in 1980 in the United States that government regulations cost business in excess of $100 billion per year. If we assume that, proportionately to population, Canada has a similar number of regulations, then the cost to the Canadian economy is approximately $10 to $11 billion annually.[19]

Since the rules and regulations issued by the government are not subject to regular review, they tend to remain long after they have served their purpose. Nevertheless, businesses must adhere to them. Staff is required to keep track of regulations and do the paperwork, while a business that overlooks regulations may face fines, as well as court costs and associated legal fees. This increases business operating costs.

For example, Dow Chemical in the United States set out to measure the costs of meeting U.S. federal regulations, and found that the total cost to the company in 1977 was $268 million, 83% higher than in 1975. While the company acknowledged that some costs are worthwhile and help to improve the environment, to make plants safer, or to benefit society in some way, many others are "unnecessary or excessive" and have "triggered confusion, indecision . . . , slowed innovation, postponed or prevented construction."[20]

What is business doing about the situation? Although many executives complain, most continue to comply. Some companies, however, are protesting. For example, the president of Dow Chemical in Canada flatly refused to comply with a request by the then existing Centre for the Study of Inflation and Productivity to provide information about the company. He explained precisely why he believed the efforts of the centre to be counterproductive. Dow was preoccupied with government regulations because it had embarked on a major program of capital expansion — approximately $1 billion in plant and other commitments — to produce petrochemicals in Alberta, even though it was facing falling profits. The company felt it did not need the added expense of complying with new regulations, particularly after committing to an investment of that size.[21]

What Should Government's Role Be?

While some intervention is clearly a necessity, government must examine its role carefully to ensure the long-term health of Canada's economy. It must control inflation by reducing expenditures; it must also ensure that the private sector is given the necessary incentives to invest in the productive capacity of the country by allowing business to make adequate profits. Government should remove unnecessary rules and regulations, and reduce its involvement in areas where private firms could be more effective. The article "Government's Role Needs Clarifying," by Charles Garneau, an economist for the Canadian Manufacturers Association, outlines what government should do to clarify its role in the economy.

When this article was written in the late 1970s, there was great concern about where the economy was going. The deficit was rising, yet government implemented new programs which were often criticized for not being properly thought out. Ever more regulations for business continued to pour out of Ottawa. High inflation hurt business and individuals. While this situation has changed considerably, the article still offers food for thought about government's role in the economy.

Government's Role Needs Clarifying

A long-term plan for the role of the government in the economy is needed to identify the exact areas in which more or less government intervention is needed, and to provide greater certainty concerning the government's role in the economy. Specifically, the plan should cover a period of approximately five years, and be revised on an annual basis. To this end, we should declare a 12-month moratorium on the role of the federal government in the economy — with no major changes made (either up or down) in taxation, spending, or regulation.

During this period, within the context of a task force such as we had on national unity, and with the help of the work done on financial management by the Lambert Commission and the Economic Council of Canada's study on regulations, interest groups could put forward their views on the form and extent of government intervention.

That task force should be charged with making specific recommendations on the role of the government in the economy. Only then should any government consider major changes to the status quo. A go-slow approach is needed — despite the strong anti-government current that has developed in Canada, the U.S., Britain and elsewhere in the past few years.

The thrust of the conservative argument (a good example is William Simon's book, *A Time for Truth*) is that by hindering producers with rules and regulations and by transferring wealth from certain individuals to others, the state stifles economic growth.

Evidence to support this argument ranges all the way from the performance of the U.S.S.R. and certain European economies to the energy crisis and the financial problems of New York City. In all cases, poor results are ascribed to state intervention. Indeed, steps in Eastern Europe and in China to introduce certain mar-

ket mechanisms to improve economic performance add fuel to the argument.

But as important as it is to emphasize the relationship between individual freedom and economic growth, it's also important to stress the relationship between equality of opportunity and individual freedom.

To not strive for conditions in which all people can compete on an equal basis makes a mockery of individual freedom. This implies the state take measures to guarantee a minimum level of health, education and welfare to all its citizens. In addition, the state should seek to reduce the inequalities generated by inherited wealth and attack entrenched economic power not based on efficiency considerations.

State intervention may also be required to ensure that the full social costs and benefits of a transaction be taken into account. Thus, the government has had to move in the area of environmental pollution to ensure that the spillover effects of production be acknowledged. Intervention may also be needed to increase the amount of information available on new products and production processes — government research in occupational health being a case in point.

The situation of natural monopoly (such as Bell Canada) may also require state intervention to ensure that the consumer reaps the benefits of economies of scale. In addition — and as is generally accepted — government intervention is needed to smooth out the peaks and troughs of the economic cycle, as well as to help absorb external shocks to the Canadian economy, such as the energy crisis and the moves toward free trade.

The point is, there is a trade-off between the individual freedom that is such a spur to economic growth, and ensuring that the economy works for the benefit of everyone, as efficiently as possible. The purpose of a task force such as I propose would be to define, in much more specific terms, where that trade-off takes place.

SOURCE: Charles Garneau, "Government's Role Needs Clarifying," *The Financial Post*, June 1979. Reprinted by permission of the author.

BUSINESS AND GOVERNMENT IN CANADA: THE FUTURE

Many thought that the 1987 stock market crash was a repeat performance of the 1929 crash that was followed by the Great Depression, but after a few months the crash was largely forgotten, and blamed primarily on computer trading. It is also important to point out, however, that economic conditions in the 1980s are significantly different from those that existed in 1929. Although many complain about big government, its very size helps to stabilize economic activity. It is a big employer and a huge buyer of goods and services from the private sector. Social Security and UIC programs were not around in the early 1930s, but the many income maintenance programs that exist today provide people who are jobless or otherwise incapacitated with purchasing power. The serious recession in the early 1980s affected only about 15% of the population. To keep our confidence in our financial system there are many legal and regulatory safeguards, such as deposit insurance, which virtually guarantees that one's savings are not destroyed by an economic disaster. The stock exchanges also have to cope with many regulations, and investments are considerably safer today.

Government involvement in social and economic management is here to stay. It is not likely that the size of the government sector will decline appreciably: it will probably continue to increase over time. But what exactly should the government's role be?

The Royal Commission on the Economic Union and Development Prospects for Canada was created in 1982 to provide some of the answers. It was to assess Canada's economic potential and recommend national policies to achieve long-term growth, as well as examine government institutions and study the division of power between Ottawa and the provinces. It was also to study generally ways of improving relations between governments, business and labour. In its report, the commission set out eight major problems facing the Canadian economy and 60 possible ways of confronting them. The issues for debate included a guaranteed annual income, more emphasis on scientific and technical training, and a voluntary "social contract" among various sectors of the economy to foster harmony and limit wage and price increases.

Whether or not these recommendations will be acted upon remains to be seen. The philosophy of the party in power, influenced by the general mood of the citizenry, affects social and economic government policy. At the moment there seems to be a trend not only in Canada but throughout the industrialized world of letting the private sector operate without extensive government regulations and red tape. In other words, there is a growing belief that government should provide a climate conducive to the growth of the private sector. The focus is still on creating jobs not through government programs, which are costly and temporary, but through permanent jobs created by the private sector. Ultimately, a healthy private sector would produce more tax revenue for government due to greater business profits and employment.

Thus, the role of the federal government is changing, particularly from that of a direct job creator to facilitator of job creation. That is, rather than instituting job creation programs, the government may offer more tax incentives and grants to encourage the growth of private industry and thereby create new jobs. Incentives to lure companies to locate in regions of high unemployment will probably also continue.

In general, the trend seems to be toward deregulation, as shown by the new transportation legislation and the new competition act. Government wants to remove regulations that have been costly to business and that may have hindered its development. Deregulation may also have some undesirable effects, such as less legislation to protect consumers. Furthermore, as has been demonstrated by the deregulation of the airlines in the United States, while prices for air travel have dropped, aircraft maintenance has become suspect. Travellers are spending more time waiting in airports as direct service has been reduced in favour of feeder service to major hubs. We may find other problems with deregulation as time progresses.

Foreign investment is more welcome again in Canada, and Investment Canada, the agency in charge of overseeing foreign investment, does not have the clout nor the inclination to reject foreign takeovers and investment as did its predecessor, FIRA. The revision of the tax system also shows that the government is interested in making the tax system fairer. It hopes that its efforts will result in increased individual effort, and stimulate the entrepreneurial spirit to create jobs and ultimately greater revenue for the government. It hopes also to reduce the underground economy.

The Free Trade Agreement between Canada and the United States was the primary issue of the 1988 federal election. Although both opposition parties and a number of other critics are intensely opposed to implementation of the agreement, most economic think-tanks in Canada and many respected economists agree that it will give Canada significant advantages. Eight of the provincial premiers are behind it, and polls indicate that the majority of Canadians in every region also support it. Large and small businesses and their respective associations are strongly in favour of the agreement, as is the Canadian Consumers Association. The Macdonald commission on the economy suggested in 1985 that "the most significant and long-term effect of free trade would be the strengthening of national unity and the removal of one of the most persistent and corrosive sources of regional alienation in Canada's political history. . . . It is difficult to think of any other act of Canadian public policy that would have so comparably healing an effect."[22]

Canada is the only industrialized country not in a free trade group. Without the Free Trade Agreement Canada would soon stand alone against protectionist U.S. legislation as well as a protectionist European Economic Community and Japan. Canadian business leaders are pleased with the agreement, expecting the opening of new markets for them. It should also help consumers by reducing or eliminating the tariffs from some goods. Nevertheless, the Free Trade Agreement is also likely to threaten many Canadian industries that have only been able to thrive because of tariffs against imported goods, such as the textile and shoe industry. Some of these industries may not be able to survive in their present state which could mean the loss of jobs for some Canadians.

Whether Canada should establish a formal industrial strategy is still being debated. Canada must deal with the impact of international trade and with the competitiveness of industries within Canada. *Ad hoc* policies and special aid to industries that have little chance of becoming competitive without government protection or aid can be detrimental to the economy. This special aid not only raises prices for Canadian consumers, it also uses up capital for development and expansion of new industries that may have a competitive advantage in trading with other countries (see the article "An Industrial Strategy for Canada" in this chapter).

Some predicted that the 1970s and 1980s would bring Canada closer to socialism, but that does not appear to be the case. Many people are beginning to see the problems a welfare state can cause in terms of efficiency and productivity of the economy. Canadians are realizing that government cannot solve all social and economic problems. Government is now telling us that we will have to rely more on ourselves or on other institutions in the future to overcome personal and economic difficulties.

An Industrial Strategy for Canada?

Debate has been ongoing as to who should develop an industrial strategy for Canada. Should it be left to private business according to the dictates of the marketplace, or should it involve the hand of government?

An **industrial strategy** is a set of government policies that directly affect the pattern of industrial development in the country. This may include joint funding between government and industry for research and development, programs to stimulate high-risk investments through low-interest loans or other means of funding, help in developing overseas markets and in modernizing facilities at home. It may include the encouragement of mergers to enable the industry to compete internationally because of economies of scale. It may also include retraining of workers affected by restructuring specific industries, or establishing training programs to correct skill shortages. It almost always includes the subsidization of exports or protection of selective imports to protect domestic industries.

In Japan for example, industrial policy has been carefully developed over the long-term, while in Canada and in the U.S., policies have been implemented on an *ad hoc* basis, or as a response to a particular crisis. In either case, it appears that the marketplace alone cannot be relied upon to establish a competitive national industrial structure because of market imperfections. Although individual investors may be successful in maximizing the return on their investment, this action may not yield the best return for a country as a whole. Individual investors are generally more interested in short-term returns, while a country must plan its industrial structure for the long-run.

How can a successful industrial strategy be developed? Countries that have developed successful strategies have adhered to the following principles:

1. The market and not government should dictate investment initiatives. Government should take the public point of view to ensure that certain important areas receive the proper funds such as research and development, development of high-risk projects, skill development, and so on.

2. Public money should not be used to bail out dying companies or companies near bankruptcy unless they are necessary for the country in the long-run and they can be restructured and become competitive.

3. Industrial policy agencies should have a small staff who consult boards of experts from universities, industry, professions, unions and the financial community.

4. Initiatives for investment projects and most of the funds should come from industry. Government agencies do not have, nor should they try to have the expertise to initiate investment ideas. Only in developing the infrastructure — transportation systems, for example — should government be the primary investor.

5. Policies should be set so they are flexible when applied to

different types of businesses. The competitiveness of each business depends on different factors which should be taken into account by government policies. While costs may be a problem for manufacturing industries, for example, it may be marketing or distribution for other firms.

6. The government's role should vary depending on the strength of private firms in a particular industry. In the case of a strong private sector, government should only provide secondary support, as compared to an industrial sector where the private firms are weak. In either case, government action should be in line with market forces instead of acting counter to them.

There are political risks in establishing an industrial strategy because some funds will be wasted and misused and various political pressure groups will force funds to be directed to unworthy projects or to serve special interests. Nevertheless, the risk of not developing an effective industrial strategy, resulting in economic stagnation, is far greater.

SOURCE: Ira C. Magaziner, "Troubled Times Demand an Industrial Strategy," *The Canadian Business Review*, Spring 1983, p. 28. Reprinted by permission.

NOTES

1. K. Stegemann, "Canadian Non-Tariff Barriers to Trade," in K.J. Rea and J.T. McLeod, eds., *Business and Government in Canada: Selected Readings*, 2nd ed. (Toronto: Methuen Publications, 1976).

2. Giles Gherson, "Competition Law Discord: Business lobbies Tories to back off on reforms," *The Financial Post*, June 15, 1985. p. 1. curtailed.

3. For an overview of the National Transportation Legislation, 1986, consult the booklet, *Freedom to Move: The Legislation*, published by Transport Canada (#TP 7749). Transport Canada also has a series of pamphlets available covering all aspects of the new Act.

4. The changes to Canada's transportation regulations brought on by the National Transportation Act and the Motor Vehicle Transport Act, as well as the changes from the previous regulations under the Canadian Transport Commission, are shown in this pamphlet: *Freedom to Move in a New Transportation Environment* (Ottawa: Minister of Supply and Services, 1988), Cat No. T22–74/1988E.

5. *Ibid*.

6. D.K. Jackson, "Trucking faces up to challenge of deregulation," *The Financial Post*, November 8, 1980.

7. Richard Blackwell, "Telecom booms despite tangle of red tape," *The Financial Post Telecommunications Special Report*, p. 41.

8. Richard Blackwell, "Bell pleads case for rate revamp," *The Financial Post*, November 2, 1987, p. 8.

9. "Foreign Control of Canadian Corporations Declines," INFOMAT (Ottawa: Statistics Canada), January 15, 1988. Cat. 11–002E.

10. David K. Banner, *Business and Society: Canadian Issues* (Toronto: McGraw-Hill Ryerson Ltd., 1979), pp. 259–60.

11. Sally Pipes, Michael Walker, and Douglas Wills, *Tax Facts #4*, Published by The Fraser Institute, 1984 period.

12. "The Canadian Weekend Poll," *Canadian Weekend*, Oct. 27, 1979.

13. Madelaine Drohan, "Probing the depth of a hidden economy," *The Financial Post*, February 8, 1988, p. 15.

14. *Ibid.*

15. See John Greene, "Wilson retreats to never-never land," *The Financial Post*, January 18, 1988, p. 15. See also Hyman Solomon, "Sales tax Tories' next challenge," *The Financial Post*, December 21, 1987, p. 19.

16. From a speech by Richard Rohmer reported in the *Vancouver Sun*, Sept. 23, 1975.

17. Robert L. Perry, *Treadmill to Ruin* (Toronto: Maclean-Hunter Ltd., 1977), p. 61.

18. Speech in the House of Commons by Joe Clark, Leader of the Opposition, Feb. 2, 1977.

19. *Ibid.*

20. Dean Walker, "Hitting Out at Government," *Executive*, Sept. 1979.

21. *Ibid.*

22. "If the deal is scuttled," *The Globe and Mail*, August 10, 1988, p. A6. See also Diane Francis, "A job for the hacks and bagmen," *Maclean's*, August 15, 1988, p. 9.

CHAPTER SUMMARY

Throughout Canada's history, government has been a major force in stimulating industrial development through tariff and non-tariff barriers against foreign imports, together with various industrial and natural resource development incentives. Today government provides services ranging from mediation and arbitration in labour disputes to bank loans and consulting services for small businesses. But government promotion of business is only one side of the coin. It also tries to protect the public through competition legislation and rules regulating the conduct of business in society. Government has also established various commissions to oversee business activities such as transportation and communication, and to review all investments made in Canadian companies by foreign operations. In addition, where private business is unwilling or unable to supply essential services, various levels of government have established corporations to provide them.

To finance their operations, the various levels of government depend mainly on personal and corporate income taxes, sales taxes and property taxes. In addition to providing revenue, taxes play an important role in fiscal policy. Fiscal policy refers to the particular fiscal program that constitutes a carefully chosen combination of adjustment of tax and expenditure levels relative to each other to combat a specific economic problem.

Another tool that government uses to manage the economy is monetary policy, which means controlling the money supply to achieve specific economic results. When the economy is in recession, an increase in the money supply lowers interest rates and makes borrowing less expensive both for businesses and private individuals. This is intended to increase business investment and the demand for consumer goods and services, which in turn should increase employment. As business profits improve and employment increases, government revenue also increases because of higher tax revenue. Conversely, when inflation threatens, reducing the money supply by raising interest rates makes the cost of borrowing more expensive, thereby reducing investment and the demand for consumer goods and services. With less pressure on the existing productive capacity of the economy, prices are less likely to rise and inflation may be reduced. Monetary policy is more effective in combatting inflation than in lifting an economy out of a recession.

In the past two decades government expenditures at all levels have increased dramatically, far exceeding government revenues, particularly in the last decade. A large part of these expenditures were due to the establishment of social programs and programs to support government economic policy. This excessive government spending contributed greatly to high inflation in the latter half of the 1970s and the early part of the 1980s. It also increased the government bureaucracy and confronted business with many rules and regulations about its conduct. While inflation was finally brought under control aided by the serious recession in the early 1980s, it can reappear anytime, particularly when the economy is in a boom period.

The greatest challenges facing the federal and provincial governments include keeping inflation in check, reducing excessive government spending, reducing the deficit and restoring confidence in the Canadian economy. Deregulation and privatization are attempts to reduce regulations and red tape for business and revitalize business performance. Tax reform is intended to make the tax system fairer and encourage individual effort and the entrepreneurial spirit, which should ultimately result in greater employment and more revenue for the government to reduce its deficits. It is also hoped that the Free Trade Agreement will provide new markets for many Canadian firms and reduce prices of some consumer products. The present government believes these measures will help Canada's vibrant economy to continue. However, some believe that Canada can overcome its economic problems only by implementing a carefully designed industrial strategy.

KEY TERMS

Tariff barriers
Non-tariff barriers
Quantity restrictions
Import quota
Production subsidies
Temporary adjustment assistance
Selective use of government
    suppliers
Department of Regional Industrial
    Expansion (DRIE)
Department of Consumer and
    Corporate Affairs
Industrial designs
Copyright
Trademark
Patent
Statistics Canada
Federal Business Development
    Bank (FBDB)
Counselling Assistance to Small
    Enterprises (CASE)
Small Business Information
    Service (SBIS)
Automated Information for
    Management (AIM)
Combines Investigations Act
Competition Act 1986
Competition Tribunal Act (CTA)
National Transportation Act 1988
Motor Vehicle Transportation Act

Deregulation
Department of Communications
Canadian Radio-Television and
    Telecommunications Commission
    (CRTC)
Public ownership/Crown
    corporations
Privatization
Investment Canada
Revenue taxes
Regulatory taxes
Income taxes
Corporation taxes
General sales tax
Property tax
Estate tax
Gift tax
Fiscal policy
Fiscal program
Monetary policy
Bank of Canada
Cash reserves
Open market operation
Bank rate
Prime rate
Consumer interest rates
Federal deficits
Net public debt
Consumer Price Index (CPI)
Industrial strategy

REVIEW QUESTIONS

1. Why is government involvement in a capitalistic economy more necessary today than it was in Adam Smith's time?
2. Why has the federal government of Canada been so heavily involved in the economy since Confederation?
3. How can government promote business by placing a tariff on imported goods? What is the major drawback to imposing tariffs on imported goods?
4. What are some of the major non-tariff barriers? How do they operate?
5. Why does the federal government provide industrial development incentives to private firms?
6. Distinguish between industrial designs, copyrights, trademarks and patents.
7. Why does government believe that it must control business?
8. How can government ensure competition between firms through anti-combines legislation? What are the major provisions of the new Competition Act? What are the powers of the Competition Tribunal?
9. What are the functions of the National Transportation Agency, the CRTC and Investment Canada?
10. What are the major revenue taxes for each of the three levels of government?
11. What is fiscal policy? How can government help to level out business cycles through manipulation of tax rates and government expenditures?
12. Why was the Bank of Canada established? What is monetary policy? How can the Bank control the money supply?
13. What does the expression "growth of government" refer to? How has government growth in Canada affected business? How has it affected private individuals?
14. What is meant by industrial strategy? How can it help a country's economy?

DISCUSSION QUESTIONS

1. Comment on the following statement: "Competition legislation is preferable to government regulation."
2. Do you think that government should extend its aid to private business? Why or why not? Explain.
3. In what ways are government regulations beneficial to business?
4. Identify some specific cases in which large-scale government involvement has been beneficial to business and society in Canada, and others in which it has been detrimental.
5. If the Canadian government developed an industrial strategy, what should it take into account?

CASE 12–1 The Privatization Drive

The Canadian Trade Union movement has been watching with growing concern the privatization of hitherto public and quasi-public organizations.

Governments, not just in this country, but on a world wide scale, are increasingly turning the services they have traditionally provided to the public over to the private sector. Such activity is undertaken in the belief that a decrease in spending and size will lead to the decrease in public sector deficits and to greater productivity at home and abroad.

Privatization can take many forms. It can be the outright sale of government assets, or de-nationalization as it is known in Britain. Domestic examples include de Havilland, Canadair and Teleglobe Canada.

Deregulation, where specific operating controls are lifted and firms operate more autonomously, has been characteristic recently of the airline industry both here and in the United States.

Finally, privatization can take the form of full or partial contracting-out of services such as municipal garbage collection.

Why Labour's concern? Their resistance is part economic, part ideological. In the latter instance, labour, in concert with the New Democratic Party, has traditionally favored a balanced mix of public and private business ownership, similar to many of the Social Democratic countries of western Europe.

Proponents of privatization point to the increased benefits that occur when firms are removed from the insulated and artificial world of the public monopoly and made to compete in the private sphere — greater cost efficiency and competitiveness with an attendant reduction on the drain of the public purse.

Labour, however, with some justification, points out that little evidence has been gathered to suggest that the result of most privatization efforts to date has been simply to shift the costs from taxpayers generally to the specific user of the service.

Labour's other main argument is quality of service. It has been shown that since the break-up of AT&T and deregulation of the airline industry in the United States, telephone service complaints and flight delays have increased significantly. Simply, the service and cost benefits one might associate in the dismantling of state-run services are illusionary.

These arguments have some validity, but in the final analysis, economic self-interest would perhaps make the most compelling argument for the position they take.

As an organization loses the protection of a government imposed monopoly through divestiture, deregulation or contracting out, it is compelled to evaluate its position in light of its new status in the private sector. Facing a competitive business environment, perhaps for the first time in its life, the organization must effect cost-cutting measures. Labour, the costliest component in any service business, comes under close scrutiny and, inevitably, the payroll is hit through layoffs, wage reductions or both. The employees' weakened state can only mean the same for the incumbent trade union as membership (read dues) declines. As with any institution, a drop in revenues can put some unions at the brink.

This argument may lack the romantic appeal in society's optimal business ownership mix, but then, most self-interest explanations do.

SOURCE: Martin Bermingham, "Privatization: Unions balk at it due to self-interest," *Canadian HR Reporter*, May 2, 1988, p. 7. Reprinted with permission.

QUESTIONS

1. What are the suggested benefits of privatizing government-owned services? The alleged problems?
2. According to the article, why are unions so adamantly against privatization?
3. List and discuss the advantages and disadvantages of privatizing the following:
   a) A Crown corporation such as de Havilland, Air Canada, or Teleglobe;
   b) The highway maintenance service of a province;
   c) The post office;
   d) Hospitals and ambulance service.
4. What in your opinion should be operated by government and what should be left to the private sector?

CASE 12–2 How About a Tax on Food?

To tax, or not to tax, food — that is no longer the question.

In fact, it has not been the question since last December when Finance Minister Michael Wilson emerged from a meeting with his provincial colleagues and announced that neither food nor prescription drugs and certain medical devices would be covered by a proposed new sales tax under discussion.

Despite those assurances, even the hint that the Commons finance committee might recommend a tax on food caused a furor in Ottawa last week that made front page news across the country.

In the end it was much ado about nothing. The committee did not make a recommendation either way on the treatment of food, saying only that the new tax should have as few exemptions as possible and that if necessities are taxed, the affected groups should be compensated.

But the violence of the reaction reinforced what Wilson and his provincial counterparts already knew — to make the proposed new sales tax they are working on politically palatable, food could not be included.

The result will be a more complicated tax containing some of the same problems as the antiquated federal manufacturers' sales tax the new tax is supposed to replace.

Lines will have to be drawn between what is and isn't food. Are potato chips considered food? Is a candy bar?

The finance committee wanted to avoid those definitional hassles. It urged the government to follow the example of New Zealand, where a broad-based goods and service tax, with almost no exemptions, has been in place since late 1986.

Clearly, having no exemptions is the most attractive option from a technical point of view. And for a while it seemed that Wilson was leaning in that direction.

But that was before he saw a public opinion poll commissioned by his department and conducted last year by Decima Research Ltd.

That poll indicated that 71% of the respondents were very uncomfortable with the idea of taxing groceries. That percentage grew to 75% among female respondents and 80% among senior citizens.

Faced with such opposition, Wilson had to reconsider.

The final push came when some provinces made the food exemption a condition of their participation in a joint federal-provincial sales tax. Wilson prefers a joint tax over a federal-only tax that would have to be levied on top of provincial retail taxes.

Even with the decision on food out of the way, technical and political hurdles remain as negotiators for Ottawa and the provinces attempt to hammer out a joint sales tax to replace provincial retail sales taxes and the federal manufacturers' sales tax.

And while the provinces have not officially agreed to participate in a joint scheme, there is enough interest on their part to keep the negotiations going.

Officials will continue to meet through the spring and summer and by fall they hope to have a framework that could be discussed at a meeting of ministers.

If all goes well and legislation is introduced soon after, it will be at least a year and probably $1^{1}/_{2}$ years after the legislation is passed before the new sales tax begins.

The long delay between phase one of tax reform, unveiled last December, and phase two does not sit well with the business community. The burden of the current federal sales tax falls unevenly, discriminating between imports and domestically produced goods and between similar domestic goods. Some of these inequities are addressed in current legislation designed temporarily to patch up the old tax.

In addition, the current federal tax only covers about one third of manufactured goods in Canada. Business would like to see a lower rate applied to a broader range of goods and services, which were not previously covered by the federal tax.

But there is another reason they would like to see phase two come sooner. In phase one, corporate taxes were increased as a percentage of tax revenue as Wilson moved some of the tax burden to corporations from individuals.

Business is hoping that in phase two the corporate surtax will be lifted and that sales tax revenues will become a larger part of the pie.

SOURCE: Madelaine Drohan, "Rumors of tax on food put Ottawa on edge," *The Financial Post*, March 21, 1988, p. 5.

QUESTIONS

1. In terms of raising revenue for the government, what are the advantages and disadvantages of each of the following: personal income tax; a comprehensive national sales tax.

2. In your view, should food be taxed? Why or why not?

3. What are the federal government's reasons for wanting to include all services and goods including food as taxable items in the comprehensive national sales tax? Explain.

4. What would be the effects on the economy and on individuals of eliminating the personal income tax, and raising all government revenue through sales taxes.

CASE 12–3 Service Fee Proposals Shock Banks

The Commons finance committee tabled a bill yesterday that would set a precedent by forcing financial institutions to eliminate certain service charges. The bill drew a furious response from banks who vowed to fight it.

Robert MacIntosh, president of the Canadian Bankers Association, called the committee's 34-page report schizophrenic and accused committee members of a string of misleading statements.

In the House of Commons, Finance Minister Michael Wilson said he was interested in the report which calls for consumer protection measures to be written into the Bank Act, but refused to comment in detail or endorse the proposals pending further study.

Junior Finance Minister Thomas Hockin, who was not in Ottawa, said in a telephone interview the report was "comprehensive and useful" and that he was now in a position to present his own conclusions on the issue within weeks.

The Finance Department, banks and the committee concur on the need for new regulations governing the notification of personal banking fees levied by banks and other financial institutions.

But the banks rejected outright the committee's proposal that they be forced to fix certain charges — such as those for closing accounts, innocently depositing a bad cheque, and for maintaining accounts that fall under a minimum balance — at zero.

Sources say the committee's proposals on regulating some service fees appeared to present a dilemma for the Government, which has been committed to financial deregulation. But they said Mr. Hockin's office would not rule out some regulation of fees that hit hard at the poor.

The committee's proposals, being put forward in a private member's bill submitted by committee member Paul McCrossan, also call for changes in fees to be disclosed 30 days in advance in writing and 60 days in advance if the bank decides to make the notification through posters.

Banks would also be required to notify customers as to which type of account was best for their particular needs.

Violations of the Bank Act would carry a maximum fine of $100 000, up dramatically from $1000 at present.

The committee also wants an ombudsman's office to be set up within the Office of the Superintendent of Financial Institutions to look into complaints over service charges and report annually on their findings.

The New Democratic Party, while agreeing with the bulk of the recommendations, decided to issue a minority report that advocates a one-year freeze on service fee changes.

It also wants the Government to set up an independent Financial Services Ombudsman to deal with complaints because it says the Superintendent's office is too preoccupied with solvency of financial institutions.

Mr. MacIntosh told a press conference: "We're angry with the fact this report is full of misleading distortions."

He said the committee's report was schizophrenic because while saying competition already existed among financial institutions, it also said it is necessary to regulate service fees.

Banks were willing to go further to provide information on service charges, and did not have problems with a mechanism for hearing consumer complaints, he said.

But he rejected the committee's interventionist approach on fees "which is totally inconsistent with the philosophy of the Government." He said acceptance of the zero-fee proposals would be the first time any industry in Canada had been ordered by government to provide free services.

The committee's report failed to mention that about four million senior citizens and youth already have basic, no-charge accounts, and that banks offered similar accounts to others as well, he said.

The CBA will fight the bill by lobbying the Government, he said.

Toronto-Dominion Bank spokesman Susan de Stein said her bank was "astounded, incredibly angry and frustrated" with the committee report.

She said it would put banks at a disadvantage against non-bank competitors, like co-operatives, trusts and loan companies, many of which are provincially regulated and would thus not be covered by the private member's bill.

Though banks have argued fixing any charges even at zero would constitute collusion under the Competition Act, Mr. McCrossan said Consumer Affairs minister Harvie Andre had assured him amendments would be made if necessary to accommodate any steps that would benefit consumers.

SOURCE: John Kohut, "Service fee proposals shock banks," *The Globe and Mail*, Tuesday, June 7, 1988, p. 1.

QUESTIONS

1. Do you agree with the finance committee's report about regulating service charges? Why or why not?

2. In view of the fact that many Canadians are dependent on banks to a greater or lesser degree, is the government justified in insisting on the banks establishing a basic account for low income earners and doing away with some of the service charges. What regulations if any should the government impose on the banks? Discuss.

3. How can the government justify the proposed regulations on the banks on the one hand, while at the same time proclaiming that it is in favour of deregulation of the private sector? Discuss.

International Business

The Financial Post

CHAPTER OUTLINE

CHAPTER PREVIEW

In Chapter 13 we look at business operations beyond the borders of Canada. After examining the reasons why countries trade with one another, we focus on Canada's major imports and exports, together with its chief trading partners. We will examine the many restrictions and barriers to international trade — tariff and non-tariff, social, economic, political and legal — as well as the various international agencies, multinational trade communities and government programs that have been established to facilitate trade.

In addition, we look at international finance and the problems associated with balance of payments and currency fluctuations. Then we consider multinational corporations and their importance to international business. The chapter closes with a discussion of the issue of foreign investment in Canada, along with some of its advantages and disadvantages for Canadians.

LEARNING OBJECTIVES

After reading this chapter you should be able to explain:

1. Why countries trade with one another;
2. Some of the major barriers to international trade;
3. The efforts that have been made to facilitate international trade, in particular the services provided by the Canadian government to help and encourage Canadian firms to trade internationally;
4. The basic concepts underlying international finance — balance of trade and balance of payments — and the problems caused by currency fluctuations;
5. The characteristics of multinational corporations, and the benefits and disadvantages for both host and home country;
6. The extent of foreign investment in Canada and its benefits and disadvantages to Canadians.

Foreign trade is not new. The earliest tales tell of adventurers setting off with their wares across the oceans of the world — despite fears that they might drop off the edge at any time. Throughout the Middle Ages itinerant merchants struggled along muddy roads to sell their goods in town markets, while traders in the medieval capitals of Venice and Florence conducted their foreign trade with a flair perhaps unrivalled even today.

Although foreign trade has occasionally been restrained because of war, trade restrictions or tariff barriers, the desire for foreign goods has never abated. The reasons are various. Goods from other countries may be less costly; some are perceived to be of better quality, and others simply are not otherwise available. Moreover, with the improvement of communication and transportation systems we are more aware of the products available in other countries, and are able to obtain them more readily.

International trade is big business, approaching $3 trillion annually and growing every year. Almost half of all such trade stems from a small group of nations including the United States, West

Germany, Japan, the United Kingdom, France, Italy and Canada. The U.S. accounts for over 70% of Canada's trade, and we in turn are their main customer. Unfortunately for Canada, two thirds of our total imports are manufactured goods, while two thirds of our exports are products of primary industries, which employ only about 10% of the labour force.

WHY DO COUNTRIES TRADE WITH EACH OTHER?

As noted above, some imported goods can be sold at lower prices than if they were produced in Canada. Many of our garments and textiles, for example, come from countries in the Far East. With lower labour costs than in the West, Hong Kong and Taiwan can produce garments much more cheaply, and thus sell them at lower prices.

However, a more fundamental reason for trade is the fact that virtually no country in the world can produce all the products that its people want. Canada cannot grow coffee or bananas, so those products must be imported from other countries. Other nations such as Japan and West Germany have developed superior technology in certain areas, making them leaders in the production of industrial machinery, cameras and electronic products. However, these countries lack raw materials, which they must therefore import from countries such as Canada.

Thus, virtually every country enjoys some advantage in the production of certain products which can be traded to other countries for the goods that they in turn have an advantage in producing. The fact that international trade makes some goods available at lower prices than if they were produced in the home country is central to the concept of absolute and comparative advantage.

Absolute and Comparative Advantage

To clarify the concepts of absolute and comparative advantage, let us suppose that all industrialized nations depended on a specific raw material that only one particular country could supply. That country would have an **absolute advantage** in the production of the material. Now let us suppose that one of the industrialized countries makes a technological breakthrough in extracting the raw material from sea water. Suddenly our hypothetical supplier nation loses its absolute advantage. However, if it can continue to produce the material at a lower cost than its new competitor can, it may still have a comparative advantage.

As this example shows, an absolute advantage in the production of a particular good can disappear quickly as technological and economic conditions change. Rather than relying on an absolute advantage, therefore, it makes sense for a nation to concentrate on maintaining a **comparative advantage**. Accordingly, it should produce and export those goods which it can produce at low cost, and import those goods which it can produce only at high cost. For example, although both Canada and Taiwan are able to produce shirts, lower labour costs in Taiwan mean that a shirt made there can be sold in Canada at a much lower price than a shirt produced in Canada. In turn, Taiwan may need certain raw materials or agricultural products that Canada can produce at relatively low cost. Trading these goods with one another would benefit both countries. It follows that if all nations adhered to the principle of comparative advantage, more goods would be available for everyone at lower prices.

However, the principle of comparative advantage is not always applied in international trade, and sometimes political considerations enter the picture. Particular domestic industries may be protected from foreign competition for political reasons through tariffs on imports. A country might choose to produce some goods, despite a low comparative advantage, in the interest of military or technological secrecy. In other instances, economic considerations influence trade. For example, eastern Canada imports foreign crude oil from Venezuela and the Middle East while western Canada exports crude oil to the United States, because at present no facilities exist to transport western crude oil to Quebec and the Maritimes.

Nevertheless comparative advantage remains the prime consideration in foreign trade. Some highly industrialized nations such as West Germany and Japan import raw materials and food stuffs, and export manufactured goods. Countries with large populations such as China and Taiwan tend to specialize in the production of labour-intensive products for export to industrialized countries where labour rates are much higher. Most of their imports consist of food products and capital goods, in contrast to countries like Canada, which export raw materials and food commodities, and import manufactured goods. Table 13.1 lists the major categories of Canadian exports and imports and some of the major commodities or products within each category. By comparing the amount of imports and exports in various categories of goods, we can see how the principle of comparative advantage works for Canada. Figure 13.1 shows imports and exports in the major commodity categories, graphically. In the first three categories Canada exports significantly more than it imports. In the fourth category — end products, meaning manufactured goods — however, Canada's imports are significantly greater than its exports.

TABLE 13.1
Selected exports and imports, 1986, by commodity category

Exports by category ($'000 000)		Imports by category ($'000 000)	
Food, feed, beverages &			
tobacco	**9 510**		**6 541**
Meat & fish	3 395	Meat & fish	1 065
Cereals & preparations	1 034	Coffee	401
Wheat	2 835	Fruit & vegetables	2 374
Crude materials, inedible	**15 328**		**7 267**
Metal ores & concentrates	3 477	Metal ores & concentrates	1 868
Crude petroleum	3 774	Crude petroleum	2 886
Natural gas	2 482	Coal	744
Coal	1 851		
Fabricated materials	**38 366**		**19 979**
Lumber & plywood	5 187	Chemicals	5 840
Fertilizers	1 135	Yarns & textiles	2 104
Wood pulp	4 072	Plastics	1 961
Newsprint	5 667	Paper & paperboard	924
Chemicals	2 609	Fabricated materials	4 695
Non-ferrous metals	7 372		
End products, inedible	**52 691**		**76 984**
Industrial machinery	3 419	Motor vehicle engines & parts	18 059
Trucks & tractors	5 089	Passenger automobiles	15 609
Passenger automobiles	17 670	Machinery	10 910
Motor vehicle parts	11 055	Office machines	4 446
Office machines equipment	1 456	Communications equipment	5 080
		Aircraft & engines	3 029
		Printed materials	1 469
Total merchandise exports,		**Total merchandise imports,**	
1986	**116 561**	**1986**	**112 678**

SOURCE: *Canadian Statistical Review* (Ottawa: Statistics Canada), December 1987, Cat. no. 11-003E. Reproduced with permission of the Minister of Supply and Services Canada.

Canadian Foreign Trade

If a country consistently imports more than it exports, it will eventually encounter financial difficulties in terms of its balance of trade and balance of payments. These factors will be discussed in more detail later in this chapter. At present it is enough to realize that countries must balance their imports against their exports. In practice, most countries endeavour to keep their level of exports above that of imports, though on a worldwide scale the value of exports and imports between all countries must balance. Canada has been

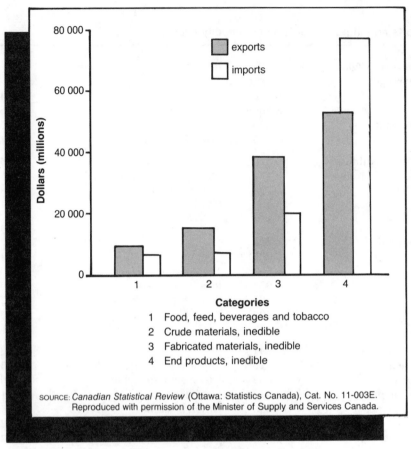

Figure 13.1 Comparing export and import categories, 1986

fortunate in that exports have generally exceeded imports. Figure 13.2 shows Canada's balance of trade for the years 1955 to 1987. The balances are generally positive.

Principal Trading Countries

Although Canada trades with most nations of the world, six of its customers account for 85% of exports, with the United States alone taking almost 77%. In the case of imports, Canada buys almost 85% of its products from six countries, with the United States accounting for almost 69% of total imports. A list of Canada's leading trade partners is shown in Table 13.2.

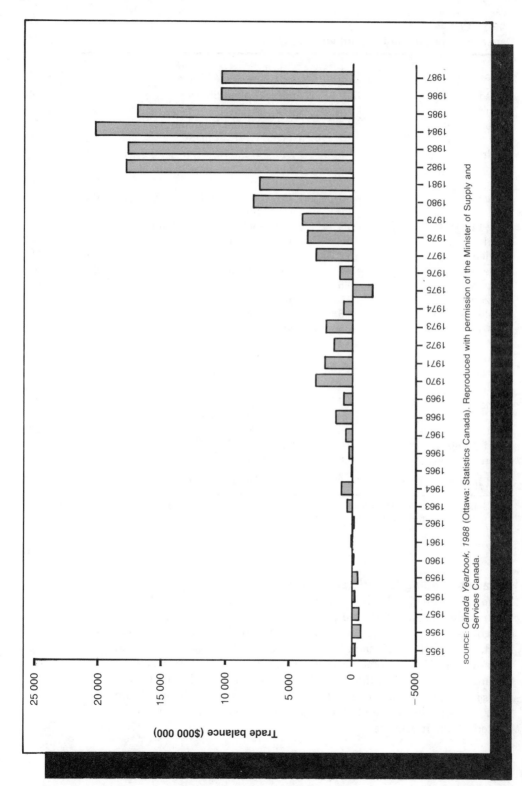

Figure 13.2 Canada's balance of trade, 1955–1987

TABLE 13.2
Canada's principal trading partners, 1986

25 Top Sellers	%	('000 000)	25 Top Buyers	%	('000 000)
United States	68.7	77 668	United States	77.3	93 182
Japan	6.7	7 625	Japan	4.9	5 934
United Kingdom	3.3	3 724	United Kingdom	2.3	2 718
West Germany	3.1	3 452	West Germany	1.1	1 317
South Korea	1.5	1 750	U.S.S.R.	1.0	1 222
Taiwan	1.5	1 744	People's Rep. of China	0.9	1 108
Italy	1.5	1 670	France	0.8	1 009
France	1.4	1 584	Netherlands	0.8	1 002
Mexico	1.0	1 179	South Korea	0.8	967
Hong Kong	0.9	1 042	Belgium-Luxemburg	0.7	844
Brazil	0.7	821	Brazil	0.7	787
Sweden	0.7	788	Italy	0.6	709
Netherlands	0.6	694	Australia	0.5	653
Belgium-Luxemburg	0.5	621	Taiwan	0.5	604
Switzerland	0.5	592	Venezuela	0.3	417
People's Rep. of China	0.5	566	Mexico	0.3	404
Venezuela	0.5	516	Cuba	0.3	365
Australia	0.4	505	Switzerland	0.3	357
Spain	0.4	440	India	0.3	353
Nigeria	0.3	368	Hong Kong	0.3	329
South Africa	0.3	341	Sweden	0.2	247
Singapore	0.2	211	Saudi Arabia	0.2	216
Iran	0.2	209	Peurto Rico	0.2	208
Peurto Rico	0.2	195	Turkey	0.2	203
Saudi Arabia	0.2	187	Algeria	0.2	191
Others	4.0	4 482	Others	4.3	5 149
Total Imports	**100.0**	**112 974**	**Total Exports**	**100.0**	**120 495**

SOURCE: *Market Research Handbook*, 1988 (Ottawa: Statistics Canada). Reproduced with permission of the Minister of Supply and Services Canada.

Canada's Leading Exports and Imports

In the list of Canada's leading exports and imports shown in Table 13.3, motor vehicles and parts are prominent in both export and import categories. This is largely a result of the Canada-U.S. Auto Agreement, which allows Canada to produce a share of automobiles and parts for the U.S. market; in turn, many of the cars purchased by Canadians are made in the United States. Crude petroleum also appears in both columns since eastern Canada imports crude petroleum from the Middle East and Venezuela, but exports crude oil to the United States in the west.

TABLE 13.3
Canada's leading exports and imports, 1986

Exports ($'000 000)		Imports ($'000 000)	
Passenger automobiles	17 670	Motor vehicle engines	18 114
Wood and paper	17 237	Passenger automobiles	12 842
Motor vehicle engines and parts	11 055	Food	6 506
Food	9 371	Chemicals	5 840
Crude petroleum	3 776	Special industrial machinery	5 798
Chemicals	5 473	Computers	4 195
Trucks	5 089	General purpose machinery	3 402
Iron and steel	3 620	Aircraft engines and parts	3 029
Industrial machinery	3 419	Trucks	2 960
Telecommunications equipment	2 516	Crude petroleum	2 886
Natural gas	2 476	Iron and steel	2 202
Aircraft engines and parts	2 381	Textiles	2 104
Coal	1 851	Precious metals	1 868
Office machines	1 456	Wood and paper	1 744
Sulphur	1 113	Farm machinery	1 728
Copper ores	593	Televisions	914
Nickel ores	476	Coal	744
Farm machinery	464	Live animals	159
Textiles	355		
Live animals	349		
Tobacco	134		
Total exports	**120 495**	**Total imports**	**112 974**

SOURCE: *Market Research Handbook, 1988* (Ottawa: Statistics Canada). Reproduced with permission of the Minister of Supply and Services Canada.

BARRIERS TO INTERNATIONAL TRADE

There are always some barriers to be overcome when Canadian companies attempt to sell their products in other countries. Some problems are due simply to lack of experience, and may be easily solved as firms become more accustomed to dealing in foreign markets. However, others may in fact prove insurmountable. Some typical problems of both kinds are discussed below.

Economic, Social and Cultural Barriers

Fortunately, the culture and social values of Canada's largest trading partner are similar to our own. Trade with the United States is particularly easy since our main exports there are primary products and specialty capital goods. Even if we were selling consumer goods, however, we could safely assume that most products suitable for Canadians would also appeal to Americans. With the appropriate product, sales would almost certainly be assured.

Other countries, however, may present problems. Cultural and social customs in France, Venezuela and Italy, for example, differ markedly from our own, and these differences could seriously hamper sales of some manufactured products. The promotional approach usually used in Canada may not work in these countries.

In some cases, even the name of the product must be changed, since a term accepted in North America may have an entirely different connotation or meaning elsewhere. For example, General Motors was puzzled when its Chevrolet Nova failed to sell in Puerto Rico. After some probing the company discovered that the name Nova sounds like "no va" — "it does not run." Sales improved noticeably once the car was renamed Caribe. In another instance, the reason sales of Colgate-Palmolive's new Cue toothpaste were low in French-speaking countries was that "Cue" was also the name of a well-known porn magazine.[1] On the other hand, Volkswagen gave careful consideration to the problem of names before introducing its successor to the "Beetle" to the North American market. By calling it "Rabbit," Volkswagon hoped the name would suggest exceptional handling qualities. In Germany and other European countries, however, a similar car was sold under the name of "Golf," while a less luxurious model not available in North America was called the "Polo" — both names suggest well-known sporting activities. The sound of a name as well as its meaning to people in a particular country are important considerations when it comes to product names, particularly for automobiles.

Economic conditions may also influence the purchase of an imported product. A convenience good in Canada may be a luxury item in a foreign country. An electrical appliance common in Canada may be too expensive to operate where energy is costly and in short supply, while many disposable products popular in North America are far too wasteful for less affluent nations.

Moreover, the imported product may not meet the needs of foreign customers. For example, North American cars were cherished in Europe in the 1950s and 1960s, but few could afford to drive them because they used too much gasoline; the cars were also too large to manoeuvre in the narrow streets of many European towns.

Exporters of manufactured goods to countries with entirely different cultural backgrounds and economic conditions may find the barriers to trade insurmountable at times. However, since Canada's major exports are primary products, we encounter few of these particular problems.

Legal and Political Barriers

When a firm conducts business in a foreign country it must be familiar with both the laws of the buyer nation and the international laws regulating trade between countries. In some areas laws may be more stringent than in Canada; in other areas they may be more lax. For example, while bribery is considered unethical in North America, it is common practice elsewhere. Property ownership, on the other hand, may be subject to much stricter regulations in other countries than in Canada. Cartels, such as OPEC, which combine to fix a common price for their product, are prohibited in Canada, but they are accepted in some countries. Moreover, various aspects of business may not have the same protection elsewhere that they have in North America. In the case of patents, for example, a foreign corporation may be legally able to copy a product and sell it at a lower price, to undercut the import without paying royalties to the company that owns the patent. In addition, each nation has its own trade restrictions, tax laws, and requirements for imports and exports.

Politics can have unpredictable consequences for foreign marketing as well. Sudden political upheavals such as the 1979 uprising in Iran may result in boycotts of certain products and physical destruction of property owned by foreign companies. However, political problems have been minor for Canadian companies.

Most legal problems in international trade can be avoided since Canadian government agencies and services can provide exporters with the necessary legal information. On the other hand, a business has little control over political problems; it must accept the risk as one of the hazards of dealing in a foreign country.

Tariff and Trade Restrictions

Foreign trade offers many benefits, but it can also be detrimental to a country's economy. Low-priced foreign-made goods can harm domestic industries that have higher labour costs, and people employed in those industries may lose their jobs. Another serious problem is the negative balance of trade that results when people are buying

Import/Export at Halifax harbour

too many imports, and the country is not exporting enough. To remedy these problems, the federal government uses tariffs and import restrictions. The imposition of a **tariff** makes imported goods as expensive as similar goods produced in Canada; an **import restriction** limits the amount of a certain product that may be imported, to ensure that domestic industry retains an adequate share of the total demand for particular goods.

While tariffs and import quotas can be defended in cases where a domestic industry is struggling to become established, or where an existing industry needs help in adjusting to international competition, they are nevertheless barriers to trade. Unless they are monitored constantly as to their usefulness in particular cases, they tend to become permanent. Then consumers suffer, since they are forced to pay higher prices. Moreover, tariffs and import restrictions may have negative consequences for domestic industries, since the incentive to improve efficiency in production and service to consumers is reduced when producers are sheltered from competition.

Although tariffs and import quotas are the major means of restricting trade, other methods also exist. Occasionally, some goods are banned from import completely under an **embargo**, a type of restriction often used against another nation as a political weapon. To prevent another country from selling its products in Canada at prices well below cost — a practice known as **dumping** — the federal government has enacted anti-dumping laws. These allow the government to impose an **anti-dumping** duty on such imports equal to the difference between the price of the product dumped and the regular price of similar Canadian goods.

As we have seen, cultural, social, political and legal differences present many obstacles to free trade between countries. Considering how important trade is to most nations, the addition of further barriers such as tariffs and import quotas may seem counterproductive. The arguments for and against protecting domestic industry and jobs are often debated, and the advantages of dropping trade barriers between countries are frequently discussed. Let us look at some of the efforts that have been made to reduce trade barriers among countries globally.

EFFORTS TO FACILITATE INTERNATIONAL TRADE

It is a paradox in international trade that the same countries that put barriers in the way of imports also attempt to encourage their own exports. Most countries realize barriers to trade are self-defeating, because other countries can retaliate. This is particularly true in the case of Canada, which depends heavily on the export of raw materials to other countries. Thus, government is torn between two competing objectives. On the one hand, it should protect domestic industries and jobs against lower-priced imports; on the other hand, it realizes the necessity of exports and the benefits of trade to a country's standard of living.

Nevertheless, it does appear that most countries are making an effort to reduce trade barriers. Various international agencies and agreements have been created to encourage international trade. Some countries have established free trade areas to facilitate the free movement of goods between countries. And the federal government sponsors a number of agencies designed to aid Canadian companies in establishing international markets and exporting their products.

International Agreements and Agencies

Among the best-known international agreements to help freer trade are GATT, the World Bank, the International Monetary Fund, and various multinational trade communities. The Canada-U.S. Auto Agreement, better known as Autopact, and the Free Trade Agreement, are two significant trade agreements for Canada and the United States.

The General Agreement on Tariffs and Trade (GATT)

Perhaps the most ambitious program to encourage free trade was the General Agreement on Tariffs and Trade signed in 1947. To reduce the level of tariffs on a worldwide basis, approximately 100 countries signed the agreement. Canada was one of the major forces in initiating GATT, despite strong ties to the Commonwealth and preferential tariff arrangements between Commonwealth nations. Canada pledged not to initiate any new tariff arrangements with Commonwealth countries beyond those already existing.

A major provision, the **most favoured nation clause**, states that any reduction in tariffs between any two member nations must be extended to all other participants in the agreement. Subsequent negotiations have led to further agreements, reducing tariffs in the industrialized countries from an average of 40% when GATT was signed, to about 4%-5% today.

In 1986 the Uruguay round of GATT talks got underway, receiving impetus from the visible and growing imbalances in trading patterns, and the strong protectionist mood of the U.S. Congress. Among the major issues being discussed is the elimination of subsidies by the year 2000, particularly on agricultural products. Another major issue is the establishment of rules about the trade in services, investment, and intellectual property, which are becoming increasingly important in world trade and are more and more the subject of trade disputes. The article, "GATT Struggles with Middle Age," provides some of the history of GATT and discusses some of the issues facing multilateral trade.

Agricultural subsidies were the critical issue when the 96 member nations of GATT met for a four-day midterm session in Montreal in December 1988. This session resulted in a bitter deadlock between the United States and the European Community (EC). The U.S. wanted GATT to eliminate all farm subsidies over an indefinite time period. They said that subsidies distort world trade and cost consumers an estimated $262 billion a year. EC representatives opposed the complete elimination of the subsidies, although they agreed to a reduction. Complete elimination of farm subsidies would mean abandoning 12 million European farmers, which would be unbearable from a social and political point of view.

With the stalemate on farm subsidies, many delegates felt that progress towards more liberalized global trade had suffered a severe setback. Tentative agreements already signed were also threatening to come undone, as when Brazil and Argentina and three other developing nations threatened to undo accords reached in twelve other areas. There were also other unresolved issues of agriculture and intellectual property rights which the GATT director general, Arthur Dunkel, promised to resolve for the meeting scheduled in Geneva in April 1989.

Nevertheless, there were some breakthroughs on the lowering of tariffs on tropical fruits, and delegates undertook to draft a framework agreement for further negotiations on trade in services such as banking, insurance, advertising and legal services. While major breakthroughs were not achieved, many delegates nevertheless believe that even a small step towards freer world trade is a step in the right direction.

GATT Struggles with Middle Age

Forty years ago in Geneva, in October 1947, 23 rich and poor nations signed the General Agreement on Tariffs and Trade, a fair trade charter intended to open up the world trading system and avoid any repetition of the protectionism that deepened the slump of the 1930s.

Now, approaching middle age, GATT is in trouble. Its rules are bent, flouted or ignored on all sides. Great swaths of trade in areas such as agriculture and services are outside its discipline. Import restrictions are rising. GATT is handling the largest number of trade complaints in its history.

Worried by the threat of chaos in world trade, GATT ministers last year launched a new round of multilateral negotiations. The Uruguay Round is more ambitious and complex than any of the seven rounds which preceded it. It is designed to overhaul the whole structure of GATT, revamp its rules, extended fair trade principles to new areas, give GATT itself more teeth and, above all, cut tariffs.

"The goal is to liberalize the trading system and make GATT more credible," says Michael Samuels, the U.S. ambassador to GATT in Geneva. If that goal isn't reached, GATT has no future, he warns.

GATT's problems date almost from birth. The original signatories of the agreement thought they were putting in place just one part of the International Trade Organization which would police an open trading system and regulate international competition in such areas as restrictive business practices, commodities, investment, even employment.

The Bretton Woods conference of 1944 envisaged the ITO as the third arm in a triad of powerful international institutions to supervise the postwar economic order, along with the International Monetary Fund and the World Bank. But the draft ITO charter ran into opposition in the U.S. Congress and was never ratified. Only GATT remained — a treaty without an organization.

Its small secretariat, with 350 people, runs the treaty on behalf of the 95 members, who make decisions through a tortuous and long-winded process of negotiation and consensus.

But, in some areas, GATT has worked well. Tariffs have tumbled — from an average of 40% when the GATT was signed to about 4%-5% today in the industrial countries. Trade in manufactured goods has multiplied 20-fold. GATT's membership accounts for nearly nine tenths of all world trade.

But in the mid-1970s, as economic growth slowed, unemployment climbed and the West faced ever-stiffer competition from Japan and other developing countries in their traditional markets, the defects of GATT became increasingly apparent.

"GATT's main success — the big reduction in tariffs — has also been one of its main flaws," says Samuels. "It hasn't been able to come up with an effective way of tackling less visible barriers to trade."

Nations have increasingly turned to non-tariff barriers such as subsidies or awkward government regulations to keep imports out. Or they have made voluntary bilateral deals to restrict exports, such as Japanese autos in the U.S. market.

GATT rules also don't cope adequately with agriculture, now the subject of acrimonious trade battles between the U.S. and the European Community. Their competitive export subsidy war on grain and other products — the U.S. and EC each spent about US$25 billion last year on farm support — has had a devastating impact on efficient non-subsidized farmers elsewhere, including those in Canada and Australia.

A U.S. proposal in the Uruguay Round to eliminate subsidies by the end of the century has received an unenthusiastic response from the EC and Japan.

Nor do the rules embrace services, which account for more than a quarter of total world trade, or investment or intellectual property (patents, copyrights), which increasingly figure in trade disputes.

Negotiators in the Uruguay Round have just begun to come to grips with these issues, and with how to bolster the GATT's enforcement role, which is seen as essential to the credibility of the system.

The U.S. is keen on turning GATT into a modern-day ITO but other countries are unlikely to let that happen. They want to keep GATT firmly under members' control, while giving the secretariat more freedom to identify wrongdoers and bring them to book.

That is likely to mean a more streamlined disputes settlement procedure and removal of the right of the offending country to vote a ruling against it. Many GATT members favor the proposal, detailed recently by Sylvia Ostry, Canada's chief trade negotiator, for regular surveillance of countries' trade policies, including their consistency with GATT rules. And members will probably agree to more ministerial involvement in GATT's work, which they see as enhancing the role of trade policy in national economic decision-making.

The U.S.-Canada free trade pact signed earlier this month could help point the way for negotiations in Geneva, especially for provisions on services such as banking and investment. But the pact has aroused concern that the proliferation of free trade agreements could undermine the basic

GATT precept of non-discrimi-
nation — treating all trading
partners on equal terms. But
Samuels point out that the accord
was conceived after a disastrous
GATT ministerial meeting in
1982, when it looked as though
the new trade round would never
be launched.

Samuels argues that the U.S.
is no longer thinking in terms of
bilateral deals. "Bilateralism and
plurilateral agreements might
serve a purpose if the Uruguay
Round fails. But multilateralism
is where our vision and efforts are
concentrated."

SOURCE: Frances Williams, "GATT struggles with middle age," *The Financial Post*, October 26, 1987.

The Canada-U.S. Auto Agreement

The Canada-U.S. Auto Agreement was established to remove restrictions, including tariffs, on the trade of automotive products between the two countries. The agreement gives duty-free access to the Canadian market to manufacturers that meet two conditions: broadly, that they produce at least as much as they sell here, and that the Canadian value-added (CVA) content of those vehicles equals or exceeds 60%. The Canadian tariff at the time the pact was signed was 17.5%. Successive reductions since then have brought it down to 9.2%. The agreement also lifted tariffs on vehicles entering the U.S. market so long as they contain at least 50% North American content. The U.S. tariff, however, is now just 3%.[2]

While the pact guaranteed Canada a fair share of the North American auto market, it has actually resulted in chronic trade deficits for Canada for many years. For example, for the 12-month period ending March 1980, the deficit under the Autopact was $3.3 billion — Canada imported $3.3 billion more in auto parts and finished cars than it exported to the United States. As long as U.S. consumers continued switching to smaller, more fuel-efficient, imported cars, Canada had trouble selling its large cars to the U.S. consumer.[3]

The turnaround came in October 1981, when Canada moved into a monthly automotive surplus. In 1982 it experienced its best year when exports to the United States were $2.85 billion greater than imports. The trend continued with further surpluses in 1983 and 1984, primarily due to the cheap Canadian dollar.

Although the Autopact is not threatened by the Canada-U.S. Free Trade Agreement, economic conditions have changed to such an extent since the agreement was signed in 1965 that commercial considerations greatly outweigh the tariff penalties that would be imposed should either side breach the agreement. For example, if the cheap Canadian dollar rises against its U.S. counterpart, or wage rates in U.S. plants drop substantially below Canadian wage rates, it is unlikely that the Autopact and its tariff penalties would keep American investment and jobs from shifting to the American side.

With tariffs scheduled to be reduced further because of the current Uruguay round of GATT negotiations, the agreement's effects will be further reduced. What is more likely to protect the Canadian auto industry is a Canada-U.S. alliance to force foreign car makers to accept a high (60%) local content in vehicles produced in North America.[4]

The Canada-U.S. Free Trade Agreement

The Canada-U.S. Free Trade agreement signed in October 1987 is the most significant agreement between these two countries. The agreement came into force on January 1, 1989. It was ratified by the United States Congress in July 1988, and by the United States Senate a month later. In Canada a general election was called primarily over the Free Trade Agreement. While the Canadian population appears to be split for and against the agreement, the Progressive Conservatives nevertheless achieved another majority in Parliament. Shortly

Canadian Press

Imported cars arriving in Vancouver

after the election the Free Trade Agreement was debated in the House of Commons for passage by the beginning of 1989. The agreement, in line with provisions of the GATT, has the following objectives:

1. To eliminate barriers to trade in goods and services;
2. To establish predictable rules, secure access and fair competition;
3. To reduce significantly impediments to cross-border investment;
4. To establish effective procedures and institutions for the joint administration of the agreement and the resolution of disputes;
5. To lay the foundation for further bilateral and multilateral cooperation to expand and enhance the benefits of the agreement.

When the agreement comes into force it will eliminate some tariffs immediately. Further tariffs will be eliminated in five equal steps, most starting on January 1, 1989. Finally, some will be eliminated in ten steps, most also starting on January 1, 1989.

Goods that originate in Canada and in the U.S. will qualify for the new tariff treatment. For goods incorporating offshore raw materials or components, there must be sufficient change made in either country in order to qualify for the treatment. This may mean that a certain percentage of the manufacturing cost will have to be incurred in the country of origin. Both parties have agreed to maintain the basic rules of GATT to regulate quantitative restrictions on imports or exports. Any existing quantitative restrictions will be eliminated either immediately or according to an agreed-upon timetable.

The Debate About Free Trade

There has been considerable debate already about the Free Trade Agreement. Those who oppose the agreement outright claim that it will result in a loss of jobs for Canadians and a loss of sovereignty. Charges have been made that Canada's social welfare system will have to be dismantled, and that ultimately it will lead to annexation to the United States.

Increasingly, however, Canadians are seeing the agreement as necessary for Canada's future. The Macdonald Commission believes it would strengthen national unity because it would be beneficial to the West, the Maritimes, and Québec and remove regional alienation caused by economic disparity. Many economists and business leaders, most premiers and a large proportion of Canadians in general are behind the agreement.

Exports to the United States are vital to Canada's prosperity, but the U.S. has been hit hard by its open-door trade policy. Americans believe that foreign-based producers have had easy access to the U.S. market while at the same time using various techniques to limit American penetration of their own markets. Furthermore, few restrictions limit foreigners from investing in the United States, but

U.S. companies face many restrictions when they want to invest abroad. Canada, for example, established the Foreign Investment Review Agency and the National Energy Program in the 1970s primarily to limit American investment in Canada. Many Americans also believe that foreign governments provide support to some of their industries that amounts to indirect subsidization of exports. Therefore, general protectionist legislation designed to curb foreign trade practices that the United States considers harmful to its own interests could be disastrous on Canada's economy in the absence of a free trade agreement with the United States.

That the Free Trade Agreement is necessary for Canada does not mean that the agreement actually struck is a good one for Canada. Some critics argue that Canada did not get an acceptable agreement, that the dispute settlement procedure is not adequate, that it ties Canada's hands in discriminating against foreign investors and foreign buyers of our energy, and that it threatens Canada's political and cultural independence.

Richard Lipsey, respected economist, lecturer, author, and now senior economic adviser at the C.D. Howe Institute in Toronto, tries to answer the above criticisms in an open letter to three of Canada's premiers and the two leaders of the opposition, Ed Broadbent and John Turner. The following are excerpts from that article entitled "Four Questions for Free Trade Critics."

Four Questions for Free Trade Critics

With respect to the criticism that Canada did not get an acceptable agreement, Mr. Lipsey says that . . .

Rejection of the agreement on the grounds that Canada obtained neither exemption from U.S. trade remedy laws nor a dispute settlement panel that could judge the fairness of U.S. laws seems to us to verge on judging the deal on the basis of unfeasible objectives. Canadians must judge the deal on the merits of what we got, rather than against unreasonable expectations of what we might have got.

With respect to the criticism that the dispute settlement procedure is not adequate, Mr. Lipsey says the following:

What Canada got in dispute settlement is not an empty shell. U.S. congressmen have been reluctant to pass trade bills that name individual countries. Contrary to Premier Peterson's view, the U.S. having to name Canada in any new legislation is a significant accomplishment. Furthermore, the requirement eliminates the "sideswipe" problem. No more will Canadian delegations have to rush to Washington to plead exemp-

tion from a new U.S. law aimed at Europe or Japan that inadvertently hits Canada because U.S. legislators forgot about our existence.

Prior notification of changes that affect Canada is of such value that one worries about discussing it too loudly. We urge those who think otherwise to study how often U.S. legislators use the tactic of attaching important amendments to a bill about to be passed on a day when the few legislators in attendance fail to notice what they have done. The infamous "full allocated cost provision" on anti-dumping was passed that way.

Canada obtained many other things from this new procedure. Most can be summed up by saying that Canadians have obtained an objective process instead of a subjective one. To turn it down seems to opt for an alternative that is substantially worse, and to make less likely agreement on future mutually advantageous changes in trade laws.

That Canada's hands are tied in discriminating against foreign investors and foreign buyers of our energy, is answered as follows:

One of the main causes of the heat of the debate is that the great battles over the nationalist policies of the 1970s are being refought today in the context of the trade agreement. These are battles over matters of real substance.

Many of the nationalist policies were discredited by the end of the 1970s. FIRA was abandoned, both because there was consensus that discouraging foreign capital was not in Canada's self-interest, and because *times had changed.* Canada is now a major foreign investor and the home base of many Canadian multinationals. In the 1990s, the U.S. may react to the large amount of foreign ownership in that country. Canada's problem then will be how to preserve its enormous stake in the U.S. shop.

Almost unnoticed, and before it becomes an issue, the agreement gives national treatment to *our* investment in *their* country. This safeguards us from having them do to us in the 1990s what we did to them in the 1970s. This

is a forward-looking achievement that should not be thrown away lightly.

In the 1970s, many countries, including both Canada and the U.S., set the domestic price of energy below the world price. This policy was discredited, because it prevented the necessary adaptation to shortages from the demand and the supply side. The energy crisis ended when countries allowed their domestic prices to rise to the world price, encouraging expansion in output and economization in use. Many of those taking part in the current debate have not accepted the conclusion to which all governments had come by the early 1980s: denying reality by pricing scarce resources below world prices is wasteful and counterproductive.

We feel that the domestic aspects of the agreement on energy also need to be addressed. On the surface, these seem to apply a very healing balm to the sores created by the National Energy Policy. It gives the west and Québec what they have always wanted: secure access to the U.S. market for their oil, gas, and electricity.

Premier Peterson says he is bothered by the supply-sharing arrangement. Yet we cannot expect the U.S. to accept free entry of Canadian energy in times of glut, if Canada reserves the right to discriminate against the U.S. in times of shortage. So if you want to keep the latter right, you must deny the west and Québec the former privilege.

Canada has also agreed not to sell energy in its domestic markets at a price lower than in the U.S., which effectively means not below the competitive price in

North American markets. If Ontario and other provinces reject this, what are they saying to the west? That the west can bear the brunt of the recession caused by low world prices of its resources, but, if world prices recover, other provinces reserve the right to force the west to sell below world prices? Sounds like heads the east wins, tails the west loses.

Finally, Mr. Lipsey answers the criticism that the agreement threatens Canada's political and cultural independence.

One group, which appears to include the leader of the Opposition, John Turner, argues that rejecting the agreement is the price of being Canadian — a price we would pay without hesitation, if that were the choice. Those who hold this view have an obligation, however, to explain what there is about the agreement that threatens Canada's political sovereignty or national identity. We find it hard to perceive reasoned arguments behind these assertions.

Other nations have preserved their political independence, their distinctiveness, *and their very different levels of spending on social policies* as full members of free trade areas, or even much tighter associations such as the European Community.

Margaret Atwood worries we may get U.S. "crime rates, health programs and gun laws." The vision is terrifying if there is any reason to take it seriously: Copenhagen turned into Hamburg! We only hope that those who take it seriously will spell out the mechanisms whereby trading more freely with the U.S. will turn us into Americans.

No one needs to apologize for strong emotions over their country's future. What is becoming hopelessly confused, however, is passion about ends, and passion about means. Canadians are right to be emotional about being and staying Canadian. But we owe it to ourselves to be rational in assessing the best ways to do so. Perhaps you have perceived some strong rational argument we have missed as to how the agreement will jeopardize our national identity. If so, we feel you should share it with the public.

These are not rhetorical questions. Unless they are answered, it is hard to make a reasoned assessment of your plea to reject the agreement. Clarification of the questions we have posed will enhance the public debate and assist Canadians in making an informed choice on the free trade issue.

SOURCE: Excerpts from Richard Lipsey, "Four questions for free trade critics," *The Financial Post*, November 9, 1987, p. 18.

ISSUE: Will Free Trade with the United States Benefit Canada?

How will the Free Trade Agreement affect Canada? Cultural subsidies — to the arts or the Canadian Broadcasting Corporation — will not be affected. However, the tax provisions that protect border broadcasting stations would have to go, with some being negotiable. The consequent economic upheavals would also be modest compared to the exchange rate swings of recent years because the treaty will be phased in over a period of 10 years. As the Canadian experience shows, when multinational agreements are made to drop tariff rates, less protection usually does not wipe out whole industries. Instead, companies abandon certain product lines which would be uncompetitive and specialize in others where they can gain larger markets.

The United States also stands to gain from a free trade deal with Canada. One of the most important is that a deal including trade in services could be used as a precedent in multinational negotiations. Furthermore, the United States would want to prevent further restrictions on investment in Canada.

There will be some dislocation and some people will have to move to areas where new jobs will be available. Some regions, such as Ontario, could be hit harder than others. The domestic clothing, textiles, and possibly the shoe manufacturing industry would probably suffer and could even disappear unless they become competitive with similar industries in the United States. Even if they did not survive, however, they would be replaced by new industries with a competitive advantage thanks to Canada's natural resources, its highly educated labour force, and its great amounts of capital equipment.

At the same time, Canada would likely remain an exporter of natural resources such as lumber, agricultural products, and minerals.

With free trade, manufacturers in both countries could plan bigger production runs, which would reduce costs and consequently prices for consumers. Canadian business, so long protected by tariff walls, would have to become more competitive. Canadian unions would have to compete with American unions, especially in areas where U.S. wages are lower.

The Canadian west would probably benefit from lower prices as new north-south trade relationships would be established. There would be new markets for western raw materials, while some manufactured goods would be less expensive for consumers. At first, prices of imported products would probably drop anywhere from 5% to 25%, depending on the tariff on the imported product. Eventually, however, the Canadian consumer would reap even greater benefits in terms of reduced prices due to expanded markets for producers and industry specialization in production. Thus, free trade could well contribute to a significant increase in our standard of living.

Whatever the effect might be, we may not have a choice. Canada is being increasingly shut out of the European Community. It is also getting harder to compete with low-wage Pacific Rim countries. Canada must become more competitive. The best way to become more competitive is to be forced to face greater competition.

SOURCE: See David Stewart-Patterson, "Study urges U.S. free trade pact," *The Globe and Mail*, Thursday, May 16, 1985. See also, Economic Council of Canada, *Looking Outward: A New Trade Strategy for Canada*, 1975.

The World Bank and the International Monetary Fund

In 1944, the United Nations sponsored a conference attended by 44 countries at Bretton-Woods, New Hampshire, to ensure world financial order after World War II. This conference resulted in the establishment of the International Bank for Reconstruction and Development, known today as the World Bank, and the International Monetary Fund. The **World Bank** was to make long-term loans to countries requiring aid for reconstruction or to third-world countries, while the **International Monetary Fund (IMF)** was intended to provide low interest loans to member nations who were experiencing difficulties in their balance of payments — which means that the outflow of funds to other countries is greater than the inflow.

International currencies compete in the money market

The IMF became an important vehicle in stabilizing international trade. Members pledged to keep the value of their currencies within certain limits in relation to others; for the sake of uniformity, all member currencies were related to the price of gold. Rather than actually transferring gold from one country to the other, however, the American dollar — a strong currency which was also pegged to gold and convertible to gold — was generally used to even out the international balance of payments.

In 1968, however, IMF member countries with a balance-of-trade surplus began converting their American dollars into gold. By 1971 the run on U.S. gold stocks had become so severe that President Nixon declared the U.S. would no longer allow the conversion of American dollars into gold. An effort was made to set new currency exchange rates in 1971, but the run on the U.S. dollar continued as speculators exchanged their dollar holdings to other currencies — German marks, Swiss francs and Japanese yen. The resulting surplus of American dollars on the world money market caused the currency to drop in relation to others, particularly the mark and yen.

With the demise of the Bretton-Woods Agreement in 1971 and the failure of efforts to establish another system of fixed exchange rates, by 1973 most countries had **floating currencies**, in which the value, or exchange rate, of a particular currency is determined by world supply and demand. While the IMF forbids members to manipulate their currencies to make exports cheaper and thus create employment at home, they are allowed to intervene in the world money markets to maintain the value of their currencies against unusual market pressures. If any currency experiences too much downward pressure, which could seriously affect trade with other nations, the government usually steps in to create a demand for its own currency and force the price up by buying it in the open market.

As an alternative to letting their currencies float, nations can set their exchange rate in terms of **special drawing rights (SDRs)**. SDRs represent the market value of a collection of 16 major world currencies and thus provide a more stable measure of the value of a particular currency than, for example, the U.S. dollar. SDRs were first created in 1969 to provide reserve assets and allow the world monetary system to expand as necessary without relying on the actual amount of gold available or on the U.S. dollar. At that time SDRs were valued in terms of gold — one SDR was equal to one dollar and 35 SDRs were equal to one ounce of gold, which is why they are also known as "paper gold."

The IMF and the World Debt Crisis

Had the world listened to 20th-century economist John Maynard Keynes, perhaps the current debt problems of third world countries might have been avoided. Keynes wanted the IMF to be a global central bank capable of creating its own money. But his visionary ideas were not accepted and the IMF became instead a vehicle for helping member nations deal with balance-of-payment problems and thus stabilize their currency. However, the IMF has become a last resort lender to many developing countries. In return for loans, the IMF has imposed stringent measures on the economic management of nations, including controls on currency deval-

uation, tax increases, government spending and monetary growth. While the immediate impact may be harsh, the long-term goals may mean sustainable growth and high employment. Unfortunately, many third world nations are politically unstable. The austerity measures imposed by the IMF as conditions for loans may lead to hunger, poverty and dangerous political instability.

Many of the loans to third world countries over the past decade have come from commercial banks in industrialized countries. The loans were needed partly because of economic mismanagement, but also because of global factors such as hugh oil bills,

worldwide recession, slumping commodity prices and high interest rates. However, many nations are unable to meet the repayment schedules laid down by the commercial banks. Most of these nations need to borrow more money just to meet the interest payments. A number have threatened with default on their loan repayments unless new methods can be found to reduce the debt burden.

The repayment problems have brought the policies of the IMF into question. Critics say that the IMF makes no distinction between deficits caused by government policies and those beyond its control. They also contend that the IMF is more concerned with reduction of inflation than with employment, which is a wrong tack in third world nations. Another criticism is that the IMF wants countries with a high debt load to suppress consumer demand. While this may work with a few countries, taken on a continent or global basis it would severely restrict international trade, particularly hurting developing countries who rely on exporting their products.

The IMF argues that the major problems lie not with the austerity measures it imposes, but with the countries themselves. The nations come to the IMF as a last resort when no other lenders are willing to give them loans and when imbalances in payments have reached crisis levels. In addition, the countries experience severe economic problems partly because of economic mismanagement and partly for the reasons mentioned earlier — global recessions and high interest rates. The IMF helps but is criticized for the resulting problems. Officials say that the IMF does not impose austerity measures — reality does. A country usually comes to terms with its economic problems and then turns to the IMF for funds. They insist that without austerity conditions, these countries would have no hope of ever getting their economy in order, nor of repaying the funds to the IMF. The end result would be even worse for the nations.

The IMF has little room to provide further help under its present mandate. It was never meant to be a lender of last resort. Private banks will also not provide further loans to countries who are already threatening with default. Some experts say that commercial banks should never have begun deficit financing. This is a role reserved for international institutions perhaps along the lines advocated by Keynes. Nevertheless, there is as yet no strong will for massive reform. However, it is also unlikely that any of the massive debtor countries will default on their loans. The reason was spelled out by a Brazilian official who said that it would mean living in an isolated economy and a poor one at that. Aircraft, ships and foreign holdings would be seized until the entire debt was repaid — not a good prospect.

SOURCE: "Third World Lightning Rod," *TIME*, July 2, 1984, pp. 31–2.

Multinational Trade Communities

When the **European Economic Community (EEC)** was founded with the signing of the Treaty of Rome in 1957, the ultimate intent was political unity of the countries on the continent. The **Common Market**, as it is also known, is an economic union that has eliminated tariffs and custom restrictions, and there is free movement of goods, services, labour and investment within the EEC bloc. However, the countries involved may raise a common tariff barrier or other trade restrictions against non-members.

The EEC, which came into being January 1, 1958, originally included six countries: France, West Germany, Italy, Belgium, Luxembourg and the Netherlands. It was joined in 1973 by Denmark, Ireland and the United Kingdom. Greece joined in 1981, and both Portugal and Spain joined in 1986. A supranational European Commission referees disputes and sets guidelines for the removal of discriminatory practices. Most EEC states are in the European Monetary System of fixed exchange rates.

The **European Free Trade Association** was established on May 3, 1960, primarily to counteract the establishment of the EEC. The original members of the **European Free Trade Area (EFTA)**, also known as the "outer seven," were Austria, Finland (an associate member from 1961 to 1985), Denmark, Iceland, Norway, the U.K., Sweden and Switzerland. The U.K. and Denmark left in the early 1970s to join the EEC and Portugal left in 1986 for the same reason. The association had three objectives: to achieve free trade in industrial products between member countries, to assist in the creation of a single market embracing the countries of Western Europe, and to contribute to the expansion of world trade in general.

The EEC and EFTA has concluded many trade deals similar to the proposed deal between Canada and the United States. When the EEC was formed there was concern that France would swallow Belgium, in view of their shared border, common language, and huge population imbalance — 55 million to 10 million. These fears have not been realized.

The EEC subsequently negotiated a number of bilateral free trade treaties with individual members of the EFTA. Almost all tariff and non-tariff barriers were removed. Exemptions were made for agricultural quotas, but services and investment were not included in the agreements. Interesting to note in this case is that the adjustment to these free trade deals went smoothly and painlessly, even between unequal economic partners. Austria was particularly worried about its neighbour, West Germany, whose population is eight times larger than its own, and which has branch plants inside Austria to overcome the high tariff walls established to protect Austrian industry. When tariffs were removed over five years, however, as often as not, Austrian industry benefited.[5]

Many other trade associations exist in addition to the EEC and the EFTA, as Table 13.4 shows. In the future, more may come into being, or existing ones may merge. The fewer trading blocs there are, the easier international trade becomes, as arrangements can be made with overall trade regions rather than with individual countries.

Canadian Government Services and Programs

The Canadian government has established a number of services and programs to identify and develop export markets for Canadian products and services throughout the world and to help finance sales. This assistance is provided through the **Department of External Affairs** and the **Department of Regional Industrial Expansion (DRIE)**.

TABLE 13.4
Multinational trade associations

Name	Membership	Date of Origin
The Andean Group (also called the Andean Common Market)	Bolivia, Columbia, Ecuador, Peru, Venezuela	1969
Arab Common Market	Iraq, Jordan, Syria, Egypt	1965
ASEAN: Association of Southeast Asian Nations	Indonesia, Malaysia, Philippines, Singapore, Thailand, Brunei	1967
CACM: Central American Common Market	Costa Rica, El Salvador, Guatemala, Honduras, Nicaragua	1960
CARICOM: Caribbean Common Market	Antigua, Barbados, Dominica, Grenada, Guyana, Jamaica, Montserrat, St. Christopher-Nevis-Anguilla, St. Lucia, St. Vincent, Trinidad and Tobago, Belize, Bahamas	1966
CMEA: Council for Mutual Economic Assistance (also called COMECON)	Bulgaria, Czechoslovakia, East Germany, Hungary, Mongolia, Poland, Romania, USSR, Cuba, Vietnam, Yugoslavia (partial participant)	1949
East African Community	Kenya, Tanzania, Uganda	1967
EEC: European Economic Community	Belgium, France, West Germany, Italy, Luxembourg, the Netherlands, Denmark, Ireland, United Kingdom, Greece, Spain, Portugal	1958
EFTA: European Free Trade Area	Austria, Norway, Sweden, Switzerland, Iceland, Finland	1960
LAIA: Latin American Integration Association	Argentina, Bolivia, Brazil, Chile, Colombia, Ecuador, Mexico, Paraguay, Peru, Uruguay, Venezuela	1960
URUPABOL	Bolivia, Paraguay, Uruguay	1981

SOURCE: *The Statesman's Yearbook, 1986-87* (London: MacMillan Press Ltd.).

Programs and services are offered by both departments, but DRIE, with its 10 regional offices in Canada, is the first point of contact in Canada for firms wanting to do business abroad. The Regional Trade Offices counsel exporters on how to approach export marketing, including export pricing, financing, documentation, transportation, insurance, and other relevant government assistance programs and services. The trade development officers give advice on export market opportunities and, as appropriate, refer businesspeople to contacts in Ottawa and posts abroad. Numerous publications for exporters or potential exporters are available through DRIE's regional offices. These include:

- A Guide for Canadian Exporters
- Canada's Export Development Plans
- Market Studies of the U.S.A.
- So You Want to Export
- Promotional Projects Program
- Commodity Books
- Businessmen's Directory of Trade Representation Abroad
- CANADA EXPORT

Following are some of the services and programs offered through the Department of External Affairs.

Market Advisory Service

Export information and market advice is provided through **Information:DEA**. The Export Information Centre gives Canadian businesses access to programs and services available to exporters. If the information is not immediately available the enquirer is referred to the appropriate division. The **International Trade Data Bank** provides data on the imports and exports of developed and developing countries, broken down according to the type of commodity and the country of origin. The information is compiled by the Statistics Office of the United Nations.

Trade Commissioners

Trade commissioners provide commercial representation abroad, together with locally-engaged commercial officers. They provide a useful link between foreign buyers and Canadian exporters. They offer Canadian businesspeople assistance in

- identification of export opportunities;
- assessment of market competition;
- introduction to foreign businesspeople and government officials;
- advice on terms of pay, claims assistance, and after sales service;
- assistance with tariff problems or difficulties with foreign import restrictions, including advice on labelling and marking regulations;
- market studies for publication.

Of particular advantage to exporters is the trade commissioners' knowledge of regional, social and cultural environments, business practices and business personalities. The service has 88 posts around the world and 10 regional offices in Canada.

Export Insurance and Guarantees

The **Export Development Corporation (EDC)**, a federal Crown corporation, provides a wide range of insurance and bank guarantee services to Canadian exporters and arranges credit for foreign buyers to facilitate and develop export trade. The EDC offers export credit insurance to protect Canadian businesses in the event that, through no fault of their own, a sale is not completed. It also provides long-term loans to foreign purchasers of Canadian goods and services, as well as a foreign investment guarantee to protect Canadian business investment abroad from changes in government policy, civil war, revolution or expropriation. When foreign buyers require advance payments or security bonds, the EDC protects the exporter through risk insurance, so as not to discourage exporters from pursuing foreign markets.

Export Market Development

The **Promotional Projects Program (PPP)** is designed to encourage export markets through three major trade promotion techniques: trade fairs, by providing exhibition services on a shared-cost basis; trade missions, by covering travel and other costs for outgoing missions to negotiate trade agreements and for incoming missions to promote Canadian products and capabilities; and trade visitors, by covering travel and living costs for influential foreign representatives and technical trainees.

To encourage firms to enter new export markets or expand existing ones, the federal government has established the **Program for Export Market Development (PEMD)**. This program has various sections, each designed to meet a specific type of marketing need that will contribute to increases in Canadian export sales. The program includes, for example, a sharing of bidding costs on specific projects outside Canada, market identification, and participation in trade fairs abroad. It also helps Canadian companies bring potential foreign buyers to Canada and helps Canadian exporters undertake a sustained marketing effort in a foreign market by establishing facilities on location.

The **Cost Recoverable Technical Assistance Program (CRTA)** is designed to improve Canada's performance in marketing Canadian goods and services abroad through the use of Canadian government experts. However, the major focus is to involve Canada's private sector.

The **Grain Marketing Bureau** provides information, direction and assistance to individuals and firms involved in marketing, handling, processing and market development to improve the efficiency of the marketing system. The objective is to expand trade activities with respect to grains, oilseeds and similar products, and to achieve greater market and income stability in this area.

Selling to Foreign Governments

Assistance in selling to foreign governments is provided by the **Canadian Commercial Corporation (CCC)**. This Crown corporation helps Canadian firms obtain primary contracts for government projects, many of which are linked to aid for developing countries and are therefore financed by the **Canadian International Development Agency (CIDA)**. This agency administers Canada's international development assistance program, which involves over 70 countries. Many grants and loans to developing countries are tied to the purchase of Canadian goods and services. CIDA also administers the Industrial Cooperation Program which is designed to promote and increase the involvement of the Canadian private sector in the industrial development of third world countries.

Other Assistance

The **Duty Drawback Program** is designed to help Canadian manufacturers compete with foreign manufacturers both at home and abroad by refunding customs duties and sales taxes paid on imported materials used in the manufacture of goods subsequently exported. The **Remission of Duty Program** applies to goods sent abroad for further processing which cannot be done in Canada. When goods cross several borders, customs arrangements can be made in advance through the **Carnet System**, details of which can be obtained through the **Canadian Chamber of Commerce**. The Department of External Affairs also makes exporters and importers aware of the requirements of the **Export and Import Act**, and review and approves (or denies) export or import permit applications. It also establishes policy relating to the control of exports and imports into Canada for reasons of national security, foreign policy or supply.

INTERNATIONAL FINANCE

Two key concepts related to international business and finance are balance of trade and balance of payments. While any country would naturally prefer that both of these balances be positive, such is not always the case.

TABLE 13.5
Federal assistance available for marketing products and services in foreign countries

Program or Service	Purpose and Description	Form of Assistance
EXPORTING		
Trade Commissioner Service (TCS)	Provides liaison services in foreign markets; identifies Canadian foreign market opportunities for producers: assists with foreign rules and regulations.	Advice on markets, opportunities, access requirements.
Regional Trade Offices	Provide information on foreign markets and market access, especially on U.S.A.	Advice and publications.
Export Development Corporation (EDC)	Provides financial assistance to export sales through loans, loan guarantees, insurance and surety guarantees.	Credit insurance—up to 90% of losses caused by non-payment. Loans, loan guarantees—provided when needed to foreign purchasers of Canadian goods and services. Foreign investment guarantees—investor requires 15% co-insurance. Surety and performance guarantees.
Promotional Projects Program (PPP)	To encourage export sales through trade fairs outside Canada, trade missions, trade visitors. Companies invited to participate by ITC.	Shared-cost exhibition service: travel and other costs for missions and visitors.
Program for Export Market Development (PEMD)	To assist Canadian firms to enter new or expand existing export markets, through participation in foreign capital projects, visits to/by foreign buyers, trade fairs, export consortium assistance.	Grants of up to 50% of cost, repayable if increased export sales result.

Corporation (CCC)	foreign governments.	contracts to Canadian suppliers.
Canadian International Development Agency (CIDA)	Canadian procurement under international development assistance program.	Bilateral aid tied to purchase of Canadian goods and services.
International Trade Data Bank	Provides trade data for 41 major trading countries.	Operates on a fee-for-service basis.
Customs Drawbacks	Returns duty and taxes on materials re-exported.	Duty and tax remission.
Carnet System	Allows advance customs arrangements for goods crossing several borders.	Carnets sold in Canada by Canadian Chamber of Commerce.
Management Advancement Program	Increases competence of managers in international business.	Courses developed at universities.

SOURCE: *ABC Assistance to Business in Canada* (Ottawa: Federal Business Development Bank, 1987).

Balance of Trade

The **balance of trade** is the difference between a country's imports and its exports. Foreign trade is not a one-way street where a country only exports goods to other nations; virtually every nation in the world also imports goods from other countries. If Canada were to export more during a certain period than it imported, it would have a positive or favourable balance of trade. If, on the other hand, imports were greater than exports, Canada's balance of trade during that period would be negative, or unfavourable. On the whole, countries endeavour to maintain a positive balance of trade whenever possible, but this obviously cannot be the case on a worldwide basis, as exports and imports between all countries must balance.

Balance of Payments

The **balance of payments** refers to the flow of money into and out of the country. Canada's total balance of payments consists of two components — the current account and the capital account. Each account is further divided as follows:

Current Account

Merchandise trade balance:	The difference between exports and imports.
Services trade balance:	All monetary exchanges between countries that do not involve goods — tourism, loans, gifts, funds transferred between banks, and interest and dividends paid to other countries.
Transfer payments:	Funds transferred between countries through inheritances, pensions and immigration.

Capital Account

Canadian claims on non-residents:	The net flow of funds due to Canadian direct investment abroad, and purchases of foreign stocks and bonds by Canadians. Also includes international currency reserves, bank transactions with non-residents, and some other claims.
Canadian liabilities to non-residents:	The net flow of funds due to foreign direct investment in Canada, and the purchase of Canadian stocks, bonds, and government of Canada money market instruments by foreigners.

The balance of payments is the difference between a nation's total monetary payments to foreign countries and its total receipts from foreign countries. Figure 13.3A shows Canada's international balance of payments since 1968. It has generally been negative, due largely to interest and dividends paid out as a result of foreign investment in Canada, and government and corporate borrowing abroad. On the other hand, Canada's merchandise balance of trade has generally been positive, offsetting the negative services trade balance. Figure 13.3B shows Canada's current account balance after all monetary inflows and outflows are combined. Table 13.6 shows the components of Canada's international balance of payments.

Currency Exchange

We have already discussed the floating currencies that exist in the world today. When it is no longer tied to an absolute value such as gold, the value of a country's currency fluctuates on the world money

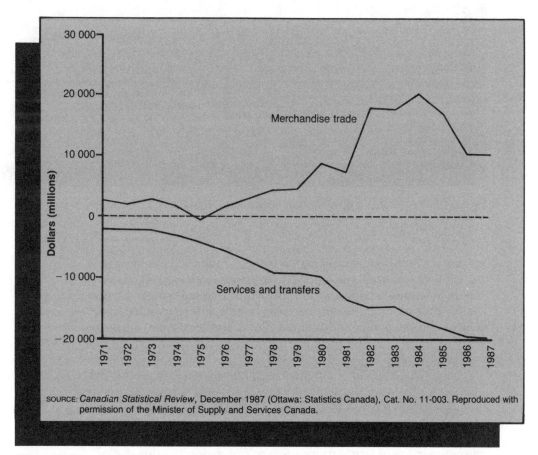

SOURCE: *Canadian Statistical Review*, December 1987 (Ottawa: Statistics Canada), Cat. No. 11-003. Reproduced with permission of the Minister of Supply and Services Canada.

Figure 13.3A Canada's balance of international payments, current account 1971–1987

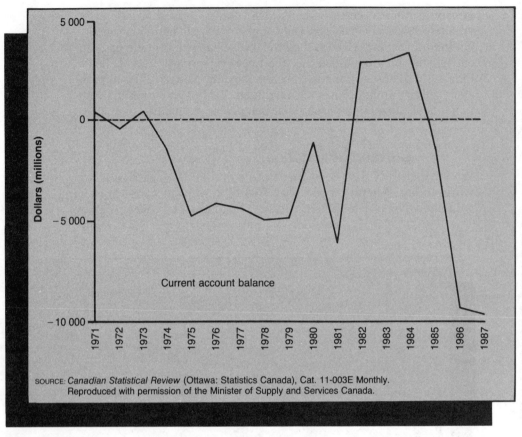

Figure 13.3B Canada's current account balance, 1971–1987

market according to supply and demand, in much the same way as the value of corporate stocks fluctuates on the stock markets. If investors believe that a company is sound and represents a good value, demand for its stock causes the price to rise; similarly, if a country is in sound financial condition and has a healthy economy, people eager to invest in it will push up the value of its currency in relation to others.

For example, a Canadian company intending to expand its own operation into West Germany cannot simply take Canadian dollars and use them to buy assets there. Rather it must sell Canadian dollars and buy West German marks on the world's currency markets. Such demand for West German marks, provided it is sustained, would cause the value of that currency to rise in relation to others.

TABLE 13.6
Summary of Canadian balance of international payments

	1986	1987
Current account balances		
Merchandise	10 388	10 341
Non-merchandise		
Services	− 4 253	− 5 343
Investment income	− 16 886	− 16 671
Transfers	1 482	2 073
Total non-merchandise	− 19 656	− 19 942
Total current account	− 9 268	− 9 601
Capital account		
Canadian claims on non-residents, net flows		
Canadian direct investment abroad	− 4 521	− 6 009
Foreign portfolio securities	− 2 412	− 1 855
Other claims	− 5 128	− 4 859
Total Canadian claims, net flow	− 12 060	− 12 723
Canadian liabilities to non-residents, net flows		
Foreign direct investment in Canada	1 550	4 361
Canadian portfolio securities	24 500	14 740
Other liabilities	− 771	7 915
Total Canadian liabilities, net flow	25 279	27 016
Total net capital flow	13 219	14 293
Statistical discrepancy	− 3 950	− 4 692

SOURCE: *Canada's International Investment Position* (Ottawa: Statistics Canada), Cat. no. 67-202. Reproduced with permission of the Minister of Supply and Services Canada.

A stable currency is desirable because fluctuations in its value can affect a nation's overall economy. If the value of the Canadian dollar falls, for instance, our exports will become less expensive in other countries. As a result, export sales would probably increase, helping to create jobs in Canada. And as imports will be more expensive, Canadians may switch from buying imported products to buying more domestic products, further increasing employment in Canada. On the other hand, if people continue to buy the higher-priced imported goods, then the drop in the value of the dollar would contribute to inflation.

There are other effects when the currency value drops. The cost of money borrowed from other countries by government and corporations in Canada will increase, since more Canadian dollars are required to pay back the loans and interest. Foreign investment in

Canada may also be affected as property and shares in Canadian corporations become less expensive in relation to other currencies.

A rise in the value of the Canadian dollar will have the opposite effect. Exports will become more expensive in other countries, which may lead to a drop in exports and a loss of jobs in Canada, while a corresponding drop in the price of imports may result in greater demand for them and consequent loss of sales and employment in similar domestic industries. And while a rising currency value will make it less expensive for government and corporations to repay principal and interest on foreign loans, Canadian property and corporate stocks would become more expensive for foreign investors.

The Fall and Rise of the Canadian Dollar

Over the years, the value of the Canadian dollar has fluctuated, as shown in Figure 13.4. The rise in the Canadian dollar *vis-à-vis* the U.S. dollar in the early 1970s was due largely to trade surpluses and capital inflows. The early 1970s was a period of heavy foreign investment in Canada and heavy borrowing, primarily from the United States, by Canadian corporations and governments at all levels. As U.S. dollars were converted into Canadian funds, demand for Canadian currency caused a rise in the value of the Canadian dollar against the U.S. dollar. Once this period of borrowing had subsided, pressure on our dollar ceased, and the currency's value dropped back to its previous level. After 1975 Canada experienced a large capital outflow which, together with poor economic performance and high inflation, caused the Canadian dollar to drop to a very low point in 1982.

Since the mid 1980s, however, the Canadian dollar has started to rise rather dramatically against the U.S. dollar. The underlying reason is Canada's economic performance, one of the strongest in the industrialized world. In addition, Canada has had relatively high interest rates in bond and money markets, and the Bank of Canada is always ready to fight inflation when necessary, both of which make Canada a desirable place to invest, which has pushed the value of the dollar upwards (see Case 13–2).

Some economists predict that the Canadian dollar will be at US $0.83 in 1989. They believe that Canada's economic growth will continue to be strong, that the free trade deal will provide a big boost, and that inflation will continue to be moderate. Others say that the Canadian dollar will head down once the interest rate differential between Canada and the United States narrows. They believe that the Canadian dollar will be back at US$0.78 in 1989.[6]

Canadian companies are neither thrilled nor upset with the rising Canadian dollar. They have learned to live with it either by cutting

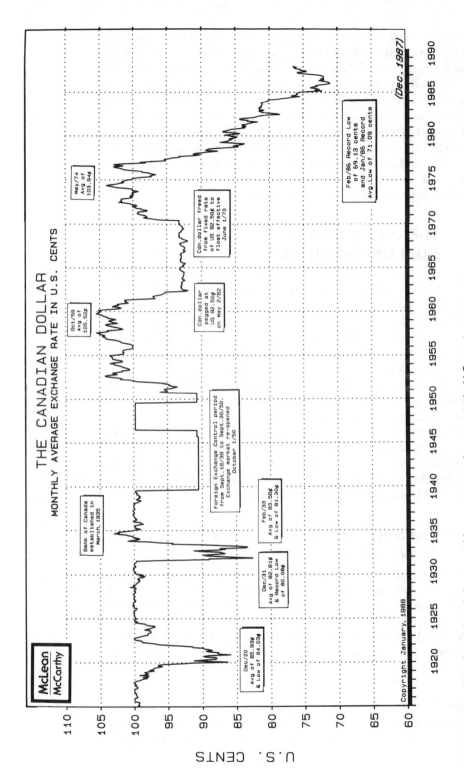

Figure 13.4 The Canadian dollar; monthly average exchange rate in U.S. cents

SOURCE: Reproduced by permission of McLean, McCarthy & Company Limited.

costs or by limiting their currency exposure through future contracts. Companies such as CAE Industries Ltd. have a policy of keeping costs in line, instead of relying on a cheap dollar to maintain the firm's competitiveness. Many resource companies have adapted to currency fluctuations, but have also been fortunate in that the prices of their products have risen, thus offsetting the impact on their earnings of rising currency exchange rates. One economist suggests that the competitiveness of many Canadian companies would be threatened if the Canadian dollar hits US$0.85. This would be particularly hard on small and medium-sized firms, which might have to consider spending money on new technology to remain competitive.[7]

THE MULTINATIONAL CORPORATION (MNC)

Multinational corporations are often simultaneously welcomed and despised. Third world nations in particular tend to see MNCs as the "imperialistic weapons" of industrialized countries, and even at home the MNC is often viewed with suspicion. The sales revenues of large MNCs may exceed the total revenues of some small countries. With operations scattered throughout the world, their business manoeuvres often resemble a game of chess in which each move is carefully calculated to achieve the greatest economic gain. They apparently owe allegiance to no one, and their major interest seems to lie in achieving their own objectives.

At the same time, multinational corporations are also praised for bringing much-needed technology to third world countries, educating the labour force, training management and creating jobs. By bringing together different cultures, ideas and ideologies, MNCs may also contribute to better international relations.

Characteristics of Multinational Corporations

A multinational corporation is one with operations in two or more countries, although it is classified as belonging to the country where the head office is located. Ownership may be widely distributed throughout the world, or the stock may be closely held in the home country. Similarly, international operations may be managed either by the home office or by locally recruited managers, particularly middle- and lower-level managers.

Evolution of the Multinational Corporation

MNCs pass through various stages of development. Initially, a firm may simply **export** products to other countries. Then as exports become more important to its operation, the company may establish an **exporting department** or hire the services of an **export agent**. As an alternative to exporting greater quantities, a domestic company may also enter an agreement by which a foreign company will manufacture a particular product under licence. This **foreign licensing** is often used to circumvent tariff barriers, trade restrictions or high shipping costs. Since local licensees are familiar with their country's social, economic, cultural, political and legal situation, they may also be of considerable aid in marketing the product.

A more advanced stage is that of **foreign marketing**, when the parent company controls a foreign sales office and sales force. The products may be manufactured in either the home plants or in foreign countries, by licence or through contract. Once the company has reached the foreign marketing stage, it is a small step to **producing in the foreign country**, either by building its own plant or by buying out an existing firm. The major automobile manufacturing companies have reached this stage in international business operation, with manufacturing plants in many countries producing either entire automobiles or parts which may then be shipped elsewhere for assembly. The basic objective is to keep production costs as low as possible.

Managing the Multinational Corporation

In addition to the problems usually encountered by management in a domestic firm, a multinational corporation operating in another sovereign state also faces several factors over which it may have very little control. While the regular business functions of production, finance, marketing and personnel are necessary in all foreign countries, they may be strongly influenced by particular cultural, social, legal and political factors.

Table 13.7 shows some of the factors that managers of multinational corporations must keep in mind in planning for international operations, in contrast to domestic planning.

To minimize the impact of foreign social, cultural, political and legal factors, MNC management is usually decentralized. Planning authority and decision-making regarding daily operations of the foreign subsidiary are left to managers largely recruited from the host country. Familiar with local customs and language, they can readily deal with local politicians and government administrators.

A second level of management coordinates the various subsidiaries and business functions on a geographical basis. This task may be shared jointly by foreign managers and those from the home office.

Tying together global operations, however, is left to top management. The head office establishes the MNC's long-range goals and objectives and the long-range strategies required to achieve them.

TABLE 13.7
Differences between domestic and international corporate planning

Domestic Planning	International Planning
1. Single language and nationality.	1. Multilingual/multinational/multi-cultural factors.
2. Relatively homogeneous market.	2. Fragmented and diverse markets.
3. Data available, usually accurate, and collection easy.	3. Data collection a formidable task, requiring significantly higher budget and personnel allocation.
4. Political factors relatively unimportant.	4. Political factors frequently vital.
5. Relative freedom from government interference.	5. Involvement in national economic plans; government influences business decisions.
6. Individual corporation has little effect on environment.	6. "Gravitational" distortion by large companies.
7. Chauvinism helps.	7. Chauvinism hinders.
8. Relatively stable business environment.	8. Multiple environments, many of which are highly unstable (but may be highly profitable).
9. Uniform financial climate.	9. Variety of financial climates ranging from over-conservative to wildly inflationary.
10. Single currency.	10. Currencies differing in stability and real value.
11. Business "rules of the game" mature and understood.	11. Rules diverse, changeable, and unclear.
12. Management generally accustomed to sharing responsibilities and using financial controls.	12. Management frequently autonomous and unfamiliar with budgets and controls.

Source: *Columbia Journal of World Business* (New York: Trustees of Columbia University, July-Aug., 1970). Reproduced by permission.

Benefits Offered by Multinational Corporations

A corporation that expands its operation to other nations benefits both the home country and its foreign hosts. One major immediate benefit, particularly for third world nations, is the transfer of the MNC's technical expertise. A multinational corporation provides technology, capital, jobs, and training for workers and management. If the corporation is large, its impact on the host's standard of living may be significant.

The benefits to the home country are somewhat less obvious. When a corporation establishes its operation in another nation, the withdrawal of capital from the home country could result in a loss of jobs. However, this situation is often only temporary. Eventually the home country may benefit from lower prices for imports from the foreign hosts, where labour costs are generally lower or raw materials more abundant. Moreover, MNCs open up markets to other domestic corporations, allowing greater production and therefore lower prices for the people at home.

In the long run, it is hoped that the greatest benefit from MNCs will be the bridging of cultural and social barriers and easing of international tensions that may come about as people come in contact with each other through economic institutions. However, this benefit can be expected only if MNCs conduct themselves in a socially responsible manner, and refrain from exploitation of their hosts.

Disadvantages of Multinational Corporations

Like any individual in a foreign country, a multinational corporation must respect and adjust to the customs of the other culture; otherwise, relations between them will become strained. For example, an MNC that gains the major share of a market may make it difficult for local businesses to compete. This new competition may eventually benefit the inhabitants, but it can cause hostility if it is introduced without due concern for social customs and cultural factors. Any attempt to monopolize the market and sell at higher prices would obviously be resented. Finally, where a foreign company has become a major economic force employing many local people, many may fear that the company will eventually withdraw once it has exploited their labour and raw materials, leaving the nation's economy in jeopardy.

On occasion MNCs have been accused of political involvement in foreign countries, whether by backing an established dictatorship to the detriment of the people or by supporting splinter parties to bring down an elected government. Such political involvement may be entirely for purposes of economic gain, but it may also represent an attempt by the MNC to protect its basic interests. For example, an unstable government may threaten **expropriation** (take-over) of the firm's assets — faced with such a loss, a large corporation would have to act to safeguard its property.

In other instances a nation's sovereignty may be infringed upon when local subsidiaries of MNCs are compelled to adhere to foreign policy decisions imposed by another government. Foreign subsidiaries may be prevented from dealing with certain nations. This was the case when Canadian subsidiaries of American corporations were unable to sell to Cuba or Communist China because the American government had forbidden any of its corporations to deal with these countries.

Finally, MNCs may drain capital out of the country in the form of interest, dividends and fees of various types. Sometimes this flow of funds out of a foreign country represents profits generated by capital borrowed in the host country. To counteract this net outflow of money, some countries have set up **exchange controls** to limit or ban the exchange of local currency for that of another country. The MNC must then reinvest its profits in the host country or produce products that can be shipped out of the country as exports.

The MNC and Foreign Investment in Canada

As discussed in Chapter 2, foreign investment has played a major role in Canada's industrial development since Confederation. Most of the initial foreign investment, from England, was used to develop Canada's primary industry and a transportation system to facilitate exports of staple products such as wheat and timber. By the 20th century, however, the United States replaced England as the dominant foreign owner of Canada's primary and manufacturing industries. In this discussion we will use **foreign investment** and **foreign ownership** synonymously; the term **foreign control** will be used in reference to corporations in Canada which are either wholly or partly owned by companies with headquarters elsewhere effectively controlling the operation of the Canadian subsidiary.

Foreign investment in Canadian industry has been encouraged in the past by a tax structure beneficial to foreign business, and through generous federal and provincial government subsidies for foreign companies to establish in economically depressed areas. In addition, Canadian financial institutions were eager to lend money to established foreign firms, particularly to U.S. companies, because they represented a lower risk than inexperienced Canadian companies. Other attractions for foreign firms included virtual freedom from pollution restrictions, abundant natural resources and energy, and a stable political structure. Once established, foreign firms were practically assured of profits, since many of the industrial sectors were almost entirely free of Canadian competition.

As Figure 13.5A shows, foreign long-term investment in Canada increased considerably from 1955 until 1984 and totalled $272 billion at the end of 1984. In 1985, U.S.-controlled companies continued to hold a dominant position. They represented 71.5% of the assets,

75.6% of the sales and 85.9% of the profits of all foreign-controlled firms. Nevertheless, the foreign-controlled share of assets declined by 0.8 percentage points to 23.4%. This compares to a peak of 37.0% in 1971; since that time, foreign ownership has decreased steadily with the majority of the decline originating in the mining and petroleum industry. In this industry, over the past 21 years, foreign-controlled assets declined from 99.7% to 42.1%, much of it due to some large acquisitions of Canadian-controlled companies such as Petro-Can. Since 1965, U.S.-controlled firms have accounted for 96% of the overall decline in the share of foreign-controlled assets.[8] Figure 13.5B shows foreign direct investment in Canada in 1987 by industry group.

During the 1970s, the extent of foreign ownership of Canadian industry had become an issue with politicians and labour leaders, and through the press the debate was transferred to the general public. Politicians and labour leaders charged that economic decisions affecting Canada were being made by corporations in foreign countries. A net outflow of capital from Canada and the possibility of political, economic and cultural assimilation were further grounds for concern. Since almost 80% of all foreign ownership in Canadian industry is American, most of the criticism was directed at the United States.

The federal government's response to the foreign ownership issue was passage of the Foreign Investment Review Act (FIRA) which came into effect in December, 1973. As outlined in Chapter 12, the Act had two major objectives:

1. To review most acquisitions in Canada that could transfer control of Canadian businesses to non-residents.
2. To review the establishment of new businesses by non-Canadians who either do not already have a business in Canada, or do not have one to which the new operation would be related.

Today FIRA is known as Investment Canada and its mandate has been changed so that it acts as a monitoring agency only. Since the change in its role, it has not prevented any foreign take-overs. Obviously, any government intervention in foreign ownership in Canada must take into account both the disadvantages and the advantages to Canadians. Some of these are discussed below.

Benefits of Foreign Investment in Canada

Has foreign investment benefited Canada? Undoubtedly foreign investment and consequent ownership of Canadian industry has had some effect on economic growth. In terms of actual capital inflow into Canada, the benefit has been minor — 90% of the funding for

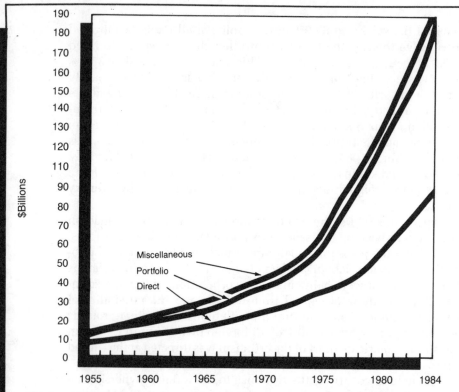

NOTE: Foreign long-term investment comprises primarily portfolio investment (share ownership in Canadian companies) and direct investment (direct ownership of Canadian companies). Portfolio ownership does not necessarily mean control of the company unless a majority portion of the shares are foreign owned.

Figure 13.5A Foreign long-term investment in Canada by type of investment

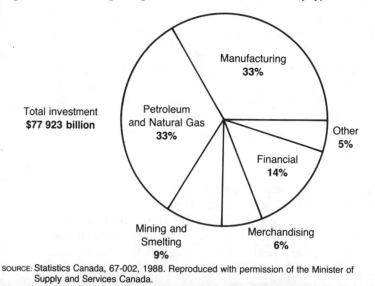

SOURCE: Statistics Canada, 67-002, 1988. Reproduced with permission of the Minister of Supply and Services Canada.

Figure 13.5B Foreign direct investment in Canada, 1987, by industry group

capital investments by U.S. corporations has come from within Canada, of which 70% comes from retained earnings (earnings not distributed to shareholders).[9] Other factors have assisted Canada's economic growth, however. Most fundamental, perhaps, was the increase in entrepreneurial spirit essential to a private enterprise economy. In addition, various new technologies, patents and processes, along with managerial expertise, have been brought to Canada from outside. Entrepreneurs who invested in Canadian production facilities have also opened markets for Canadian products worldwide through the export of many of the goods produced.

A major benefit of foreign investment in Canada, however, has been its contribution to the development of a manufacturing industry, steering Canada away from complete reliance on staple and primary exports, which provide few jobs and make the economy vulnerable to fluctuating world markets and prices for primary products. Since manufacturing provides more jobs than primary industry, it gradually raises the level of total personal income, which in turn increases demand for manufactured products. Thus as the increase in total production contributes to overall economic growth, it also increases the standard of living.

Another direct benefit of foreign investment in Canadian industry was the introduction of mass production techniques largely developed in the United States. These techniques have helped to reduce the prices of manufactured products. In many instances the competition for existing Canadian companies provided by foreign-owned firms has also led to lower prices for the Canadian consumer. Finally, all levels of government have benefited from the additional revenues in corporate taxes from foreign-owned subsidiaries, as well as the increase in overall economic activity.

Disadvantages of Foreign Investment in Canada

One major disadvantage of foreign investment is the net outflow of funds from Canada in the form of dividends, management fees, licence fees and royalties. As discussed earlier, this outflow can affect the balance of payments and the exchange rate, with serious ramifications for the country's general economic condition.

Moreover, despite the increase in manufacturing noted above, much of the foreign ownership in Canada still involves the development of primary industry. The oil, mining and forest products industries depend largely on unskilled labour, with upper level management and technical experts usually brought from the foreign country. Few of the jobs created are permanent, and once the resource is depleted, the firm may move on. Nevertheless, in the past our governments have offered subsidies to foreign corporations to develop these industries in Canada, providing generous tax benefits and other financial incentives.

The third major disadvantage in foreign investment is the possibility that it may lead to a reduction in Canadian sovereignty and a loss of decision-making control over the nation's economic future. While some claims may be exaggerated, American-owned Canadian subsidiaries have in the past been forbidden to conduct business with certain countries even when Canada itself maintained diplomatic relations with them. In addition, foreign control of certain Canadian companies may leave major economic decisions to shareholders outside the country. Given that much of this control over Canadian affairs resides in the United States, many fear that Canada is gradually becoming assimilated — socially, economically and politically — into our southern neighbour.

Solutions to Canada's Foreign Ownership Dilemma

One solution often heard is "buy back Canada." What would the consequences of such an action be? First, it would mean channelling already scarce Canadian capital into the purchase of outstanding shares in existing Canadian companies which are already producing jobs, and which would not add to new capital stock, productivity or total production. The federal government embarked on this course of action to reduce foreign ownership in the oil industry. In 1981, through Petro-Canada, it bought the Belgian-controlled Petrofina Canada Inc. for $1.46 billion, to be partly financed through a tax levied on gasoline. The purchase was attacked as contributing to inflation because of the increases in gas prices. However, the primary criticism was that the company siphoned off capital from Canadians. Rather than being used to buy existing refineries and gas outlets, the critics argued that the investment should have gone to search for new sources of oil or energy, or to help develop new industries to create jobs.

Several questions have to be answered if a **buy-back** of foreign-owned industry were to be done on a large scale. How much capital would be left to invest in new ventures to create the new jobs that will be required in the future? Would there be capital available to replace outdated and worn-out machinery and equipment, to raise the present level of productivity and increase total production? Where would we obtain capital for projects that are particularly crucial because of the world energy crisis: to find new supplies of crude oil, develop the tar sands and discover new sources of energy, for example?

Canadians have to consider that a buy-back Canada policy could reduce our economic well-being. In addition, there are other questions. If we did buy back the physical assets of foreign-owned corporations, how could we buy their technical and managerial expertise? How could we ensure continued access to the major world markets, particularly in the United States?

What are the possible solutions to Canada's foreign investment dilemma? Rather than inviting foreign corporations to establish in Canada, we could manufacture products under licence or in joint ventures. Instead of giving subsidies to foreign companies, our governments could help domestic companies finance new ventures in Canada. Financial institutions for their part could put more faith in Canadian entrepreneurs and make loans for business more readily available. On the other hand, results could be detrimental if we resort to tariff barriers and other forms of protection from foreign competition, or if we continue to support industries, such as textiles and shoe manufacturing, which are inefficient. The onus could be put on these industries themselves to modernize their plants and equipment and thus become more productive. We should develop those skills and products that give us an international competitive advantage, and then export those products or services through our own multinational corporations.[10]

Canadian Multinational Corporations

Foreign-based concerns, however, are not the only MNCs operating in Canada. In fact, a number of multinational corporations doing business in other parts of the world are headquartered in Canada. One Canadian MNC, Brascan Ltd., was established in 1912 as Brazilian Traction, Light and Power Company. Known in Brazil as "Light," it was once the largest private industry in that country. In 1978 the Brazilian government purchased the Brazilian assets of the Canadian firm, but until that time most of the company's profits were taken out of Brazil to finance diversification in other companies in Canada and elsewhere. Other large Canadian MNCs are Moore Corporation which produces business forms and related products; Noranda, a company in mining and smelting operations; and Bata Shoe Company, which makes shoes in over 90 countries.

Canada has also become active in foreign investment elsewhere, particularly in the United States. Figure 13.6A shows Canadian direct investment abroad from 1979 to 1987. Each year shows total direct investment in all countries as well as the portion of total investment that was made in the United States. Total Canadian direct investment abroad in 1987 amounted to $55.556 billion. Of the total direct investment abroad, 68% or $37.824 billion was in the United States. Figure 13.6B shows how Canadian direct investment abroad was broken down by industry group.

The flow of funds southward began with the Liberal government's energy policy: its struggle with the provinces regarding resource ownership and taxation contributed directly to the exodus of resource companies out of Canada. Other incentives for Canadian

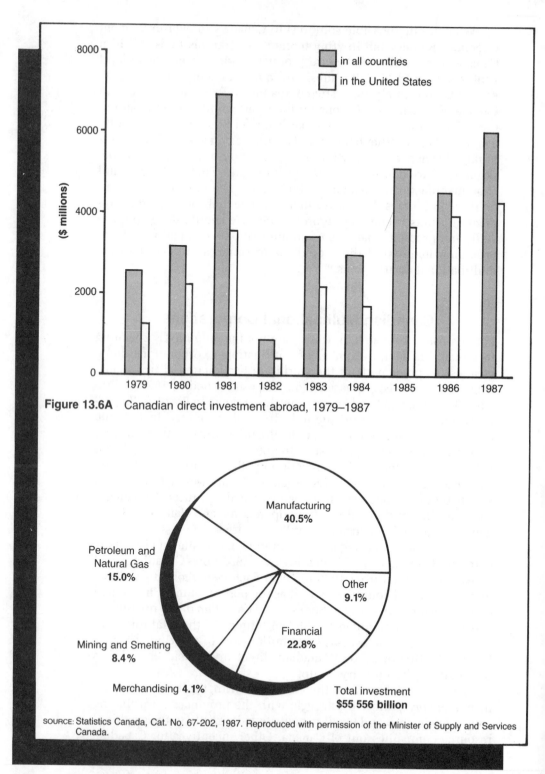

Figure 13.6A Canadian direct investment abroad, 1979–1987

Manufacturing
40.5%

Petroleum and
Natural Gas
15.0%

Other
9.1%

Financial
22.8%

Mining and Smelting
8.4%

Merchandising **4.1%**

Total investment
$55 556 billion

SOURCE: Statistics Canada, Cat. No. 67-202, 1987. Reproduced with permission of the Minister of Supply and Services Canada.

Figure 13.6B Canadian direct investment abroad, 1987

business to move south resemble those that first drew foreign investment here — new markets, lower labour costs, fewer government regulations, and business incentives in the form of lower corporate taxes and low-cost financing. Many states also have low construction costs, numerous industrial parks, and a pool of labour easily trainable and under little union influence — right-to-work laws in a number of states allow workers to choose whether or not they will join a union. Today, many business executives believe the climate in the United States is healthier, particularly for resource companies dealing in natural gas, petroleum and coal.[11]

Although the Progressive Conservative government has virtually dismantled the National Energy Policy and made a number of other policy changes in an attempt to lure back investment capital, change does not occur overnight. With the free trade deal, it is also difficult to forecast what will happen with regard to capital flowing into and out of Canada. With tariff barriers gone, Canadian companies will be able to operate in Canada, yet sell to a huge American market. On the other hand, it might be worthwhile to move the manufacturing plant to the United States where the greatest market exists.

Although many business leaders believe that Canada's long-term future is assured because of resources and technology, in the short run, government policies are thought by some to have disturbed the economic climate. Resources were used to shore up economic and social policies that drained Canada financially, creating huge deficits and a national debt that may never be reduced. Yet some social programs and policies have represented a significant improvement in the quality of life in Canada. It is important to consider the trade-off between economic growth on the one hand, and the implementation of social programs on the other.

NOTES

1. David J. Freiman, *The Marketing Path to Global Profits* (New York: AMACOM, a division of the America Management Association, 1979), pp. 41–2.
2. Andrew Coyne, "Domestic firms still want content quotas," *The Financial Post, Special Report on the Auto Industry*, February 23, 1987, pp. 33–44.
3. "Why we're losing out on autos," *The Financial Post*, March 29, 1980, p. 1. See also, "A push to attract more auto production," *Business Week*, June 16, 1980, p. 76.
4. Fred Blaser, "Auto Pact's been irrelevant for years," *The Financial Post*, July 6, 1987, p. 6.
5. Andrew Coyne, "Other nations play free trade, and win," *The Financial Post*, October 12, 1987, p. 38.

6. Ted Jackson, "Economists split on how long surge will last," *The Financial Post*, March 21, 1988, p. 4.

7. Fred Lebolt, "Panic missing as companies see C$ rise eat away profit," *The Financial Post*, March 21, 1988, p. 4.

8. "Foreign Control of Canadian Corporations Declines," *INFOMAT* (Ottawa: Statistics Canada), January 15, 1988. Cat. 11–002E. See also Statistics Canada, 1984, Ottawa: The Minister of Supply and Services, Cat. 67–202, pp. 31–5; A.E. Sofarian, "Some Myths About Foreign Business Investment," in David K. Banner, *Business and Society: Canadian Issues* (Toronto: McGraw-Hill Ryerson Ltd., 1979), pp. 286–90.

9. Banner, *op. cit.*, p. 261.

10. Sofarian, *op. cit.*

11. John Van der Feyst, "Exodus! The Flight of Canadian Capital," *Canadian Business*, Dec. 1976.

CHAPTER SUMMARY

International trade is an important element in the Canadian economy — almost one quarter of what we produce is exported. Trade is also essential to other countries, as few can produce all the goods required by their people. According to the principle of comparative advantage, nations should export what they can produce most efficiently and import what they cannot produce or can produce only at high cost.

Despite the necessity for international trade, however, a number of barriers exist. Many governments have recognized the disadvantages of these barriers, and have combined to establish agencies and agreements such as the World Bank and the International Monetary Fund. Several countries have also joined together in trade communities of various types. The Canadian government offers a variety of programs and services to assist Canadian manufacturers in finding and developing markets in other countries.

International trade and international finance work hand in hand, and both can affect a country's balance of payments. Although Canada has generally enjoyed a favourable balance of trade, the balance of payments since the latter part of the 1970s has been unfavourable, largely because of the outflow of funds in interest and dividend payments to foreign investors. Government and corporate borrowings abroad have also been contributing factors. An unfavourable balance of payments can affect the value of a nation's currency and its ability to borrow in the world money markets.

International business can operate on several levels, from simply exporting products to owning facilities in other countries and producing there. Multinational corporations are those with operations in more than one country. MNCs are often resented by host countries because of their power to control markets and prices, as well as their occasional interference in a nation's internal affairs and politics. However, MNCs also offer many benefits — expanding world trade, bringing technical expertise to third world countries, training workers, and creating new jobs, foreign customers and investment opportunities.

Foreign investment has played an important role in Canada's economic development, helping to establish both primary and manufacturing industries. In the 1970s many Canadians were afraid that excessive foreign ownership of industry would interfere with Canada's sovereignty and hasten its social, economic and political assimilation into the United States, Canada's major foreign investor. In response to these fears the federal government established the Foreign Investment Review Agency to monitor and control foreign investment. In the 1980s foreign ownership, particularly in the mining and petroleum industry, has declined substantially, a decline attributable in large part to the acquisitions by Canadian-controlled companies. FIRA was also abandoned because there was increasing realization that discouraging foreign investment was not in Canada's self-interest. Furthermore, in the 1980s Canada has become a major foreign investor in the United States and the home base of many Canadian multinationals.

KEY TERMS

Absolute advantage

Comparative advantage

Exports

Imports

Cartels

General Agreement on Tariffs and Trade (GATT)

Tariffs

Import quotas

Embargo

Dumping

World Bank

International Monetary Fund (IMF)

Currency exchange rates

Floating currencies

Special Drawing Rights (SDRs)

Common Market

European Economic Community (EEC)

European Free Trade Area (EFTA)

Trade Commissioner Service

Export Development Corporation (EDC)

Canadian Commercial Corporation (CCC)

Canadian International Development Agency (CIDA)

Balance of trade

Balance of payments

Merchandise trade balance

Services trade balance

Multinational corporation (MNC)

Foreign licensing

Foreign marketing

Expropriation

Exchange controls

Foreign investment

Foreign ownership

Foreign control

REVIEW QUESTIONS

1. Why do countries trade with one another?

2. Distinguish between absolute and comparative advantage. For what goods does Canada have a comparative advantage in producing and selling to other countries?

3. Why is comparative advantage not always the basis underlying foreign trade?

4. List and describe five major barriers to international trade.

5. What is the purpose of the GATT? What are the major problems with the GATT today?

6. What was the purpose of the Canada-U.S. Auto Agreement? Why might the agreement not be very effective in the future?

7. What are the objectives of the Canada-U.S. Free Trade Agreement? What appear to be the major advantages to Canada of free trade with the United States?

8. Why were the World Bank and the International Monetary Fund established? How has the IMF become entangled in the world debt crisis?

9. What is meant by a floating currency? What are SDRs?

10. Distinguish between a common market and a free trade area.

11. What are five major ways in which the federal government encourages exports of Canadian goods? Why is the government interested in expanding foreign markets?

12. Explain how it is possible for Canada to have a favourable balance of trade, but an unfavourable balance of payments.

13. Outline the major categories that make up Canada's total balance of payments. Distinguish between current account and capital account.

14. Why is a stable currency desirable?

15. Explain the effect on a country's economy of the value of its currency rising against those of others.

16. Outline the major characteristics of a multinational corporation. How do MNCs establish themselves in other countries?

17. What are some of the difficulties in managing a multinational company as compared to a domestic company?

18. Why would certain governments, particularly those in third world countries, encourage foreign corporations to locate there?

19. What are the advantages and disadvantages of foreign investment in Canada?

DISCUSSION QUESTIONS

1. Debate the following statement: "Canada should have free trade with the United States."

2. Why does the government restrict trade through tariff and non-tariff barriers, while actively encouraging exports to other countries? Explain.

3. Discuss the following statement: "The benefits of multinational corporations to international business and international development outweigh their disadvantages in all respects."

4. Should MNCs be controlled? How might this be done?

5. Discuss the following statement: "We should reduce foreign ownership in Canada by buying back shares held by foreigners in Canadian corporations."

CASE 13–1 The Beer and Wine Industry and Free Trade

When the free trade agreement between Canada and the U.S. comes into effect there will be winners and losers. Many Canadian businesspeople support free trade and believe that the numbers of losers would be relatively small. However, one industry that believes it will be an

---

early casualty is the Canadian wine industry. According to a study prepared for the free trade negotiators in 1986, at the present time the wine industry is neither price nor quality competitive with European and U.S. wines. It is a small industry, employing about 3200 people mainly in Ontario, British Columbia and Nova Scotia. In 1986 it produced about $225 million worth of wine. The industry claims that under the free trade deal, U.S. wineries will increase their Canadian market share from 10 per cent to as much as 50 per cent.

The Wine Institute, which represents a majority of California's wineries, called for retaliation against Canadian beer and whisky exports to the U.S. unless Canadian trade negotiators agree to end federal import tariffs and the high provincial sales markups on imported U.S. wine.

The brewers also fear that their $2 billion industry may be sacrificed for a free trade deal with the U.S. Government officials have promised that a free trade deal will include a transition period to allow for changes in regulations and tariffs. The brewers, however, are concerned that Ottawa will not provide sufficient adjustment time for their industry to adapt to the new trade environment.

The large-scale American breweries have the capacity to serve the Canadian market three times over, at significantly lower cost than those of the Canadian makers. While Canadians show some brand loyalty, if offered lower priced American beer, many Canadians would switch, according to brewery officials. Brands such as Coors, Budweiser, and Miller could quickly increase their share of the Canadian market to 40% from the present 15% under a free trade deal. This would result in 8000 of the industry's 20 000 workers losing their job.

SOURCE: Adapted from "Potential victims of a trade pact," *Maclean's*, August 10, 1987, p. 23.

QUESTIONS

1. Ignoring the Free Trade Agreement for the moment, can you suggest reasons for and against government protection of an industry, such as the wine or beer industry, which would not otherwise be able to compete against U.S. and European imports?

2. When the Free Trade Agreement comes into effect, the case suggests that the American breweries have the capacity to serve the Canadian market three times over, at significantly lower cost than Canadian brewers. What might the Canadian breweries do to stay in business?

3. If the Free Trade Agreement comes into effect and in fact hurts the wine industry, does the federal government have an obligation to help the industry and affected workers? If so, what might the federal government do?

CASE 13–2 The Dollar's Power Trip

Its rise and fall is always a mixed blessing. But for Canadians who have grown accustomed to living with a low-valued currency, the dollar's recent surge in the foreign exchange markets has been a welcome change. The Canadian dollar nudged the 80-cent (U.S.) mark last week, closing at 79.53 cents — the first time since February, 1984. The currency's new surge marked an abrupt change from its sluggish performance in recent years. The dollar has climbed eight cents since late 1986, when it hovered near 72 cents after plunging to a record low of 69 cents in February, 1986. Indeed, during the past two years, it has rebounded strongly, posting a gain of 10 cents against the U.S. dollar. Said Hugh Williams, senior manager in the Bank of Nova Scotia's foreign exchange department: "There's a lot of confidence among foreign investors about Canada's economic prospects."

Among the driving forces behind the Canadian dollar's strength is the perception of an enormously improved Canadian economy. The international view of Canada's economy started to improve as prices for such commodities as nickel and forest products began to strengthen last year. As well, economists attribute the Canadian dollar's steady ascent to our leading rate of economic growth compared with that of other industrialized nations. The Paris-based Organization for Economic Co-operation and Development predicted that this year Canada's economy would outperform those of all other major industrialized nations except Japan. At the same time, interest rates in Canada are higher than in the United States, which attracts foreign investors who want a higher yield for their money. Indeed, the economy's strong performance attracted $4.4 billion in direct foreign investment last year.

Offshore buyers' demand for Canadian currency is growing steadily stronger. Economists say that when the 78-cent level was achieved on Jan. 20 speculative pressure started forcing the dollar up further as buyers anticipated a continuing increase in the currency's value. Williams predicted that the Canadian dollar would hit 80 cents before the end of the first quarter, and some economists say that they expect the dollar to reach 81 cents by the middle of the year and jump to 83 cents by the end of 1988.

Many Canadians will likely soon experience tangible results from the currency's upward movement. The dollar's rise against the greenback will make most U.S. imports cheaper. And Canadians vacationing in the United States or in any country that uses the greenback as its prime currency will also get more value for their dollar. At the same time, the Canadian dollar has fallen, along with the greenback, against other currencies, including the West German mark and the Japanese yen. This means that European imports and vacations will be more expensive.

But many Canadian exporters will eventually find it more difficult to sell their goods in the United States because a stronger dollar will make their goods more expensive. It is usually at least six months before a change in a currency's value affects the volume of imports and exports, but at some point U.S. buyers might turn to cheaper domestic or foreign suppliers for goods and services traditionally imported from Canada.

The dollar's rebound may also force the Conservative government to alter its monetary policies. Finance Minister Michael Wilson and Bank of Canada governor John Crow are under increasing pressure to lower Canadian interest rates to a point closer to those of the United States. Because short-term interest rates are about 2.5 percentage points higher in Canada than in the United States, foreign investors seeking high yields are favouring Canadian bonds and treasury bills — sustaining demand for the dollar.

But some economists say that the high rates are no longer necessary to keep the dollar strong. As well, they say, lower rates would stimulate domestic economic activity, keeping the dollar high. Meanwhile, officials in Wilson's office said that the interest rates have been effective in keeping inflation down. They added that, because the economy continues to perform solidly, Wilson is reluctant to lower rates.

In fact, lower interest rates might weaken the dollar if foreign investors began looking for better returns elsewhere. According to Williams, if interest rates are lowered it may create an expectation that the dollar will stabilize, or fall, and foreign demand could drop off dramatically. If that happens, Canadians might experience higher inflation because they would have to pay more for imports as the dollar fell. But last week the central bank increased its lending rate slightly — a clear sign that the government's resolve has not softened.

SOURCE: Theresa Tedesco, "The dollar's power trip," *Maclean's*, March 21, 1988, p. 32.

QUESTIONS

1. Explain how higher interest rates in Canada compared to those in the United States will cause the value of the Canadian dollar to rise. On the other hand, why might a rise in U.S. interest rates cause the value of the Canadian dollar to drop?

2. What impact does the rise in the value of the Canadian dollar *vis-à-vis* the U.S. dollar have on the Canadian economy? How might it affect individual Canadian citizens?

3. Explain how the Bank of Canada can prevent the value of the Canadian dollar from dropping.

CHAPTER 14

Social Responsibility and Business

Dick Hemingway

CHAPTER OUTLINE

CHAPTER PREVIEW

In Chapter 14 we examine the social responsibility of business. By now you have some appreciation of our business system — what it is, what it does, how it evolved and how important it is to our way of life. In the context of society at large, however, it is particularly important to understand the role and function of management, since it is management's values and beliefs that determine its reaction to the various issues of concern to society. When discussing social responsibility, therefore, it is not so much a question of business in relation to society as it is of management in relation to society. And management's position on social issues depends on the individual manager's view.

Thus, in this chapter we first define the concept of social responsibility and then consider the ethics that influence management's reaction to social issues. We review the arguments for and against business accepting social responsibility, before turning to some of the specific social and ethical issues of primary concern today. The chapter ends with a discussion of what society expects from business, whether business is meeting these objectives, and the ways in which business can control and measure its social responsibility.

LEARNING OBJECTIVES

After reading this chapter you should be able to explain:

1. The meaning of social responsibility, morals, ethics and laws;
2. The arguments for and against business taking on social responsibility;
3. Some of the major social issues affecting employees, consumers and the community;
4. Some of the major ethical issues facing businesspeople today;
5. The problems that business encounters in deciding how to carry out its social responsibility and measure its achievement of social objectives.

We have now reached the point in our examination of business where factual and practical matters must give way to more abstract concerns. Rather than asking how managers perform their jobs or why a particular decision is made, we will ask questions such as: "Should managers do this? Is it good or bad? Is it right or wrong?"

Questions of this nature cannot be answered by feeding information into a computer. Computers can solve many practical business problems, control production processes, compile statistical information into reports and solve arithmetical problems quickly; they can even perform sophisticated logical analysis based on specific criteria. However, they cannot determine whether a management decision — based, inevitably, on value judgments — is good or bad, right or wrong.

What is the social responsibility of business? What is the role of business in society? These questions have not always been of concern to management. A century ago business still subscribed to Adam Smith's principles of non-interference — leave business alone, let everyone pursue his own interests, and society will be best served. Undoubtedly many individuals in business today still hold the same fundamental view.

Surveying the current Canadian economic system, we find that the basic principles underlying it have not changed. We still rely on private individuals to decide what to produce; we still use the profit motive for incentive; competition is still the basic control mechanism that keeps the system in check. Nevertheless, substantial modifications have been made by government intervention in the economic system and by other groups in society such as labour and consumers. These changes came about because an increasingly mature society has demanded that business pursue social as well as economic goals. Today business owners and managers operate in a restrictive environment. Their freedom to operate has been curtailed in many areas, and demands that business adopt a more social orientation are increasing.

But business — or more specifically, management — faces conflicting objectives in this respect. Traditionally it has been management's responsibility, as hired guardians of shareholders' investment, to protect that investment and ensure the highest possible return on it. Today, while no one disputes management's duty to shareholders for economic performance, it must be fulfilled with society in mind. In other words, management's responsibility extends beyond the shareholders to employees, customers, minority groups, the country as a whole and even to other nations.

WHAT IS SOCIAL RESPONSIBILITY?

Businesses generally act in such a way as to achieve the greatest economic benefit for themselves and their shareholders. This goal may or may not take into account the impact of certain business decisions on society. When a business organization is determined to act in a **socially responsible** manner, it will attempt to anticipate the social consequences of a proposed course of action and if necessary modify it, even if it means lower profits.

However, it is often difficult to judge how society will be affected by a course of action prior to its implementation. An example is the issue of nuclear power. Many nuclear power plants are built by private companies using private investment funds, and the shareholders of these companies want a return on their investment. Moreover, unless Canada can rely on other sources of power, the economy as a whole will continue to depend on the oil-producing countries, which can throw it into instant turmoil by cutting supplies or raising prices. Yet in the present stage of technology nuclear accidents cannot be ruled out. Given the gravity of both considerations, should the management of these private companies be involved in the crucial decision as to whether to build such plants at all? Or should the judgment be left to politicians? Then business managers would simply be responsible for building the plants and operating them as efficiently as possible — in other words, fulfilling their responsibility to consumers by keeping the price of energy as low as possible, and to shareholders by ensuring them a reasonable return on their investment.

Business managers have a responsibility to be cost-efficient, both in operating these plants and in building them. But what if the concern for costs results in construction flaws which may ultimately contribute to a serious accident? What is management's social responsibility in this instance? Obviously, if flaws were consciously permitted, the company was not acting in the best interest of society and will pay for its negligence through heavy fines or lawsuits. But what if the accident happened inadvertently?

Social responsibility is never a clear-cut, black and white issue. Certainly business must be socially responsible, but what is considered responsible behaviour hinges not only on the situation but also on society and the individuals concerned. Socially responsible behaviour is therefore closely tied to personal ethics, morals and laws.

LAWS, MORALS AND ETHICS

Society establishes safeguards for protection against behaviour by individuals which may cause harm to other individuals or society in general. All individuals and businesses must conduct themselves according to the **laws** of society — rules established by elected officials which generally reflect the values of society at a particular time — or face the penalty for non-compliance. Unfortunately, the system of laws is complex and often difficult to interpret, even for judges. Thus it is not always clear whether or not individuals are breaking the law when they conduct their activities.

When it comes to social responsibility, businesspeople face not only the laws of society, but moral and ethical questions as well. Moral and ethical rules and behaviour are generally deeply rooted in tradition and religion and reinforced by the family and educational institutions. A **moral code** is the standard of current acceptable personal behaviour in a society, while **ethics** is the study of moral behaviour — what is morally right. In ethics, social behaviour is examined from the standpoint of what is best for society. Some organizations and professional associations in fields such as medicine and the law have thus established ethical codes that specify the behaviour expected of their members.

BUSINESS ETHICS

A formal **code of business ethics** would specify how every businessperson should behave in a particular situation. Unfortunately, in business there is no such universally accepted code. What is considered acceptable varies from one individual to another, and from one society to the next. For example, while in Canada it is considered unethical to obtain a business contract through bribery, the practice is common and accepted in many other countries.

Thus, the quest for a common set of business ethics — agreeable to all individuals and applicable in all situations — has so far been unsuccessful. Nevertheless, most individuals do strive to maintain a high standard of behaviour, and many companies establish their own internal ethical codes. A high percentage of the businesspeople questioned in one survey stated that they would rather go bankrupt than resort to behaviour contrary to their own conscience.[1] Still, the drive for profit, especially in a highly competitive situation, can put extreme pressure on executives to ignore ethics at times.

DOES BUSINESS HAVE A SOCIAL RESPONSIBILITY?

There are certain instances in which few would argue against business fulfilling its social responsibility. Pollution of the environment, for example, can no longer be tolerated. Therefore, government has

"Before we begin this month's board meeting, does anyone want to break down and confess to any high level wrong doing, bribe taking, price fixing or what have you?"

SOURCE: Cartoon by Henry Martin. Reprinted, by permission of the publisher, from "Executives Under Siege: Strategies for Survival," by George S. Odiorne, *MANAGEMENT REVIEW*, April 1978, © 1978 by AMACOM, a division of American Management Association, p. 12. All rights reserved.

stepped in to legislate what organizations must do to avoid pollution — though as we will see later, pollution control still depends for the most part on voluntary action by businesspeople.

Other issues are less clearly defined, however. What is a company's responsibility to long-term employees who are no longer useful to it? Should it be obliged to take care of them, or can they be let go? What is a company's social responsibility regarding the quality and possible danger of the products that it puts on the market? In both instances ethical considerations certainly come into play. And while most managers would probably agree that they have a responsibility to employees and customers, some might indeed place business performance and profitability first.

The Case for Business Assuming Social Responsibility

The major argument for business assuming some degree of social responsibility is based on the notion that inasmuch as a firm is a "corporate citizen," its relations with society are similar to those of an individual citizen. In the eyes of the law a corporation is an artificial person and therefore has certain rights — it may produce goods and services as it sees fit and deal with the proceeds as it wishes. At the same time, the corporation also has certain responsibilities. Since it uses air, water and land which are the joint property of society, it must ensure that its use of these resources is careful and conscientious, that it does not endanger society, and that the environment is disturbed as little as possible. If a business persistently ignores society's demands in these areas, its charter may be withdrawn.

Another persuasive reason for business to accept its social responsibility is to keep government rules and regulations to a minimum. Some businesspeople now realize that unless they assume their social responsibility voluntarily, they will be forced to accept it through increased legislation. As many believe they are already subject to excessive government intervention, it is in their own interest to take on greater responsibility.

One factor that may facilitate an increase in social responsibility is the growing trend toward separation of ownership from management. Most large corporations today are run by professional managers who have at most a small share of ownership in the business. Hence there is less pressure on managers to be concerned exclusively with economic performance, and some social costs could be included as part of the overall costs of doing business. Moreover, as responsible private citizens, business managers should use their professional expertise and power when possible to do something about issues of concern to society.

A final major argument in favour of business accepting its social responsibility is based on the power enjoyed by large corporations. With power comes the responsibility to use it wisely. Large corporations such as General Motors and IBM have total sales revenues greater than those of many small nations, and this fact alone creates an obligation to behave responsibly toward the society that has fostered their growth.

The Case Against Business Assuming Social Responsibility

One well-known American economist believes strongly that since a business is not a social organization but an economic institution, its primary responsibility is to its shareholders. Milton Friedman, author of *Free to Choose*, says that business should concentrate on its economic objectives. Human, material, and financial resources should be used efficiently and effectively to maximize profits through the production of the goods and services that society needs and wants — social obligations are discharged through the payment of taxes to government which is better equipped for evaluating social needs. In fact, Friedman is not so much against the idea of social responsibility in business as he is opposed to business taking on activities that fall outside its primary function and for which it is ill-equipped to do a good job. Unfortunately, this view does not take into account two major factors. First, business uses resources such as air and water that must be shared with the rest of society; if they are improperly used, society may suffer. Second, Friedman's system also assumes that competition between firms is great enough to keep corporate behaviour in check — a situation that rarely exists today.

Another argument questions the manager's right to decide unilaterally on how to dispose of shareholders' property — in this case, money — without their consent. After all, shareholders take risks when they invest in a company, and they should be adequately rewarded. Moreover, many shareholders, especially those who are retired, depend on their dividends from share ownership for survival. Even if shareholders did give managers the authority to use some profits for social purposes, are managers competent to judge which social projects are desirable?

Those who oppose business taking on social responsibility also cite the competitive disadvantage — companies that spend money for social projects must charge higher prices for their products than companies that do not. While this argument may be true in the short run if profits are adversely affected by social projects, in the long run the resulting customer good will would lead to increased sales. Moreover, increased acceptance of social responsibility could eventually reduce existing pressures to change the current business system because it does not meet society's needs.

Finally, some argue that firms that accept social responsibility actually take on a more powerful position in society than they should have — social and economic power becomes concentrated in the hands of a few individuals who subscribe primarily to business values. Is business equipped to decide on the social projects to be undertaken? Or should such decisions be left to politicians with a mandate from the people? Perhaps the financing of such projects should be left to government, which can collect revenue from all citizens to carry out the programs judged essential for society.

While there are valid arguments on both sides of the issue, today business does appear to be gradually accepting more social responsibility. The change is slow, as it requires a major shift in management's philosophy and its priorities. Somehow business must achieve a balance — remaining a profitable economic institution, essential to our material well-being, and at the same time safeguarding the health and welfare of individuals in society.

SOCIAL ISSUES

In its continuing quest for profit, business comes into contact with three major groups — employees, customers and the general community. Today, members of each of these groups believe that business has a responsibility to them beyond simply providing them with goods and services and jobs. We now examine the nature of this social responsibility.

Social and ethical issues are similar and closely related. However, social issues generally are rather broad in scope and may affect all businesses, while ethical issues tend to concern the behaviour of individual managers and businesses. We discuss ethical issues later in this chapter.

Business and its Employees

The days of the Industrial Revolution, when people were often considered to be easily replaceable cogs in a machine, are over. Today, most businesses realize that people are a very important resource, and that simply handing them a pay cheque is no longer adequate. Generally employees now desire a great deal more from their jobs, looking to the firm not only for satisfaction of their social needs, but for self-esteem — the satisfaction which comes from contributing to the operation of the business — advancement and personal development. Some organizations simply cannot satisfy all these needs, however hard they try; others do not even make the attempt.

For those firms that have recognized their responsibility towards their employees and can do something about it, human resource development has become a major objective. In Canada quality of work-life programs have been introduced by many companies in an effort to shift authority, decision-making and responsibility down to the lower levels of management and employees. The West German experiment in placing workers on the management boards of companies is discussed in Canada and the United States, even though actual implementation in North America may be far in the future. Where possible, the jobs of assembly-line workers are being upgraded to make them less monotonous. Many employers are also making a serious effort to hire members of minority groups.

Business is beginning to realize that employees are better motivated and more productive when they know where they are going and what their specific responsibilities are, in addition to being fairly rewarded for their efforts. Even those who object to the acceptance of social responsibility by business could find little fault with the maintenance of physical resources such as plant and equipment. Today business is acknowledging that the maintenance of human resources is equally important.

Business and Consumers

Although it is often said that "the consumer is king," that view is not always reflected in the way that business treats its customers. The quality of consumer goods and services is often poor; products break down too soon and services are inadequate. In the past the customer had little recourse against these problems. Consumers today are better educated, and demands for more information, safer products and better performance are beginning to have an effect.

The consumer movement which began in the 1960s probably took its greatest impetus from Ralph Nader, whose book *Unsafe at Any Speed*, describing the safety hazards of the General Motors Corvair car, was the first major criticism aimed at a giant firm. Consumer groups formed since then have been responsible for the passage of a wide range of protective legislation in the areas of quality, packaging, labelling, advertising and warranties.

One of the major consumer-producer issues is product safety. Each year millions of people in North America are injured as a result of harmful consumer products. Often we hear of new children's toys withdrawn from the market because of dangerous electrical and mechanical hazards, televisions and microwave ovens that emit radiation, and drugs with dangerous side effects that had gone unrecognized because of inadequate testing. One highly publicized example was the drug thalidomide, a sedative found responsible for severe birth defects. Perhaps these tragic consequences would have been prevented if the drug had been adequately tested prior to general use.

Another consumer issue concerns guarantees and warranties. Some warranties contain so many exceptions that they leave buyers very little protection; in other cases, retailers and manufacturers simply refuse to meet their warranties. Each side generally blames the other for product failure, but neither party satisfies the consumer.

Perhaps the most common object of criticism is deceptive advertising. In one well known case, a mouthwash which had long been advertised for its ability to kill germs that cause colds and sore throats was found to be no more effective than salt water. Some consumers automatically discount statements made in product advertising because they expect advertising claims to be inflated.

In Canada, however, misleading advertising is outlawed in legislation passed and administered by the Bureau of Consumer Affairs. The bureau prepares proposals for common legislation regarding packaging, labelling, weights and measures, and hazardous products, in addition to handling consumer complaints and inquiries and promoting the consumer movement in Canada. Still, the question remains as to how much business should be forced to do through legislation, and how much it should do voluntarily.

Business and the Community

No doubt the most serious matter faced by business regarding the community is pollution of the environment, a problem which we now discuss in some detail before turning to more general issues.

Environmental Pollution

Like the consumer movement, the environmental protection movement began in the early 1960s when Rachel Carson's book *Silent Spring* revealed the uncontrolled use of pesticides and their effect on the environment. Suddenly people's eyes were opened to the smog over their cities, to polluted waters killing aquatic life, to the noxious fumes lingering in the atmosphere, and to the almost unbearable noise of our cities. The public became aware of the term ecology, the study of the fragile relationship that exists between water, air, soil and life on earth.

Various environmental groups were formed to press for legislation enforcing pollution control. In 1971 the federal government

Environmental pollution is a major issue facing business

created the Department of Fisheries and Environment for the protection, preservation and enhancement of the quality of the environment and its renewable resources. The department is responsible for reducing existing air, water and land pollution and any new environmental hazards, as well as examining the impact on the environment of major developments on federal land. Most of the provincial governments have also introduced legislation in these areas.

While the initial legislation was passed largely in response to immediate dangers, later legislation such as the Environmental Contaminants Act is actually preventive. Under this act industry may be asked to furnish the department with information concerning contaminants and may be required to conduct tests on hazardous chemicals to evaluate their potential dangers. The government is empowered to ban or control the use or manufacture of hazardous contaminants.

Although business recognizes the problems of pollution and is generally anxious to correct them wherever possible, control is expensive; pollution control equipment may cost hundreds of millions of dollars, and eventually the consumer will have to pay for it. Even today environmental pollution is still regarded as an external cost, because in the past business was not required to control pollution and thus had no costs in this respect. Indeed, much of our material well-being to date stems from our past neglect of the environment in the production of goods. Now controls must be implemented, if not voluntarily then through government legislation. In any event consumers will pay for the cost of controls, either through higher product prices or through increased taxes.

While some forms of pollution can be prevented or at least reduced, in other cases the only solution is to suspend the activity responsible. However, our society cannot function without automobiles and airplanes; even though we cannot eliminate radiation pollution, we need the nuclear power plants. And what would be the costs of eliminating all air and water pollution?

Nevertheless great improvements can be made in some areas. Rather than dumping solid waste material, for example, much of it can be recycled to make new products. Recycling can provide energy savings of up to 60% in the manufacturing process, as the primary refining has already been accomplished. Among the materials currently being recycled are newspapers, bottles, cardboard boxes and metals; used motor oil, once discarded by service stations, is now re-refined in recycling plants and is virtually as good as new oil. The major problem with recycling is the expense of collecting, handling and transporting waste materials: it is still cheaper simply to dump refuse in a landfill site. However, the situation may improve as the costs of raw materials and energy rise.

Conservation of Energy and Resources

Our standard of living in the past has largely depended on the availability of cheap energy. With only 6% of the world's population, North America accounts for approximately one third of world energy consumption, and Canada has the highest per capita rate of consumption of energy in the world. And our consumption of energy continues to increase while new sources of oil and natural gas become ever more difficult and expensive to find and develop.

Types of Pollution

Air Pollution: The release of gases or solid particles into the air; a contributing factor in illness and agricultural and timber losses as well as property damage from rot and discolouration.

Water Pollution: The discharge of solid or liquid materials into lakes and streams from industrial establishments; makes water unfit for human consumption and enjoyment, kills aquatic life and leads to losses through the destruction of fishing grounds and the cost of extraordinary water purification measures.

Land Pollution: Also known as "aesthetic pollution"; solid wastes such as bottles, tin cans and automobile bodies and operations such as strip mining — in which the top soil is stripped away to expose the minerals beneath, particularly coal — deface the natural beauty of the land; in some cases, important wildlife habitats are destroyed.

Radiation Pollution: The disposal of radioactive material through storage either above or below ground; a severe health hazard.

Noise Pollution: Noise from industrial plants, airplanes, automobiles and so on; can cause sleep disturbances and nervous disorders.

Pesticide Pollution: The use, often excessive, of pesticides to control insects in the production of food; some pesticides have been found to cause cancer, while the side effects of many others are as yet unknown.

However, consumers are not the only ones to blame for energy consumption. There is also a responsibility on the part of business and industry to help conserve energy. The products they offer must be made more energy-efficient — automobiles are a prime example. Houses and buildings must be better insulated. Products must be made to last longer, designed for easy repair rather than replacement at the first sign of wear. Manufacturing processes must also be redesigned to use less energy.

Some immediate savings can be brought about simply by using less energy, through voluntary restraints, lower speed limits, and the use of techniques and equipment that are more fuel efficient. One novel experiment combining an old-fashioned energy source and the most modern technology is described in the article "Is That a New Age of Sail Coming Over the Horizon?"

Is That a New Age of Sail Coming Over the Horizon?

Automobiles are not the world's only gas guzzlers: deep-sea ships burn 140 million tonnes of fuel oil per year, amounting to 4.5% of total world petroleum consumption. In an effort to do something about the problem before supplies run out, corporations and governments in both Europe and Japan are researching the feasibility of sail-powered ocean vessels. Already one such ship, a 1600-ton deadweight tanker operating off the coast of Japan, has shown fuel savings of over 10%.

The Shinaitoku Maru has two rigid canvas sails which are computer controlled and operated hydraulically from the bridge. The tanker is designed to travel at 15 knots, with a normal speed of 12 knots. Under sail with a full load, a prevailing wind would push it along at 5 knots with engines making up the difference in speed. The sails automatically adjust for optimum wind power: when wind speed drops below 8 knots or rises above 40 knots, the sails are automatically retracted and the engines take over.

Other countries are also developing sail-powered ships. The British Ship and Marine Technology Requirements Board is planning to build a sailing ship with a cargo-carrying capacity of more than 750 000 cubic feet, while a team at the University of Hamburg is working on a 17 000-ton bulk carrier fitted with thin hydraulically manipulated aerofoils instead of sails.

The reason for this renewed interest in sailing vessels is obvious — the cost of fuel, which formerly amounted to 20% of the daily cost of running a conventional ship, has now risen as high as 80%. As fuel prices continue to rise we may indeed see sailing ships once again ply the oceans of the world.

NKK Corporation

SOURCE: See Alan Daniels, "Sail-powered freighters foreseen in next 5 years," *Vancouver Sun*, Oct. 2, 1980, p. E1.

Responsibility to Education and the Arts

If pollution control and conservation are matters of absolute necessity, business is also making voluntary contributions to the community. Corporations and individuals have poured millions of dollars into charitable organizations, educational programs, medical research, artistic endeavours and other projects of benefit to society. In addition, many businesspeople offer their time, physical energy, knowledge and leadership abilities to charity drives, colleges and university boards, community groups such as the Boy Scouts or Girl Guides, and other non-profit organizations.

Their motives for supporting education and the arts are many. While some obviously look for short-term business gain, others sincerely hope to make a lasting contribution. In any case, it is clear that support for education and the arts is a growing concern for many executives.

ETHICAL ISSUES

Social issues move into the realm of ethics when the individuals involved make their personal decisions for action. Whatever the broader view of society may be, an individual's decision in a particular situation will depend on his or her values: what he or she believes is right or wrong. Some of the areas in which ethical questions most often arise are discussed below.

Employment Discrimination

Some years ago, the person most likely to be hired for a managerial position was a white Protestant male, probably between the ages of 26 and 40. A younger individual was assumed to lack experience, while older people were considered to be resistant to change, impossible to retrain, or too old to go on the company pension plan. Women were largely relegated to traditional roles, usually on the grounds that they might become pregnant and leave after expensive training; in addition, women were often considered to be too emotionally unstable to handle managerial responsibility. Finally, members of minority ethnic groups were virtually barred from managerial positions.

In response to this problem, in 1971 the federal government passed legislation under the Canada Labour Code prohibiting discrimination in employment on the grounds of race, sex, religion, colour or national origin. Most provinces have passed similar legislation as well.

But can discrimination in employment be legislated away? The young still have trouble finding jobs because employers are reluctant to spend money on training. Women still have less chance of promotion than men, and are still paid less for performing equal work. Few companies provide maternity leave other than the minimum required by legislation, while pension and group life insurance plans often provide less protection for women than for men. Many employers are still reluctant to hire older workers, while ethnic minorities and native people in particular still face deep-seated prejudice.

Obviously, employment discrimination cannot be ended by legislation alone. Efforts must be made by employers, government and various interest groups to resolve the problem through education and incentives. But it also involves a question of personal ethics on the part of the employer. Is it right to pay a man more than a woman, when both are performing the same job? Is it right to hire a white applicant on the grounds of colour alone, when a native candidate is equally qualified for the job? Should age alone restrict an experienced worker from gainful employment? In the end the decision is determined by the employer's own conscience.

Relations with Labour Unions

The establishment of a union is almost invariably a struggle. When management agrees to bargain, it is often with reluctance, and not always in good faith as the law prescribes. In most cases the attitude is one of mutual distrust and confrontation: "us versus them."

Even if the practices employed in the struggle are not actually illegal, they are often ethically questionable. Often unions resort to strikes and management to lockouts when significant economic loss could be prevented through further discussion. Illegal practices are deliberately adopted in order to force the other side to seek an injunction, which costs time and money. If management hires strikebreakers — people who are prepared to cross a picket line and work in place of regular employees — riots can follow. In short, little is spared by either side in attaining their objectives. Does the end justify the means?

On the other hand, economic hardship could often be prevented if both sides trusted each other and shared information openly. In Europe, representatives of labour are placed in the boardroom and given voting rights — little can be hidden, and major decisions are made jointly.

However, neither labour nor management accept the European model as workable in North America. Unions claim they are only interested in improving wages and working conditions for their members, not in running businesses. Management is adamant about retaining its rights. Concerned about the amount of union influence in the decision-making process, and alarmed about the future as labour costs increase, management fears increased union encroachment on its rights.

Acceptance of Voluntary Government Restraints

From time to time, the government asks business to observe voluntary restraints, such as raising prices or discontinuing trade with another country because the Canadian government finds that country's internal policies objectionable. When the action requested conflicts with a firm's immediate interests, ethical considerations must enter into the decision. What is a firm's responsibility in a case such as South Africa, which practises apartheid? Should a Canadian company that has spent considerable time and money to establish a business in, or trade relations with, South Africa pull out of that country at a great loss, because the prime minister asks Canadians not to deal with that country due to the way it conducts its internal affairs? Furthermore, government's reasons for supporting voluntary restraints may conflict with the personal convictions of the individual businessperson.

Responsibility to Developing Countries

What is the responsibility of Canadian businesspeople involved with a developing country through exporting or importing, or the establishment of a corporation there? Should they simply consider the profit that can be made from doing business with that country, or should they be concerned with offering fair wages and good working conditions? Many foreign governments have accepted exploitative practices by multinational companies in an attempt to gain the investment and jobs for their people. Should a Canadian business offer the workers a better deal than their own government demands?

Involvement in Politics

Should business contribute to political campaigns? Should it offer financial support to individual politicians? No doubt business has more money available for the purpose of influencing the political process than any other group in society, and supporting politicians who have business' interests at heart may be detrimental to other sectors of society. Is it ethically proper to exercise that power?

MANAGEMENT PHILOSOPHY

In our discussion of the relations between business and society so far, we have generally treated the two as if they were separate. However, the managers who make business decisions are also members of society. Since individual managers read the same books, watch the same movies, hear the same news and vote at the same polls as other people, their ethics are likely to be closely aligned with those of the majority of society.

Conflict can arise, however, when an individual works for an organization whose top management holds beliefs that differ from those of society in general. Top management's philosophy spreads throughout the organization, and individual employees who do not share those beliefs may be torn between their own principles and the demands of management. When individuals depend on the organization for their livelihood, their business behaviour may not reflect their personal ethics, and such conflicts can cause tremendous stress.

Management philosophy refers to the values and ideas that shape management decisions, whether or not managers are conscious of them in their day-to-day operations. The philosophy of top management within each firm determines how the business will respond to the social and ethical issues raised in this chapter.

MEASURING SOCIAL RESPONSIBILITY

In general, the sequence of steps involved in fulfilling social responsibilities resembles any other business operation. Management must decide which social projects have priority; to do so, it must be in tune with the needs of society. Once particular social objectives have been chosen, managers must plan and implement the programs to achieve them. Finally, they must determine how well those objectives have been achieved.

Parameters of Social Behaviour

We cannot establish standards, or parameters, for socially responsible behaviour as we can for economic performance, simply by drawing up a budget. Rather, while management will obviously be guided by its own ideas and values, it must also listen to the needs and wants of other groups in society, including consumers, labour unions, government, environmental groups, educational institutions, social organizations and minority groups. Clearly no company can meet all the demands placed upon it, but it can select those objectives considered most important by the majority.

Once the social objectives to be achieved have been clearly formulated, priorities must be set by viewing the objectives in terms of both their importance to society and the availability of company resources. Then the firm can take steps to include those objectives in both short- and long-range operating plans.

The Social Audit

Just as a financial audit is required each year, a company should also make a social audit of those areas of its operation which have a social impact. The **social audit** is a self-assessment of a firm's social performance.

A number of critieria may be used to take a social audit, but two are in general use. First, a company may either list the expenditures made in implementing social programs or simply describe verbally how they were implemented. In this case none of the benefits of the social programs are shown. The second type of social audit resembles an inventory, in which a company lists what it is doing in each major social program, or is not doing in an area where there is a need for social action. Companies that reject the term social audit because it implies a virtually impossible quantification of social activities may prefer terms such as "social report" or "social statement."

WHERE DO BUSINESS AND SOCIETY STAND TODAY?

Clearly the future of our business institutions will depend on how well they are able to integrate their economic objectives with the objectives of society as a whole. Never have managers been more concerned about the impact of their business decisions on the well-being of society, if only because they know that unless they assume responsibility voluntarily, society will force them to do it through government legislation.

Top management's prime consideration, of course, is still the shareholders, and most social projects must still be somehow equated to profitability, rather than simply stated as a benefit to society. Nevertheless the trend toward greater social responsibility in business has begun, and is unlikely to be reversed unless our society's material well-being takes an unforeseen drop, in which case economic objectives might again become dominant.

NOTE

1. George A. Steiner, *Business and Society*, 2nd. ed. (New York: Random House, Inc., 1975), p. 216.

CHAPTER SUMMARY

For a business firm to survive today, it must conduct itself in a socially responsible manner. Even though it is primarily an economic institution, business must take social, political, and ethical considerations into account along with economic and market factors. On occasion, a course of action which might have meant great economic benefit for the firm and its shareholders must be modified in view of possible adverse consequences for other sectors of society.

Debate continues as to the extent of business' social responsibility. Some believe that a firm's duty is limited to the efficient production of goods and services, leaving government to handle all other social concerns with the taxes collected from business. Others believe that since business is a part of society, it must respond more directly to the needs of that society.

Major social issues today concern the relationship between business and employees, consumers and the community. Some social issues also give rise to ethical questions — what is right and wrong in relation to society's interests. Major ethical issues faced by managers include the full utilization of human resources, discrimination in hiring, product safety, truthful advertising, relations with unions, adherence to government rules and regulations, political involvement and relationships with developing countries. How individual managers deal with these social and ethical issues depends largely on the firm's overall management philosophy.

KEY TERMS

Social responsibility	Environmental pollution
Morals	Ecology
Moral code	Recycling
Laws	Ethical issues
Ethics	Management philosophy
Consumer movement	Social behaviour
Social issues	Social audit

REVIEW QUESTIONS

1. Why does society today demand that business assume greater social responsibility?
2. Explain the concept of social responsibility.
3. Distinguish between morals, ethics and laws.
4. Explain the meaning of business ethics.

5. What are the major arguments for and against business taking on more social responsibility?
6. What is the responsibility of business toward its employees? Toward consumers? Toward the community?
7. Distinguish between social and ethical issues.
8. What measures could be taken to reduce employment discrimination, apart from legislation?
9. How does management philosophy influence individual employees' business ethics and their reaction to social issues?
10. How should a firm decide which social issues to pursue? How can it measure its achievement of these objectives?

DISCUSSION QUESTIONS

1. Does business have a social responsibility? Explain fully.
2. What do you think is the responsibility of business to the consumer regarding product safety and quality?
3. Do you think business managers should adhere to an established ethical code in the same way that doctors and lawyers do? If so, what should be included in this code?
4. Do you think that a standard code of business ethics would be compatible with a competitive business system such as Canada's?

CASE 14–1 Latent Hazards: Who Pays?

Approximately 1200 people who have lived on or near the Love Canal in Niagara Falls, N.Y., have sued the Hooker Chemical and Plastics Corp. for damages of up to $15 billion. Although the company has not used the canal since 1953, when it deeded the property — along with all risk and liabilities for its use — to the local school board, the toxic chemicals it began dumping there in the early 1940s are now held responsible for an alarming incidence of disease in the area.

The company denies any responsibility on the grounds that it gave warning of the presence of the chemicals in the contract of sale. While that warning could absolve Hooker of liability as far as the board is concerned, the law does not allow for contracting out of liability to a third party. Other questions also remain to be tested in court. Should the company have continued to monitor the seepage of chemicals? Was the warning adequate in this case?

Love Canal is not the only case in which the consequences of past activities have become apparent only many years later. Naval shipyard workers who were required to work with asbestos during World War II have since attempted to sue the U.S. government for compensation. However, the government is not liable for injuries or illnesses resulting from war: thus the plaintiffs sued the companies that made the asbestos for alleged negligence in producing a dangerous product. By 1984, roughly 25 000 cases had been brought against about 100 producers. So far approximately 7000 cases have been either lost or settled with $400 million in damages paid out and legal expenses amounting to another $500 million. One major company, the Johns-Manville Corp. declared bankruptcy in 1982 to try to sidestep the claims. Similarly, the Dow Chemical Co. is now involved in suits arising from the U.S. military's use of a chemical defoliant for which Dow manufactured one of the ingredients: Vietnam veterans blame the chemical, Agent Orange, for cancer, liver abnormalities, nervous disorders and birth defects in their offspring. The potential number of people who may have been injured through the actions or products of various companies is estimated in the tens of millions.

In response to the increasing potential for injury resulting from latent hazards, some states have already adopted a rule of absolute liability. Under this rule, a company marketing a dangerous product is assumed to be aware of the hazards associated with its use, even if they were not recognized at the time of sale. Thus, failure to give warning automatically establishes liability.

SOURCE: See *Business Week*, June 16, 1980, pp. 150–51; *Newsweek*, May 28, 1984, p. 69.

QUESTIONS

1. What responsibility, if any, do you think the companies concerned have to the individuals who have been injured?
2. What, in your opinion, is the central problem presented in this case? How might this problem affect companies in their research and marketing of new drugs for presently incurable diseases?
3. Can you suggest any solutions?
4. Do you think government should absolve itself of blame, as it has done? If government did not absolve itself, payment for damages would come out of the public purse; do you think this is justified?
5. What questions of ethics, if any, are involved here?

Part Five

Business in Canada:
The Future

It has often been said that the only constant is change. Having examined business and its development in the Canadian environment to this point, we can be certain that it too will change. The particular twists and detours on the road ahead can be the subject of endless speculation. Nevertheless it should be possible to make some reasonable predictions about our general direction.

In Chapter 15 we attempt to forecast some of the social, economic and technological changes most likely to affect business in Canada in the next decade. We also discuss some of the challenges facing managers in the future and offer a little guidance on career planning and job search techniques.

Business, Management, and the Future

© Jay Brousseau/The Image Bank Canada

CHAPTER OUTLINE

A WORD ABOUT PREDICTING THE FUTURE
    Change, Change, Change
    Methods of Predicting the Future
MAJOR CHANGES BASED ON CURRENT TRENDS
    Population Changes
    Life Style Changes
    Economic Changes
    Technological Changes
OUR FUTURE CANADIAN BUSINESS SYSTEM
THE MANAGER OF THE FUTURE
YOUR CAREER IN BUSINESS
    Business Environments
    Choosing a Career
    Knowing What You Want to Do
    Finding Your Job: Beginning a Career Plan

CHAPTER PREVIEW

In Chapter 15 we briefly consider two opposing projections for Canada's future, and then examine the means by which such predictions are made. Although computer models are probably the most sophisticated techniques used, others such as trend analysis are also used to forecast changes in population, technology, economics, and life styles. We then discuss how these changes may affect Canadian business and management in the future.

We conclude the chapter with a brief discussion of career planning and introduce the job search process to help students prepare for their future business careers.

LEARNING OBJECTIVES

After reading this chapter you should be able to explain:

1. Why it is necessary for businesses to make forecasts about the future even though all aspects of life are undergoing rapid change;

2. Some of the methods used to predict the future;
3. Some major changes based on current trends;
4. Some key factors that may affect Canada's future business system;
5. The job search process.

Our examination of the present Canadian business system in the preceding chapters has shown that it works, if at times imperfectly. Some business concepts and practices are subject to debate; others are not fully developed and require further research.

We have also looked at the past, and in hindsight we realize that affairs might have been conducted better, with less hardship to the mass of society. Unfortunately we can do nothing about the past, except to use it as a guide for the future. Perhaps that is the major reason for studying history — to examine the impact of events on society and see how they influenced the future.

Speculating on conditions at the turn of the next century is a popular activity today. What will Canada be like in the year 2000? Barring any nuclear holocaust or natural catastrophe, we can describe two scenarios at opposite extremes.

Scenario No. 1

Inflation in Canada is out of hand: now into triple digit figures, with the prices of goods and services doubling or tripling every year. Not many people are really concerned about monetary inflation, however, since few goods and services are even available for purchase. Basic necessities are provided by government, which takes most of the money that anyone earns. Other goods and services are only available on a barter basis, as no one wants the rapidly devaluating Canadian dollar.

Unemployment in the year 2000 is somewhere between 30% and 40%. However, whether an individual has a job or not, the comprehensive welfare system takes care of all Canadians with a guaranteed annual income which at least allows them to buy basic necessities. Those who are employed are slightly better off, but only because they can purchase a few more of the basic items. Few can afford to buy goods for recreational and leisure activities, which have become virtually nonexistent. The major affordable activities are reading, television and walking, or community services and education. Gasoline prices are high, and it is difficult to travel anywhere since most automobiles are in extremely poor condition — service, when available, is both poor and extremely expensive.

Economic activity in Canada has dropped to the point of negative growth. Productivity is extremely low because machines and manufacturing plants are outdated and in disrepair. International trade in manufactured goods has virtually ceased, although our raw materials and food products are in great demand throughout the world. Unfortunately, most of Canada's productive capacity is in foreign hands, owned by multinational corporations. Canadians benefit little because foreign corporations bring in their own labour and management, while any profits made are quickly converted into valuable raw materials for export elsewhere. Although the government has instituted exchange controls, Canadian funds still slip out of the country in great amounts. As a result the balance of payments is worse than ever, and the value of the Canadian dollar has shown a severe drop against some other world currencies. The Canadian dollar is worth only half of the American dollar, but neither currency is well regarded on foreign exchange markets, where three U.S. dollars are required to buy one German mark.

Scenario No. 2

In the year 2000 inflation is no longer a problem in Canada. The Canadian dollar is strong, as investors from all parts of the world are anxious to invest in the nation's economy; productivity is high, thanks to huge investments of capital in Canadian industry. Most monotonous, routine jobs are now mechanized, but where workers are still required, they receive handsome benefits for performing tedious work.

Most people work only twenty hours per week and spend their free time in leisure activities or in furthering their education. Universities and colleges have expanded tremendously, and the quality of education has risen as scholars are attracted to Canada from all over the world. This has resulted in a significant increase in inventions, discoveries, research and development. In fact, several major energy breakthroughs were made in Canada — first in tidal and solar energy and then in fusion power, providing Canada and the world with unlimited sources of energy.

Although unemployment is almost non-existent, ample social welfare services are readily available in Canada's highly productive economy. Many of the improvements in Canadians' standard of living can be directly attributed to cooperation between business, government and labour in joint management of the economy.

Which of these scenarios will be true by the year 2000? Probably neither. In all likelihood we will continue on some middle course. Inflation may be higher or lower than at present; some problems will have been resolved, but new issues will occupy our time. In any event, as some changes will certainly occur, let us consider how they might influence our business system in the future.

A WORD ABOUT PREDICTING THE FUTURE

By "predicting the future," we do not mean to suggest gazing into a crystal ball or searching out an oracle: we mean the reasonably accurate forecasting of future events on the basis of current trends. However, trends may change direction quite suddenly — a rapidly growing economy may come to an abrupt halt when oil prices double; a single technological innovation can create an entirely new industry almost overnight. Imagine what a new source of cheap energy might do for all countries, industrialized and developing. What would it mean to the North American economy if a new battery were developed capable of storing and providing the energy output of a tankful of gasoline? When we base our vision of the future on current trends, any sudden developments can make many or all predictions obsolete.

Change, Change, Change

Another reason for the difficulty of predicting the future is the rate of change itself. According to Alvin Toffler, whose book *Future Shock* was published in 1970, the rate of change accelerates because technology feeds on itself with each successive development. Thus, change in each future period will be much more dramatic than in the last. To illustrate this acceleration, Toffler points out that if the 50 000 years of human existence are divided into 800 lifetimes of approximately 62 years each, the first 650 of them were spent in caves; writing has existed for only the last 70 lifetimes, and only during the last six did writing ever reach the masses; by far the majority of the material goods we know today were developed in the present lifetime.[1]

With the pace of change quickening at such a rate, business and managers must learn to adapt. Resistance to change may be a common problem, but it is one no businessperson will be able to afford. Managers must be able to deal quickly with change in every aspect of the business environment — technology, economic conditions, life styles and society at large. While managers must have an ever-increasing store of knowledge to draw on, they must also be prepared to discard outdated information and replace it with new; they must be well-trained and willing to be retrained as necessary. Above all, they must be prepared to deal with any change as it arises.

Methods of Predicting the Future

Several methods are available for predicting the future. While different techniques can result in different predictions, that uncertainty may be useful if it prevents us from focusing on a single future possibility to the exclusion of all others.

TREND ANALYSIS: In trend analysis we assume that what has happened in the past will continue to happen in the future in more or less the same way.

DELPHI METHOD: In this method, a variety of experts are polled independently about a particular question. All are then shown the results of the total poll and asked to reassess their original forecasts in the light of the other opinions.

SCENARIO: A scenario writer chooses a single possible future situation at a given point in time, then traces the sequence of events that might lead to that future.

MODEL BUILDING: This scientific approach uses computers, statistics and other data to create a model. By varying the data employed, a number of alternative futures can be postulated.

SEAT-OF-THE-PANTS TECHNIQUE: Science fiction writers often create alternative futures through a combination of research and personal knowledge mixed with imagination and intuition: in many instances their predictions have come true.

While any of these techniques can be used, futurists should also challenge the projections of others in order to clarify the bases for their own forecasts and prevent visions based solely on imagination. Forecasts should be plausible, describing a future which could conceivably develop out of the present. All assumptions must be clearly stated, and all aspects of the scenario must be consistent — one part must not contradict another. Above all, forecasts should cover a specific number of years, so that the direction and speed of changes affecting society can be assessed.

MAJOR CHANGES BASED ON CURRENT TRENDS

A number of future changes based on trends in population, life styles, economic conditions, technology and society are already evident in Canada. Perhaps the major agent for change is advancing technology. New discoveries in science are often used to develop new products or methods of operation. This can create entire new industries and shift education requirements, as with the development of the computer. Advances in medicine and medical technology affects the health and age of people, consequently extending their lifetimes. This has an impact on business in terms of the products demanded by an older group of people. It is essential that all managers recognize these trends and understand how they might influence the future operation of their organizations.

Population Changes

How many people can this planet hold? In a book entitled *The Limits to Growth*, researchers built a computer model of the world based on five global factors: population, agriculture, production (industrial output), non-renewable resource depletion and pollution generation.[2] According to this model, if present growth trends continue, the limits to growth on this planet will be reached sometime in the next 100 years. By the year 2000, it is estimated that the population will have expanded from the present 5 billion to 6.3 billion. Much of this population growth will occur in developing nations, however; the growth rate in industrialized countries will be much slower, in some instances approaching zero growth.

What will happen to Canada's population in the 21st century? Academics who study demographic trends generally predict a bleak outlook for Canada. Early in the next century Canada's population will begin to age rapidly, and then slowly dwindle, all because of a declining birth rate. An immediate problem is the large number of senior citizens that will have to be supported by fewer and fewer workers. This will greatly affect the social welfare system and the labour market in Canada.

While some experts believe that Canada will be able to adjust to the change without it's having too much effect on the standard of living, others are deeply concerned. They insist that Canada's sovereignty and ultimate survival as a nation will be at stake unless the trends are reversed. If the population shrinks, so will demand for goods and services, greatly slowing the economy. The market for new homes would be almost eliminated and schools would have fewer students. A major question is what effect a shrinking population would have on innovation and research and development, since these areas generally derive from younger rather than older groups.

What can be done to head off this catastrophe? Canada must look to immigration for more people. Another approach is to provide more incentives to families to have more children. For example, Québec's concern about its low fertility rate resulted in a program of cash payments to families — a $500 bonus for the first and second child and a $3000 bonus over two years for a third child. Québec hopes to raise its fertility rate from 1.4 children per fertile woman to 1.8

in five years. This would mean an extra 20 000 babies in 1993 bringing the annual total to 100 000. Nevertheless, because of the high cost of raising children, the scheme is not likely to create a mini baby boom in Québec, but it will provide some incentive to expand families. Perhaps other creative ways can be found to prevent the predicted population decline.[3]

Grim Projections for Canada's Population

- At the peak of the baby boom in 1959 the fertility rate per woman was 3.9 babies. Since then it has dropped steadily to 1.67. A fertility rate of 2.1 is required to ensure that the population remains stable. Canada's rate has been below this rate for 17 years.

- The fertility rate is expected to drop further to 1.4 or less. In Québec it is already at that level and most major cities in Canada are close to that level.

- If the current trend of 1% growth per year continues, Canada's population will peak at approximately 33 million in the year 2031 and then stabilize at that level. If the fertility rate drops, the population is expected to peak at about 28 million in about the year 2013 and then decline. There is a possibility that Canada's population could drop to 12 to 16 million by the middle of the next century.

- There will have to be an increase in immigration, depending on the fertility rate, to about 300 000 by the turn of the century and then rising to 500 000 just to maintain the present annual population growth of 1%.

- The median age in Canada will rise from the current 31 to 43 (48 if the fertility rate drops) by the year 2031.

- There will be a shift from the youth population to senior citizens, the latter group almost tripling in size. If the fertility rate drops, 27% of Canadians will be over the age of 65 by the year 2031 compared to only 11% in 1986. Over the same time period the proportion of Canadians under age 17 will drop to 15% from 26%.

- The labour force will continue to increase in size until 2006, when the first baby boomers reach retirement age. After that it will begin to decline from one to two percent every five years.

SOURCE: Adapted from Joan Bryden, "Greying of Canada promises to burden next generation," *Vancouver Sun*, June 4, 1988, p. B2.

Managers must consider how this potential change in population growth in Canada and the increasing world population will affect their business. They must ask themselves, for example, what products or services they will offer to a growing world population: should they concentrate on providing wheat and other natural resources, or on manufacturing, or information processing?

And what about the changing age structure of the population? Will the upward shift in age be beneficial or detrimental to our economy? As people age they will require more medical and hospital services, which will be a drain on the economy. Some firms that are primarily catering to younger age groups will have to be concerned about a drop in demand for their products. On the other hand, the aging population will provide business with opportunities to offer new products and services.

Life Style Changes

Life style refers to the way people live and work, how they spend their leisure time, what their hobbies and other interests are, including their personal philosophy. Individuals' life styles normally change as they grow older, leave school, take a job, marry and have children. When changes occur in the life style of an entire society, they can have a tremendous impact on the future of individual business organizations.

There has been a continuous increase in the amount of leisure time available to Canadians. Although the 40-hour workweek is still the legal standard, many people today work only 35 hours and some even less. Furthermore, for many individuals the amount of vacation time has increased, often supplemented with leaves of absence for various personal reasons. People also live longer than in the past, and many retire earlier. Many opportunities exist for business to provide goods and services for a leisure-oriented society.

Another essential factor in overall life style is the family. Individuals are now marrying later in life and having fewer children. At the same time, the divorce rate has been rising and may rise further still as divorce becomes easier to obtain, resulting in more single-parent families. Among those families that remain intact, the proportion of women working will most likely continue to increase through the 1990s. Social values and behaviour can change quickly, however, and it is possible that the above trends will be reversed. In any case, business must be prepared to adjust to these life style changes.

Education is another major influence on life style. As people become better educated, they question the values and beliefs of the previous generation. For example, during the 1960s and 1970s many young people abhorred the emphasis on the acquisition of material goods, and instead put more emphasis on the quality of life. In the 1980s, however, as the baby-boom generation entered middle age, the trend appeared to be reversing with a renewed emphasis on economic growth and traditional values. Education also becomes more important as technology advances since knowledge becomes quickly outdated. Old jobs disappear and new jobs are created. Thus, lifetime learning is becoming increasingly accepted.

Canadian life styles have changed with the continuous increase
in the amount of available leisure time

For a time the increasing cost of energy, especially gasoline,
appeared to have a major impact on life styles and the economy.
People moved closer to their place of work, or sought to find ways
of working at home. Great emphasis was placed on the development
of rapid transit systems. The auto industry was turned upside-down
as it attempted to meet the needs of commuters with smaller, more
fuel-efficient cars. Energy shortages are still lurking in the background, and political events can once again make the cost of energy
a major concern. But as computers and more sophisticated communications systems are developed, the need for many people to
commute to their place of work at all may gradually diminish.

Social values and behaviour can change quickly, however, and
any of the trends mentioned above can be reversed. In any case,
business must be prepared to adjust to these life style changes.

Owing to the enormous impact of life-style changes on many
businesses, marketers of consumer products have turned to life style
research to determine clusters of homogeneous buying behaviour,
allowing them better to meet the needs of their customers. Rather
than simply classifying consumers according to age, an attempt is

made to establish certain life style characteristics in order to compare how individuals with various characteristics behave in the marketplace. As life style research becomes more important it will be refined and become a major marketing research tool.

Economic Changes

The growing interdependence of world nations can have severe effects on the economies of many countries. For example, the 1973 Arab oil embargo that shocked the industrial world, contributed to high inflation, unemployment, and subsequently to slow economic growth. Then came the 1982 recession, which had a severe impact on many small firms, causing an unusually high number of bankruptcies. The recession also created considerable unemployment, which affected many individuals and families.

As much as our governments attempt economic management, we will likely not escape recessions, although deep depressions, such as the Great Depression of the 1930s, are unlikely to happen again. On the other hand, structural changes in the economy will likely affect many individuals over the next few decades. This may be due to international competition and advancing technology that makes existing processes or products obsolete. Since we are today economically interdependent with many nations, as currency values rise and fall, inflation and interest rates in Canada can be affected.

Will the future bring us renewed high inflation, perhaps in double digits? Will we be able to maintain our exports upon which so many Canadians depend for their livelihood? Will there be other energy shortages?

These questions are not easy to answer because world events that affect economies are difficult to forecast, but they underline the importance of business people having a good understanding of our business system, economics, and particularly of how world events can affect Canadian businesses and individuals. No business firm can isolate itself from economic forces. Managers must be aware of them and plan either for survival or for taking advantage of any opportunities that present themselves.

Technological Changes

We can expect technological change to continue to accelerate in the remainder of the century. In Chapter 7 we discussed the automated factory and its potential to produce any kind of product almost immediately. While this undoubtedly is some years away, more and more of the manufacturing jobs, particularly those that are repetitive and boring, will be performed by machines or robots.[4] Powerful computers will guide robots through dangerous or monotonous operations. Although new production methods and other advances in technology can cause great unemployment in the short term, in the long run greater employment should result. However, retraining will require money, and large pockets of unemployment may be with us for long periods of time. Furthermore, with rapid technological change, knowledge becomes outdated quickly, making education in itself a lifetime occupation.

As it has in the past, the introduction of new technology will give rise to other changes and perhaps entirely new industries. Some of these changes will become evident in new and more efficient production techniques. The greatest boon to Canada — provided we seize the opportunities as they arise — will be the creation of new

The Financial Post

Innovations in technology — a solar power collector on the
Sunoco building in Toronto

jobs from new industries. A prime example is the field of communications. With the development of the Telesat telecommunications satellite, Canada became a leader in the communications industry. Today communications is a $10 billion industry, with various sectors expected to grow by 8% to 25% per year. The job creation potential of this industry is tremendous, judging by the United States, where half of all jobs are classified as information jobs. Even though many of these people are not directly involved in producing communications equipment, the potential of this industry is evident.[5]

Although Canada obviously lacks the resources to challenge the United States in areas such as space technology, we can make a significant contribution to various technological advancements provided we have the necessary entrepreneurial spirit and moderate financial resources. One of our greatest achievements in space technology is the robot arm, Canadarm, used in the U.S. space shuttle. Canada's plans to become involved in building the space platform in the 1990s will contribute considerably to our expertise in space technology.

OUR FUTURE CANADIAN BUSINESS SYSTEM

Although the trend is toward less government involvement in the private sector, the size of government will not diminish significantly, if at all, and its influence in the economy will likely grow. Canada is blessed with abundant natural resources and an educated labour force. Under normal circumstances we should enjoy one of the highest standards of living in the world, but we are also faced with some towering problems. The federal and provincial government deficits are enormous. The federal deficit alone requires one third of every tax dollar to meet interest charges. Unless this deficit is reduced, funds may not be available to continue with the major government programs unless taxes are increased. This in turn could cause an economic slowdown and further aggravate unemployment. Furthermore, structural unemployment from continued automation could increase, which would require large amounts of money for retraining and for care of the unemployed.

What will business do? An overriding concern for many Canadian firms is increasing productivity in order to retain our competitive position in the world. Canadian managers are studying Japanese management techniques, but as we found in Chapter 6, these techniques are not likely to work in Canada. Perhaps the emphasis will have to be on quality, satisfying customers and placing renewed value on the employee. Another alternative is increased automation of many operations, particularly in the factory. However, increased automation will aggravate unemployment: it would then become important to encourage the entrepreneurial spirit and make it easier for individuals to open new businesses to generate new jobs.

The Free Trade Agreement with the United States will occupy Canadian discussions for many years. It has many detractors as well as many defenders. Small business appears to be for it, as it will open new markets for them in the United States. At the same time, some Canadian businesses that have lived behind the protectionist wall may be severely hurt, including the wine and beer industry, textiles and shoes. This does not mean that these industries will not survive, but they will certainly have to change their manufacturing techniques and other methods of doing business. In short, they will have to become more competitive and productive.

If the agreement comes into effect in 1989, it could be the beginning of a common market with the United States, and Central and South America. This would not happen immediately. Over the next several decades, major moves toward such a trade pact will likely develop. Ultimately, the agreement may be the forerunner of an American economic union, similar to what the European Economic Community will establish by 1992. If we are to compete with other trade blocs, such as the EEC and the communist countries, a common market extending over the entire continent may eventually prove to be a necessity.

The world is changing fast. Major developments in arms reductions have been accomplished by the two superpowers. More disarmament is bound to happen. The more peaceful the world becomes, the more third world nations will be concerned with increasing their standard of living. They will insist that money be invested in machinery and equipment to provide them with more goods and services, not new missiles and guns. Utopian perhaps, but the world cannot remain an armed camp forever. There are too many poor people in this world: as they become aware of what the industrialized countries have, they will not be satisfied with their lot. Rather than starting a war, they will demand that their leaders provide them with a better life. This is where industrialized countries like Canada can enter with their expertise in technology and business and provide help. It could be an exciting and profitable time for many young business people.

Another area for improvement is in the relationship between business, labour, and government. Although the European idea of worker representation might not be accepted by management in Canada today, this view could change quickly as social and economic developments make better cooperation between business and labour a necessity. Even if collective bargaining remains the union's primary method of getting its share of the economic pie, some changes in the system will be required.

First, strikes are an expensive luxury for our economy — they reduce total output and seldom allow the injured parties to recoup their losses. Although unions will retain the strike weapon, government may increase its use of back-to-work legislation, particularly in vital sectors of the economy. Eventually, continued government intervention in settling labour disputes is bound to lead to reform.

Second, both unions and management will be obliged to become more responsible toward society. Each side will have to open its books to the other, to allow the other side to determine for itself what can reasonably be expected. In cases where this approach still does not produce a settlement, unions may resort to the more sophisticated ways of pressuring the employer to concede, such as advertising, picketing and boycotts. Unions may also demand joint management of pension funds, which currently amount to more than $50 billion, and insist they not be invested in companies that condone anti-union practices or violate health and safety regulations. As the trend toward employer associations for management continues, bargaining will become industry-wide under government supervision. Perhaps unions will suffer in numbers of members if economic conditions do not improve quickly as more and more workers leave their union to work with non-union firms.

THE MANAGER OF THE FUTURE

The manager of the future will be a professional: well educated, with a broad knowledge of the social sciences such as psychology, sociology and economics. Highly developed conceptual skills will be required to analyze increasingly rapid changes in the environment and their effect on organizational plans and operations. Managers will have to be able to adjust quickly to change if they are to protect their organizations from loss and take advantage of new opportunities as they arise. Adequate time for decision-making will be another luxury that few will be able to enjoy.

Moreover, although workers will be more affluent, many may still be required to perform monotonous jobs that offer little satisfaction for their higher level needs. Good communication skills will be essential for managers, to listen to their employees and provide them with the necessary motivation. Depending on their level in the organizational hierarchy, some managers must also be prepared to deal with subordinate managers who are themselves dissatisfied, while others may be required to handle demands for collective bargaining from the lower levels of management.

Professional managers must be capable of working closely with a variety of groups in their own business organizations and in society at large. Since an increasing number of decisions will be made by work groups and committees, managers must know how to conduct themselves with groups. The ability to cooperate will be essential in relations with others outside of the organization as well, whether they be consumers, government administrators, union leaders or politicians.

Indeed the use of committees for decision-making may be one of the greatest problems facing managers in the future. For a committee to reach a consensus, a great deal of time is often required, yet in many cases the rapidly changing environment demands almost instantaneous action. Individuals who can be flexible enough to listen to many competing views, yet are able to obtain a consensus quickly enough for action, will be the most effective professional managers.

Another major challenge for managers, today and in the future, will be coping with Canada's *Charter of Rights and Freedoms*, which came into effect April 17, 1982. The charter may outlaw many current business practices, particularly those relating to employees. Because it has such broad implications, it will take years to determine its many ramifications for business. The future manager will have to be aware of the extent of the charter and work within its constraints.

YOUR CAREER IN BUSINESS

Although you have many courses to complete before you graduate, assuming you are aiming for a business degree or diploma, it is not too early to think about your future career. In the remainder of this chapter we review briefly some of the advantages and disadvantages of going into business for yourself, and of joining a small or a large company. Then we look at the process of getting a job. This section is not meant to be an extensive treatise on career planning, résumé writing and how to conduct yourself in an interview. It is simply meant to introduce you to the job search process. You are asked to give some thought to what you would like to do when you finish your course of study, what skills you have now and what they will be in the future, and some tips and ideas about how to approach finding the job that, at least initially, may be suitable for you.

Business Environments

When you graduate with your business degree or diploma, you can choose to go into business for yourself, or you can find a job with either a small company or a large company. Let us briefly review each of these business environments.

Going into Business for Yourself

Going into business for yourself means you are the boss. You do not have to answer to anyone else or live up to anyone else's expectations. Nevertheless, you must cater to customers and cope with the competition. There are also government regulations, which can be costly and time-consuming to deal with, not to mention frustrating. In terms of income, as a successful entrepreneur you can potentially make far more money than if you work for someone else.

On the other hand, running your own business is demanding. A business owner can seldom have a nine-to-five job. Long hours are normal and if the business fails you could lose everything. Nevertheless, being in business can be exceptionally challenging and rewarding and give the owner a good reputation in the community.

Before starting your own company, however, you must think about the knowledge and experience you have in running your own company. Another major consideration is the availability of financial resources. You may want to postpone starting your own business until you have gained some business experience in a small or large company.

Joining a Small Company

Students generally think of large companies when they look for a job, but a small company can provide many of the same advantages in terms of salary, insurance, pensions and other benefits. However, the pay scales may not go as high as those in larger companies.

A major advantage of joining a smaller company is that you feel nearer to the top because there are fewer levels of management. People also have a stronger sense of identity with the company because they have a better idea of the problems facing the firm as well as its successes.

Working in a small firm will probably give you more direct exposure to solving business problems and give you broader experience in a variety of fields. This is in contrast to a large company, where you are in a particular department, such as accounting or marketing, but interact little with other departments and get little chance to learn.

Another advantage of being in a smaller company is the fewer rules and restrictions that you will face, and fewer reports to make to superiors. Nevertheless, some rules and regulations must exist even in a small company.

Finally, a small company will not hire as many graduates: therefore, there will be less competition for the available jobs and for future promotion. On the other hand, there will be fewer opportunities for promotions as well.

Joining a Large Company

Working for a large company has many advantages, including higher salary and benefits and more opportunities for promotion. Larger firms can also provide more job security than smaller ones, and can usually weather much more severe recessions without laying off employees. Another advantage is the ability to transfer to other departments and acquire experience in advertising, marketing, sales, production, and so on. A job is more interesting when one can move from one department to another and learn new ways of doing things, or take advantage of training and development programs to further one's learning. Large companies also often provide their employees with free goods and services, discounts, specials, promotions, trips, and so on, that smaller companies cannot provide. Last, but not least, there is generally more prestige involved in working for a large well known company. It can impress friends and relatives who may not have heard of a smaller company.

There are also disadvantages, however. The size of the company makes it easy to get lost and forgotten among the hundreds, sometimes thousands, of managers. Climbing the corporate ladder may seem like a hopeless task. The feeling of insignificance one gets from making seemingly small decisions can be disheartening.

Frustration may also come from the many rules and policies that large companies have and that must be followed. Finally, large companies may require frequent moves around the country. Transfers are a sign that one is not forgotten and may mean a path to promotion, but they can also be tough on a family.

Choosing a Career

In choosing a career, you must pay particular attention to yourself. What are your likes and your dislikes? You must make sure that you match your aptitudes and skills with your interests, otherwise you will struggle in your job and not do well.

You should pick a company, large or small, where you can learn. This provides satisfaction and interest and prevents you from becoming stale and set in your ways. You will also be ready for new job opportunities when they come along, or for establishing your own business.

Having a good boss is another important factor, particularly to individuals who are new in the work world. A boss who is a good manager can teach you good management skills. He or she should be willing to help you become a good manager and take pride in seeing you develop. Guard against those who are incompetent, selfish, and uninterested in their subordinates. Usually these individuals are interested only in furthering themselves by exploiting their subordinates, and will not give recognition to others.

Finally, make sure you are in a career that is rewarding and gives you a feeling of accomplishment, of doing something that is worthwhile. If the paycheque is the only reward you get out of your job, it is time to look for something else.

Knowing What You Want to Do

How often do people graduate from a course of study or a program having little idea of what they really want to do? They wander aimlessly through college and university recruiting centres, hoping to get a job, any job.

Many graduates do find a job and eventually most settle into something that they like. However, finding a suitable job is so much easier if a few logical steps are followed and if the job seeker does some planning.

First, perhaps most important, is to find out what you would like to do. What are your interests? You should ask yourself, "What really turns me on about a job?" After all, if you want to excel at something, you have to be keenly interested in it. Unfortunately, what we would really like to do is often not immediately available to us, but if it is business-oriented, then perhaps through hard work we can eventually achieve it.

You should also look ahead to the future, perhaps 15 years down the road. How would you like to live at that time? What do you want to do then? What are some of the personal values that you hold? Perhaps most important of all, what do you really think you can accomplish?

Understanding yourself is important, because you can then channel your energies of finding suitable employment into those directions. Even if you have to accept a job that is not exactly in your field of interest, you can always look at it as a learning experience. Make a change at a later time if you so desire, when you have gathered some experience.

Finding Your Job:
Beginning a Career Plan

As a graduate, especially one with very little work experience, finding work in a job related to your area of study is a challenge. There are a few things to remember.

First, the new graduate's "job search" process should start when you begin the course of study. Perhaps now is the time to do so if you are reading this text for a course in your first year. Once you complete your program the emphasis changes to self-assessment and the development of job leads.

Another thing to remember is that job search skills are not an innate talent. They are a combination of interpersonal and organizational skills that require a great deal of effort to develop.

The job search process shown in Figure 15.1 contains basic elements that have remained constant for decades. If this process is to be an effective tool you should constantly update the various elements in it. Although you can deviate from this process if you wish, you will make very little progress unless you understand and are willing to work at all of the elements of your search. The skills that a job search requires should become integrated with one's career, the process being part of career planning.

The Job Search Process

Figure 15.1 shows the job search process and its five major sections:

1. Pre-job search preparation
2. Developing job leads
3. Job search management
4. Interview management
5. Job maintenance

We will briefly discuss each of the sections to give you some idea of the process involved in getting a job.

1. Pre-Job Search Preparation

Few graduates can expect to have the perfect job waiting for them when they graduate. In most instances it takes planning and considerable effort to contact potential employers. The following should be completed as part of the pre-job search preparation.

Self-assessment. This first step is to develop an indicator to show your potential employer what personal qualities you possess. As a recent graduate, you lack experience, but a potential employer knows that. You can overcome that deficiency by showing that you are positive in your outlook and have lots of energy and drive. That is how you will gain experience quickly and that is what your potential employer wants to see. Some positive action words are shown in Table 15.1 that you can use in your dealings with potential employers. Put them into your letters or into your résumé.

Skills inventory. During your time in school and the workplace you have developed many personal skills that could be real advantages to an employer. You should compile a list of these skills and select those that you want to highlight in a résumé or letter of employment. Table 15.2 provides a list of personal skills. Look through it and pick out those that you think you have acquired.

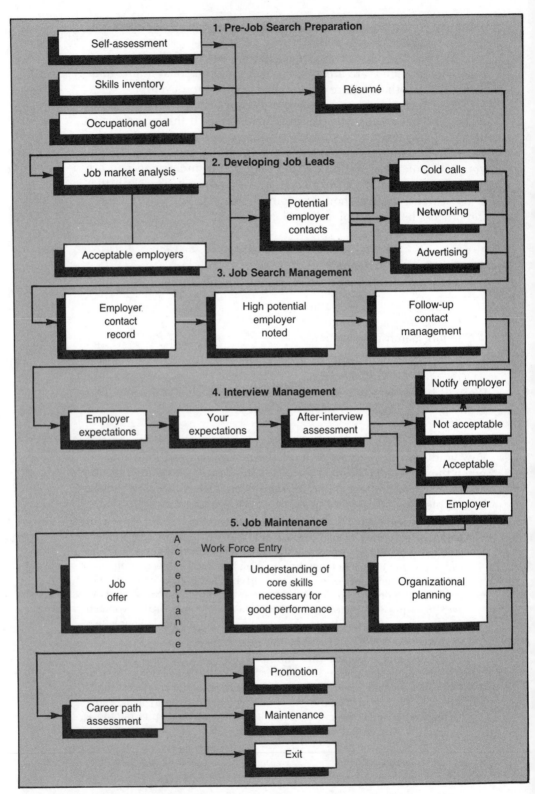

Figure 15.1 Employment flow chart

TABLE 15.1
List of active words

Competent	Profitable	Managed
Successful	Positive	Directed
Capable	Complete	Supervised
Resourceful	Investigated	Initiated
Qualified	Designed	Created
Versatile	Developed	Organized
Proficient	Maintained	Trained
Efficient	Built	Worked
Knowledgeable	Established	Led
Consistent	Communicated	Coordinated
Experienced	Processed	Analyzed
Productive	Participated	Improved
Effective	Sold	Repaired
Stable	Engineered	Employed
Well educated	Implemented	Expanded
Wide background	Controlled	Achieved
Equipped	Guided	Specialized
Accomplished	Administered	

Occupational goal. It is difficult for a graduate to know what job to apply for. To find rewarding employment in your area of interest requires matching your skills and interests with the job titles used by employers you would like to work for. List those titles, based on the information you have gained from potential employers and other sources.

The résumé. After completing the above steps you should have enough information to put together one of your most valuable tools — your résumé. If you have a number of diverse occupational goals you may need more than one résumé. Keep in mind, however, that you have time constraints. It may be impossible at this stage to conduct an effective multi-directional job search.

Figure 15.2 shows a sample, chronological résumé. This type of résumé is the one preferred by businesses employing recent graduates. There is a large degree of flexibility with this format, but keep in mind the following considerations to avoid giving an incorrect impression about yourself.

    i. **Title Page**. Optional. However, if you feel it provides the proper tone for your résumé, use it.

    ii. **Career objectives**. This is also optional but suggested for most résumés as it shows the potential employer that the applicant has thought through his or her goals and has matched them with the needs of the employer.

TABLE 15.2
A list of personal skills

Administering programs	Interviewing people
Advising people	Inventing new ideas
Analyzing data	Listening to others
Arranging social functions	Locating missing information
Assembling apparatus	Managing an organization
Auditing financial statements	Mediating between people
Budgeting expenses	Meeting the public
Calculating numerical data	Monitoring progress of others
Checking for accuracy	Motivating others
Classifying records	Negotiating contracts
Coaching individuals	Operating equipment
Collecting money	Organizing people and tasks
Compiling statistics	Persuading others
Confronting other people	Planning agendas
Constructing buildings	Planning organizational needs
Coordinating events	Preparing materials
Corresponding with others	Printing by hand
Counselling people	Problem solving
Creating new ideas	Programming computers
Deciding uses of money	Promoting events
Delegating responsibility	Protecting property
Designing data systems	Raising funds
Dispensing information	Reading volumes of material
Displaying artistic ideas	Recording scientific data
Distributing products	Rehabilitating people
Dramatizing ideas or problems	Repairing mechanical devices
Editing publications	Reviewing programs
Enduring long hours	Running meetings
Entertaining people	Selling products
Estimating physical space	Serving individuals
Evaluating programs	Setting up demonstrations
Exhibiting plans	Sketching charts or diagrams
Finding information	Speaking in public
Handling complaints	Supervising others
Handling detailed work	Teaching classes
Inspecting physical objects	Updating files
Interpreting languages	Writing clear reports

Career Objective

To work in a company's information processing department and eventually manage the department. To further educate myself in computers and business data processing as required.

Personal Information

Name: William Charles White
Address: 222 Rosebank Street
                 Lakeland, Ontario
Telephone
number: 666-8888

Education and Training

Academic: Grade 12 Matriculation
                 Campbell College
                 2712 King Street
                 Towers, Prince Edward Island

                 Business Management with major in Data
                     Processing
                 Inland College
                 Winnipeg, Manitoba

Job Experience

May 1988
to present   Programmer

                 Developed a customer appointment
                 schedule for NU-Software. Worked
                 mostly on my own. Occasional
                 demonstrations required for customers.

                 Salary: $18 000/year

July 1987 to
April 1988   DBase programmer

                 I was engaged in programming for a
                 small electronics company that was
                 computerizing the parking industry. My
                 specific task was to develop report
                 formats for the industry.

                 Salary: $17 000/year

July 1986 to
June 1987   Sales clerk

                 Computer retail store. Sales of
                 hardware and software. I was
                 responsible for customer service and
                 inventory control.

                 Salary: $13 900/year

Scholarships
and Awards: Government Grant/Scholarship for both
                     years at college.
                 Elizabeth Henning Memorial Scholarship

Affiliations: Member, Inland College Alumni Association

Other Activities: Tennis, Skiing, Music

References: Academic and work references available on
                 request.

Figure 15.2 A sample résumé

iii. **Personal information**. This section follows career objectives and should provide the reader with basic personal information, such as your address.

iv. **Education and knowledge**. Besides giving a history of your educational background, this section allows you to emphasize the relevant items from your skills inventory, experience and knowledge. This section is the place to pull it all together, especially as a lead-in to your employment history, if you have one.

v. **Employment history**. This section indicates where you have previously worked and acquired your listed skills. You should provide a reverse chronological description of what you did in each job. If you do not have a work history, then keep it short.

vi. **Scholarships and awards**. As a student, this is very important. If you have achieved anything that might set you apart as a high-quality student, the reader must know the details and when these achievements were made.

vii. **Affiliation**. Are you, or have you been a member of any club, group or association? Any potential employer views this as an indication of the level of professionalism and commitment he or she can expect from the applicant.

viii. **References**. Do not list them. Say that they are available on request and then have them ready for the interview. This allows you to select the references most appropriate for the potential employer.

ix. **Introductory letter**. The letter is meant to create a favourable impression on the employer, introduce the résumé, and obtain an interview with the employer. The letter must mention your present job or area of activity, field of interest, training and experience, knowledge of the company and the job desired. It should also emphasize that you are available for an interview with the employer and mention the attached résumé.

Your résumé must make a good first impression on the person reading it. It must be well set up on the page, and the type must be evenly dark. Use a new ribbon. Furthermore, your grammar and spelling must be impeccable. Read your résumé as if you were the employer. If you don't like what you see, change it until you are satisfied.

If you can develop your résumé with a word processor you are ahead of the game. A word processor allows you to edit your résumé easily; change the information around as desired until you are satisfied that it reads well. If you want to make changes later it is a minor task because you can store the résumé on disk and recall it when you need it. Similarly you can store any letters you have written to various potential employers and recall them to alter the content as required for each application.

2. Developing Job Leads

You may have heard about the hidden job market. It simply means that about 80% of the jobs available are not advertised. You must go and find them. To do so you must approach the job search systematically.

Job market analysis. First you must decide what industries you want to work in, to ensure that you have not left a good potential job market out of your area of search.

Acceptable employers. Once you have decided on the industry you must decide on the employers you would like to work for. This is also known as targeting. Out of the thousands of possible employers you can only talk to a few. Do not waste your time on mass-mailouts. Use your time wisely. Research whom you want to work for and then put them on your contact list.

Potential employer contacts. Now you are ready to take action. First, you should use all the personal contacts you have, also known as **networking**. You may find them surprisingly willing to help. Second, do some "**cold calls**." They are useful, but require more research and time on your part in order to get to the person responsible for hiring you. Third, look at **job advertisements**. While they may ask for experience you do not have at the moment, they can be a source of employment later or may be able to refer you to other potential employers.

3. Job Search Management

As you are gathering information about employers you must keep track of it so that you can compare information about employers and follow up on promising employers.

Employer contact record. As soon as you finish a conversation, make notes of names and details of employment possibilities. This information is of critical importance to you.

High potential employers. You must continually pick out those employers that promise a high probability of employment from those that do not, while continuing to make new contacts.

Follow-up contact management. As your job search matures you should spend more and more time talking to those potential employers who show an interest in you, have a job you are interested in, and, most important, have a reasonable opportunity for vacancy. Establish a mutually agreeable time and date for your next contact and follow through. This is an excellent way to demonstrate your organizational skills and motivation to the potential employer.

4. Interview Management

When you sit down with an employer, be organized: know the job, the company background, and be prepared to ask some questions. Be sure you understand the following:

Employer expectations. Whom does the employer see as the ideal person for the job?

Your expectations. Did the employer's statements about the job match what you expected to hear?

After-interview assessment. Prepare a balance sheet of the positive and negative aspects of the job. You must make a decision of whether or not you will accept the job if you receive an offer.

- If there is not an acceptable position, notify the employer. There may be a job in the future, and as a budding professional you must demonstrate your skills to everyone you come in contact with.

- If the position is acceptable, notify the employer of your impression of the position and thank him or her for the interview. How you conduct your post-interview follow-up can influence the interviewer to hire you.

5. Job Maintenance

Job maintenance is an ongoing activity once you are employed. Success on the job provides the basis for future promotion, either within the company or with another employer. If you are a recent graduate, you first job is critically important in that it allows you to demonstrate your skills and abilities. Job maintenance involves the following:

Understanding of core skills. As your time on the job increases, you will develop a better and better understanding of the skills required to be successful in that particular job and in the company.

Organization and planning. How are you going to succeed and advance? Act on the knowledge you have of your job. If further study is needed, enrol in the necessary courses. If other direct knowledge of the company is needed, explore all options available in gaining that knowledge.

Career path assessment. Ultimately, you must decide whether or not you wish to remain in your present job or change careers. To avoid any negative experience on the job, ask yourself what your priorities are. Do not be surprised if your priorities have changed, and if they have, it is up to you to adapt to the change.

NOTES

1. Alvin Toffler, *Future Shock* (New York: Bantam, 1970), pp. 13–14.
2. Dennis L. Meadows, *The Limits to Growth* (New York: Universe Books, 1972).
3. Joan Bryden, "Greying of Canada promises to burden next generation," *Vancouver Sun*, Saturday, June 4, 1988, p. B2.
4. Richard Blackwell, "Full automation getting nearer as more plants go on-line," *The Financial Post, Special Quarterly Report*, June 29, 1985. This entire section provides many examples of computerization in factories and where Canada stands in manufacture and use of robots.
5. Glynnis Walker, "Why we're struggling in communications," *The Financial Post 1980's Outlook*, Jan. 5, 1980, p. 10.

CHAPTER SUMMARY

Forecasting and planning for the future is a major task of management, to ensure the organization's achievement of its goals and objectives, and even its survival. Accelerating changes in virtually all aspects of society, together with rapid technological development, make forecasting difficult. Nevertheless, certain societal trends which will affect business are evident, including changes in population, age structure, life style, economics and technology.

No doubt changes will also occur in the relationships between business and government, labour, and society generally. The manager of the future will need to be highly educated, and willing to adapt to new situations in order to effectively manage an organization subject to numerous outside pressures.

Choosing a business career is difficult. One of the most important tasks for potential business graduates is to determine their aptitudes and skills and match these with their interests. Opportunities for graduates exist in both large and small companies, although each has advantages and disadvantages. Starting one's own business is also an alternative. To ensure that the business will be successful, the graduate must obtain the business knowledge and management experience, which is best done by working a number of years in one or more small or large firms.

To find that first job a graduate should follow the job search process, which consists of five steps: pre-job search preparation, developing job leads, job search management, interview management, and job maintenance. Students should begin the job search process when they begin their course of study, rather than wait until graduation. This will allow them to acquire a considerable amount of knowledge about various companies, and determine their own aptitudes and interests as they are progressing through their course of study. When the time comes to begin the actual job search the graduate can concentrate on getting the right job with the right employer.

KEY WORDS

Trend analysis	Life style
Delphi method	Life style research
Scenario	Job search process

REVIEW QUESTIONS

1. What do we mean by forecasting the future?
2. Why is the world changing much more rapidly as time goes on?
3. What are the five major methods of predicting the future? Why should we not rely on only one method?

4. Why is life style research becoming an important tool for business?
5. How will some of the changes in life style affect business?
6. What will be the impact on business of anticipated population changes? Of changes in the age structure?
7. What is a key advantage of joining a small company? A large company?
8. Why should students begin the job search process when they first begin a program of study rather than wait until they graduate?
9. Briefly describe the key elements of the job search process. Why is a résumé of critical importance?

DISCUSSION QUESTIONS

1. How will technological changes in computers and communications affect individuals? What are some of the business opportunities that may arise as a result of these changes?
2. How will private business be affected by a continued increase in expenditures by the public sector?
3. Write a scenario describing your view of Canada in the year 2000.
4. What major technological advances do you anticipate over the coming decades? How may they affect business and individuals?
5. How may business be affected by changes in Canada's political system in the next ten years?
6. How may technological changes affect the jobs and careers of business graduates?

Index